TRIBAL TATTOO
ENCYCLOPEDIA

RAD[illegible] [illegible]SA

TRIBAL TATTOO ENCYCLOPEDIA
RADOMÍR FIKSA

www.tetovani.eu
First press

Graphic edit: Patrik Fujera

ISBN: 978-80-87525-78-4

CONTENT:

´AATANGA – To be shining, flashing; brightness (often said of tattooing), Bellona island.

´AGA´AGA´(´ANGA´ANGA) – to alleviate the pain of one being tattooed and to keep him from fainting , Bellona.

´AGO GANGI – Sky chest, an honor, reference to the taukuka chest tattoo, Bellona.

'AGO GUA – term for men with taukuka tattoo on chest and back, Bellona.

A TOTO - three-day rest periods called days of blood (a toto) after each tattooing process, so that the operation covered from two weeks to four months, Marquesas.

A´AHU – To burn, smart, hurt, as new tattooing, Bellona.

AALLNEQ – the tattoo pigment, was made from the soot (aallneq) of seal oil lamps which was taken from the bottom of tea kettles , St. Lawrence Island.

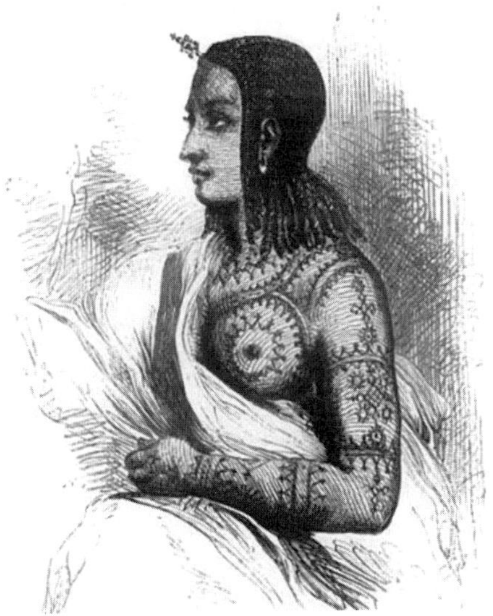

Tattooed lady from Life in Abyssinia book by M. Parkyns

ABE – the tattooist's Y-shaped blade, Yoruba, Afrika.

ABIKU– Abiku is a Yoruba word that can be translated as "predestined to death". It is from (abi) "that which possesses" and (iku) "death". Abiku refers to the spirits of children who die before reaching puberty; a child who dies before twelve years of age being called an Abiku, and the spirit, or spirits, who caused the death being also called Abiku. This child was tattooed on the shoulder with three commas so that he might be given exemplary care during a rebirth.

ABIPONES – People from around the Paraguayan Chaco, women practiced tattooing.

ABYSSINIA TRIBE – Abbysinia is the older name for today's Ethiopia. The men seldom tattoo more than one ornament on the upper part of the arm, near the shoulders, while the women covered nearly the whole of their bodls with star lines, and crosses, often rather tastefully arranged.

ACACIA – coniferous tree in Egypt. The Romans allegedly used his bark as part of the tattoo color. The bark was mixed with the rock, bile and then water and leek juice added.

ACHOMAWI TRIBE – Tattooing was done on women's faces, with three thin lines on the chins and a few lines on the cheek. Men occasionally had a series of small points running from their eyes through the temple. Men had their noses pierced so they could wear a shell or bone ornament through the nose.

ACROCLADIA TRIGONARIA – sea hedgehog, from whose spikes the tattoo

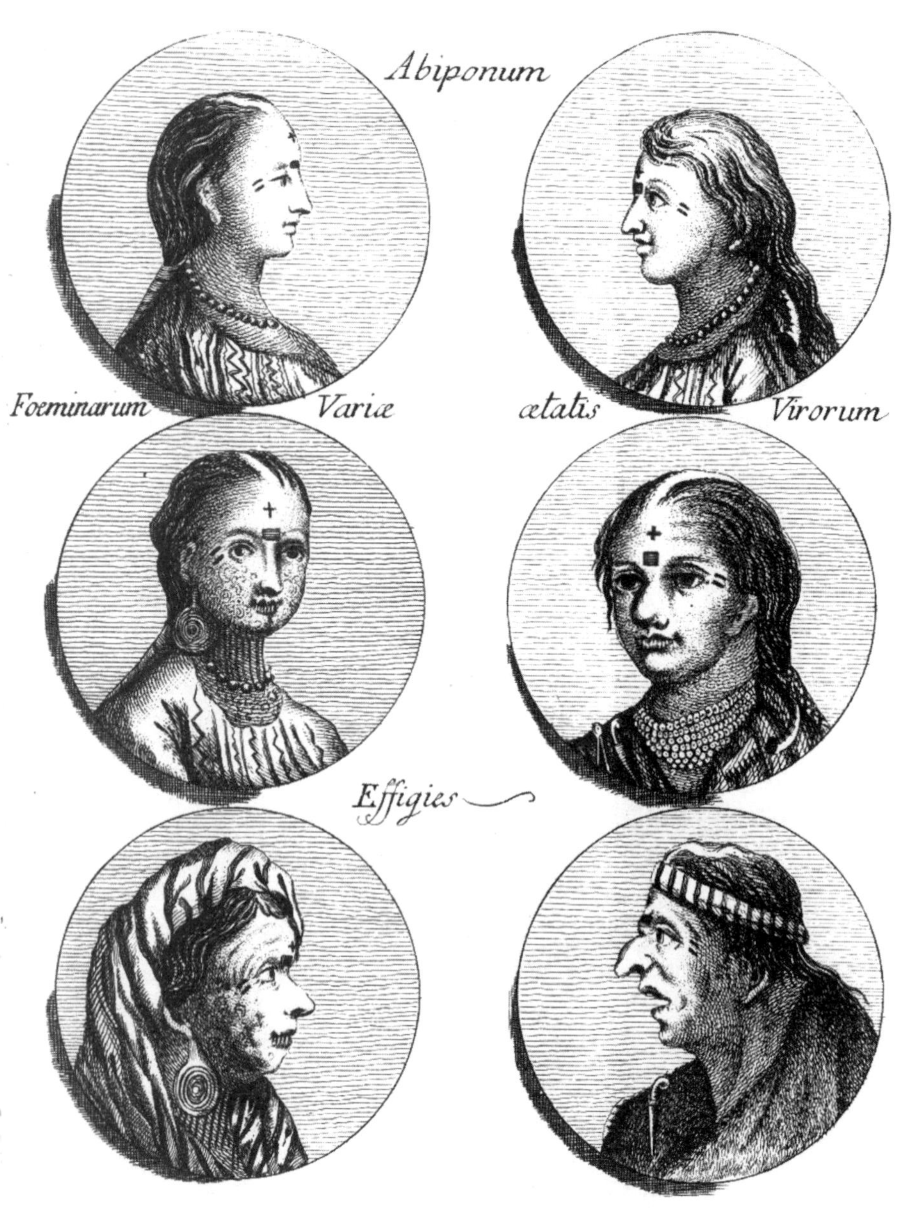

Abipones

tools were made in the Marshall Islands.

ADABO - Barracks from Madagascar used Adabo (Ficus cocculifolia, subspecies Sakalavarum) for tattoo color.

ADASIYA – Gypsy tribe practising tattoos. The Adasiyas who came from Tunisia were known for their palm reading and decorating techniques, including tattoos.

ADMIRALITY ISLANDS – Peoples tattooed with rings round the eyes and all over the face, and in diagonál lines over the upper part of the front of the body, the lines crossing one another so as to form a series of lozenge-shaped spaces.

ADUMBA - Tattooing is also a preparatory rite for both males and females to enter another state of passage called the adumba. This is a dance ceremony of the retreating men, who beat the gongs suspended from human jawbones, and encircle the women, who mark time without locomotion and revolve in place to face the warriors dancing around them. In any Kalinga dance, physical contact among the dancers is taboo. During the adumba, the women wear the kain adorned with platelets of silver and colored stones, creating an impact on the sight and sound of the dance. The tattoos also make them attractive to the men and vice versa. The adumba is the event where the women can find a potential mate, and this rite of adumba is an indication that a woman is of marrying age and capable of bearing a child. They are already considered marriageable after they complete the ceremonies, Batek.

ADUPI – process for tattoo, Hidatsa Indian tribe.

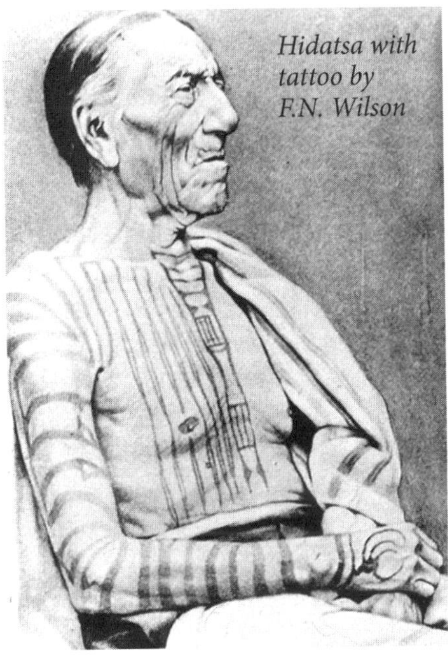
Hidatsa with tattoo by F.N. Wilson

ADŽI – a term in Japan for the touch of the artist's personality penetrating the work. The artist approaches the calligraphic character as a violinist to score. The aim is to balance the composition, the rhythm, the subtlety of the power and, above all, the adventure.

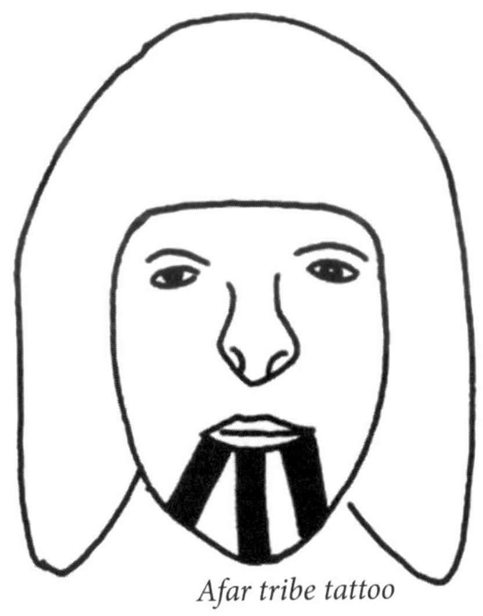
Afar tribe tattoo

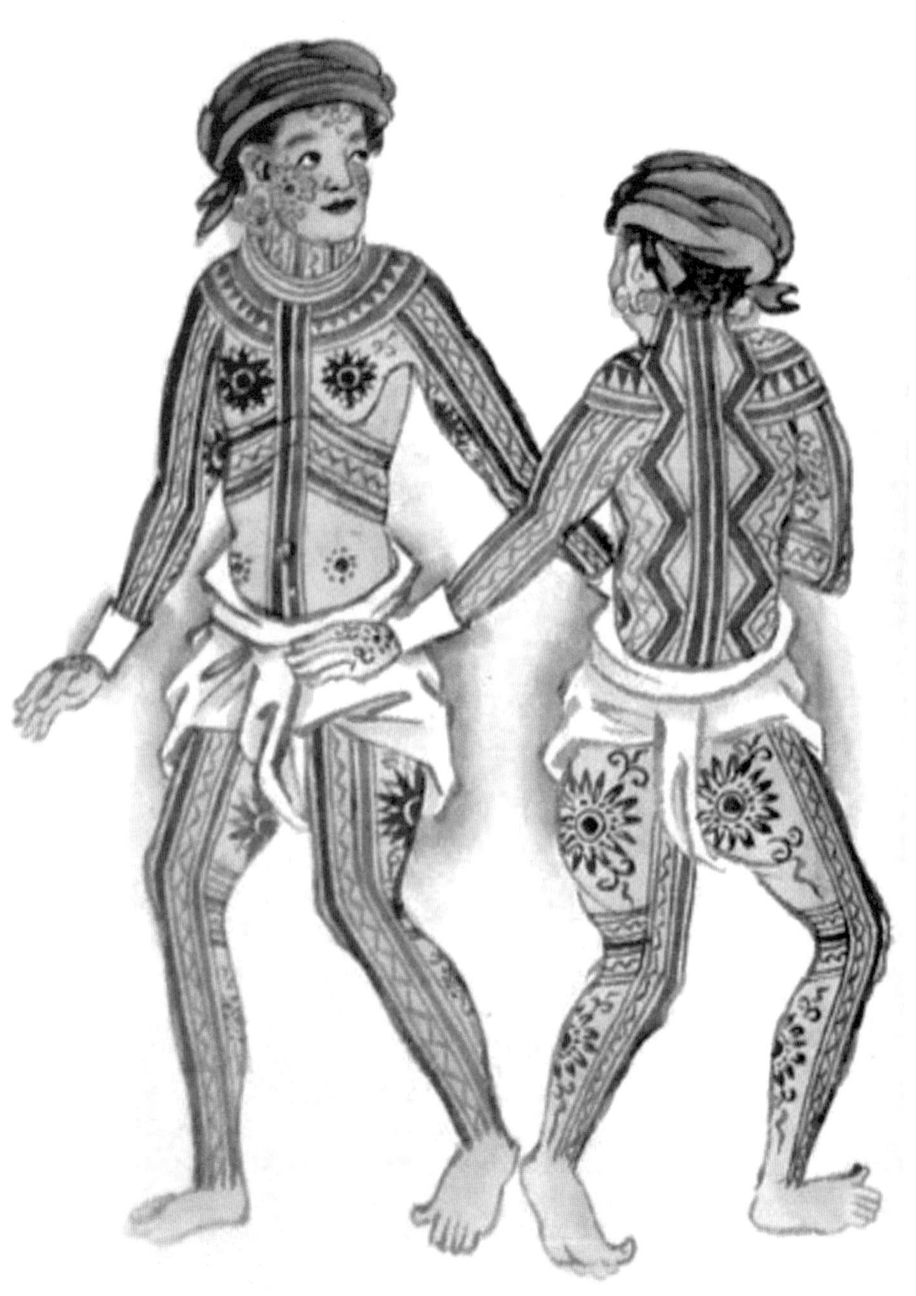

Adumbaa

AFAR TRIBES - are an ethnic group of more than one million people, inhabiting predominantly the Danakilian desert in the Ethiopian, Etritree and Djibouti districts of the African region. Women are traditionally tattooed in their faces. In particular lines forming arches under the eyes and on the chin.

AGHTUQAAYAK, ANNA - (Qayaghhaq) the name of the last tattooed woman (according to their customs on the legs, cheeks, chin, hands and wrists) of St. Lawrence Island, who died in 2002 at the age of 96 years.

AGOFERE - After tattooing about an hour or two the completed portion of the pattern is washed with water and afterwards rubbed with the leaf of a certain croton (agofere). This leaf is freshly picked and held over a fire for a short while to make it more pliable, Santa Anna.

AGURU - sap used for thinning tattooing paste, Bellona.

AHETJAM - body art markings, called lousham in Arabic or ahetjam in Tamazight, are no longer considered to be a pious Muslim practice and as a result very few younger women will carry these tattoos. At one point, these tattoos were tribal markings of status and beauty, symbols that were borrowed from the complicated designs in the rus.

AHI KAURI- The fire at which the pigment (ngarehu) was prepared, was known as an ahi kauri, the term kauri being applied to the prepared soot (awe), Maori.

AHI TA MOKO - The ahi ta moko, as the tattooing rite was termed of yore, was an exceedingly tapu affair when the subject was a person of importance; for it meant interfering with the body of a tapu person, and the shedding of his, or her, blood. The operator would also be stained with the blood of such sacred person, Maori.

AHI TA NGUTU - The ceremony of tattooing the lips and chin of women is known as ta nguta, or ahi ta ngutu, or taanga ngutu. This ahi ta ngutu is a sacred fire and the tattooing of the eldest daughter of a chief was an extremely tapu function, but not so that of the younger daughters, the law of primogeniture being strictly upheld by the old time Maori, the eldest of either sex being the most important and tapu members of a family. A human sacrifice was sometimes made in order to give force, renown, prestige to the tattooing of such a girl, as also for the piercing of her ears (pokanga taringa), Maori.

AHKOOMOOS - was probably the last woman from the Pepeekesis Reserve (North America) to wear tattooed lines from mouth to chin, the widow of Chief Little Black Bear, who died around 1913.

AI– AI - Various colour shades could be derived by mixing them together. As in the case of prints, indigo (ai) was made by boiling old rags originally dyed with indigo, a common practise in the Edo period. Mixed with beni, a transparent red extracted from the safflower (benihana), this blue could be made into violet; if mixed with seiko (stone yellow) a light green could be obtained. For red, occasionaly benigana (presumably derived from Bengal) was used, a pigment made from iron sulfate and green vitriol. Because of its poisonous

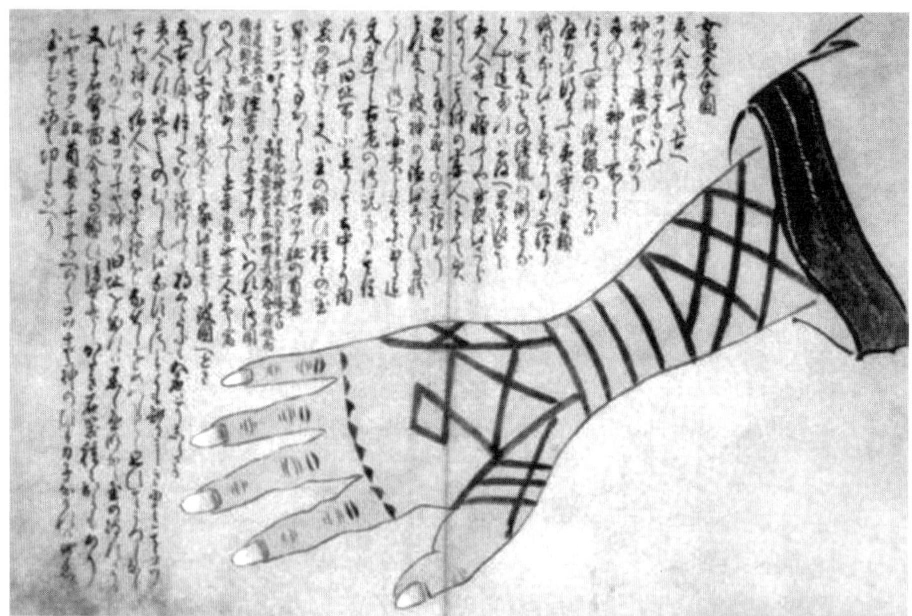

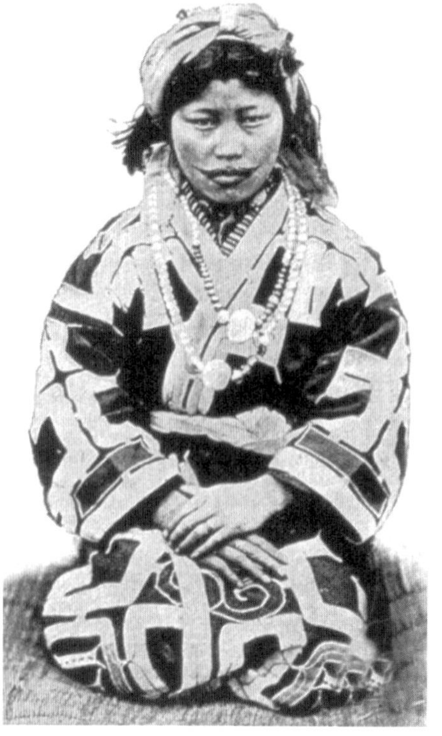

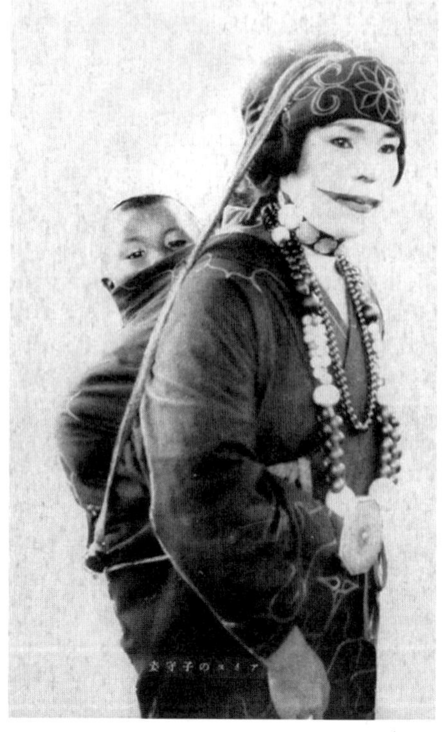

Ainu

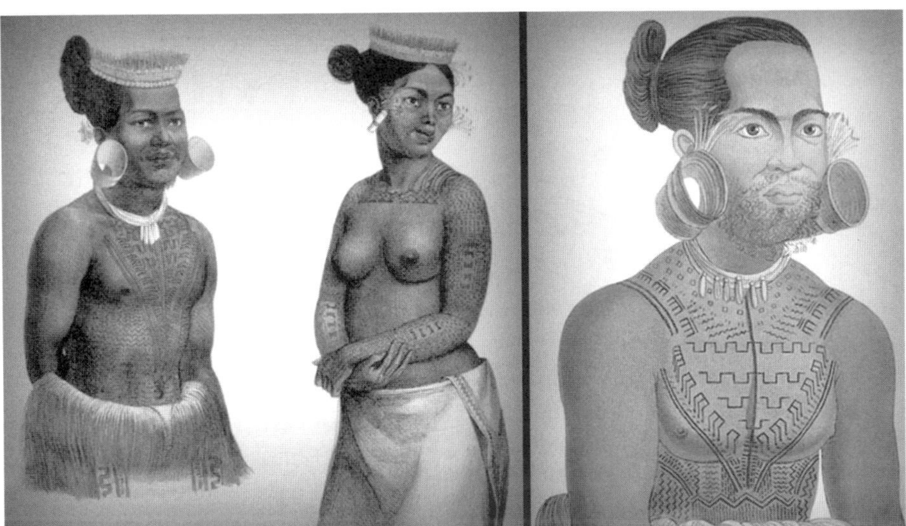

Ailin-Glaplap

components it was applied sparingly, Japan.

AI URI – term for tattoo in Daui district, Papua New Guinea.

AILIN-GLAPLAP – Atol on Marshall Islands. Exist legend that God Lowa sent down two men to Ailinglaplap to tattoo all that been created - the birds and animals, fishes, humans everything. Everybody on earth had to come to Ailinglaplap to be tattoed. That´s how each kind of thing has its own markings. And that´s why the highest-rank tattoos were for chiefs, and different onew were for women, and then commoners and animals.

AINU PEOPLE - The Ainu ("human" or "people") are an indigenous people in Japan native to the regions of Hokkaido, Northern Tohoku, and Karafuto, among others. As part of their ancestral tradition, Ainu women had the custom of getting tattoos on their bodies, including their lips. For the Ainu, the tattoo was perceived as a symbol of beauty, a

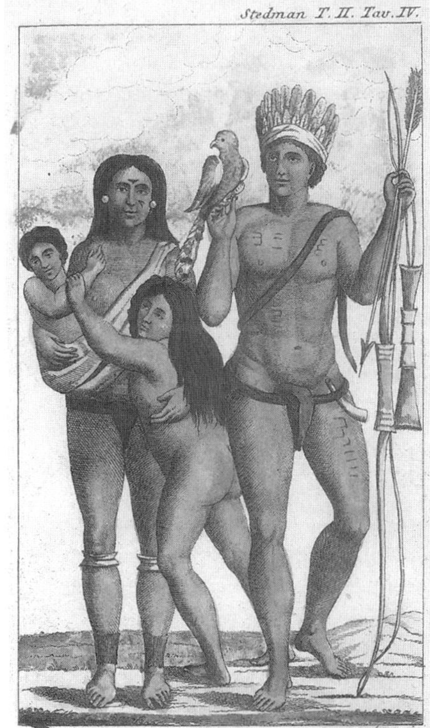

Akawayo

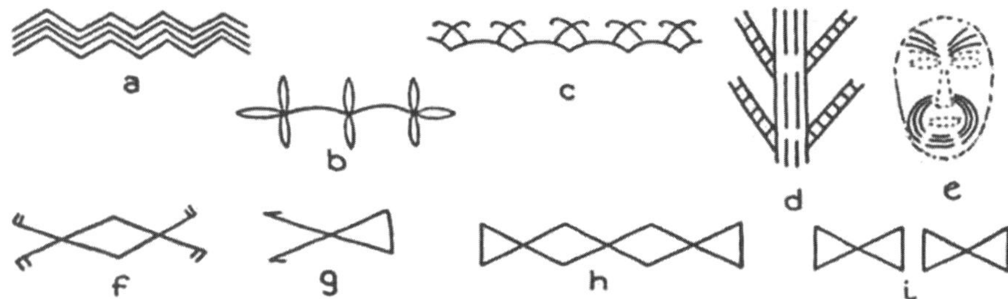

Motifs from Aitutaki Islands: a- papavaro; b- parepare; c- ruru; d- manuta'i; e- tatatao ;f- puapua-inano; g- komua; h- paeko; i- punarua

talisman and an indispensable tool to prepare their body for after death. However, the traditional tattoo was legally prohibited by the Japanese government in 1871, in an attempt to force Ainu to follow a "Japanese lifestyle". As the result, Ainu women reduced the use of tattoos on their bodies, progressively changing their concept of beauty and losing an important part of their ancestral tradition.

AITUTAKI ISLANDS - also traditionally known as Ara'ura and Utataki, is the second most popular island in the Cook Islands.

AJA´SOVIN – term for tattoo, Chippewa Indians.

AKA – a tribe from Northeast India, the Naga area, women practice tattoos.

AKANZA – tattoo (Hausa language), Nigeria.

AKAWAYO - the proper name of Kapong, an ethnic South American Indian in southern Guyana. They plucked eyebrows and this place was dark tattooed. So they even decorated the corners of their mouths.

AKAZUMI – Different color shades could be obtained by mixing. Red mixed with black, resulting in a brown shade, called akazumi, Japan.

AKEBONO MIKIRI – Akebono means „daybreak", this somewhat ambiguos border gradually becomes less intense in color, just the rays of the sun, Japan tattoo.

AKOTTO – The Australian word akotto or kotto, is also found as the name of Polynesian tattooing, where the instrument is also called kotto.

AKU MAEBA – expression for: my tattoo with the name of tattoo artist, Bellona.

ALASKAN ESKIMO - whale´s tail is s favourite device among the Alaskan Eskimo for carving on ivory or wooden

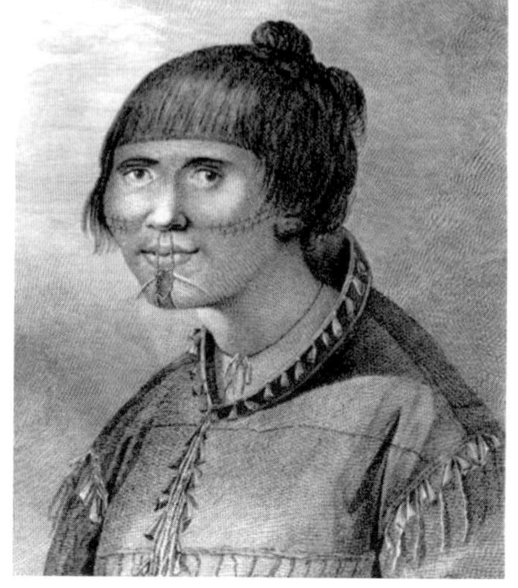

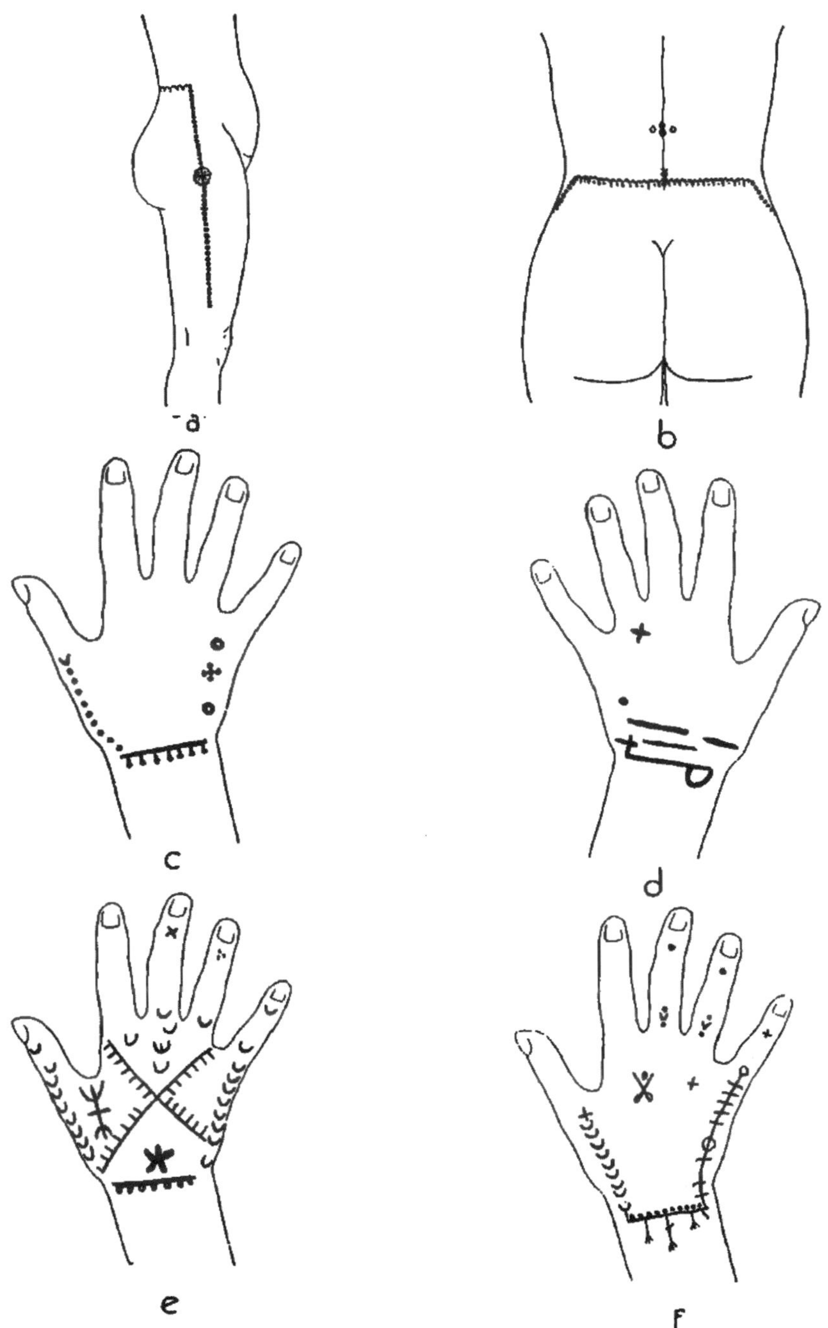

Tattoos of Arab men and women. A, B, woman of Albu Muhammad; C,D, men of Albu Muhammad; E, woman of Shammar tribe; F, man of Dulaim tribe

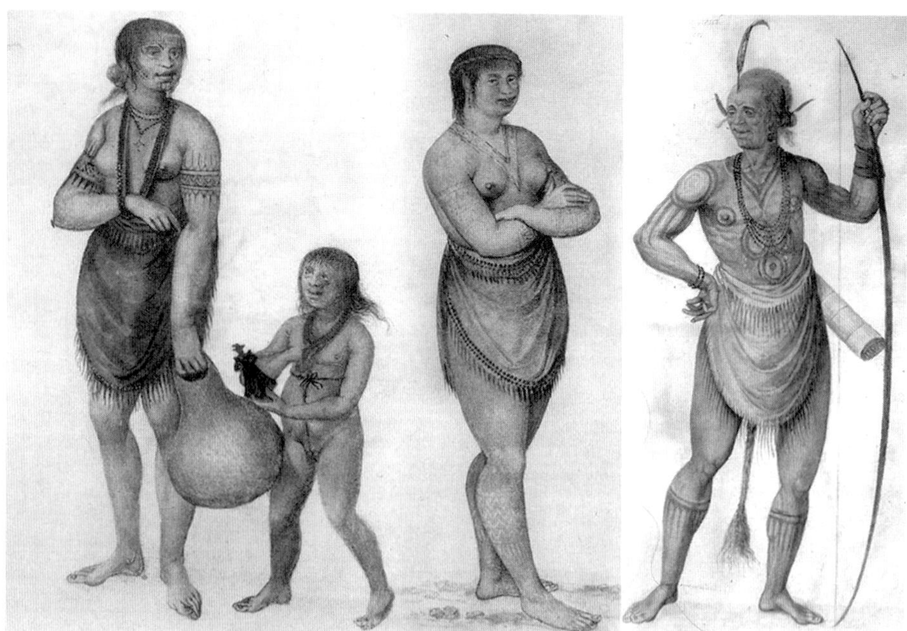

John White Painting of Algonquian Indians, 1585

implemented and for tattooing on their person and for charms.

ALBU MUHAMMAD – a tribe in the territory of today's Iraq, widespread tattoos among women.

ALEURITES MOLUCCANA – The tattoo color was produced from the soot of the candelnut (Aleurites Moluccana), Samoa.

ALEURITES TRILOBATA - The tattoo pigment was made from roasted nuts (Aleurites trilobata) in Polynesia.

ALEUT PEOPLE - These people had tattoos in the form of intricate ornamentation on the cheeks and under the nose down to the chin. The tattoos and piercings of the Aleut people demonstrated not only their accomplishments in life but their religious views. Their body art was thought to please the spirits of the animals and make any evil go away. The body orifices were believed to be highways that evil entities traveled through. By piercing their orifices, the nose, the mouth, and ears, they would stop evil entities, "Khoughkh", from entering their bodies. Body art also enhanced their beauty, social status, and spiritual autority.

ALGONQUIN INDIAN - The Algonquian are one of the most populous and widespread North American native language groups, withtribes originally numbering in the hundreds of thousands. Today, thousands of individuals identify with various Algonquian peoples. Historically, the peoples were prominent along the Atlantic Coast and into the interior along the St. Lawrence River and around the Great Lakes. This grouping consists of peoples who speak Algonquian languages.

ALIFURU – a tribe of Molucca islands, practiced tattoos.

ALLEN TRICIA - Anthropologist and tattooist Tricia Allen has harnessed centuries of knowledge about Hawaiian tattoos and has created this fascinating, comprehensive reference book about Hawaiian tattoo, that can be enjoyed by both tattoo enthusiasts and cultural scholars. Tattoo Traditions of Hawaii describes the evolution of Hawaiian tattooing as an art and science tracing it from its early roots in ancient Polynesia; presents motif, meaning, placement, tools and techniques along with personal observations and commentary in meticulous and graphic detail.

ALOE VERA - Aloe vera is a succulent plant species of the genus Aloe. An evergreen perennial, it originates from the Arabian Peninsula, but grows wild in tropical, semi-tropical, and arid climates around the world. It is cultivated for agricultural and medicinal uses. The species is also used for decorative purposes and grows successfully indoors as a potted plant. Aloe vera is an effective, natural and safe remedy that will allow you to take care of the new tattoo so it will heal in the right way.

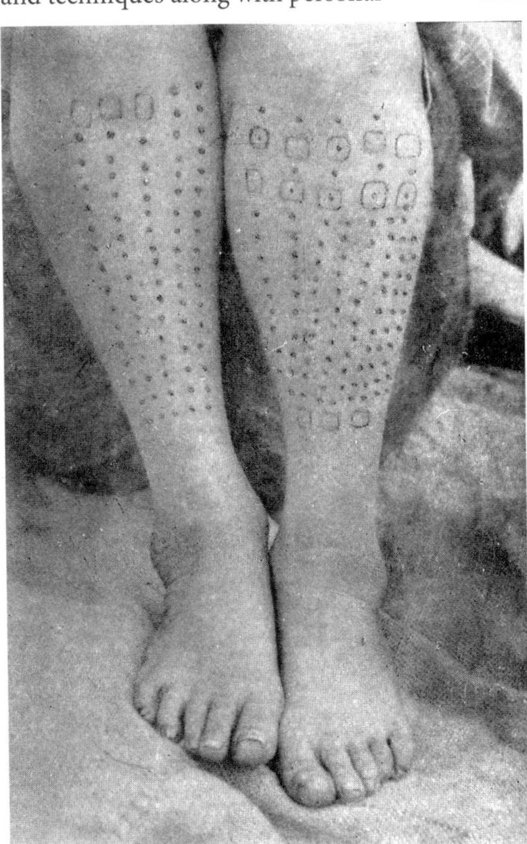

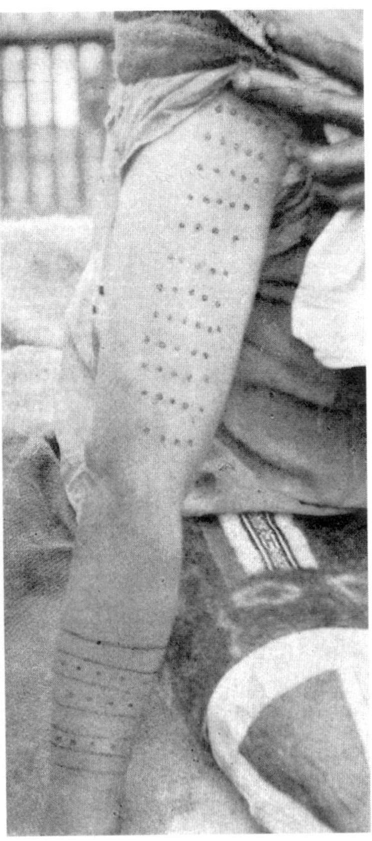

Ammassalik womans

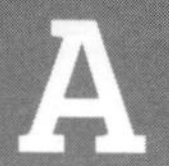

AMAHUKA – the tribe of the Amazon, as a tribal sign, tattooed a stripe across the nose.

AMBARU – young men and girls become Ambaru (beautiful) when undergoing tattoos, Kalinga.

AMBON – island in the Moluccas archipelago, the people there practiced tattoos.

AMH´ALA NI – The local name in Dargi amh'ala ni', which means 'donkey milk', used as a part of tattoo color, Dagestan.

AMHARA PEOPLE – tribe near Bhar Dar, Ethiopia, women practice tattoos.

AMAHI AMA - the process of preparing carbon black for tattoo ink, Marquesas.

AMMASSALIK – all the women are tattooed, having a couple of short lines between the eye-browns and one just below the root of the nose, and also a few short lines on the chin. The arms and hands and, to some extent, the legs are more or less tattooed with rectilinear figures and small strokes, which often cover considerable areas. Some women are also tattooed on and between the breasts. The men are very seldom

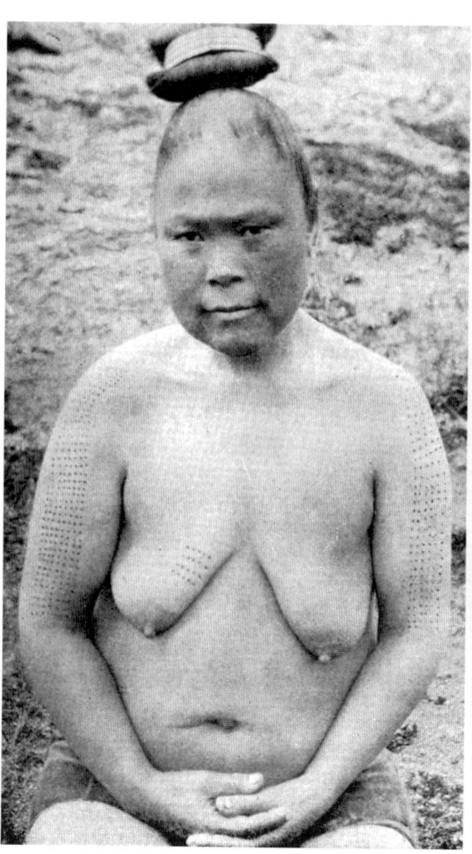

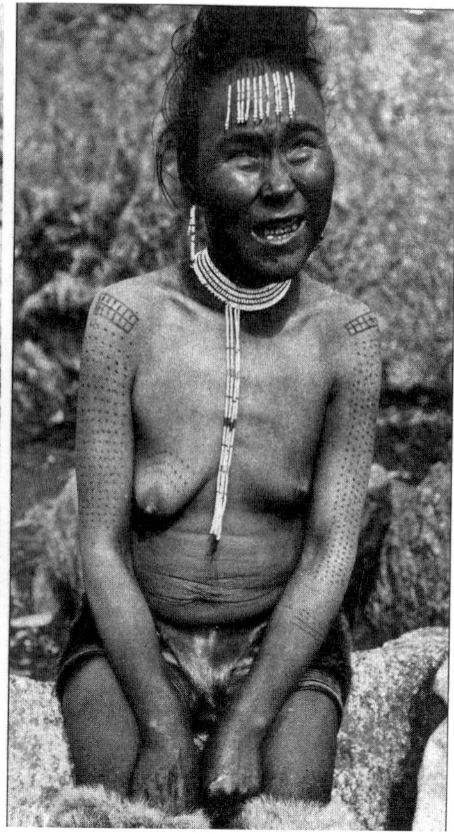

Ammassalik womans

tattooed, and then they only have a few small lines on their arms and wrists. Sometimes they have also a few lines in the face by way of ornament.

AMOCA – Description of the preparations of a native to be mokoed: He lay upon his back, with his head resting upon the knees of the operator, who sat upon the ground, and for whose guidance the instended form of the amoco had benn previously traced in black lines upon the patient´s face.

ANÂ-MURI - (behind the star) God of fish and fishermen, pillar of tattoo, Polynesia.

ANADASIYA - nomadic gypsies who performed tattoos, Tunis.

ANDI PERI – name for the tattoo method, Ainu people.

ANIHO – papyrus aniho, is an ancient Egyptian papyrus named after its owner, who was a more unknown dignitary Ani. It was founded sometime during the 19th dynasty during the New Kingdom. This document states that the god Osiris is tattooed all over his body with a small pattern, which indicates that the ancient Egyptians used tattoo. They wanted to resemble the gods, who, according to legend, were also tattooed.

ANO LE TUA – In the first tattoo session the height to which the tattoo will rise is decided (Ano le Tua), this is always such that the top of the design will show above the lavalava. Then theva'a, pula tama and

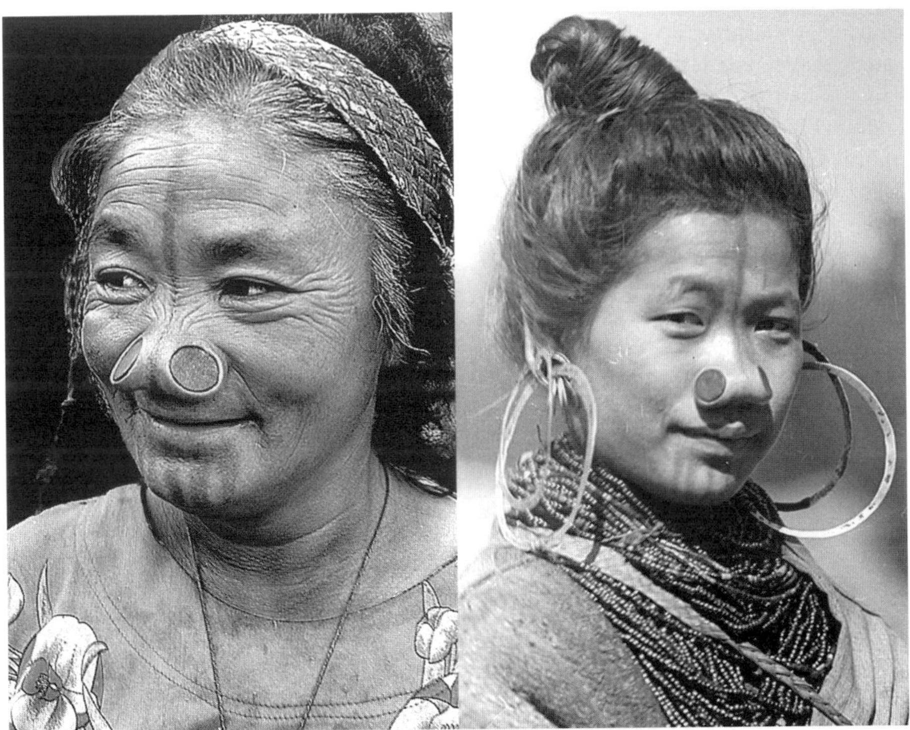

Apatani womans from North East India, with traditional facial tattoos and nose plugs, beaded necklaces and large hoop earrings

pula tele are outlined and the design filled in, Samoa.

ANU – mallet, which beat the chisel into the tattoo, it was an ordinary stick ofcoconut wood, island of Mangaia.

ÄO – tattoo, Marshall Islands.

AOTEAROA - Maory term for New Zealand.

APATANI TRIBE – The Apatanis are a major ethnic group residing in the valleys of Ziro in Arunachal Pradesh, in northeastern India. The tattoos, called tiipe in the Apatani language, on a woman usually run from the top of the forehead to the tip of the nose, complemented by five strips starting from the edge of the bottom lip to the end of the chin. Some also pierced their noses and over the course of time larger nose-plugs made of cane called yaping huto would be placed. The ink that was used, is basically soot (called chinyu) collected from the bottom of heavily-used cooking utensils. And no fancy tattoo needles here; what was used as a 'needle' was made by tying together a bunch of three-headed thorns called iimo-tre. A small stick hammer called empiia yakho helped produce the necessary pressure to pierce the skin and hammer in the ink.

APIAKÁ – Amazonian tribe who live in western Brazil. Men were tattooed by women who used tucum thorns. The pattern consisted of three lines extending

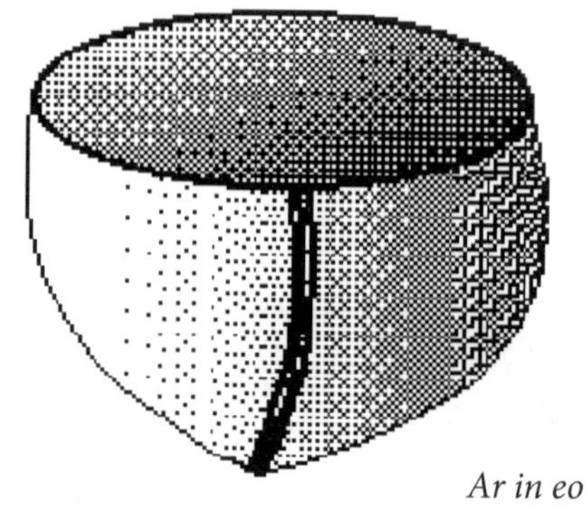

Ar in eo

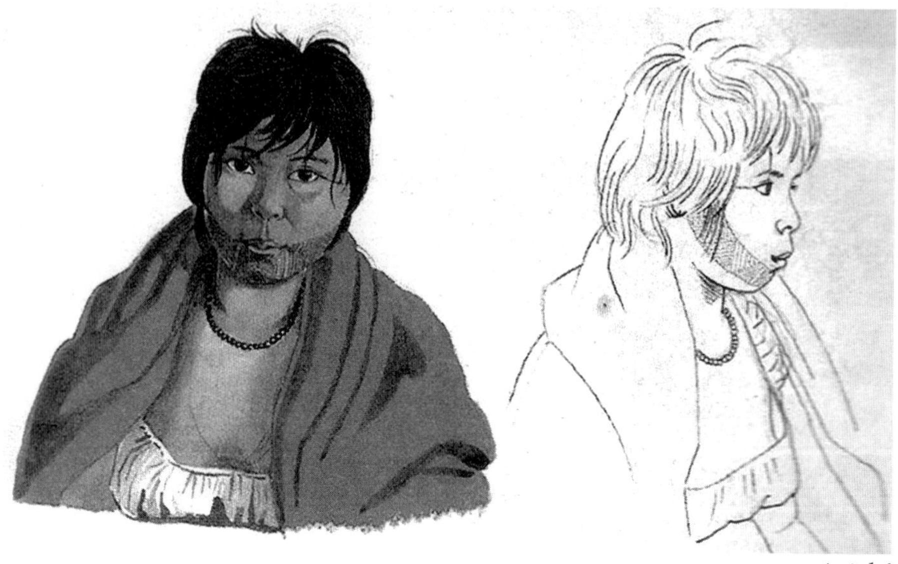

Apiaká

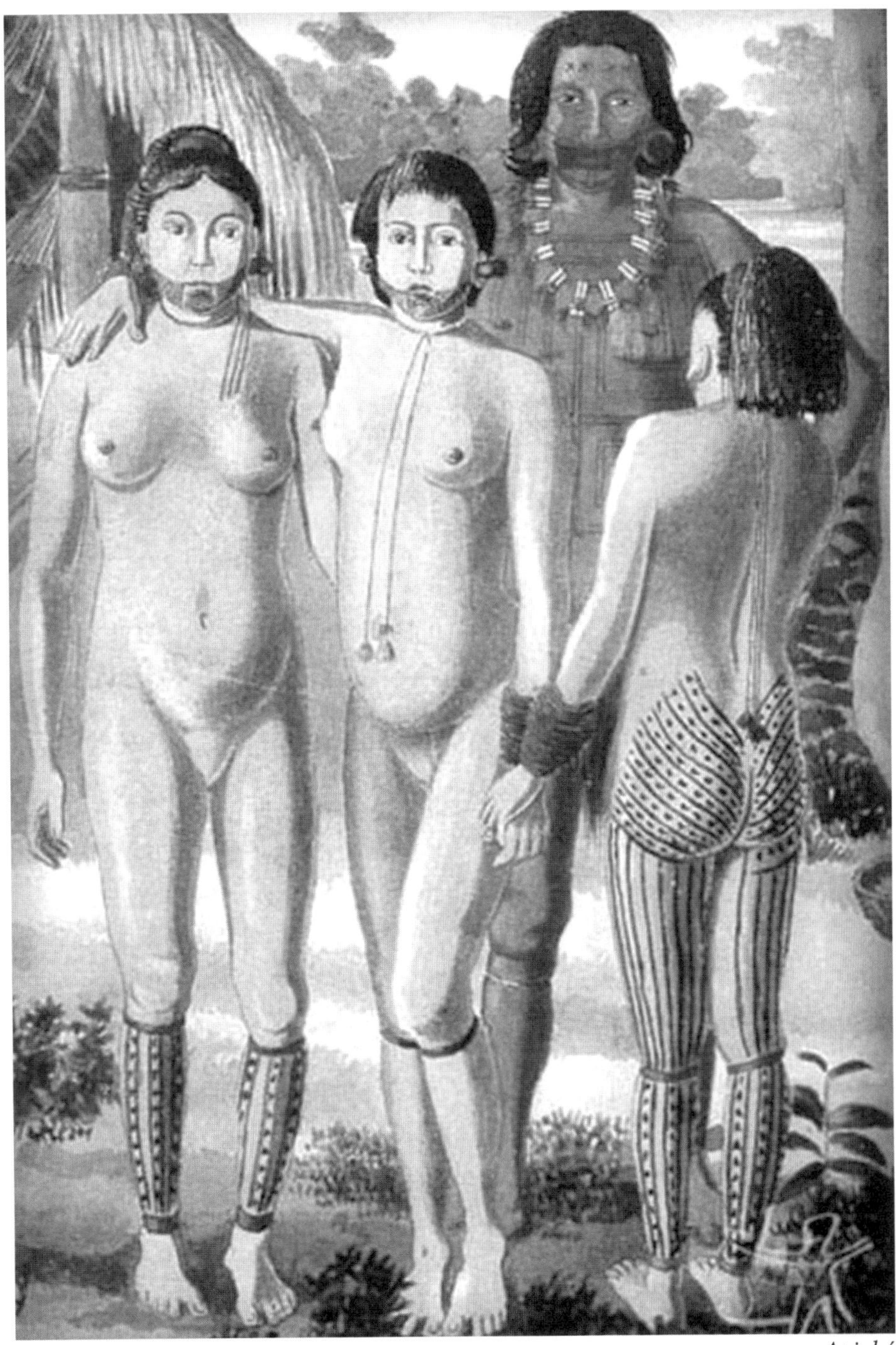

Apiaká

from each ear, one to a little below the nose, one to a corner of the mouth, one to the chin. At the age of 14, the tattooing was completed with a rectangle around the mouth, a symbol indicating that the wearer could eat human flesh. The designs tattooed on the body are said to have illustrated their war and hunting deeds. According to Florence, these included parallel right angles on their chest and abdomen, and crude representations of animals, fish, men, and women on their arms and legs. A young man had the figure of a jaguar (?) on his right arm and a man on his left. The women's tattooing was done after marriage, and consisted only of a rectangle on the chin, with a band running to the ears.

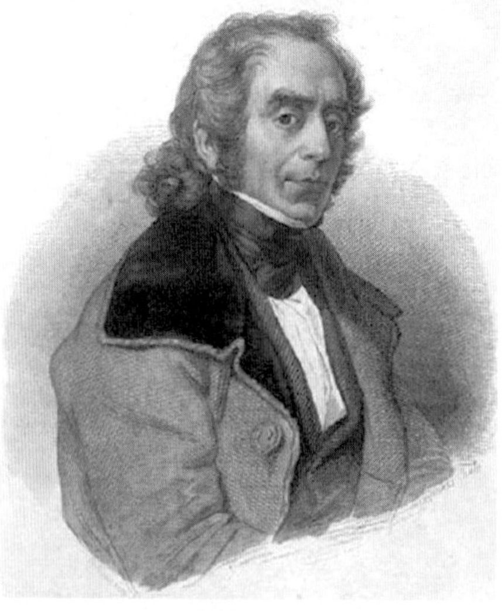

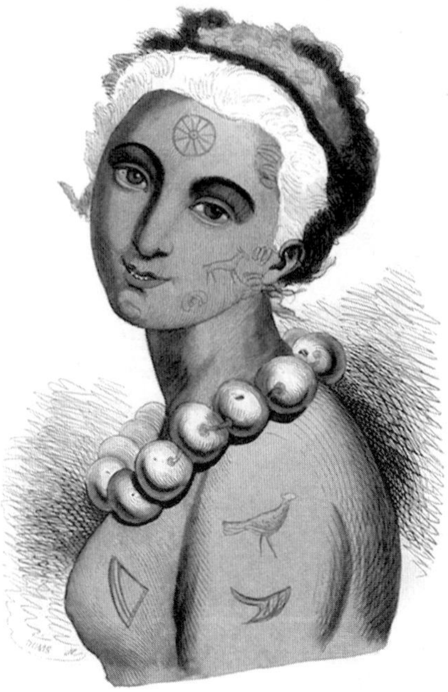

Tattooed girl by Jaques

AR IN EO – large container for tattoo color, half of coconut shell to dip tattoo chisel, Marshall Islands.

AR IN JEJE – The pigment container consisted of half a coconut shell. Two types of containers are distinguished, large ones (ar in eo)to dip in the tattooing chisel and small ones (ar in jeje) for the drawing brush, Marshall Islands.

ARAGO, JAQUES – 1790 – 1855, a French writer, traveler and painter who wrote about the Hawaiian tattoo.

ARAPAHO – The term Arapaho is a Crow word signifying "tattooed on the breast." Their tribal mark was three equidistant blue punctures on the breast. The fingers of one hand touch the breast in different parts, to indicate the tattooing of that part in points.

AREOI - or Areoitx, a secret society which originated in Tahiti and later extended its influence to other South Pacific islands. To its ranks both sexes were admitted. The society was primarily of a religious character. Members styled themselves descendants of Orc-Tetifa,

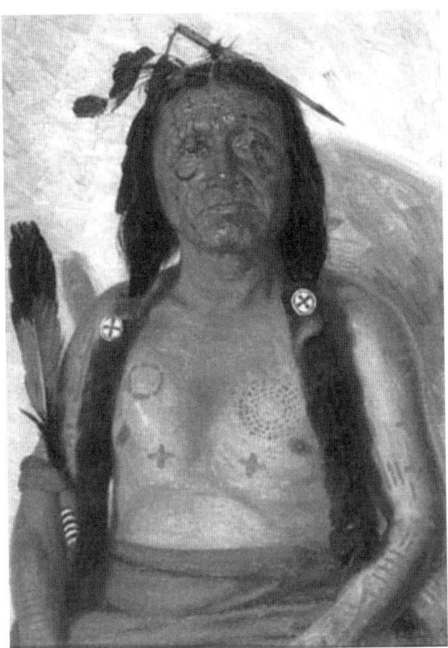

Chief Black Coyote, Arapaho Tribe

the Polynesian god, and were divided into seven or more grades, each having its characteristic tattooing. Chiefs were at once qualified for the highest grade, but ordinary members attained promotion only through initiatory rites. The Areois enjoyed great privileges, and were considered as depositaries of knowledge and as mediators between God and man. They were feared, too, as ministers of the taboo and were entitled to pronounce a kind of excommunication for offences against its rules. The chief religious purpose of the society was the worship of the generative powers of nature, and the ritual and ceremonies of initiation were grossly licentious. But the Areois were also a social force. They aimed at communism in all things. The women members were common property; the period of cohabitation was limited to three days, and the female Arcois were bound by oath at initiation to strangle at birth any child born to them. If, however, the infant was allowed to survive half an hour only, it was spared; but to have the right of keeping it the mother must find a male Areoi willing to adopt it. The Areois travelled about, devoting their whole time to feasting, dancing, and debauchery, varied by elaborate realistic stage presentments of the lives and loves of gods and legendary heroes.

ARII RII – chieftains in Tahiti. During the baptism of the chieftain's firstborn child, all members of the Arii nui clan made several deep incisions into their forehead at the appointed moment. They joined the blood that busted out from the wounds together and blend it with coconut milk. Then everyone dipped a palm twig into this red-white fluid and smeared a face of the new born with it.

ARIKI – paramount chief, high chief, chieftain, lord, leader, aristocrat, first-born in a high ranking family - qualities of a leader is a concern for the integrity and prosperity of the people, the land, the language and other cultural treasures (e.g. oratory and song poetry), and an aggressive and sustained response to outside forces that may threaten these, New Zealand.

ARIKI MAU - as in Polynesia, on Rapa Nui was tattooists - specialists overseen by ariki mau - an untouchable sacred figure.

ARIOI – see ARIORI

ARIORI– a secret community in Polynesia. This community was established on the Raiatea island by the Great God Oro himself who entrusted this great task to his brothers Urutetefe and Orotetefa. In his book The Last Days of Paradise, M. Stingl wrote: “What do Ariori do? On the first glance, they were some kind of a huge all-Polynesian nomadic society. They were visiting individual Polynesian island with their large fleet and performed diverse performances showing tales about the lives and deeds of legendary founder God Oro and other gods, legendary chiefs and Polynesian seafarers. Every Polynesian man or woman could become the member of the community. Airori were divided into several classes which differed in clothing, but especially the extent of tattoo. A novice (Poo) – a candidate – had no tattoos. Ohemara – the members of the second class – were allowed to have a circle tattooed around their ankles. Otoro – the members of the third class – had a line tattooed on the left buttlock cheek. Nuova – the fourth class – its members had two to three small figures tattooed on one of their shoulders. The members of the fifth class were entitled to tattoo the whole lower part of their bodies. The sixth class had a right to tattoo their arms from shoulders to finger tips. The seventh class was the last one and their members could tattoo their legs from the knees below.

ARIOI´I - social class in Tahiti, term for clan leaders, and tattoo motifs corresponded to this, which they could have tattooed. There were 8 degrees -

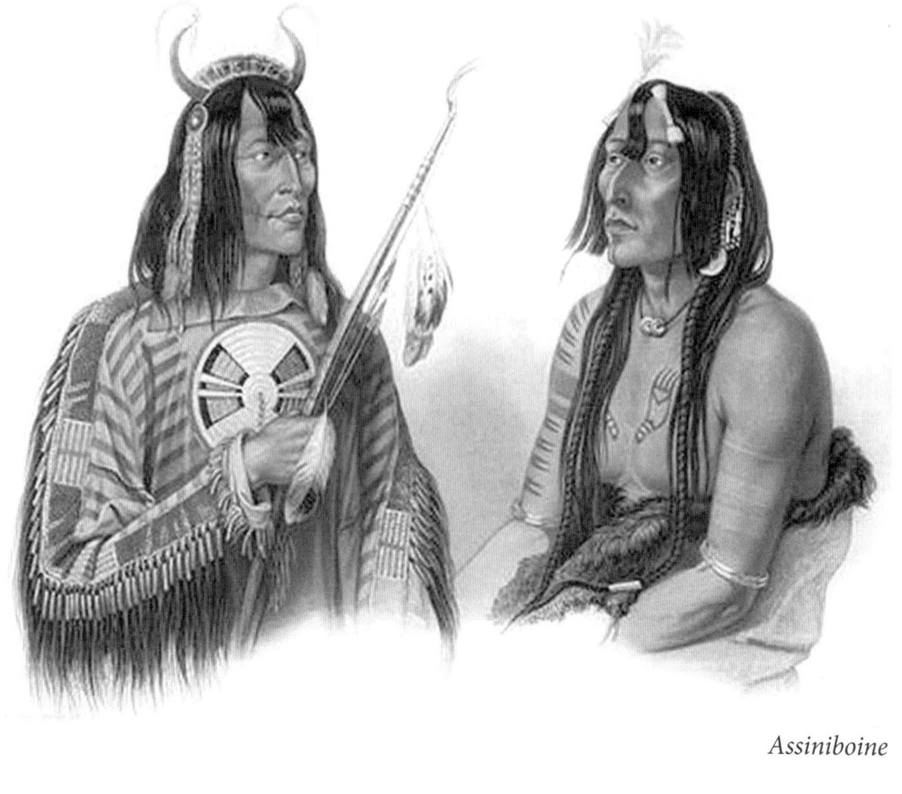

Assiniboine

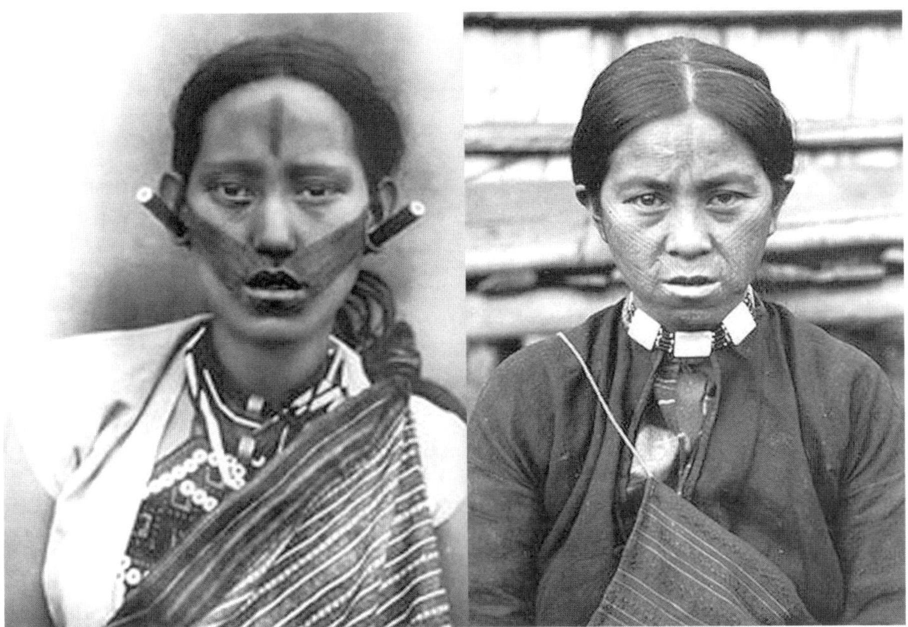

Atayal tribal woman (right) from Taiwan with tattoo on her face as a symbol of maturity, which was a tradition for both males and females. Atayal women with intricate facial tattooing, ca. 1900 (left)

I.Avae Parai, II. Harotea, III. Taputu or ha'aputu, IV. Oti'ore, V. Hu'a, VI. Atoro., VII. Ohe mara a VIII. Tara tutu.

ARJAN – Thai tattoo master.

AS-HUDSK – tattooed in lines (striped), North American tribe.

AS-TLETL – tattooed, North American tribe.

ASÁF – a term for a bird whose bones were used for the tattoo comb – see NIN ÁNIS

ASAI-HIKAE– see HIKAE

ASHLUSLAYS - tribe on the Loir Rio Pilcomayo tattoo the girl at puberty, but never the boys.

ASS-SAS-SOOT – term for tattoo, Cree, North America.

ASS-SAS-SOO-WAYO – tattooing process, Cree, North America.

ASSINIBOINE TRIBE – Tattooing is much practised by all these tribes, and a great variety of figures are thus painted, sometimes in spots on the forehead, stripes on the cheeks and chin, rings on the arms and wrists.

It is usually done on females at the age od 12 to 14 years, is only exhibited on them in the form of a round spot in the middle of the forehead, stripes from the corners and middle of the mouth down to the chin, occasionally tranversely over the cheek, and rings around the wrist and upper parts of the arms. Men are tattooed entire after having struck their first enemy, but smaller marks of this kind are also only ornamental. The material employed and the modus operandi are

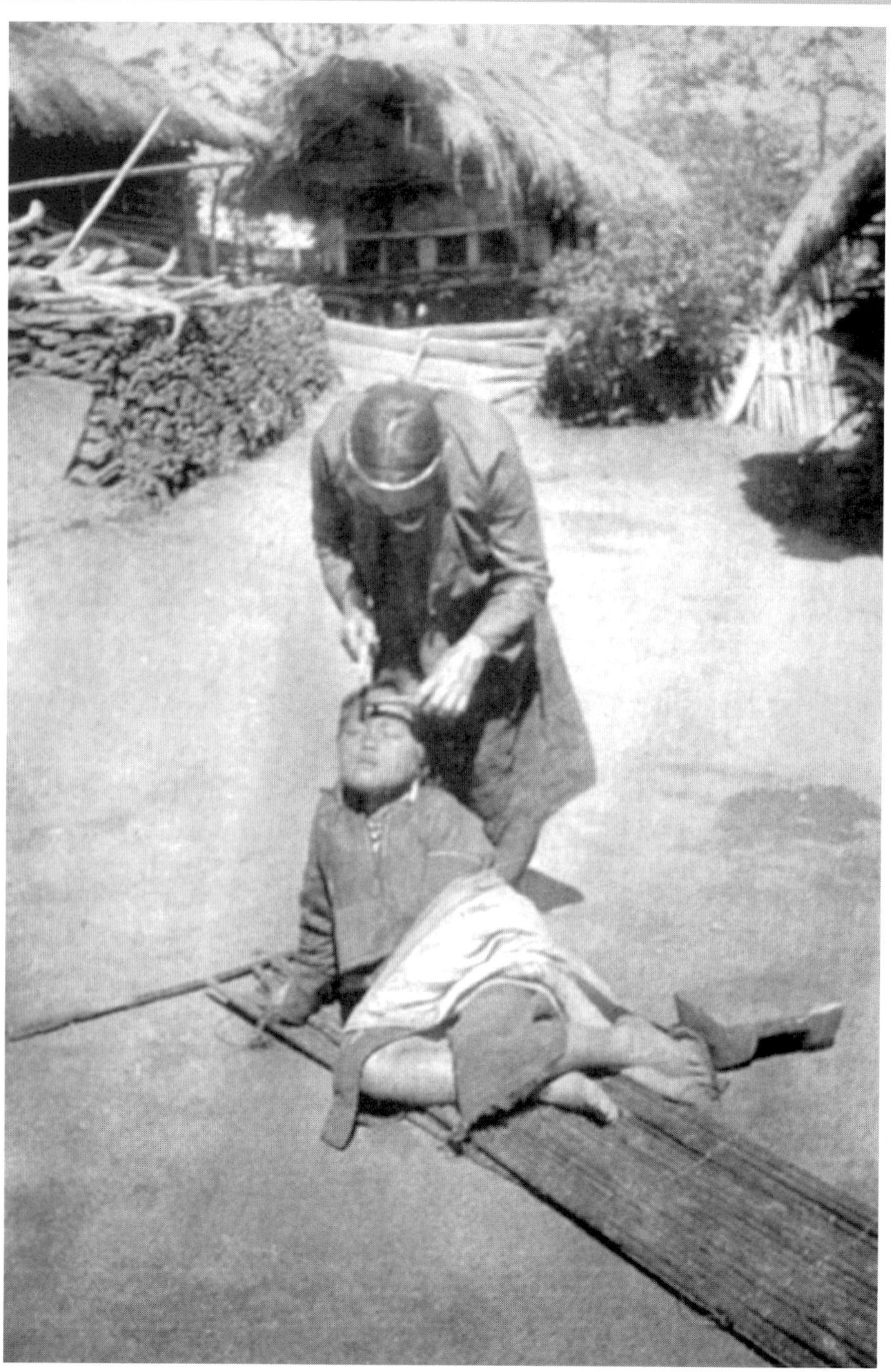

An Atayal tattooist at work with atok, 1910

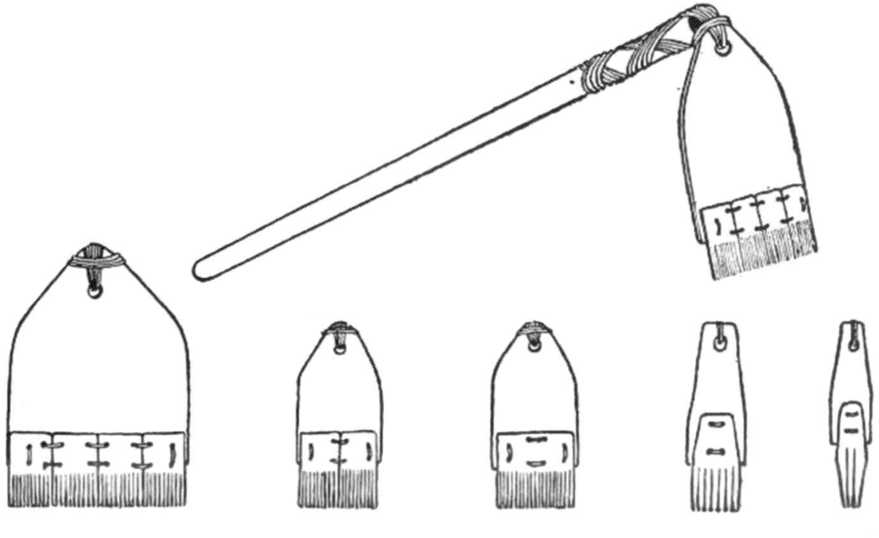

Au

as follows: Red willow and cedar wood are burned to charcoal, pulverized, and mixed with a little water. This is the blue coloring matter. From four to six porcupine quills or needles are tied together with sinew. There are enveloped in split feathers; wrapping with sinew, until a stiff pencil about the size of a goose quill is had, with the quills or needles projecting at the end. One of the priests or divining men is then presented with a horse and requested to operate. At the same time a feast of dried berries is prepared, and a considerable number of elderly men invited to drum and sing. When all are assembled the feast is eaten with much solemnity and invocations to the supernatural powers.

The person to be tattooed is then placed on his back, beign stripped naked, and the operator beign informed of the extent of the design to be represented, proceeds to mark an outline with the ink, which, if correct, is punctured with the instrument above albed to, so as to draw blood, filling up the punctures with the coloring matter as he ges along, by doping the needles therein and applying them. The drumming and singing is kept up all the time of the operation which, with occasional stops to smoke or eat, ossupies from two to two and a half days, hen the whole of the breast and both arms are to be tattooed; and the price for the operation is generally a horse for each day´s work.

AST-LETL-SHID– I tattoo, North American tribe.

ASTIKTON – {to astikton} is probably for {to me estikhthai}: but possibly the meaning may be, "those who are not so marked (not tattooed) are of low birth."

ATA or AETA PEOPLE – only account of tattooing among the Ata tells that they used a short knife that "cuts" or "incises" ("pretty deep cuts or incisions") instead of punctures, Philippine.

A

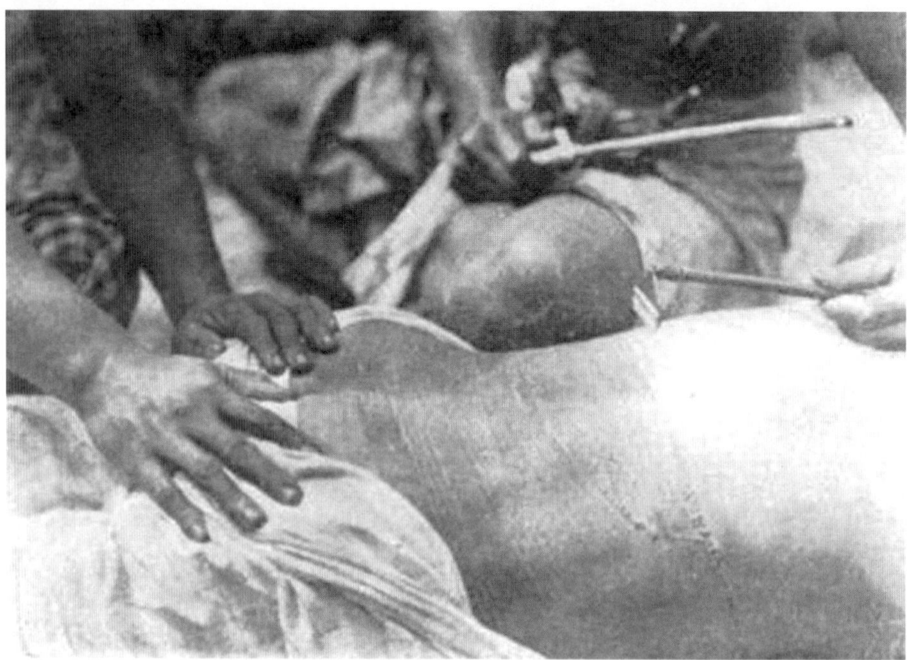

A: Tattooing process: artist holds tattooing instrument in left hand and mallet in right ;patient shows scabbing on back from previous stage of tattooing; assistant holds cloth

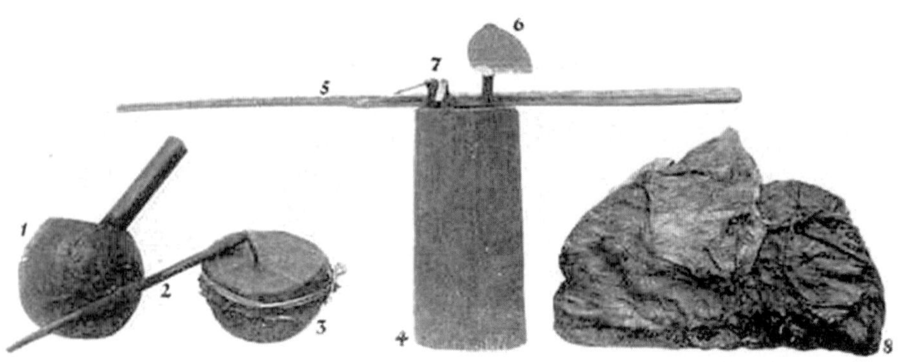

B: Tattooing implements: 1, coconut mortar with wooden pestle for preparing pigment; 2, medium-sized tattooing comb (au songi aso tetele); 3, palette of green talo leaf tied over half coconut shell; 4, cylindrical instrument container (tunuma) made of pandanus wood; 5, tattooing mallet (sausau) made of coconut leaf midrib, with handle on the left cut away for grip; 6, large au tapulu instrument for filling in the dark areas; 7, two small au fa'atala instruments for making dotted lines; 8, old bark cloth used as sponges after dipping in water.

ATAATA MAI TE TAUKUKA - the chest tattoo gleams, Bellona.

ATA PANGARA – men who displayed the star as a sign of their bravery were known as "ata pangara." See MADU

ATA NGORA - men who displayed the star as a sign of their bravery were known as "ata pangara" or people of renown and belonged to the "ata ngora" class. See MADU

ATAGA – shard used in tattoos (wiping soot with it?), Motu tribe.

ATAHU - when the tattoo was completed, the priest came and recited a spell called atahu, the Maori.

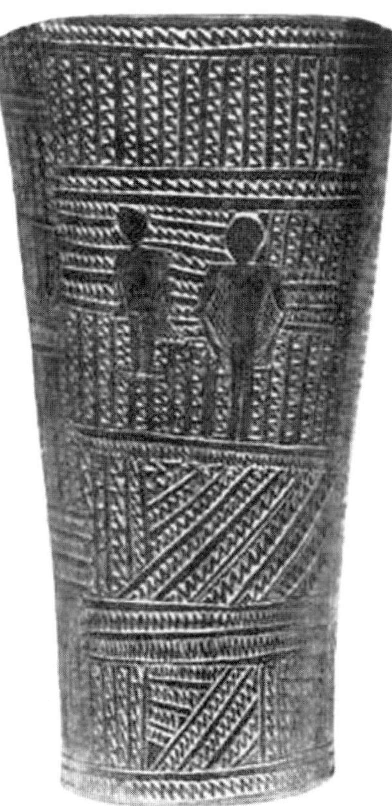

Ato laupaogo

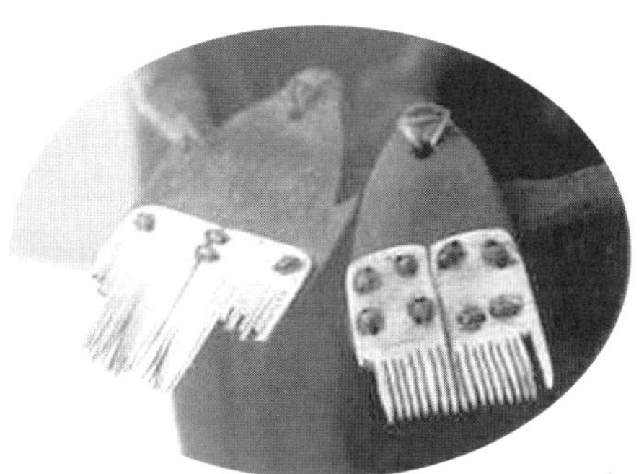

Autapulu

ATAYAL TRIBE – indigenous groups in southern Asia, practise fascial tattooing. Tattoos were once given only by male tattooists known as patasan. The family of the youngster would discover the date for the tattoo in a dream, which would be interpreted by a shaman. The tattoo would then be given with tree thorns – which were bundled together and lashed to a stick called an atok, which, then tapped into the skin using a hammer called a totsin, would open the skin.

ATE – part of tattoo mallet. A small two-pointed bone of any seagull (suri na manu) is inserted in a length of reed (ate) and lightly tapped with a small stick made of any hardwood Santa Anna a Santa Catalina.

ATOK– The tattooing was performed using a group of needles lashed to a stick called atok tapped into the skin using a hammer called totsin. Has 4 to 16 needles arranged in a row and attached to a wooden rod of about 1.5 cm in diameter and 15 cm in length.

ATSUGEWI – see ACHOMAWI

AU - The handle ('au) is made of fau and ranges in length from about 9.5 inches in the smallest instrument to 11.75 inches in the largest. The handle is rounded or elliptical in cross section for most of its course. In the smallest instrument it is 0.3 inches in diameter and 0.4 inches in the largest. The proximal end of the handle is cut away on the under surface for 3 to 3.5 inches for about half its thickness. This gives a flat under surface for the grip and renders the handle less liable to roll in the hand during the operation. The distal end is cut away slightly on the under side to form a slot for the upper end of the turtle shell plate. When the plate is fitted in position, its front surface lies flush with the end surface of the handle. Some handles are made of thin bamboo.

AUFA´AILA – see next

AU FA´ATALA –The au fa'atala, or au mono, is the narrowest instrument. In five instruments measured, the width of the bone plate ranged from 5.5 to 7 mm. and the depth from 22 to 26 mm. The turtle shell plate ranged from 6 to 7 mm. in width and 32 to 45 mm. in depth. The width between the points of the outside teeth ranged from 3 to 4 mm. and the number of teeth from 4 to 6. The overlap between the two plates is from 11 to 13 mm. The implement as its name implies is used for making points (tola) or dots. It is also the instrument used for measuring off the commencement of the work on the back, Samoa.

AU MIRO – painted pattern, Maori.

AU MOGO - This small mallet is used to make very tiny marks.

AU SONGI ASO LAITIITI - tattoo instrument in Borneo. Had a bone plate 22 mm. deep and 9 mm. at its widest part. The turtle shell plate was 28 mm. deep and 9 mm. wide. The overlap between the two was 11 mm. The width across the teeth was 6 mm. and the number was 10. The instrument was used for making fine lines.

AU SONGI ASO TETELE – tattoo instrument, Borneo, measured, the bone plate ranged in depth from 20 to 31 mm. and in width from 15 to 20 mm. The turtle shell plate ranged in depth from 30 to 50 mm and in width from 15 to 20 mm. The width across the teeth ranged between 13 and 17 mm and the number of teeth from 14 to 20. The overlap was

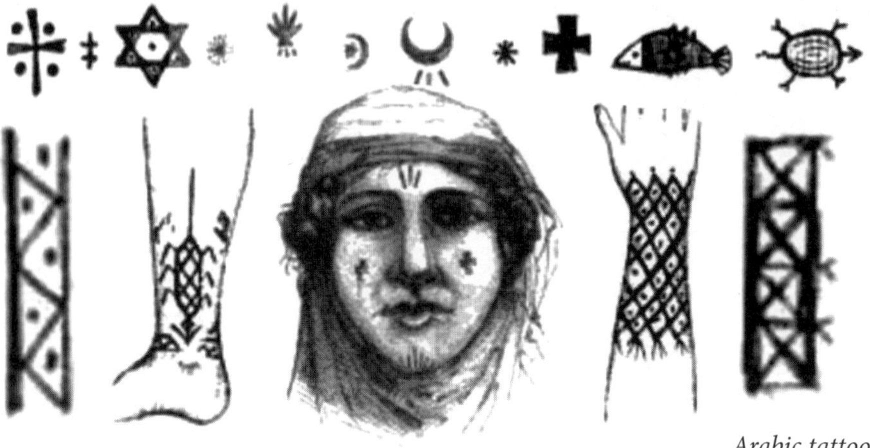

Arabic tattoo

11 to 14 mm. The use was for making the wider or thicker lines.

´AU TA - term for hand tattoo tools, Samoa.

AUSOLO - are the assistants that work with the tattooist while receiving a traditional Samoan Tatau (Pe'a). There are often four assistants: two holding the person, one stretching the skin, and one wiping the blood away with a damp cloth.

AUSOLO - are the assistants that work with the tattooist while receiving a traditional Samoan Tatau (Pe'a). There are often four assistants: two holding the person, one stretching the skin, and one wiping the blood away with a damp cloth.

AUSOGI´ASO LAITITI – a tattoo comb used for making thin lines, Samoa.

AUSOGI´ASO TELE – a tattoo comb used for making thick lines, Samoa.

AUSONI´ASO - (pestle soni), a tattoo comb for line aso.

AUTAFA – see AUTAPULU

AUTAPULU - Of the two au tapulu measured, the bone plates were 17 and 19 mm. deep and 53 and 55 mm. wide. The turtle shell plates were 63 and 68 mm. deep and 53 and 56 mm wide. They were 49 and 52 mm. in width across the teeth and there were 41 and 46 teeth. The overlap between the two plates was 9 mm in both instances. The greater width of the au tapulu is obtained by joining three or four sections of bone together. It is used for filling in the field in the dark parts of the tattooing. Of the four types of implement, the au songi aso tetele is the one in most use. Though there are four main types of instrument, the artist may have more than one variety of each by using different widths of even the same type, Borneo.

AUTUFUGA– tufuga normally had up to six assistants ('autufuga). Each one had a particular responsibility. One apprentice mixed the pigments, another wiped the blood, and another kept the tool black with pigment. One assistant ensured that the ta tau combs remained sharp, another stretched the client's skin, and another uttered chants to instill the necessary courage in the patient so that he would endure the sacred designs of his fellow men and ancestors, Samoa.

AVAE PARAI – the highest degree of society ario'i, literally "black legs" or "stained feet". Their sign was a tattoo that led from heel to groin. The black-legs were also called arioi maro ´ura or ‚red-feather-girdle Arioi'. This referred to their privilege of wearing a red cloth, imitative of the red-feather girdle which signified the highest chiefly status.

AWA – root from which is the prepared drink kava.

AWE – soot (for tattooing) , Maori.

AWEMBA - The Awemba make large crosses on the back, reaching from the top of the blade-bone on either side to the point of the hip on the opposite side. As a rule, both sexes are tattooed, and the tattoo marks certainly serve both among the Anyanja, the Wa-yao, and the Wankonde to distinguish tribe from tribe.

AWHETO HOTETE – A charcoal of the burnt and powdered resin of the kauri pine, or a charcoal made of one of the many kinds of veronicas, was used as a pigment for tattooing. Maori knew of the Awheto Hotete, or vegetable caterpillar, which was burned and powdered.

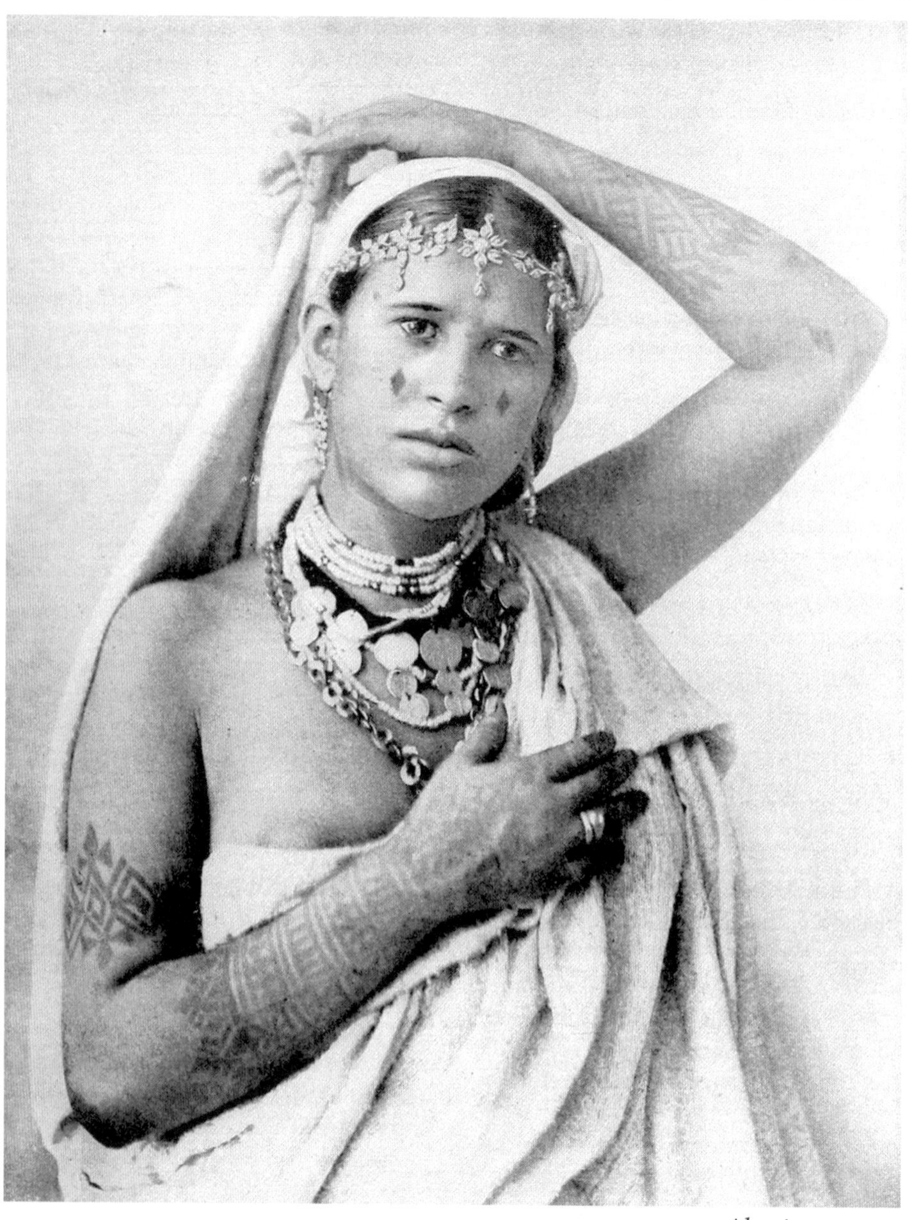

Algerian woman

AYHASSOWE- tattooing, Objiway tribe.

AZANDE TRIBE - the Western branch of the Azandé, who have adopted the lateral tattoo mark of the race they have conquered, the Mobanghi.

AŽAF– bird bones (Tachypetes) used to make tattoo needles, Mortlock Island.

BA- THONGA - A tribe living in East Africa. Young tribe girls are tattooed on the shoulder and abdomen. The shoulder is decorated with triangles, while the abdomen is decorated with more elaborate designs.

BA´E ´UNGI or B.UGI – tattooed legs; one with tattooed legs, Bellona.

BADAGA - All the women are tattooed on the forehead, Nilgiri mountaind, India.

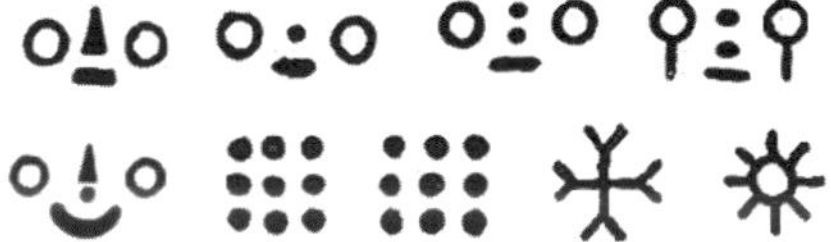

BADNIN – tattoo master in Baiga tribe was known as Badnin.

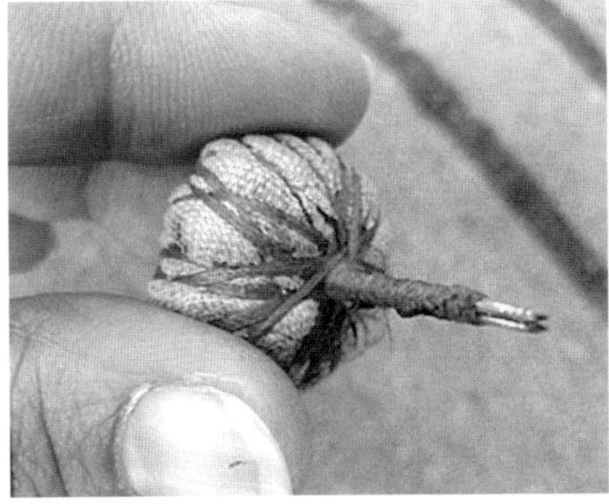

BAIGA – tribe of central India is one of the most primitive tribe of India. Tattooing is an integral part of their lifestyle.The body of a Baiga women is extensively tattooed. There is a specific tattoo for every part and the tattooing is done by people of Badi-Badanin community.

BAIKABOKU - special Japanese tattoo paint in the shade of plum blossom (Plum Flower Ink).

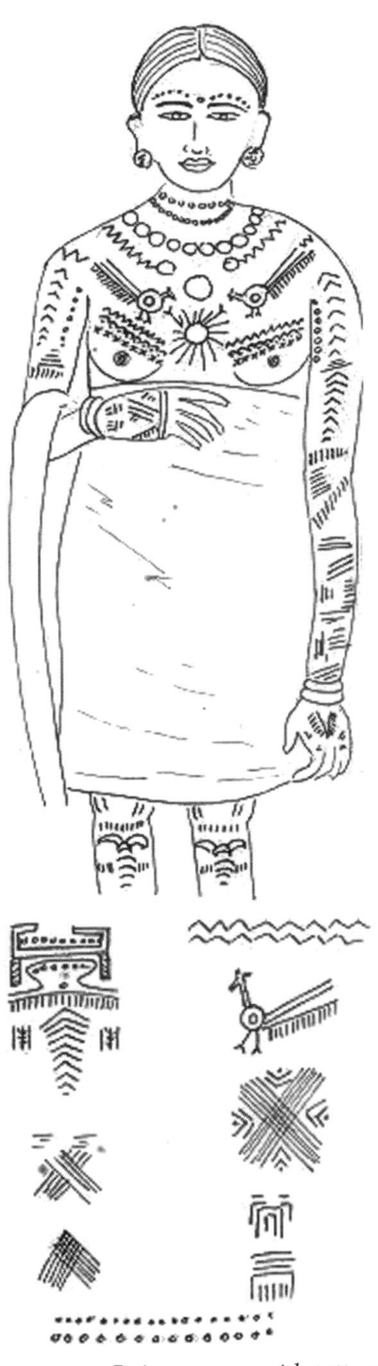

Baiga women with tattoos

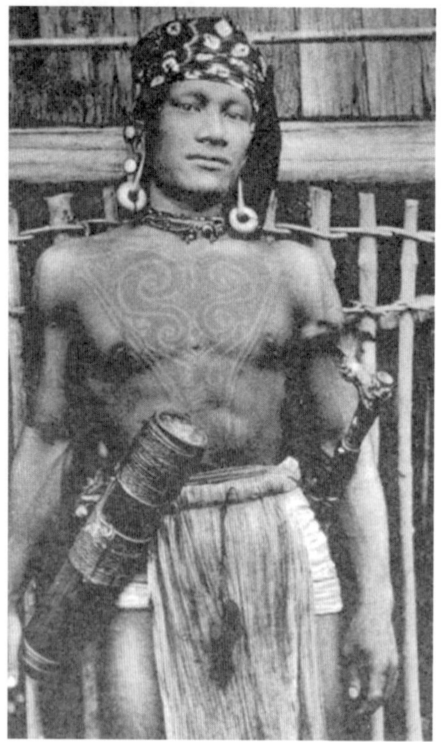

Baketan

BAKANGA PEOPLE – an African tribe whose members use several body modifications. Tattoos, scarification – in women mainly in the face – and teeth sharpening. In his book Mezi nejmenšími lidmi světa (Among the Smallest People in the World), Pavel Šebesta describes: "A dental technician had two tools: a tiny chisel and a pounder. A patient stretched out on his back, rested his head on a log, closed his eyes, strummed Sanzi on a zither between his legs. The technician would gently chop off his teeth to look like small needles, other times to be just slightly pointed." According to the Bakangas, they do it to not look like animals. Women also pierce their upper lip and insert a round ivory disc into it. Šebesta wrote: "Even at the earliest age, the girls' upper lips are pierced. With terror in my eyes, I once saw how midgets proceeds during such operation: several women gathered around a girl, about 12 years old. They held her so tightly she cannot move at all, while an old woman pierced her upper lip with an oiled spike. The little one screamed out of pain. No sooner than the hole was open, the women started to pass thin and gradually thicker banana stalks through there, until it was finally possible to pass a coarse shaft of an arrow, at the end of which a transverse stick was attached, so that it did not fall. In a similar way, women pierce their earlobes, into which they

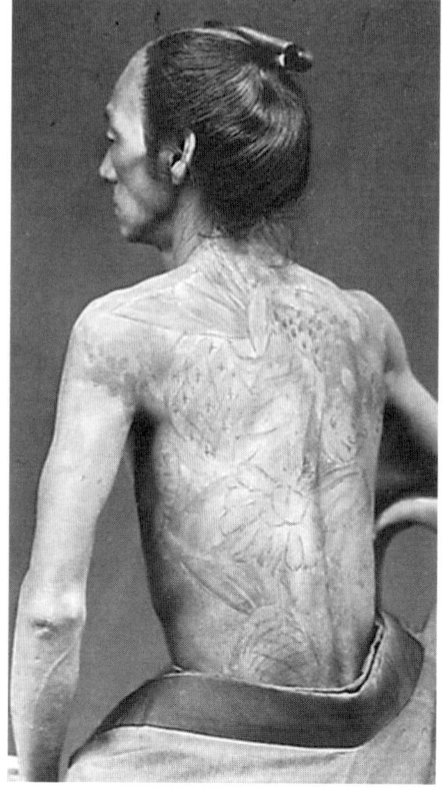

Bakuto

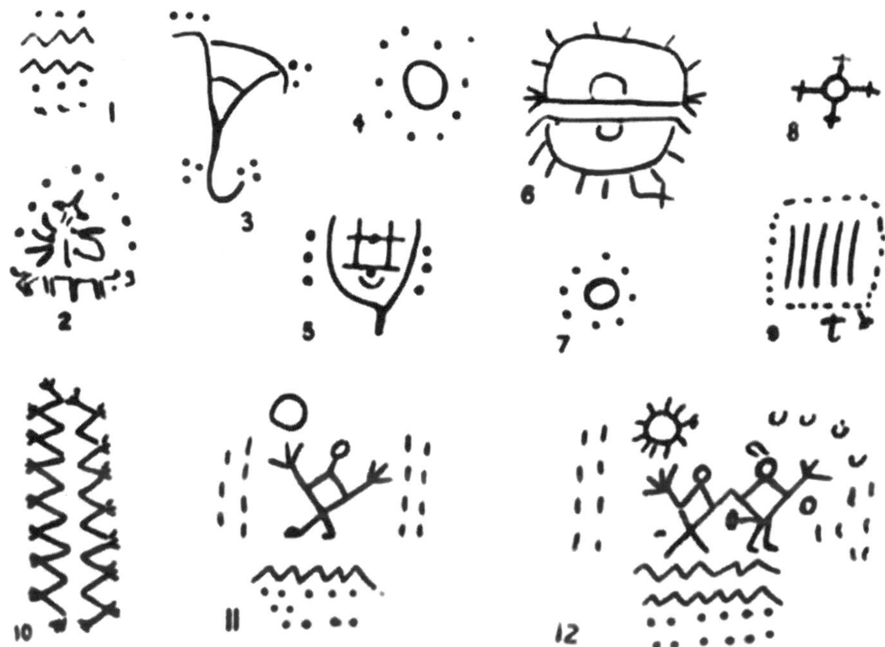

No. 1 measured 7 cm, from top to botám, the strokes represent a skorpion, and dots jasmine flowers. No. 2 represents „flowers", No.3. on the left forearm, represents a skorpion and some stars. No.4, also on the left forearm, represents the moo nand stars. No. 5 is known by the name Kattari. No.6, of uncertain signifikance, was tattooed on the left forearm. No.7, which closely resembles No.3 on the right forearm of the same individual. No. 8, 9, and 10are unexplained. No.11, tattooed on the left deltoid, represents a man, the moon, stars, and a necklace. No. 12 was tattooed on both shoulders of one man.

insert leaves as a decoration. Time after time, I met men and women who had a porcupine spike passed through their nasal septum. As most Pygmy people, all Bakanga men are circumcised.

BAKETAN - (also known as Bukitan) is a small tribe living in the state of Sarawak, Malaysia and East Kalimantan of Indonesia. They are found in Bintulu district of Sarawak. Not many of these people are left due to intermarriages with other tribes.

BAKUTO - were itinerant gamblers active in Japan from the 18th century to the mid-20th century. They were one of two forerunners (the other being tekiya, or peddlers) to modern Japanese organized crime syndicates called yakuza.

BANA – The native name for the tattooing is bana. Gojjias people, India.

BANAWE – Banaue (or alternatively spelled as Banawe), officially the Municipality of Banaue is a 4th class municipality in the province of Ifugao, practised tattooing, Philippines.

BANGALA – an african tribe, used free

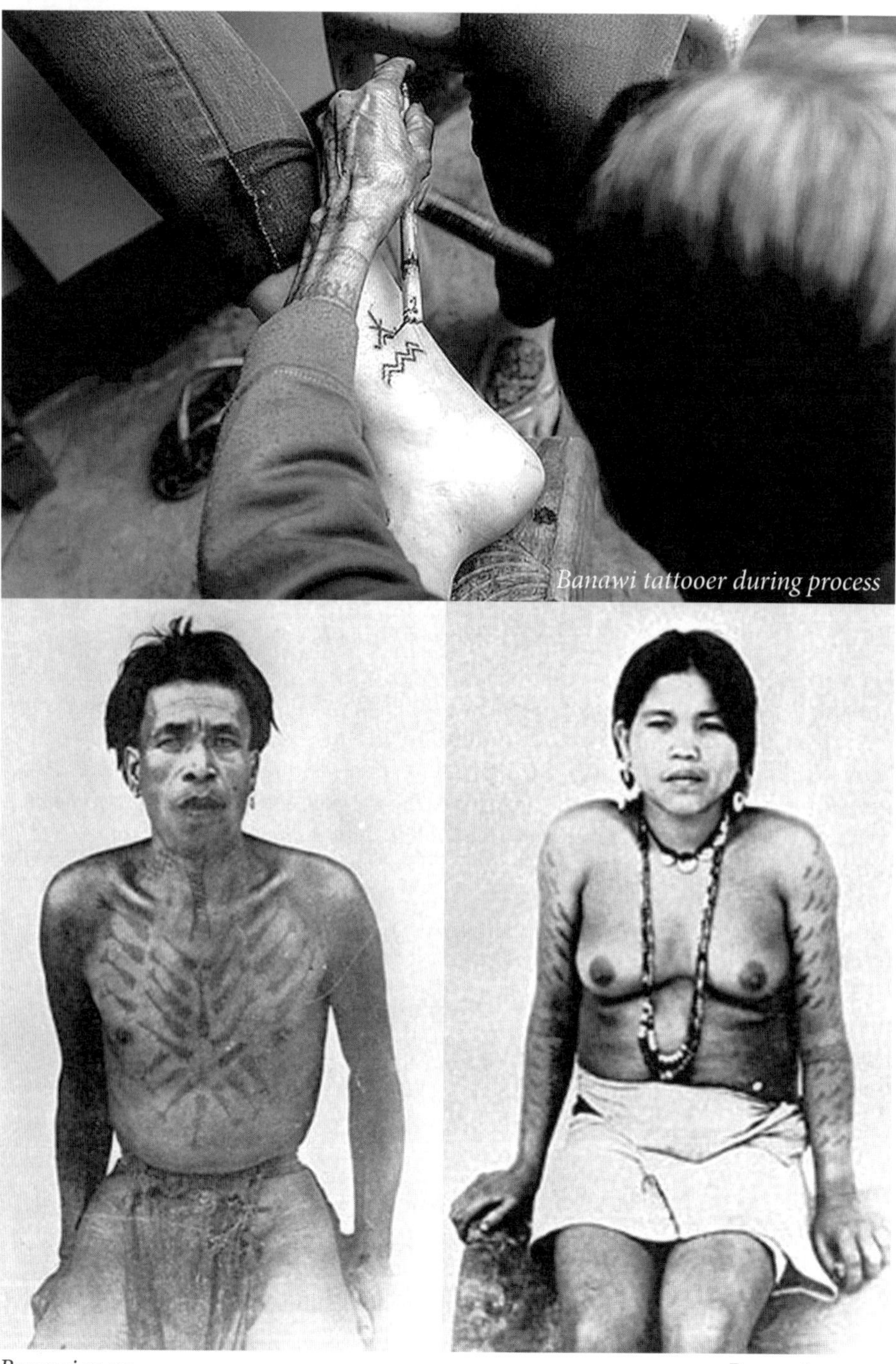

Banawi tattooer during process

Banawi man

Banawi woman

kinds of tattooing among them. 1. A Single line of elliptical punch-marks running from temple to temple just above the eye-brows. 2. A cock´s comb running from the tip of nose insome, and from between the eye-browns in others, to the crown of the head. 3. A cock´s comb as above plus a palm-leaf on each temple. The second and third tattoos were seen singly and together on men and women, boys and girl, from age of théty-five downwards. Bangale tribe of the Upper Congo River.

BANJARA – gipsy tribes, from the waist upward, they tattooed their skin with flowers.

BANKS, JOSEPH - Sir Joseph Banks (1743-1820), naturalist and patron of

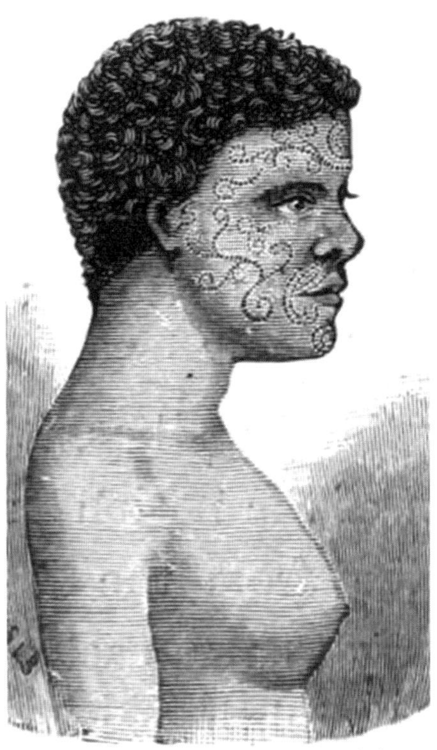

Bashilange

science, was born on 13 February 1743 at Westminster, England. He made collections and observations at Rio de Janeiro, Tierra del Fuego, Tahiti, and during the survey of New Zealand. They took full advantage of landings on the eastern coast of Australia, especially at Botany Bay (28 April–5 May 1770) and at Endeavour River (17 June–3 August).

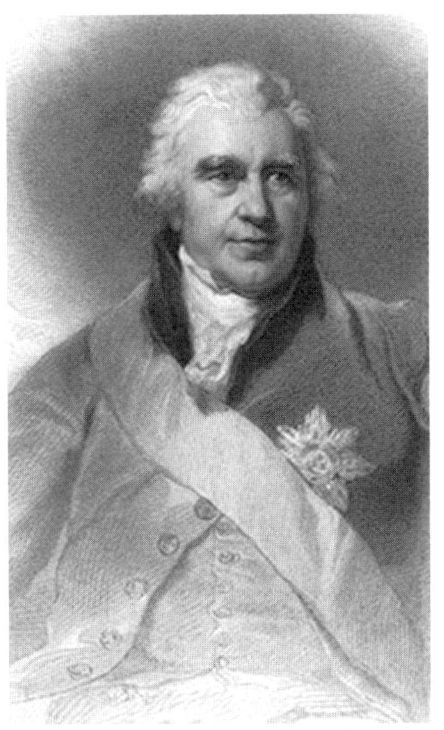

Joseph Banks

BAPOTO - African tribe practicing scar-tattoo. Three rows of lines that are the size of a pea, descending from the root of the hair to the end of the nose.

BARAKA – Many traditional forms of tattoo can be associated with the indigenous Berber peoples. Living in Morocco, Algeria, Libya, Tunisia, and

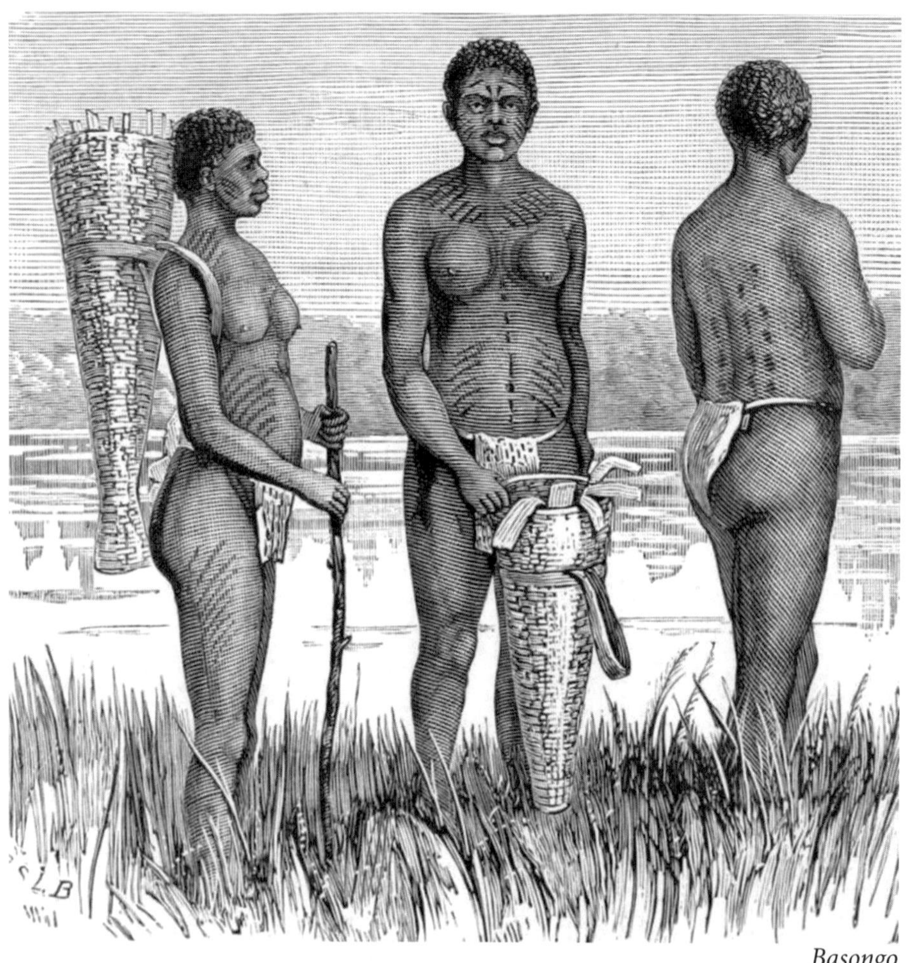

Basongo

Egypt, the Berbers are Muslims who follow a specialized branch of that religion, but one that retains elements of atavistic animism: a belief that supernatural energy (baraka) resides in all things. Berber tattoo designs hold the sacred energy of baraka which can be used to deal with the darker forces of life, to cure illnesses and to protect oneself against spirits called jnoun (singular: jinn).

BARAWAN - is a tribe living in Borneo. The same name is given to their traditional tattoo design, which was placed on a man's chest or shoulders.

BASHILANGE TRIBE – A tribe from the Congo, men wear a spiral-shaped chest scar tattoo, marking fertility and the ability to enter into marriage. Women also practiced tattoos.

BASMAH - Method of producing a tattoo pigments, Berbers. see KOHL

BASONGO – ethnic group in Congo

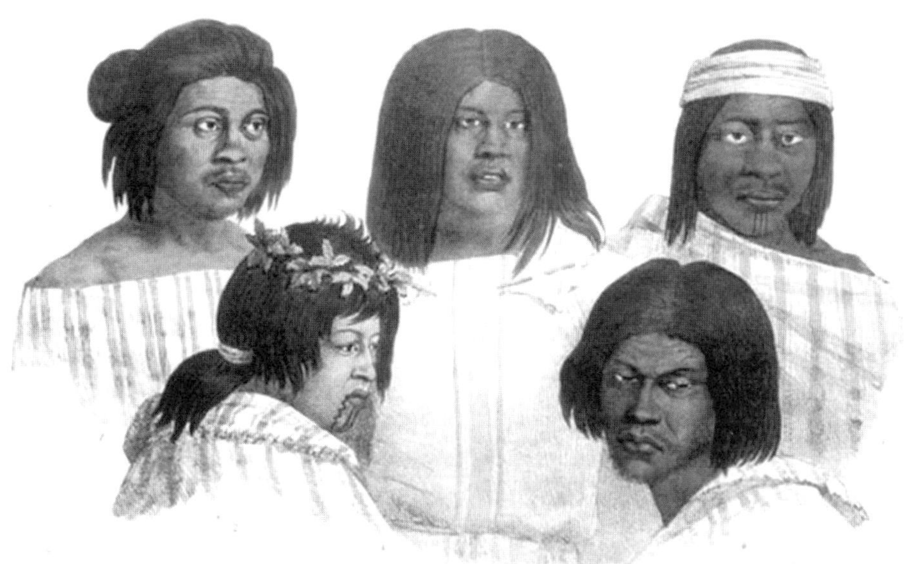

Bayogoula

near the Kasai river practicing tattooing and chiseling teeth.

BASTAR – tribes practicing tattoos, India.

BATANGA – D.G. Rutherfor wrote: Tattooing evidently originated in certain marks being applied to the face and other parts of the body in order to distinguish the members of one tribe from those of another. The same marks would be used for both sexes, but as the tendency to ornamentation became developer, they would be apt to observe some artistic method in marking them. The men tattooed their children at an early age, but as the girl approached a marriageable age they addend, on their own account, various ornamentations to those already existing. As example that tattooing in its later stages is regarded as an increase of beauty, West Tropical Africa.

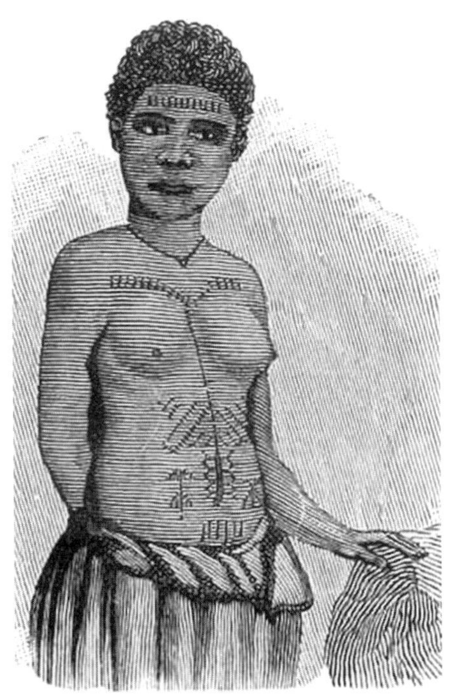

Bateke

BATEKE TRIBE - The Teke people (Tio/Bateke) are an amalgamation of

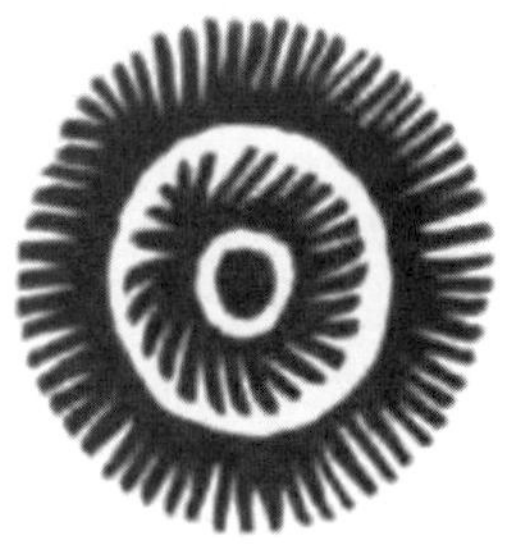

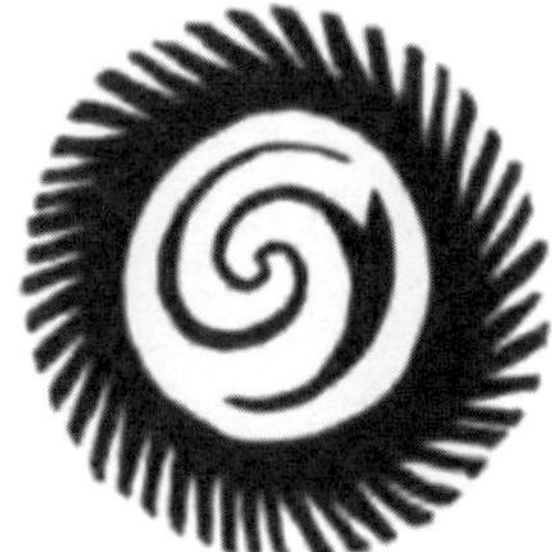

Berawan motifs

agriculturalist, skillful fishermen and powerful river-traders as well as Kiteke-speaking ethnic group of Central African Bantu origins. They practice tattoos. In particular, longitudinal cuts on both sides of the face, close together.

BAWANG DAHA – Lake of Blood, Dayaks, Borneo. If a man died in battle and was tattooed, he was allowed to live near Bawang Daha in the afterlife.

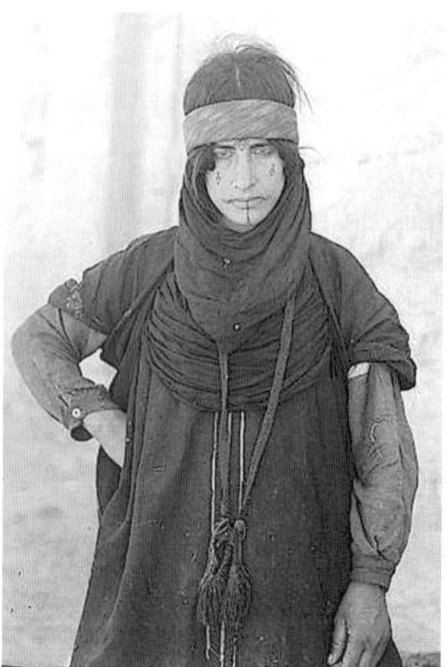

Tattooed Bedouin woman of Alkarak, Jordan, 1907

Untattooed people were unlucky.

BAWDITHADA - The most potent and dangerous magical tattoo a Burmese culd wear the Bawdithada. The bearer of this tattoo would be permanently protected from swords of firearms, and would be the strongest, fastest and bravest man in the world.

BAYAKA PEOPLE – see AKA

BAYOGOULA TRIBE – some had the body tattooed and marked with black on the face and breast, North America.

BAZOKO TRIBE - Their tattoo is very distinctive, almost exclusively reserved for the face; it is composed of large points delimiting the lips in parallel lines and covering the chin and forehead, Congo.

BEDOUIN - women tattooed themselves all over their bodies – wrists, ankles, breasts, thighs – facial tattoos were the most significant as they were visible to the public. Tattoos were most commonly located on several significant spots on the face: dots or symbols above or between the eyebrows, dots on the nose, beauty spots on the cheek and lines and symbols below the lip and on the chin. Tattoos traditionally symbolised protection in battles and wars as well as from spirits and the evil eye. In some

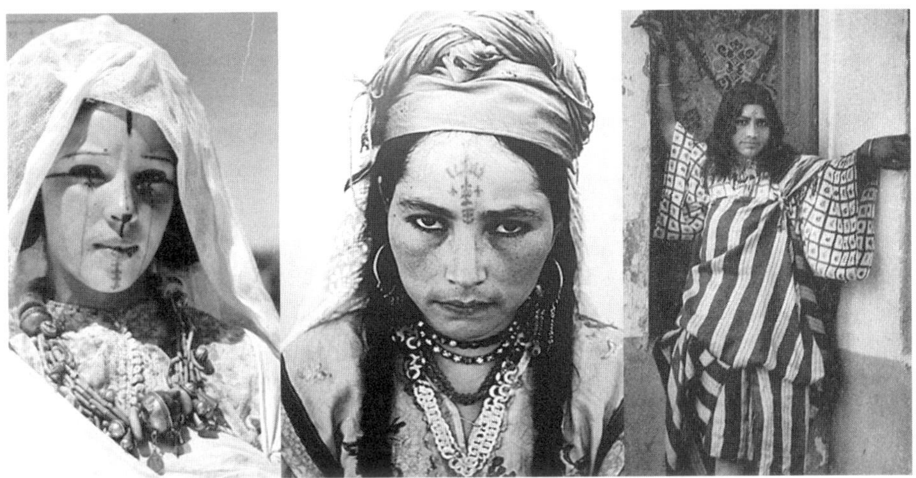

Berber women with tattoos

areas, tattoos were also used for medical purposes; many believed that a combination of dots on the side of the head or above the eyes would heal aches and pains and prevent disease.

BECHIS or BETSIS - The tattooing on the women's faces was different among each tribe or group in this general region, and the Coast Yuki show that they form no exception to this rule. They used fine marks in considerable quantities on the cheeks and chin, but did not employ heavy wide chin-tattooing as did some other tribes. Tattooing was called betsis or bechis and was done only on women both before and after puberty.

BELABELA = tattoo, Sinaugolo Island.

BELLA BELLA – Indian tribe practised tattooing, northwest US coast.

BELLA COOLA – Indian tribe practised tattooing, northwest US coast.

BELTLALA – the name for the tattoo in the Akusha area, Dagestan.

BERAWAN TRIBE - They are part of the Borneo-Kalimantan people cluster within the Malay Peoples affinity bloc. This people group is only found in Malaysia. Their primary language is West Berawan. The primary religion practiced by the Berawan is ethnic religion. Ethnic religion is deeply rooted in a people's ethnic identity and conversion essentially equates to cultural assimilation.

BERBER CULTUR - women were historically tattooed facially. In times pre-dating the arrival of Islam in North Africa the practice was widespread. However since the arrival of the Islamic faith, the belief that to alter a creation of Allah is haram (forbidden) has lead to the almost complete decline of the practice. For important ceremonies and celebrations henna or Harquus are often used to replace the significant symbolism of the tattoo, but on a temporary basis. The placement of Berber Tattoos was often around openings in the body(eyes, nose, mouth, navel and vagina) or upon surfaces of the body which may be perceived as vulnerable (the feet and the hands). These areas of the body were perceived to require protection from the 'Jnoun' (bad spirits) which may try to enter her body and possess her. Many tattoo designs were of a style and placement on the body so as to offer protection from the evil eye. Indeed the name for Berber tattoos is 'Jedwel'- meaning Talisman. Tattoos would be relevant to rites of passage and added at key stages of life.

BES - The earliest known tattoo with a picture of something specific, rather than an abstract pattern, represents the god Bes. Women, especially musicians and dancers, were sometimes depicted with images of the dwarf god Bes on their thighs, in addition to the more traditional geometric patterns. The Egyptians worshipped Bes as a protector of women in labor, children, and the home.

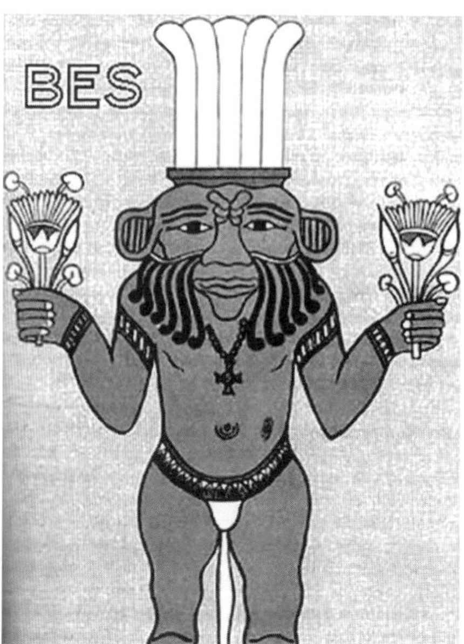

BHUMIA – tribe practicing tattoos in the form of lines and points on the face, and elsewhere on the body, belongs to the Baiga Grou, India.

BIANCHI, ROBERT S. - Respected and quoted expert (Egyptologist) to Egyptian tattoos.

BINI WOMEN – The general mark was a tattoo of three parallel cuts about half an inch long, and placed close together upon both cheeks about half way between the eye and the corner of the mouth. Some added to this ʹbeauty-spotsʹ on the middle of the forehead, vertical lines of similar marks above the eyebrows, and free stripes, or rather broad shallow scars, from above the breast to the stomach.

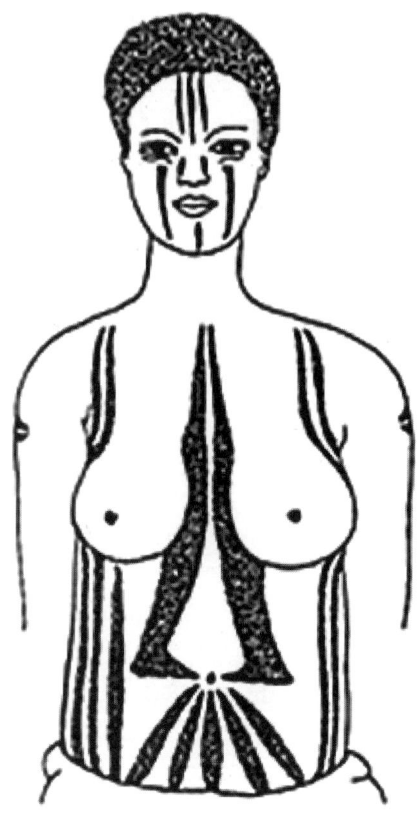

Bini women

BLIGH, WILLIAM – (born September 9, 1754, probably at Plymouth, county of Devon, England—died December 7, 1817, London), English navigator, explorer, and commander of the HMS Bounty at the time of the celebrated mutiny on that ship. He wrote about Tahiti tattoos in his diaries.

BOAS, FRANZ - pioneer of modern anthropology. Often called the "Father of American Anthropology." You can read about Inuit tattooing ih his books.

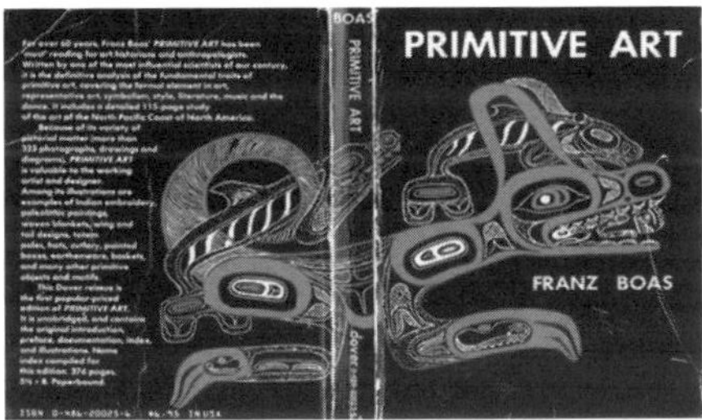

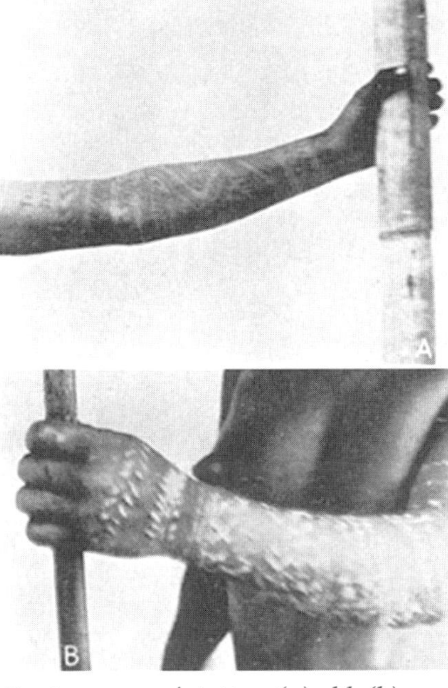

Bontoc woman's tattoo. (a) old; (b) new

BODI PEOPLE – a tribe belonging to the

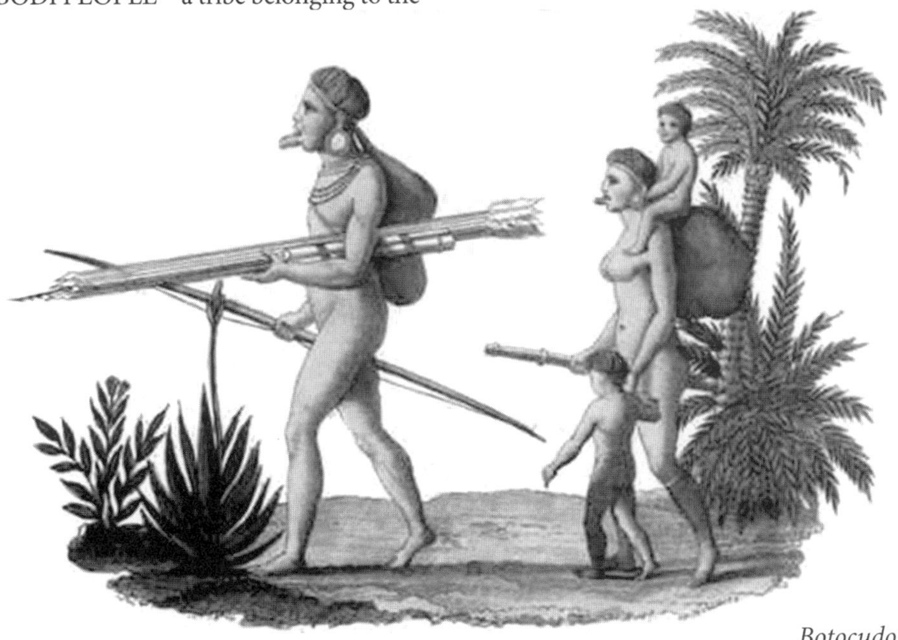

Botocudo

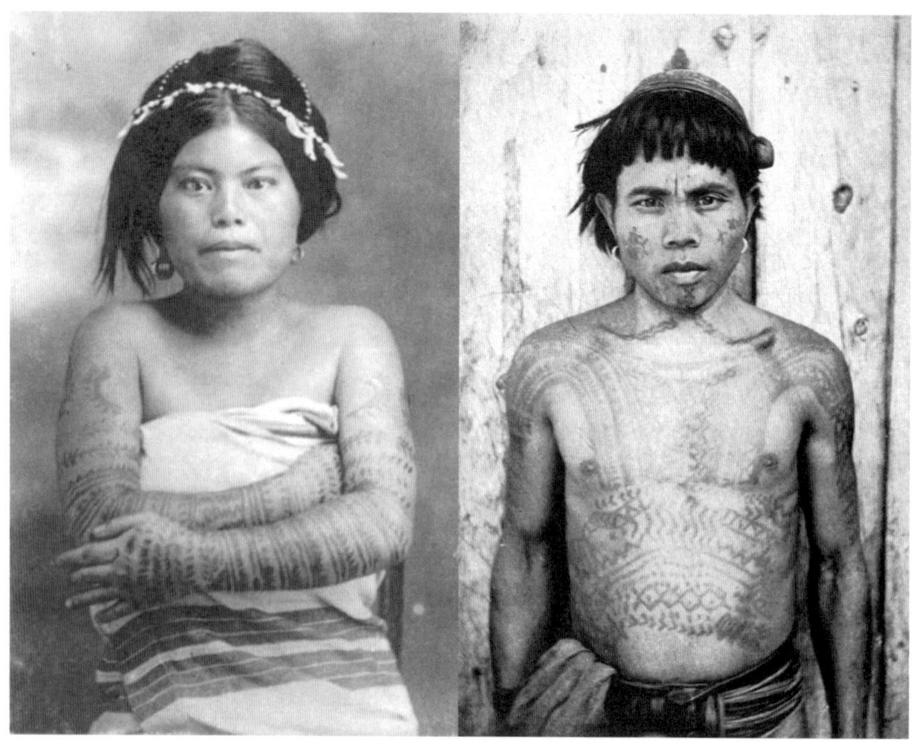

Bontoc

ethnics as the Surma people and the Mursi people. They live naked or half-naked in the bush near the Omo River. Instead of lip plates, they use only a "lip plug". The Bodi's traditions are also different. The most significant one is breeding of so-called "dancing bull". It is a bull chosen at a young age from a herd. Scarification is made on his whole body and throughout his life, he is given a maximum attention. His head is decorated by a special halter with huge boar tusks. On festive occasions, men take those "chosen" bulls and dance with them.

BÖGNI, - During the entire tattooing period, the words emman "man" and körä "woman" were not allowed to be pronounced, but the men had to be called jalak, the women bögni., Marshall Islands.

BOKASHI - Japanese tattoos are distinguished by bokashi or shading-off of a pattern.

BOKUSEKI – calligraphic style of the Buddhist sects known as Zen in Japan and Ch'an in China. This calligraphic form sprang directly from the transplantation during the 12th and 13th centuries of Ch'an Buddhismto Japan, in which country it became known as Zen. Bokuseki became a part of the major artistic flowering associated with Zen Buddhism during the Muromachi period (1338–1573), at which time calligraphy was regarded as an essential cultural

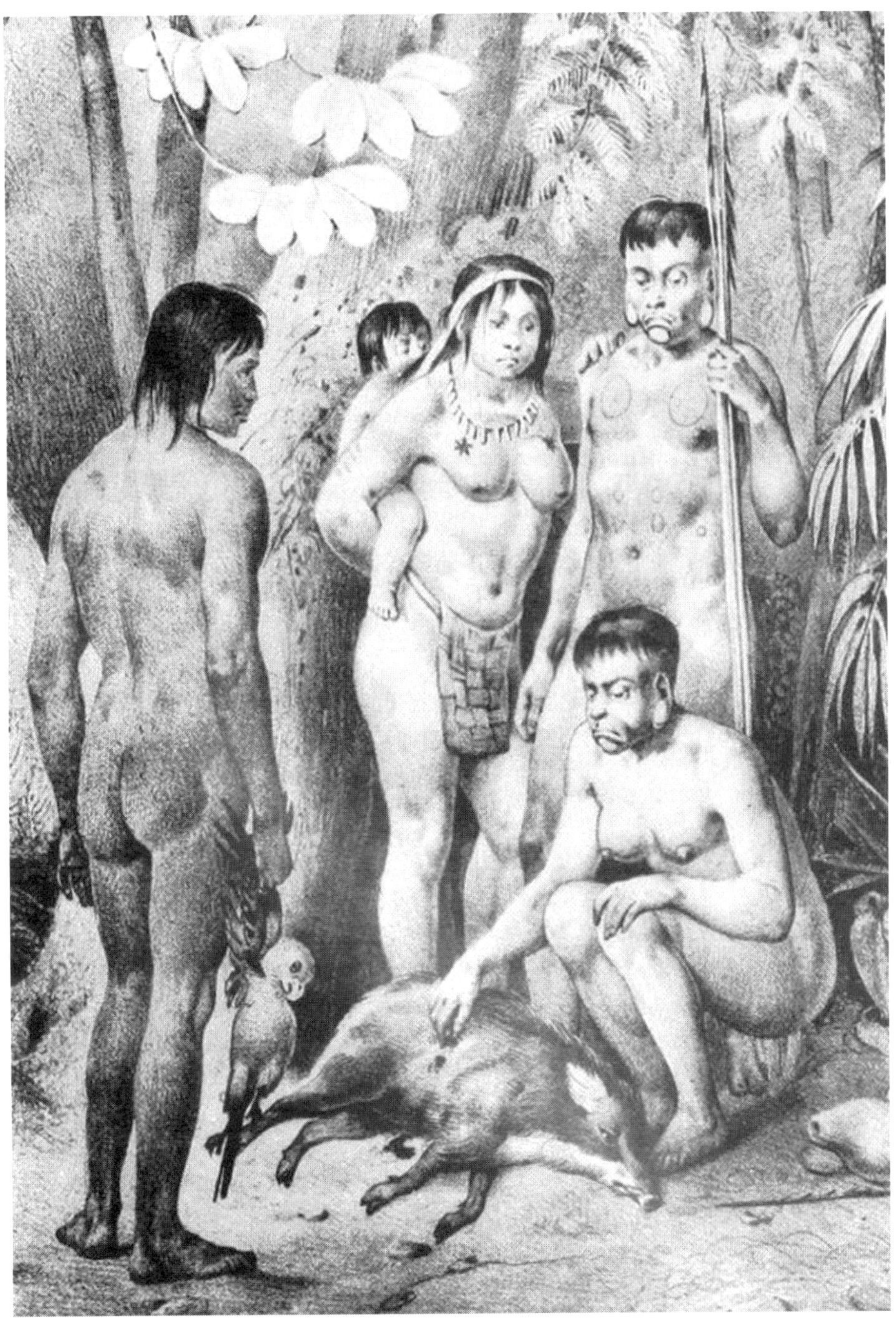

Botocudo

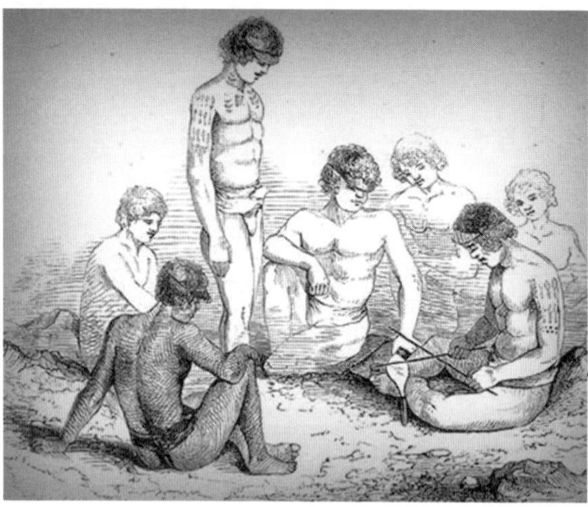

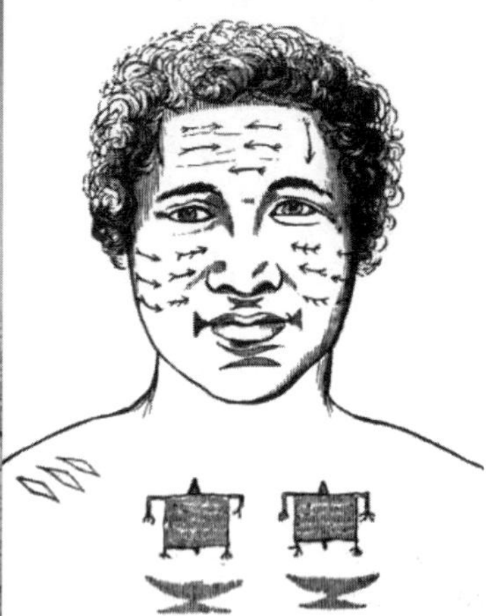

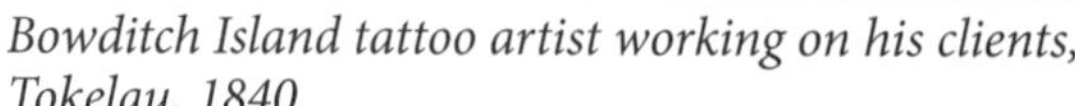

Bowditch Island tattoo artist working on his clients, Tokelau, 1840

Bowditch Island

accoutrement of a distinguished Zen monk.

BOKWI – For the duration of the ceremonies the normal terms for men (mmaan; leo) and women (kora,lio) were emo (tabooed), and the women of men about to be tattooed were called bokwi, while the men of women about to be tattooed were called jomij. A completely tattooed male was also called jomij, Marshall Islands.

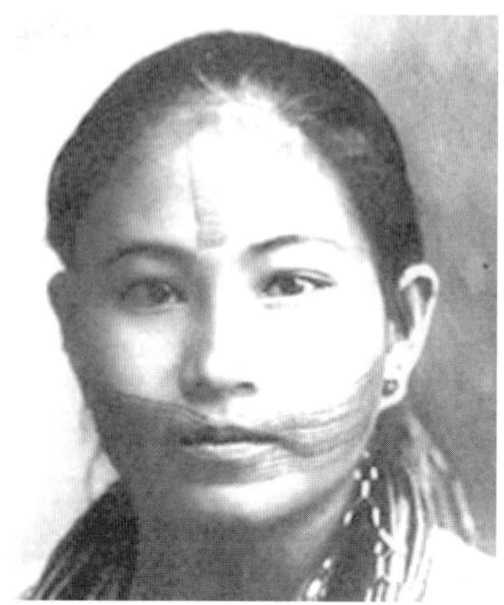

Bunun woman with facial tattooing, ca. 1900

BONOTIA - term for people with komplete tattoo, Karibati tribe.

BONTOK TRIBE – In Bontoc, tattooing was done using ten needles attached to a piece of a water buffalo horn. A similar instrument was collected by Alexander Schadenberg, a German pharmacist who made several expeditions to the Cordilleras between 1886 and 1889. This instrument consisted of a thin piece of carabao horn bent at right angles and furnished on the shorted end with sharp pieces of wire. According to Schadenberg, these needles were placed against the skin and driven in by a stroke with a wooden hammer. When about twenty strokes have thus been made, the wounds were rubbed vigorously with soot. The soot was obtained by burning resinous wood, and a pot was held over the flames to collect the soot. The Bontoc Igorots recognize free kinds of tattoos. First, that

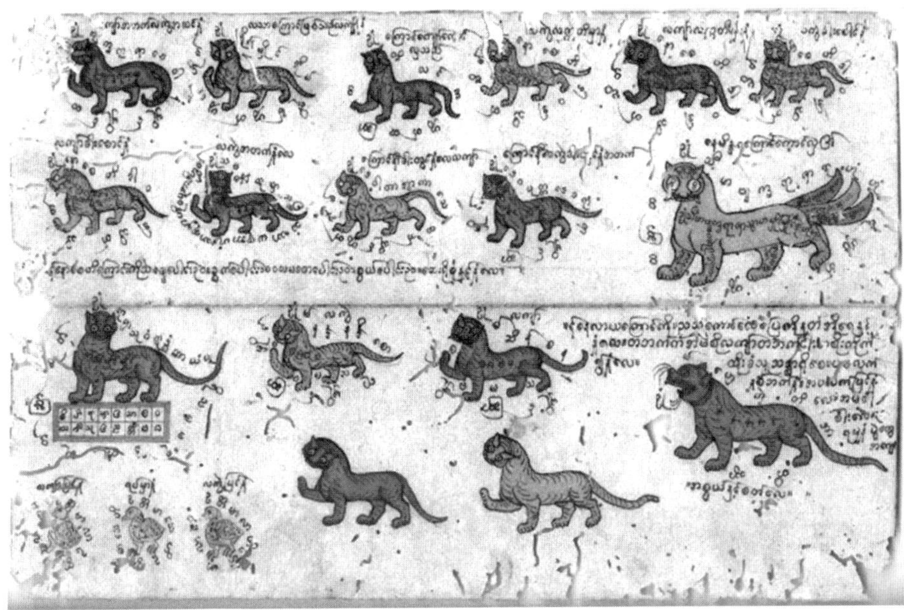

Burnese tattooing manual

on the breast, usually running upward from each nipple, curving out on the shoulders and ending on the upper arms. This indicates that the person so marked has taken ahead. Second, the tattoo on the arms of men and women. Third, all other tattoos of both sexes. The woman was tattooed only on the arms.

BOTOCUDO PEOPLE - South American Indian people who lived in what is now the Brazilian state of Minas Gerais. Practised of tattoo and piercing.

BOUGAINVILLE, LOUIS ANTOINE DE (1729-1811) - was a French admiral and explorer. A contemporary of the British explorer James Cook, he took part in the Seven Years' War in North America and the American Revolutionary War against Britain. Bougainville later gained fame for his expeditions, including a circumnavigation of the globe in a scientific expedition in 1763, the first recorded settlement on the Falkland Islands/Islas Malvinas, and voyages into the Pacific Ocean. Bougainville Island of

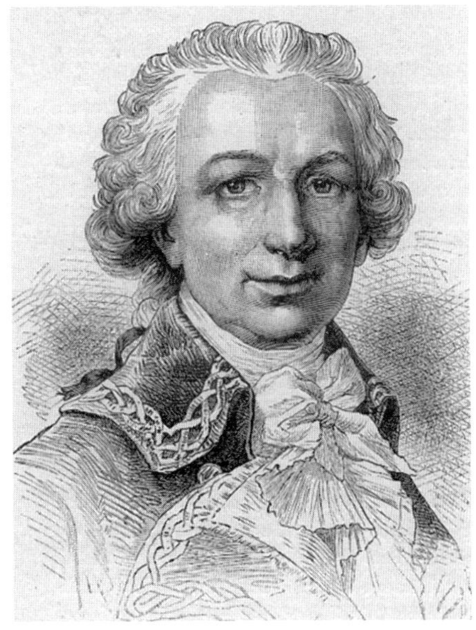

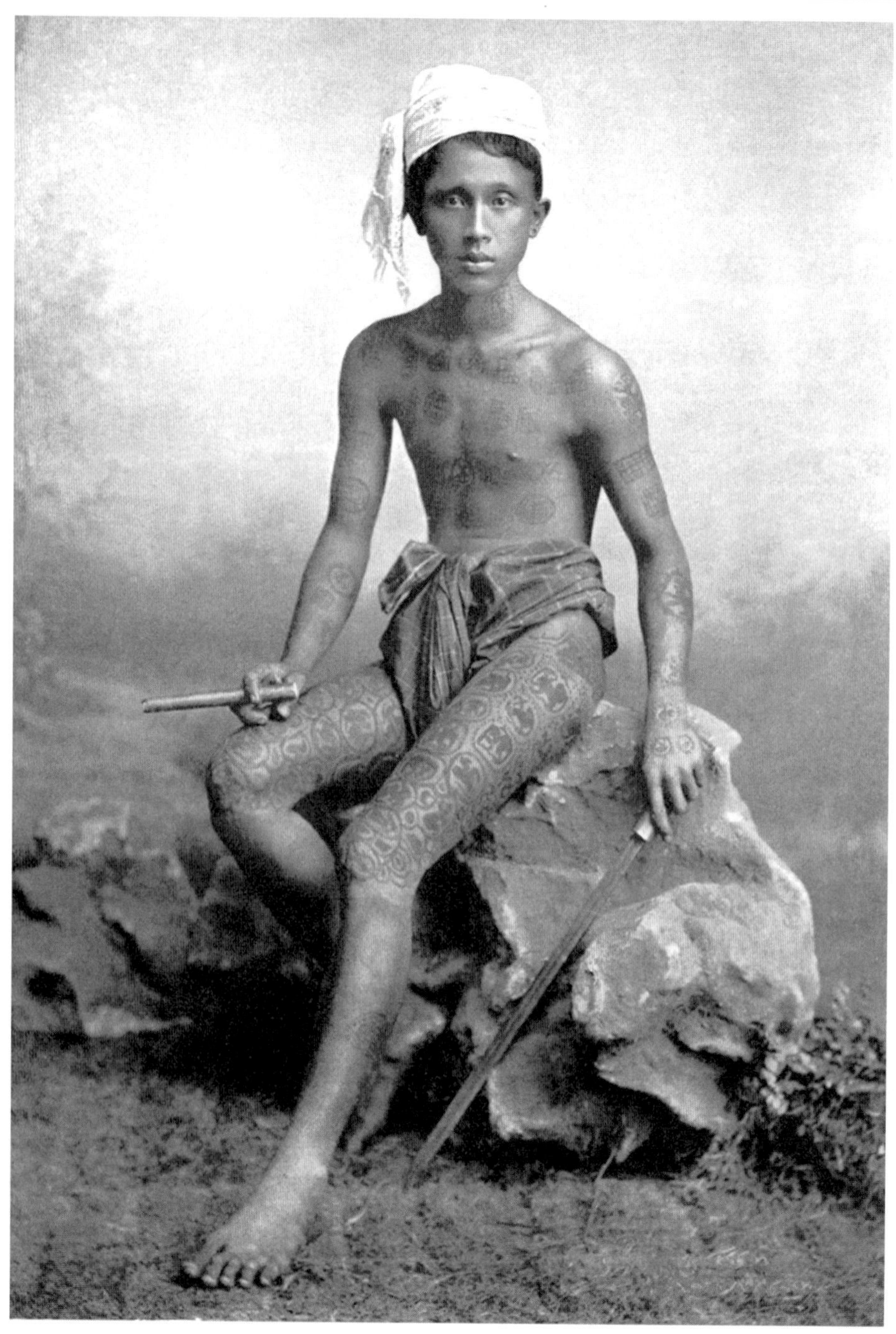

Burmese tattooing

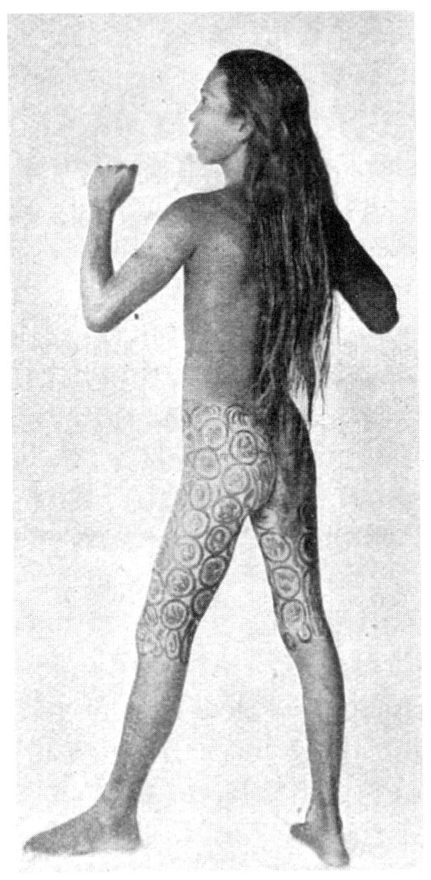

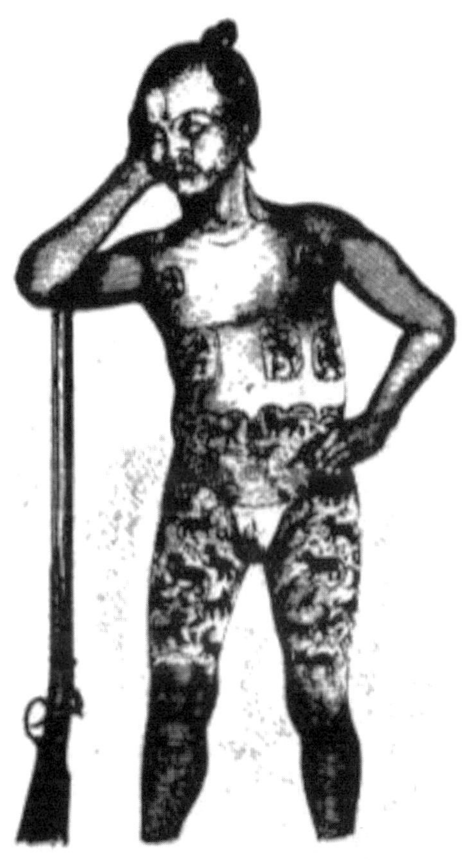

Burmese tattooing

Papua New Guinea as well as the Bougainvillea flower was named after him.

BOWDITCH ISLAND - Fakaofo, formerly known as Bowditch Island, is a South Pacific Ocean atoll located in the Tokelau Group.

BU-MA-FA´-TĚK– term for a person who understands tattoos, Bontok.

BUMARU – with tattooing a woman becomes a bumaru (beautiful) tribe of Kalinga.

BUNGAN – wooden cabinet in which it was stored tattoo equipment, Borneo.

BUNINEMID - The mat to cover the face, Marshalls Islands.

BUNNEMIJ – A woven ornamented mat (bunnemij) to cover the face during the tattooing ceremony, Marshall Islands.

BUNUN - historically known as the Vonum, are a Taiwanese indigenous people and are best known for their sophisticated polyphonic vocal music. Practise of tattooing.

BURIK – The name of one of the wild and independent tribes of the island of Luzon, and province Abra, inhabiting the northern portion of the Western Cordillera. They tattooed the whole of the upper portion of the body, so as to represent the figure of a chat-of-mail, on which slender fact some Spanish writers have jumped to the conclusion that they are the descendahts of inslanders of the Pacific, driven by story on the coast of Luzon.

BURMESE PEOPLE - Burmese males are tattooed on their thighs and frequently on other parts of the body. Often tattoo marks are traced as charms against lethal weapons. Professional thieves frequently have a cat tattooed on each thigh. One cat they pat on entering the house they are about to burgle, the other on emerging with their booty. Burmese women are not tattooed.

BUSSADI - Only in very exceptional cases is the lusam tattoo made with a knife blade (bussadi).

BUSAO – Pacific tribe practising tattoos.

BUTIT HALAP – The time at which to begin tattooing a girl is about the ninth day after new moon, this lunar phase being known as butit halap, Kayan tribe.

BUWA KAIN – tattoo pigment made by combining charcoal with the juice of an herb collected near the village called buwa kain ('tattoo medicine') which together produced a thick black liquid, Maisin.

BUWA – tattooing (bua, buwa) was female-focused and signified a girl's transition from childhood into a marriageable young woman, Maisin tribe.

BUWA SE-TA - Tattooing may be called kisevi, but frequently people say buwa se-ta (she applied tattoos), Maisin, Papua New Guinea.

BUZU – a tribe from central Nigeria practicing facial tattoos.

CABRI, JEAN BAPTISTE - French deserter, Jean Baptiste Cabri was living in the Marquesas Island with his native wife and his extensive tattoo collection for some years before he was discovered in 1804. Discovered by a Russian explorer, George H. von Langsdorff, Jean was convinced to make the long journey back to Europe with him to start an exciting new carem. Returning first to Russia, Cabri enjoyed some success exhibiting himself and telling tales of his life with the 'savage people' of the islands. He not only exhibited himself in Russia but also toured Europe. However, his career declined quickly and he died in 1812 (or 1818 according to some sources) with little remaining fame.

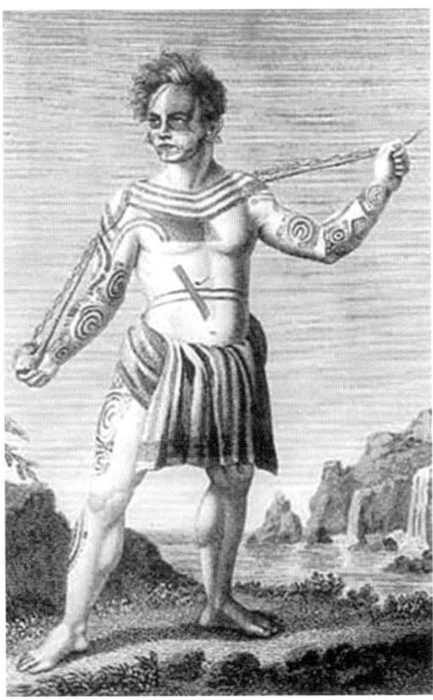

CADUVEO - The Kadiwéu are an indigenous people of Brazil. The Kadiweu are also known as the Cadiguebo, Cadioeo, Caduveo, Caduvéo, Caduví, Cayua, Guaicuru, Kadiveo, Kadivéu, Kadiweu, Kaduveo...

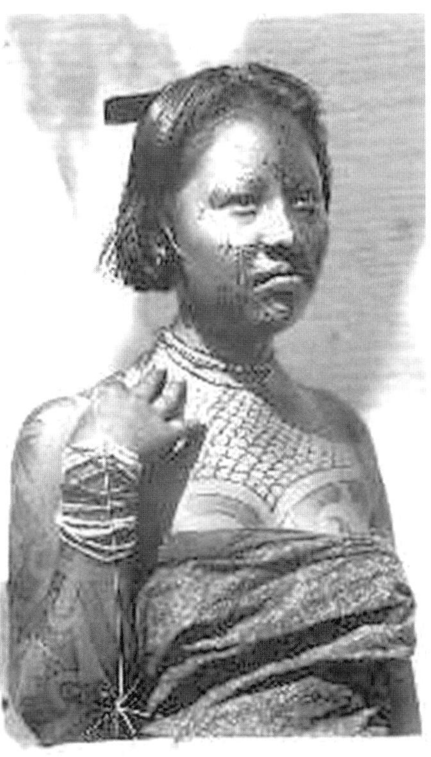

CALDERÓN LANDA, DIEGO DE – was a Spanish bishop living on Yucatán, an inquisitor and an author of writings on the Mayan civilization. He was born on 12th November 1524 in Cifuentes, Spain. He died on 29th April 1579 in the age of 55 in Mérida, Mexico. Among others, he commented the Maya's decorating as follows: "Those, who had do this, painted the appointed spot and then cut it; the interaction of blood and dye leaved permanent traces on the body. Due to the pain, this intervention was being performed in steps. Then they would

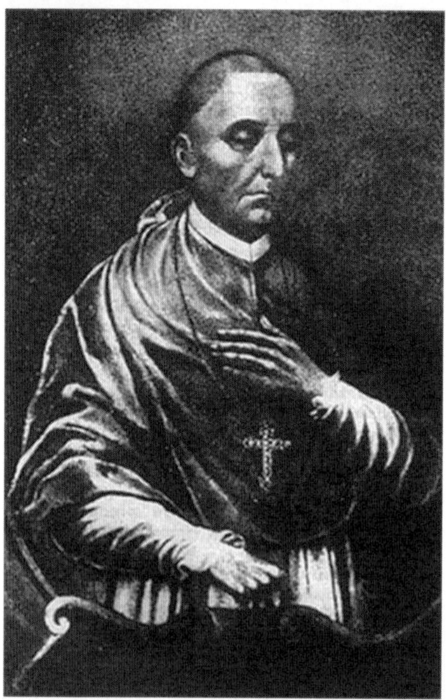

Diego de Calderón Landa

suffer from diseases for the painting would become inflamed and suppurated. Despite all that, they mocked the untattooed."

CALOPHYLLIUM INOPHYLLUM – tree native to Southeast Asia. It occurs mainly in Polynesia. He often appears in Hawaiian songs. His seeds were used as one of the components of dyes for tattoos in Polynesia.

CANIBOS TRIBE– Rio Ucayali, eastern Peru, worn scar-tattooing. The scars are small points or spots which are applied two and two along the outsider of the arm from the wrists to the shoulders. Young men frequently had the skull full of long deep scars.

CAROLINE ISLANDS - (or the Carolines) are a widely scattered archipelago of tiny islands in the western Pacific Ocean, to the north of New Guinea. People practised tattooing.

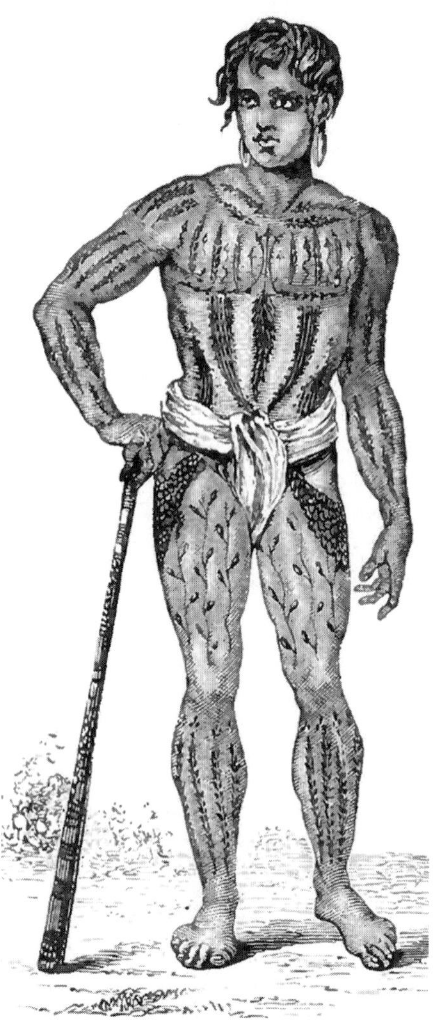

Tattoos from the Caroline Islands

There are two different methods of tattooing. One is tattooing by incision (scar-ornament, cicatrization), by cutting or burning the skin. The other is tattooing by puncture (or simple tattooing), inserting pigments in punctures to mark the skin

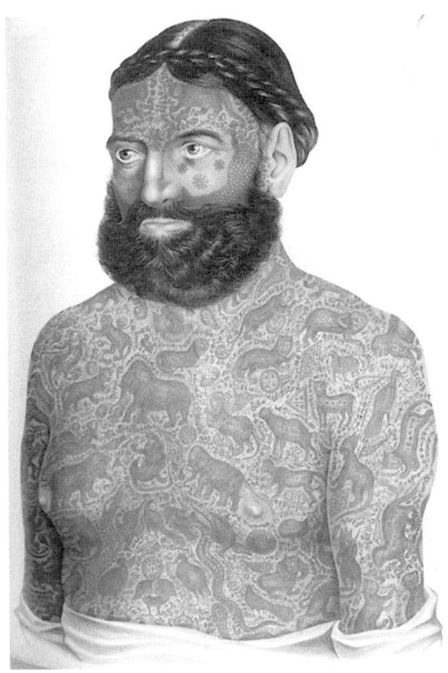

Constentenus Alexandrinos

with various patterns, which form a permanent ornament for the skin.

CASAS GRANDES - a village, Chihuahua, Mexico, an archaeologist found here clay jugs (1200-1450 CE) with various marks on the bodies and limbs, especially on the faces, apparently representing tattoos or paintings.

CEHŁGAY - tattoo tool, "white stone". A sharp sliver of quartz was used for various purposes, including as a knife for tattooing, Hupa Indian.

CIJINGO - Another type of tattoo in Sub-Saharan Africa is known as cijingo, in combination with a cross. Cijingo denotes a spiral brass bracelet.

CINGELYENGELYE - The cruciform tattoo with triangles on the forehead is known as cingelyengelye in Sub-Saharan Africa. Originally, cingelyengelye occurred as a necklace in the form of a cross, cut from tin plate, and worn by the Chokwe as an amulet. During the 17th century, Capuchin monks from the Order of Christ of Portugal had distributed medals in the form of a cross throughout Chokwe country, and this cross was probably the prototype for cingelyengelye.

CIQING – old term for tattooing, China.

CIZI – another old term for tattooing, China.

CON-NAH-TAH– the tattoo color was obtained from the ash of the blueberry bush, con-nah- tah [kanata], The Tlingit Indians.

CONIBO TRIBE – Pano tribe form Amazon. Practiced facial tattooing.

CONSTENTENUS ALEXANDRINOS - or "The Greek Albanian," (April 17, 1833 - ?) was a circus performer in the late 1800s. A man who was tattooed over his entire body, he was a famous traveling attraction who claimed to have been kidnapped by Chinese Tartars and tattooed against his will. His surname was sometimes spelled as Constantenus and Constantinius. He was also known as Djordgi Konstantinus and Georgius Constantine.

COOK, JAMES - British naval captain, navigator, and explorer who sailed the seaways and coasts of Canada (1759 and 1763–67) and conducted three expeditions to the Pacific Ocean (1768–71, 1772–75, and1776–79), ranging from the Antarctic ice fields to the Bering Strait and from the coasts of North America to Australia and New Zealand. Captain James Cook recorded

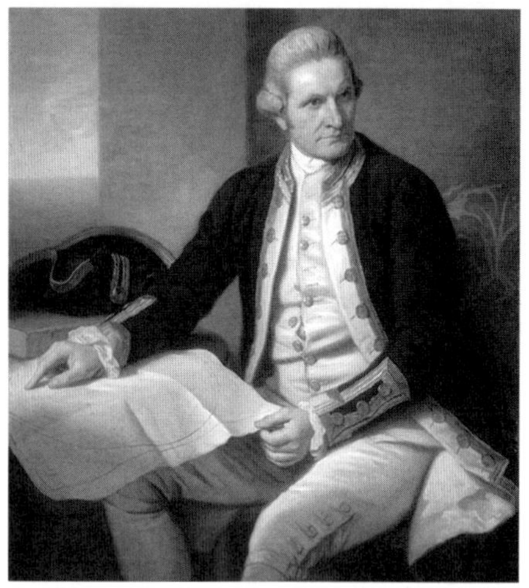

James Cook

tatau as the Tahitian term when he arrived there in 1769, although tatau is not the only word for this art form. In some French Polynesian Islands and some Cook Islands it was known as nana'o.

COOK ISLANDS - are a self-governing island country in the South Pacific Ocean in free association with New Zealand. It comprises 15 islands whose total land area is 240 square kilometers. Tattooing was forbidden in the Cook Islands after the arrival of missionaries but has recently become popular again.

COOS TRIBE - are an indigenous people of the Northwest Plateau, living in Oregon. They live on the southwest Oregon Pacific coast. Practised tattooing. At their puberty ceremony, young women received rows of dots near their wrists. According to Coos and Alsea informants, this was done to symbolize that a young woman was ready to cook on her own and have hands strong enough for all her tasks.

COPTICS - are an ethnoreligious group indigenous to North Africa who primarily inhabit the area of modern Egypt, where they are the largest Christian denomination in the country and in the Middle East. Copts are also the largest Christian denomination in Sudan and Libya. Many Copts have the cross tattooed as a sign of faith on the inside of their right arm at the wrist. Many Copts resort to a tattooer at a Coptic "mulid" (the annual feasts in honor of the Holy Virgin).

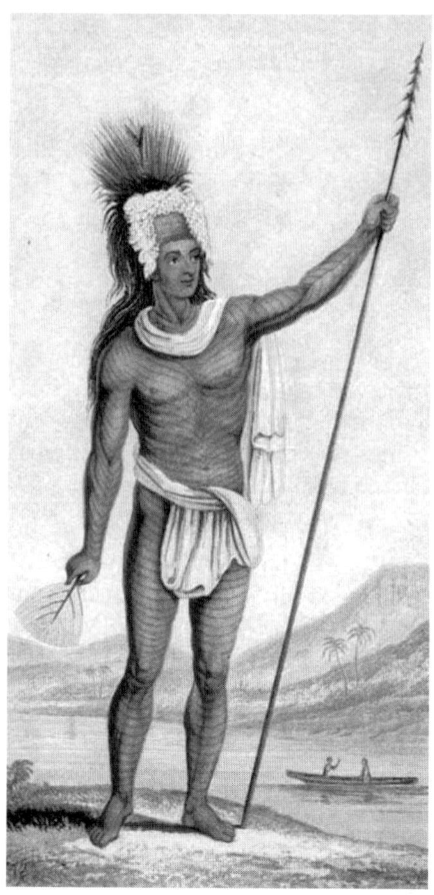

Te Po chief of Rarotonga, Cook Islands

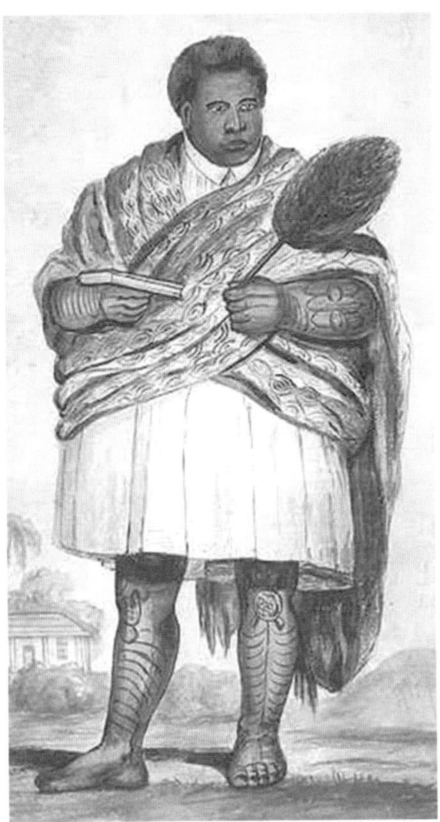

Cook Ilands, Makea Pori Ariki, Chief of Te-au-o-tonga, Rarotonga (1837)

CORDYLINE TERMINALIS – The tattoo ink on Rapa Nui was made out of natural products, primarily from the burning of Ti leaves (Cordyline terminalis) and sugar cane.

COROADO TRIBE - Among the Coroado, both sexes were tattooed by a method not reported elsewhere in South America except for the Tehuelche : The skin was pinched between the fingers, and with a needle and a thread wet with pigment it was stitched through in circular designs or in crude representations of animals and birds, South American Indians.

COWICHNA TRIBE – is the band government of the Cowichan, a group of Coast Salish peoples who live in the Cowichan Valley region on Vancouver Island, practiced tattooing.

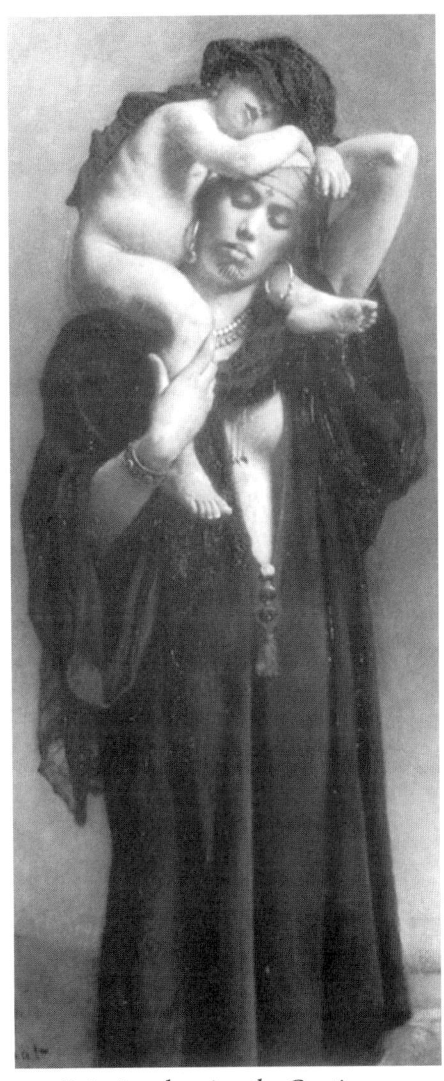

Painting showing the Coptic woman

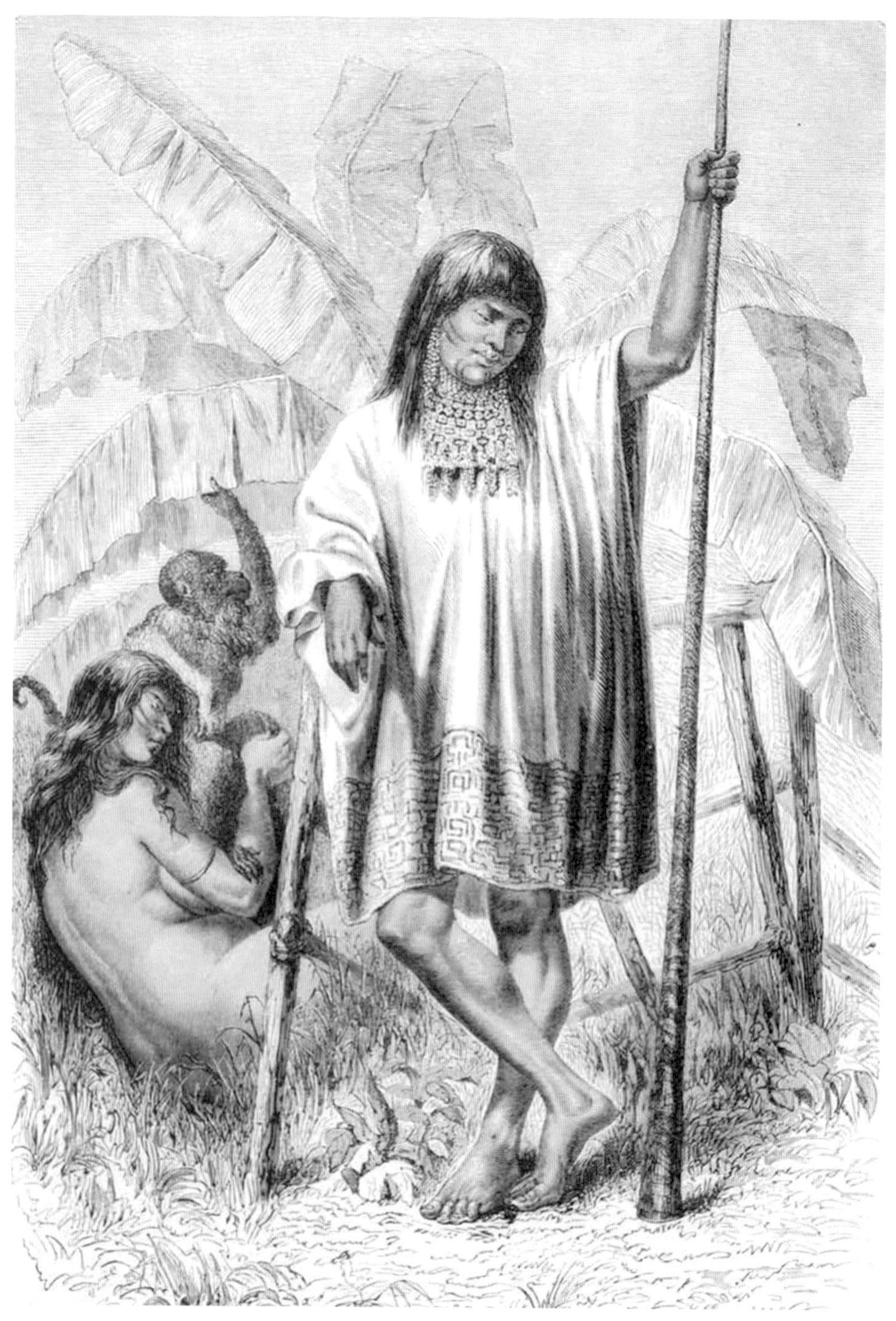

Conibo

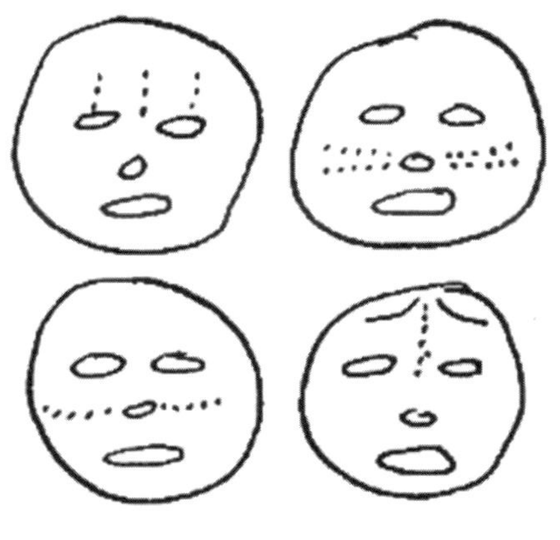

Coos

CREE INDIANS– Formerly practised both tattooing and skarification. Some of women tattooed free perpendicular lines, which were sometimes double: one from the centre of the chin to that of the under lip, and one parallel on either side to the corner of the mouth. Tattooing was performed by charring birchbark or wood and rubbing it on a thread which is fastened to a needle and the design sewed under the skin, the pigment making it permanent.

CROW TRIBE - The Crow, called the Apsáalooke in their own Siouan language, or variants including the Absaroka, are Native Americans, who in historical times lived in the Yellowstone River valley, which extends from present-day Wyoming, through Montana and into North Dakota, where it joins the Missouri River. PractiSed tattooing. The term Arapaho is a Crow word signifying "tattooed on the breast." Their tribal mark was three equidistant blue patterns on the breast.

CRUITHNEACH – Scottish Gaelic name for Picts.

CUCUTENI - In 1981, more than 20 ceramic human figurines reclining on chairs and bearing elaborate incised decorations were unearthed in northeastern Romania. They, and many other figurines like them—such as the one pictured at right—were made by a people we know today as the Cucuteni culture, which lasted from 4800 to 3000 B.C. in what is now Romania and Ukraine. Some scholars have interpreted these lines as representations of body modification. "They could be tattoos," says San Francisco State University archaeologist Douglass W. Bailey. "Some say they are clothes, or they could represent something else we don't understand. We will never know for sure, but in a sense, that's unimportant. What's important is that they were using the surface of their bodies to communicate ideas, whether they related to membership in a group or individual identity." He notes that earlier Paleolithic figurines such as the Venus of Willendorf were unmarked, and that incisions on the bodies of figurines only appear after the beginning of the Neolithic, when ceramics were first made and decorated. "In the Neolithic, people were incising pots by taking a sharp point and cutting away the clay," says Bailey. "If the pot was a metaphor for the body, that process of engraving could have also been seen as tattooing." While the practice might have existed in Paleolithic times, there is no evidence for tattooing before 7,000 years ago. Perhaps it was only after the first pots were decorated that people began to contemplate making permanent changes to their own skin's appearance.

CUKIHARI – coloring, Traditional Japanese Tattooing.

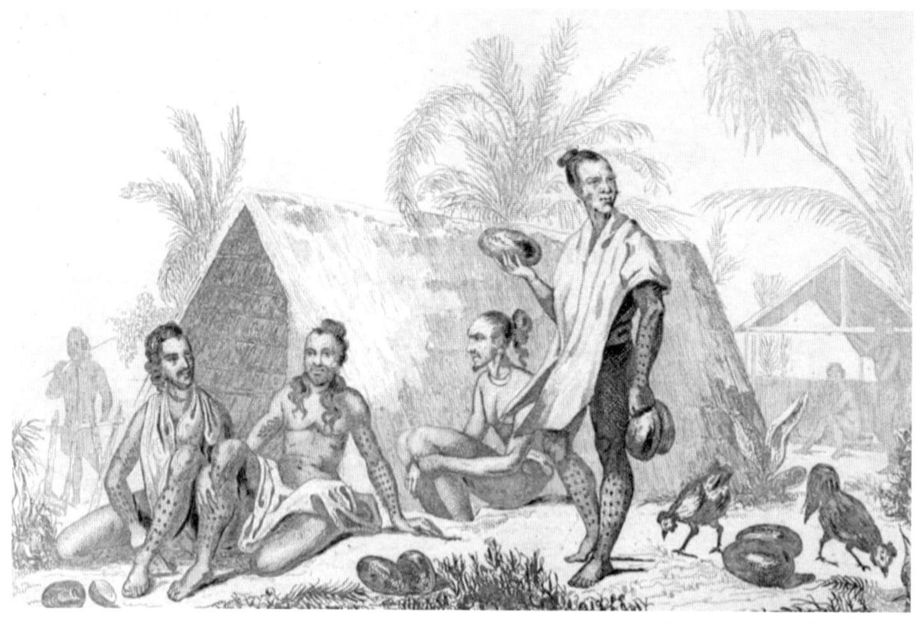

Caroline Islanders tattoo

CUMSHAWAS – or Cum-sha-was, Indian tribe , Queen Charlotte's Islanders, practiced tattooing.

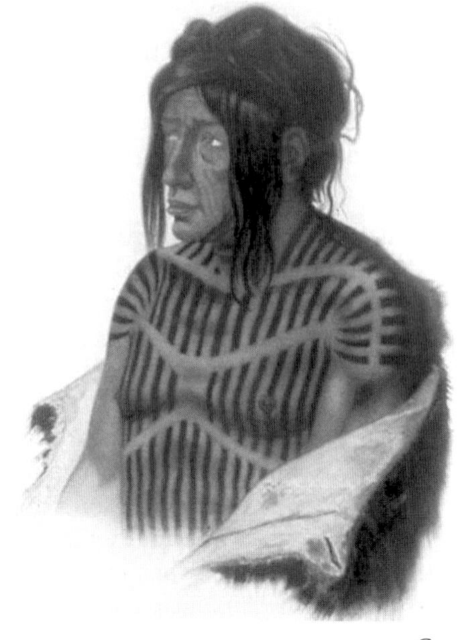

Cree

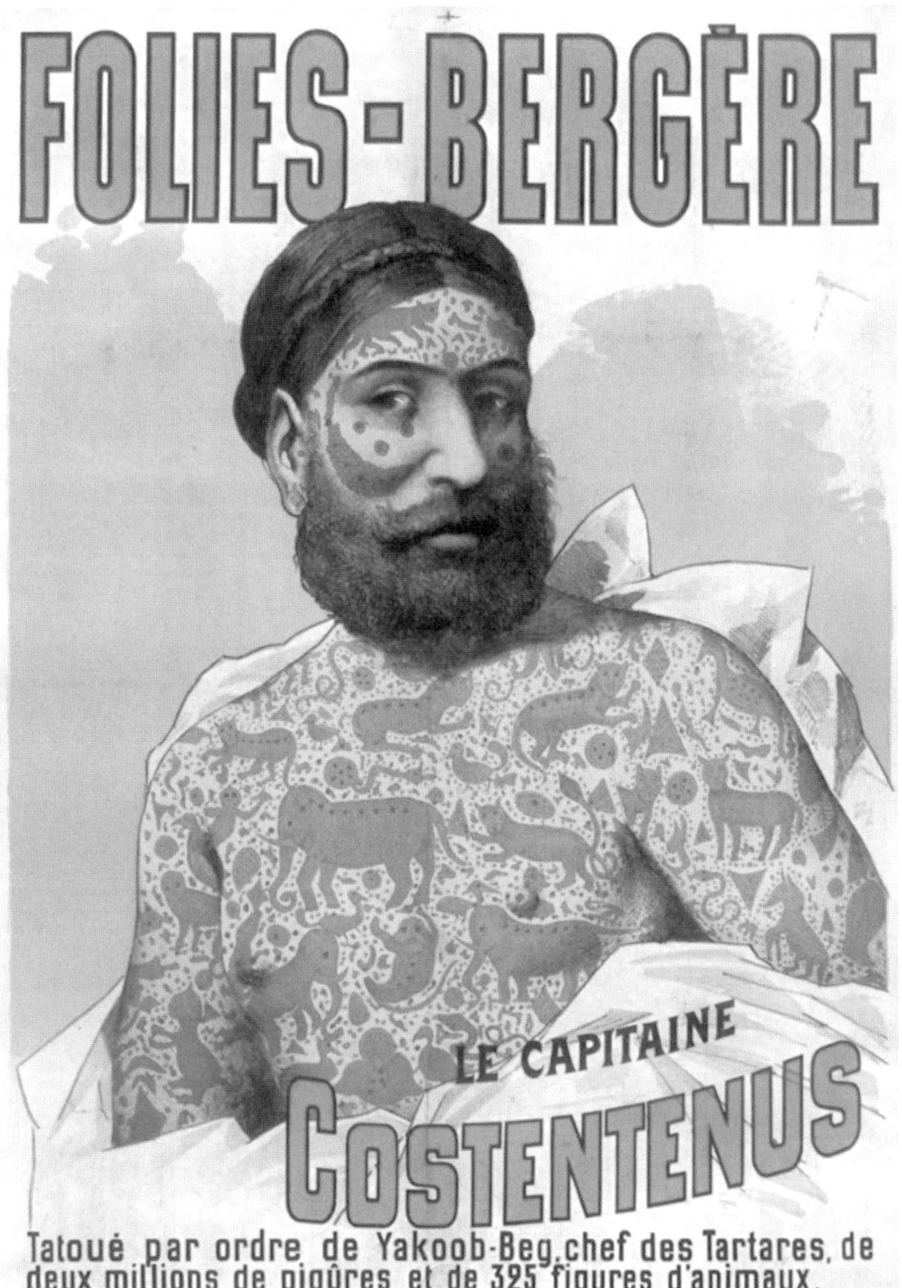

Constentenus Alexandrinos

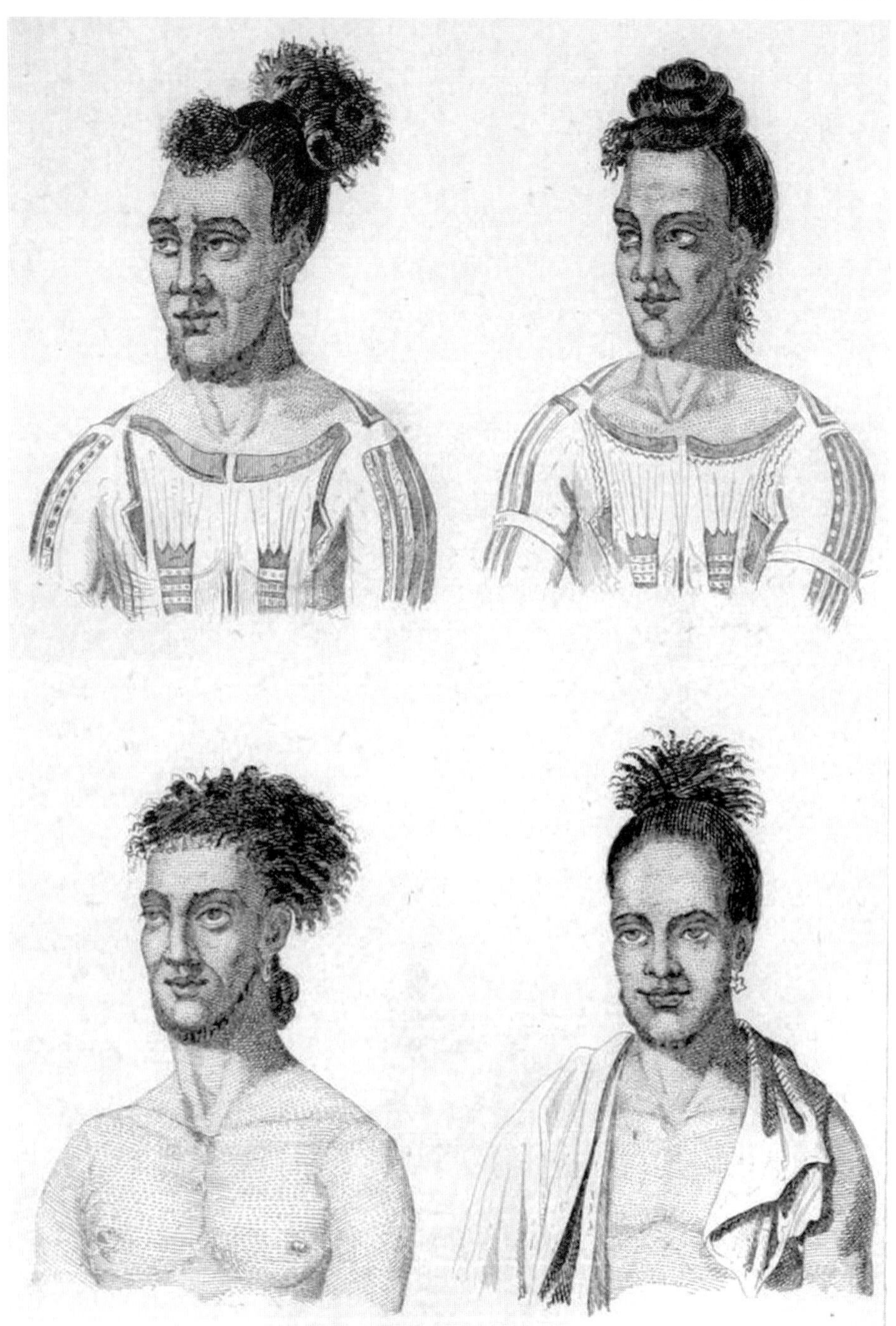

Tattoos from the Caroline Islands

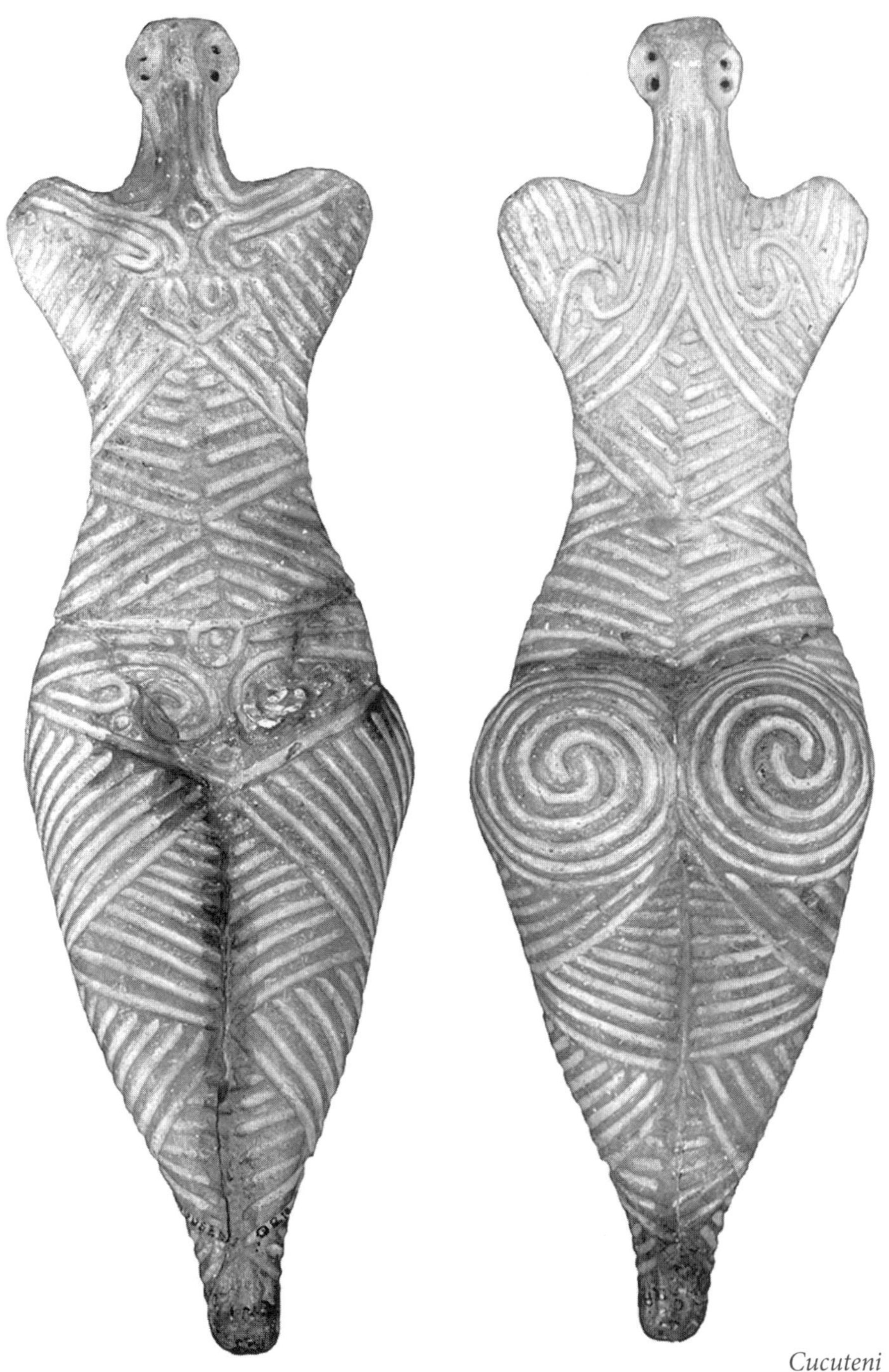

Cucuteni

D´URVILLE, JULES, SEBASTIEN CESAR DUMONT (1790–1842) - was born on 23 May 1790 at Condé-sur-Noireau, a village in Normandy, France. His father was Gabriel François Dumont, sieur of Urville and an hereditary Judge; his mother, née Jeanne de Croisilles, was of a noble French family. The d'Urvilles, because of their aristocratic connections, took refuge after the French Revolution in a secluded part of Normandy. Here, after the death of his father, Jules was educated by his mother's brother, a churchman of wide learning. Later he

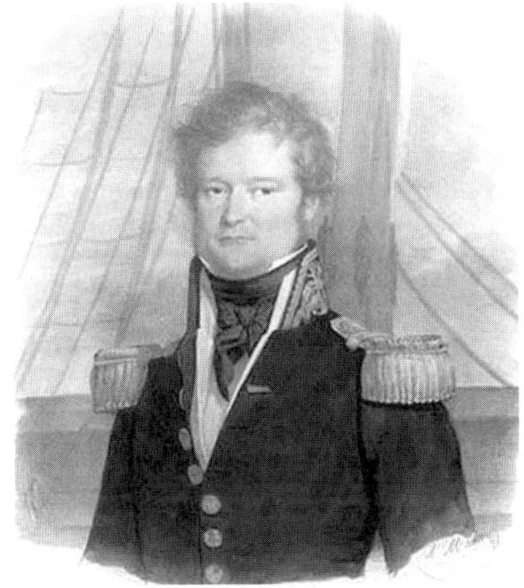

attended the Lycée Malherbe at Caen. In 1807 he entered the Navy. A student by talent and inclination, he devoted himself to learning, both in the humanities and natural sciences. In 1815 he married. In 1820, while on a visit in a French naval vessel to the eastern Mediterranean, he was instrumental in procuring for France a Greek statue which had been found on Melos – the Venus de Milo.

In 1822–25, while serving on the Coquille, he surveyed the Falklands, Tahiti and other Pacific islands, and New Holland (W Australia). In 1826–29 he commanded the Astrolabe in a voyage around the world; searching for the ill-fated La Pérouse expedition, he explored Fiji and many other islands of Oceania, the New Zealand coast, and the Moluccas. With the Astrolabe and the Zelée he made a second circumnavigation in 1837–40, and in 1840 he penetrated the ice pack south of New Zealand and discovered the Adélie Coast region in Antarctica.

DAGGAGAH – Nearly all tattooing among the Arabs of Iraq is done by women, mostly professionals. It is not a hereditary profession, but any woman who has the skill and inclination can become a daggagah or tattooer.

DAI PEOPLE – The Dai people of China have an ancient tattooing tradition. Both

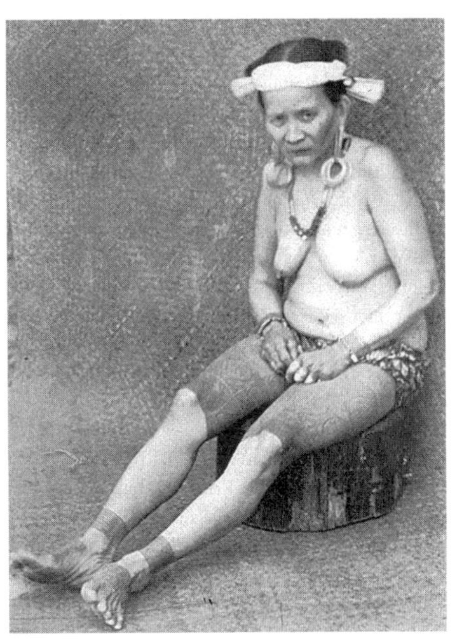

Dayak women with tattoos

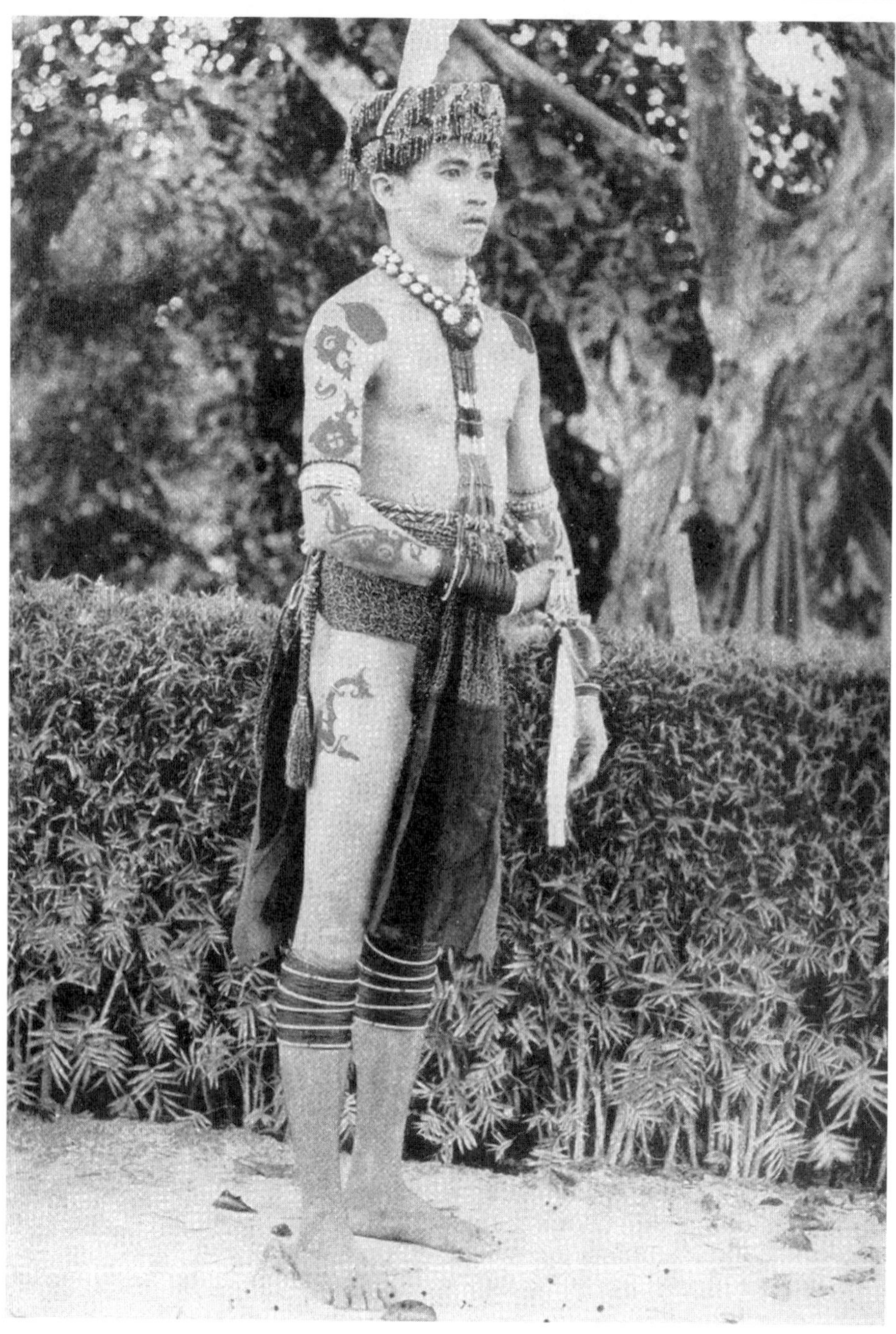

Dayal boy

men and women among the Dai are tattooed. Dai women are generally tattooed on the backs of their hands, their arms or have a small dot tattooed between their eyebrows.

"Frogs' legs are decorated, men's legs should be decorated if they want to be called men," is an ancient proverb among the Dai ethnic group of Xishuangbanna, in Southwest China's Yunnan Province. For them, especially the elderly men, a tattoo is not a special way to show contemporary fashion but a centuries-old practice. A tattoo is called sangmen in Dai language and most local men have tattoos on their bodies.

DAKOTA TRIBES -the Dakota people are a Native American tribe and First Nations band government in North America. They compose two of the three main subcultures of the Sioux people, and are typically divided into the Eastern Dakota and the Western Dakota.

Thruston wrote: the tattoo marks on the faces of two of the chief figures are significant. I find, from a series of rude drawings or „counts“ of the Dakota Indians, illustrating the fourth annual report of the Bureau of Ethnology, that the principal chiefs of the Dakotas were marked by free tattoo line of paint across their cheeks; and that, in the Indian picture writings, the holding of a war club or pipe was a sign of authority, and indicated that these special chiefs had at some time led independent war parties. According to the interesting pictograph presented, the chiefs among the mound builders of Tennessee had four lines of paint, or tattoo marks, on their faces upon occasions of ceremony. The prevalence of this custom among the pottery markers of Tennessee and Arkansas may also be established by testimony, independently of the pictured stone.

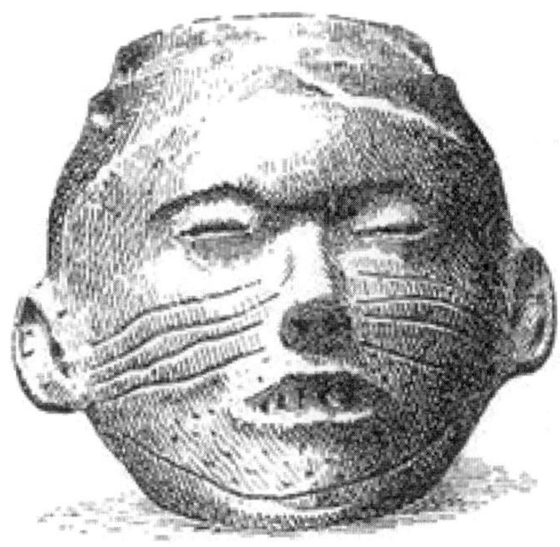

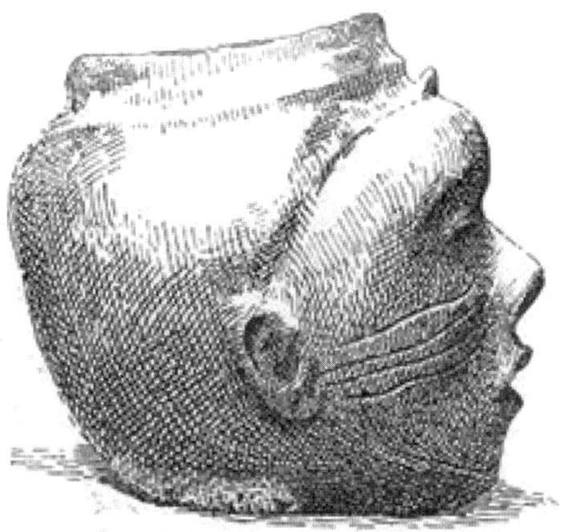

Dakota

DAQQ – Al-washm is the most common Arabic word for tattooing, but words like daqq (from a root meaning to strike or knock) , dagh, khal and sham are also used when referring to this practice.

DAWA - tree, from the burning of its nuts is obtained ash for tattoo ink, Fiji.

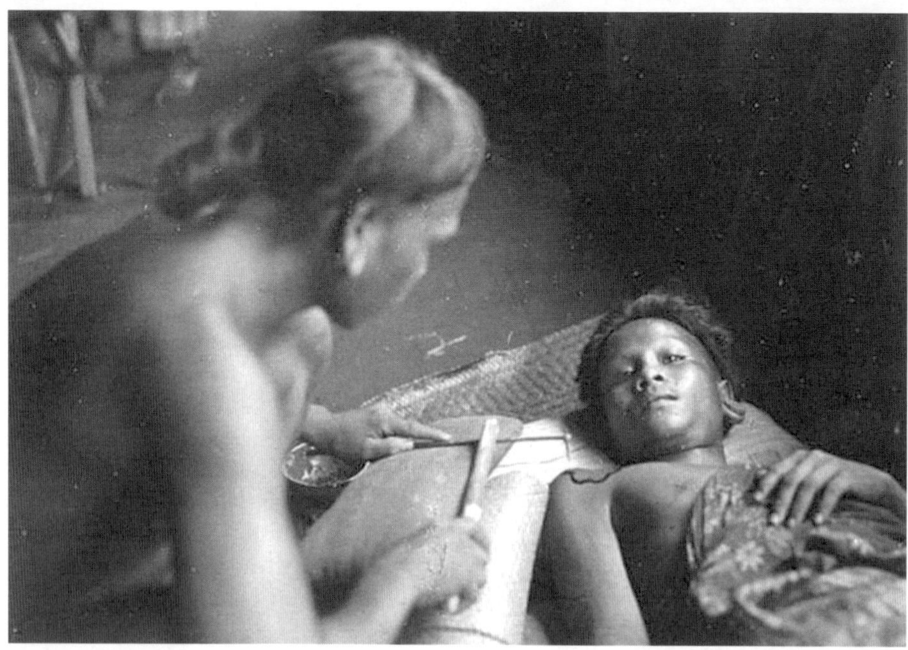

Dayak tattoo process

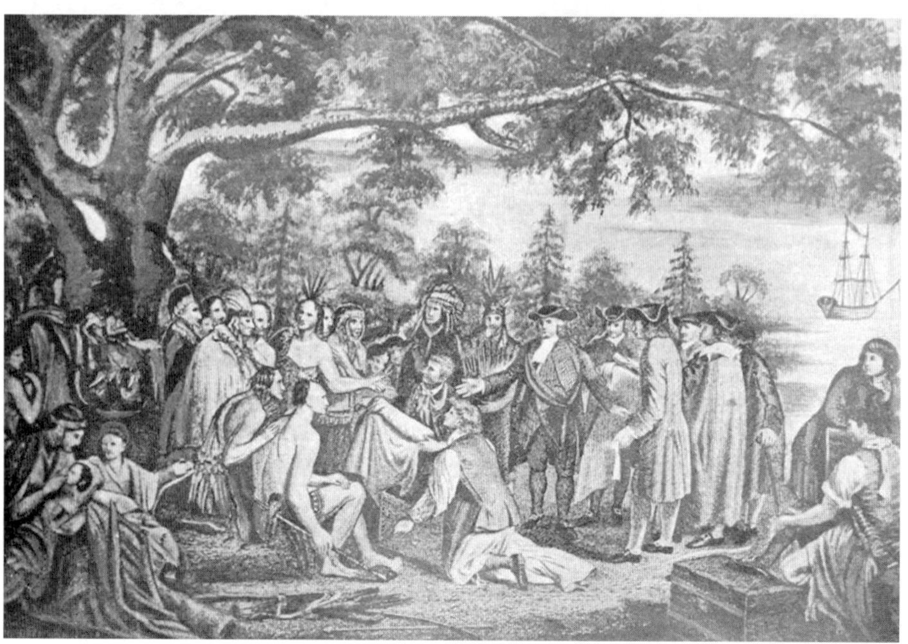

Delawar

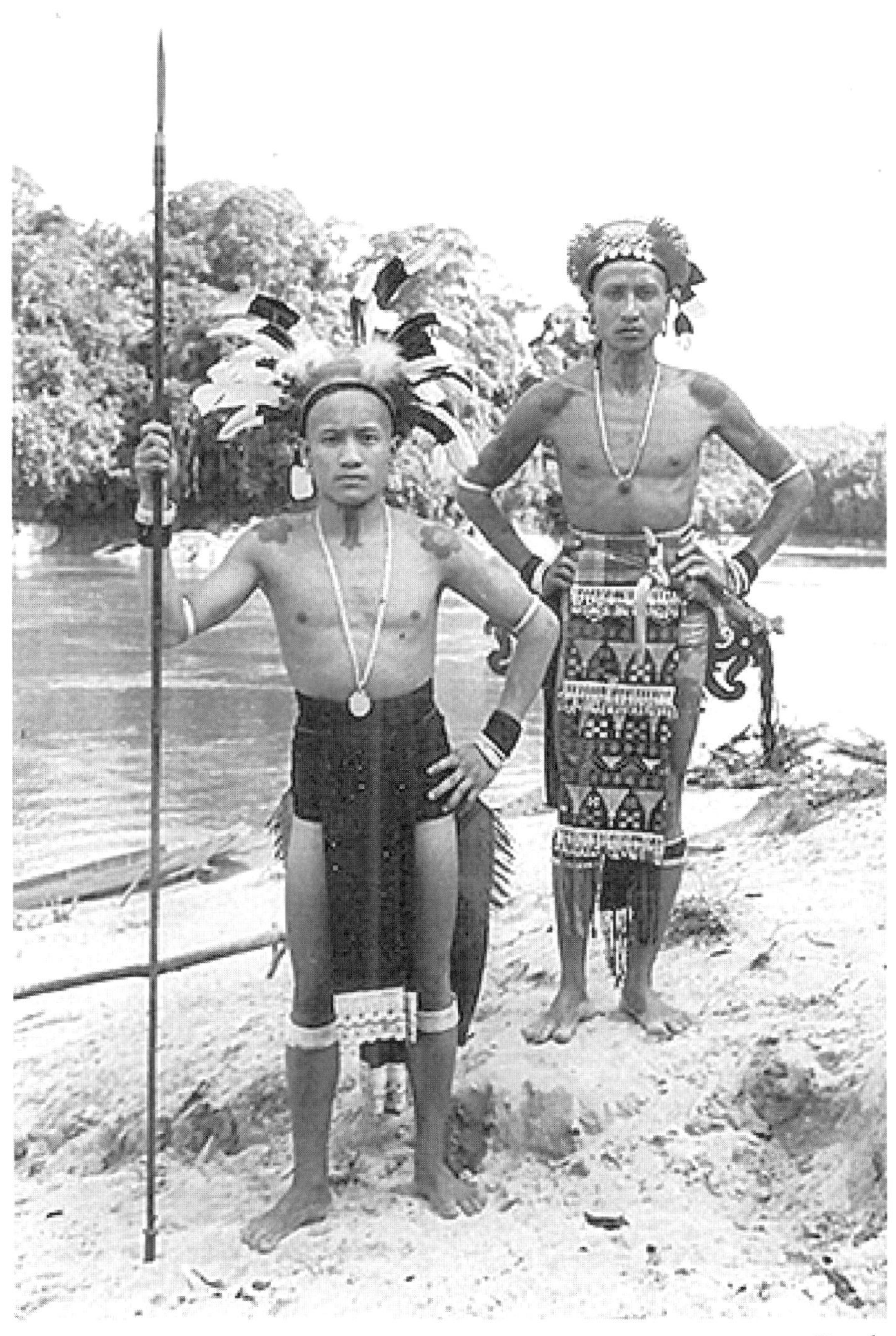

Dayaks

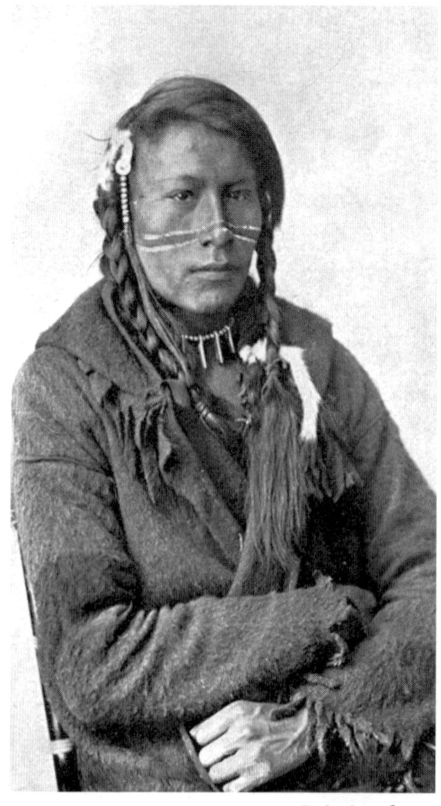

Déné indian

DAYAK – is a generic term used to categorize a quite large group of indigenous peoples of the island of Borneo. The island is in fact divided between three countries: Indonesia, the Malaysian Federated States of Sabah and Sarawak, and Brunei Darussalam. Traditionally, Dayak tattooing was performed in a sacred ritual among gathered tribe members. Soot from lamp lamps or charcoal pots and cauldrons, used as a dye. The ingredients are collected and mixed with sugar and stirred in such away. Thorns of orange trees that are long enough and the level of sharpness adequate, used as a tool to merajah.Duri can be used directly or clipped to a sprig of wood for the handle so as to resemble a hammer. The orange tree spines are dipped in "ink" with soot and sugar, then start the tattoo thrust into the skin according to the desired motif.

DELAWAR TRIBE – tattooing was also frequent, among the Delawares at least and there are accounts of some of the old men who even at a much later time then this were covered with figures representing their exploits in war. See LENAPO too

DELTLUNLISHANTE - name for tattoos in the areas of Gapshima and Shukty, Dagestan.

DENÉ INDIANS – a tribe that lived in Canada and on the coast of the Pacific Ocean, it belongs to the Cree group. Tattoo was very widespread among them, and not only on the chest, arms, and legs, as with various neighbouring tribes, but also on the face. In general, face designs were lines, one or two parallel ones, on cheeks, forehead, temples, chin or came from the corner of the mouth and they were not a totem ones. They also used symbols like crosses, fish, and birds and so on. A grizzly symbol was highly respected, and during its creation, many ceremonials feasts took place. Forearms were mainly the spots for a personal totem sign; an animal seen in a dream. The marks on arms and legs were sometimes used as a spell against weakness; in this case, only one or two lines formed them. Symbols on faces were usual symbols for otters, fish, birds, beavers, a branch in the water, mountains, martens, lizards, caribous.

DEQ – Kurds (people of the Middle East) have long practiced tattooing, known as deq.

DERUNG PEOPLE – see DRUNG TRIBE

DESAI– see RABARI

DEWA – a permanent mental component of an individual, Sumba island. Girls were tattooed since puberty, which was a symbol of the fact they can reproduce and they were born again as adults and so they are full members of the company and they can be considered as "complete persons in a new skin". It was about that time that their new state of an adult person was further strengthened by the fact that they start to teach how to weave and grain sieve. As a proof of continued fertility, buffalo designs were tattooed after the birth of her first child to demonstrate not only her ability to give a new life to her husband's house, but also the fact that now she is a part of husband's "buffalo house." This tattoo suggested that its carrier has strengthened not only her "Dewa" as a fertile woman, but also husband's "Uma" and it proves the fact that the woman is a new lineage which represents a new generation of the relation between "The ones, who provide wives" and "The Ones, who accept wives" groups, and so create a "buffalo house" or the "Buffalo Uma" which formed the basic unit of the Laboy society.

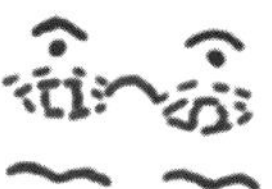

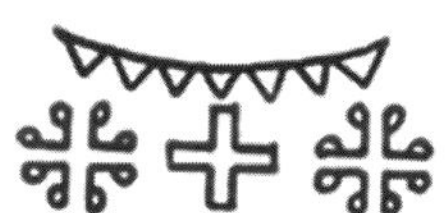

Diamialuka

DEWASI – see RABARI

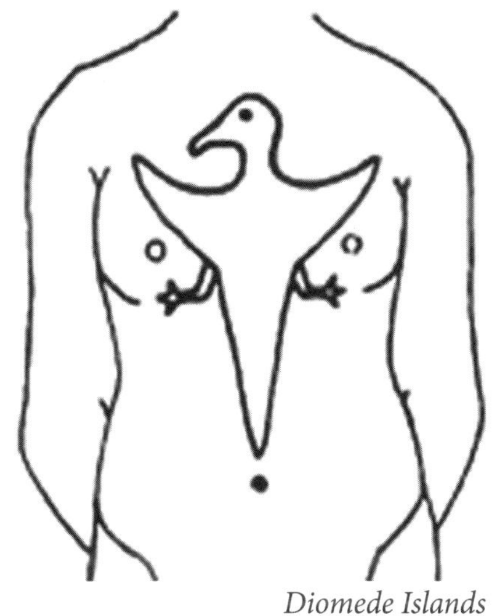

Diomede Islands

DHARBA - (Poa cynosurides) juice used in tattooing, India.

DIABOLO INSTINCTU – devil's marks, the designation of the Irish Church for tattoos. This church explicitly banned tattoos at the Caucuth´s synod in Northumberland in 787 AD. She did so apparently for his pagan associations.

DIAMIALUKA – The name for the tattoo, the Bara tribe, Madagascar.

DIAOGING – decorative tattoo according to Chinese records from the 19th Century.

DIJU = tattooed, Onjo, Collingwood Bay, New Guinea.

DINEMBO – Macedonian term for tattoo.

DINKA PEOPLE - are an ethnic group of Sudan, practiced scar tattooing.

DINURAS – those who do not have a tattoo are considered weak and unlucky for the tribe. Kalinga chant: "Awad kad

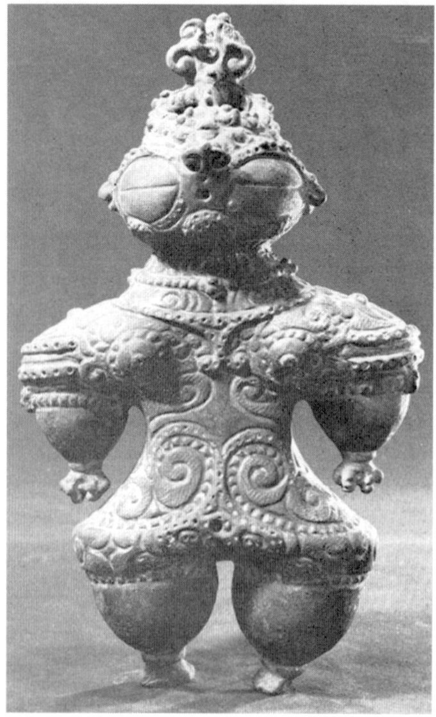

Dogu

da dinuras, (shame on women with no tattoos)".

DIOMEDE ISLANDS - are located in the middle of the Bering Strait between mainland Alaska and Siberia, which borders with the Chukchi Sea to the north and the Bering Sea to the south. 9.3 km (5.8 mi) to the southeast is Fairway Rock, which is generally not considered part of the Diomede Islands. A Diomede island man was observed with a mark on either cheek, close to the mouth, another on each temple, and two more on the forehead. Boys of twelve a raven tattooed on breast and the feet of the same bird on a leg.

DJABON IGAN – The implement (djabon ´igan) used in tattooing consisted of a stick usually a twig of a tree or bush, into one end of which three or four needles had been inserted - occasionally the needles were tied around the stick, Chippewa tribe.

DNEMBO - The Makonde word for tattoo is dnembo and it means design or decoration.

DO-EY– term for tattooing, Tsemai tribe, Southern Ethiopia.

DOGU -The origin of tattooing in Japan

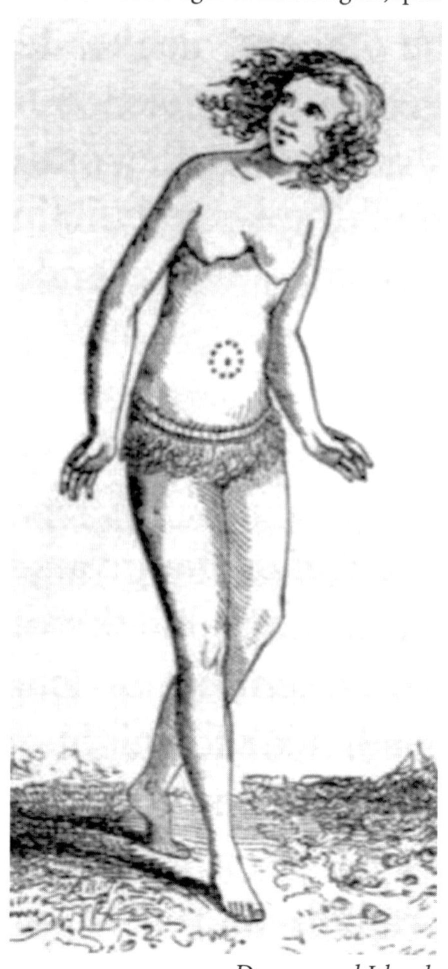

Drummond Island

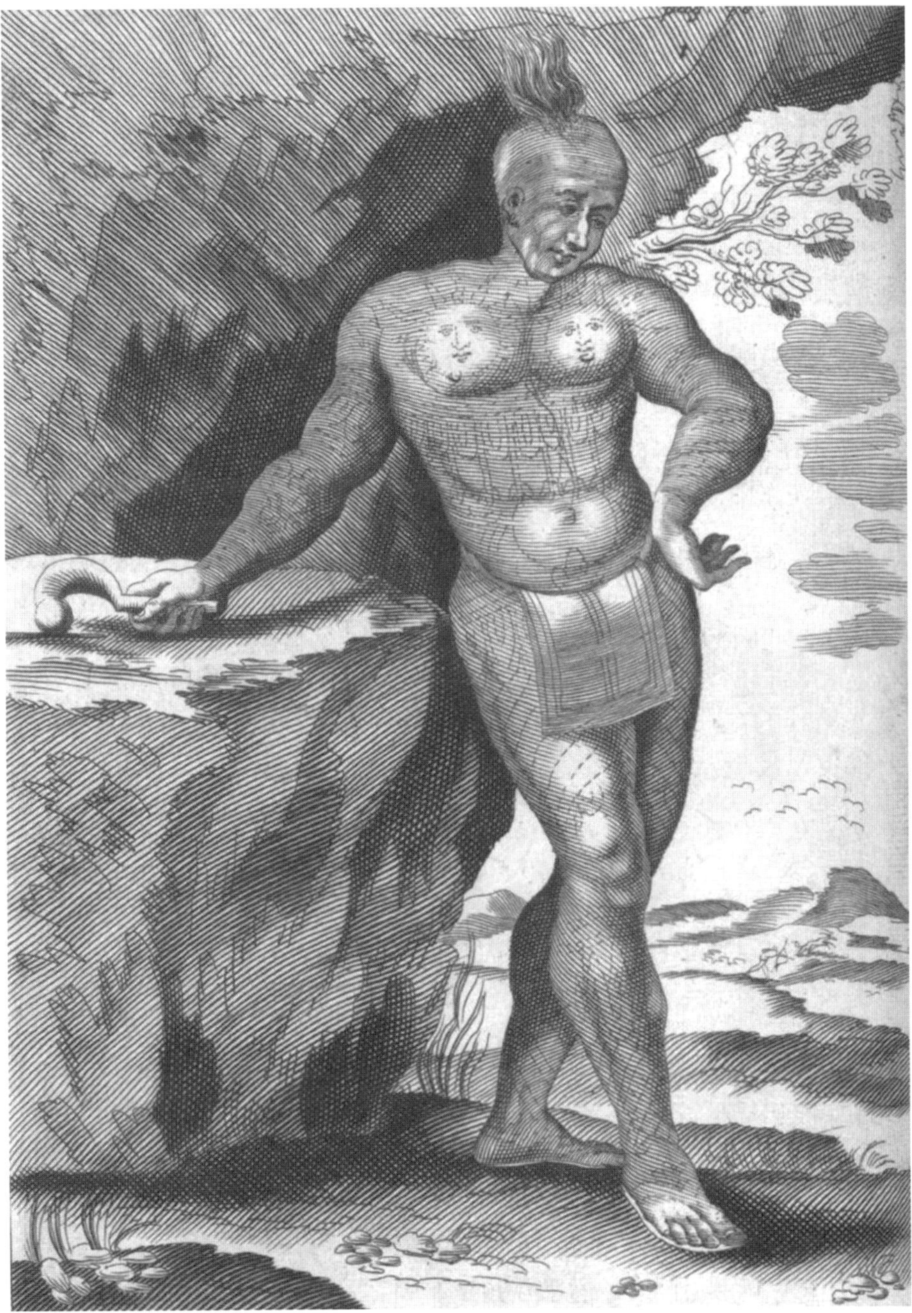

Engraving of a heavily tattooed North American Indian wearing a loincloth by Francois du Creux

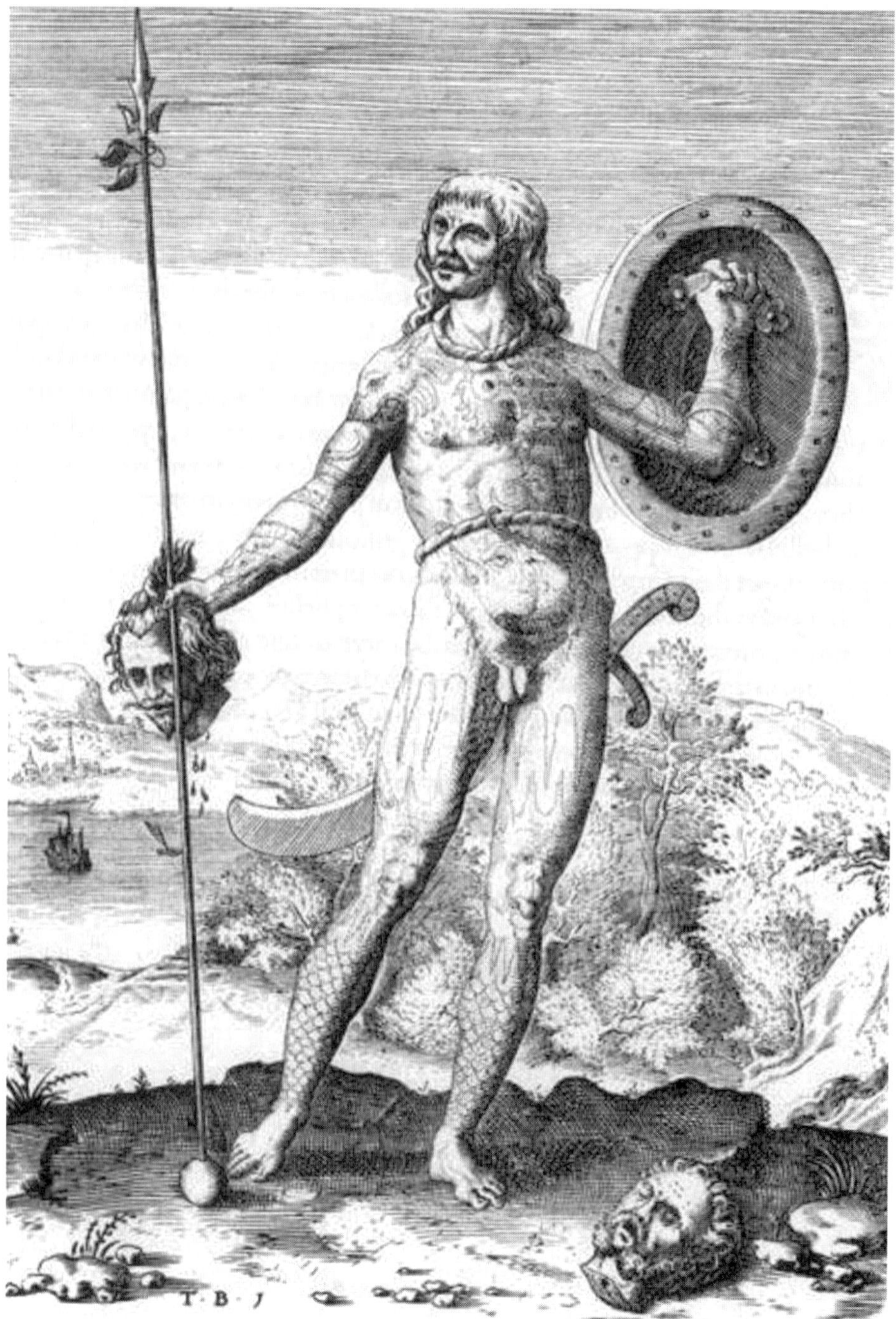

The Picture of One Picte - Theodor de Bry's engraving of an imagined Pict

has been traced back to the Jomon period (10,000 B. C. ~ 300 B. C.). Jomon means "pattern of rope." Many ceramic pots with markings of rope were found in that period. Clay figurines produced in this period are called dogu. Scholars consider that some dogus show tattoo-like markings on their faces and bodies. The oldest dogus whose faces have a depiction of tattooing were found near Osaka in 1977. They are estimated to date from dated the fifth century B. C. (Richie,1980). During the Yayoi period (300 B. C. ~ 300 A. D.) clay figurines with tattoo markings were also found.

DORSET CULTURE (800 B.C. – 1300 A.D.) – Parallel engraved lines, usually in a vertical position, are a characteristic feature of the face tattoo on carvings from the Dorset culture. Even though the Dorset period was long, most of the art from the Central and Eastern Canadian Arctic belongs to the Middle Dorset phase, which is dated around the year 500 A.D. A wooden mask found at Button Point on the Bylot island appears to have two sets of four beveled, parallel lines on the chin and similar patterns can be found on one of two 28 human faces carved into a caribou antler from the area on the Abverdjar island at the northern part of the Fox Basin. A small mask made of talc found near Igloolik has two parallel lines on both cheeks.

DRUMMOND ISLANDERS - A few were tattooed very lightly, and in some it was scarcely distinguishable. Those that were so adorned had it from the breast to the ankles, consisting of short oblique marks, an inch or two in length, drawn paralle a quarter of an inch apart: there was a space both before and behind, of three inches wide, from the neck down, that was uncovered. No tattooing was seen on the face and arms.

DRUNG (or DERUNG people) – In the mountains of Southwest China's Yunnan Province lives one of China's least known and smallest ethnic groups, the Drung people. Formerly, the women used to tattoo their faces when they reached the age of twelve or thirteen. The tattoos of some women resembled masculine mustaches.

DUSUN PEOPLE– the men only tattoo. The design in simple, consisting of a band, two inches broad, curving from each shoulder and meeting its fellow on the abdomen, thence each band diverges to the hip and there ends; from the shoulder each bands runs down the upper arm on its exterior aspect; the flexor surface of the forearm is decorated with short transverse stripes, and, according to one authority, each stripe marks an enemy slain.

DU CREUX, FRANCOIS (1596-1666), priest and historian, was born in 1596 at Saintes, a town midway between Rochelle and Bordeaux in France. He illustrated his book, you can find tattooed people in this picture.

DUK DUK - is a secret society, part of the traditional culture of the Tolai people of the Rabaul area of New Britain, the largest island in the Bismarck Archipelago of Papua New Guinea, in the South Pacific. Only males could belong to Duk-Duk. As membership of such a society is a title of respect, those who have been initiated sometimes adopt a pacticular body or facial mark.

EGYPT – among the females of the lower orders, in the country-towns and villages of Egypt, and among the same classes in the metropolis, but in less degree, prevails a custom somewhat similar to that above described: it consists in making indelible marks of a blue or greenish hue upon the face and other parts, or, at least, upon the front of the chin, and upon the back of the right hand, and often also upon the left hand, the right arm, or both arms, the feet, the middle of the bosom, and the forehead: the most common of these marks made upon the chin and hands are here represented. The operation is performed with several needles (generally seven) tied together: with these the skin is pricked in the desired pattern: some smoke-black (of wood or oil), mixed with milk from the breast of a woman, is then rubbed in; and about a week after, before the skin has healed, a paste of the pounded fresh leaves of white beet or clover is apllied, and gives a blue or greenish colour to the marks: or, to produce the same effect in a more simple manner, some indigo is rubbed into the punctures, instead of the smoke-black, ets. It is generally performed at the age of about five or six years, and by gipsy-

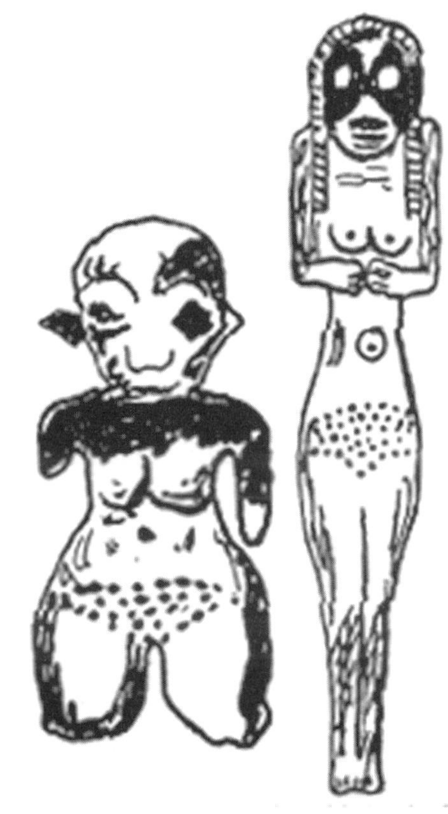

Egyptian bone sculptures from the archaic period. The marks may have been painted or tattooed. They probably date from the 1000 BC period

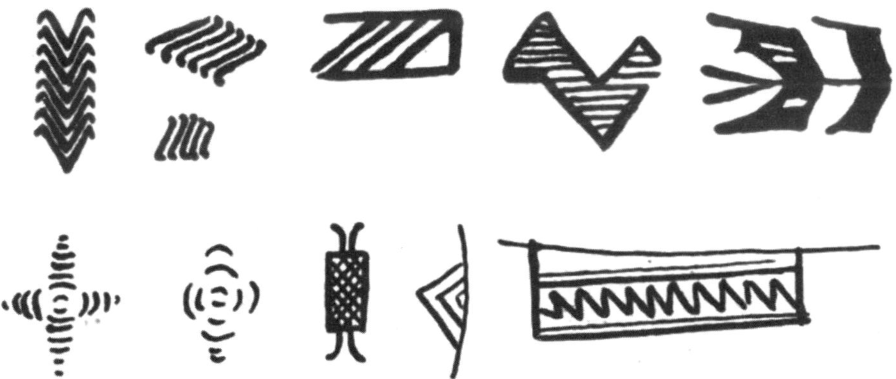

Tattoo marks of primitive Egyptians compared to Libyan

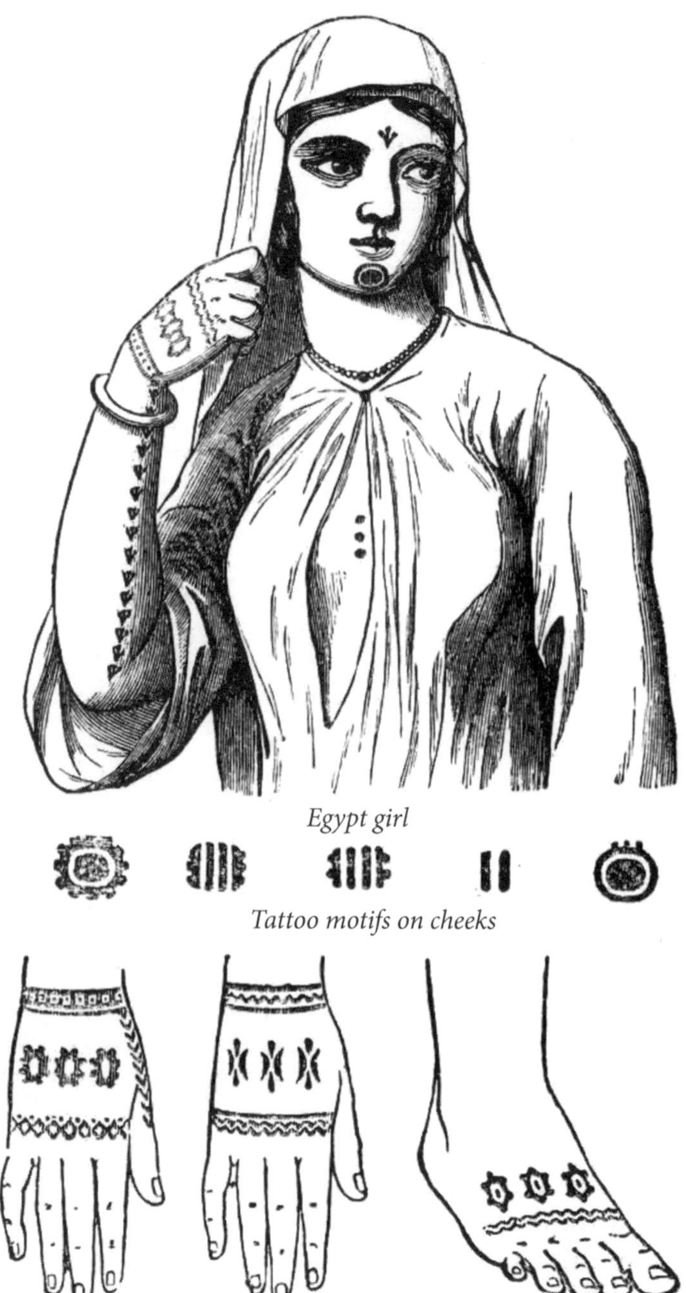

Egypt girl

Tattoo motifs on cheeks

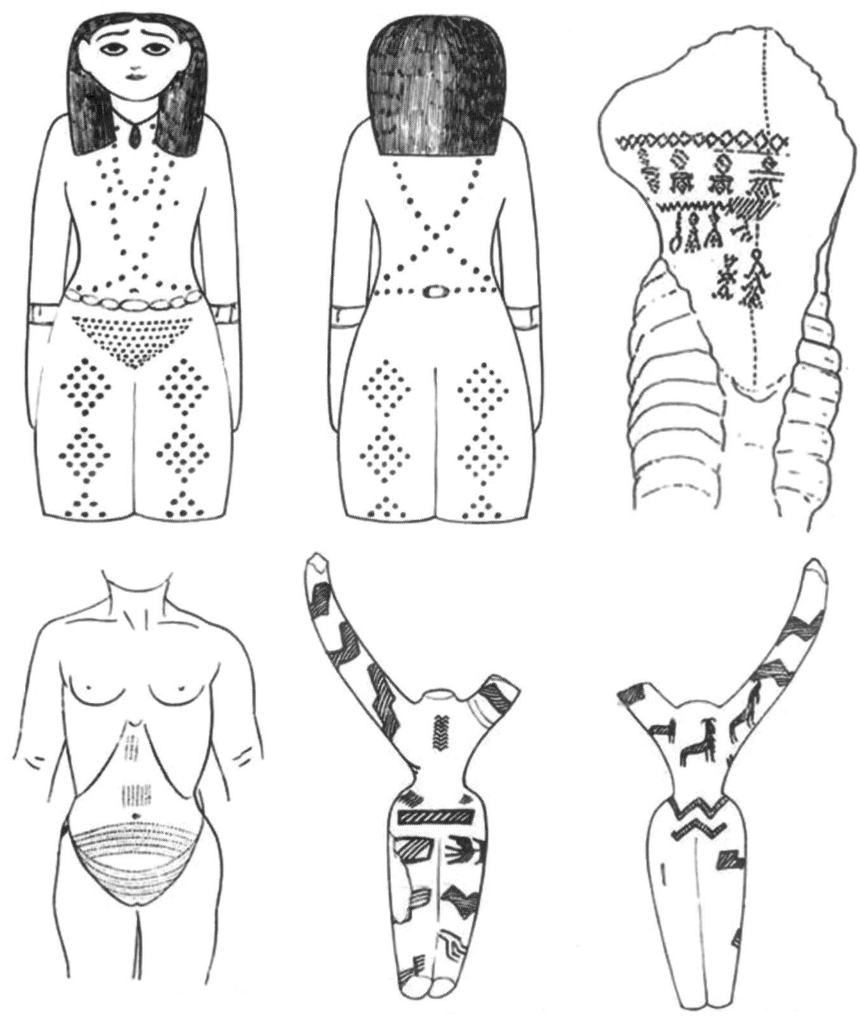

Egypt tattoo

women. The term apllied to i tis „dakk" or „daqq."

EIMEO– tattooing in, Society Islands.

EKUT– term for tattoo performed with a knife without a handle, Pangwe tribe.

ELLICE ISLANDS - The tattooing was in great variety on the body; but in all, the arms were tattooed alike, for there it varied only in quantity. On the body it was frequently extended across the back and to the abdomen; and in many, the bodies and thighs were tattooed down as far as the knee.

EMISHI - (also called Ebisu and Ezo), meaning the "Shrimp barbarians", constituted an ancient ethnic group of people who lived in parts of Honshu,

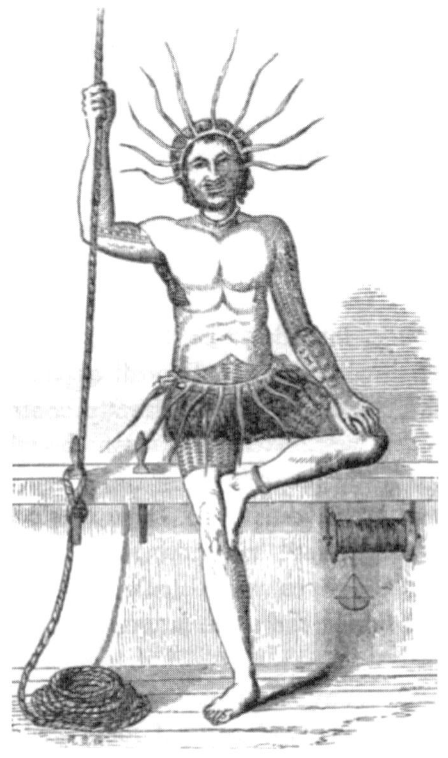

Ellice Islands

especially in the Tohoku region, referred to as michi no oku. See AINU.

EMLAPLAP – Tattooing houses, after the divination and presentation of sacrifices to the gods of tattooing, a large tattooing house did built. Marshall Islands.

EMU OIL - The emu is a large, flightless bird, native to Australia. It is also farmed there as well as in the United States, Canada and Europe. Emu oil prepared from the fat of this bird and is used to make medicine. People use emu oil for conditions such as high cholesterol, dry skin, wound healing (tattoo), sore muscles, and other conditions, but there is no good scientific evidence to support these uses.

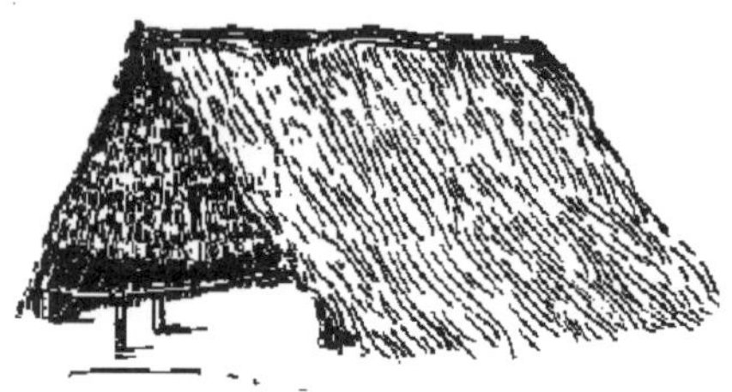

Emlaplap

ENCABELLAO – see SECOYA

EO– tattooing, general name,Marshall Islands.

ESKIMO TRIBES - are the indigenous peoples who have traditionally inhabited the northern circumpolar region from eastern Siberia (Russia) to across Alaska (of the United States), Canada, and Greenland. The two main peoples known as "Eskimo" are: Inuit and Yupik. Practised tattooing.

ESTICHTAI - among the Thracians (4th - 5th centuries BC), those who were "marked", ie tattoos, were considered to be of noble origin.

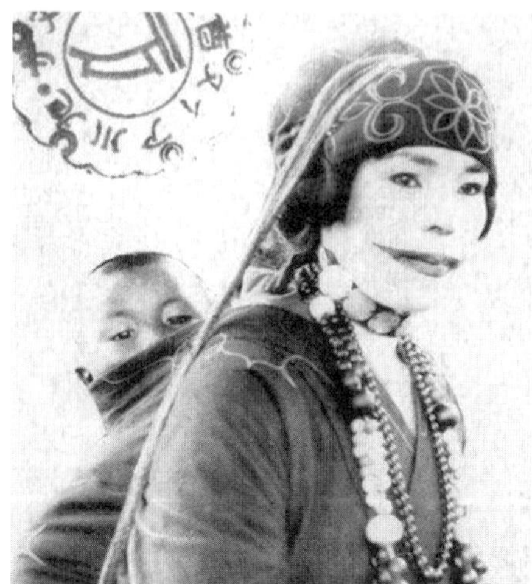

Ainu woman

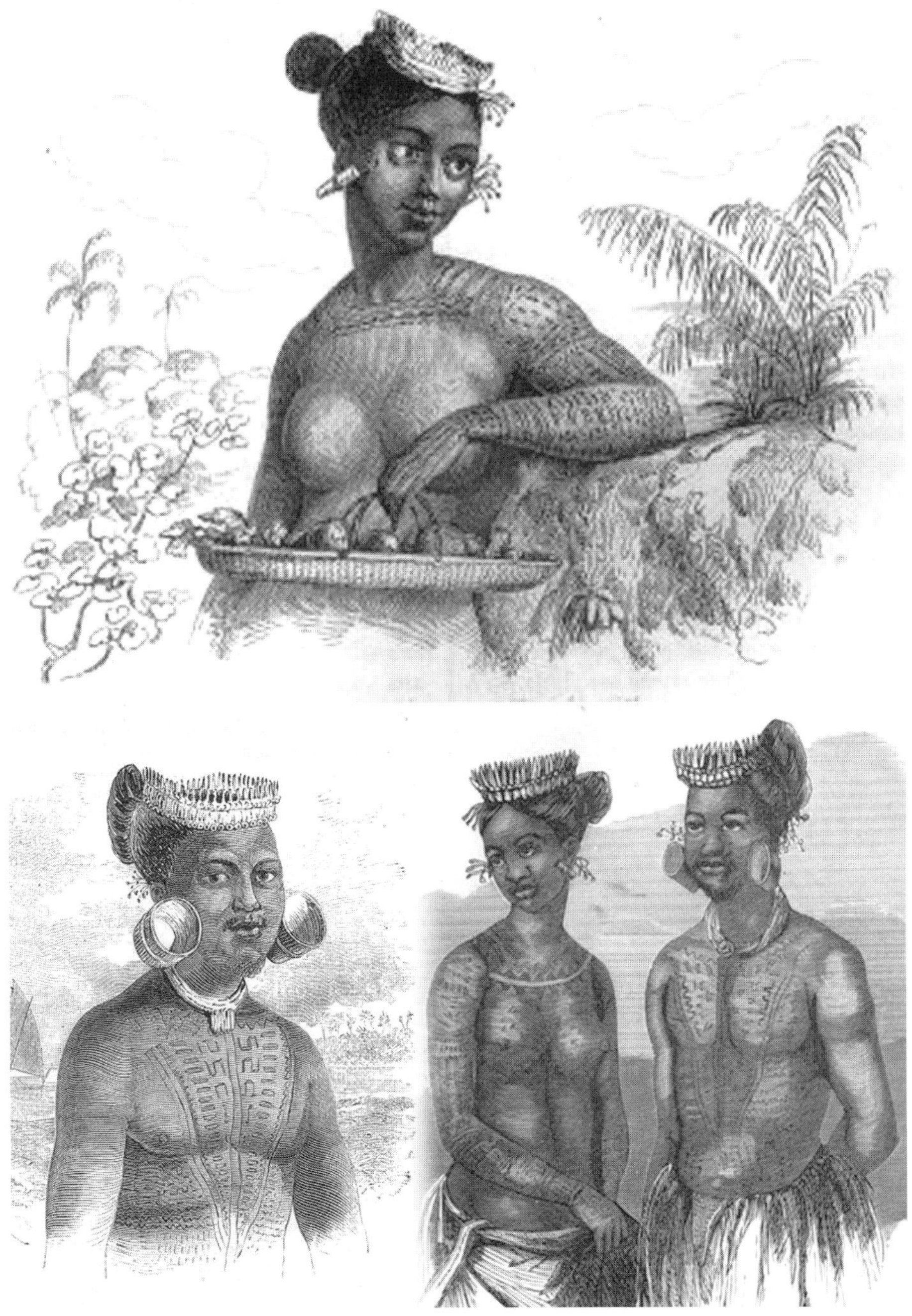

Eo

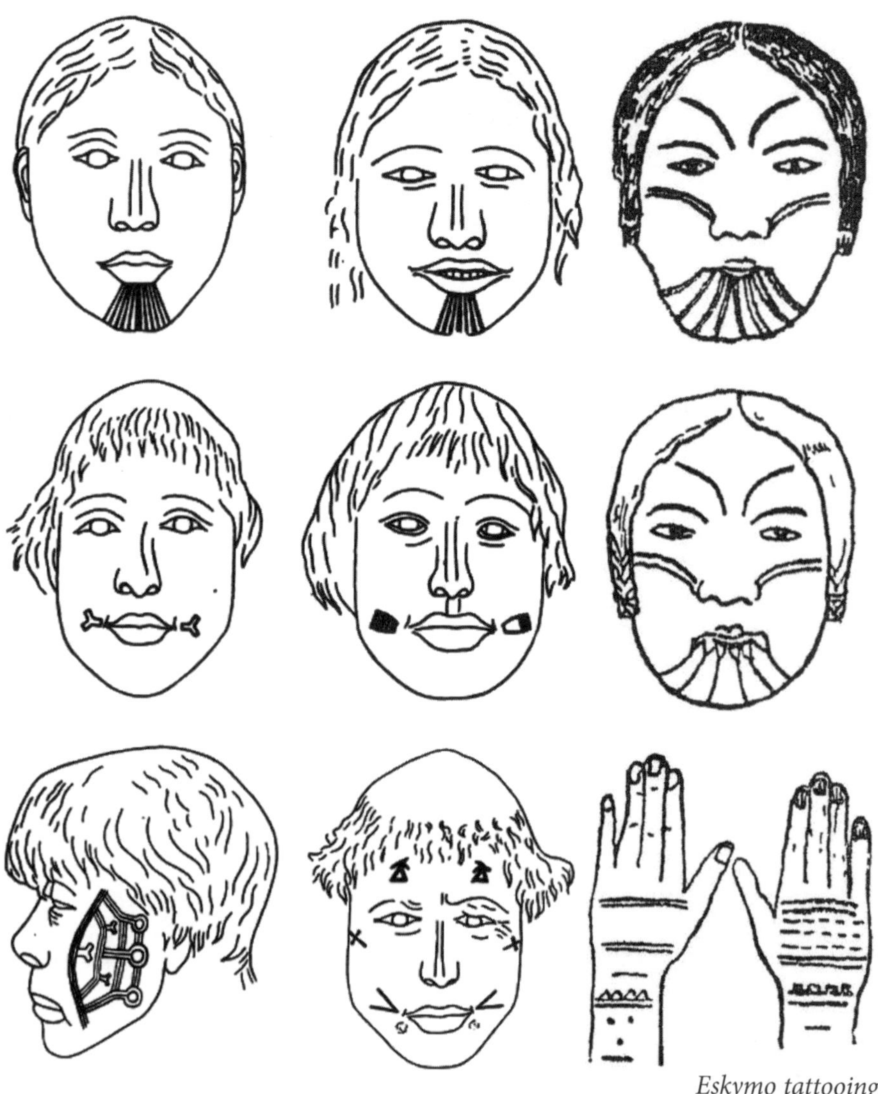

Eskymo tattooing

EVENKS - (also spelled Ewenki or Evenki based on their endonym Ewenki(l)) are a Tungusic people of Northern Asia. In Russia, the Evenks are recognized as one of the indigenous peoples of the Russian North, with a population of 38,396 (2010 census). In China, the Evenki form one of the 56 ethnic groups officially recognized by the People's Republic of China. Facial tattooing was very common.

EZODŽIN - original name for Ainu people from the 7th Century. See also AINU

FA´EPO´A - a small house called fa´epo´a was built next to the family house for the girl's tattoo and the whole family lived in it during the operation, Marquesas Islands.

FAKARAKEI - None of the fakafoiika (tattoo) motifs is generally considered to represent any specific fish. Nor are the projections on them seen as fins, tails and heads, but are simply described as fakarakei or decorations, Tikopia.

FAKATARA - The (tattoo) cuts were made from both the front and back of the blade. The teeth forming the cutting edge are called fakatara, the same name as is used for the toothed pattern carved on bowls and other artefacts, and also in tattoo patterns, Tikopia.

FANGONGO REFU - During the tattooing operation, the black pigment 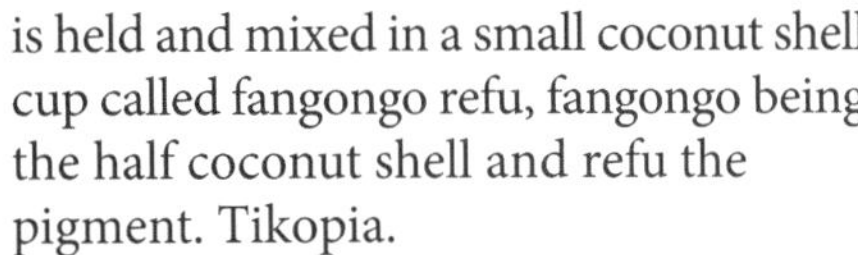 is held and mixed in a small coconut shell cup called fangongo refu, fangongo being the half coconut shell and refu the pigment. Tikopia.

FANJAITRA – tattoo needles, Sakalava tribe.

FAŊOŊO TUKI REFU - a small cup of coconut shell (cup for pounding tattoo pigment), Tikopia.

FANS TRIBE - The King of the Fans was painted his body by red color, and was also covered with body-drawn tattoo-marks.

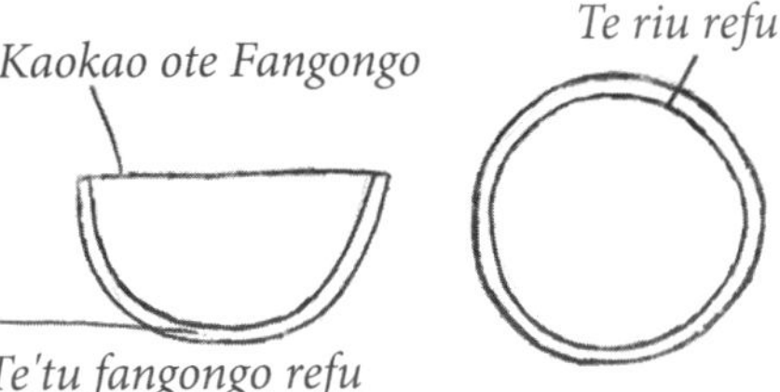

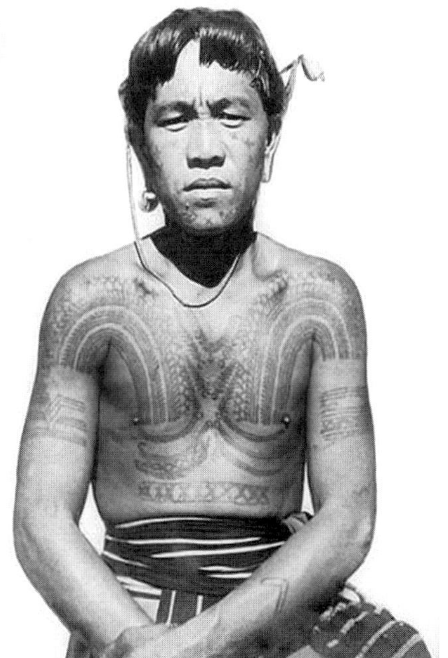

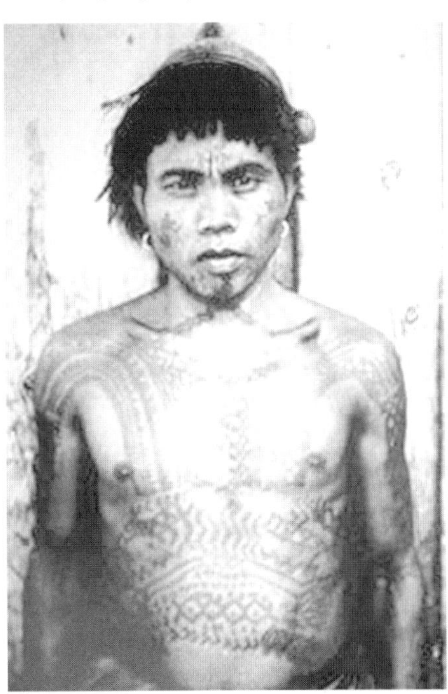

Fa'-tek

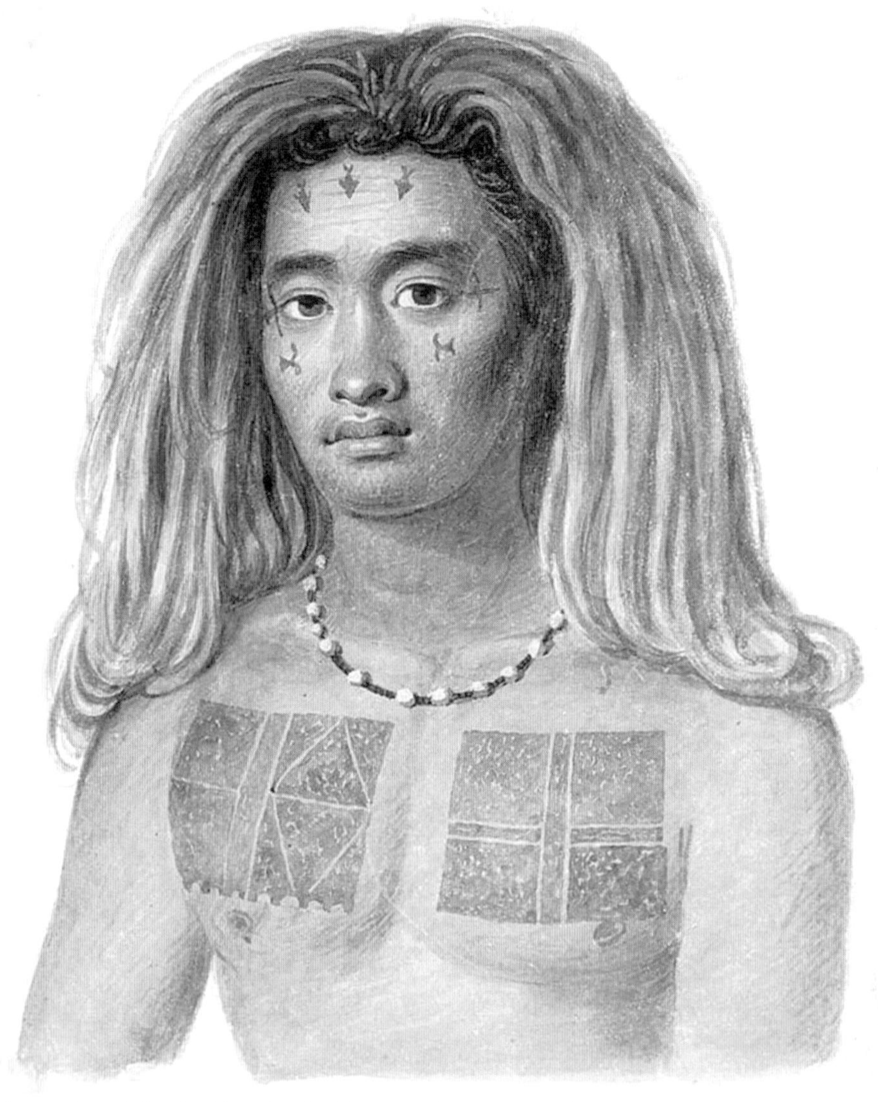

This native of the Pacific island of Tikopia has rectangular chest tattoos which are thought to have been inspired by flags of passing sailing ships, which were considered symbols of power by indigenous peoples. Dates to 1827

FARUFER – for both sexes on Songosor the main decoration of the body was rich tattos farufer, Palau.

FÁTAK – The bontoc Igorot men tattoo (fátak) upper arms, chest and face, with all kinds of fantastic designs.

FA-TĚK – (fatek) tattoo in Bontok tribe language, Filipiness.

FATUKE - is a file made from one of the large spines of a sea urchin and is used for sharpening the fatakara or serrations on the cutting edge of the tattooing chisel. The file, the sea urchin, and its spines are all called vatuke too.

FEOKI– During the entire tattooing process, the girls had to cover their face with a piece of cloth whenever leaving the house. Especially boys and men were not allowed to see their faces, and as a consequence were not allowed to enter the tattooist's house. In the more distant past the girls would cover their entire head and a large part of their bodies with a large tapa (bark cloth), called feoki, while more recently girls would often use a towel.

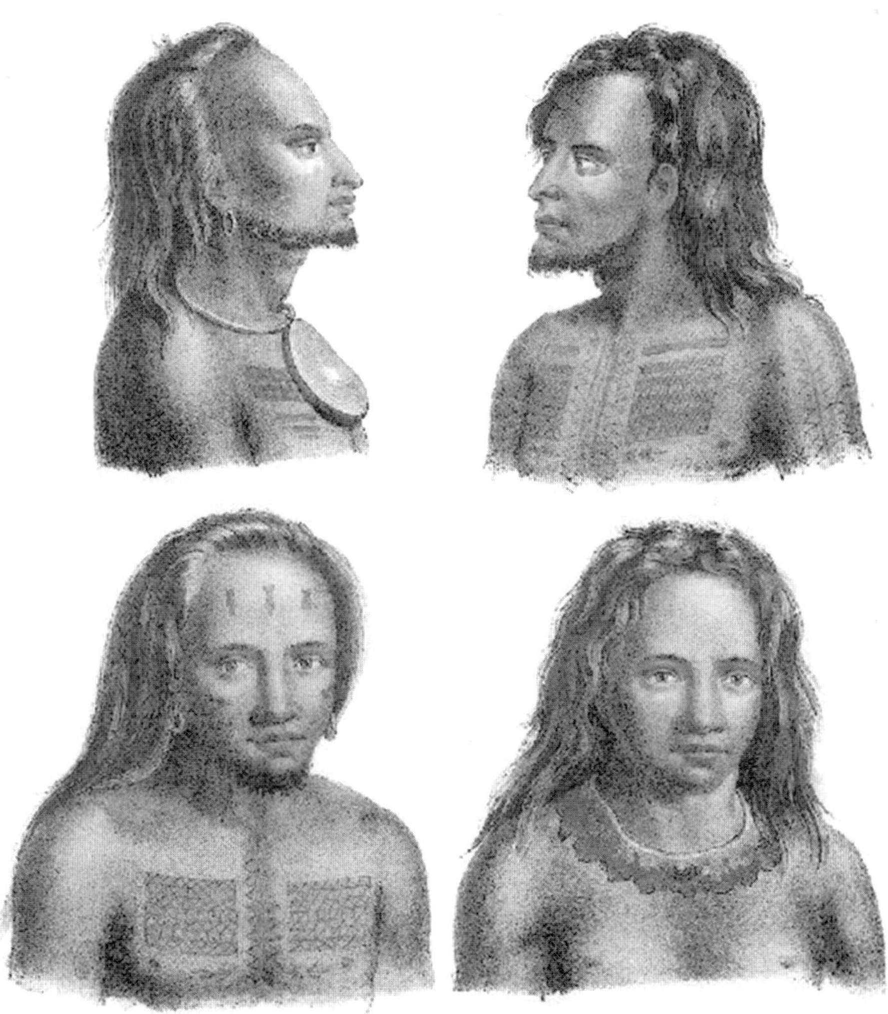

Tikopia tattoo

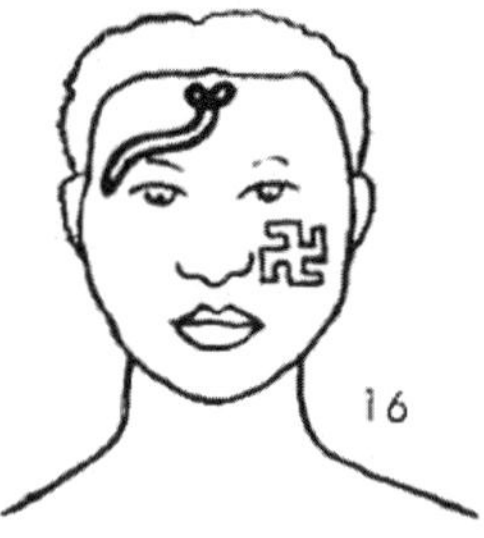

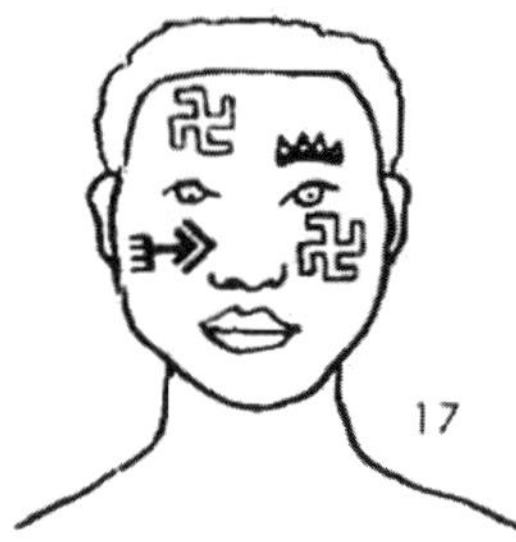

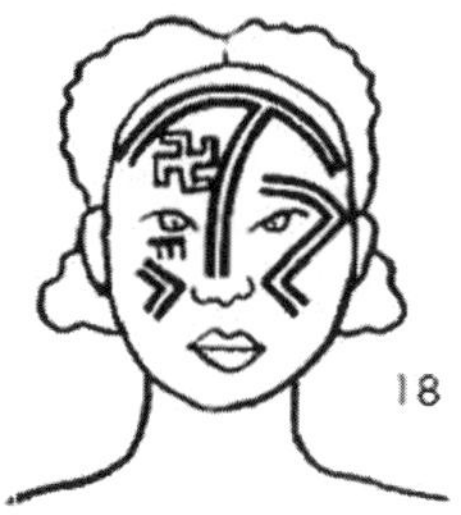

Fanjaitra - Sakalava tattoos

FÉRIFER – the tattooing is called "Férifer" and is practiced extensively in both sexes, Caroline Islands.

FETAU – nuts (Calophyllum inophyllum), a part of tattoo pigment burning process. See TE REFU

FETAU MARO – the dry nuts.

FIEMINA - The tattooed drawings are ornaments, fiemina, and they add: they are "ornaments of the elders," fieminan taolo, Sakalava tribe.

FIEMINAN´ TAOLO – see FIEMINA

FIJI - is an island country in Melanesia in the South Pacific Ocean. Tattooing was called qia. Shortly before puberty, every Fijian girl was tattooed. This was not for ornament, for the marks were limited to a broad horizontal band covering those parts that were concealed

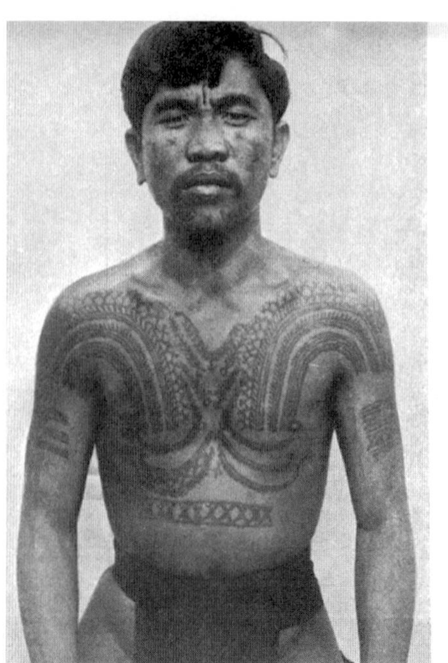
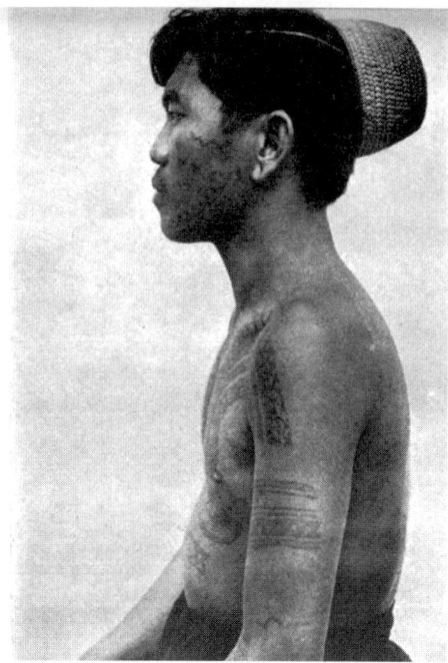

Elaborate Bontoc Igorot tattoo, ca. 1900. Sometimes Bontoc facial tattoos also represented totems, usually of animals, which were protective in nature

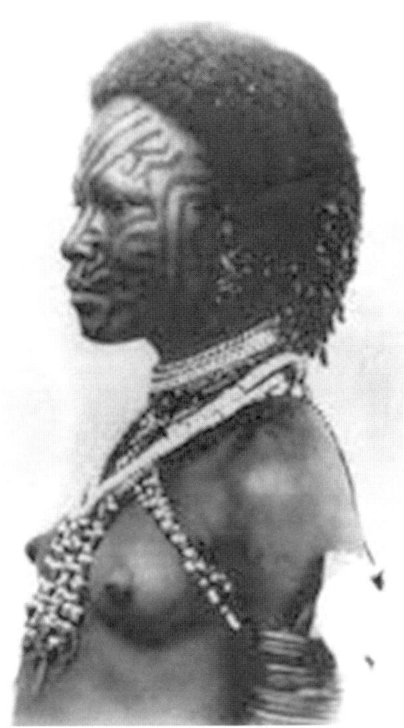

Women's Facial Tattooing among the Maisin of Oro Province, Papua New Guinea

by the liku, beginning about an inch below the cleft of the buttocks and ending on the thighs about an inch below the fork of the legs. The pattern covered the Mons Veneris and extended right up to the vulva.

In addition to this tattooing, barbed lines and dots were marked upon the fingers of young girls to display them to advantage when handing food to the chiefs, and after child- birth a semicircular patch was tattooed at each corner of the mouth. The tattooing of the buttocks had undoubtedly some hidden sexual significance which is difficult to arrive at. It is said to have been instituted by the god Ndengei, and in the last

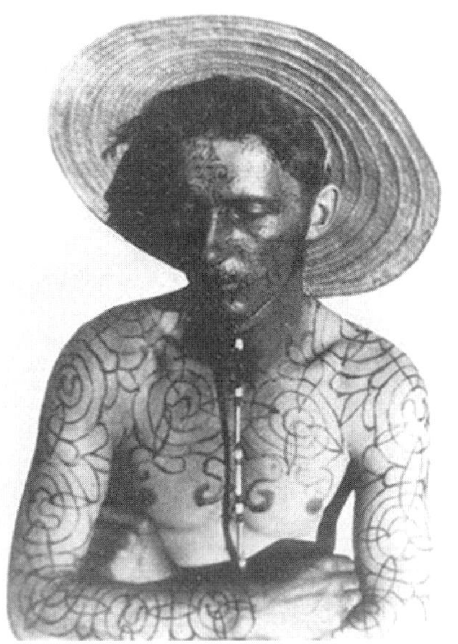

Alberto Vojtěch Frič

journey of the Shades an untattooed woman was subjected to various indignities.

FORMÁNEK, JOSEF – a successful Czech writer and traveller who became famous for his stays with the Mentawai tribe. During these visits, Frománek gained artefacts for his planned exhibition. He has had a ritual Mentawai tattoo done all over the upper body, which represents a primeval forest and the Sun – the life giver – using geometric patterns.

FORMOSA - Taiwan- also Formosa, is an island in Southeast Asia. People applied tattoos.

FRIČ, ALBERTO VOJTĚCH (1882 - 1944) – a Czech geographer, botanist, traveller and writer. South American Indians called him KaraiPukú, means Tall Hunter in English. In Europe, he was also known as the Cactus Hunter. Frič

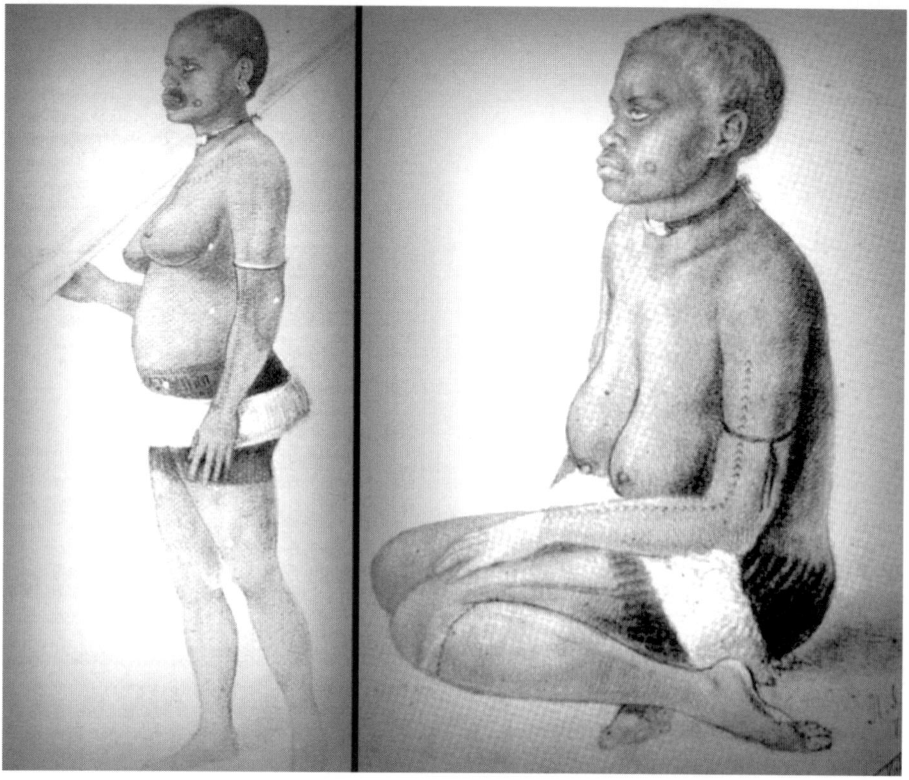

Fijian woman with facial and body tattoos, 1870

visited America and Brazil several times; often he went to places where even Brazilians themselves did not dare to step. He focused on the study of tropic plants and after he returned back to Prague, he organized several successful lectures. Most likely, he was the only European who managed to contact local Indians and gain authority from them. In 1943, Frič's crucial work in the field of ethnography came out – South American Indians – in which he described the traditions of the local Indians.

FROBISHER MARTIN - English sailor, in 1577, Martin Frobisher brought Inuit natives from the Americas to England, and they were covered in tattoos.

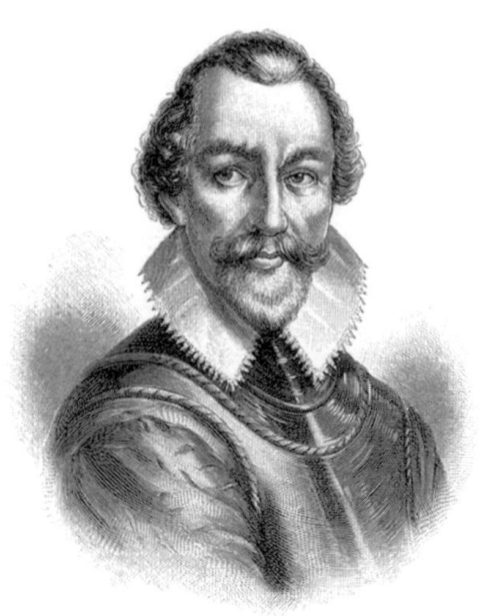

Martin Frobisher

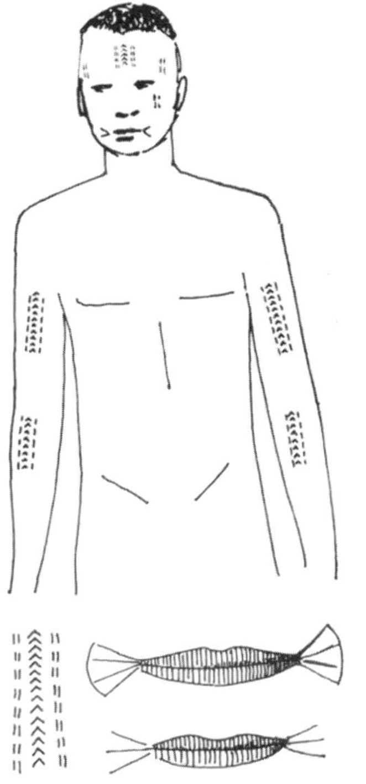

Fulbe: Distribution and drawings of tattoos.

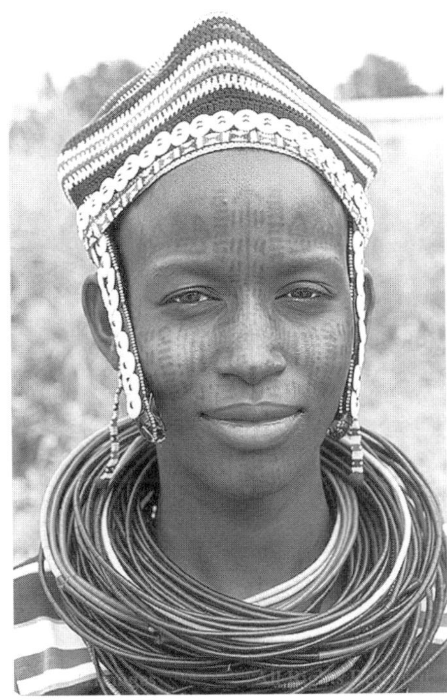

Fulani with traditional tattoo

FULANI – see FULBE

FULBE PEOPLE– a tribe or a community living in West and Central Africa. Their location can be identified by many various names they have been given. Depending on how their names got into European languages, they are called Peuls or Peuhls, Masins, Fula or Fulani. They also use the names of lesser groups which are considered as a part of the whole like Bororo, Toukoleur or Fuuta. Upon the CuraSalé feast, men embellish their faces, besides that, both men and women decorate their faces with tattoos.

FULA– see FULBE

FUMAFĂTEK – tattooer, Bontoc Igorot.

FUNAFUTI - The atoll of Funafuti, Ellice group. People were tattooed their arms being covered, from the shoulder to the wrist, with small curved figures or zig-zag lines. They had this tattooing also on the body, extending from the armpits to the waist, and down, until the whole body was encompassed in the same manner.

FUTI KI RUNGA – see SAU KI TUA

FUUTA – see FULBE

GA-OUA-OUÉ – a term for tattoos in the Neo-Caledonian language.

GAHO - To draw a tattoo outline, Bellona.

GACHAU –tattooing, Yap Island.

GACHOW – a type of tattoo from the island of Yap, designed for ordinary members of the community.

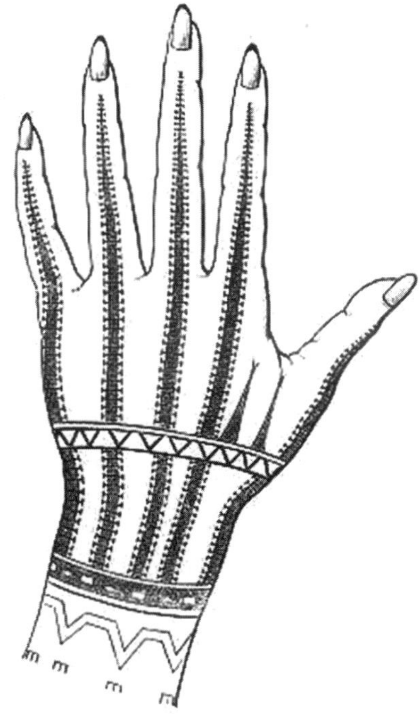

GAL – sketch of a tattoo, Fais Island.

GALIBIS – a tribe from the Mexican region, A.T. Sinclair wrote: that the Galibis still tattoo the feet, half the legs, the forearms, and other parts of the body, and also retain some other very peculiar customs of their ancestors.

GAMA MEA - formerly for handles of tattooing needles, Bellona.

GAMAN – term used for tattooing prevalent in the Kyoto-Osaka region, meaning „endured“ or „perseverance“, originating from the fact that pain had to be endured and perseverance demonstrated while being subjected to the process of tattooing.

GAMBANG - steel needles, Kalinga.

GAN.GAN – colored powder rubbed into the tattoo punctures.

GAPSHIMA – a group of people from southern Dagestan practicing tattoos.

GARANKE - Tattooing among the Bambara is performed by old women who belong to the caste of leather workers, the garanke. See GWELE, N´ZEGENE or NYI-SUSU

GASHING – The Andamanese peoples, who also practice tattooing by means of gashing.

GATODA – The girl to be tattooed goes into the forest and scrapes resin or gum from some bleeding place in the bark of the trunk of a tree, a Barringtonia bearing edible almonds, called gatoga. Having collected enough she returns to her home. Early the next morning she lights the gum and catches the soot in the concave stem of a fresh coconut leaf. This soot the girl scrapes into the half shell of a coconut, and mixes it into a paste with a little water. After three days she squeezes the juice of the fruit of the tree aguru into the paste to thin it and make it suitable for tattooing. Bellon, Santa Anna and Santa Catalina, Solomon Group.

GEEMUGI – three, white sap of the trunk is smoked black for torches (pugu) and formerly for tattooing dye, Bellona.

GEISHI = apply tattooing, Japan.

GEISHIN - was a technical name used for convict tattoos in Japan since the 17th century until its extinction in 1870. Convict tattoos were probably nothing new in the Tokugawa period. Already in the Jomon period (10,000BCE-300), there are records about Japanese interested in the practice of aesthetic tattoos, but also in convict tattoos. However, with an emphasis on the Confucian ideology in the Tokugawa period, the convict tattoo became not only a brand of crime, but it was also a contempt for one's family. Confucian doctrine says that "protecting one's body means to worship god." In the Tokugawa period, long black stripes on forearms were used for marking criminals and many scientists believe that the beginnings of Japanese body suits (tattoos all over the body that look like clothing) are based on recovery of the body by tattoo wearers.

GENIPAPO (too Jenipapo - Genipa braziliensis) – Once upon a time, the Kaduvej patterns supposedly used to be tattooed, but later prevailed the painting with the juice from the fruit of the jenipapo tree. Unlike faint, over sweetened tropical fruit, its pulp, including its loquat-looking stone, is sour like a lemon, refreshing and thirst-quenching, yet no one eats it. It is because its juice that turns everything that it comes in contact with – hands, lips, teeth, tongue – blue and it lasts three-four weeks to get rid of it. Some Indian tribes use this property for tattoos – but a pattern like this, which may not necessarily be always done perfectly stays with a man to his death. For this reason, it is better to use the paint just for painting. Indian women smudge the squeezed transparent green juice using a stone in a bowl and blend it with pulverized charcoal, so it is possible to control the even application of paint and do the painting by a "brush" made of chips from bamboo bark. After several hours, charcoal is washed away, the juice slowly oxidates on the air and by the following day, a beautiful, blue cyan ornament, which colour is more intense day by day, begins to appear. After several weeks, when the painting begins to fade, it is possible to change the pattern or repair it until it is absolutely perfect.

GI HOT – designation for a tall man (scalp holder) who is tattooed on both sides of the face with a T-shaped motif, Osage.

GIHNI – Tattoo instrument. They are extremely simple and consist of Gihni and Iboki, the knocker. Gihni consists of a about 1 3/2 long thorn, which is cut off with a piece of the branch in such a way that the latter forms the natural stem. Papua New Guinea.

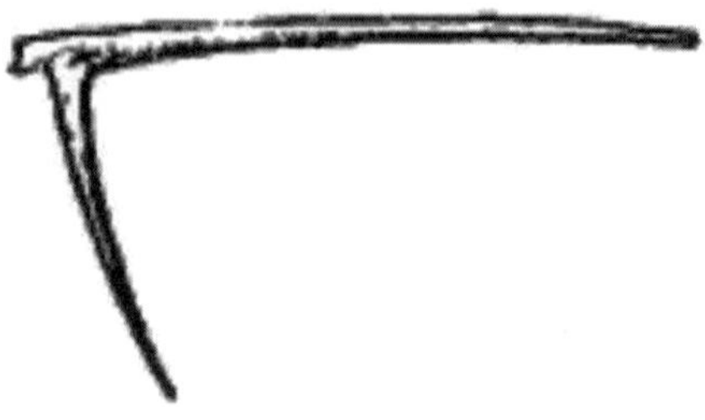

GILBERT ISLANDS - The Gilbert Islands (Gilbertese: Tungaru;formerly Kingsmill or King's-Mill Islands) are a chain of sixteen atolls and coral islands in the Pacific Ocean about halfway between Papua New Guinea and Hawaii. They form the main part of Kiribati ("Kiribati" is the Kiribati rendition of "Gilberts").

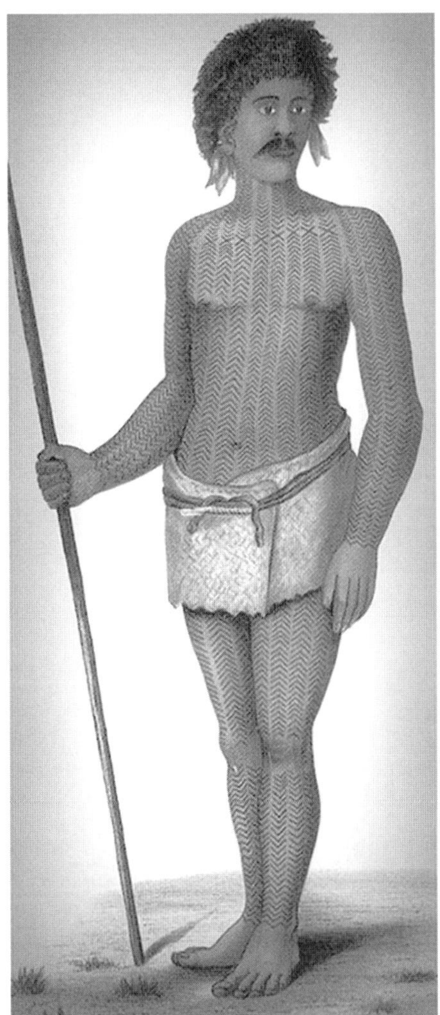

Heavily tattooed man of Gilbert Island, 1880

Peoples practised tattooing.

GILYAKS–see NIVKH PEOPLE

GINI– tattoo needle attached to iboki, Papua New Guinea.

GIOLO - known also as "Prince Giolo", as he used to be called, was one of the first people (if not the first of all) who tried to expose his tattooed body for earnings. In 1961, William Dampier received Giolo in London with an intention to make profit from his exhibition so he would be able to pay a debt. Dampier heavily invested into the propagation of the exhibition, which was eagerly expected by English audience, including the king and queen. Among other claims, he alleged that Giolo's tattoo protect him against snake poisons.

GISHIWAJINDEN - The custom of tattooing in Japan is described in the third-century Chinese account Gishiwajinden. This is the oldest record mentioning Japan. Japan is called Wa, and the custom of tattooing is mentioned as: The men of Wa tattoo their faces and paint their bodies with designs. Long ago they decorated their bodies in order to protect themselves from large fish. (They are fond of diving for fish and shells) Later these designs became ornamental. Bodypainting differs among the various tribe. The position and size of the designs

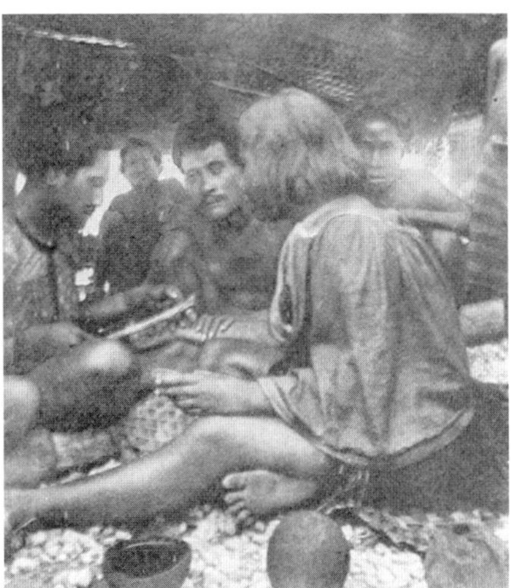

Tattoo process - Gilbert Islands

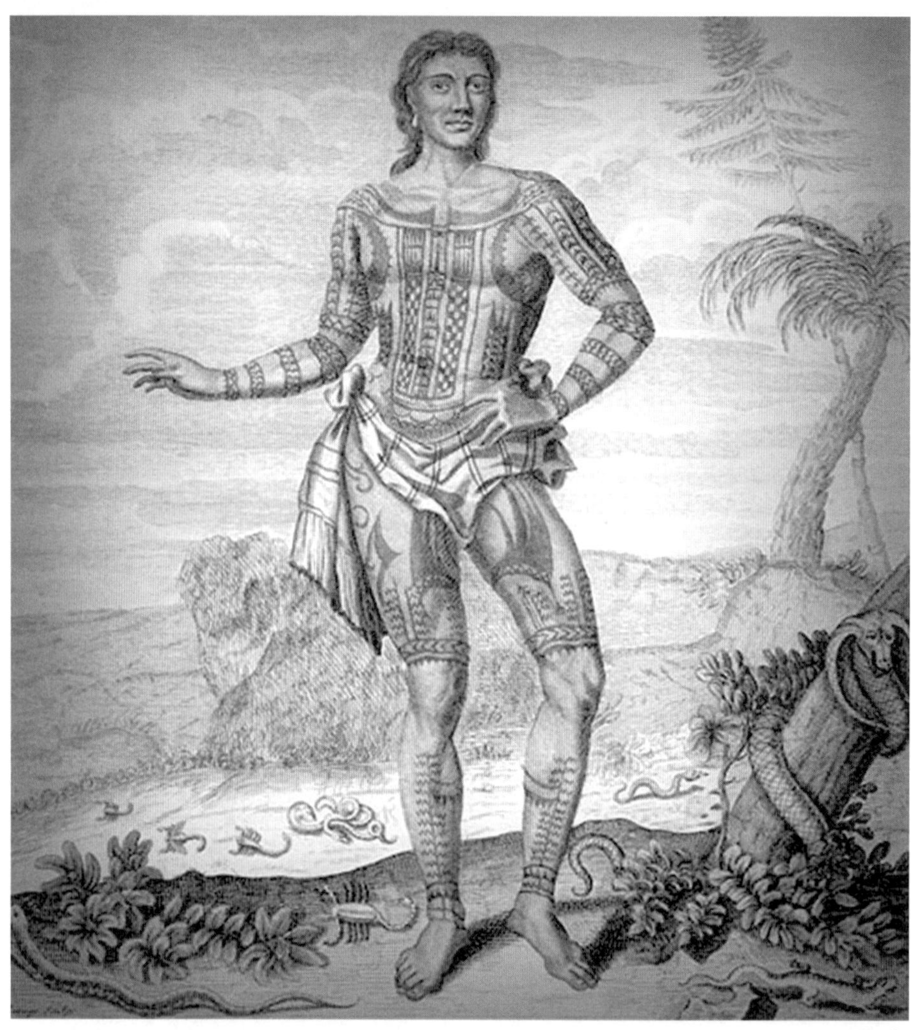

Giolo

vary according to the rank of individuals.

GISI –The Kankanay (group in the Luzon region of the Philippines) use the tattoo implement gisi and is a piece of wood to which is attached a set of needles, made of thorns. The needles are then tapped into the skin using a mallet.

GNATU - bark that was used to wipe tattoos, Tonga Island.

GOBBIAT – The Mentawai tribe (Indonesia) applies not only permanent tattoos (titi), but also gobbiat, painting the face with paint.

GODNA–Women of the Baiga tribe of Madhya Pradesh are known for their art of tattooing or Godna. This practise has been an integral part of the Baiga culture for women of the tribe. This art form instils a sense of pride among the women.

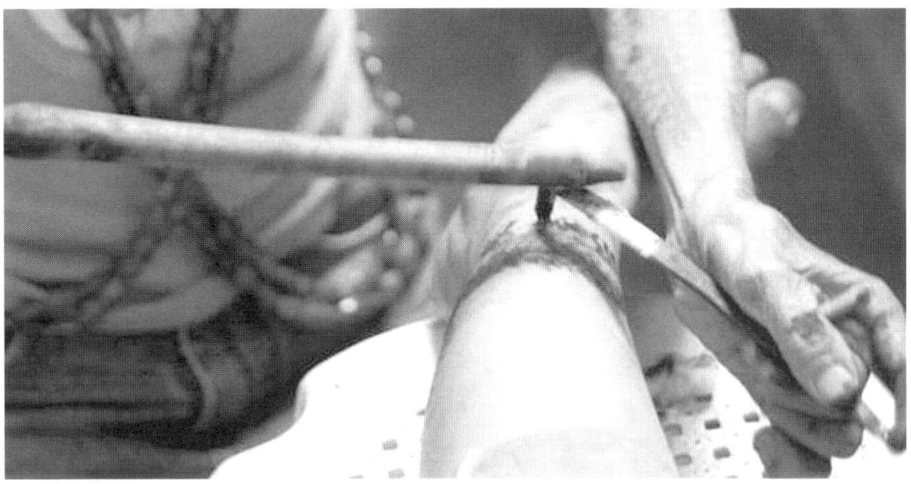

Gisi

The women feel incomplete without their godna.

GODHARINS - The women who work as tattooing artists belong to the Ojha, Badni and Dewar tribes of Madhya Pradesh are called Godharins.

GOLDIE, CHARLES FRDERICK - (October 20, 1870 - July 11, 1947) was a New Zealand artist who painted tattooed Maori.

GONZALO DE, GUERRERO – probably the first white man tattooed by a Mayan method (mention from 1511). He first became a prisoner, a slave, and then he converted. He got married and fought

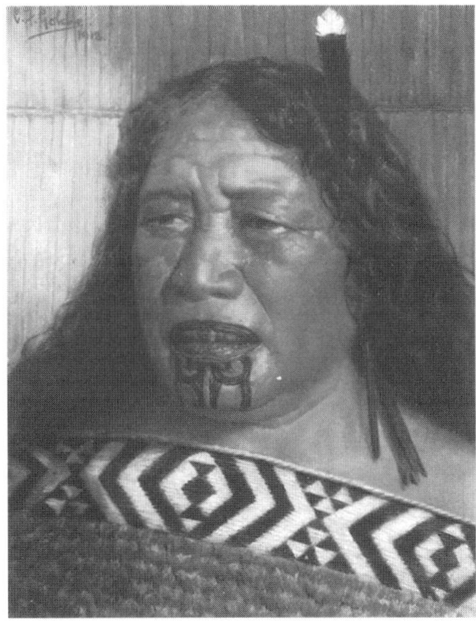

Goldie art

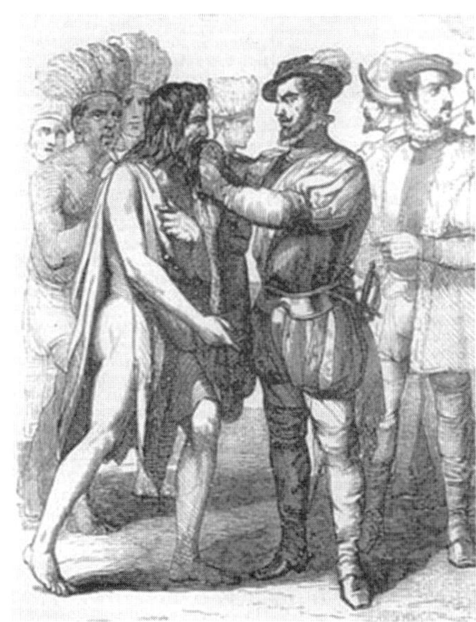

Guerrero de Gonzalo

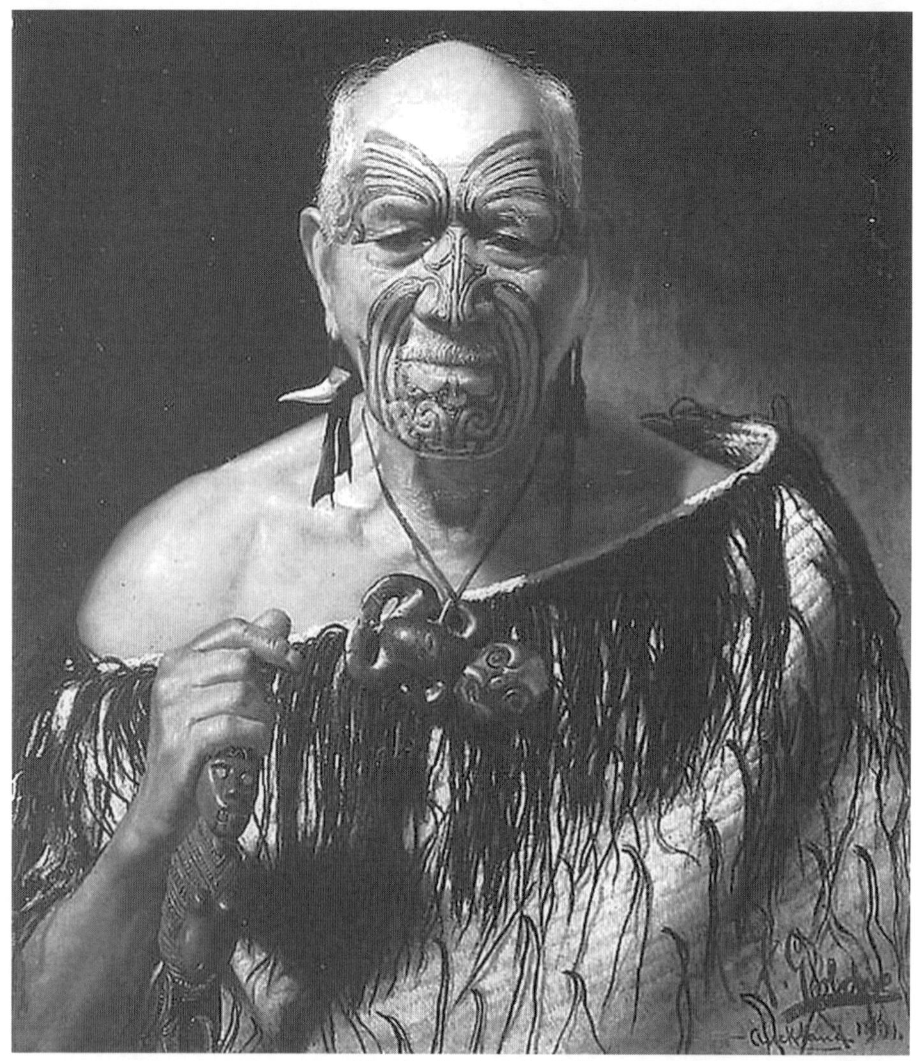

Charles Frederick Goldie - image of a tattooed Maori

against Spanish conquistadors. When he got a chance to get back to his mother country, he responded: "… fare thee well, for I got my face tattooed and ears pierced." In 1536, the Spanish were attacked near the Honduras coast and after a won battle; they found a body of a white man between the Indians' cadavers. It was Guerrero.

GORDÉMĚL - the handle, it was passed through a hole in the little slab (madál), Palau isl.

GORO –or GURO – to tattoo, Shilluk people, Afrika.

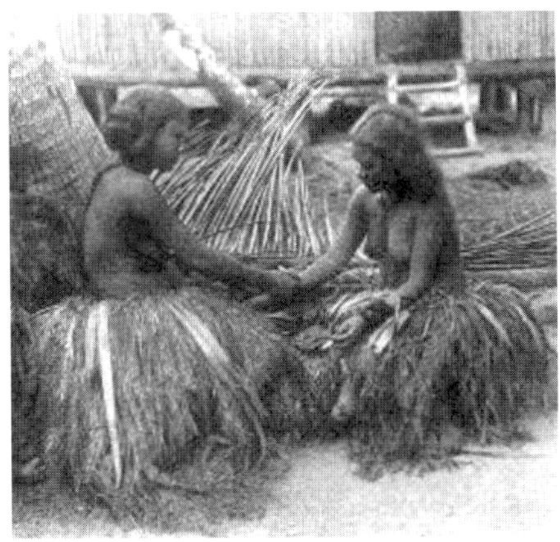

Götau tattooing

GÖTAU – is the native name for the art or tattooing, Yap.

GREENLAND MUMMIES - In 1972, a group of mummies was found at two burial grounds in the area of Qilakitsoq in Greenland. Greenland mummies are the best-preserved body remains found in Northern America. They dated back to the half of the 15th century. This period relates to the Thule culture in the Arctic, which was a former form of the modern Inuit culture.

In accordance with Inuit traditions, mummified women had facial tattoos. The tattoos consisted mainly of curves on foreheads and cheeks. The basic forehead pattern was arched over and between over the eyebrows, as if in an "M" shape. The lines on cheeks started from the bottom of outer corner of the eyes and diagonally stretched to nostrils. The chins of three mummies were

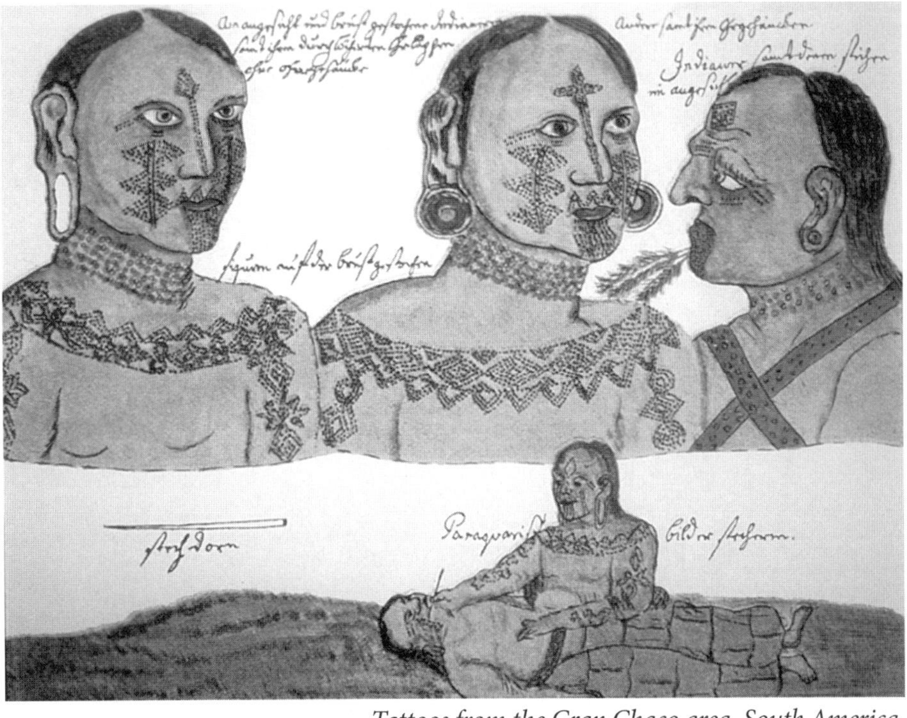

Tattoos from the Gran Chaco area, South America

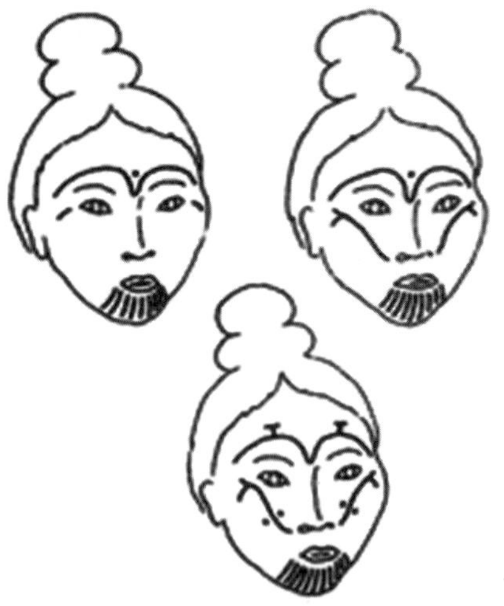

Reconstructions of the Qilakitsoq mummies

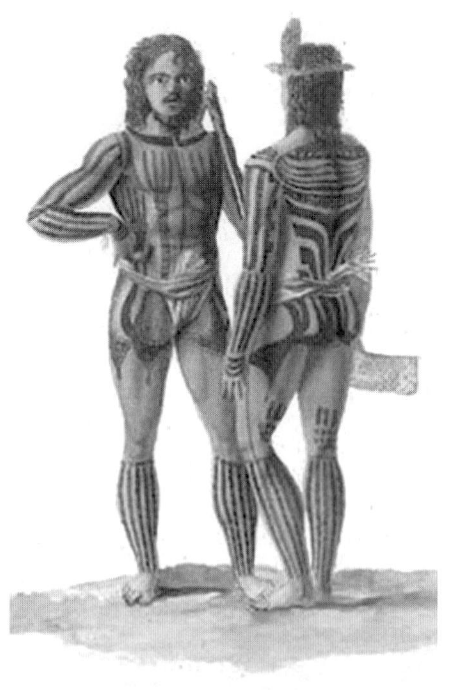

Guam, 1819

decorated by a group of vertical lines. Some bodies also had dots on foreheads and cheeks.

GUAM CULTURE - The culture of the Marianas Islands, including Tinian, Saipan, Rota, and Guam, reflects

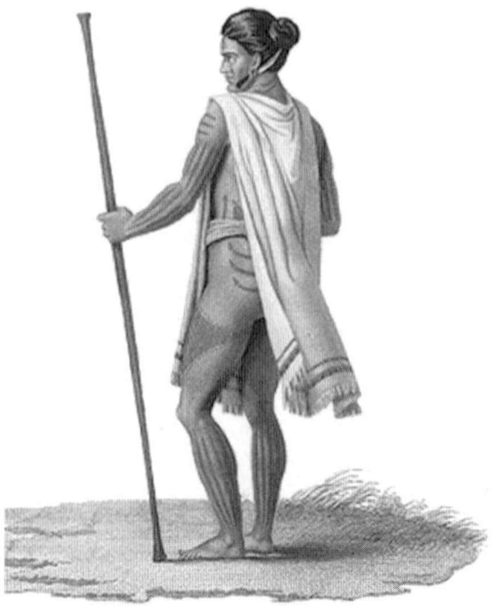

Guam Men by Jacques Arago

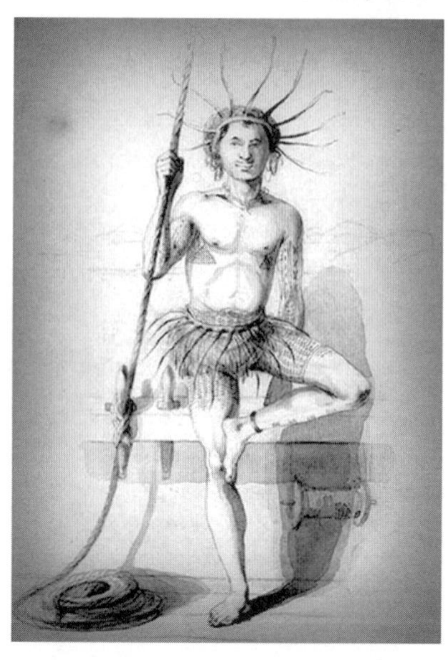

A man from the southern part of the Gilbert Islands, 1840

traditional Chamorro customs in a combination of indigenous pre-Hispanic forms, as well as American, Filipino, Spanish and Mexican traditions.[1] The Chamorro people have lived on the Micronesian island of Guam for nearly 4000 years, and have cuisine, dance, fashion, games, language, music, and songs of their own.

GUAYCURÚS – Paraguayan, Bilovian and Argentine Gran Chaco. They custom of pulling off the eyelashes, ear-ornaments, tattooing and scarification used,

GUISIT – Several scholars have documented the process of tattooing among the people in the Cordilleras. An early account, by Fray Perez, narrates that the process of tattooing was done "with three needles joined, the points of which are millimeter apart like steps, and dipped in a liquid somewhat like ink, made of pig's bile and soot, which mixture, called guisit, they introduce into the skin in the same way as vaccination among us, and it causes inflammation so great that it prevents them from being able to work for some days, which inflammation is always accompanied by a high fever. Among the drawings of animals, the figure of the lizard predominates all of them," Burik tribe.

GUWAR– Atayal name for a scraper that wipes blood from tattoos. It was mostly made of reeds.

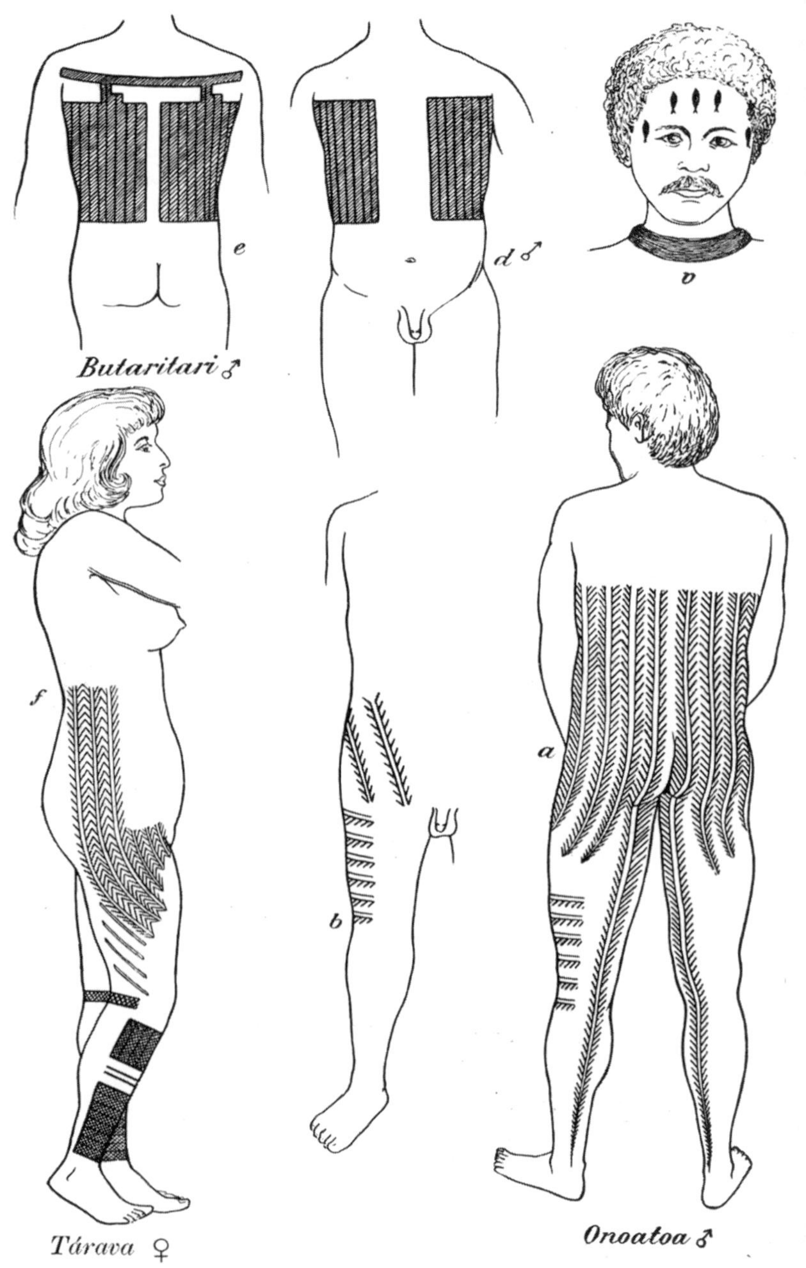

Pictures: Gilbert Islands - a, b, c - man of Onoatoa; a from the back, b from the front, c calf from the inside; d, e - Man of Butaritari; d from the front, e from the back; f - wife of Tárava; g - Woman's calf from the inside on Tapitúea; h, i - female arm and leg of Makin;

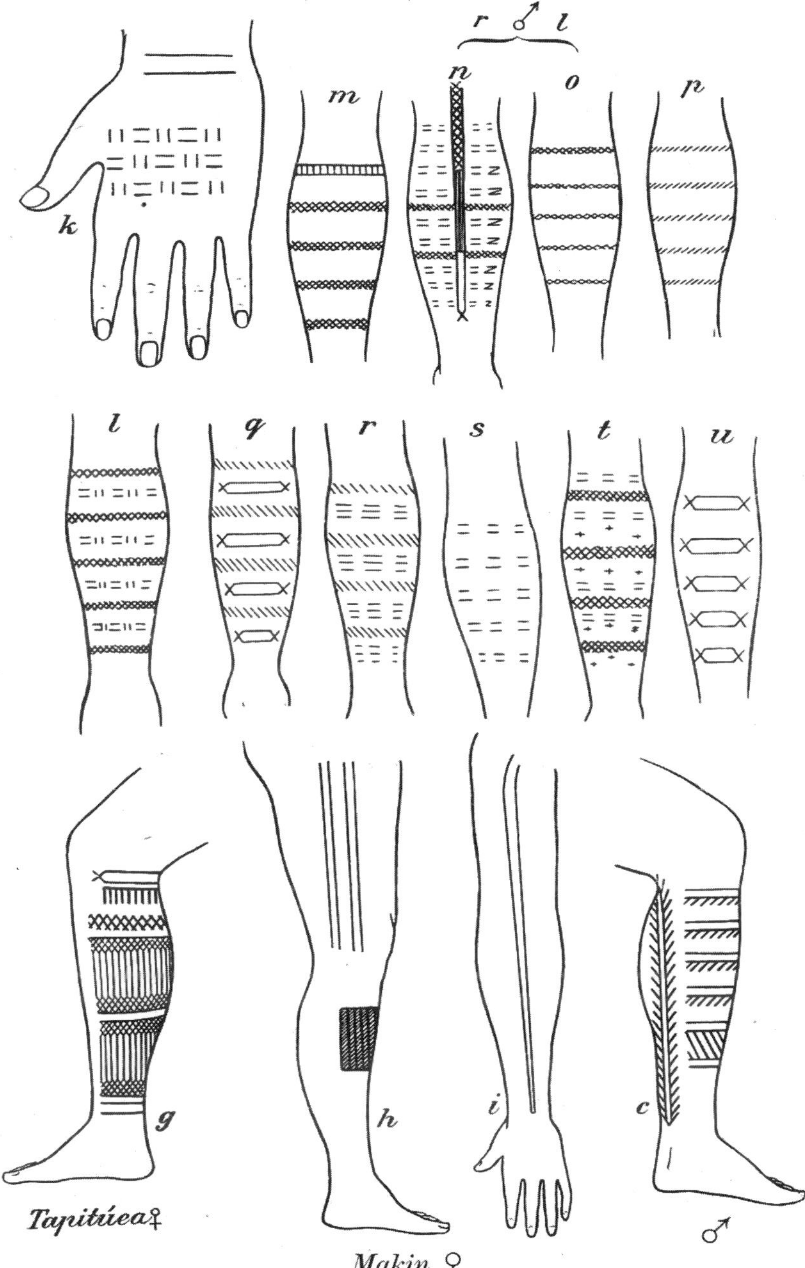

k, l - Back of the hand and inner arm of a girl from Tapitúea; m - forearm of a girl from ibid.; n, o - right and left forearm of a man from ibid; p-u - insides of girls' forearms on Nonuti; v - Face of a man with fish from Apamama

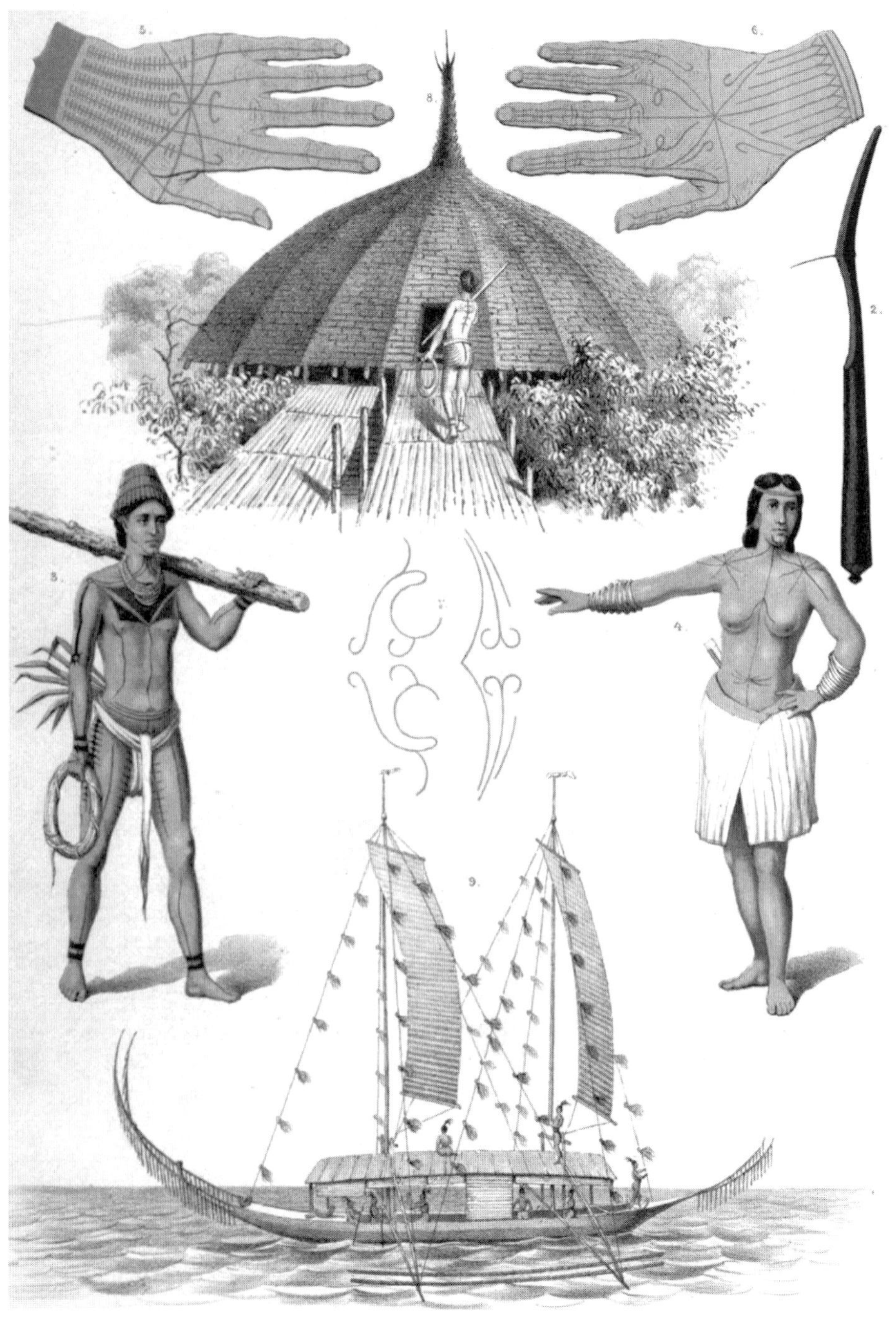

Guyana Indians and their tattoos

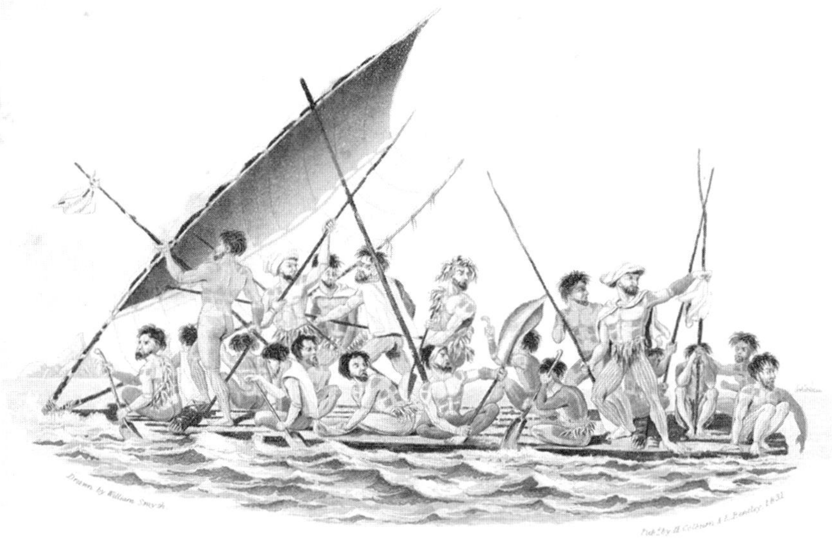

A Raft Of Gambier Island

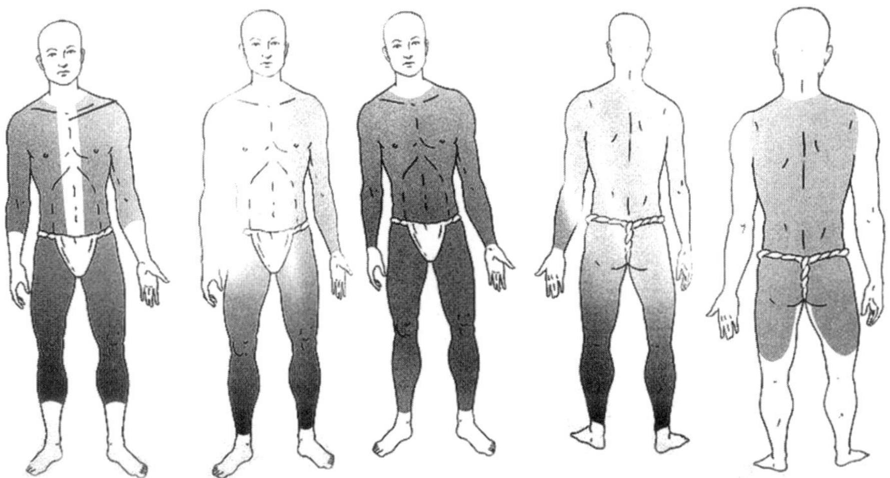

Japan
The style with a strip of leather in the middle is called munewari.
7/10 sleeves and legs with v-shaped spots on the inner thighs and inner biceps (katabori) is called "shishibu munewari"
Full sleeves and full legs with a stripe in the middle are called "soushinbori munewari"
5/10 sleeves with a skin strip in the middle and on the thighs are called "Gobu" or "Gobu munewari"
No sleeves with a full back to the back of the thighs are called "Kame no koh" (turtle)
Full coverage is called "Donburi soushinbori"

HAIDA - are original people of the Pacific Northwest Coast. Their homelands are the islands near the coast of southeastern Alaska and northwest

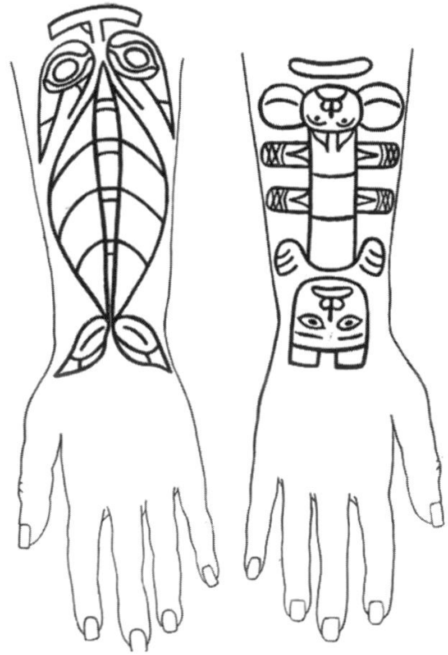

British Columbia, particularly the Haida Gwaii archipelago and Prince of Wales Island. The Haidas painted their faces with different colors and designs for

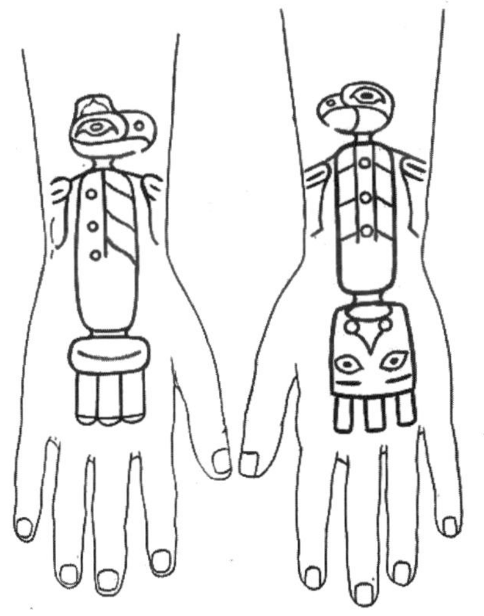

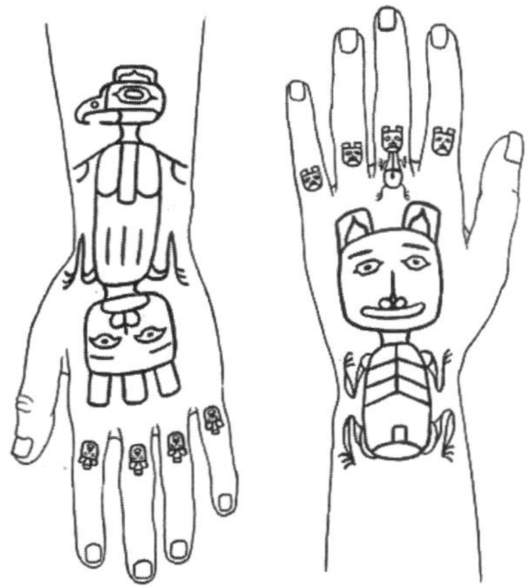

different occasions, and often wore tribal tattoo designs of stylized animals.

HAI-DA-MAS-A – black tattoo ink, Haida.

HAILTZAS - North American Indian tribe from around the Bella Coola River, practicing tattoos.

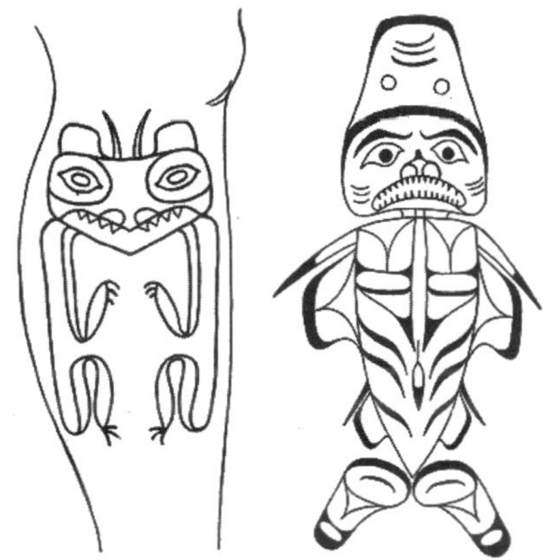

HĂJI - A.T. Sinclair wrote: The pious duty of every good Moslem is to make the pilgrim- age to Mecca, and many also go to Medina. Thousands go every year and from all parts of the Mohammedan world, even from Turkestan, India, and the Far East. So here as at Jerusalem, it

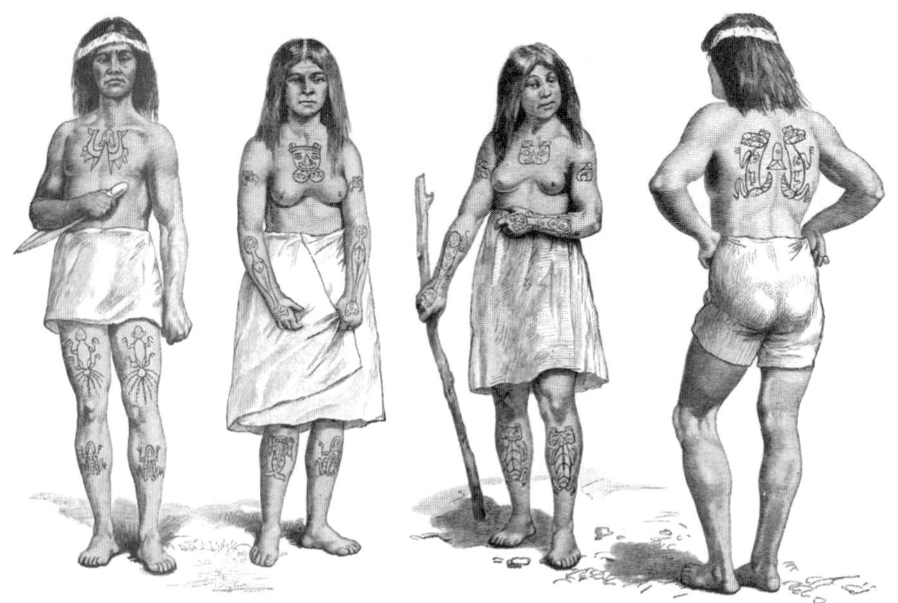

Haida

is now as for centuries the custom for all pilgrims to be tattooed, with the date of pilgrimage, name or initials, and holy devices. Some Africans whose skin is too dark to show tattooing have three gashes made on the right cheek, which were the tribe mark of Mohamed and were born eby him on his cheek. Such a Moslem pilgrim is called in Turkish Hăji, and this word applied hence to such tattooing

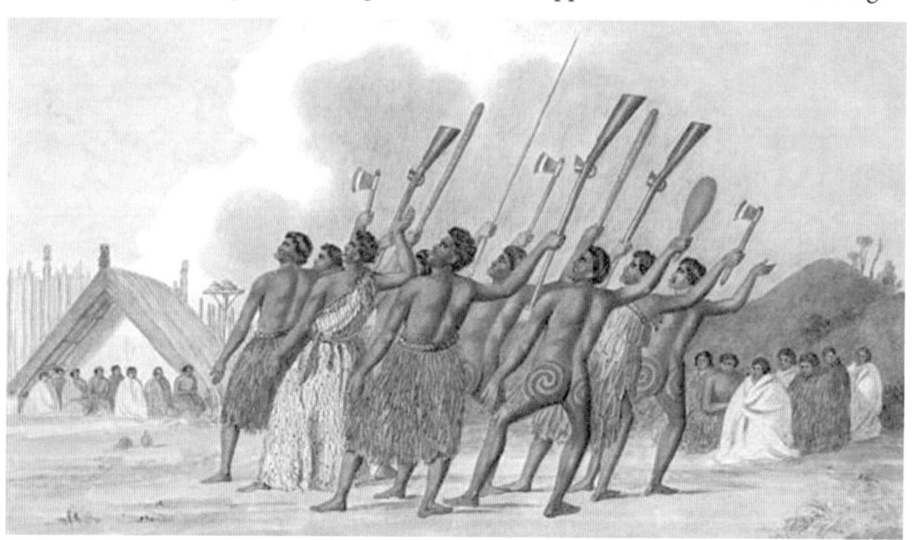

Haka

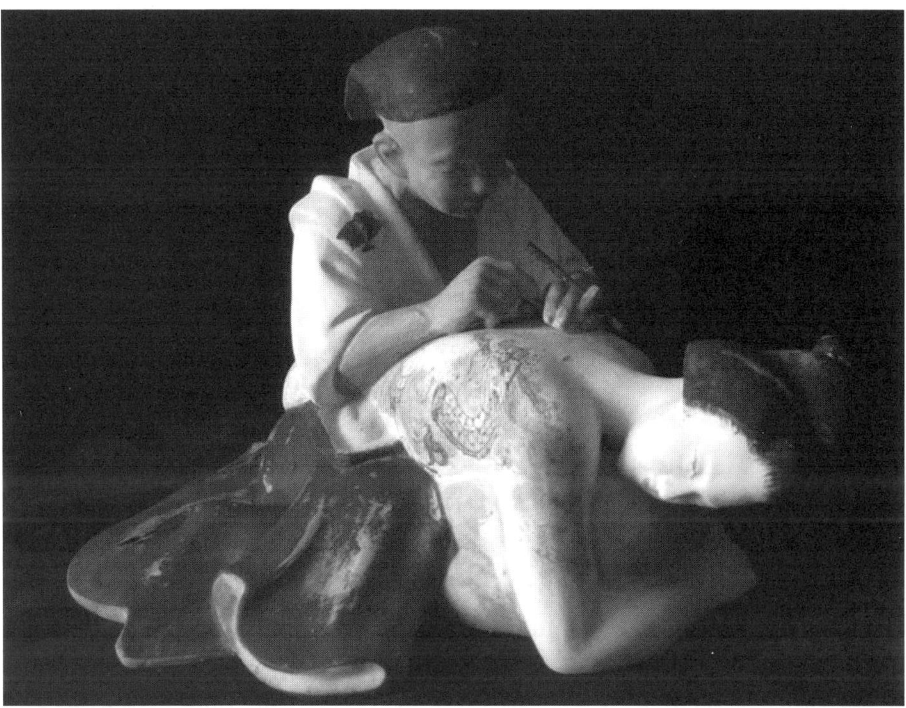

Hakata

made in Mecca is now the only word for any tattoo mark. Sometimes I have seen a spot at the root of the thumb of a Turk made when a boy, but he always still applied the word haji to it. It is contrary to the Koran to be tattooed, and as the Turks are very strict Mohammedans few are marked otherwise.

HAKA – (Maori: "dance") Maori posture dance that involves the entire body in vigorous rhythmic movements, which may include swaying, slapping of the chest and thighs, stamping, and gestures of stylized violence. It is accompanied by a chant and, in some cases, by fierce facial expressions meant to intimidate, such as bulging eyes and sticking out of the tongue. Though often associated with the traditional battle preparations of male warriors, haka may be performed by both men and women, and several varieties of the dance fulfill social functions within Maori culture.

HAKATA– the Hakata doll's porcelain skin is synonymous with beautiful skin for Japanese women. In Japan, archeological evidence indicates that simple biscuit fired dolls were consumed at Buddhist temples in Hakata and Kamakura in the 12th century. In the year 1600, Lord Nagamasa Kuroda came to Hakata province to become its governor, and many artists and craftsmen were summoned by his side. The ceramic dolls that emerged at this time are the root of Hakata dolls. In the late 19th century, prominent artists such as Soushichi Masaki boosted the reputation for Hakata's doll making.

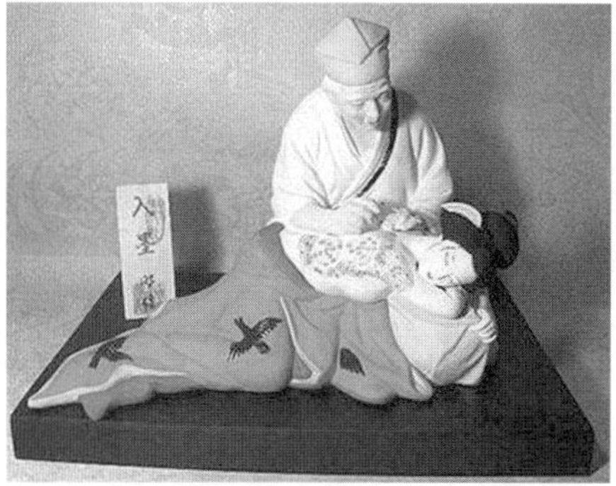

Hakata

HALACH UINIC – Halach Uinic was the head of a city-state in the Mayan civilization. In his book Indians Without Tomahawks (Indiáni bez tomahawků), M. Stignl states: "A Real man differed not only from the public, but also from lower ranked members of the ruling class, firs and foremost by his splendid clothes: a beautiful big crown – headband – made of feathers of rare birds, colourful sandals, nephrite rings, etc. His face was richly

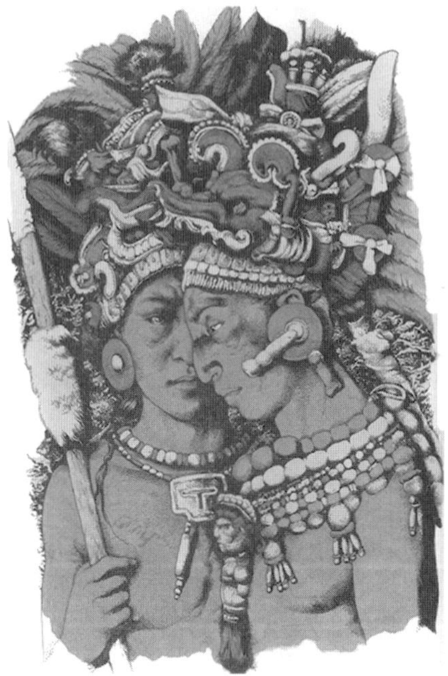

covered in tattoos and a large fake nose. The nose should represent a beak of an eagle. Other parts of his face and the whole body were also embellished or intentionally deformed to highlight the exclusiveness of the Real man. Teeth were sharpened and adorned by inserted nephrite plates, ear lobes were pierced and elongated by inserting a turkey egg. Men even deformed their penis"

HALIB UMM AL-BINT – Many people hold that the soot must be moistened with halib umm al-bint, the milk of a woman nursing a daughter, which has magic properties, but others say that is it not good, and water or kerosene, Berber people.

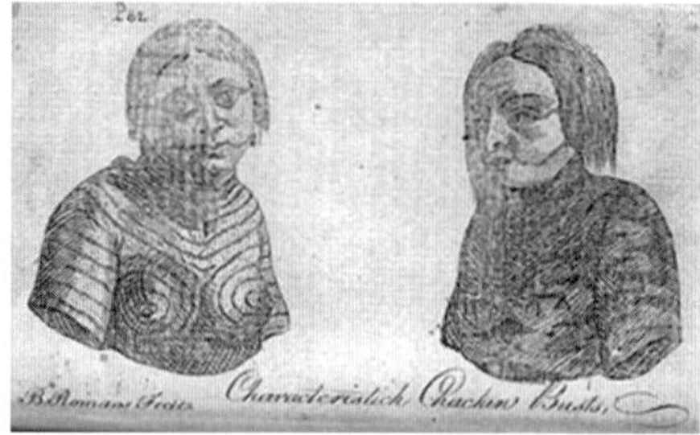

Hanchahale

HAMER– also HAMAR. Tribes from southern Ethiopia, practicing tattoos, scarring and body painting.

HANCHAHALE – Choctaw tattooing (hanchahale) was practised by both men and women, but only to a very limited extent. An women had lines of tattooing extending from the corners of her mouth across both cheeks to her ears. The method of tattooing practised was follows: A needle was used to puncture the skin and soot caused by a fire of yellow pine was rubbed over the surface. This was then wiped off and more soot rubbed in, to make certain that all the

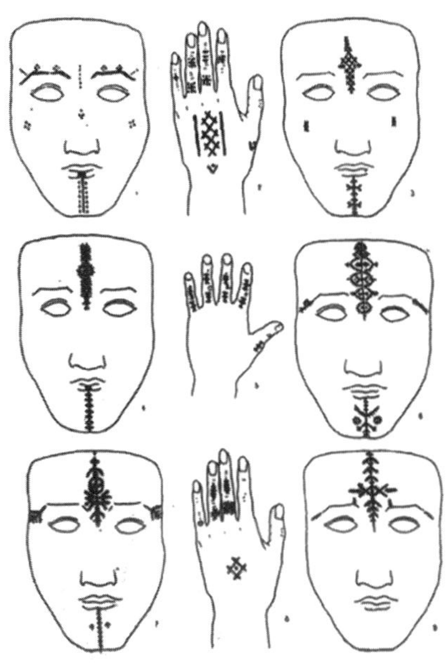

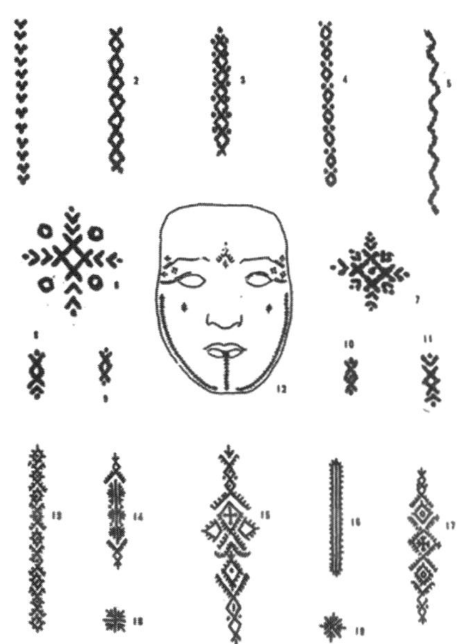

Hargus - motif patterns

punctures were filled. The soot gave a bluish tinge to their dots. No other substance or color ever employed.

HANE BARI - technique, which is less painful but requires an even greater skill and experience of the tattoo master. This method involves inserting the needles diagonally into the skin at a particular angle and subsequently levering the tattoo shaft in such a way that the needle points are raised slightly upwards, just under the outer surface of the epidermis.

HANE BORI - see TEBORI

HANIWA - The Kofun period (300 A. D.- 600 A. D.) came after the Yayoi era. The word kofun means an old tomb. In this period, hilly tombs in many places were made, and the clay figures in the shape of dolls, horses and huts were also found in the tombs. The clay figures are called haniwa, which is the counterpart of dogu in the Jomon era. Markings on some haniwa are regarded as patterns of tattoos.

HAPU – kinship group, clan, tribe, subtribe - section of a large kinship group and the primary political unit in traditional Maori society. It consisted of a number of whanau sharing descent from a common ancestor, usually being named after the ancestor, but sometimes from an important event in the group's history. A number of related hapu usually shared adjacent territories forming a looser tribal federation.

HARGUS – or Harqus is essentially a gall ink, made from the tannic acid of oak galls and iron or copper sulfate, which produces an intensely deep black ink, lasting for a few days on living skin and permanent on parchment. It was (and is

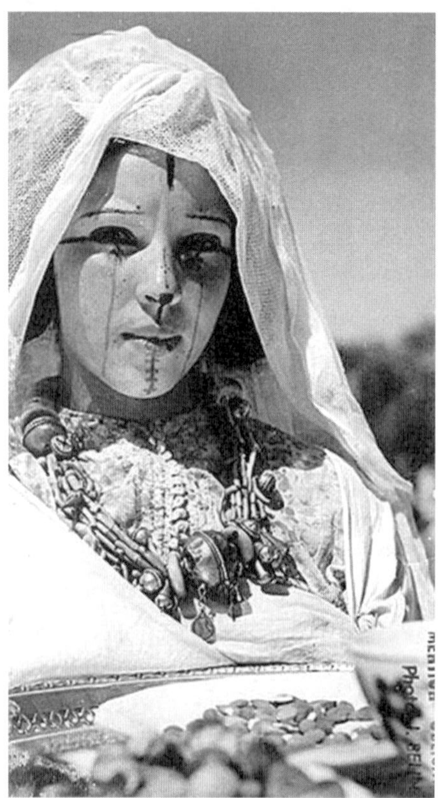

Jewish girl with harqus, southern Morocco, circa 1930

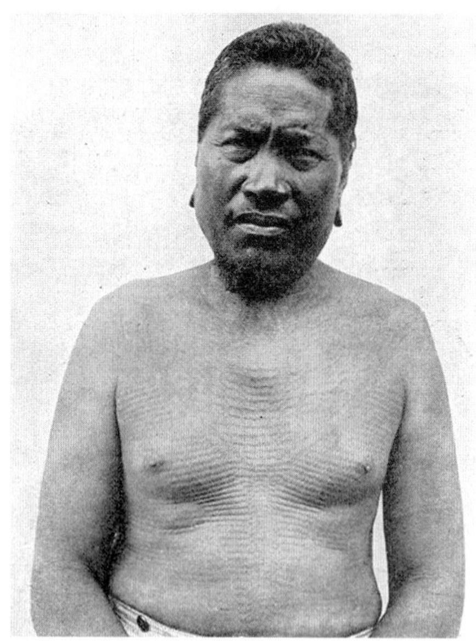

Hawaiian man with chest tattoo

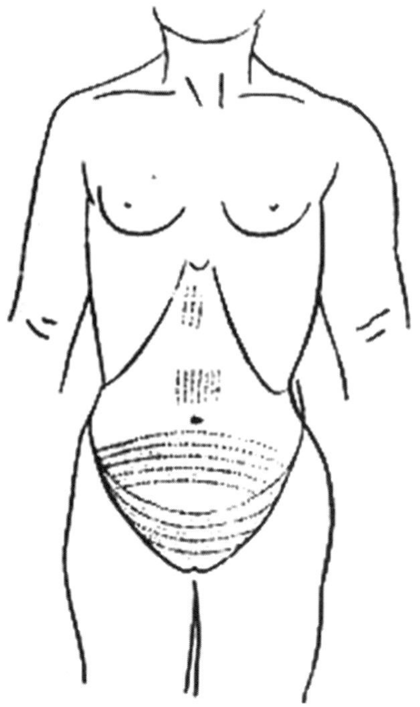

The Tattooed Priestesses of Hathor

still) used throughout the Maghreb, mainly Morocco, Algeria, and Tunisia; a similar cosmetic was also used in the Arabic peninsula, known there as khi?ab. When made at home, poorer women sometimes used just a simple mixture of soot and oil, but 'professional' recipes for ḥarqus show the variety of organic and non-organic ingredients:

"The black material which is used to make the harqous is obtained by heating (in a small and well-covered clay pan) a mixture of 'afsa (a sort of gall nut) and hadida (lead sulfate); a fine black powder

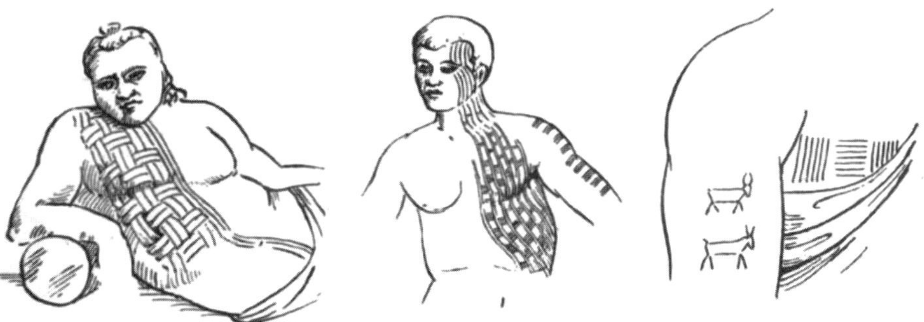

Portrait of a chief of Hawai, man of Hawai and goats tattooed on arm of man

builds up under the pan's lid; this powder is mixed with a little saliva and they then dip the end of a small walnut twig (merwed) with which they then trace the harqous. Generally the merwed is purchased on the day of 'Ashura"

"To make the ḥarqus, they place in the pot a mixture of incense (jawi), gallnuts ('afs), Ethiopian nuts (zuzt usserk), the kernels of cherry pits (mahlab), and scrape the lid of the pot with copper sulfate (ḥdida). The baqiya [pot] is then placed over a very low fire. It must be hermetically sealed... When the ḥarqus is ready, it has the appearance of a thick, black, and glistening liquid".

"The women also paint their faces with a dark colour, imitating tattoos, with a sort of gall known as iegg. This gallnut, ground and mixed with a little soot, burnt oleander, and oil, makes the hargous. Hargous designs are much loved by men, who consider them to give women a brilliant beauty. The greatest compliment you can pay a beautiful woman is to say of her, 'zina bela hargous,' which one can translate 'beautiful without make-up'"

"One prostitute [from Rabat] burns in a small pot [touijen del harqus] a little hadida zerga [copper sulfate], hadida l-hamra [iron oxide], jawi [incense], el-iegg [galls from Pistacia atlantica], and zrouda [sweet clover seeds], and she collects the soot that forms under the lid".

HARI - needles, varying from one single needle point to as many as thirty, are attached to a handle or shaft (of wood, ivory, bone etc) by means of fine wire of thread.

HAROTEA – the second degree of the Ario´i community. Harotea (light-coloured haro tattoo mark). Filigree bars crosswise on both sides of the body from the armpits downwards towards the front.

HATETEI – dark blue tattoo of the Sheklnam tribe (Sek´nam), Tierra del Fuego, South America.

HATHOR – the name of an Egyptian princess whose mummy can be included in the Middle Kingdom (2400 - 1780 BC). Until 1991, her color marks on the skin were considered the oldest tattoos.

HAU TA - tattoo chisel handle,Tonga,

HAUMONO – small tattooing implements, Tonga.

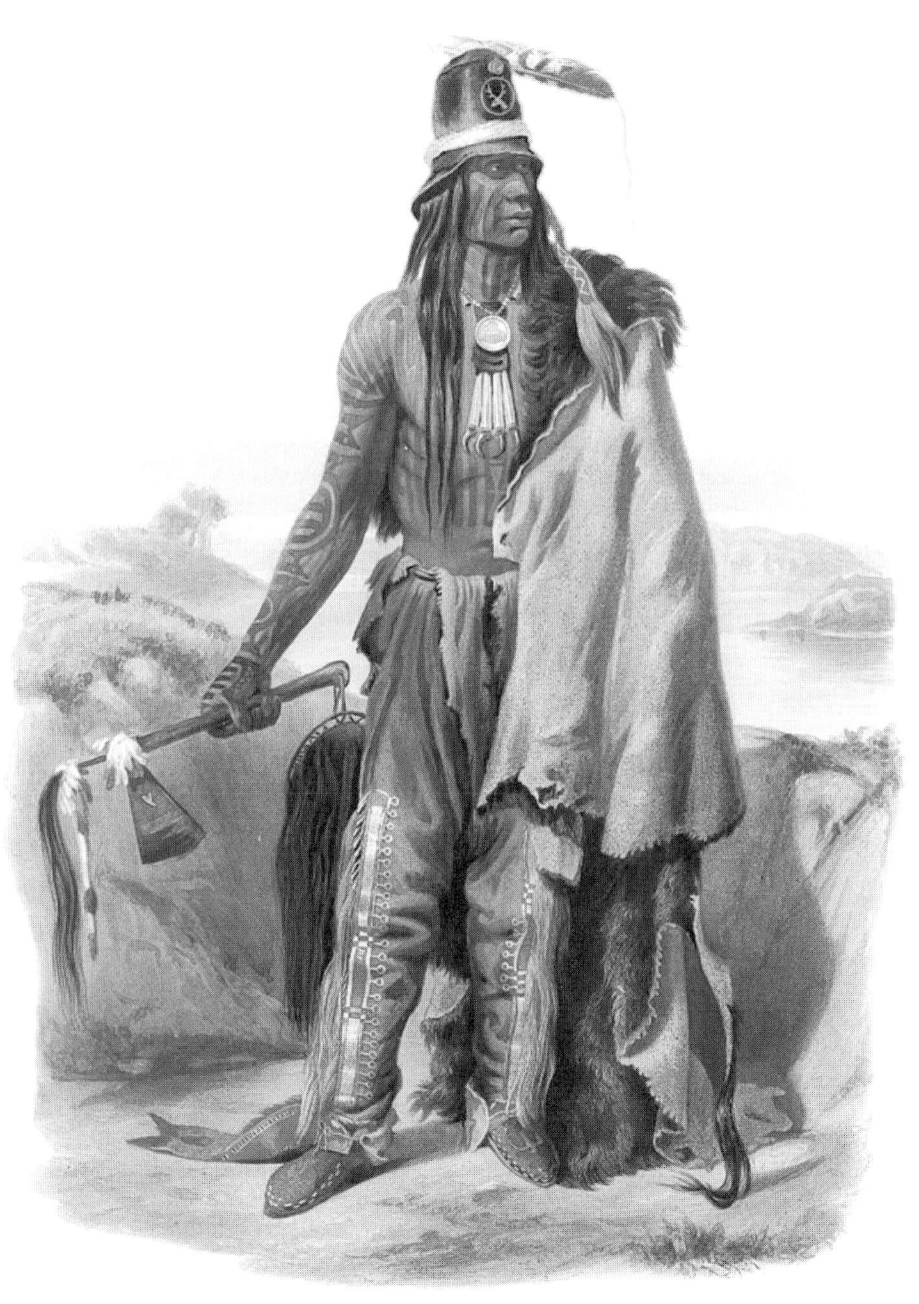

Hidatsa Chief

HAUPULU - big tattooing implements, Tonga.

HAUSAK PEOPLE - African tribe practicing scar tattoo.

HAWAIIAN ISLANDS - (Hawaiian: Mokupuni o Hawai'i) are an archipelago of eight major islands, several atolls, numerous smaller islets, and seamounts in the North Pacific Ocean. Formerly the group was known to Europeans and Americans as the Sandwich Islands, a name chosen by James Cook in honor of the then First Lord of the Admiralty John Montagu, 4th Earl of Sandwich. The contemporary name is derived from the name of the largest island, Hawaii Island.

Tattooing was very slightly developed in Hawaii and the information is exceedingly scanty. One very definite connection with rank occured, the outcast Kauwa, (slave) class were tattooed on the forehead. Property marks tattooed on the persons of the lower classes, and tattoo marks served as a badge to distinguish the retainers of different chiefs. These statements may refer to the same phenomenon, the branding of the Kauwa. The chief were all tattooed on the tongue in the case a death in the royal family.

The designs were of two types, free realistic representations and very simple geometric patterns.

HE MAHOE – The mallet was sometimes termed 'he mahoe', and had a surface that could be used for wiping away the blood, Maori.

HELI´I – tattoo hammer, Solomon Islands.

HENRY, ALEXANDR – fur trader,

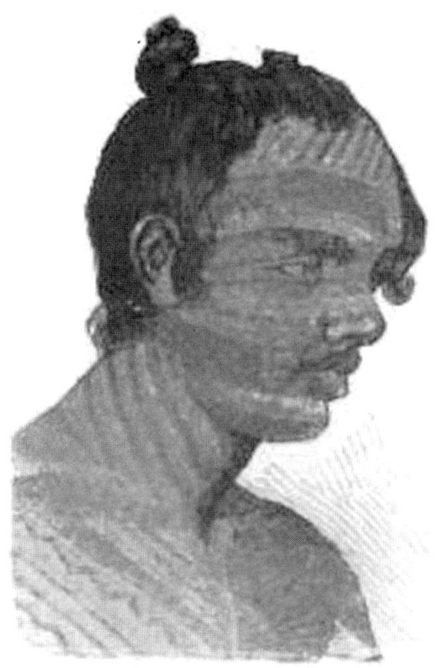

Hiva Oa

explorer, and writer. About Mandans wrote: Most of the women have their faces tattooed in a very savage manner, lines a quarter of an inch broad passing from the nose to the ear, and down each side of the mouth and chin to the throat. This disfigures them very much; otherwise, some would have tolerably good faces. Some tattooing is done to beautify the face, but at other times it is the disfiguring mark of a fit of jealousy in the husband.

About Cree: The men in general tattoo their bodies and arms very much. The women confine this ornamentation to the chin, having three perpendicular lines from the middle of the chin to the lip, and one or more running on each side, nearly parallel with the corner of the mouth.

HETAU – a tree, from the burning of its nuts, ash for tattoo ink is obtained, atol Sikaiana.

HIDATSA – The Hidatsa are a Siouan people. They are enrolled in the federally recognized Three Affiliated Tribes of the Fort Berthold Reservation in North Dakota. Practised tattooing: The marks consist of numerous parallel bands on one side, or over the entire of the chest and throat, and over one or both arms.

HELI΄I – Tattoo hammer, Leuneuwa, Solomon Islands..

HINAEREEREMONOI – the native account of the origin of tattooing. Hina, the daughter of the god Taaroa, bore to her father a daughter, who was called Apouvaru, and who also became the wife of Taaroa. Taaroa and Apouvaru looked steadfastly at each other, and Apouvaru, in consequence, afterward brought forth her first-born, who was called Matamataaru. Again the husband and the wife looked at each other, and she became the mother of a second son, who was called Tiitiipo. After a repetition of this visual intercourse, a daughter was born, who was called Hinaereeremonoi. As she grew up, in order to preserve her chastity, she was made pahio, or kept in a kind of enclosure, and constantly attended by her mother. Intent on her seduction, the brothers invented tattooing, and marked each other with the figure called Taomaro. Thus ornamented, they appeared before their sister, who admired the figures, and, in order to be tattooed herself, eluding the care of her mother, broke the enclosure that had been erected for her preservation, was tattooed and became also the victim to the designs of her brothers. Tattooing thus originated among the gods and was first practiced by the children of Taaroa, their principal deity. In imitation of their example, and for the accomplishment of the same purposes, it was practiced among men. Idolatry not only disclosed the origin but sanctioned the practice. The two sons of Taaroa and Apouvaru were the gods of tattooing.

HINU - Before the coming of the tuhuna, the father of the opou had prepared the pigment (hinu). The preparation of this was a very tapu operation, the man making it being forbidden all relationship with women during the period; and, it was necessary for a virgin to aid him in the work. The shells of the ama nut (Aleurites triloba) were heated so as to open easily, and the kernels placed over a fire in a kind of pocket of stones which allowed the smoke to ascend through a small passageway in order to collect on a smooth stone (pa'e hinu). Upon this stone, a constant tapping was kept up while the soot collected to the depth of

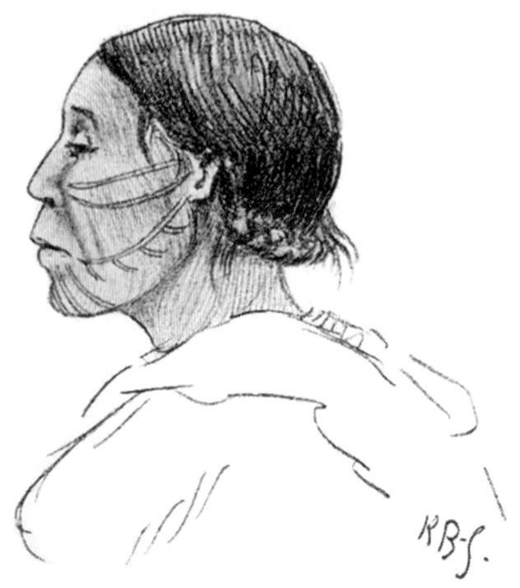

Face tattooing of Hudson Bay women

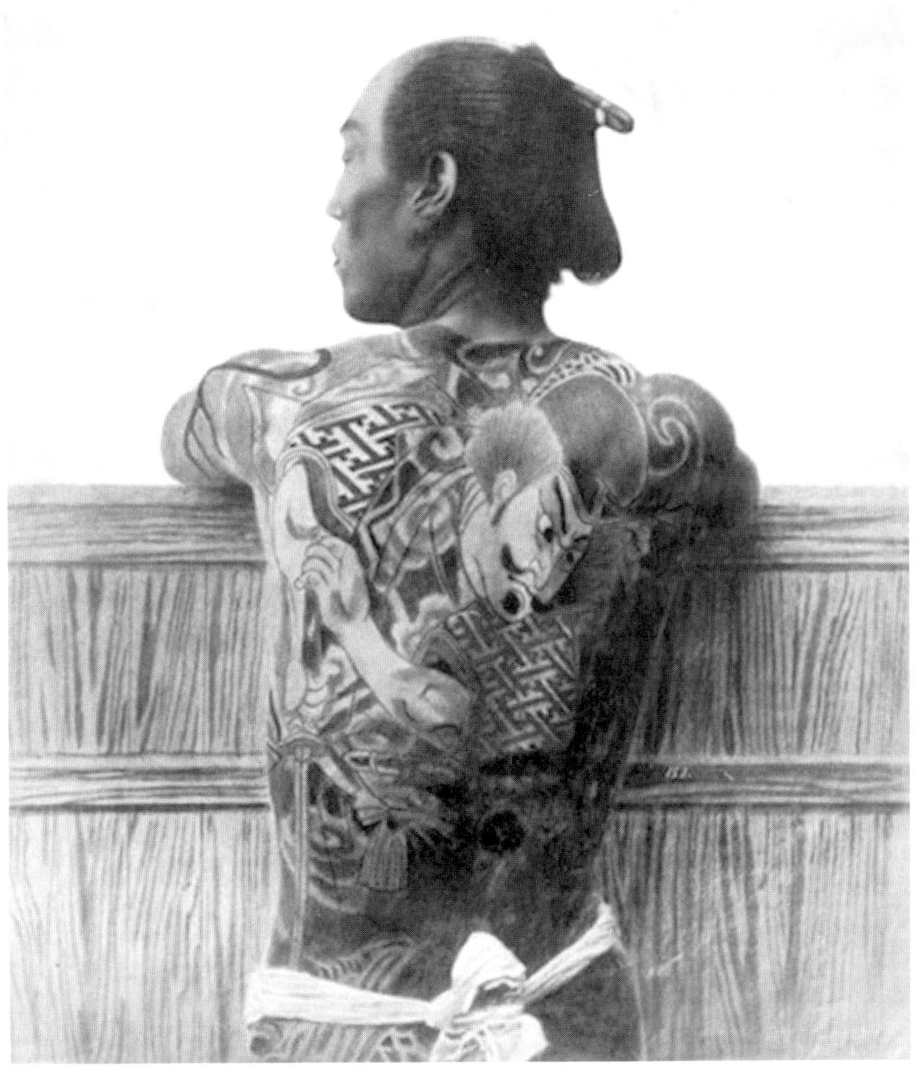

Horimono

about an inch. This process, according to Berchon, was called amahi ama. The soot-covered pa'e hinu was then placed on a banana leaf and left in the sun to dry, being kept thus until the tuhuna arrived for his work. Thereupon, the father, according to information, mixed the soot with plain water in a small coconut shell (ipu hinu) and gave it to the artist.

HIVA OA – A tattoo style widespread on the Marquesas Islands. By its arrangement, it is similar to the one from Ua Pou, it extends up to thighs though, and it represents the middle between two

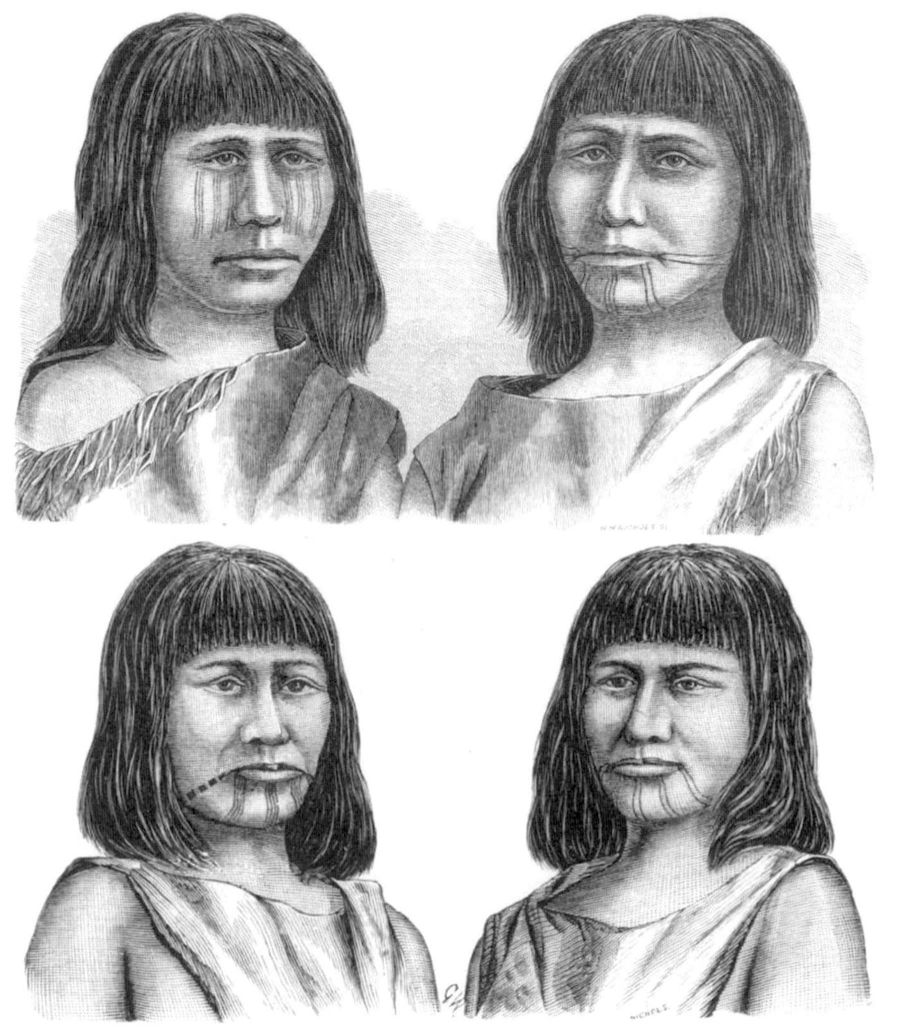

Huchnom

other styles in the treatment difficulties, the great lines turn into black curves. The style is almost purely conventional.

HOA - To mix, as water with resin (pugu) for tattooing, Bellona.

HOA-HAKA-NANA-IA – a statue from Rapa Nui in the British National Museum, which has reliefs apparently symbolizing tattoos.

HOGI- To do in parts or sections, as tattooing. Rare. Bellona.

HOHO - To be dark, as rain clouds or tattooing; to retattoo so as to darken; Bellona.

HOKUSAI KATSUSHIKA - (c. 31 October 1760 – 10 May 1849), known simply as Hokusai, was a Japanese artist, ukiyo-e painter and printmaker of the

Edo period. His art was an important source of inspiration for many tattoos.

HOO´PATH – see HUPA

HONITETU TRIBE - The Wemale people are one of the more ancient ethnic groups of Seram Island, Indonesia. The Wemale language is of Malayo-Polynesian origin and it is divided in a northern and a southern form, having variants known as Horale, Kasieh, Uwenpantai, Honitetu and Kawe. Practising tattoo.

HORI CHYO - was a traditional tattoo master in the Meiji period. According to the English tattoo artist, George Burchett, Hori Chyo tattooed a lot of British aristocrats including Duke of Clarence, Duke of York (later King George V) and Russian Tsarevich (later Tsar Nicholas II). Thanks to this, Japanese tattoos had spread to overseas countries and gained the reputation outside Japan.

HORIIRE – In Osaka, tattooing was also often called horiire – to dig in, end of Tokugawa period.

HORIMONO - **(彫り物, 彫物)** literally carving, engraving, can refer to the practice of traditional tattooing in Japanese culture; while irezumi usually refers to any tattooing, "horimono" is usually used to describe full-body tattoos done in the traditional style.

Made together with Teba, Japanese masters used traditional motifs such as peonies, dragons or the unique ukiyo-e style of human figures to create the tattoo, which makes the whole body one symbolic work. The horimino tattoos are flawless during their gaku, literally a “frame” of waves, water and wind swirls

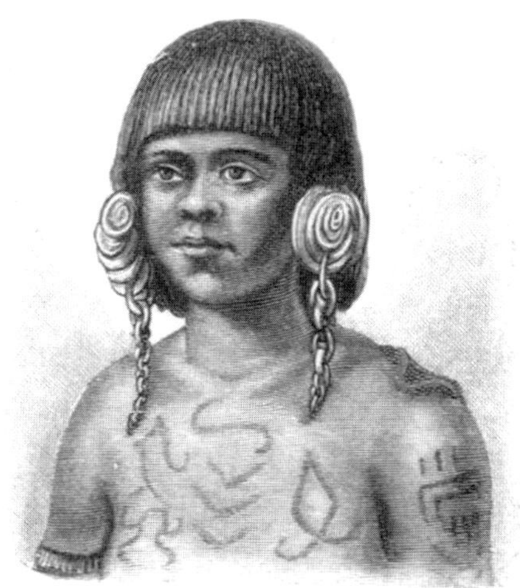

Tattooed women, Humboldt Bay

around the centre of tattoo which gives the horimino its unique appearance. Within different literature or languages, Horimino are known also as irezumi, bunshin, shisei, gaman, or hokuro. Because the name horimino includes the artistic form related to the creation of such a tattoo, Japanese tattoo masters and its wearers use the horimono term.

According to Kitamura: “For many years, tattoo masters had been refusing to use the irezumi term, in order to distance the art from the cruel practice of punishing tattoos. They started to call themselves the Horishi. The name was derived from the verb of horu – “to carve” – which was used by the ukijoe woodcut masters. Tattoos were rather called horimino, meaning “carved item”, than irezumi. The change of the name highlighted the skills necessary for tattoo artists and the close relation with the woodcut relief printing. The irezumi terms has already lost its negative meaning and today it is solely used for Japanese decorative tattoo on a high level.”

HORIŠI – term for a traditional tattoo instrument in Japan.

HOWKAN TRIBE – indian tribe in the Prince of Wales archipelago. Practiced tattoos.

HU´A – the fifth degree of the ario´i community. Literally "small". They feature tattoos in the form of two or three light marks on the shoulders.

HU TU NU– sign for tattoo master, Nag apeople, India.

HUA MIAN - to mark the face, Old Chinese term for tattoo

HUALPAI – is a federally recognized Indian Tribe located in northwestern Arizona. "Hualapai" (pronounced Wal-lah-pie) means "People of the Tall Pines." The Hualapai painted their faces for decoration (women tattooed their chins)

HUASTÉK – Mayan ethnic group, practiced tattoos, deformed their skulls and decorated their teeth with plates of obsidian or jade.

HUDSON BAY INUIT - The term Hudson Bay Eskimos is here defined as comprising there tribal groups to the west and northwest of Hudson Bay — the Caribou, Netsilik, and Iglulik — all of which, though closely related to each other physically, Linguistically, and culturally, are still sufficiently distinct to consider themselves separate units.

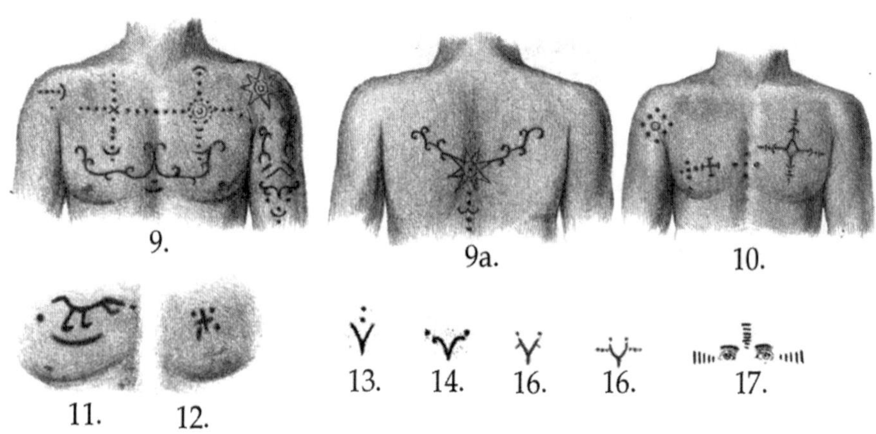

Image 9 - thoracic tattoos of the inhabitants of the Hatusua area;
Img. 9a - similarly on the back of the same person.
Img. 10 - Alfuren tattoo from the Honitetu area.
Img. 11 - Tattoo on the left chest of a man from the Kaibobo area.
Img.12 - Tattoo on the right chest of another man from Kaibobo.
Img. 13 - Tattoo on the forehead of a girl from the Murinatin area.
Img.14-16 - Tattoos on the forehead of girls from the Honitetu area.
Img.17 - Tattoo of a woman from the Honitetu.

HUÉA – ceremonies officiator, Shuar people.

HUCHNOM INDIANS - A division of the Yuki of northern California, speaking a dialect divergent from that of the Round Valley Indians. They lived on South Eel river above its confluence with the middle fork of the Eel river, or in adjacent territories, and on the headwaters of Russian River in upper Potter valley. To the north of them were the Witukomnom Yuki, to the east the Wintun and on the other sides were Pomo tribes. The Pomo call them Tatu, the whites Redwoods, from Redwood Creek

HUI ARI´I - social class in Tahiti. A term for the descendants of priests, they had special tattoo motifs.

HUI RA´ATIRA – see HUI TO´A

HUI TO´A - social class in Tahiti, by this term were termed, leaders and warriors. Their tattoo motifs corresponded to this.

HUKA-HUKA – An important part of Kuarup is the huka-huka wrestling matches. Opponents face each other, imitating the grunting of the jaguar. Matches are brief, often lasting a few seconds, and end when one of the opponents is thrown to the ground. A representative of the host village confronts an adversary of each invited village, one at a time, beginning with matches of their champions and ending with novice matches

HUKE – "Recover tattoo," Tonga.

HUMBOLDT BAY - is a natural bay and a multi-basin, bar-built coastal lagoon located on the rugged North Coast of California, entirely within Humboldt County.

HUPA (hooʻ-path) - A tribe of Indians in the Hoopa (Hupa) Valley on the Trinity River in California. All adult women among the Hupa " were tattooed with vertical black marks on the chin, and sometimes curved marks were added at the corners of the mouth." ' The men " had a set of lines tattooed on the inside of the left forearm to measure shell money. In measuring shell-money, he takes the string in his right hand, draws one end over his left thumbnail, and if the other end reaches the uppermost of the tattoo lines, the five shells were worth $25 in gold or $5 a shell.

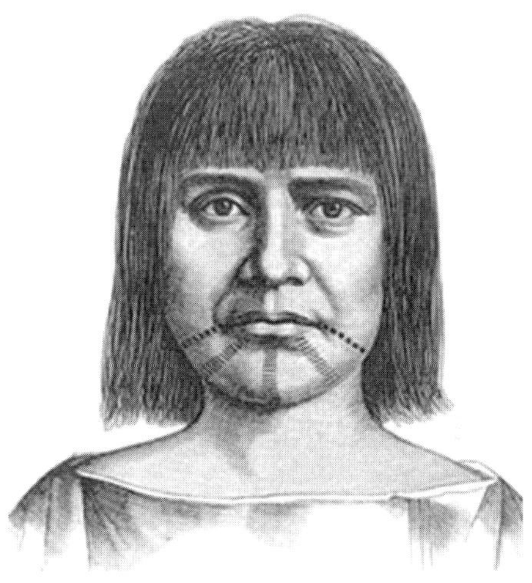

HURÓNS TRIBE - (from the French hure - head of a wild boar or huron - savage, brawler) (also Wendati, Wyandoti - inhabitants of the peninsula, islanders) by their own name Onkvaonvé (ie "True Men") are some of the indigenous people of North America tribes. The Recollect missionary Gabriel Sagard Theodat mentions that among the Hurons "Some have the body and face tattooed [gravée] with figures of serpents, lizards, squirrels, and other animals, and especially the

Petun tribe [culturally related neighbors of the Hurons], who nearly all have the bodies so covered with devices...

HUTU - two small and two large drums in a public place drummed to announce the beginning of the construction of a tattoo house and convene ka′ioi.

Handy write: Several days before the beginning of the operation, the father announced that the oho'an tiki, or special house for the occasion, was to be built. About one o'clock on the morning on which the erection of this structure was to take place, two great drums (pahu) and two small ones (hiitii) were beaten on the public festival place, to declare the be- ginning of the tapu and to summon the ka'ioi.

CH´ING-MIENWEN-SCHEN - face and body tattoos. The Ch'ing-mien compound is found in the special sense of "face branding (from crime)", Kumaso Province, Japan.

CHACO - tribe from Paraguay, the girls were ritually tattooed and were not allowed to eat meat or fish for a whole year afterward.

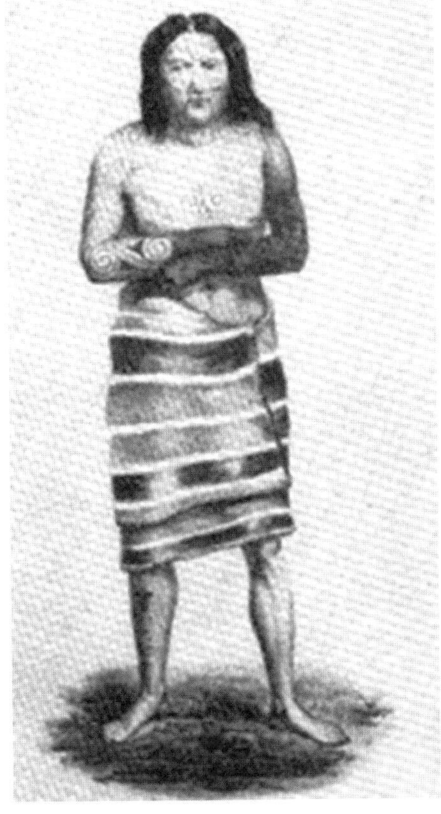

CHA-KAY´-YUM – The instrument used for tattooing is called "cha-kay'-yum." It consists of from four to ten commercial steel needles inserted in a straight line at the end of a wooden handle; "cha-kay'-yum" is also the word for needle, Bontok tribe.

CHAMACOCO - people (Ishír) are an indigenous people of Paraguay. Some also live in Brazil. The Chamacoco have two major divisions, the Ebytoso, who lived along the Paraguay River, and the Tomáraho, who traditionally lived in the forests.

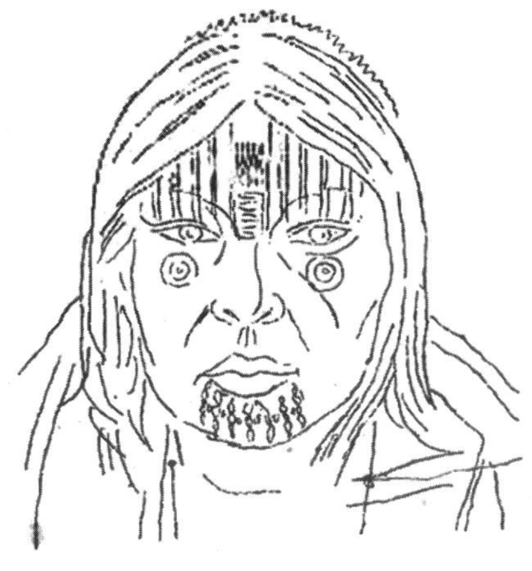

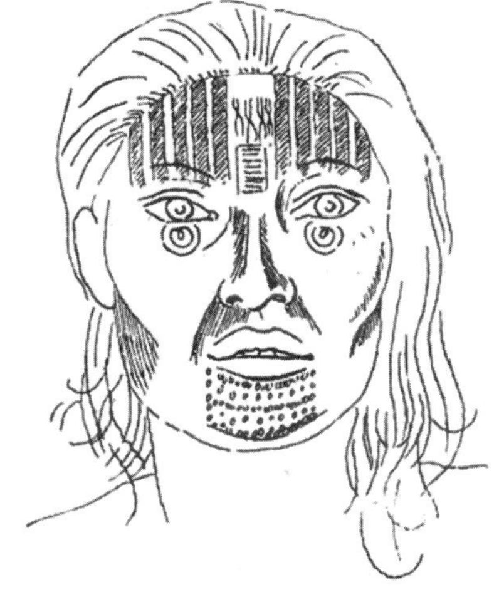

CHANG TRIBE - is a Naga of Nagaland, India. It is one of the recognized Scheduled Tribes. Practiced tattooing.

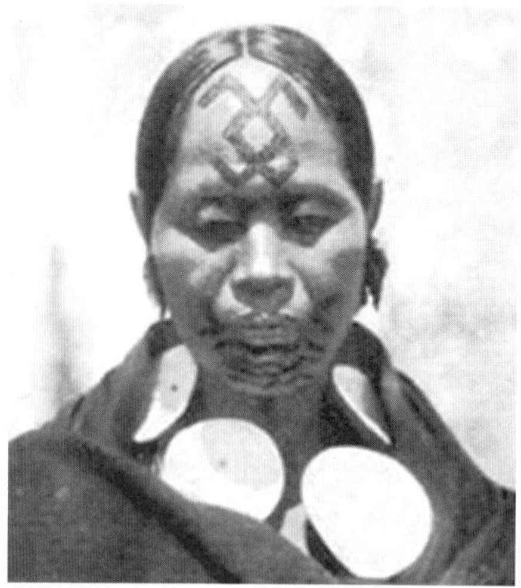

Chang woman with facial tattooing, ca. 1925

CHARRUA – A tribe probably affiliated with the Caddo confederacy, living on a North branch of Red River of Louisiana. The Charrua made great efforts to maintain as many aspects of their traditional culture as possible. These included tattooing the face with blue lines, using body paint in warfare, performing the earlobes for pendant of shell, bone, and Colorado feathers, and the use of lip plugs.

CHEN HUA - tattoo – to draw with needle, to prick pattern, Old China.

CHEROKEE - are one of the indigenous people of the Southeastern Woodlands. Prior to the 18th century, they were concentrated in southwestern North Carolina, southeastern Tennessee, and the tips of western South Carolina and northeastern Georgia. Practised tattooing.

CHESSAQUOT – Long wrote: "the war songs are sung, accompanied by a rattle being round the hawk bells, called Chessaquot, which is kept shaking to stifle the groans such pains must naturally occasion (during tattoos)"

CHICKASAW TRIBE – tattooed symbols as blue in color, with the color itself prepared from pine-pitch soot. They used

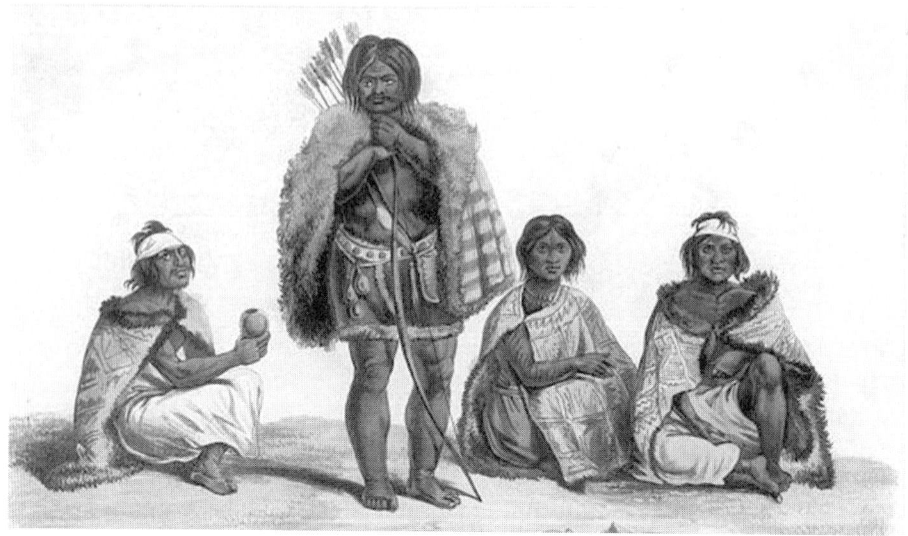

Charrua tribe

the original tattooing instrument as the sharp-toothed jaw of the garfish. The tattoo marks were inscribed on the arms and chests of warriors and described as being as „legible as our alphabetic characters are to us."

CHIMSYANS – Native American tribe from Fort Simpson and at Chathamsound, practicing tattoos.

CHIMÚ – The Chimú culture has become known for the high quality of metal works. Tattoos were found on mummies discovered in 1980, as well as traces of tattoos were found on preserved gold artifacts symbolizing hands. About 1000 - 1470 AD, Peru

CHIN- Women in this group have traditionally tattooed faces. Myanmar, Burma.

CHIN-ALL - smaller sticks for applying black or white paint for painting the motif, see CHIN-KARR.

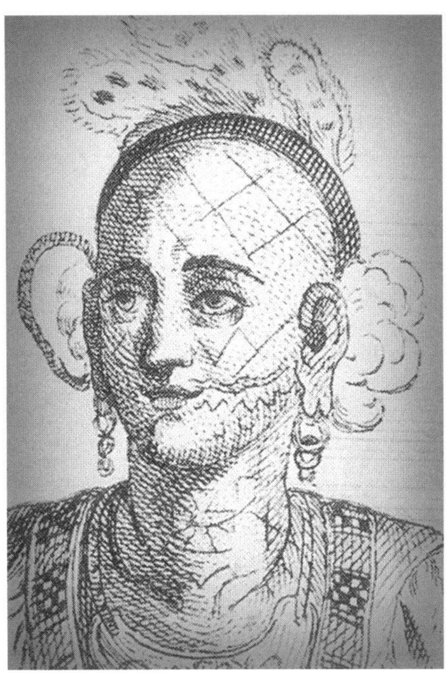

Facial tattooing of a Cherokee war leader, 1762

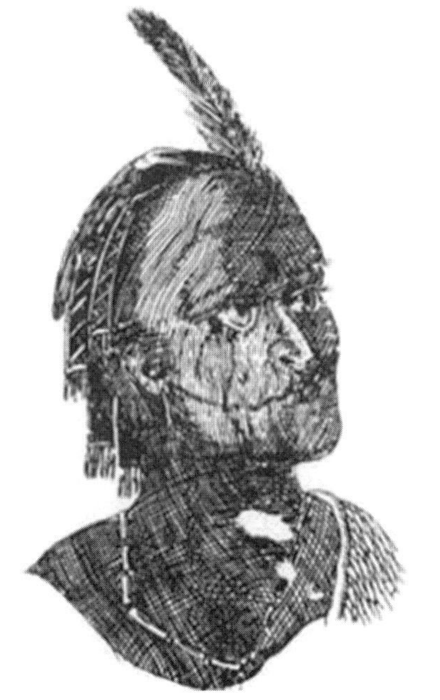

Chickasaw tribe

CHIN-KARR – black and white stripes are produced by dipping into the paint the little sticks which serve as brushes. The longer sticks (" chin-karr "), which are 4 cm. long, are used for painting on the black lines, two or three of which are applied in close proximity by means of two or three sticks which are held in the fingers simultaneously.

CHINOOKAN - peoples include several groups of indigenous people of the Pacific Northwest in the United States who speak the Chinookan languages. Part of the Chinook culture is the decorating of their bodies and faces with tattoos.

CHIPLUMBA – African tribe practiced tattooing.

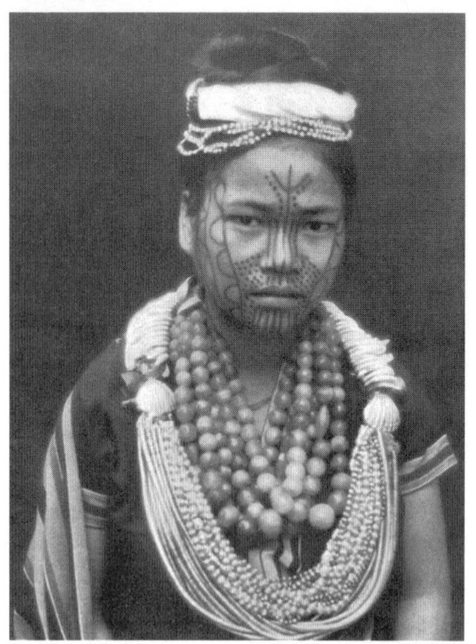

Chin girl

CHIPPEWYAN – The Chipewyan (Denésoliné or Dënesųłıné or Dënë Sułinë, meaning "the original/real people") are a Dene Indigenous Canadian peoples of the Athabaskan language family, whose ancestors are identified with the Taltheilei Shale archaeological tradition. People tattooed their faces with parallel lines on the cheek.

CHIPOPO – Makonde tattooing was a form of skin-cut tattooing. After the cuts were made with a knife-like tattoo implement (chipopo), vegetable carbon from the castor bean plant was rubbed into the cuts producing a dark blue color. The tattoos were washed with water, and oil prepared from castor beans was applied with a feather for healing.

CHOPI– African tribe, practicing scar tattoo.

CHOROTI– ethnic group, Grand Chaco. They practiced tattoos

CHOSEI – in ancient Japanese books, other names appear for tattoos, such as Chosei – carving in of blue/green.

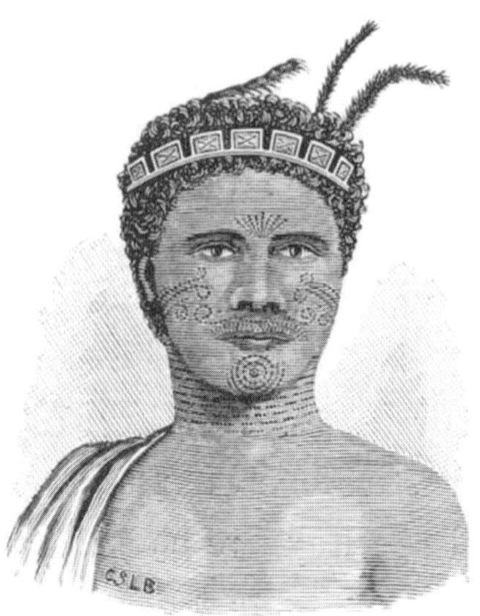

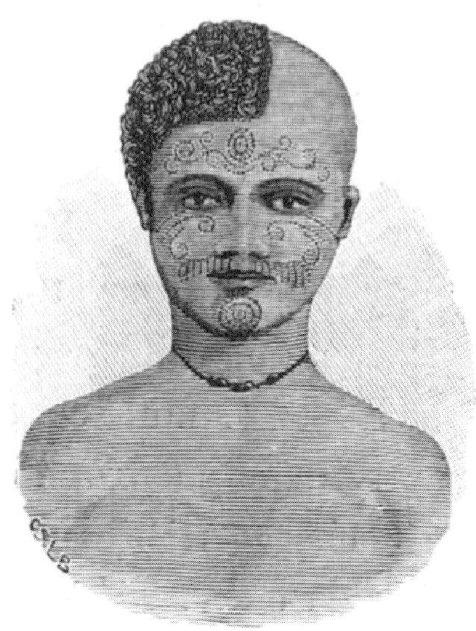

Chiplumba man and woman

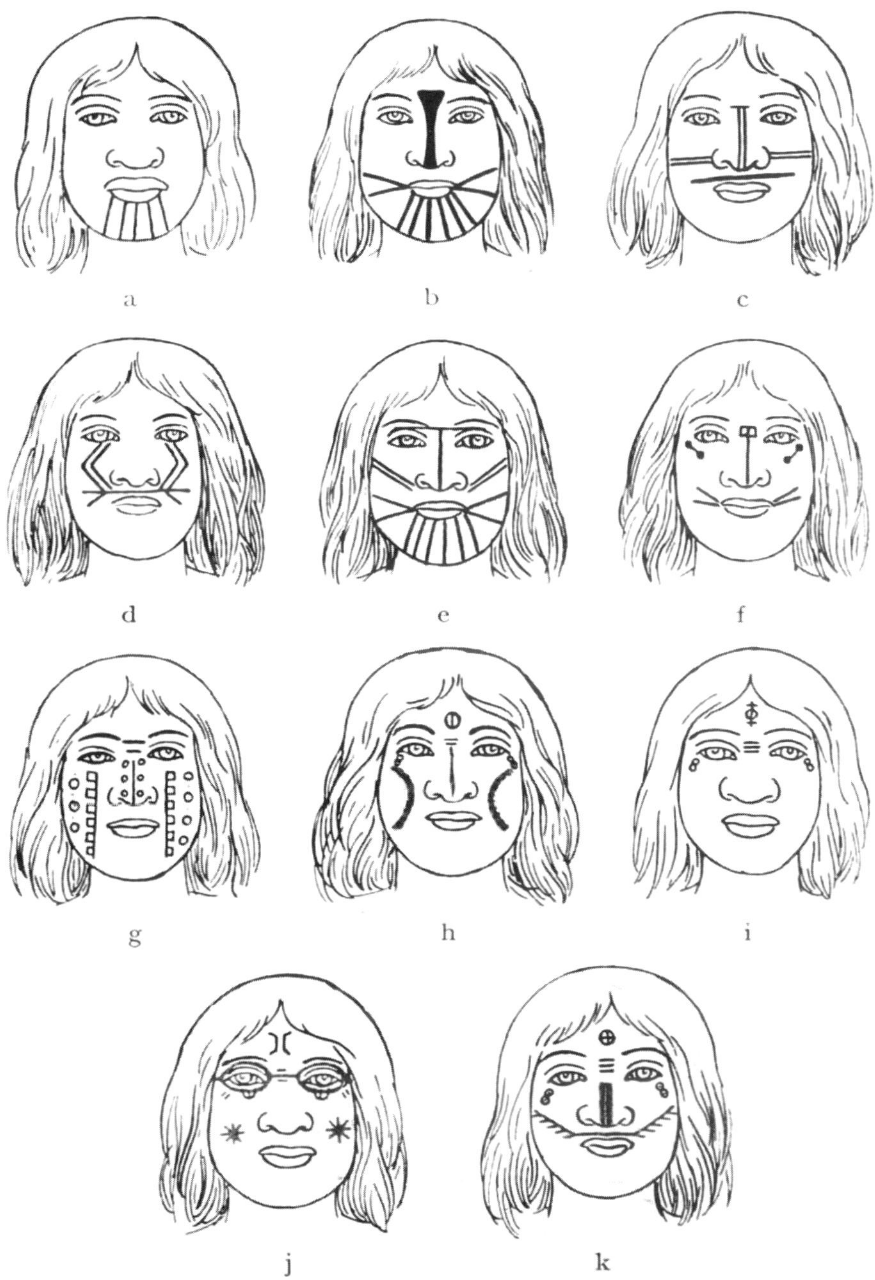

Tattoos and face painting. Chorotis. Ashluslays and Matacos.
a - about five years old girl; b - tribal tattoo typical of Ashluslay women; c - g - = men; a-g = Ashlusely; a -b tattooing; c-g = face painting; h = tattoos on the forehead and under the eyes, ; i = Matacomann, Creveau, tattooing; j-k = Chorotis, j - man, k - woman.

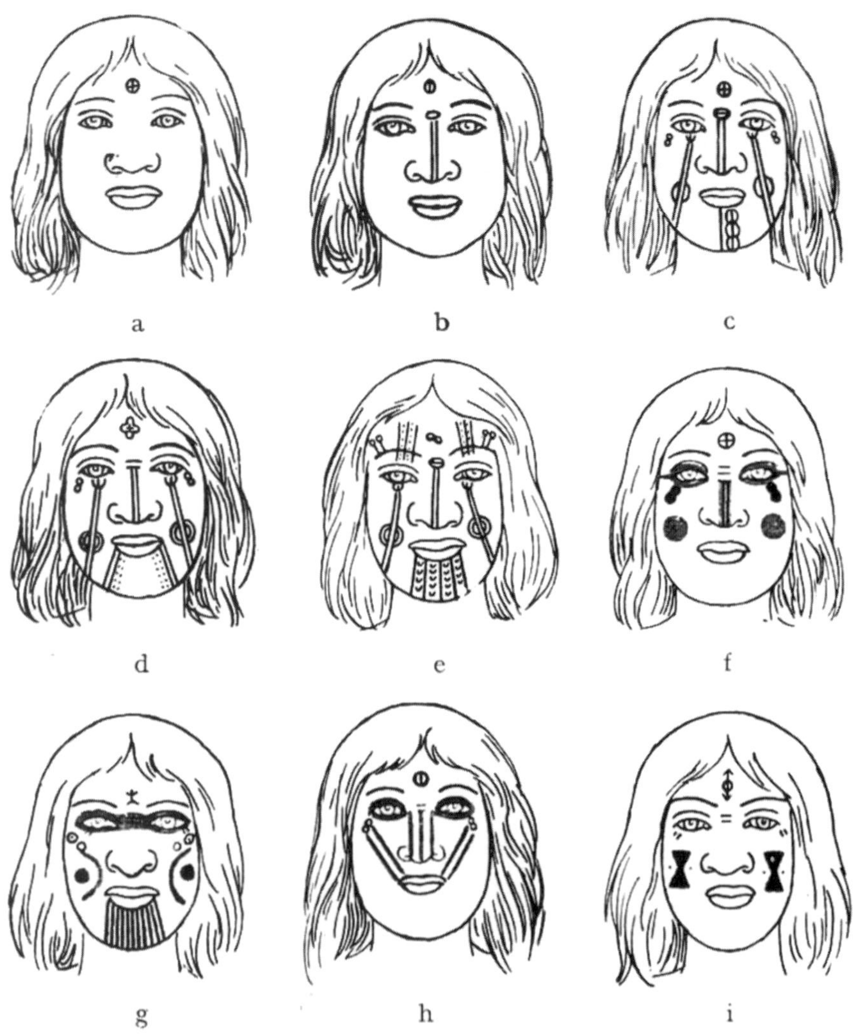

Tattooing and facepainting. Chorotis. Rio Pilcomayo. a - about five years old girl; b - about seven years old girl; c - eighteen-year-old girl; d - woman, e - woman, f - eighteen-year-old girl, g - man, h - a girl whose mother is Choroti and father Ashluslay, i - man , a - e - only tattoos; f - i - tattooing and facepainting.

CHUKCHEES TRIBE - Among Chukchees in the extreme north-east of Asia, women were commonly tattooed with a vertical line on each side of the nose and with several vertical lines on the chin. Childless women had a tattoo on both cheeks three equidistant lines running all the way around. This was considered to be a charm against sterility.

CHUN LIU CHIEN FAN - criminal wore the heavy cangue and tattooed on his left

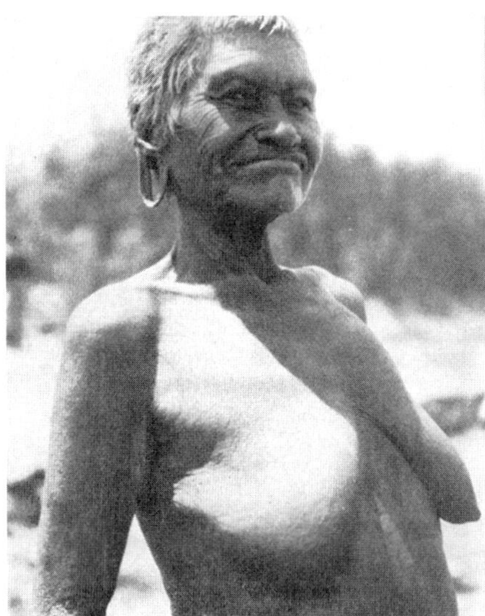
Choroti tribe woman with tattoos

temple with the crime for which he was suffering punishment. He belonged to the chun liu chien fan class of convicts, China.

CHUWIT – indigo or blueing used in making dye for tattooing, Arabs.

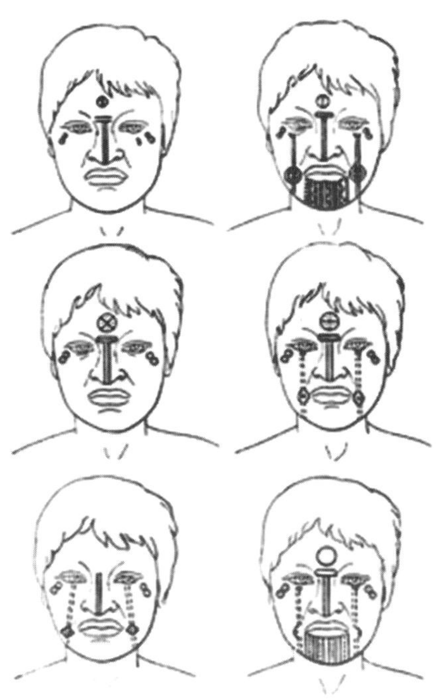
Choroti - face tattooing

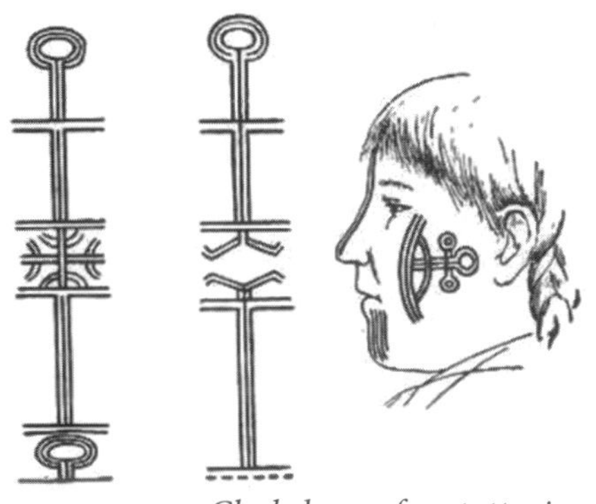
Chukchees - face tattooing

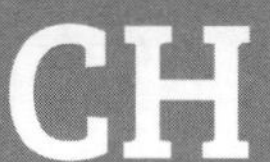

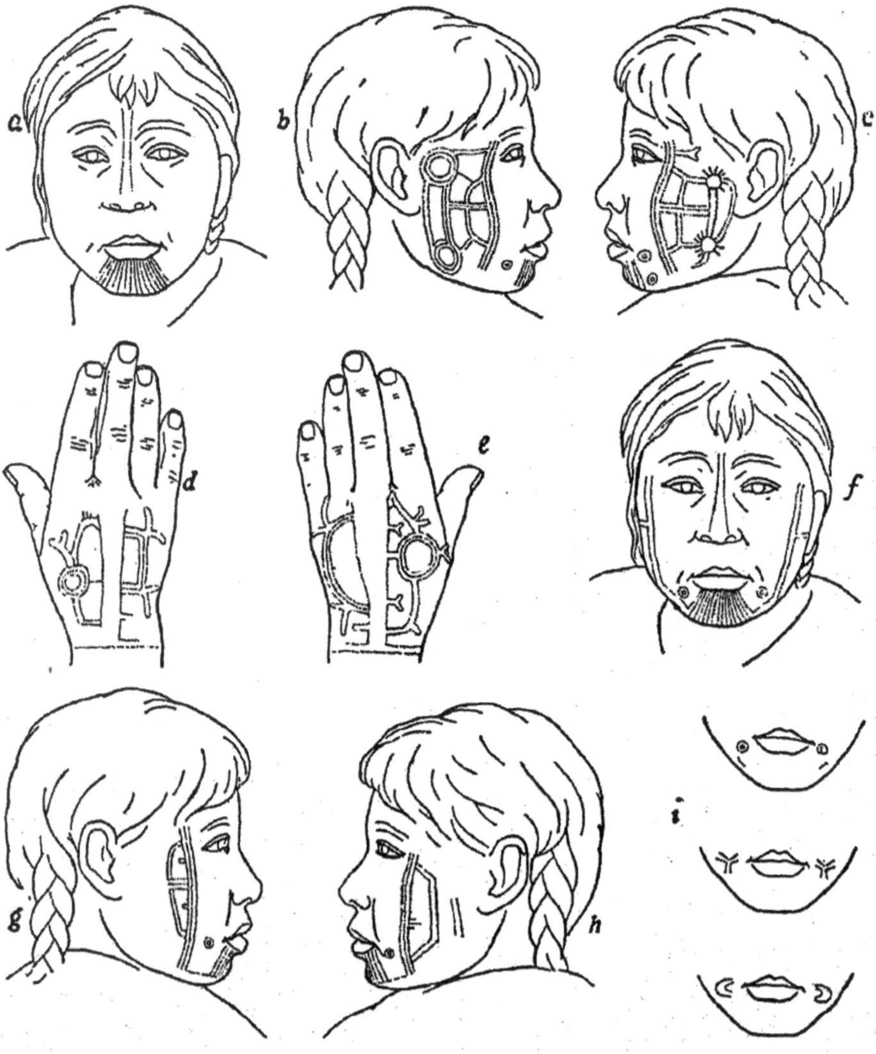

Tattooing; a) of Reindeer Chukchee Woman, b,c, d,e) of Eskimo Woman; f,g,h) of Maritime Chukchee Woman; i) of Men

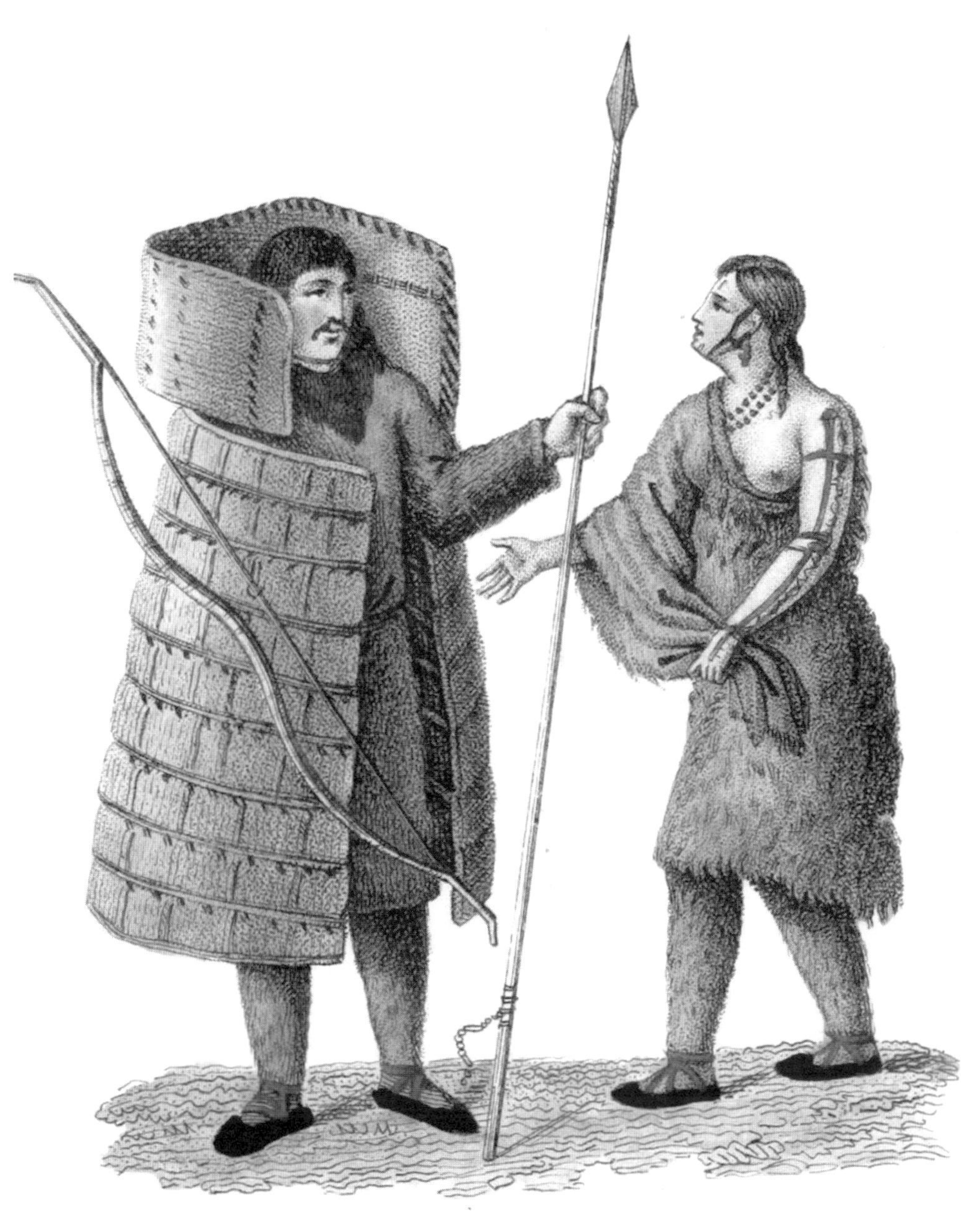

Man and woman of the Chukchees

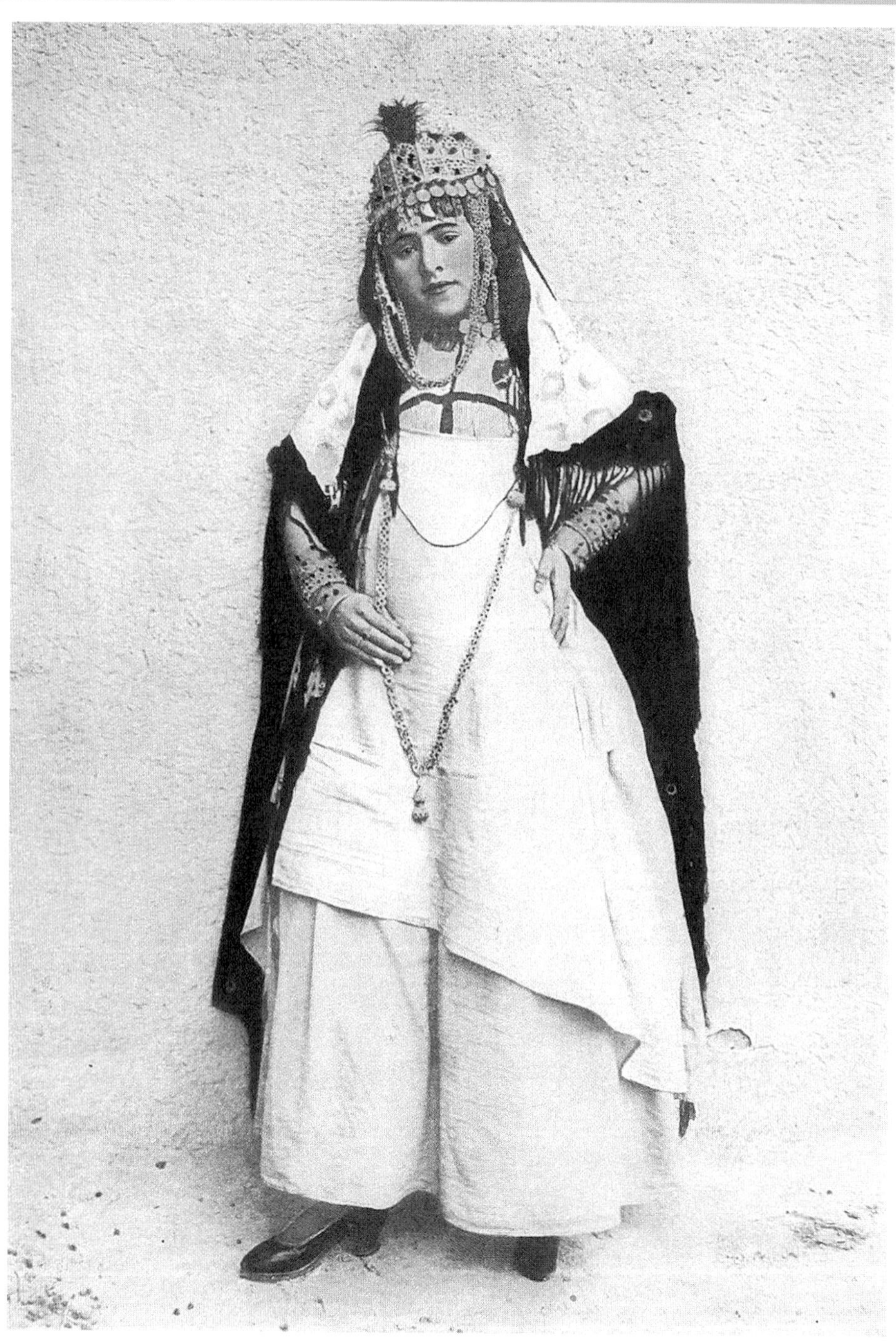

Cafes dancers with tattooed faces, Algeria

IAPALAPA – the hammers used to pat the needles into the skin were called iapalapa, Samoa.

IASI-IASI TRIBE - women, like the Maisins, tattooed their faces, New Guinea.

IBALOI - An indigenous people known as the Ibaloi once mummified their honored dead and laid them to rest in hollowed logs in the caves around what is now the Filipino municipality of

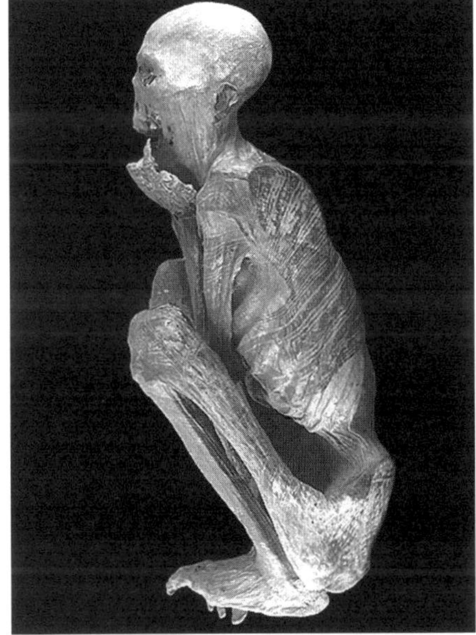

Kabayan. In life, these ancient people had won the right to be covered in spectacular tattoos depicting geometric shapes as well as animals such as lizards, snakes, scorpions, and centipedes. "According to nineteenth-century ethnographic accounts, Ibaloi head-hunting warriors revered these creatures as 'omen animals,'" says Smithsonian anthropologist and tattoo scholar Lars Krutak. "The sight of one before a raid could make or break the entire enterprise." After successfully taking the

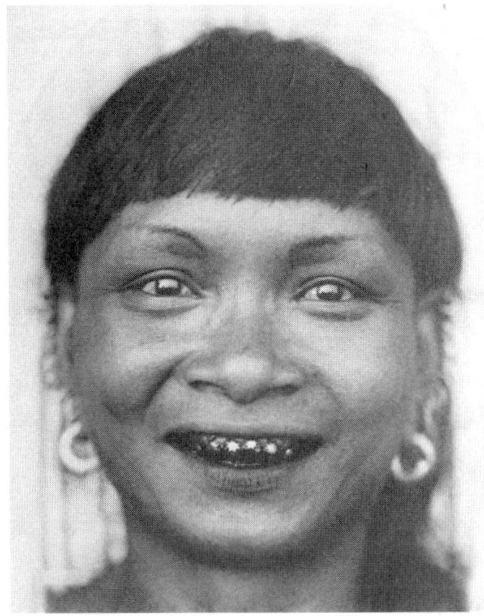

Iban with filed, studded, and blackened teeth

head of an enemy in battle, a warrior would have these propitious animals

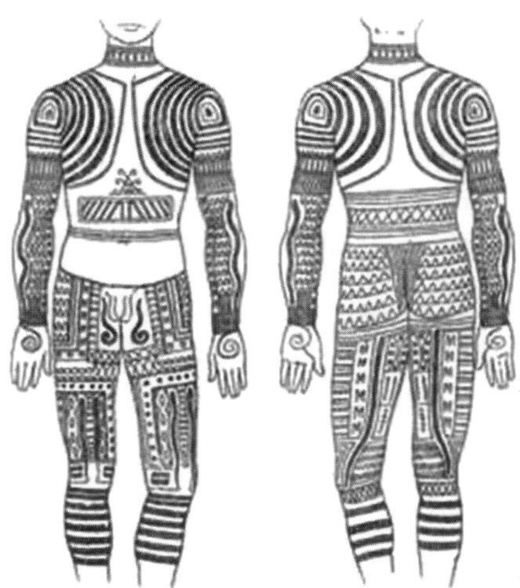

Traditional Ibaloi burik, drawing by Hans Meyer, ca. 1880. Many figurative designs such as lizards, snakes, scorpions, and anthropomorphs are incorporated into the overall burik design

Iboki

permanently etched onto his body. Some Kabayan mummies also feature less fearsome tattoos, such as circles on their wrists thought to be solar discs, or zigzagging lines variously interpreted as lightning or stepped rice fields. "All these tattoos seem to depict the surrounding environment," says Krutak, who notes that the increased attention paid to the mummies in the last decade has helped fuel a resurgence in traditional tattooing, which had largely died out. Today, thousands of people tracing their descent to the ancient Ibaloi wear designs on their skin modeled after those of their ancestors.

IBAN PEOPLE - The Ibans or Sea Dayaks are a branch of the Dayak peoples of Borneo, in South East Asia. Dayak is a title given by the westerners to the local people of Borneo Island. Both men and women wore tattoos. For young men, the first tattoo was usually the "bunga terung". This was a depiction of the flower of a local aubergine species

IBOKI – wooden tattoo tool used by Papuans from New Guinea.

IBO TRIBE - African tribe practicing scar tattoo.

IEP – A small basket to keep the implements (for tattoo), Marshall Islands.

IFIIFI – by applying tattoos, the girls "became" an adolescent (ifiifi) adult woman (susuki), Maisin tribe, Papua New Guinea.

IFUGAO - The Ifugao are wet-rice agriculturalists occupying the mountainous area of northern Luzon, Philippines. Known to the Spanish conquistadores and missionaries as the Ygolote, (Igolot, or Igorrote) and to Americans as the Igorot, the Ifugao inhabit the most rugged and mountainous part of the country. The term "Ifugao" is derived from "ipugo" which means earth people or mortals or humans, as distinguished from spirits and deities. It also means "from the hill," as "pugo" means hill.

IGIHISI – Tattoos were done by hand, with a device called igihisi, made from a piece of rattan with needles attached to one end; the tattooist hits the rattan,

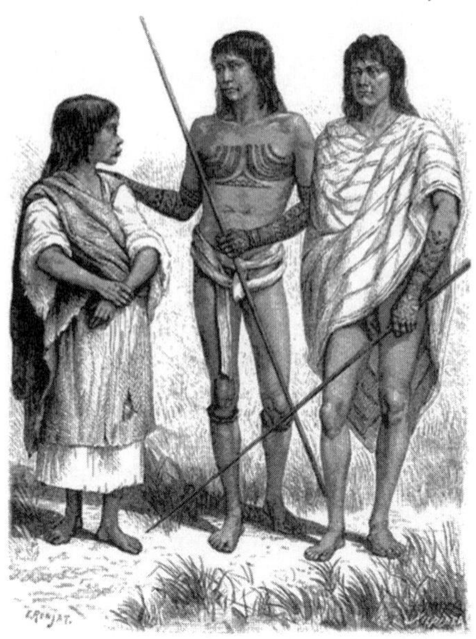

Igorot

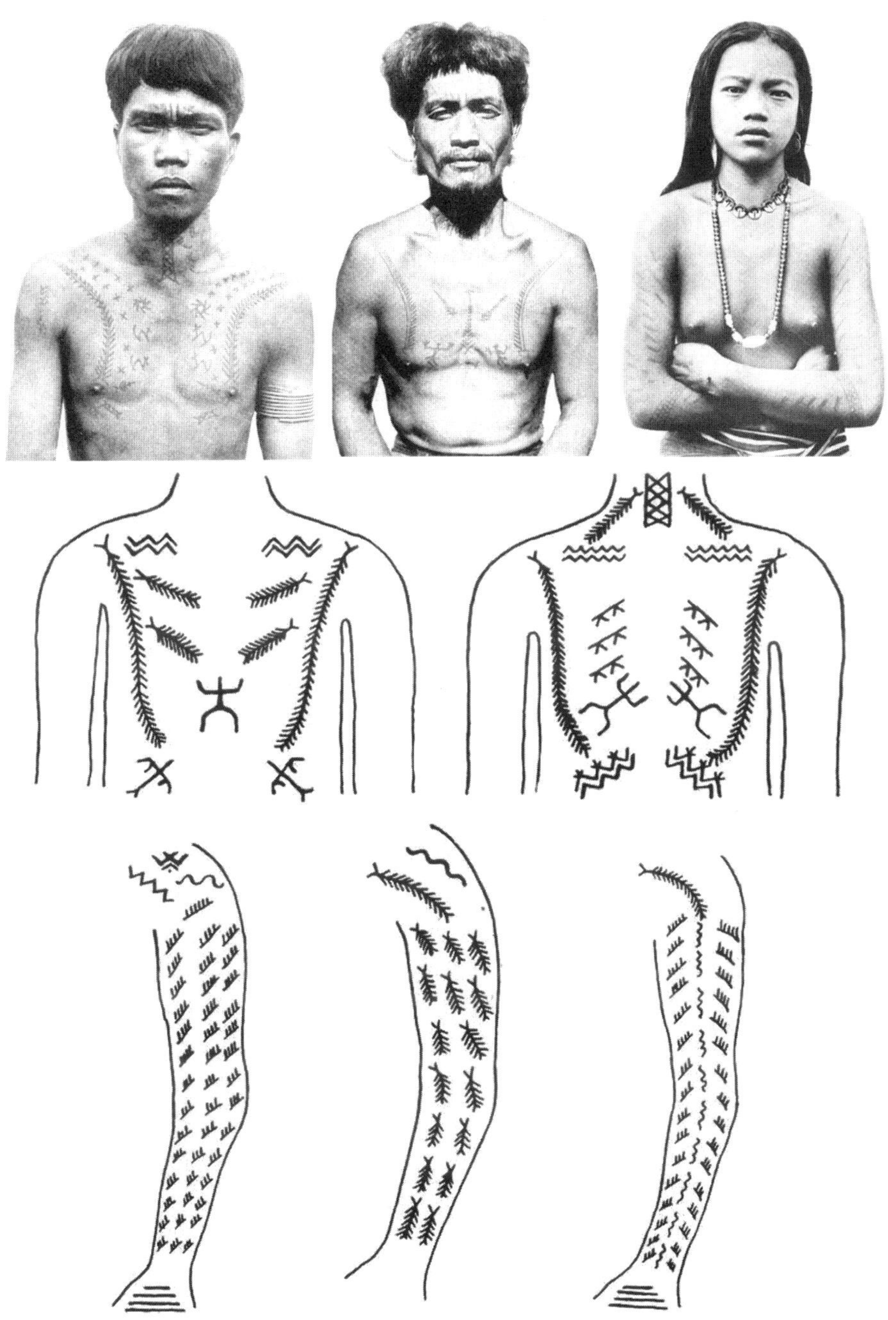

Showing typical Ifugao pattern extending high on the neck

forcing the needles into the skin, followed by dubbing pigment into the wounds, Isneq tribe.

IGOROT - or Cordillerans, is the collective name of several Austronesian ethnic groups in the Philippines, who inhabit the mountains of Luzon. These highland peoples inhabit all the six provinces of the Cordillera Administrative Region: Abra, Apayao,

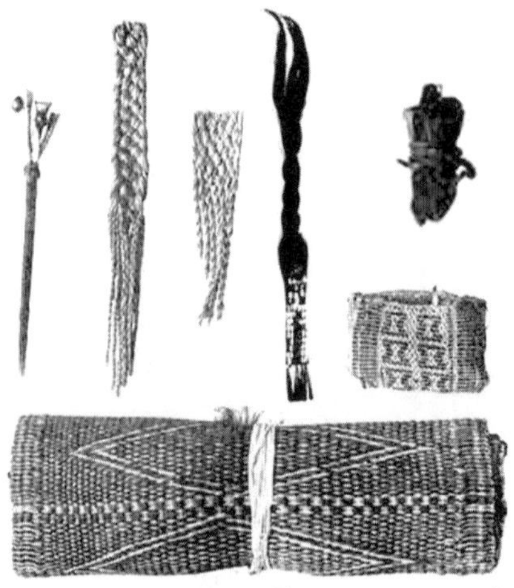

Ioway tattoo tools.

Benguet, Kalinga, Ifugao, and Mountain Province, as well as the adjacent province of Nueva Viscaya.

IHOH – the ink is called the ihoh, a pigment from the charred pinewood resin stored in a small gourd or iron case. In some cases, the ink that was used for tattooing was from the soot of the pan that turns into a fine powder mixed with water, Atayal.

ILIE´E Ilie´e (Plumbago) - a small shrub with white flowers that was used as a medicine, the juice of which served as a color for tattoos, Hawaii.

INEGEBOO – members of the Rajah tribe of Borneo practicing tattoos.

INCHUNLI – to tattoo, Choctaw language.

INCHUNWA – the mark made in branding; a stigma; a tattoo, Choctaw language.

INNU INDIANS - The Innus didn't usually paint their faces, though Innu men did tattoo patterns on their skin sometimes, North America.

INTIN - in Ponape, the world for writting would be merged in that for tattooing, or commemoration. Intin, Inting - to write, tattoo.

INTING – tattooing operation, Ponape.

INUIT - are people living near Arctic. Their homeland spreads from the northeastern promontory of Russia, through Alaska and northern Canada to some parts of Greenland. In the past, the Inuit were called "Eskimos". The "Eskimo" term comes from a mocking word of Native Americans, which possibly meant "raw-meat eater". Today, the name Inuit, which means "people" or "the real people", and comes from the language called Inuit-Inupiaq is more common. The singular of Inuit is Inuk which means "a person".

Many high-ranked Inuit and Tlingit women wear large labret piercings called tootuk or just tutu (generally speaking, the larger labret the higher family status) - these have also been symbolically illustrated in some art works. They worn jeweleries pierced in noses. Furthermore, many people from the north wear tattoos, including the facial ones (the word for tattoo in their language is tab la o'tit).

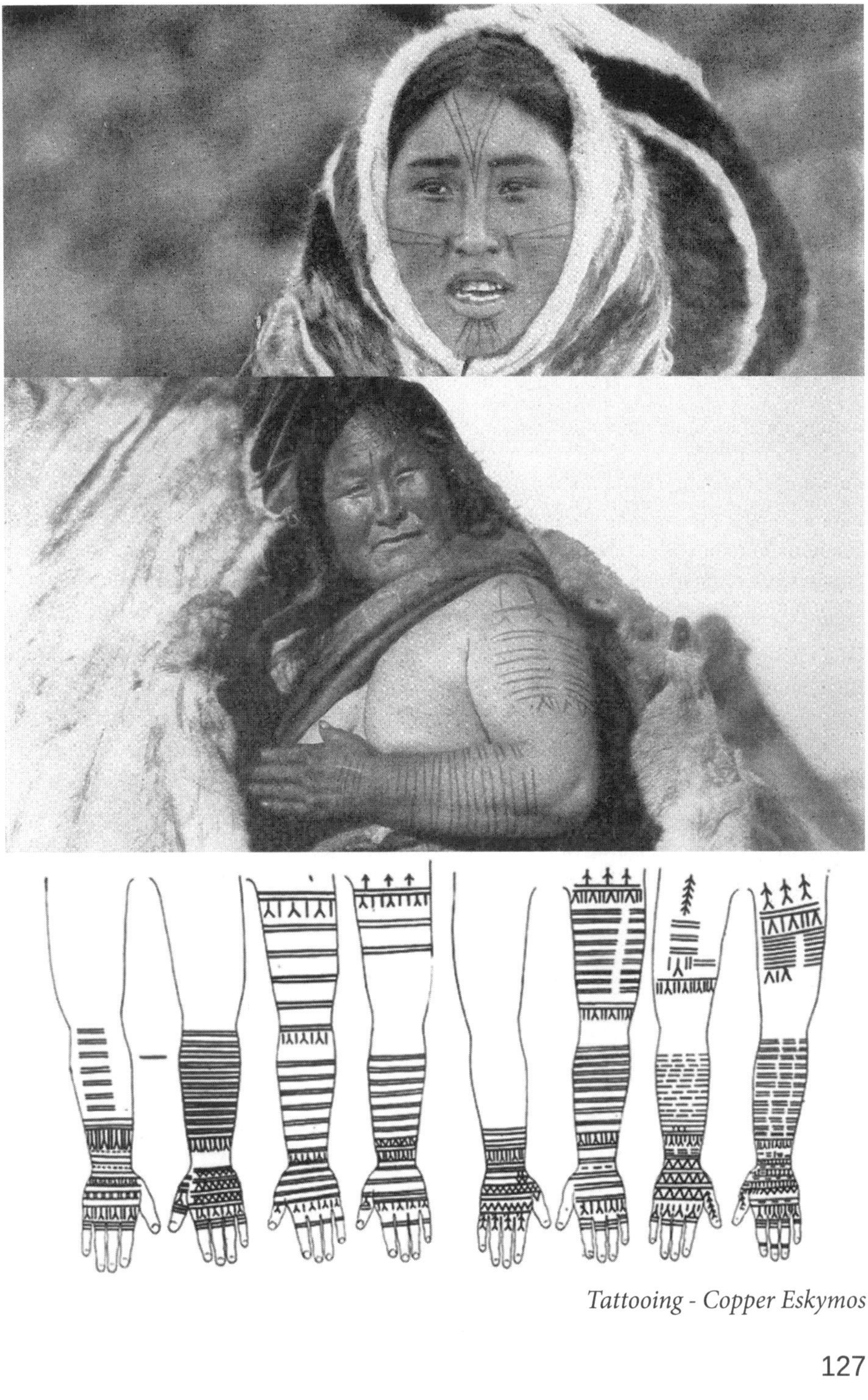

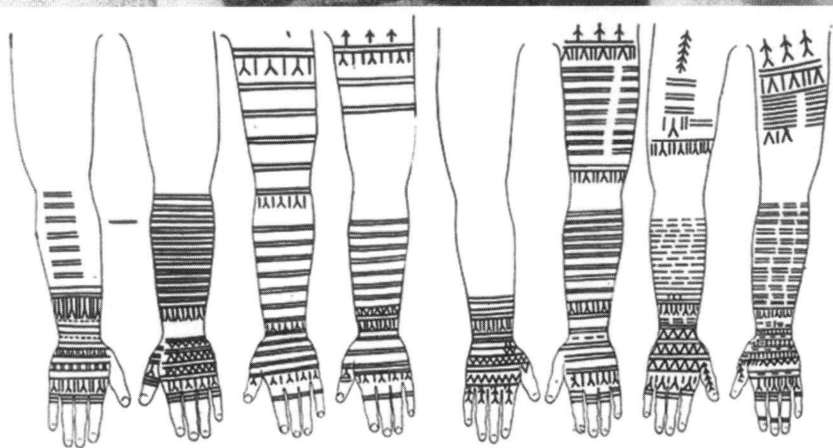

Tattooing - Copper Eskymos

Men also wear these modifications, depending on the region.

IOWAY – Tattooing was under the sponsorship of the Wind Deity, "Taje" or "Tache" (TAH-chay) (like the Lakota's "Tate", Dona). Tattooing or certain marks were not associated with certain clans, but with social status (either chief's families or war exploits). It was an important visible signal of social status. During the historic period only the highest status families had their daughters tattooed. One person said it was "like wearing a diamond." Besides young daughters of chiefly families, warriors of distinction were also tattooed. All tattoos were blue-black in color as it was charcoal made from willow that was the coloring agent. In later days they also used commercial blue pigment.

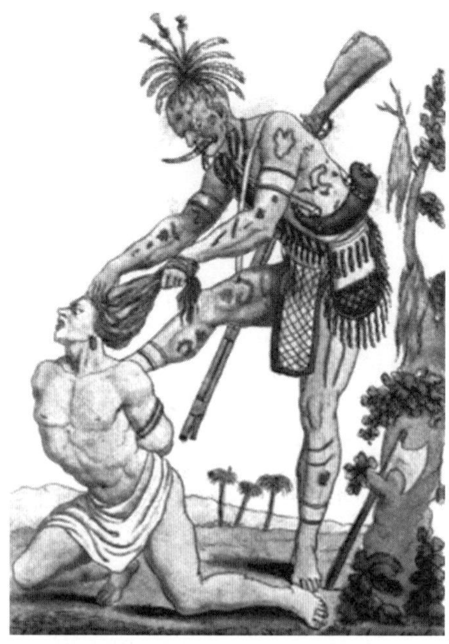

Iroquois warrior

IPU HINU - tattoo ink was mixed with the soot with plain water in a small coconut shell (ipu hinu), Marquesas.

IPU TU´U LAMA - The palette (ipu tu'u lama), is also formed out of a half coconut shell (ipu) over the opening of which a talo leaf or a mamala leaf is tied with a strip of fau bast. The pigment is dipped up on the pestle and dropped on the improvised palette. In order that the half shell may rest on the ground, the bottom or muli is chipped off or the shell may be set up between three stones to keep it level. Nowadays the talo leaf is usually tied over the end of an empty beef tin because of its flat bottom, Borneo. See AU FA´ATALA

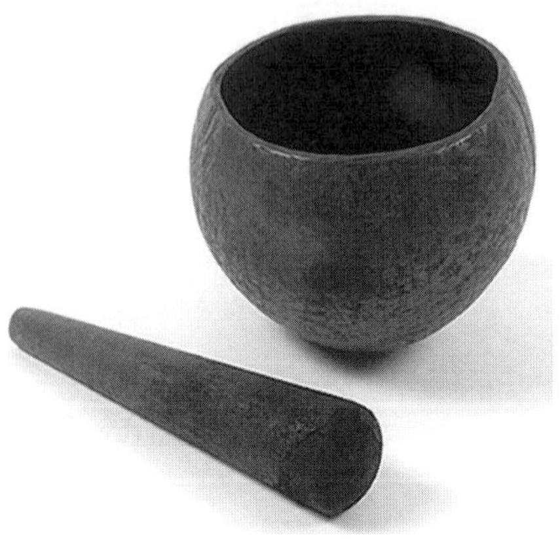

IPULAMA - A cup containing a tattoo dye. It was made from carbon black, selected from burnt llama nuts (Samoa).

IPUNIU – a cup of coconut shell, used for tattoo color, Samoa.

IREZUMI - "inserting ink, " is the Japanese word for tattoo, and is used in English to refer to a distinctive style of Japanese tattooing, though it is also used as a blanket term to describe a number of tattoo styles originating in Japan,

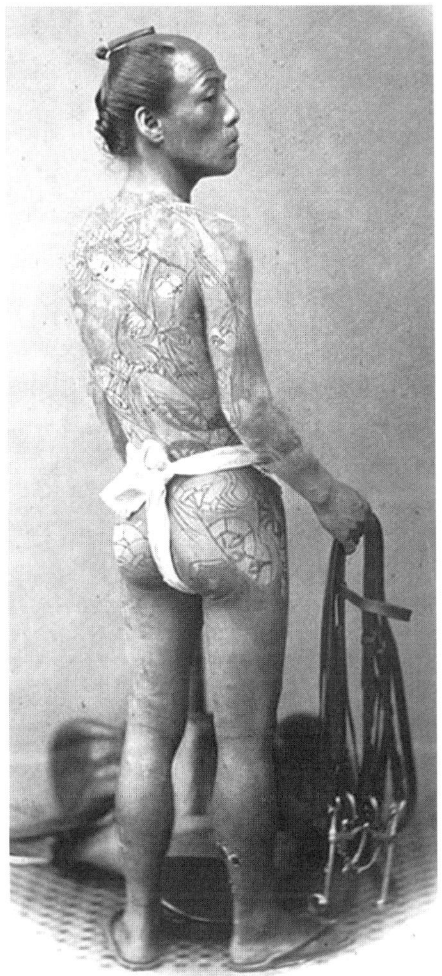

Irezumi

including tattooing traditions from both the Ainu people and the Ryukyuan Kingdom. All forms of irezumi are applied by hand, using wooden handles and metal needles attached via silk thread.

IRI – see ATAHU

IROOJ – Chief in the Marshall Islands.

IROOJ LAPLAP – the highest chief of the Marshall Islands, who was always tattooed first.

IROQUOIS - or Haudenosaunee are an indigenous confederacy in northeast North America. With figures of men and animals, they ornamented their faces and those parts of the body which were uncovered, without bestowing much pains or attention in their application.

A desire of rendering permanent these decorations of the body, suggested the

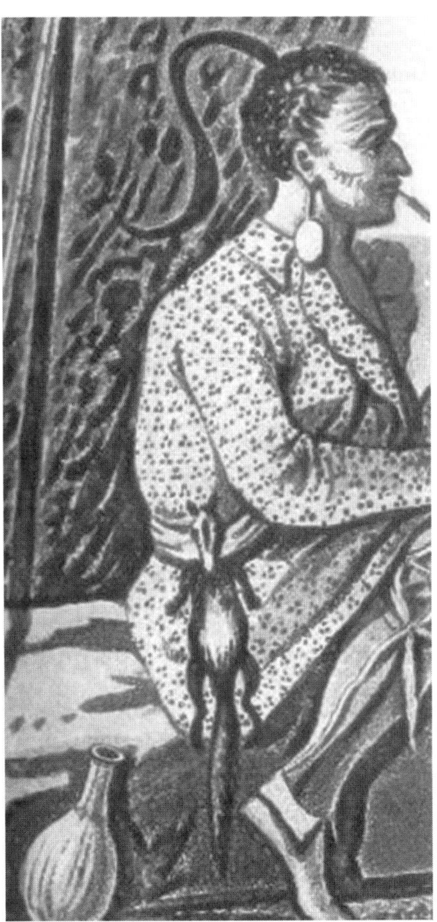

Iroquois with a tattoo on his face

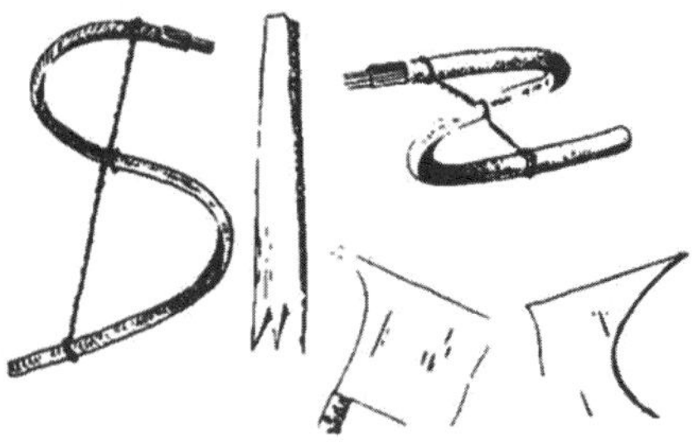

Isnag tattoo instrument

practise of tattooing, or of impressing on the human skin various fantastical figures, first sketched with coal or chalk, and afterwards pricked with sharpened point of a bone, the punctures being rubbed with whatever colour seems most to please the fancy. These operations are always painful, and often attended with some degree of fever. The figures thus engraved on the face and body, become distinguishing marks of the individual.

ISNAG PEOPLE - (also referred to as the Isneg and Apayao) are an Austronesia ethnic group native to Apayao Province in the Philippines' Cordillera Administrative Region. Their native language is Isneg (also called Isnag), although most Isnag also speak Ilokano. Practiced tattooing.

ITURU - a small basin with legs, ituru, for holding tattoo dye, Motu, New Guinea.

IVALU – The sinew (ivalu) used for tattooing usually came from reindeer tendons and sometimes from the tendons of sea mammals, like bowhead or gray whales.

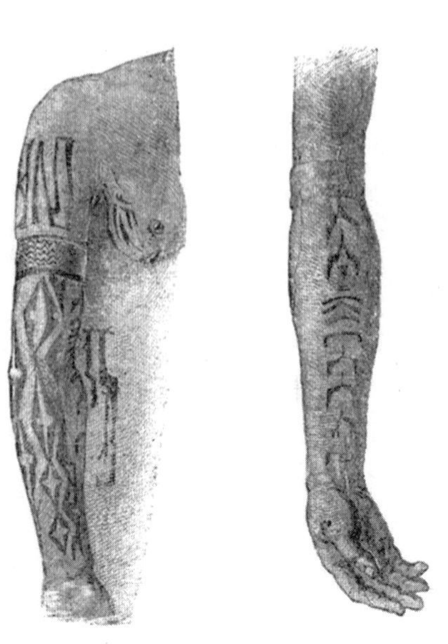

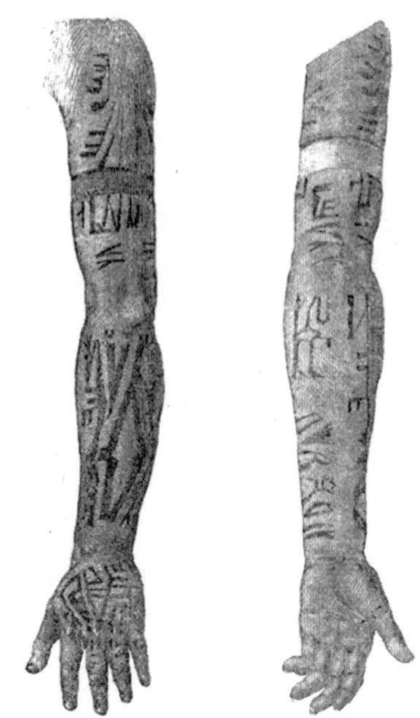

Ima patterns on the hands of Motu girls

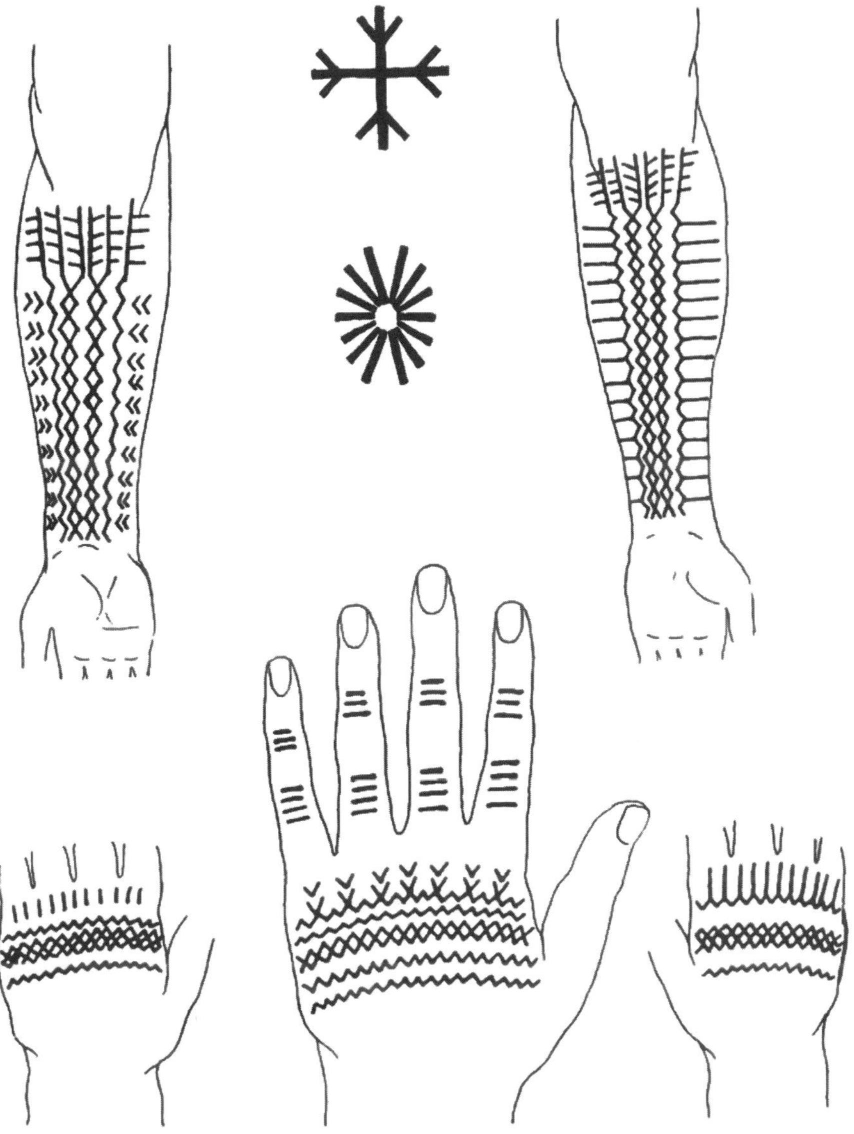

Female tattoos of the Isnag tribe

IVALUNGELQUGHRUK – In the reindeer, a bundle of tendons (ivalungelqughruk) lie underneath the skin on either side of the vertebrae or along the muscles of the back legs. These fine strands of reindeer ivalu were utilized in the tattooing of women. The ivalu procured from the back of the bowhead or gray whale was used in the tattooing of men.

IVI – tattoo tool, Magaia Island.

IVI HEANA – The flat instruments for straight lines and gradual curves were of human bone, sometimes of the bones of enemy sacrifices (ivi heana), Marquesas.

IVI-TA-TIPATIPA - In Mangaia the process of tattooing is called ta tipatipa. The instruments used correspond to those used by the New-Zealanders. The ivi'ta-tipatipa, a piece of bird's or human bone with three or more teeth, tied at right angles into a wooden handle.

IWA-NI - In preparation for tattooing, bark of the ash-tree (iwa-ni) or sometimes the spindle-wood (komke-ni) was cut into small pieces and boiled, producing an infusion of a dark greenish colour. This did not affect the colour of the tattooing, which was done with soot (pash) from birch bark. The bark was lighted under the pot and it deposited a fine soot (supash). The infusion (nire) was applied three times, before the incisions, immediately after and when the soot had been lightly rubbed in. It was supposed to be healing and perhaps also to fix the pigment, Ainu.

IWU – As part of the cultural geography of the body, iwu (tattoos) mapped out ethnic terrain and transformed the self, inscribed male and female personhood, denoted stratification by pedigree, and delineated selected occupational roles. Benin Tribe.

IZEPIULÁ – tattooing, Waurá tribe.

JADE– to beat the tattooing chisel with the mallet, Marshall Islands.

JADWAR – In Persia, the procedure (tattooing) was to rub over the place with two Chinese herbs known as jadwar and tanzu, famous for healing properties.

JAKAN – soot for tattoo color was obtained on the island of Ponape by burning the fruit tree yakan (Aleurites triloba).

JAREO – the group of women drumming and singing outside the tattooing house during the tattooing process, Marshall Islands.

JAUNDE TRIBE - Yaunde, also spelled Yaounde or Jaunde, also called Éwondo, a Bantu-speaking people of the hilly area of south-central Cameroon who live in and around the capital city of Yaoundé. The Yaunde and a closely related people, the Eton, comprise the two main subgroups of the Beti, which in turn constitute one of the three major subdivisions of the cluster of peoples in southern Cameroon, mainland Equatorial Guinea, and northern Gabon known as the Fang (q.v.). The other two main subdivisions are those of the Bulu and of the Fang proper, who live mostly in Gabon and in Equatorial Guinea.

JAZUN - a triangular or double triangle design or a crescent, Arabs.

JE ANGET NEKASSAT – tattooing process, Abyssinian.

JEDWEL - Oftentimes Berber tattoos were placed near body orifices (eyes, mouth, nose, navel,vagina) or surfaces believed to be vulnerable to the machinations of evil. For example, tattoos

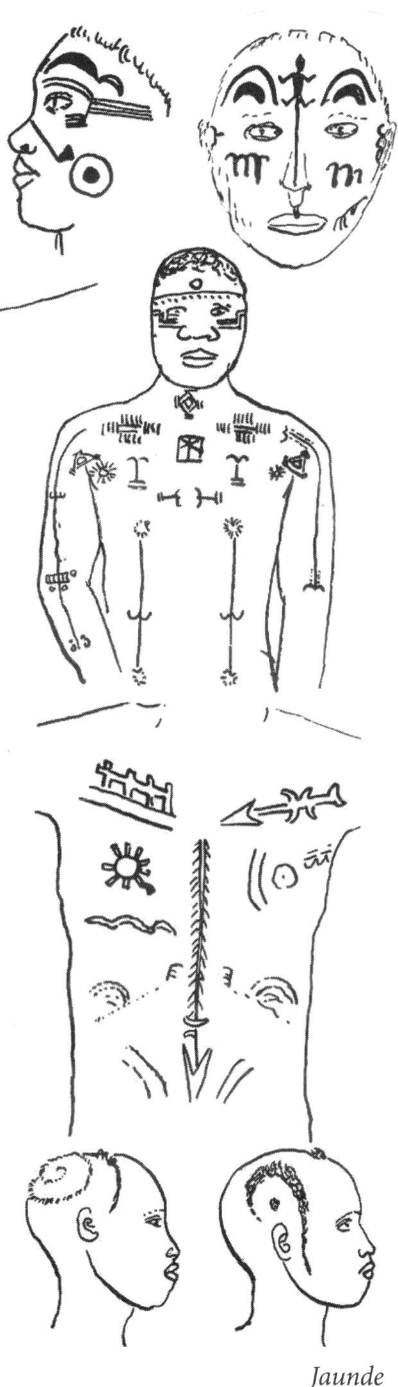

Jaunde

usually marked the feet to protect women from jnoun who attempted to enter the body through the earth. Other designs on the ankles, hands, and face were believed to protectindividuals from the evil eye. Thus, it is not surprising that many Berber tattoos carry the tag of jedwel or "talisman" (Krutak, 2010)

There are many abstract elements to Berber tattoo designs and symbols, yet many others are reoccurring , such as :

The tree – representing strength.

Seeds – representing fertility.

Frog and Spider – representing fertility and magical rites.

Snakes – representing the Phallus, fertility and healing.

Fish bones – representing water, prosperity and fertility.

The lizard – representing re birth and light.

Flies and bees – representing stamina and energy.

Diamond shapes – representing protection of personal space.

Khamsa – representing protection form of the evil eye.

JĔCHĔJÚ - rosin (like dammar), found on trees; used as a sticking material and by burning producing the soot, chan, which serves as a colouring material and for tattooing, Humboldt Bay.

JEJE – The drawing brush (jeje) consisted of the long tail feather of a frigate bird or of a central rib of a coconut leaf, often mounted on a handle made of a small stick or the thicker end of a feather, Marshall Islands.

JEMBE – tribe practicing scar tattoo, Zaire.

JEMOUN – jemoun means "to paint black with genipapo," and juices of the green, immature fruits of the genipapo tree were used at least 1,000 years ago, South America.

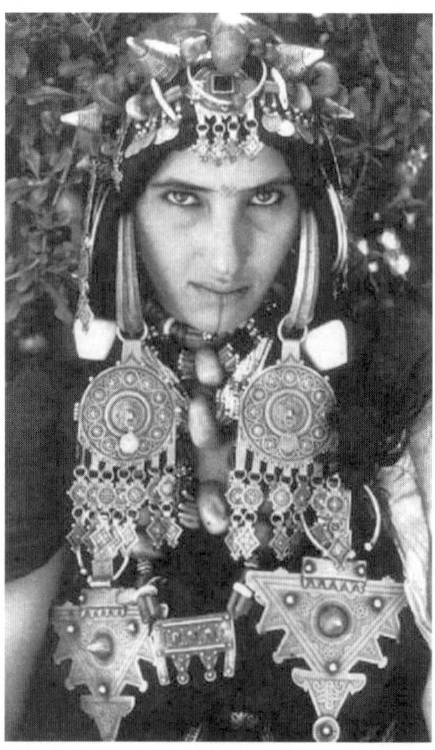

Jedwel

JIB IN JOWI – In order for a commoner man to be tattoed, one man was selected to represent his jowi (clan). If he survived the jib in jowi (torture ceremony) all males of his entire clan could be tattoed. Even if a clan member was on another island during the time the selected man passes the test, at a later time this clan member could sail to Bouj and permission would be granted by the irooj for him to be tattooed, for his clan member had survived the jib in jowi, Marshall Islands.

JINN– or the evil spirits from which the Fulani (West African tribe) protect themselves by tattoos.

JJIBUR EN KORA – Several (fine) mats to cover the freshly completed tattoo (sections) to prevent infection, Marshall Islands.

JOMIJ– For the duration of the ceremonies the normal terms for men of women about to be tattooed were called jomij. A completely tattooed male was also called jomij, Marshall Islands.

JOMON – The oldest period of traditional Japanese tattoo known (10,000 B. C. ~ 300 B. C.). Jomon means "cord-marked". Many ceramic vessels with rope marks coming from this period were found. Clay statutes created within this period are called dogu. Scientists belief that some dogus have marks similar to tattoos on their faces and bodies. The oldest dogus with facial tattoos were found near Osaka in 1977. People living on Japanese islands within the Jomon period may be distant ancestors of the Ainu people.

JORUBA - African tribe practicing scar tattoo.

JOWOS – for men, tattoos were also linked to head-hunting. After a warrior brought back the head of an enemy, a ritual called Jowosi was held to celebrate the dech and the accomplishments of the warrior. After the ritual, the warrior received a tattoo of the name of the victim.

JUANG TRIBE - The Juang women tattooed three strokes on the forehead just over the nose three on each of the temples.

JUB – The mallet for pounding in the teeth of the adze was commonly made from a straight, 20-30cm long piece of hardwood or the central rib of a coconut frond with a slightly flattened end.

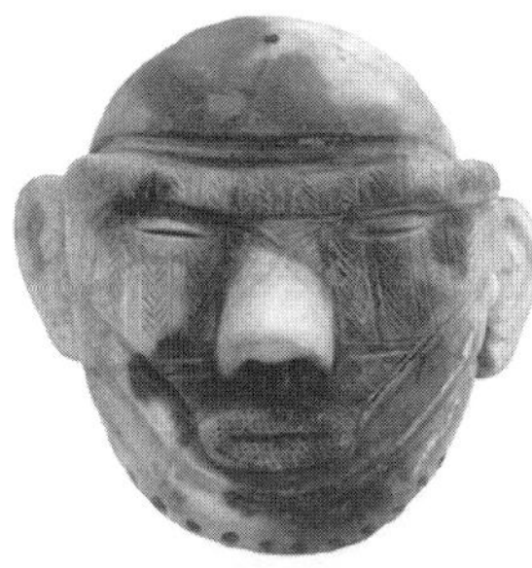

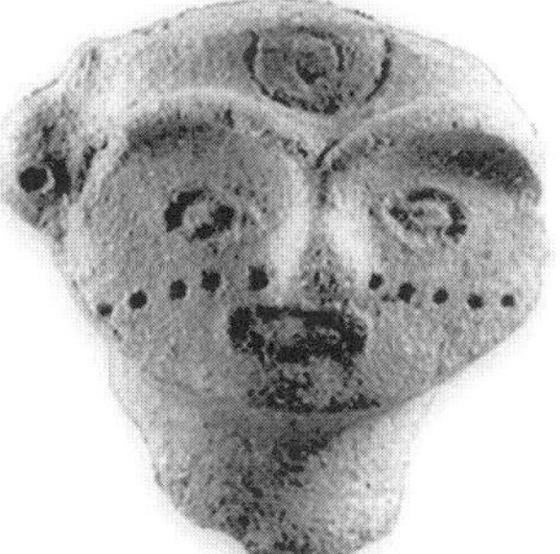

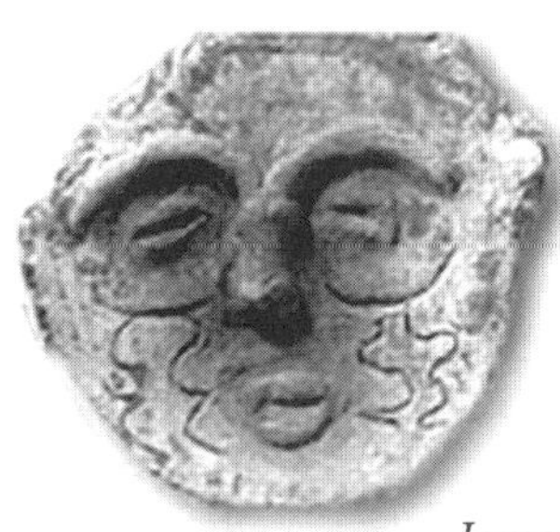

Jomon

JUGKAO - The link between tattoos and the afterlife is one that is also widespread among various groups in Southeast and East Asia. Tattoos for the Kalinga served to make one recognizable to and "worthy to live with the deceased ancestors" in the jugkao or afterlife.

JUPOT – tattoo, was done with thorns from the Tucun palm, Kayabi tribe, Amazon.

JURÍ TRIBE - The distinctive Uainumá, Jurí, and Pasé ornament was extensive facial tattooing in wide patches which covered the whole mouth region and often reached the eyes. This tattooing was begun in early childhood and

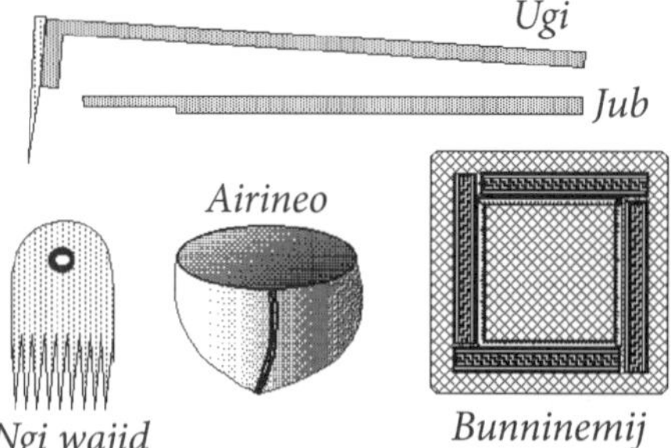

increased during life, until in old age it finally reached its perfection. The Juri owe their name, Juru-pixuna, "Black Mouth" (in Portuguese, Bocapreta) to their typical tattooing.

JURO – The ngi, "tooth", a tattooing adze, was made from a stick or piece of bamboo, about 25-30cm long, which formed the handle (juro). In its upper end, a flat piece of bone about 40mm long and 7 mm wide is inserted at right Angeles, Marshall Islands.

JUYAN - one of the ancient Chinese terms for tattoos.

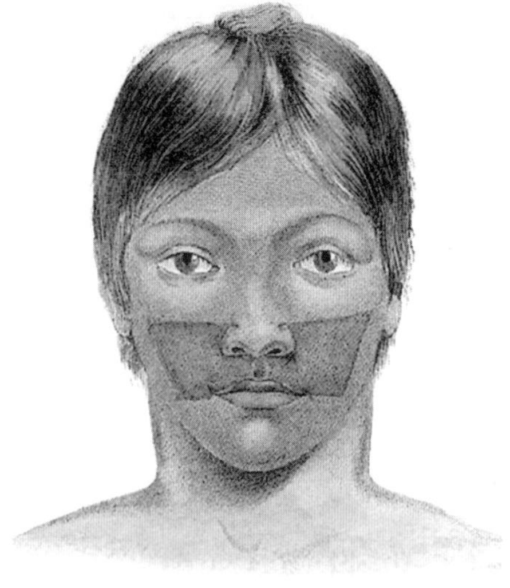

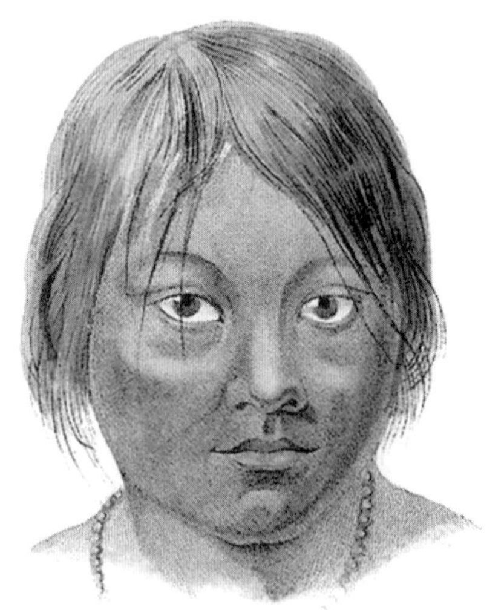

Jurí

K´AKH´NU - ('partridges'), tattoos, Laki in Kuli rayon, Dagestán.

KA´IOI – a group that built a special house for tattoos. Members of this group had tattoos from head to legs, as opposed to opou, Marquesas.

KAAHI – the ink, which he calls kaahi, was made by mixing the soot with coconut oil, Marquesas.

KABWIJERAN – payment for the tattoo, Marshall Islands.

KADJIME- The payment for tattoo (kadjime "make straight" -) took place with food and mats, Marshall Islands.

KADMO-MARNGUTTA – tattoing, Tasmania.

KADSCHALA - Another utensil used in tattooing is a kind of vegetable fiber brush used to foment the tattooed areas during healing, the same name being Kadschala, Marshall Isl.

KADIWEU TRIBE – is a tribe located in the Mato Grosso lowlands (South America) between the Paraguay River and Bodequena and Serra dos Gaviaos mountains. Tattoo belongs to their ancient arts for generations. According to Czech explorer Frič, the Kadiweu were beautiful people: almond eyes, permanent half-smile, noble expression, always kind and open-minded. Women were charming even for European standards by their deportment and skin colour resembling bronze statues of Antique or Renaissance art. "Beautiful like a Sandro Botticelli's vision," wrote another traveller in his diary ten years before Frič – an Italian Guido Boggiani (1861-1901) - when he managed to take a picture of

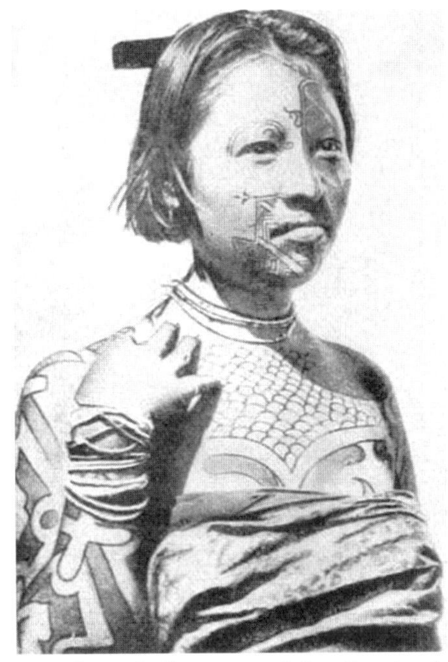

A Caduveo belle in 1895 (after Boggiani)

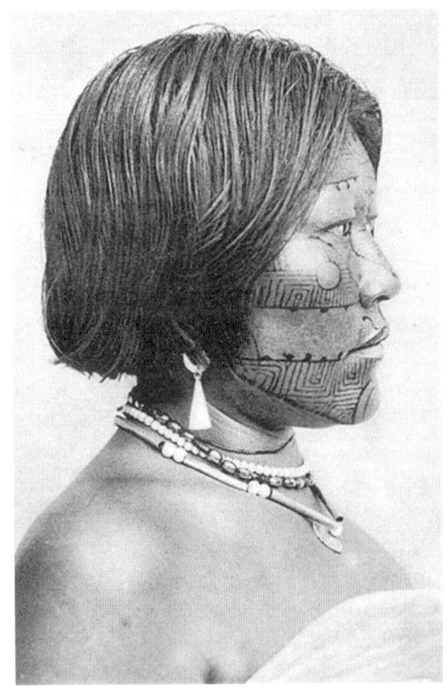

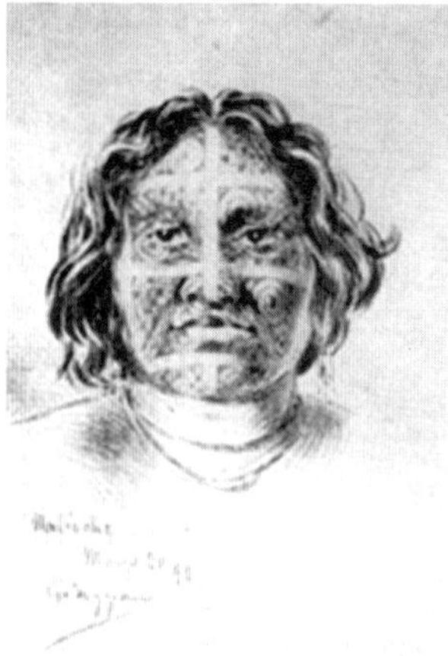

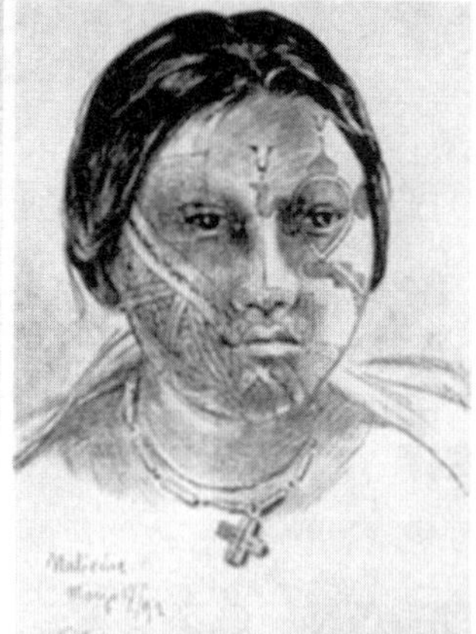

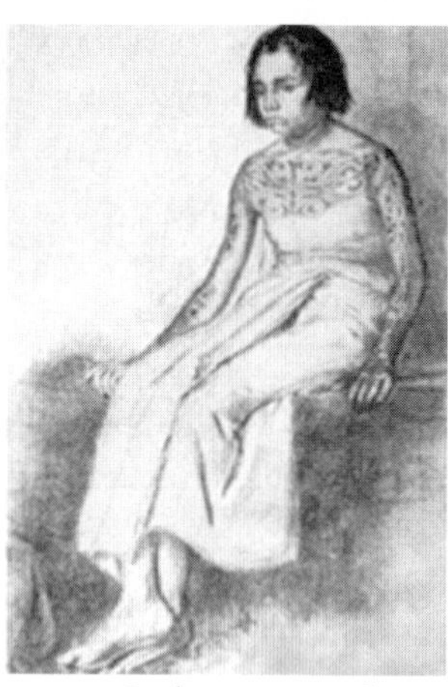

Caduveo or Kadiweu

noble Kadiweu girl decorated by marvellous symbols that have no parallel in any other culture.

According to a religious law, Kadiweu women have to wear a short haircut and pluck their eyelashes and eyebrows to not resemble an ostrich. Symbols are related to the individuality of their wearers – they do not respect the face relief by any means and often bring to mind "maps" of Chinese acupuncturists.

Frič commented on the women of the Kadiweu in a following manner: "She is not satisfied with the beauty given to her by Mother Nature – she always wants to be even prettier. How beautiful is an Indian woman who embellishes her face and the whole body with strange but elegant painting to please her husband or lover! Personally, I like it more than make-ups and powders of Prague girls and a naked Kadiweu woman, with a body covered in blue symbols, does not upset me unlike plunging necklines of ladies from higher society flirting by their artificially laced bodies."

KAESHIBARI - within the traditional Japanese tattoo of Tebori, the kaeshibari represents tattooing using tattoo needles for applying the dye. Some tattoo artists use specialized tools consisting of 3 needles for improving details. However, real professionals of Japanese Tebori are able to create everything with just one outline set, they do not need any extra tool. They can tattoo any thin or thick lines, small circles, etc. Masters of this technique tattoo create shapes smoothly from the bottom up and vice versa; from left to right, right to left. When, for example, more dye for tattooing from left to right is needed, the kaeshibari is used; the needle is shaken and turned to the other side.

KAFA – binding string for tattoo hammer, Tonga.

KAFÓ - Very often there are also small scars that come from cupping. A horn, kafo or canoe is used for this. It has an opening at the top through which it sucks in air. The hole is during the process closed with wax, the tribes of Yoruba, Adiinka and Ibadan.

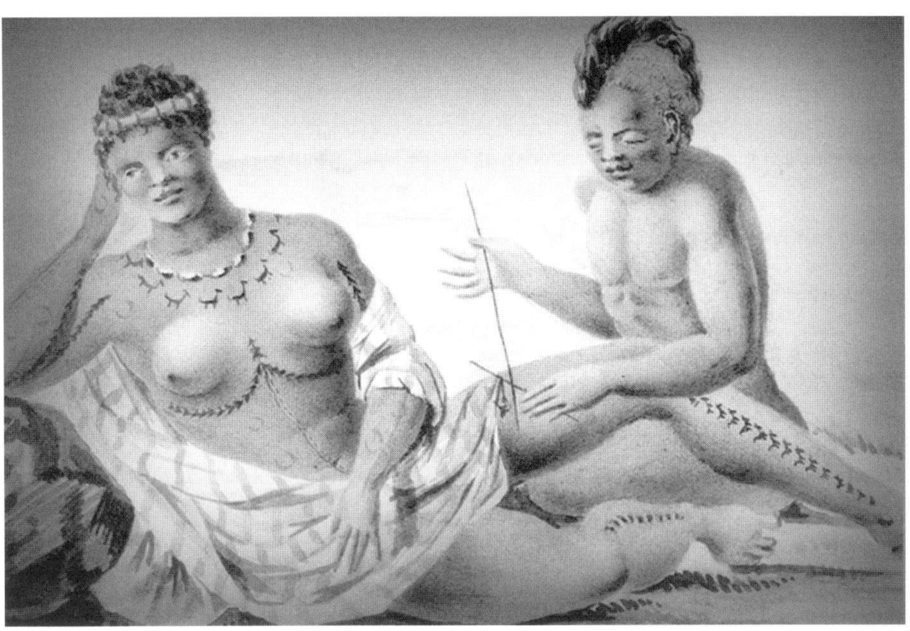

Kahuna, 1819

KAHUNA - a tattoo master in Hawaii.

KAI– tattoo hammer. For this hammer fresh sugar cane cuts, tšeu, are used.Ponape.

KAIGANI – The Kaigani Haida live north of the Canadian and US border which cuts through Dixon Entrance on Prince of Wales Island (Tlingit: Taan) in Southeast Alaska, practised tattoo.

KAIOI – a community similar to the Ariori but located on Marquesas Islands. Characteristics of this community were, among others, headhunting and obtaining human sacrifices. A member of society had to be tattooed with precisely designed patterns that were supposed to be located on a specific spot of his body.

KAJALA – A brush made of coconut or other fibers (kajala) to fan the tattooed skin during the healing process.

KAKAHO - (reed or cane) for the horizontal support of the teeth of tattoo instrument, Marquesas.

KAKATI – see KAKATOE

KAKATOE - Tattoo was chiefly applied to women, the lower legs being the main focus in Lamboya, others extending the shin and calve tattoo to the thighs, while arm tattoo was also encountered although, this was not considered essential.

KAKAU – Hawaiian expression for tattoo.

KAKAU I KA UHI – In Hawaii, the art of tattoo was called kakau i ka uhi, or to “strike on the black.”

KAKI - tattoo, Bahasa Tanah.

KAKKALAN CASTE – They were tattooed, north and central Travancore, India.

KAKUSHI-BORI - Literal translation of Kakushi Bori is “hidden tattoo”. Basically Kakushi Bori refers to the tattooed area on the inside of the upper arm (which can include the armpit) and the inside of the thighs.

KALABIT – ethnic group in Borneo practicing tattoos.

KALAMAKA – Tanal people use for tattoo color juice from the crushed leaves of the legume Kalamaka, Madagascar.

KALIČ - tattoo needles, Ponape.

KALIS - tattoo needles, Yap.

KALINGA - is a landlocked province in the Philippines situated within the Cordillera Administrative Region in Luzon. People practised tattooing.

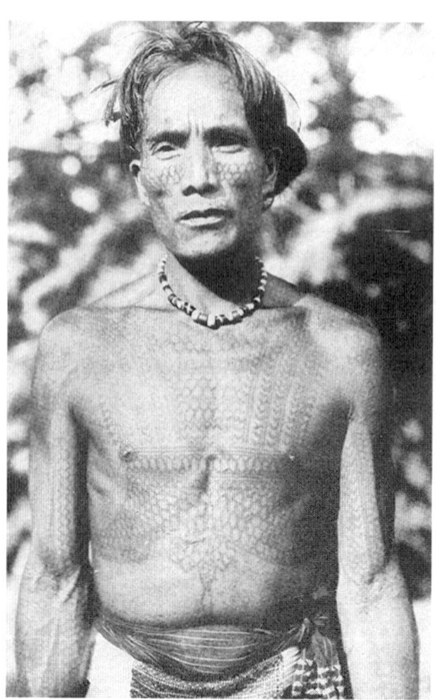

Kalinga chief

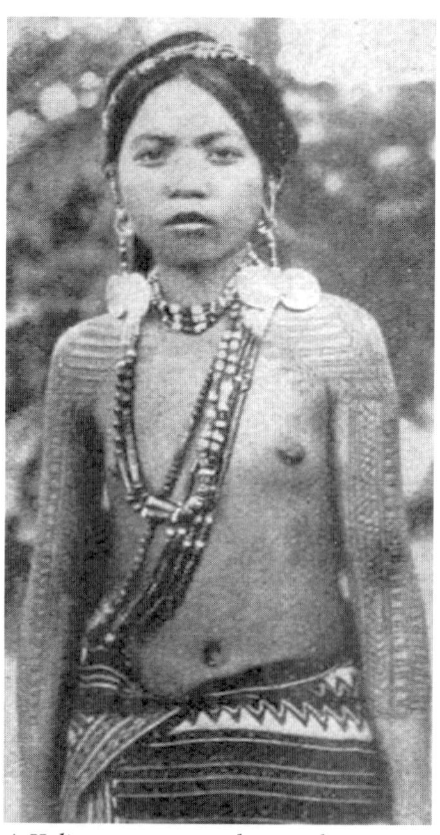

A Kalinga woman with typical tattooing

KALIZ- tattoo tool with sharp thorns of local bushes at its end. The handle of kaliz was often made of bone. Ponape, Micronesia.

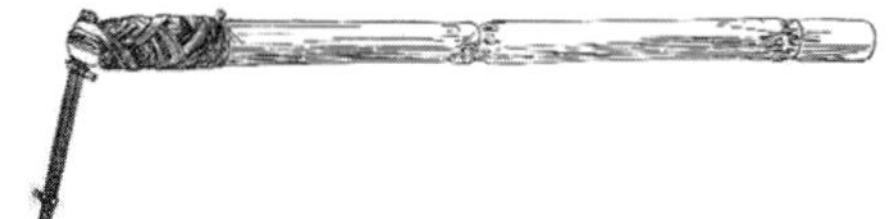

KAMADILA – Tattoo was called kamadila in Laboya, Sumba Island.

KAMARAN – After the tattoo, the tattooed person was forbidden to go public and show his new tattoo - Kamaran, Marshall Islands.

KAMI – an Indian tribe in which tattoos used to be only a female ornament.

KAMMAI – The tattoo patterns did initially applied onto the skin, using a piece of wood carved with tattoo patterns (kammai) that had been dipped in ink (merteka), Batek.

KANIRI - The dye, which was of a blue-black color, was made from the nut of the fruit of the Kemiri ("kaniri") which was burned and pounded to a fine state, presumably being mixed with water, Sumba island.

KANJI - (pronounced Hanzi in Chinese) are Chinese logographic symbols used in the font system of several Asian languages. The "kanji" word is related specifically to a subgroup of language used in Japanese, although this differentiation is often overlooked.

Kanji tattoos are one of the most popular tattoo kinds. They represent Chinese and Japanese symbols and mostly they are created by people who don't have a clue about their actual meaning. The result is that many people wear a tattoo that doesn't quite describe what they think it does. After all, most of the professional tattoo artists don't think much about these people because they got their kanji done to look cool rather than for their own personal attitude.

KANÓ – see KAFÓ

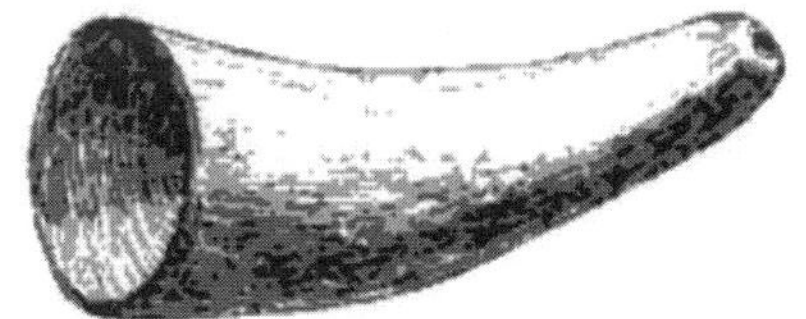

KANU ´ANGA – expression for writing, creating designs or tattoos, Bellona Island.

KANU – be patterned as with tattoos, tattoo, Bellona Island.

KANUA – to be tattooed, Bellona Island.

KANUKANU – draw tattoo motif, Bellona Island.

KANYAPPA – the operation of tattoing was performed with sharp pieces of quartz (kanayppa), by means of which raised lines and dots (bakkurta) are made on the breast, Tanzania.

KAOKAO O TE FANGONGO - The upper edge of the fangongo refu is called kaokao o te fangongo refu.

KAPA – when a Hula woman underwent the last stage of tattooing, she underwent an initiation festival called Kapa.

KAPARA – viz NARAHU

KAPI- To tap the head or body of a sick person with the tattooing needle, to tap the needle to tattoo, Bellona.

KAPULU– the largest tattoo instrument, Samoa.

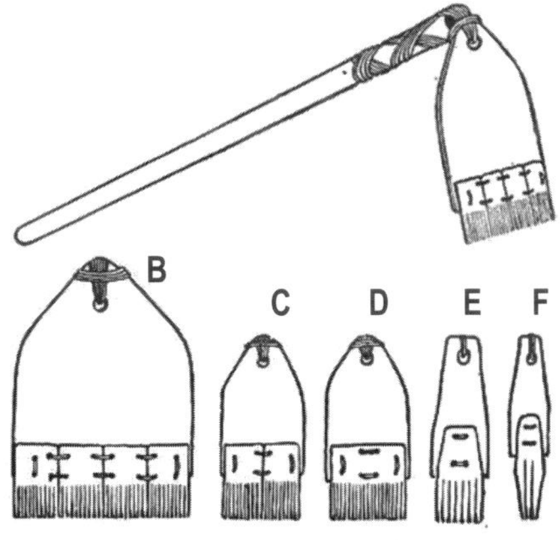

Obr. B – kapulu, C, D- songi aso, E, F – au mongo

KARAKIA – Karakia are prayers or incantations. They are generally used to ensure a favorable outcome to important events and undertakings such as tangihanga (the ritual of farewell to our deceased), hui (meetings), unveiling, etc., however they can cover every aspect of life. For example: welcoming the dawn and farewelling the day, to ensure a safe journey, for different types of illness, when undertaking ta moko (tribal 'tattoo'), when carving wharenui (meeting houses) or waka (traditional canoe), and more. Karakia, in their true essence, are ritual chants invoking spiritual guidance and protection.

KAREHU – blue tattoo pigment, Ngai-Tahu tribe, New Zealand.

KARIJÓ - (Krarajá / Guaraní) Indians tattoo the representatives of both sexes with a blue circle on their cheeks. Its perimeter is first marked with a wooden punch, then with a sharp stone. He lays a tuft of cotton on the wound. When the wound stops bleeding, they rub the juice into it, and the scar turns blue.

KAROK or KARUK – Indian tribe, present-day California. The women tattooed three stripes from lip to chin. They used stone soot, mixed with plant juice to do so.

KAS´TEL POMO - The women of this and other tribes of the Coast range frequently tattoo a rude representation of a tree or other object covering nearly the whole abdomen and breast.

KASIRI VAHORO– means non-tattooed in thelanguage of the Motu tribe.

KÁSSAQ – men with tattooed chins, carrying on solely female work, living always with women, and similarly to these having one and sometimes even two 'husbands,' Kodiaks.

KAT CLASS - In "Katha" are three general classes of tattoo: btw tattoos that create a barrier around the person that prevents animals of all sorts from biting, knives from cutting, and bullets from entering the body (kat or pik). See ACUN, YAPAYA

KATAKANA - is a purely phonetical set where every "letter" represents a sound. It differs from the Hiragana, which is another Japanese set of phonetical characters used for borrowed (foreign) words. Although katakana is sometimes used in the culture of Japanese youngsters to put emphasis on words, it is not a grammatically correct use and it is not recommended to use the katakana for tattoos, unless you are well acquainted with Japanese.

KATAKKO – term for tattoo in Wajewa area, Sumba Island.

KATALATOGA – when the tattoo pattern was bad, not according to the pattern, the Motu tribe.

KATALI – see KAKATOE

KATATU – term for tattoo in Rindi area, Sumba Island.

KATHA – Thai term for tattoo. The operation itself involves recitations and the acceptance of various precepts such as refraining from killing, stealing, improper sexula behavior, lying, and intoxication. Tannenbaum anylyze various classes of tattoo in terms of the rituals involved in administering them, their purposes, and their intersection with gender, power, and religion.

Through her study of tattooing, she shows how animist beliefs and state-sponsored Buddhism are intergrated into a single moral universe.

KATSA– term for tattoo, Betsimisaraka tribe, Madagskar.

KATSUNARI, FUKUSHI - is well known for his research on the Tokyo University including a collection and preservation of tattooed human skins. Fukushi studies, keeping and recording a collection of traditional tattoos of Japanese "Yakuza" members. The bright, vibrant colours are interesting, and the contours of the patterns with needles' punctures.

KATU – mens tattooing, Katu tribe, Laos.

KATU; KAKATU, KAUKATU (redup)- to tap or beat, as with a tattooing needle, drumstick, stone; Lakalai tribe, Papua New Guinea.

KAU AU - Handle of tattooing needle, Bellona.

KAUNASU – designation for a tattoo ink made from water and soot, the island of Tikopia.

KAURI – the wood from which the tattoo tool was made, Bellona.

- the name of a tree (Agathis australis), soot from burnt kauri resin, used in tattooing, Maori

KAUWA LAE-PUNI – Name of a servant marked in the forehead; Hawaii.

KAVA - is a slightly narcotic drink that was served before tattoo ceremonies. It is made of leached root of Piper Methysticum plant. Once upon a time, it was distributed before a war campaign or upon religious rituals. It was also offered as hospitality and accepting of it meant establishing an alliance.

KAVIGMIUT - An Eskimo tribe occupying the coast of Norton sd. and the neck of Kawiak peninsula, Alaska.

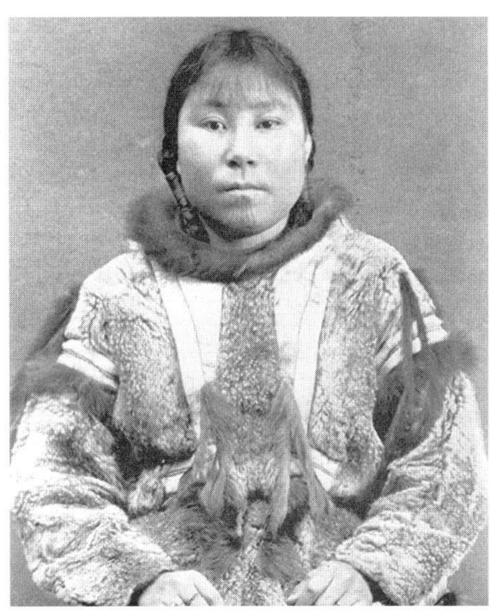

KAWARS - are mainly agriculturists preferring to live in the plains. Tattooing was common as among many aboriginal tribes.

KAYAN – tribe of Borneo. Practiced tattooing. In The Natives of Sarawak and British North Borneo you can read: The

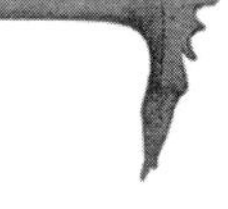

Kayan tattooing instrument

Kayans are particularly fond of tattooing; the women more so than the men. A Kayan woman is tattooed on the upper part of the hands and over the whole of each forearm; on both thighs to below the knees, and on the upper part of the feet and toes. The pattern is so close that

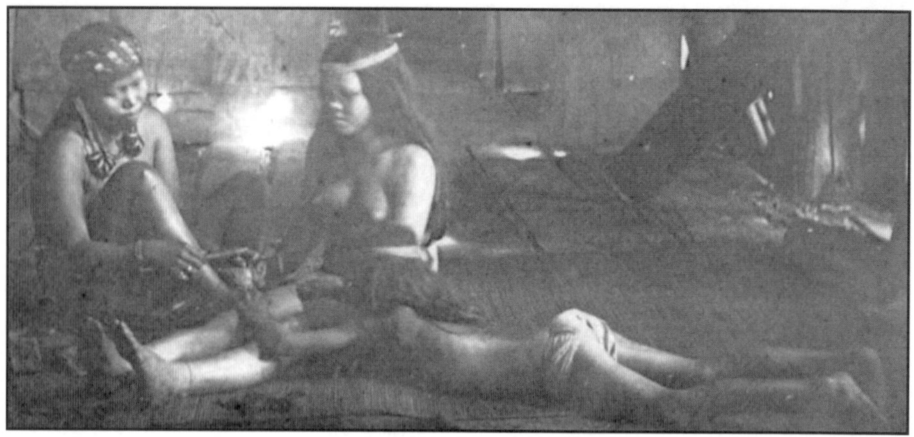

Tattooing a Kayan girl - While the skin it was kept tense by the hands of and assistant and by the feet of the tattooer, the design, which has been marked on the skin with ink-smeared wooden stals, it was pricked in by tapping on the back of the needle-holder with an iron or a wooden beater.

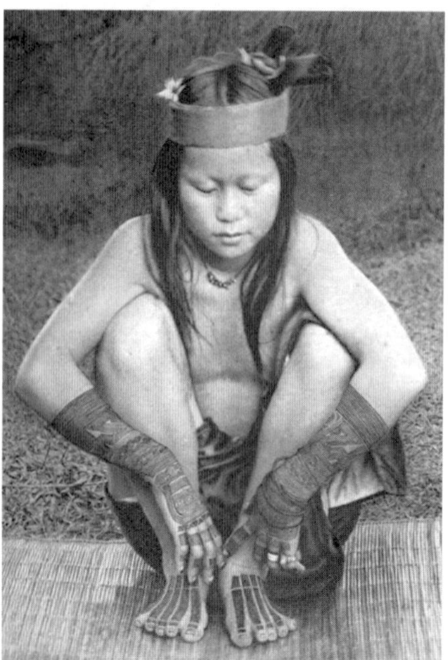

Tattooing on the forearms and feet of a Kenyah woman

at a slight distance the tattooing appears simply as a mass of dark blue, and the designs – some of which are very pretty – usually consist of a multiplicity of rings and circles. A man is suppused to tattoo one finger onnly, if he has been present when an enemy has been killed, but

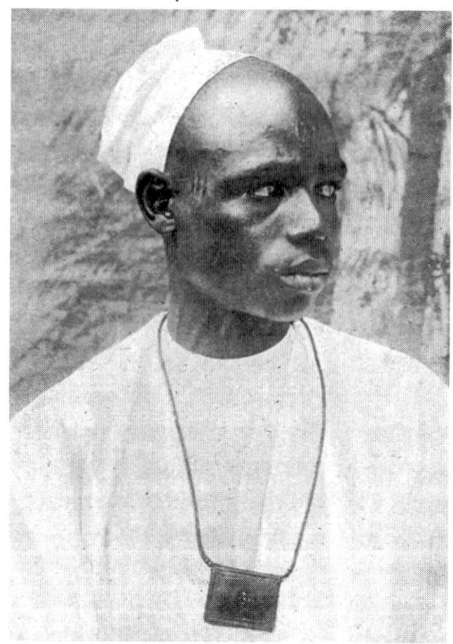

Khassonkés

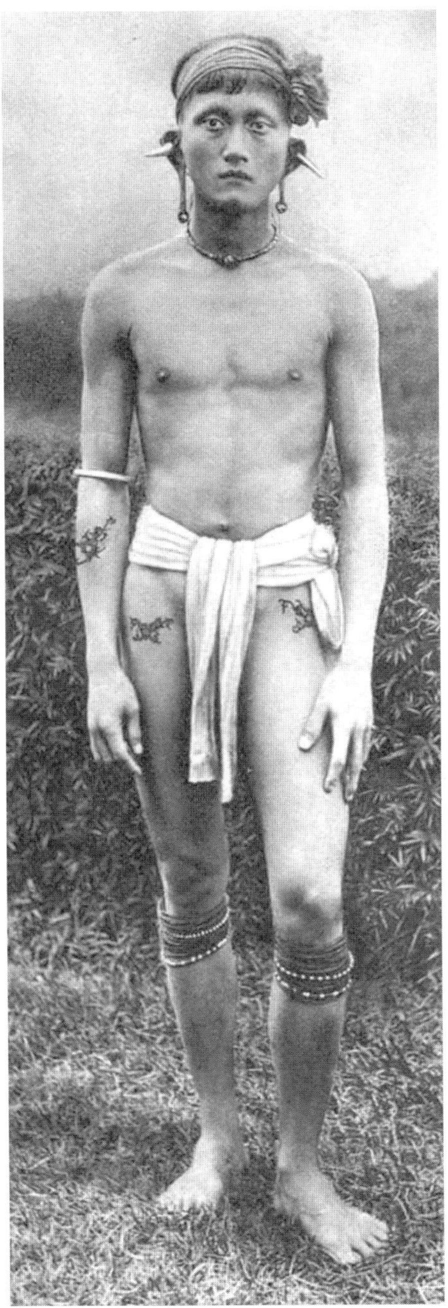

Young Kayan chief with characteristci tattoo of the Baram district

tattoos hands and fingers if he has taken an enemy´s head.“

KAYŠAPŠAP - The soft stem of the Kayšapšap plant is used as a tattoo mallet, Palau Isl.

KAZUO OGURI (HORIHIDE) - is the famous first artist – tattooist - who made his way to United States after the World War II. In 1970, he went to Hawaii to meet Sailor Jerry Collins and share the skill and history of Tebori bringing the traditional Japanese tattoo to the Western people again. As a founder of the Japan Tattoo Institute and the Tokai Tattoo Club, his contribution in the tattoo field is known all around the world and is acknowledged by various artists.

KE NIE - one of the ancient Chinese terms for tattoos.

KEDE - to carve, to tattoo, to write, Salomon Islands.

KEDE MAA – to tattoo the face, Solomon Islands.

THE TATTOOING OF THE BODY IN "SEVEN DAYS" CHRONOLOGY

The legend of the Marquesan hero Kena, describes the chronology of the tattooing of the entire body in "seven days".

- First day: tattooing of the face.
- Second day: one leg, starting from the foot and going up.
- Third day: second leg.
- Fourth day: neck and chest.
- Fifth day: ribs and arms.
- Sixth day: the back.
- Seventh day: buttocks and small additional designs.

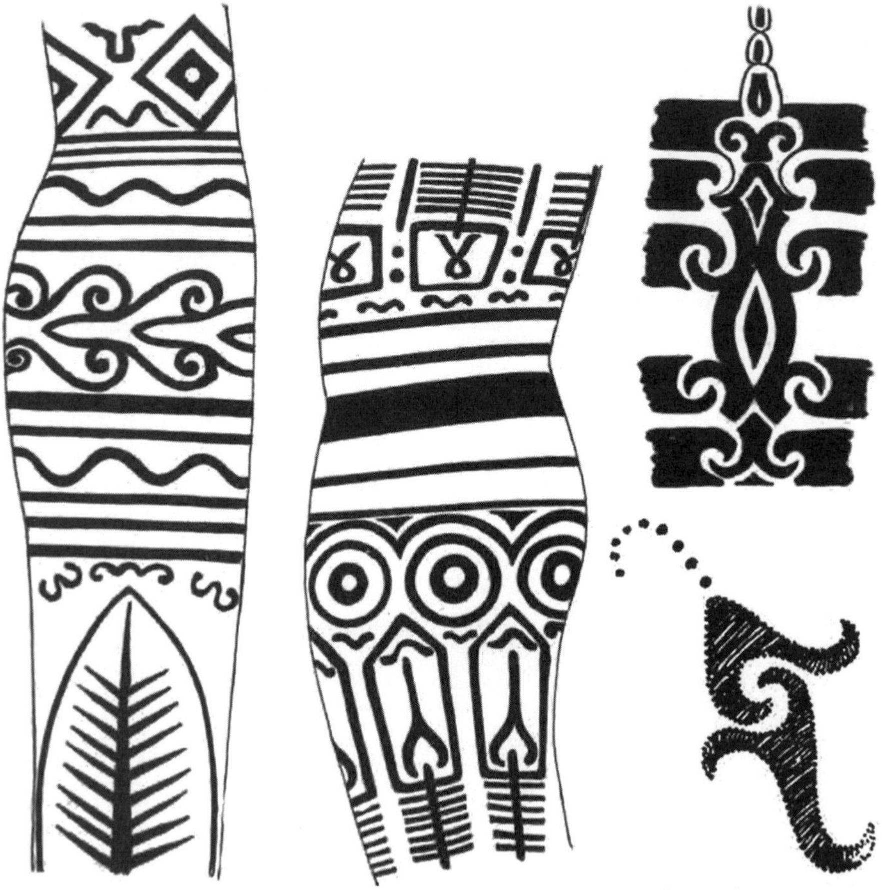

Traditional Kayan tattoo

KEDEKEDE – see KEDE

KEIBUNSHA - is the first organization dedicated to preserving and promoting the traditional Japanese hand tattoo, known as tebori. The institute, founded in 1981 by Keibunsha together with the artists Horiyoshi II, Dr. Katsunari Fukushim and writer Akimitsu Takagim publishes books, photo publications, videos.

KEKEDE–see KEDE

KELINGE or KLINGÉ – For larger tattooing patterns, Kayan tattooists used wooden stencils called kelinge. These intricately carved blocks were made by the male craftsmen of the tribe.

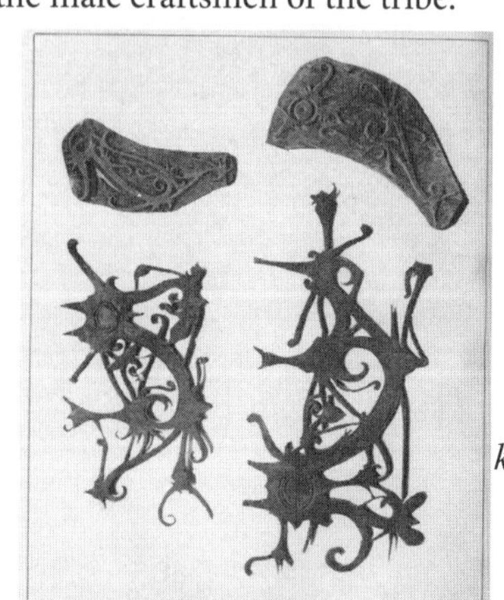

klingé

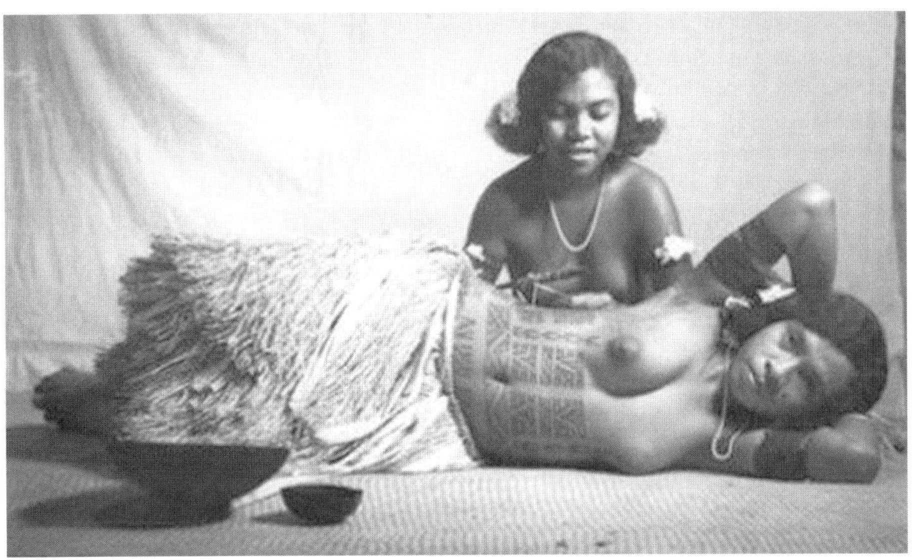

Tattooing with hammer kimama, Motu tribe, Papua, New Guinea

KHAL – Persian word for tattoo mark.

KHASSONKÉ – tribe from Senegal. Practised tattooing. Lips and gums stitched in blue.

KHEING – bamboo blade used for tattoo, Chin tribe, Burma.

KHEM SAK - Thai Metal Tattooing Spike.

KHIDAB – temporary tattoo on the Arabian Peninsula.

KHWIRHI - The type of tattoo that shows the greatest constancy over time during the late nineteenth and twentieth centuries is the incised scarification of women's epigastric area or khwirhi (belly)—i.e., the front of a woman's torso between her breasts and her navel, Mozambique.

KI-DÄ – tattoo of the Indian tribe Haida (skindegate dialect).

KIKIIOANI - Polynesian goddess of

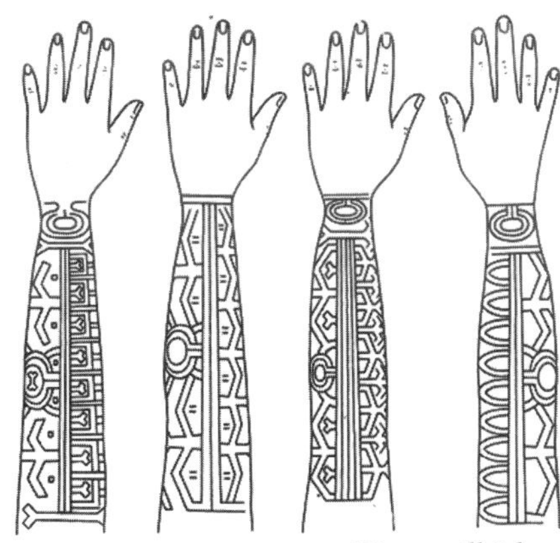

Kingsmill Island

tattoo. Kikiioani had a brother Taha Mata Kee, who she wished to tattoo. But he wasn't much into it, so she tattooed someone else. Her brother than stole her tools. Sister was desperate to find her tools and she cried, all in vain. She yelled out of her anger and since that day, it is painful to get tattooed. When the brother himself wanted to tattoo somebody, the one being tattooed couldn't bear the pain. Taha Mata Kee then came to his sister and said: "The man's dying!" His sister asked him if he has stolen her tools and he confessed. Kikiioani then asked: "Why have you taken them from me? I would have lent them to you!" The sister then took a leaf from the Noni plant, chew it, applied on the tattoo, and blew on it, by which she relieved the pain. Thanks to this, people found the painkiller and explained the origin of the pain connected with the tattoo at the same time.

KIMAMA – tattoo hammer, Maisin tribe, Papua New Guinea.

KINGSMILL ISLAND - old name of The Gilbert Islands. The young men weren´t tattooed before the age of twenty, and slaves never. The tattooing is mostly in short oblique lines, about the eighth of an inch apart. These are arranged in perpendicular rows, of which there are four or five down the back on each side of the spine, with a similar marking in front, beginning just below the collar-bone. The legs also were tattooed.

The women were tattooed in the same manner, but not so much as the men. Owing to the lightness of the lines, and the distance between them, they do not show very conspicuously. The colouring matter used is charcoal, mixed with cocoanut-oil. The instrument employed was a piece of bone, cut like a fine-toothed comb, similar to that used at the Samoan Group. Professed tattooers, who was held in great estimation, and receive very high prices; this confines the art to the wealthy and those of rank.

KIOWA INDIANS – people are a Native American tribe and an indigenous people of the Great Plains. They migrated southward from western Montana into the Rocky Mountains in Colorado in the 17th and 18th centuries and finally into the Southern Plains by the early 19th century. In 1867, the Kiowa were moved to a reservation in southwestern Oklahoma.

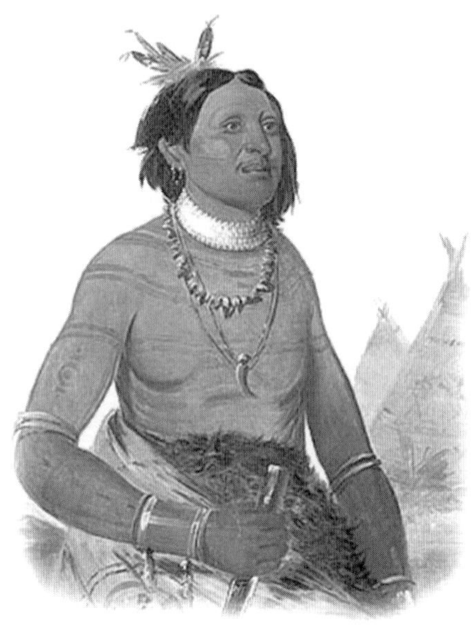

Kiowa designates them by indicating tattoo marks, stating that the women, and sometimes the men, tattooed the arms, breast, and around the lips.

KIPI– tattooing, Hidatsa tribe.

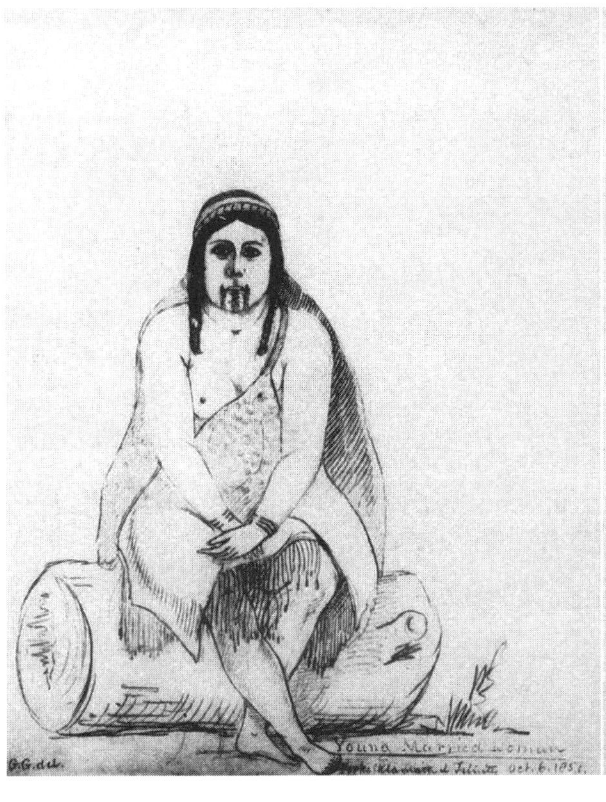

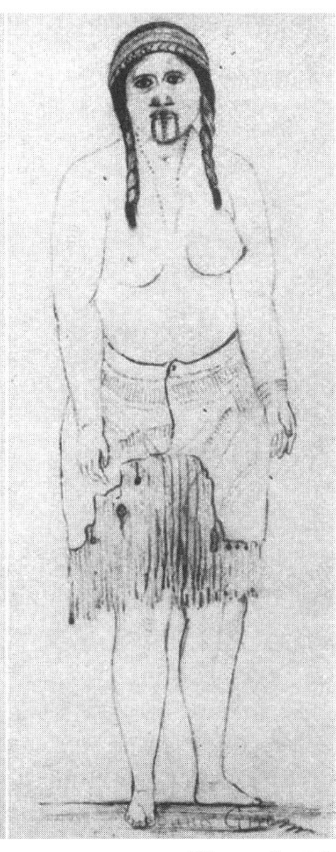

Klamath girls

KIRITUHI - Kirituhi is a Maori style tattoo either made by a non-Maori tattooer, or made for a non-Maori wearer. Kirituhi has mana of it's own and is a design telling the unique story of the wearer in the visual language of Maori art and design. Kiri means 'skin', and tuhi means 'to write, draw, record, adorn or decorate with painting'.

KISHO-BORI – „vow tattoo", practises of Japanese courtesans who "tattoo kisho bori" (promise engravings) on hidden parts of their bodies, visible only when naked or in the act of love.

KISI– tattooing tool, which was a water buffalo horn Kalinga, Philippines.

KISEVI – less-used term for tattoo, Maisin tribe, Papua New Guinea.

KIT-KÄ-GENS - carver and tattooer, indian tribe of Haida, North America.

KITOMBOKA FANJAITRA - tattoo process, see TOMBOTOMBOKA

KKATALAL KHYARB – in Dagestan, they use kkatalal khyarbe berries as the basis for tattoo color, the fruits of which provide a blue-black liquid.

KLAMATH TRIBE - women tattooed the underlip and chin; the young girls in faint lines, which are deepened and widened as they become older, and in the married women are extended up above the corners of the mouth.

KLEOMAKOAN – Indian tribe in the Prince of Wales archipelago. Practiced tattoos.

KLINGÉ – too KELINGE – For larger tattooing patterns, Kayan tattooists used wooden stencils called kelinge.

KO´INA TUHI TIKI – Festival (Ko'ina tuhi tiki; Ko'ina, feast; tuhi, show; tiki, design), which was always given to celebrate the completion of the work, and the newly decorated girls and boys donned them before their appearance on the paved floor of the festival place where admiring friends and relatives were gathered to view them, Marquesas.

KOAKIES – (Osages) who had killed a monstrous magic serpent carried the mark or impression of it tattooed on his body. Their process is this: They first draw the animal or figure with black, or gunpowder; then ' sting ' the skin in the outline with one or more needles to the blood; the figure is then washed slightly with a sponge dipped in a solution of rock salt, which mixes the blood with the black, contracting the skin and rendering the figure indelible. It is a kind of knighthood, to which they are only entitled by great actions. These marks multiply with their achievements in war.

KOBIA – healed tattoo, Bellona Island.

KODI - Tattoo was chiefly applied to women, the lower legs being the main focus in Lamboya, others extending the shin and calve tattoo to the thighs, while arm tattoo was also encountered although, according to Kruyt, this was not considered essential. Certainly Hoskins pictures a women from Kodi in western Sumba with forearm tattoo although does not mention as to whether this was the common style in that district. Kodi women also tattooed the thighs and legs. Ten Kate mentions that in the north

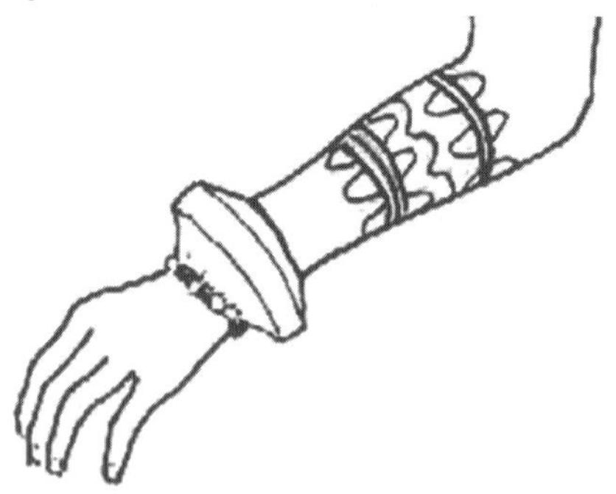

western areas as far as he could see the preference was for arms and legs with the women concentrating on the legs. Conversely, Forth says that in Rindi the lower arm was the most common, tattoo being less common on the upper and lower legs. In the Mamboru men formerly tattooed on the chest while women on the legs and thighs. In Melola in eastern Sumba, Ten Kate saw a man with both arms tattooed. Needham mentions that in Lamboya men tattooed on the chest and arms.

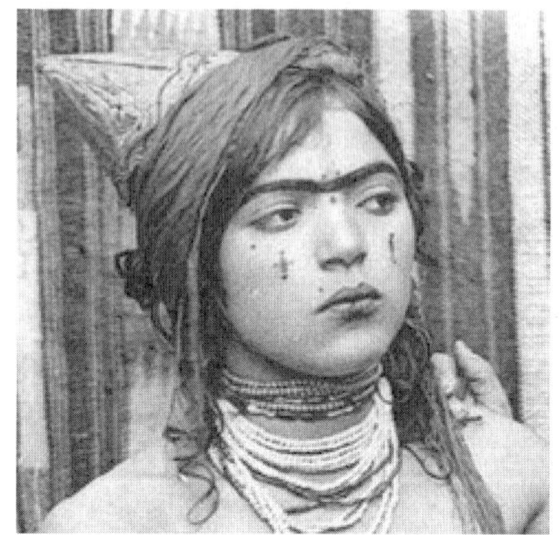

KOHL - Arab tattooing is always blue in color, and the designs are geometrical or sometimes extremely stylized representations of natural objects. There are various methods of making the pigment for tattooing, which is known as kohl or basmah, but the principle is the same, for the chief ingredient is always carbon in the form of lamp-black. The word kohl usually refers to the powdered antimony which is put around the eyes, but it is also used to mean lamp-black, which is used by the poor in the same way as the antimony. The carbon is precipitated by burning either the ordinary kerosene of lamps, or tallow, or a piece of cloth dipped in dihn, the mutton fat used for cooking. Sometimes indigo is added, or bile from the gall-bladder of an ox, which sets the dye, but the commonest method is to gather the soot precipitated on the bottom of a dish held over the lamp, and make a paste.

KOIKA TUHITIKI - a party where a new tattoo was shown, Marquesas.

KOIKO = tattooed, Mangareva.

KOL TRIBE - Kol people are a tribe in Uttar Pradesh and Madhya Pradesh, who migrated there from central India around five centuries ago. The Kol custom of tattooing on the forehead was practised by a few. The tattooing was done by the women of the Temma of brass-working caste.

KOMKE-NI - bark of the spindle-wood, see IWA-NI

KONDH – The Kondhs typically tattoo their faces and hands in a very painful process that is accompanied by song to forget the ordeal.

KOPA´G-MUT – tribes comes from Kŏk river, and păk – the designation meaning people of the great river, form the designation of the Yokon-mouth Innuit, from the same roots. They have a tattooed band Gross the face.

KORAVA – Both men and women of the Korava class wear tattoo marks of circular or semi-circular form on their foreheads and forearms. The pattern was pricked in with a bundle of four or five needles tied together. The needles and drawing-stick were kept in a hollow bamboo, and the tattooing mixture in the scooped out fruits of the bael and palmyra palm. For tattooing an entire upper extremity, at several sittings, the Korava woman would be paid from eight to twelve annas, or received food-grains in lieu of money, India.

KOŘENSKÝ, JOSEF (1847-1938) - a naturalist, teacher, traveller and collector born on 26th July 1847 in Sušno near Nové Benátky. After graduating from Realschule in Mladá Boleslav he was

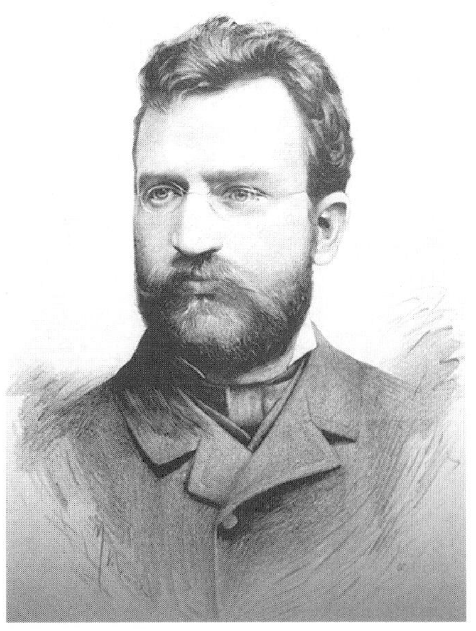

admitted to the Budeč Teacher Training Institute in Prague where he spent two years. After that, he worked during 1867-1871 as a tutor in the town of Radnice where he has a memorial on the house number 239. In 1871-1874, he lived and taught in Litomyšl where, likewise in Prague later, he focused on natural history, physics, drawing and mensuration, German language and singing. He concluded his teaching career as a headmaster at Girls' Primary and Burgher School in Smíchov, from which he retired in 1908. His main interest were natural sciences, mainly geology, mineralogy, botany, and entomology. For his lifelong work in this field and for his contributions to the popularization of natural sciences, Kořenský was awarded an honorary doctorate at the Faculty of Science of Charles University in 1927.

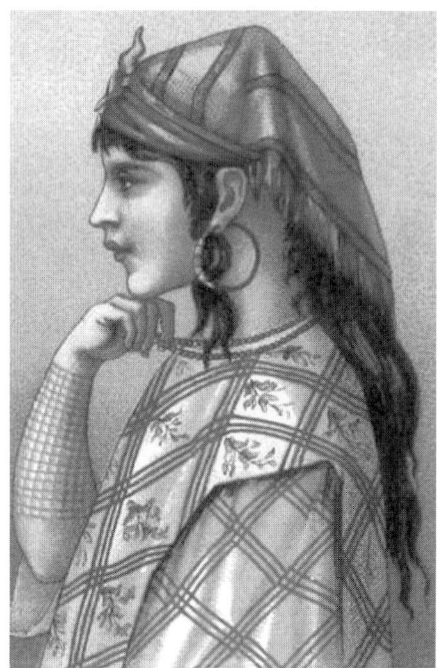

Kulughli

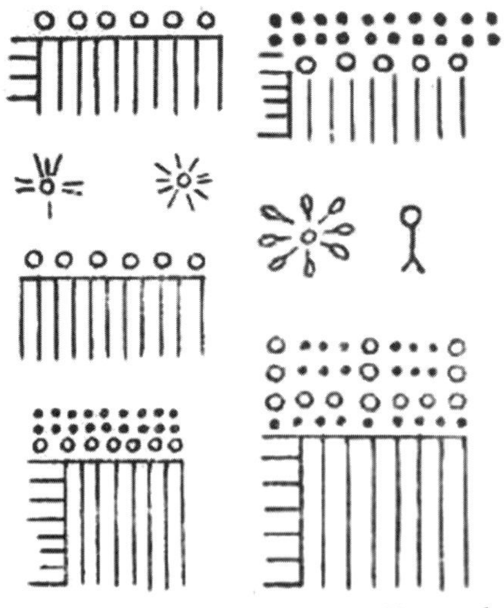

Kota tribe

KOREKORE – tattoo stick, irrespective of material used, is called korekore, Santa Anna and Santa Catalina Islands, Solomon Islands.

KORYAKS – Ornamental tattooing was practised by women only. In former times tattooing among women was widespread, which may be concluded from several myths. Thus it is related how River-Man, on turning into a woman, had his face tattooed to please Illa. See LO-KELE.

KOTA TRIBE – Todas and Kotas lived near each other before the settlements of the latter on the Nilagiri. They have system of personal ornaments and system of tattooing. India.

KOTTO – see AKOTTO

KOW´-HE or KOW´-HĚ - The material used in tattooing, instead of the usual soot from burnt stems of poison oak or other plants, was obtained by burning the pitch or resin, called kow'-he, Pomo Indians.

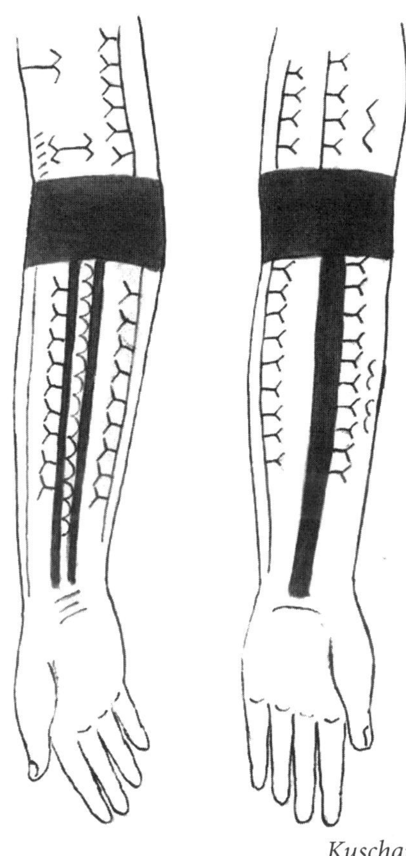

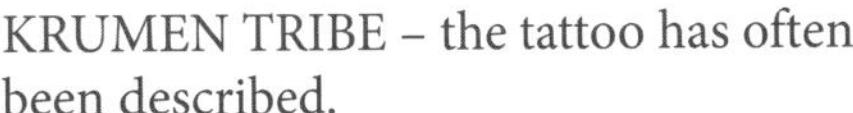

Kuschai

KRUMEN TRIBE – the tattoo has often been described.

KU-TSOGA– tattoo, Giryama tribe, East Africa.

KUARUP – see XINGÚ

KUDUIMI- caste in India, women practiced tattoos.

KUCHAVA - women who were cut repeatedly wore on their skin permanent (tattooed) proof that they had no “fear” (kuchava), Mosambik.

KUH KARLH - Common name for tattoo - "mark", tribes Tlingit.

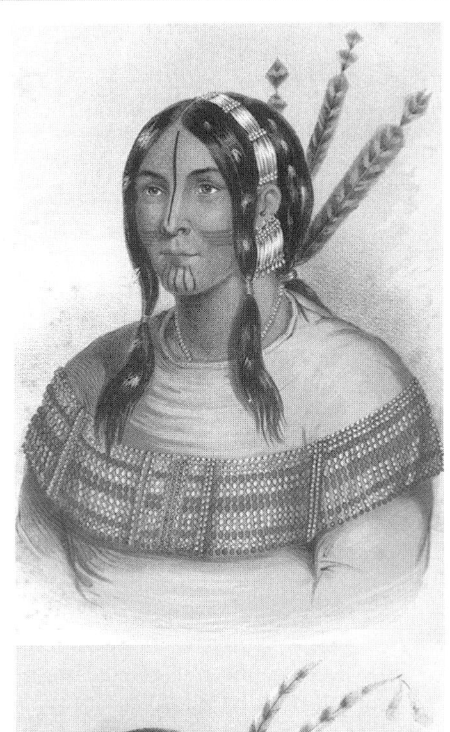

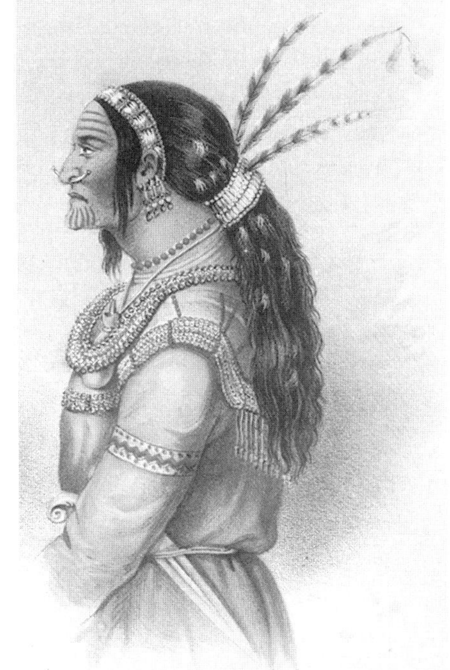

Saviah, Chief of the Gwitchin (Kutcha-Kutchin)

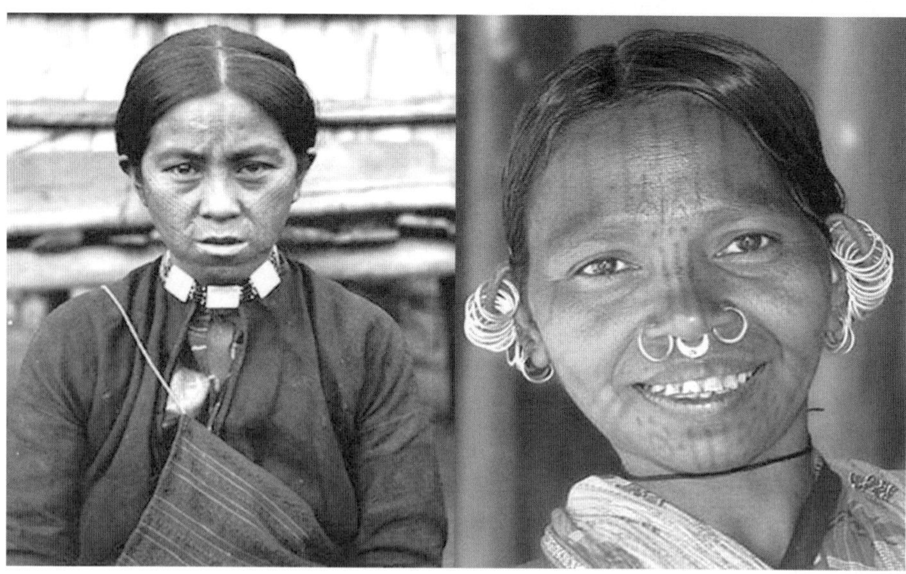

Kutia Kondh

KUH KARLH OT KUH CHUL - „sewing into the skin“ southern Alaskan Tlingit term for tattoo technique.

KUH KAY CHUL - The general name for tattooing was kuh karlh, "mark" [?], but it is said that at Yakutat it was called kuh kay chul, "sewing on the body" [kaqe'cat, "stitches"], as it was done by passing a needle threaded with stained sinew under the skin, Yukutat , Tlingits.

KUIRIGA – At the climax of the two-day ceremony, known as kuiriga, the freshly tattooed women ascended the dubu (ceremonial house) platform to prepare themselves for the forthcoming public display of their newly transformed bodls, Hula tribe.

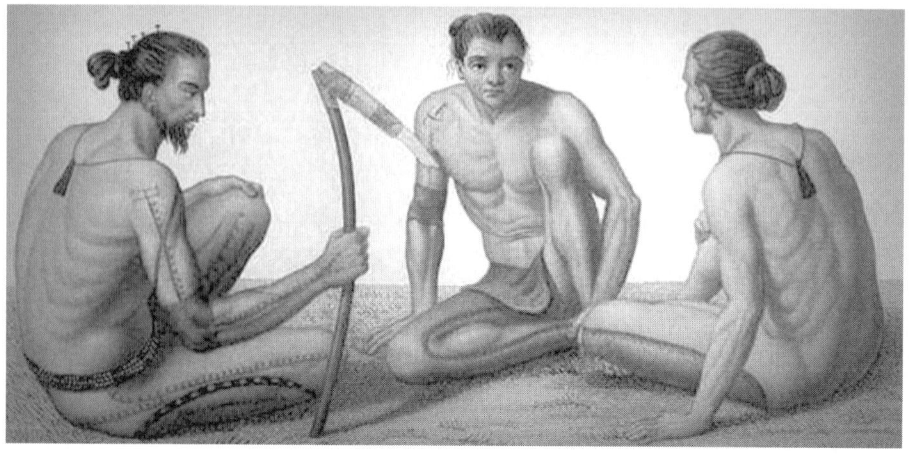

Inhabitants of Kosrae Island, Micronesia, 1820

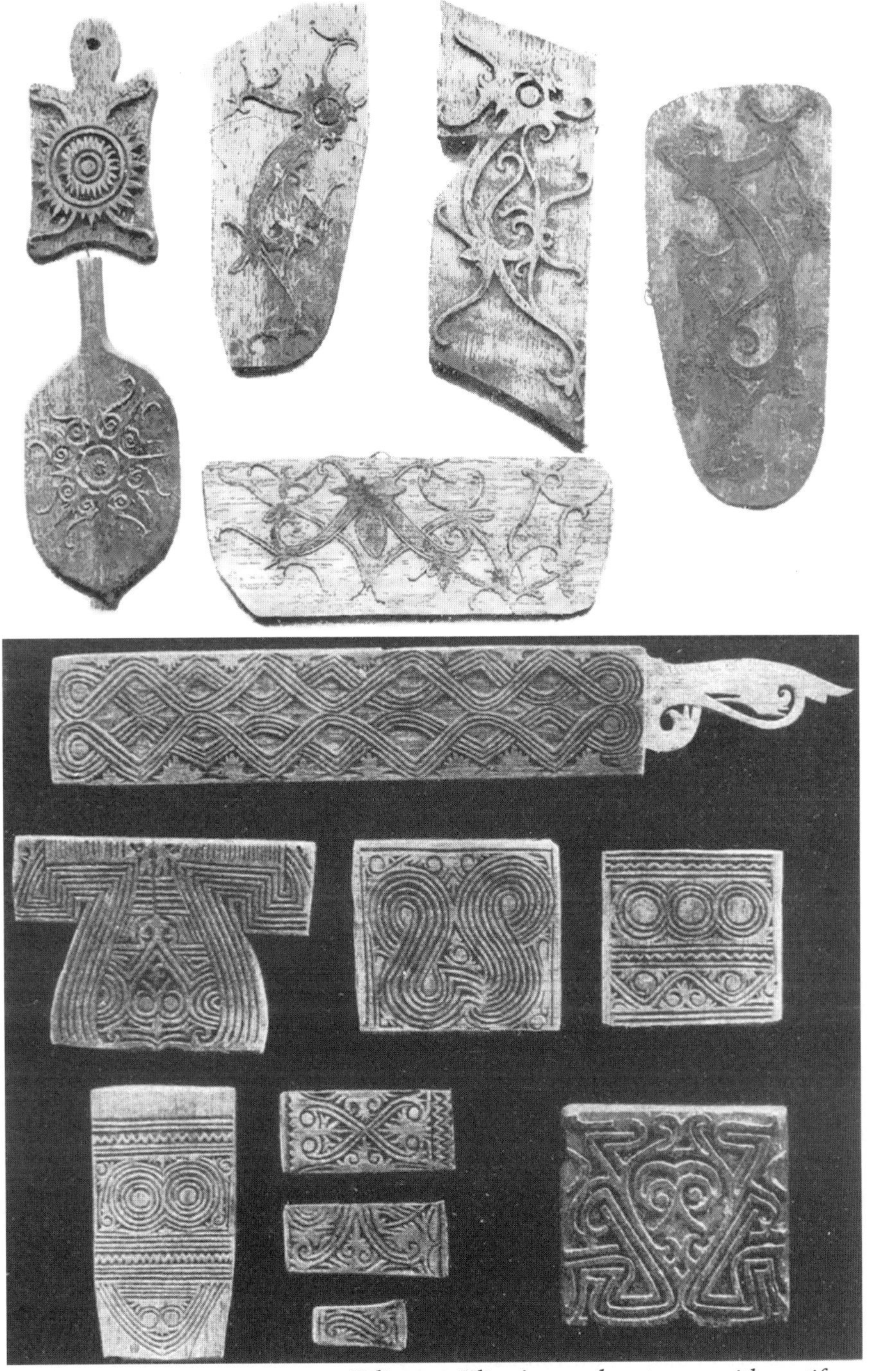

Kelinge or Klingé - wooden stamps with motif

KULMAT - to strut around showing off new tattoos, Visyans tribes.

KULUGHLI CLASS - offspring of Turkish soldiers and Algerian women, practised tattooing.

KUMI-SARA – tattooer, NUKU-ORO Island.

KUMI-TONU – tattooer, NUKU-ORO Island.

KUMEYAAY – The Kumeyaay women decorated themselves with paint and other materials. When the women are ready to be married a when they grew from a girl into a woman they would tattoo there chins with blue dots. They would also paint their faces with red stripes, yellow and white dots for special occasions.

KÚN – body tattoo, Basa tribe, Cameroon.

KUNA TRIBE – these Indians have settled in the San Blas archipelago off the northeast coast of Panama since the nineteenth century. They are characterized by special physical features. They are shorter in height, has high arched chest and an aquiline nose. Women are characterized, among others, by various decorations on face and around neck; by strings of red, black and yellow beads on legs and arms; and by an olo, which is a golden nasal ring. They say that it is a protection against evil ghosts. The nose of young girls is pierced by the olo during the ikko ina ritual. During the initiation ceremony of inna suit, bodies of young girls are painted with natural dyes. After the ritual, they are ready for the wedding. Traditionally, women tattoo a line across their forehead and nose as a sign of being married.

KUPARA - completely blackened /of a person covered with tattoos, Maori.

KURI KURI – tattooing, Bona Bona Island.

KUSCHAI – island in Micronesia, tattoos were practiced here.

KUSKOQUIM – tribes living by the river of the same name, women wore two tattooed lines on their chins, Alaska,

KUTCH - Women from the nomadic Kutch tribe in northwestern India have many very complicated tattoos.

KUTCHINS – also Gwich´in, a tribe on the Canadian-Alaska border. Men painted a black stripe across the forehead and nose, often this line was crossed by a second red across the cheeks and chin. Women tattooed their chin with black tattoos.

KUTIA KONDH – Kutia Kondh people at Kotgarh village (market). The women can be recognised by the straight lined 'tiger' tattoo in the face.

KUTIMISA - Girls who sat through the tattoo process stoically were considered "courageous" (kutimisa); Magude tribe, Mosambik.

KUTIYA – Girls who sat through the tattoo process stoically were considered "strong" or "steady" (kutiya), Magude tribe, Mosambik.

KUTRA´I – Kurdish „tattoo".

KUY-KAY-CHUL – the name for a tattoo, meaning "sewing into the body", Tlingit tribe.

KWORAFI – women of their tribe, like the Maisins, tattooed their faces, New Guinea.

L-QAYDA– Generally speaking the Berber term for tattoo is oucham ("to mark"). Tattoos were traditional or l-qayda("custom") and some motifs were rooted in the ancient Berber alphabet known as Tifinagh. The Tifinagh is a figurative alphabet derived from tools used in agriculture, sea products, and constellations.

Ł-TAČ – This is how the tattoo is called by the Hupa Indian tribe, the territory of present-day California, USA.

LA TO´AI – see HUI TO´A

LAJU NAGA – tribe living in India. Women practice tattoos on their arms and face. A facial tattoo consists of a stripe over the forehead and nose, a stripe with a ring from the mouth to the chin and from each corner of the lips to the ears, forming a kind of two triangles.

LAKATOK – a place where oblation (food) was made to the tattoo gods, Marshall Islands.

LAKHAL - in the Maghreb region of North Africa, for example, tattoos are referred to only by the name of the color, such as lakhal ("black") on the face, "a surrogate sign of beauty." See also SDAR or UCHAM AL-LAHYA

LAMA – pigment was made from the soot of burnt candle nut or lama nut, Borneo.

LAMA - n. obsol. Black dye used in tattooing, made from the fruit of the hetau tree, Takuu.

LAMANU – tattoo pigment, which was traditionally formed by water along with soot, the Motu tribe, New Guinea.

LANIDJ – One of two gods of the art tattooing on the Marshall Islands. The other is Leowudj.

LANGO PEOPLE - African tribe practicing scar tattoo.

LAPALAPA - Mallet used to pound the Au into the skin in Samoa.

LAPITA - an early Polynesian culture. Most often, it is referenced in a connection with pottery. The Lapita ceramics was characterized by carved decorations, which consisted of V-shaped elements, intertwined geometrical shapes and stylized motives resembling masks and sea creatures. It is possible to find analogous motives within tattoos all over Polynesia. The technique of carving series of shapes and needling in ceramics is even very similar to tattooed decorations. It is believed that Lapita, who came from the Southeast Asia 4 000 years ago, began to tattoo in Samoa and different variations of his work have spread a long way off to islands of South Pacific. In the beginning of 20's of the 19th century, it

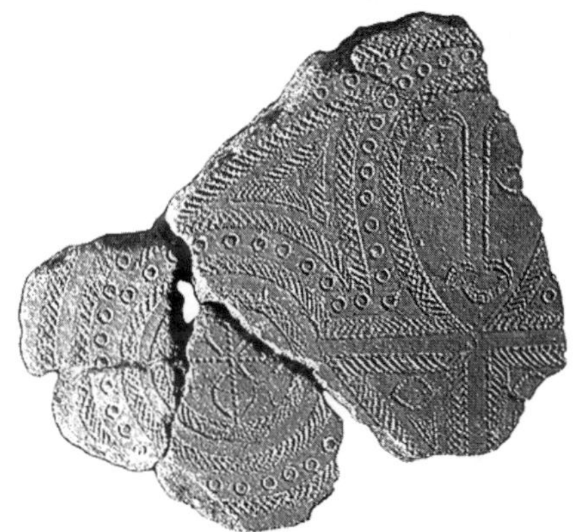

was nearly wiped out by the Europeans. Its resurrection started around 1970 and its popularity is growing strong

LASAT MATA - A small gift generically

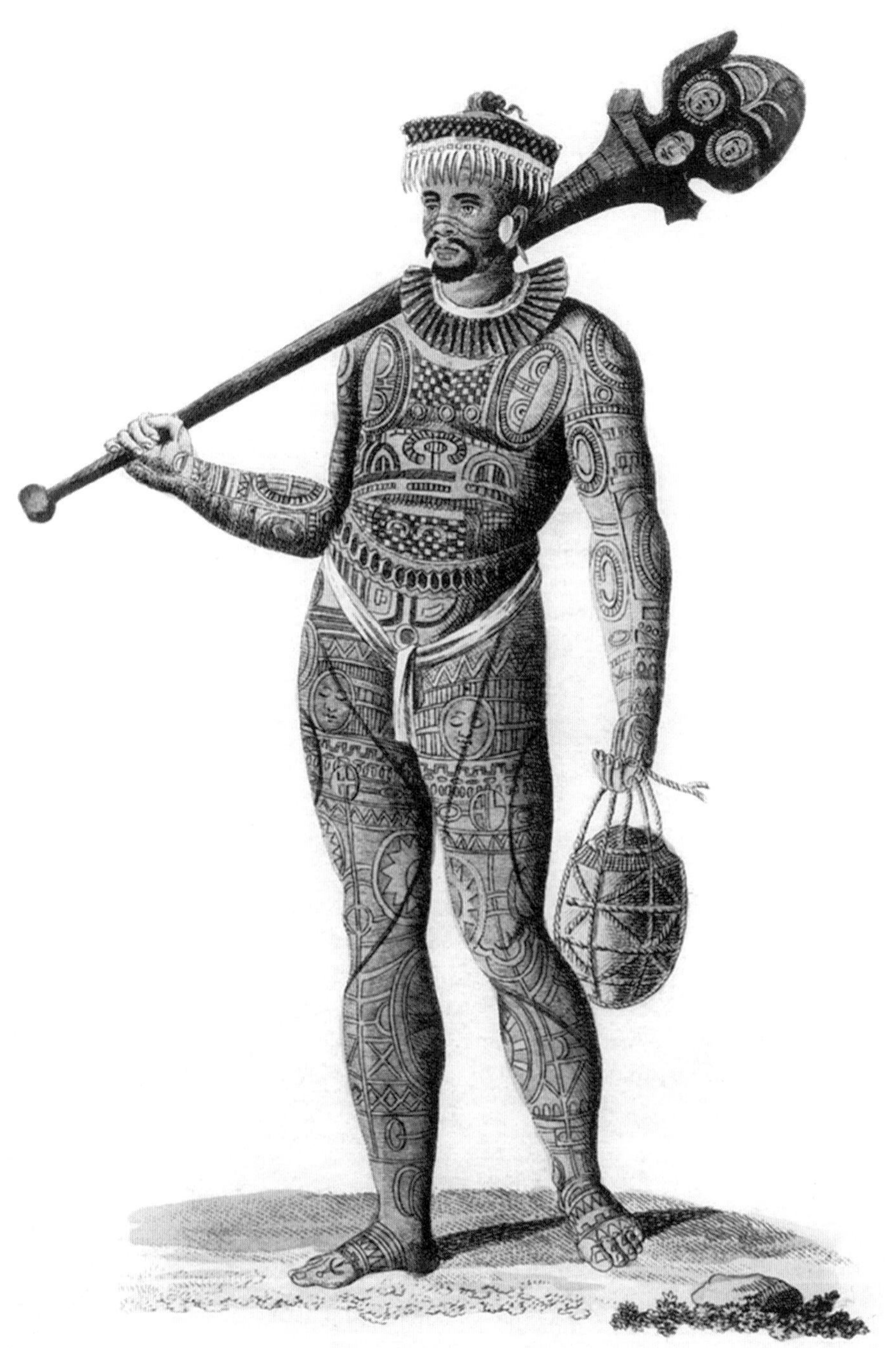

Lapita

called "lasat mata" (which may be beads or any small item) must be given to the female tattoo practitioner, and "if it were omitted the artist would go blind". In Kayan language, lasat mata literally comes from the categories "eyes" (mata) and "to wipe clean" (last).

LASKEETS – among certain tribes, the men and women tattooed the face and arms, like the Laskeets, and the Skringwai, Queen Charlotte Islands.

LAUGHLAN ISLANDS - are a remote archipelago of several low-lying coral islands situated off Milne Bay, on the eastern tip of Papua New Guinea comprising Wabola and Bolaluna Islands. Tattoos were called kutukuat and were performed by specially appointed old women.

LAULAU = tattooing , Paluan, Admiralty Island.

LAULAUSI – tattooing, Teste Island.

LAUNGI – body decorated with ornaments in Lau language, Solomon Islands.

LAUNGIA – ornament on the body in Lau language, Solomon Islands.

LAVALAVA – tattoo decoration was paid by Lavalava (cotton handkerchiefs), Ponape.

LAVEN – term for female tattoo, Katu tribe, Laos.

LEELA - tattooing, known to the Tharu as leela, is widely practiced by both men and women, although it is more commonly noted among the women.

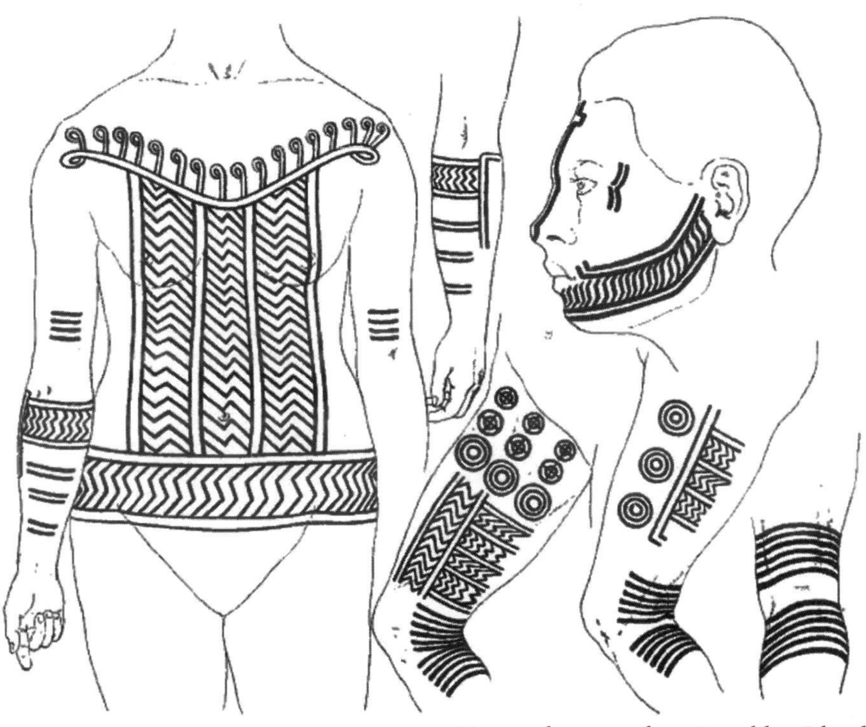

Tattooed women from Laughlan Islands

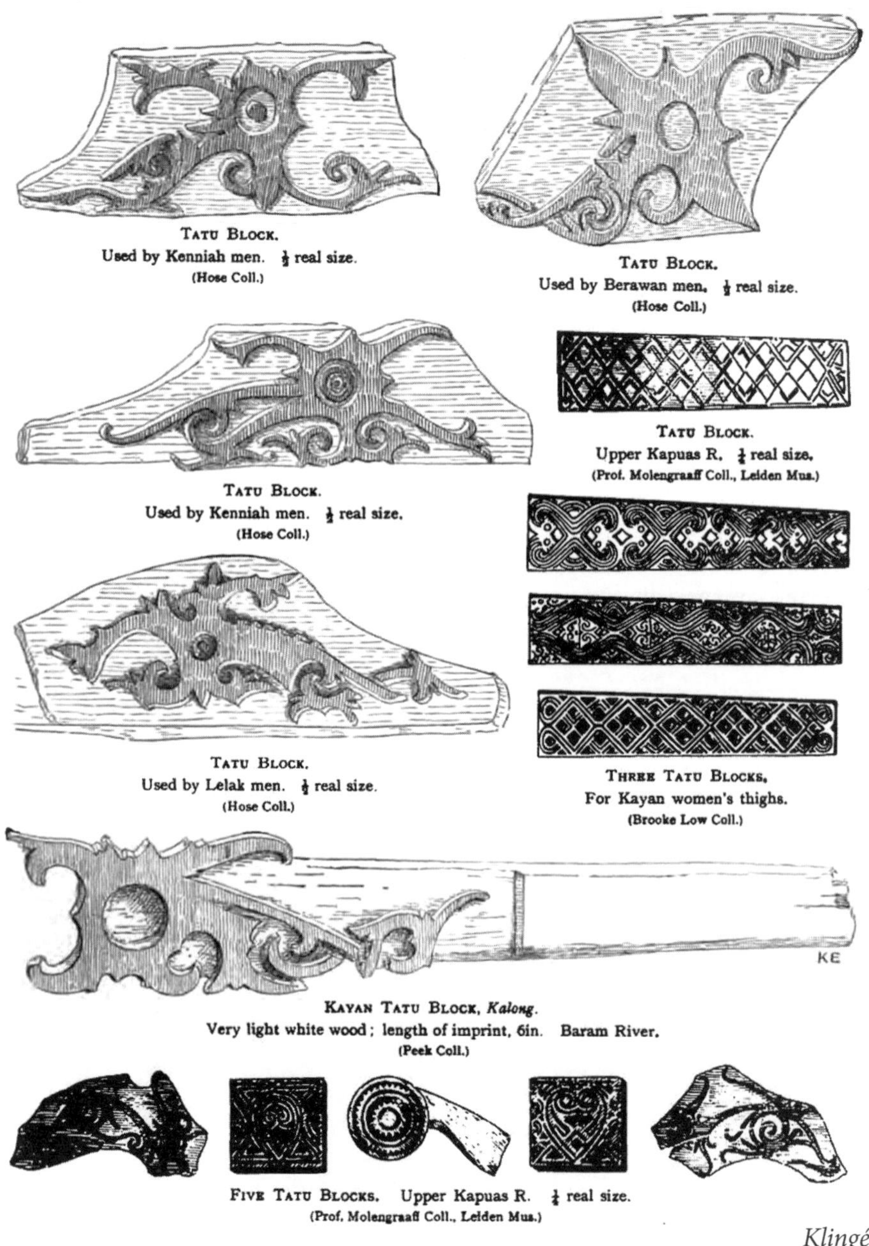

TATU BLOCK.
Used by Kenniah men. ⅓ real size.
(Hose Coll.)

TATU BLOCK.
Used by Berawan men. ⅓ real size.
(Hose Coll.)

TATU BLOCK.
Upper Kapuas R. ½ real size.
(Prof. Molengraaff Coll., Leiden Mus.)

TATU BLOCK.
Used by Kenniah men. ½ real size.
(Hose Coll.)

TATU BLOCK.
Used by Lelak men. ⅓ real size.
(Hose Coll.)

THREE TATU BLOCKS.
For Kayan women's thighs.
(Brooke Low Coll.)

KAYAN TATU BLOCK, *Kalong*.
Very light white wood; length of imprint, 6in. Baram River.
(Peek Coll.)

FIVE TATU BLOCKS. Upper Kapuas R. ½ real size.
(Prof. Molengraaff Coll., Leiden Mus.)

Klingé

Tharu women, especially the elderly, are heavily tattooed. Though the process of being tattooed is a very painful one, people eagerly and happily go in for it.

LELAK PEOPLE - Lelak is an extinct language of Malaysian Borneo. The Lelak people now speak Berawan. Practiced tattooing.

LENAPE (Dela¬war): Indian tribe lived around the Delaware River. Reverend John Heckwelder wrote: This man, who was then at an advanced age, had a most striking appearance... Besides that, his body was full of scars, where he had been struck and pierced by the arrows of the enemy, there was not a spot to be seen, on that part of it which was exposed to view, but what was tattooed over with some drawing relative to his achievements. On his whole face neck, shoulders, arms, thighs, and legs, as well as on his breast and back, were represented scenes of the variations and engagements he had been in...

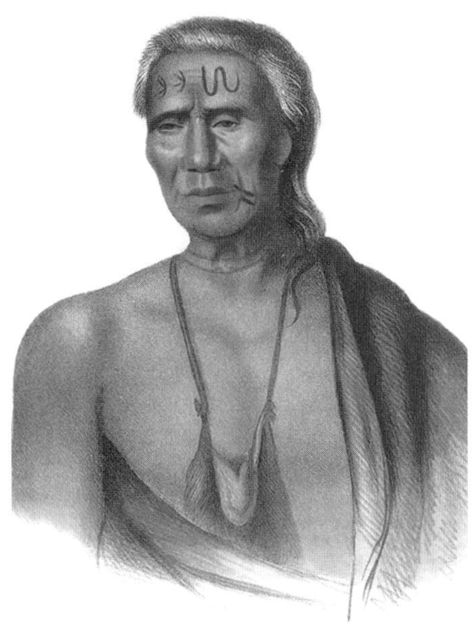

Lapowinsa, Lenape Chief

LENEIR - tattoo ink made from crushed Aleuritastriloba nut mixed with coconut oil, Pohnpei.

LENGE - African tribe, scar tattoos.

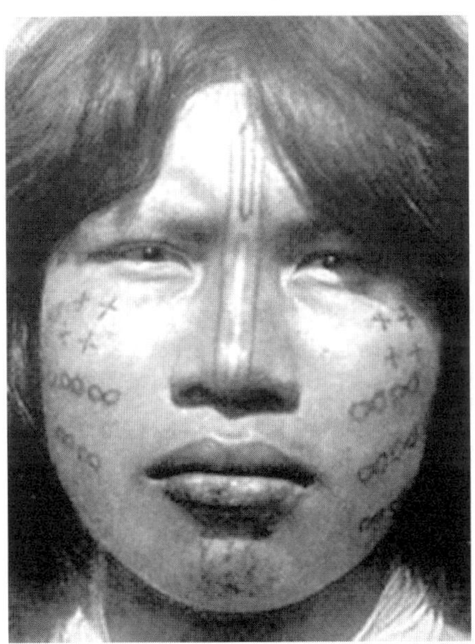

Lengua woman with facial tattoos, 1930

LENGUA - The Lengua Indians live in the Gran Chaco area of Paraguay and constitute the largest Indian group in that region. They speak a language belonging to the Maskoyan Family.

LETE BINYE – In Kodi, Sumba Island, the ceremonial sacrifice of a chicken took place before making a tattoo itself. This sacrifice was made for the spirit of a native village from where the tattooed person came from, because of the lete binye, or “the gate and the stairs” to obtain the approval of ancestors. Tattooing was a very painful procedure, not only due to spikes creating the pierced markings but also due to the ash from nuts that was rubbed into the wounds during the tattoo crafting.

LEWA DAU BATI - "expert tattooer" on Fiji, they were women.

LEWOJ – It was said that tattooing in the Marshall Islands came from the gods,

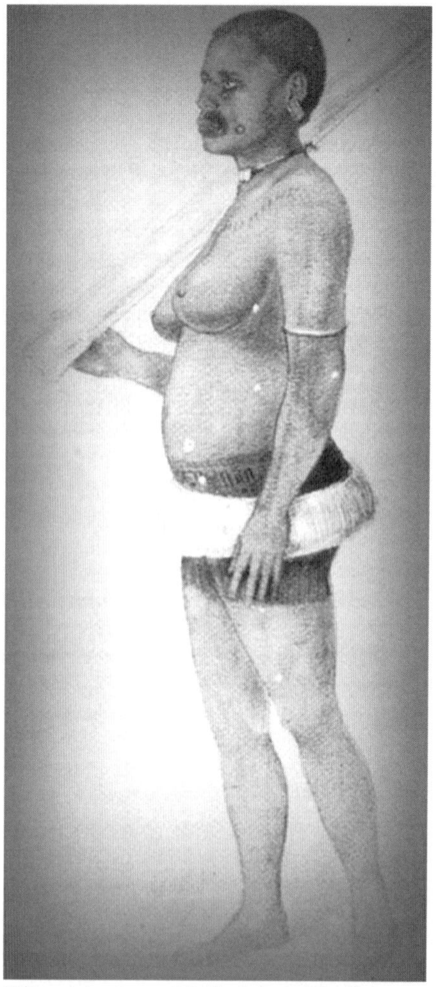
Fijian woman with facial and body tattoos, 1870

with Lewoj and Lanij, the sons of the creator god Lowa, bringing the art to the islands.

LI PEOPLE - In Hainan, tattooing has a long standing tradition among the Li ethnic people. The history of their tattoos could be traced back to 3,000 years ago. During the time the Li people were under attack from many of their neighbors, and the women would often be taken as slaves. And the Li women began tattooing their faces to protect themselves. It was thought that the tattoos would make them uglier and less likely to be insulted.

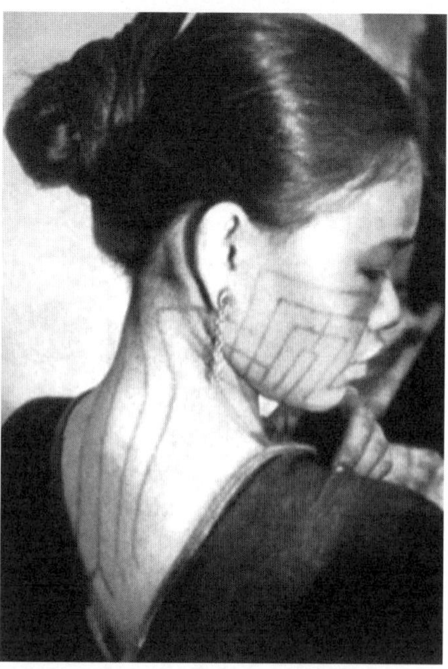
Geometric tattoos of a Basadung Li woman. The blue beauty lines down the back of the neck mark her a fit model of Ba-Sa-Dung cosmetics

LIGOBIA - I have seen (poetic praise of tattooing), Bellona.

LIL-HILA – a therapeutic tattoo in Iraq that is performed at the site of injury or pain.

LIMIAN – old Chinese term for tattooing.

LINDAUER, BOHUMÍR - also known as Gottfried Lindauer, or Lindaur (January 5, 1839 Plzeň - June 13, 1626 Woodville, New Zealand), was an artist of Czech origin who became famous for portraits of the Maori.

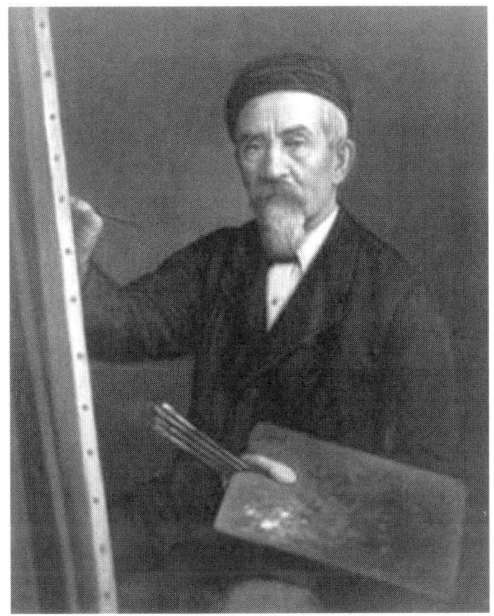

Bohumír Lindauer

LINGAYAT - Caste of India. Tattooing was confined to females. Children was tattooed in their fifth year. A round mark was pricked between the eyebrows, on the right cheek, and on the chin.

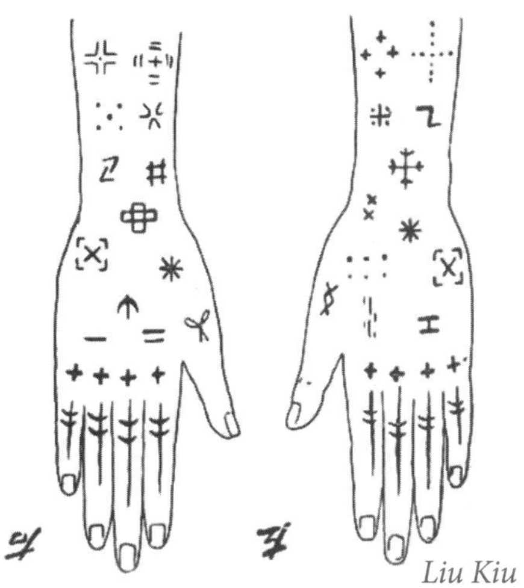

Liu Kiu

LIPOMOLIMBESU – tattooing, Congo.

LIPULUWA - a boil ; the scar left after tattooing, Yao language.

LIU-KIU – another term for Ryukyu Islands, Japan.

LOUSHEN - one of the terms in ancient

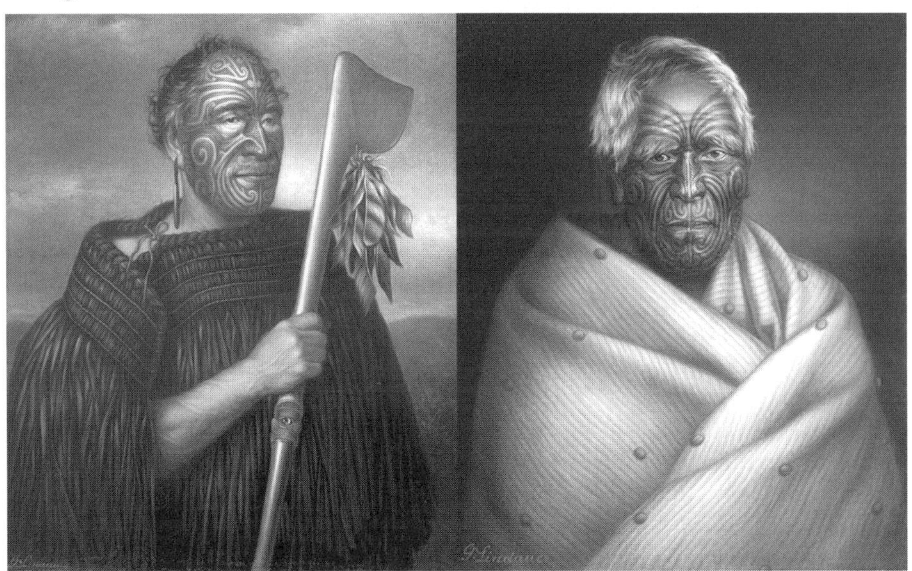

Arts by Bohumír Lindauer

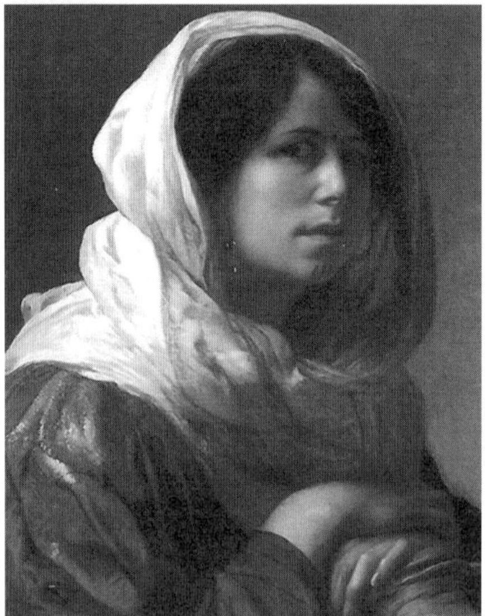

Libyan woman with tattoos on he rforehead and chin, circa 1925

China (206 BC to 220 AD) for tattoos, translated as "engrave into the body".

LOU TI - one of the ancient Chinese terms for tattoos, meaning the same as before.

LUISEII – North American Indian tribe practicing tattoos. The girls of this tribe were tattooed on the face, chest, and hands in infancy. Coal was inserted into the skin with a cactus thorn.

LUKONOR – tattooing men in.

LULU΄U - the ceremony of Lulu'u, or sprinkling, which was performed by one of the operators taking cocoanuts and sprinkling the water over each individual of their number. After this the workmen took their leave and the company separated to their homes. The bottle of water was only broken before a chief, but the ceremony of sprinkling was performed on each one of the tattooed, whatever their rank might be. This singular custom appears to have been used, as in other cases, to remove what was considered to be a kind of sacredness attaching to those newly tattooed, Samoa.

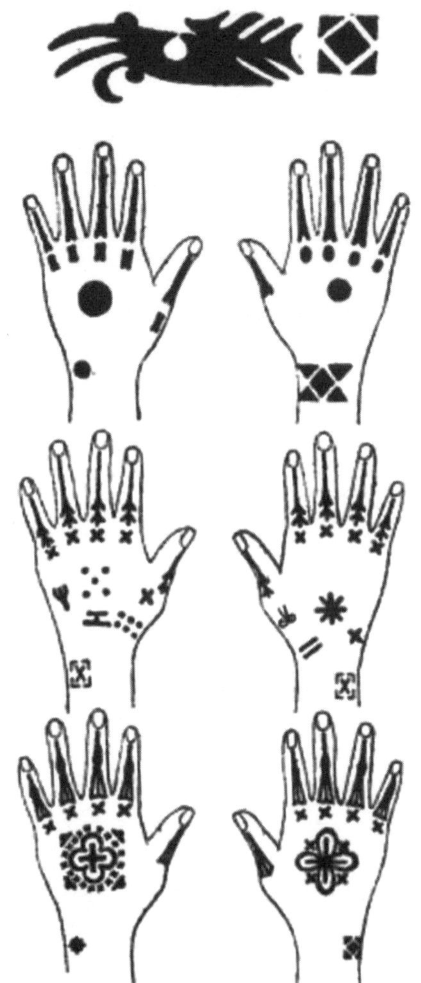

Tattoos from the Lutshu Island

LURI – tribes in Iraq. The women of the Kurdish chiefs are tattooed with fan-shaped palm leaves on their necks, three stars on their chins, one star in the middle of their foreheads and other insignia on their hands, arms and body.

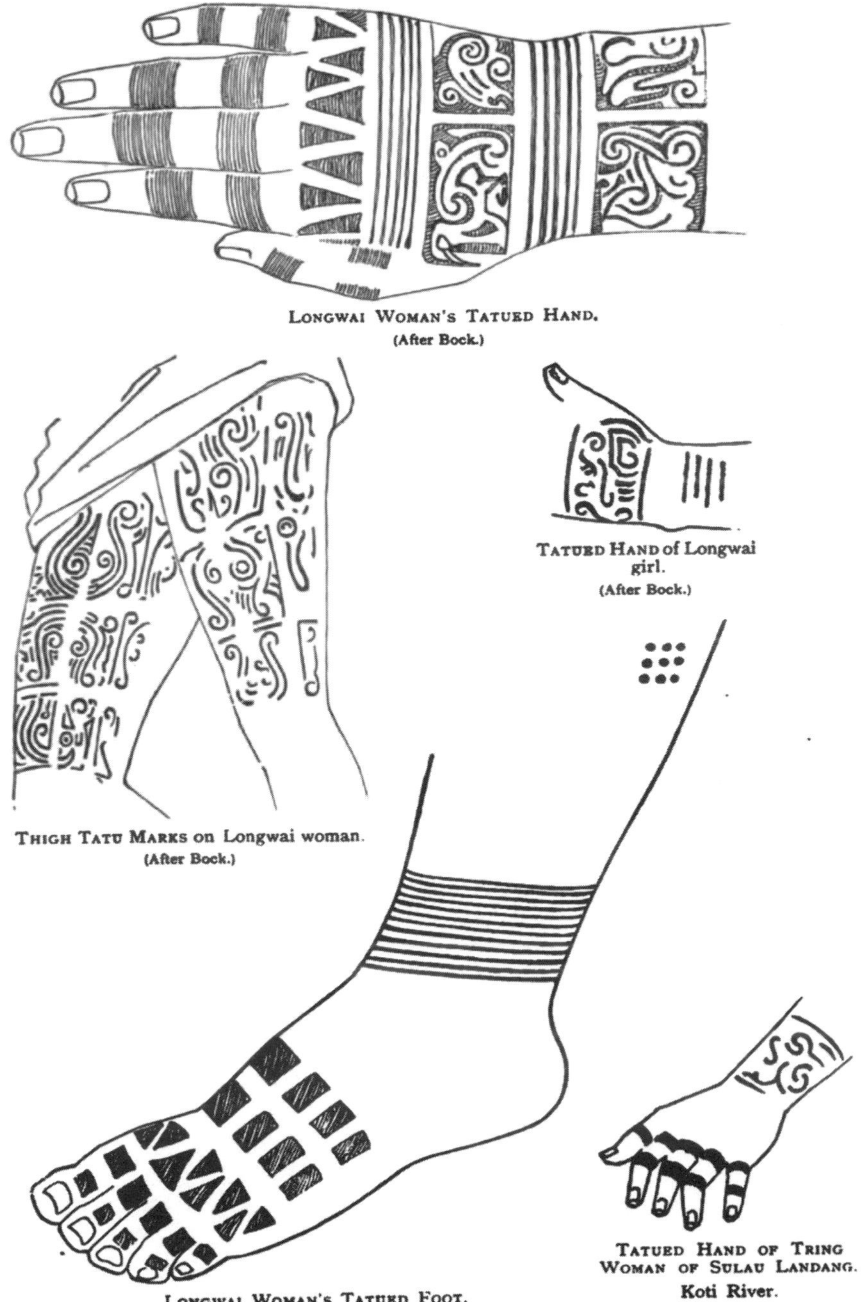

LONGWAI WOMAN'S TATUED HAND.
(After Bock.)

TATUED HAND of Longwai girl.
(After Bock.)

THIGH TATU MARKS on Longwai woman.
(After Bock.)

LONGWAI WOMAN'S TATUED FOOT.
(After Bock).

TATUED HAND OF TRING WOMAN OF SULAU LANDANG.
Koti River.
(After Bock).

MABODÉ TRIBE - these people tattoo themselves, not as we understand tattooing, but by the excision and removal of little triangular pieces of skin, the healed wound leaving permanent scars in quaint symmetrical designs, both back and front being subject to this process.

MAGA´E HAKAGONGO – offering a coconut for a chest tattoo, Bellona Island.

MAGEMAGE - see MARAMARA-ANGARI

MAHABIBO - Makuo and the north-western Sakalavas (Madagascar) use the juice contained in the fruit of the Mahabibo fruit (Anacardiumoccidentale) for the tattoo ink.

MAHDĚSI - Armenian word for pilgrim is mahědsi' (mah- death, děsi' - I saw). Hence, this name is applied to a tattoo mark done in Jerusalem. It is also spoken muksi, mukdisi, mukdesi. Since such pilgrims are virtually the only Armenians tattooed, it has become the ordinary and indeed only word for tattoo mark in Armenian. Occasionally an Armenian is seen when a boy had a dot or a minute cross made on his hand, but hardly one in a hundred. Even then, however, he calls it "mahdesi". The Armenian women as well as men make this pilgrimage and are all tattooed there in the same way.

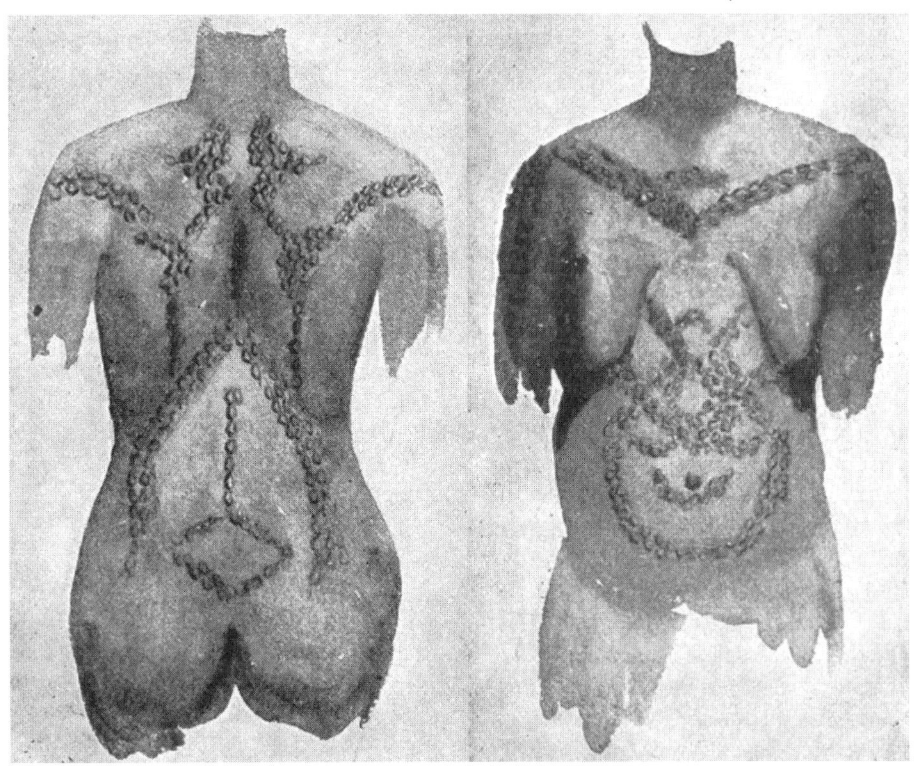

Mabodé

MAHUTA – old term for tattooing, Maori.

MACHIGUENGA - (also known as Machigenga, Matsiguenka, Matsigenka or Matsigenga. Machiguenga) come from the jungles of southeastern Peru and the border area of Peru with Bolivia and Brazil. In addition to painting the body with colors obtained from plants, minerals and coal, tattoos (face and body) are widespread.

MAI SAK - a tool used to perform a magical Sak Yant tattoo.

MAIDU – Indian tribe. Franz Boas wrote: Tattooing was practised perhaps somewhat more commonly among the Northern Maidu than among the southern members of the stock. Women were more often and more elaborately tattooed than men. As a rule, the women had three, five, or seven vertical lines on the chin. In the Sacramento Valley region two marks were also made on the cheeks, running obliquely downward from the cheek bones toward the corners of the mouth, and lines were also made on the breast. In this section and in the foot-hills, lines or dots were made occasionally on the backs of the hands. Among the Northeastern Maidu, women were not so commonly tattooed as in the rest of the area. Men occasionally had one or two vertical lines on the chin, but more commonly had a single line, about two inches in length, rising vertically from the root of the nose.

They also frequently had rows of dots on the breast, arm, or abdomen. It is said that sometimes both men and women had more elaborate designs, such as those called in basketry " flying geese " and " quail-tip. " Such designs have, however, not been seen. The method used in tattooing was not always the same. Among the Sacramento Valley portion of the Northwestern Maidu the designs were made by making fine parallel cuts with a small sharp flake of flint or obsidian, and then rubbing charcoal into the cuts so made, the charcoal used in this region for the purpose being obtained generally from the wild nutmeg (Tumion californicum Greene). Sometimes a reddish pigment was used, obtained from a roasted and pulverized rock. Designs made in this manner rarely show solid color, and the individual cuts can usually be seen. This method, among the Maidu, is restricted, apparently, to this section alone. It is also in use by the Shasta.

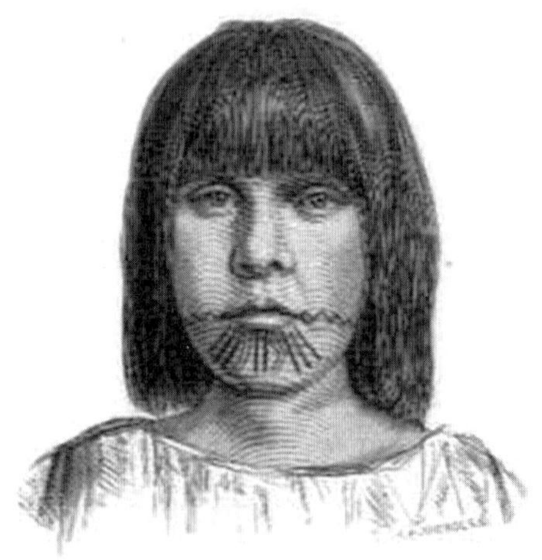

Maidu

The more common method by puncture was used by all the rest of the Maidu people. Fish bones, pine-needles, or sharpened bird-bones were used for pricking the skin. After the skin was pricked, the pigment was rubbed in, the

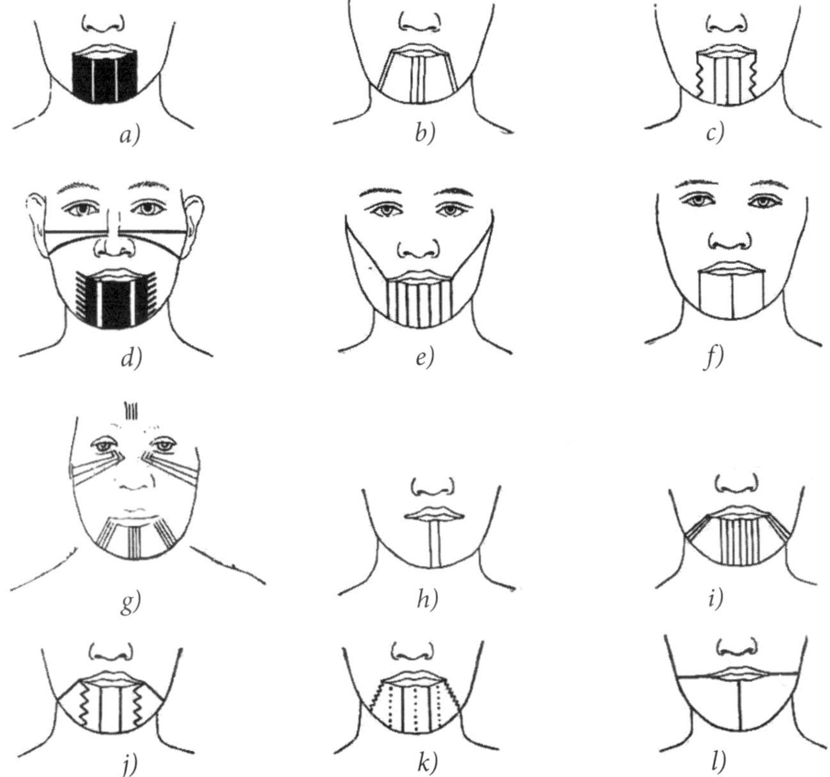

Women´s tattoo - a) Yurok and northwestern tribes; b, c) San Francisco, probably Constanoan; d) Sinkyone; e) northwestern valley Maidu; f) northeastern and southern Maidu; g) Yuki; h-l) Chuckchansi Yokuts.

pricking instrument being also dipped in the pigment while making the punctures. This process is said to be much more painful than the other; and it is said that serious illness, or even death, has followed its use in some cases. The operation was performed, as a rule, at about the age of ten or fifteen years, and was performed by any one, there being no special persons who were regarded as proficient, and no ceremony apparently connected with the matter. Girls were usually tattooed by an older woman, a relative if possible; boys were tattooed by the younger men.

MAINGOR - a Kalinga warrior, wearing a specific tattoo.

MAKAO– tattoo needles, Leuneuwa, Solomon Islands.

MAKAU – Tattoo needles made of frigate bones, Solomon Islands.

MAKAN CHIN - ethnicity, Mindat village, Chin province. Local women traditionally decorate their faces with

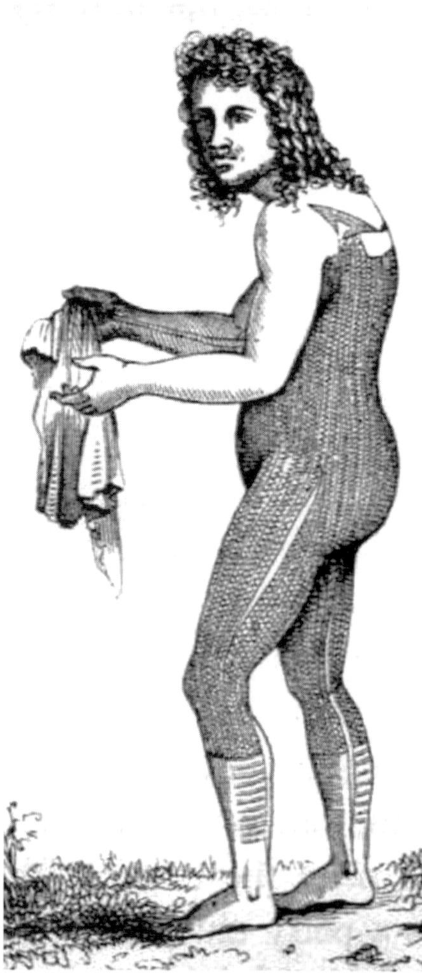

Tattoo from Makin Island

tattoos. Various ethnicities use different tattoo patterns. Myanmar (Burma). Again, this ethnic group is divided into subgroups but they have one mutual habit – women tattoo their faces. Today, of course, nobody knows precisely how this tradition had originated and so it is commonly perceived as a beautification tool. However, an old legend is connected to the tattoo, according to which a Burmese king once wanted to marry a Chinian woman, since they were the most beautiful ones within the whole kingdom. But she did not want him and so she tattooed her face to disgust him and avoid the marriage. Then, all other women started to do it as well so no king want to merry them.

MAKAUKA – tattoo style, Body completely covered with tattoos. The design consists of longitudinal lines, Tonga.

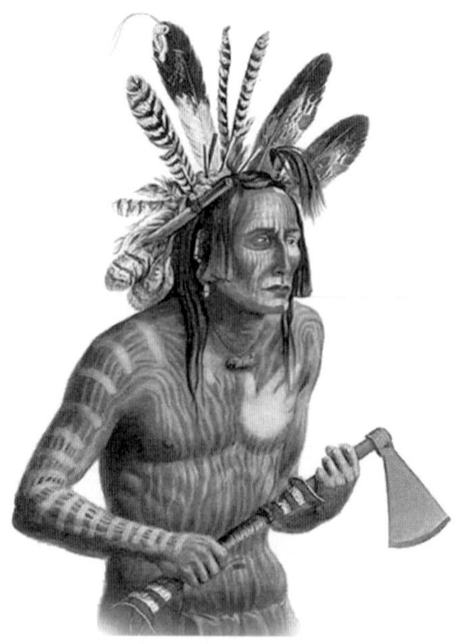

Chief of the Mandans by George Catlin

MAKDE´GOS – tattoo master, Haida.

MAKI - tattooed, Vitu Island.

MAKI - to tattoo, Lakalai tribe, Papua New Guinea.

MAKIN ISLAND - Makin is the name of a chain of islands located in the Pacific Ocean island nation of Kiribati. Makin is the northernmost of the Gilbert Islands.

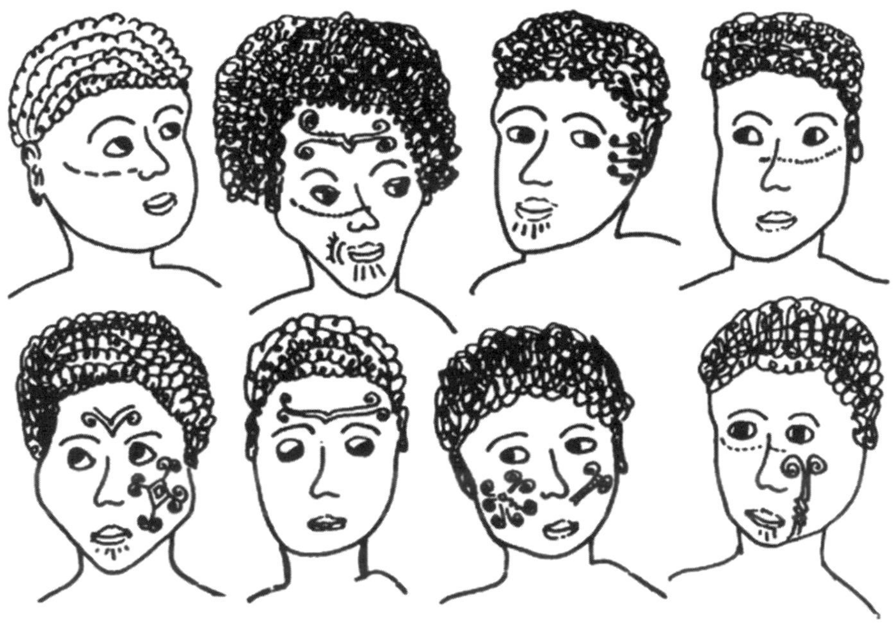

Managalasi

The men was very handsomely tattooed, of which the above cut will give a correct idea.

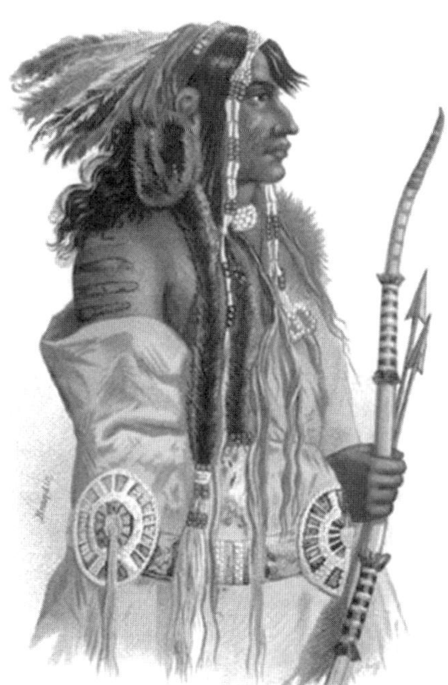

Chief of the Mandans by Karel Bodmer

MAKIRI – tattoo tools of the Inuit, Japan.

MALAT – For the fingers, the tattooist is paid a malat or short sword, Borneo.

MALIGANG – The Kayan in the early twentieth century believed that after death, tattoos "act as torches in the next world", without which their souls would be left in total darkness. Also for the Kayan, tattoos on the hands of a successful headhunter was said to allow him to be able to easily cross the single log that served as the bridge into the afterlife. This log was said to be guarded by, and incessantly disturbed by a supernatural being called Maligang, and so being tattooed facilitated a soul's crossing of it.

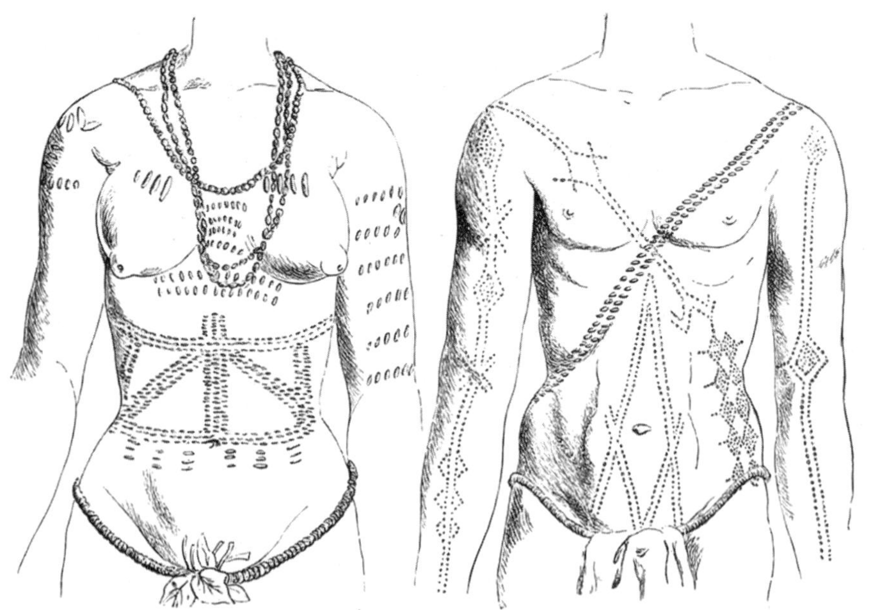

Mangbetu

MALOFIE - the real name for a traditional Samoan tattoo. According to some sources, the better-known term pe´a did not begin to be used until around 1800.

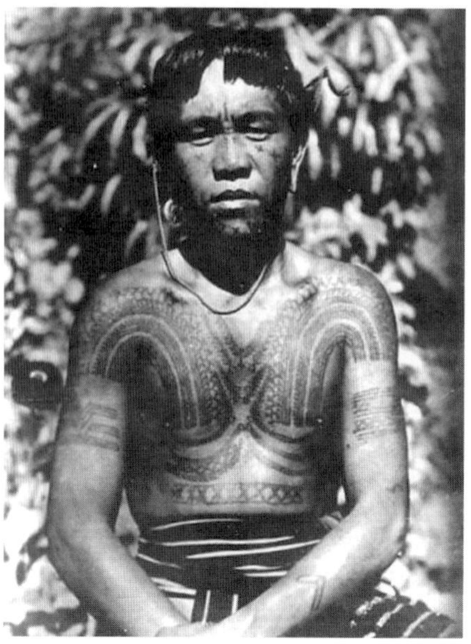

Mangkusdor

MAMBABATOK – First draws the design, or sometimes uses a wooden black to stamp the design onto the skin, and then uses the kisi and mallet to inscribe the design.

MAMOJ – The black pigment, used for both outlining the tattoo design on the skin, as well as for the application of the tattoo itself, is obtained from pounded charred coconut fibres which are then mixed with water. According to another source the pigment consists of pounded charred coconut fibres, the sap of the aerial roots of Pandanus and of a composite plant, Marshall Islands.

MANAGALASI PEOPLE - the custom of tattooing the face, torso, arms and legs of males around the age of fifteen, New Guinea.

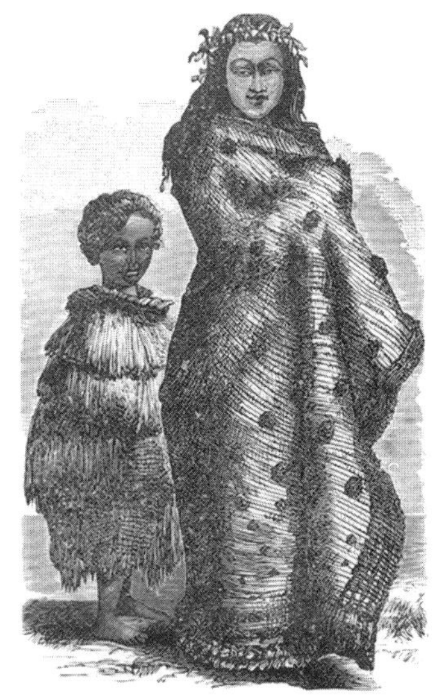

Maori woman and her son

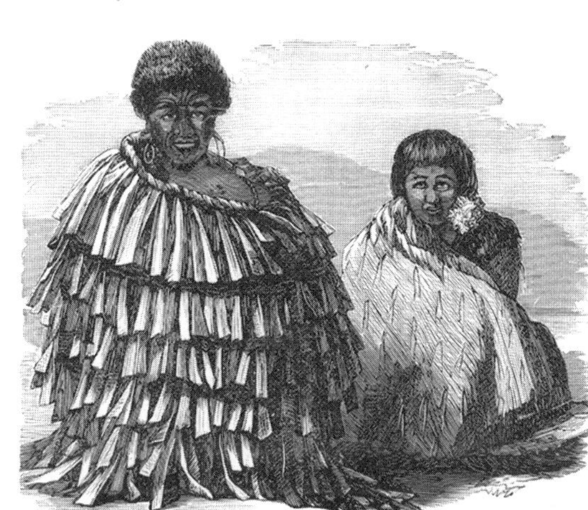

Maori chief and his wife

MANAOTOMBOKAFO (TOMBOKALANA) – Tattooer in the language of the Antandroy ethnic group, Madagascar.

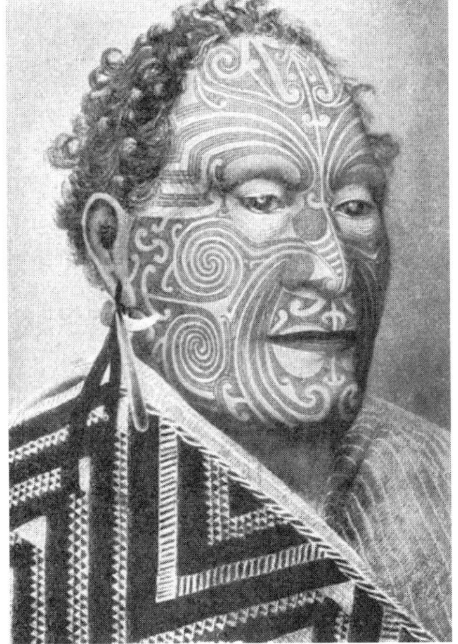

Maori chief

MANAOTOMBOKAVATSA – tattooer in the language of the Antandroy ethnic group, Madagascar.

MÁNAU– wooden mallet, part of tattoo tools, Truk Island.

MANBATEK - tattooer, Batek tribe.

MANDAN INDIANS - The Mandan, Hidatsa, and Arikara Nation (MHA Nation), also known as the Three Affiliated Tribes, is a Native American Nation resulting from the alliance of the Mandan, Hidatsa, and Arikara peoples, whose native lands ranged across the Missouri River basin extending from present day North Dakota Through western Montana and Wyoming. Mandan women had a small spot tattooed on the forehead, together with a line on the chin, while of the ment he Chin alone were tattooed, this being done on one side, or one half of the breast, or on one ar mand breast.

The Mandan tribe used a variety of dyes

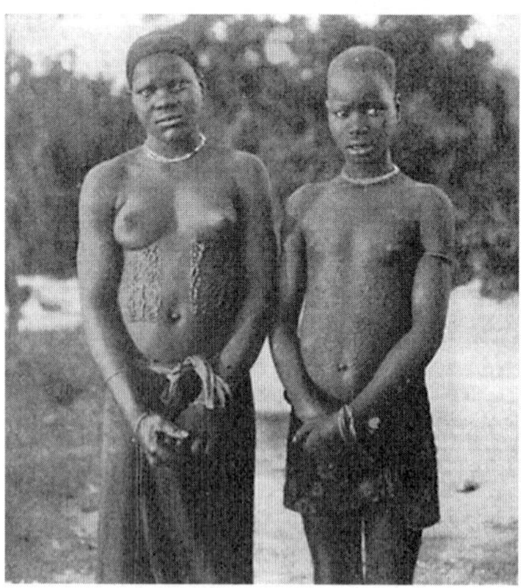

Maputju

and pigments for tattoos.

• Black Tattoos: Natural black dyes were achieved by the application of soot or bone black which was an animal charcoal produced by charring animal bones

• Brown / Reddish Tattoos: Reddish dyes and pigments were achieved by the application of ochre mixed with clay

• Blue Tattoos: Blue dyes were achieved by the application of indigo, a dye that was plentiful in North America

MANGAIA – Penis tattoos are connected to various communities. Some men of the Mangaia tribe in Cook Islands even had a picture of the vulva tattooed over their penis. However, penis tattoo was not meant for the common people. One ruler of the Tonga kingdom had the whole glans of his penis covered in tattoos to demonstrate his absolute disregard to pain.

MANGBETU - also spelled

MONBUTTU, peoples of Central Africa living to the south of the Zande in northeastern Congo (Kinshasa).

MANGEPE - The tattooist outlined the pattern, while women mangepe 'mourn, lament; groan' with pain for men, who was being tattooed, Bellona.

MANGKUSDOR – with a tattoo, a man becomes a mangkusdor (strong and beautiful) tribe of Kalinga, Philippines.

MANMANPUL – sponge, used to wipe, man, in tattooing, Mota Tribe.

MANKANI – a term for the abdomen, where women of the African tribe of Makonde were tattooed because they believed that they would gain in eroticism and thus gain supernatural power to attract men.

MANSI TRIBE - an East Siberian tribe that practices tattoos. They made perforated needles with which they stretched threads with a dye mixed with carbon black and oil. The tattoo is then done with this needle and thread.

MAORE-NI-ROPO – The whole tattoo process did probably taken from one to three years, or even longer, and the girl, or married woman, was called maore-ni-ropo, after a brightly-patterned small fish. This was used as a compliment, for a completely tattooed woman is nowadays a rarity, Santa Anna a Santa Catalina Islands.

MAORITANGA – Todays Maori who gradually discover the beauty of their roots and the Maori identity. Thanks to this, a new and active form of tattoo has appeared, mainly in urban areas: Maoritanga, to live as a Maori with ta moko. One of the expressions of this new political confidence is the increased number of the Maori who let themselves tattooed with a combination of ancient drawings complemented by new conceptions, ideas and images.

MAORI PEOPLE –inhabitants of the New Zealand practicing tattoos. The meaning of location of men's facial tattoos was as follows: the top of the forehead

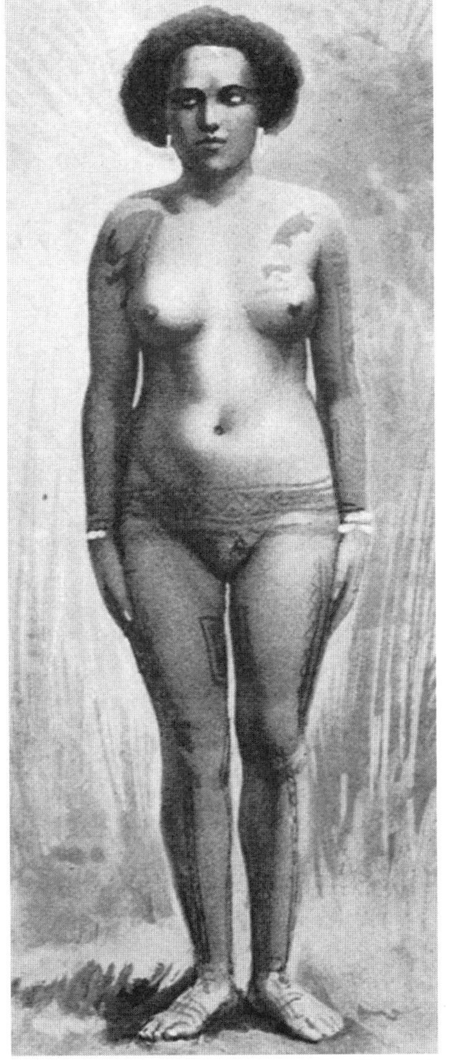

Woman from the Marquesas Islands

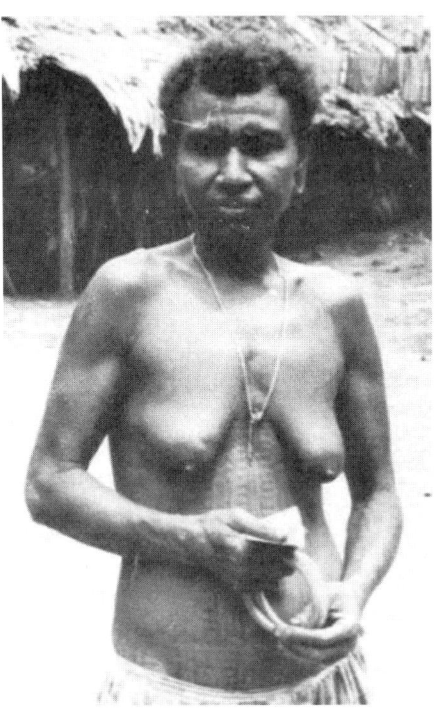

Tattooed woman, Solomon Islands

meant a rank, left and right part above the eyebrow represented status, left and right marks under eyes expressed the genealogy, left and right cheek up to the ears was reserved for a marriage, the area between the nose, eyebrow and mouth was individualized and was recognized as a signature, the space under the ears served as an expression of an occupation, the chin showed the power and strength and the parts leading to the neck social status upon the birth. Women had decorated chin; less then breasts and nose.

MAPARA - wood that is burned to form soot Awe.

MAPUTJU – African tribe practiced scar tattoo.

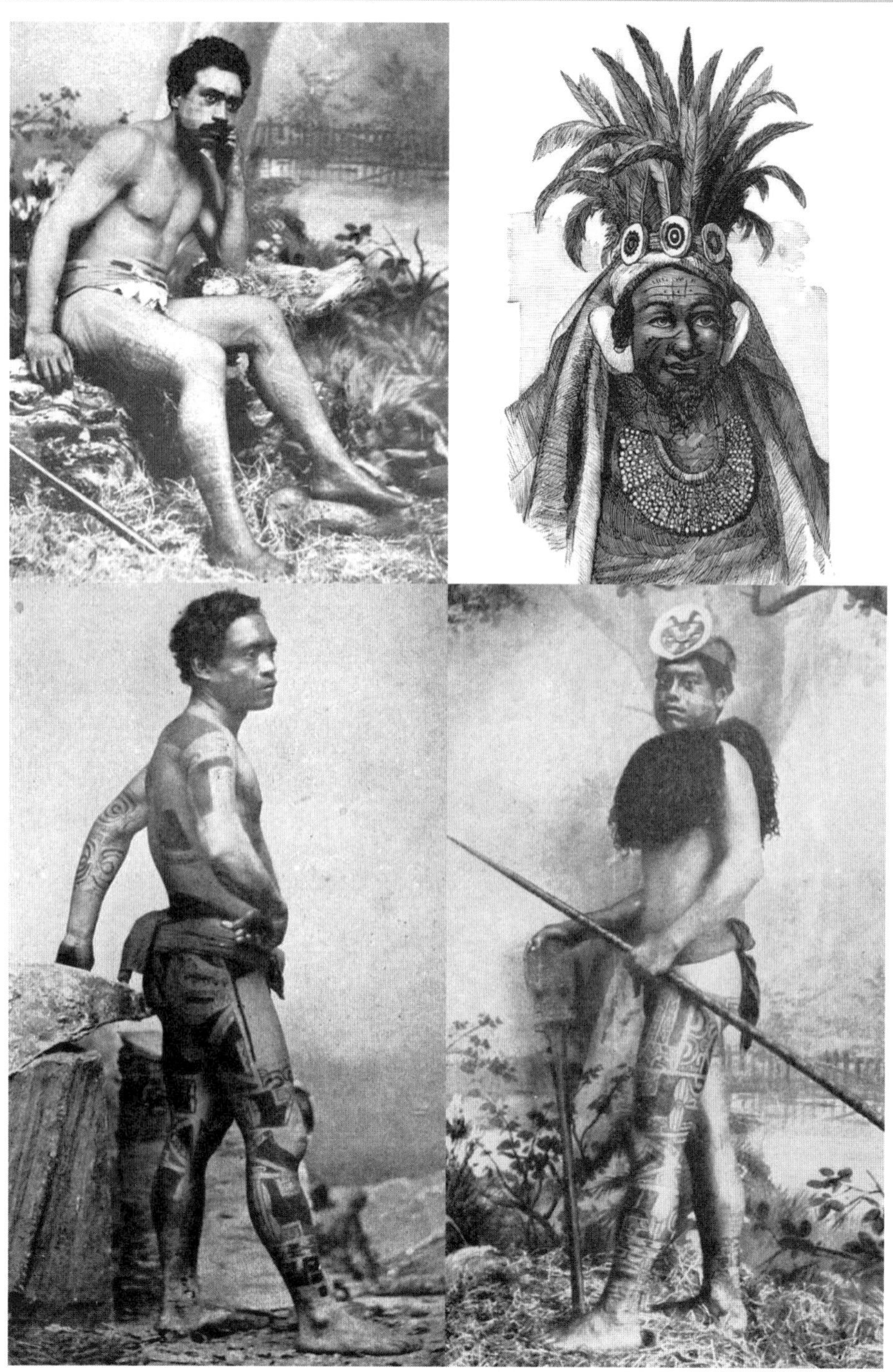

Marquesas

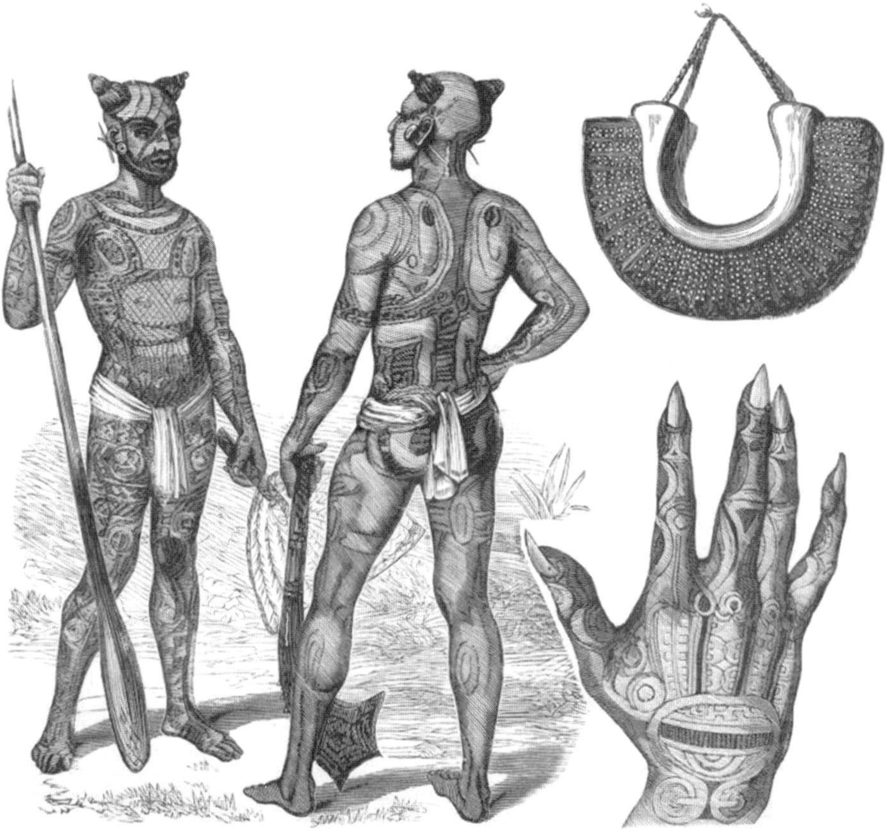

Marquesas Islands

MARAMARA-ANGARI - When dry the sap of the maramara-angari or the agatoga is burnt, the soot is collected and mixed with the juice crushed from agura fruit. This ink is punctured into the skin with a two-pronged chisel made of frigate bird bone. The chisel is tapped about one-tenth of an inch into the skin with a slender mallet made of magemage, Eastern Solomon Islands

MARA ARA - initiation house, where tattooing was done, Managalasi tribe.

MARAMARANGALI - resin used for tattoo, Santa Anna, Solomon Islands.

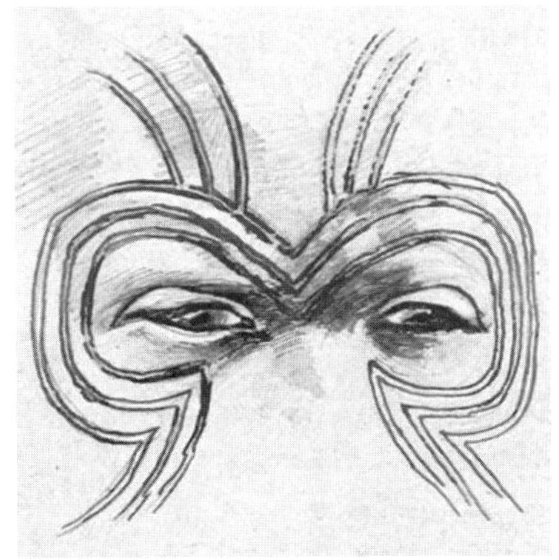

Tattoo around the eyes of a Masai woman

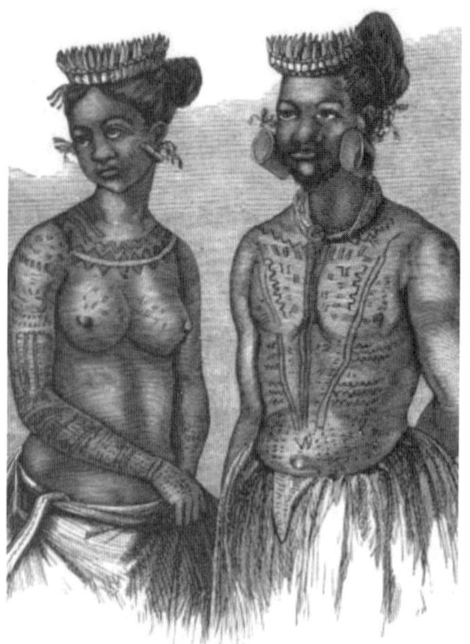

Marshall Islands

MARAUFU – initiation of young men, during which young girls from the islands of Santa Anna and Santa Catalina, Solomon Islands, could not be tattooed.

MARAUHAS – north-west Brazil tribe, wear band-ornaments round the ankles.

MARAWA-WAWE – Payment for tattoos is not a regular payment for the Maisin tribe (Papua New Guinea), but as gifts denoting "friendship" (marawa-wawe).

MARCO POLO - (September 15, 1254, Korcula Island or Venice - January 8, 1324, Venice) was a Venetian merchant and traveler who became famous for his travels in China, recorded in the book Il Milione. He was the first European to describe East Asia in more detail.

Excerpts from the Half Book:

Men's Tattooing in Vochan

After leaving Kara-jang, the traveler continues westwards for five days till he reaches a province called Zar-dandan. Its chief city is called Vochan. The people here are idolaters and subject to the Great Khan. They have all their teeth of gold–that is to say, every tooth is covered with gold. They make a cast of gold of the shape of their teeth, and with this they cover both their lower and their upper teeth. It is only the men who do this, not the women. The men also make a sort of stripe or circlet round their arms and legs with black dots. These are produced by means of five needles tied together with which they prick the flesh till they draw blood, whereupon they rub in a black ink that produces an indelible stain. And they reckon it is a distinction and an ornament to have such a stripe of black dots. The men are all gentlemen, according to their notions. They have no occupation but warfare, the chase, and falconry. All the work is done by the women, and by the other men whom they have taken captive and keep as slaves.

Extensive Tattooing on Men and Women in Kaugigu

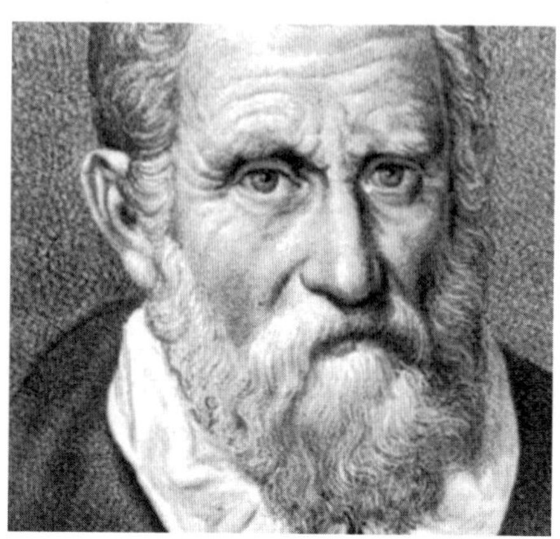

Marco Polo

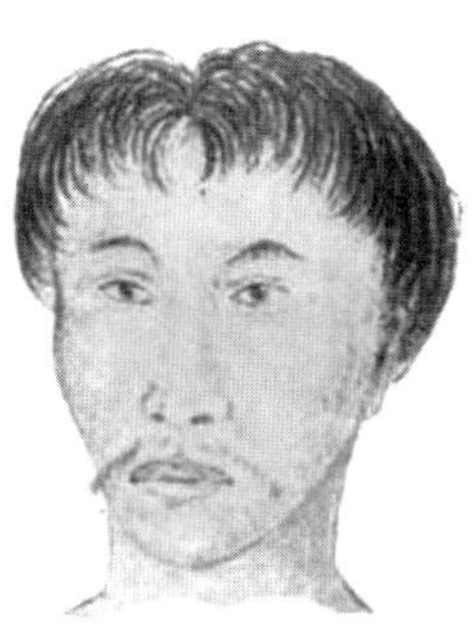
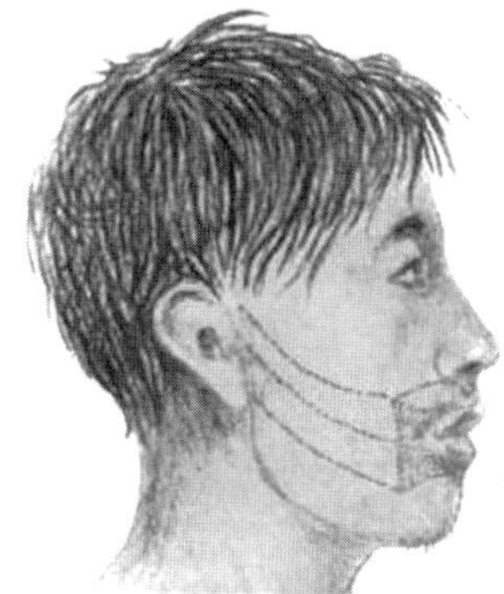
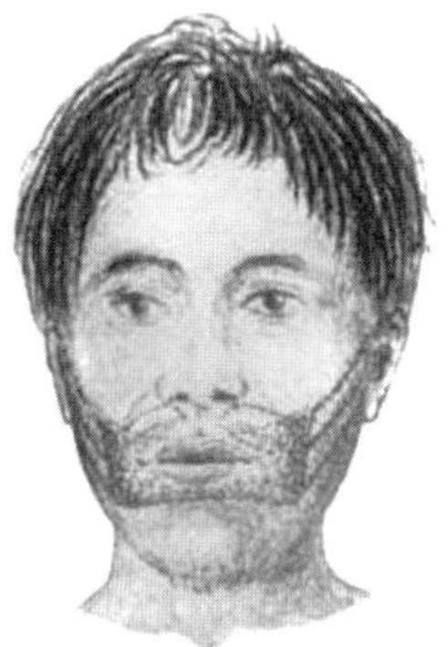

Mauhe

All the people alike, male and female have their flesh decorated in the following fashion. They have their flesh covered all over with pictures of lions and dragons and birds and other objects, made with needles in such a way that they are indelible. They make these on their faces, their necks, their bellies, their hands, their legs, and every part of their bodies. And this they do as a mark of gentility: the more elaborately anyone is decorated, the greater and the handsomer he is considered. First of all a man will have such images as he may desire sketched out in black all over his body. This done, he will be tied hand and foot, and two or more persons will hold him. Then the master craftsman will take five needles, four of them fastened together in a square and the fifth in the centre, and with these he will work all over his body, pricking out the images previously sketched. As soon as the pricks are made, ink is applied to them, and then the figure as sketched appears in the pricks. During the process the victim suffers what might well pass for the pains of Purgatory. Many even die during the operation through loss of blood.

Tattoos on Travelers to Zaiton

The people here are idolaters and subject to the Great Khan. It is a delightful place, amply supplied with all that the human body requires; and the inhabitants are a peaceful folk, fond of leisure and easy living. Many people come here from Upper India to have figures pricked out on their bodies with needles, as described above.

MARQUESAS ISLANDS - are a group of volcanic islands in French Polynesia, an overseas collectivity of France in the southern Pacific Ocean.

The extent to which tattooing was developed in the Marquesas is paralleled only by the Maori tattooing. Instruments like small adzes, made of fish bone, tortoise shell, and occasionally of human bone. The handle of the instrument was of bamboo, as also was the mallet. The blade was inserted in the handle of the instrument, a little distance from the end. The number of teeth varied from two to twelve. The soot from which the dye was made was derived from burned cocoa-nut shell or burned aleurities. The soot was collected on a small stone or in a cocoa-nut shell, and mixed with water or vegetable oil. The design was first sketched on in charcoal, and the dye was rubbed on the comb by two fingers of the operator´s right hand. The blood was wiped away with a piece of tapa.

Men were tattooed on the top of the head, the face, including the eyebrows, the inside of the nostrils, the tongue, the palms and backs of hands,arms, legs and trunks. Women were tattooed to the base of the gums, the ear lobes, behind the ears, on the curve of the shoulders, on the hands, the legs, and from the buttocks down.

MARO - Each day that the tattooing takes place the immediate kinsfolk of the patient prepare the oven and carry food to the house of the expert, with some areca nut or tobacco. When the work is done the patient goes and cultivates for a day in the orchard of the expert, making him a present of this labour. A ritual gift of the type known as maro is also prepared. It consists of a pandanus mat, a sheet of white bark-cloth, a piece of orange bark-cloth and a number of pieces of ordinary bark-cloth-ten or so. The maro is not given on the day of completion of the tattooing, but a period of days or even weeks is allowed to elapse while the kinsfolk are collecting the various items. There is no haste about the repayment as there is at an initiation ceremony. The patient himself takes only a small part in this; his elders make themselves responsible. The same is true for a woman. Since it is customary for her not to marry until her tattooing has been completed, my informants could not admit the validity of a question as to who pays for the tattooing of a married woman, Tikopia.

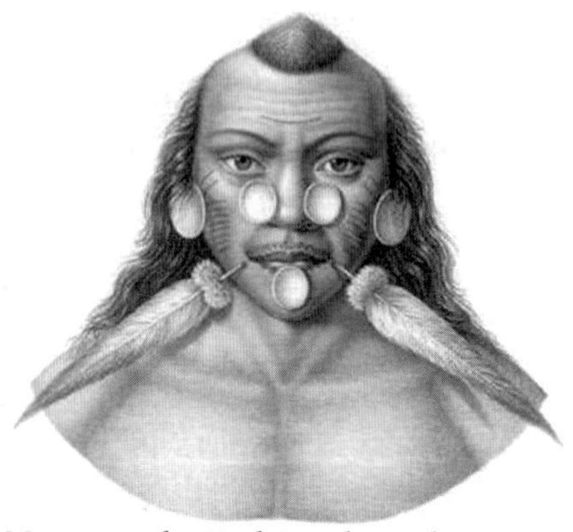

Maxuruna by Karl Joseph Brodtmann, 1827

MARSDENIA TINCTORIA R. BROWN – plant, from seeds are produced blue dye for tattooing, Dagestan.

MARSHALL ISLANDS - officially the Republic of the Marshall Islands (Marshallese: Aolepan Aorokin M̧ajel), are an island country and a United States associated state near the equator in the Pacific Ocean. Peoples practiced tattooing.

MASAI TRIBE – the Masai men do not mark of decorate their skin with patterns in scars r in tattooing; but women in the Naivasha District that parallel lines were apparently burnt on the skin round the eyes or on the forehead.

MASIN– see FULBA

MASSETS – Indian tribe in the archipelago of the Prince of Wales after Bentinck Arm, practicing tattooing.

MATACOS – Argentine and Bolivian Gran Chaco, women blacken their face, use tattooing.

MATAISAU – tattooer, Bellona Island.

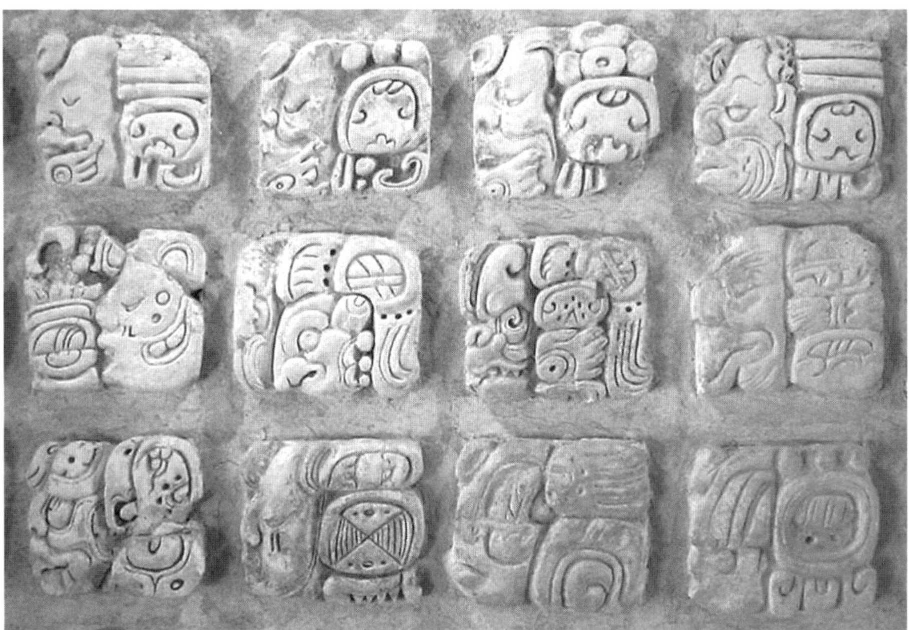

Mayan glyphs in stucco. The Mayans may have chosen one of these glyphs for their tattoos

MATAIE – tattoo ceremony, Samoa, Polynesia.

MATAILI - Before commencing work the tufunga donned his magic eye-shade (mataili), Ellice Islands.

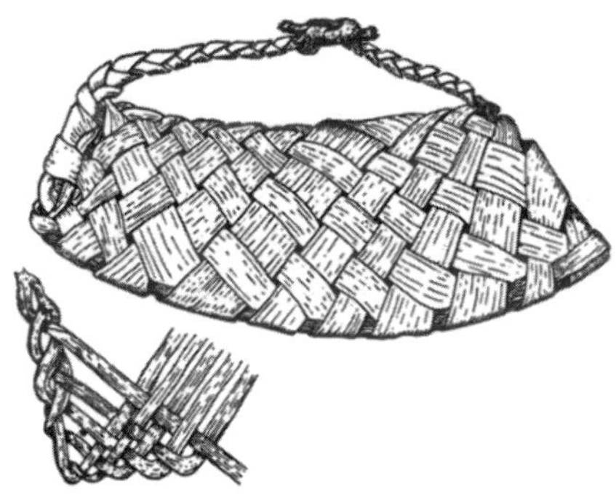

MATAMAATARU – a god in Polynesia who allegedly invented the tattoo technique with his brother Tiitiipoo. See HINAEREER-EMONOI

MATAMBWÉ TRIBES – African tribes from Kongo.

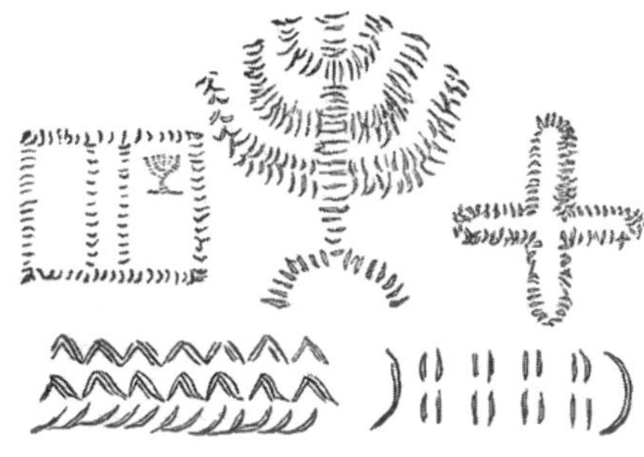

MATAORA –

• A man who was legendary inventor of tattooing in spirals.

• Mataora was the Orpheus of Maori-land, he descending to Hades (Po) in search of his wife Niwareka. In the Under-world he saw his father-in-law, Uetonga, who looked at the tattooing on Mataora´s

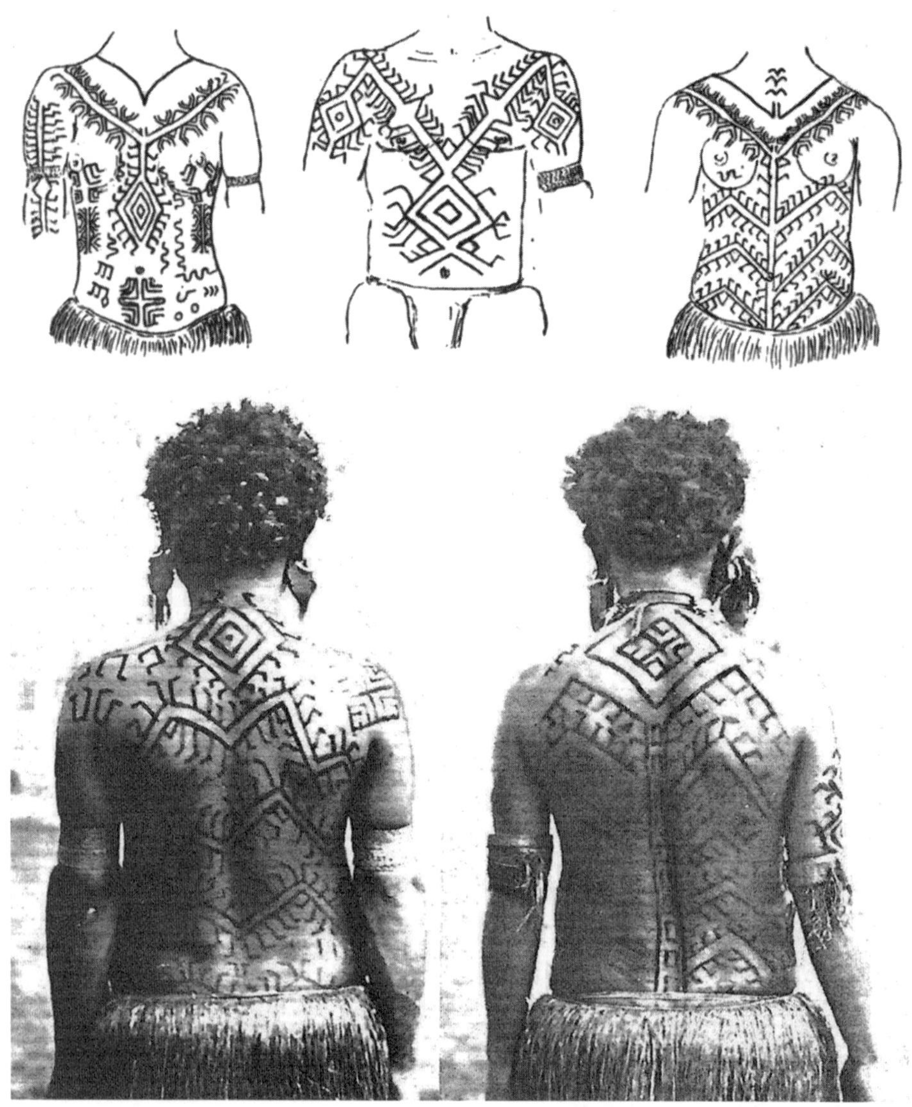

Mekeo

face and wiped it off, offering to mark him properly by puncture. Mataora consented, and was tattooed. He was nursed by his wife till he recovered, and she accompanied him back to daylight, but Mataora had omitted to leave one of his wife´s garments with Kuwatawata (the guardian of the door of Death) as an offering, so it was decreed that thenceforth no mortal should be allowed to return from the Shades to the world of light.

MATAU– is the tattooing implement. It is a small adze- like tool

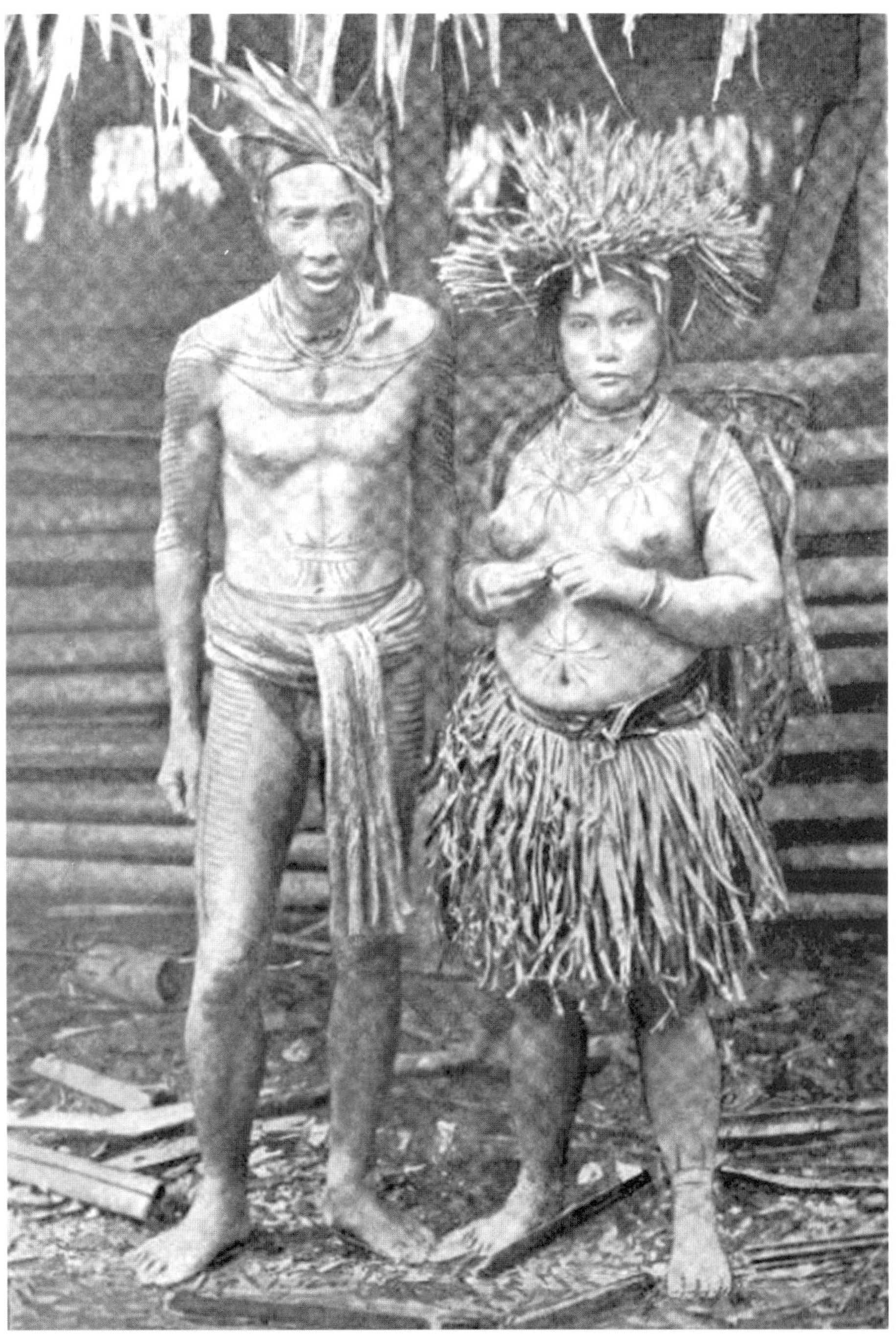

Mentawai man and woman with tattoo

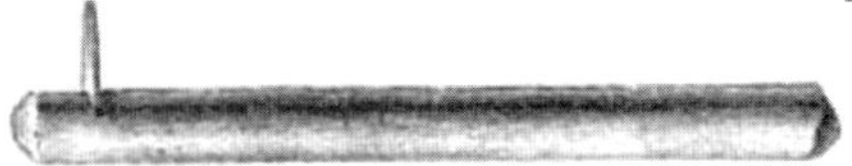

with a tiny blade made by cutting diagonally a piece of bird bone-that of the rofa, a species of mollymawk (popularly called albatross) -and sharpening the edge into five or six teeth. The piece of bone, which is about an inch-and-a-half long, is lashed like an adze-blade to a small stick about free times it is length, which is flattened and curved downwards at the haft end.

MATAU´U – tattoo tools, Sikaiana Atoll.

MATAISAU – tattooer, Bellona Island.

MATA-ORA - One who brought knowledge of tattoos from the underworld, Polynesia.

MATIS - A small group of virgin speaking Indians living in the Amazon Javari (Yavarí) Valley in Brazil. They use face painting and tattoos to help mimic the look of a jaguar. They also like the piercing of the nose and ears, in which they insert ornaments from snail shells.

MATSIGENGA - see MACHIGUENGA

MATSIGENKA - see MACHIGUENGA

MATSIGUENKA - see MACHIGUENGA

MATSÉS PEOPLE – their facial tattoos consist of lines that surround the mouth and continue along the cheeks to the ears. A bright red dye (achiote), obtained from the seeds of stromannatta (Bixaorellana's), is applied to the face and body, Northeastern Peru. See MAXURUNA

MAUÉS – north Brazil tribe, women tattooed during pregnancy. The Maué, though brave, were less warlike than the

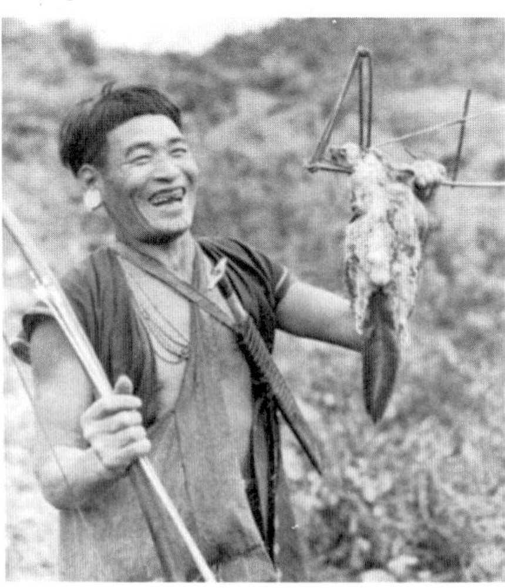

Minyong Adi man with chin tattoo

Mundurucu, with whom they warred until the second half of the 18tli century. According to Barboza Rodriguez (1882), the Maué who took part in the last fight between the two tribes had lines of black tattooing on the thorax, similar to that of the Mundurucu.

MAUZ – The name for a tree whose pitch is used as one of the ingredients to obtain a tattoo color, tribe Ghilzais, India.

MAVUTSINIMA – see XINGÚ

MAWO – In a similar context as a permanent spiritual component (see Dewa), this tattoo also confirmed that a girl inherited the ability to control tok mawo, which is identified as a perishable part of an individual (literally means "shadow"). Furthermore, this tattoo served as a form of beautification and an index of social status and distinguished humans from animals. Men did not seek

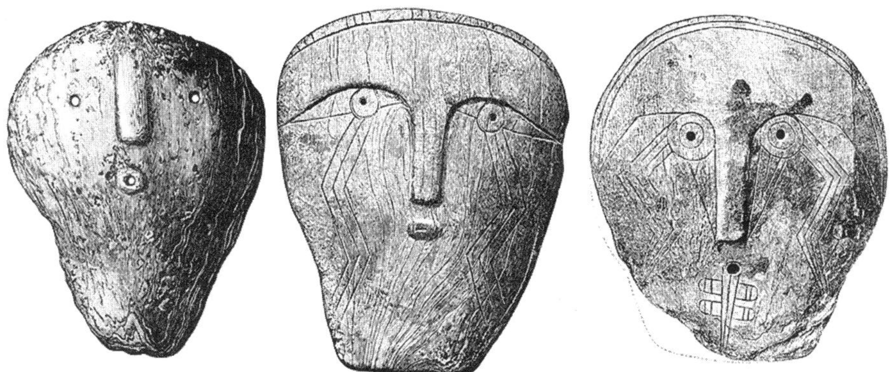

Mississippian Marine Shell Mask with lines represents the characteristic of the painting or tattooing of the clan or tribe

for untattooed women and further tattoos after giving a birth increased the social status indicators – women whose legs were completely covered in tattoos had higher social status than the others such as newlyweds who "had showed the white parts of their legs when crossing a river". The tattoo marks defined married women, and this was a cause why many young women in Kodi let themselves tattooed to avoid raping from Netherlands soldiers, when they occupied the stated area in 1911. They thought that soldiers may perceive them as married women and mothers and would let them be! Since some tattoos could be seen only by a husband of a specific women, these tattoos were a strong erotic enticement and lead to a situation when some children used insultations like "your mother has no tattoos on her thighs," which implied that it is commonly known about her and that she is promiscuous.

MAXURUNA – Another name for the Matsés tribe from the area of Brazilian-Peruvian border between the Javari and Galvez rivers. During ethnographic expeditions, this tribe was captured on canvas by a Swiss painter Carl Joseph Brodmann. This tribe experienced the first contact with the outer world in 1969 when they received missionaries into their villages. Peruvian government tried to destroy them by bombing and burning all the surrounding forests, their natural source of life. Later, thanks to the international pressure on the rainforest protection and indigenous people there, the relationships with the government improved. This tribe practiced piercing decorations, tattoos, and body painting.

MAYORUNA – see MAXURUNA

MAYA PEOPLES – are the original inhabitants of South Mexico and the northern parts of America. The term Maya indicates inhabitants of the region, who keeps specific similar culture and language traditions. Many different populations, communities and ethical groups within the Mesoamerica region are called this way. Abundance of body modifications was used in their history. Tattoos, scarification, head deformations, piercing and teeth sharpening were common. "Face and body paintings were

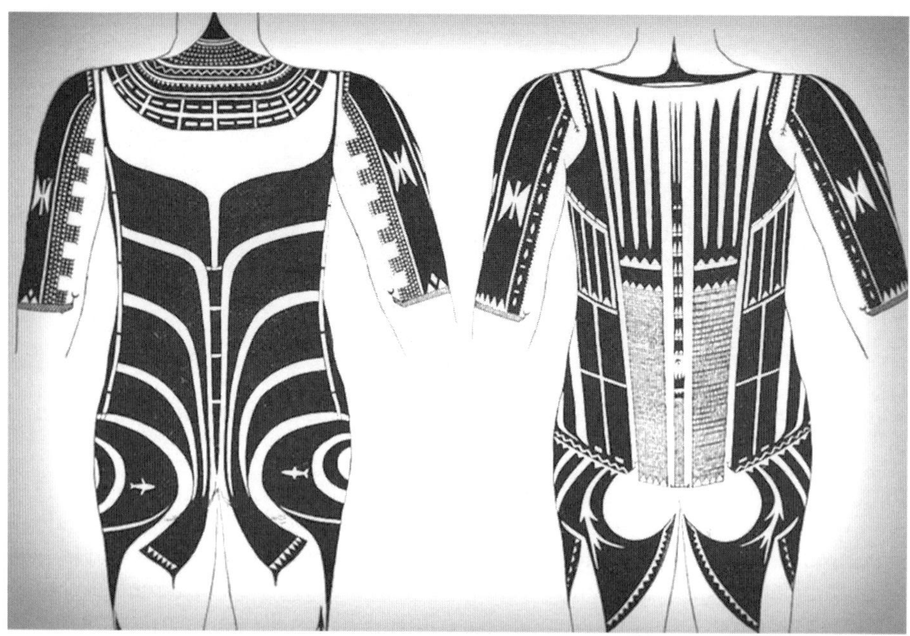

Mogmog Island man, Micronesia, ca. 1900

so common that Landa has to be an exceptionally talented observer when he managed to distinguish the original color of a man's face because men painted their bodies at every opportunity.

Black color was a color of young, single people, as well as those who fasted. Red belonged to warriors, blue to priests or the ones who were chosen as sacrifices. For elegance, fighters painted themselves red-black. In the case, that they had fallen into captivity, the greatest disgrace to them was losing badges and soot stains. It was possible to estimate the social status of the Mayas from their body paintings. Women painted their faces. Hue of red, obtained from the achiote seeds, symbolized blood and was blended with strongly perfumed ixtahte, which is a fluid amber matter with a pleasant scent and sticky properties," intends V. W. Hagen in his book Mayan Culture.

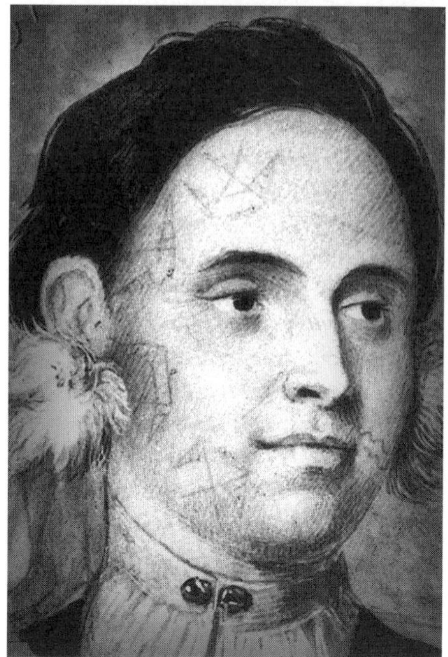

Facial Tattooing Of The Mohawk Warrior Onigoheriago, 1710

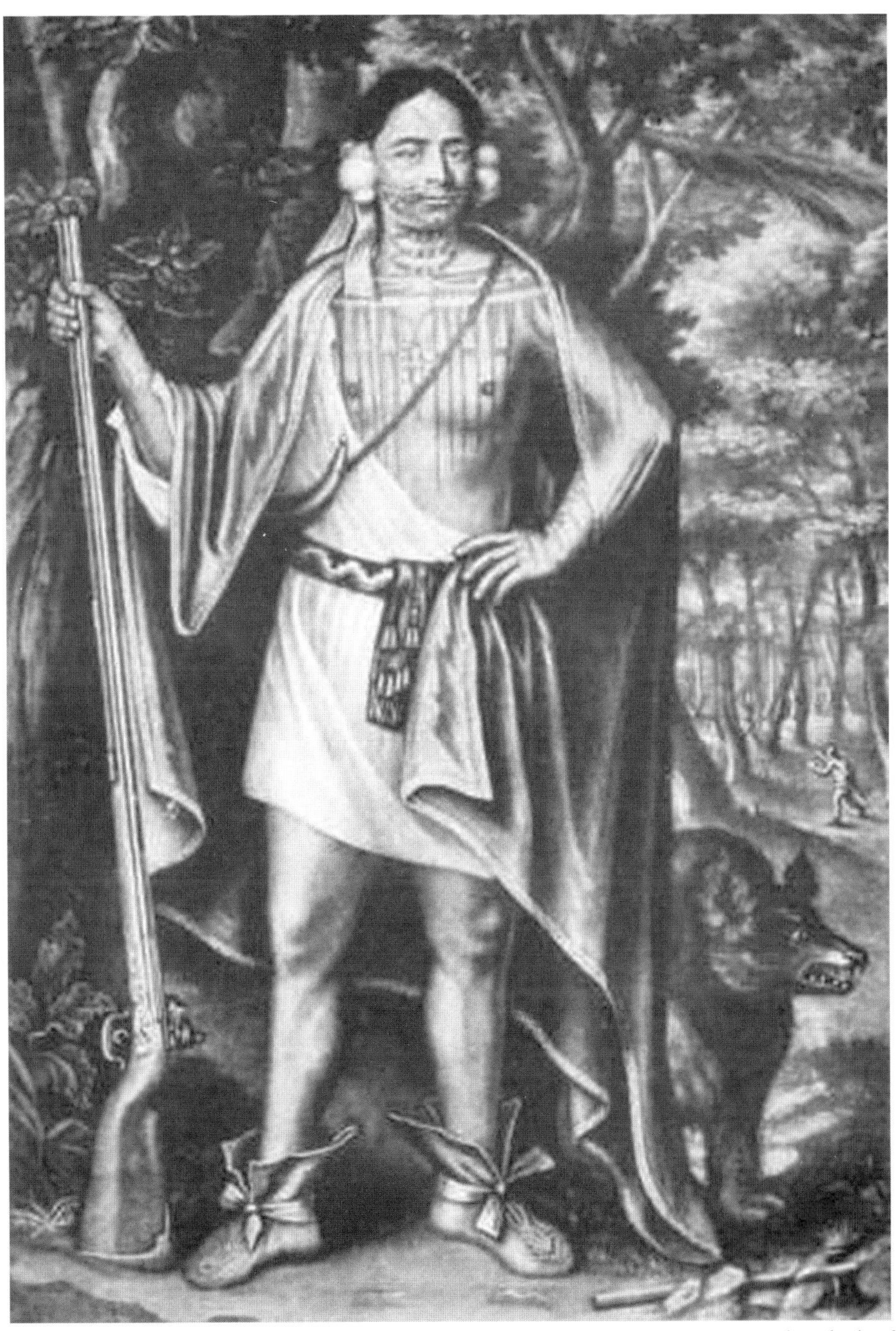

Mohawk chief

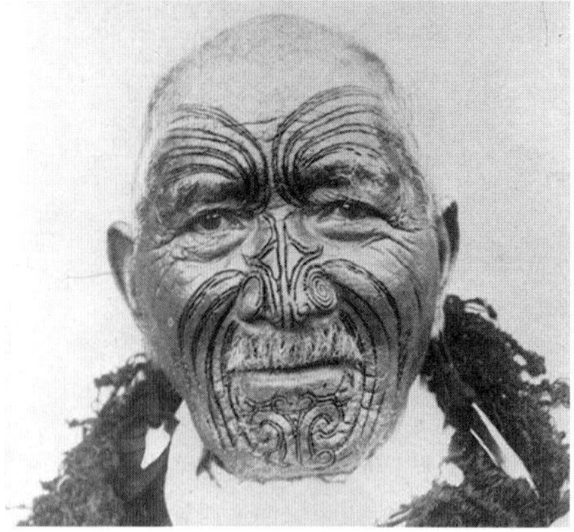

Moko

Women tattooed themselves from waist up except breast. However, women's tattoos were smoother than for men. The Mayas used to wear nose and lips decorations made of nephrite and obsidian. In lower Maya's classes, the nose and lip jewelry made of bones, wood, shells, or stone were only worn. Men also burned different scars on themselves, Morley, for example, states burning a circle on the top of the head.

The old Mayan considered foreheads skewed to the back as a sign of beauty; this deformation was achieved by pressing kids' heads between two plates whilst one was seated to the back of the head and the second against the forehead. This tradition was practiced mainly among the upper classes.

In his book Indiáni bez Tomahavků (Indians without Tomahawks), Stindl stated: "He (a man of the upper class) was decorated by rich tattoos and a giant nose. Rulers had elongated their noses by some kind of a "putty" extension, which given the desired "eagle profile" to the face. All other parts were also embellished or artificially deformed to emphasize the exclusivity of the Real man. Teeth were sharpened and decorated by inserted nephrite plates, earlobes were drilled and elongated by inserting a turkey egg."

MBATI –with an instrument called a mbati, or tooth, and a cocoanut shell filled with a mixture of charcoal and candle-nut oil, the operator first paints on the lines with a twig, and then drives them home with the mbati, which consists of two or more bone teeth embedded in a wooden handle about six inches long, dipping it in the pigment between each stroke of the mallet, and wiping away the blood with bark-cloth, while the other two control the struggles of the patient. The operation is continued until the patient can bear no more, for it is excessively painful, Fiji.

MEANA´I– tattooist's assistant, Samoa.

MEHINAKÚ TRIBE - Mehinakú women tended to have two small curved lines tattooed as armbands, a motif that also appeared in the center of pots made in their village.

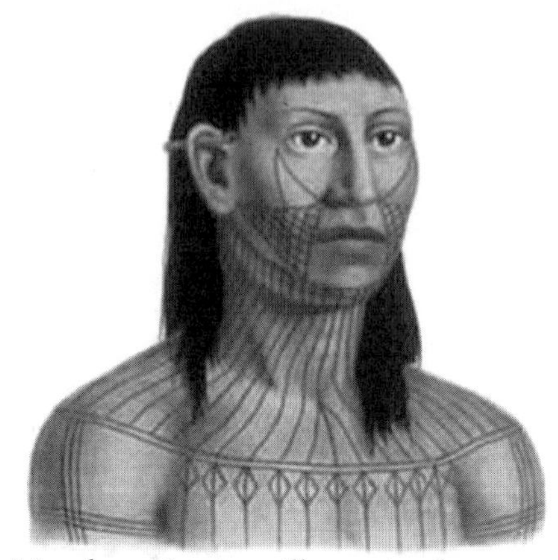

Mundurucú tattoo, illustration by Hercules Florence, ca. 1817

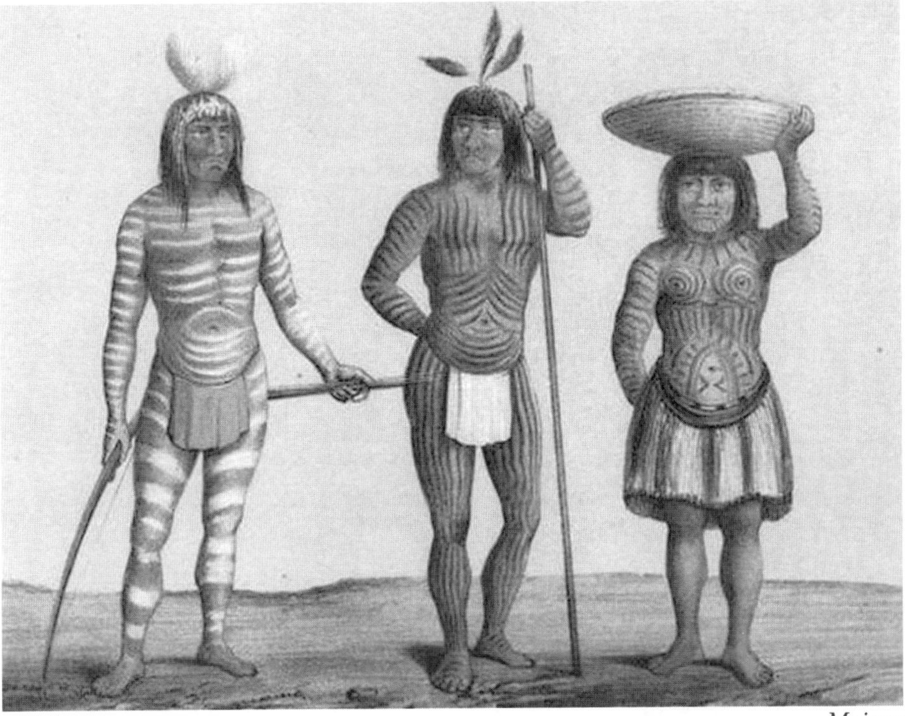

Mojave

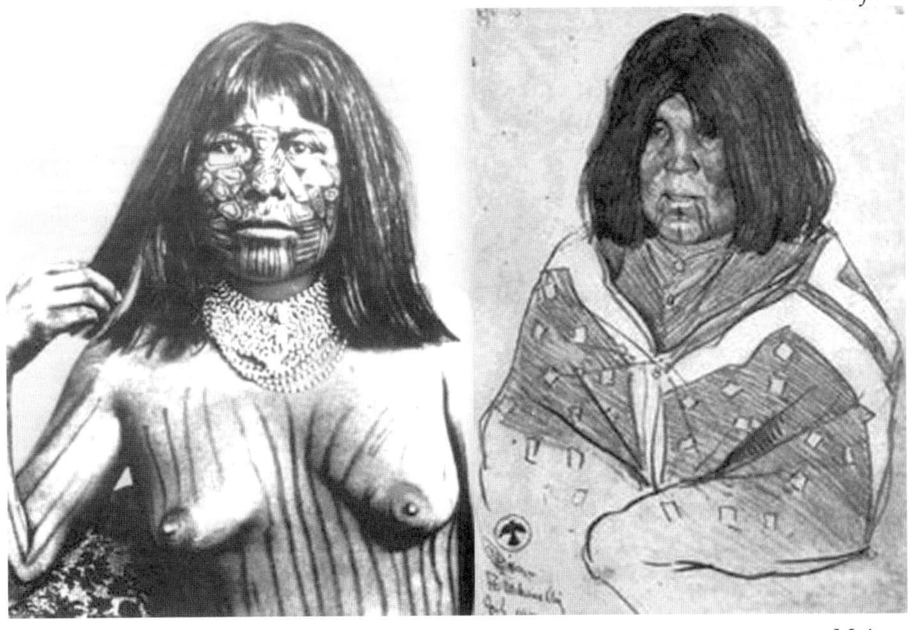

Mojave

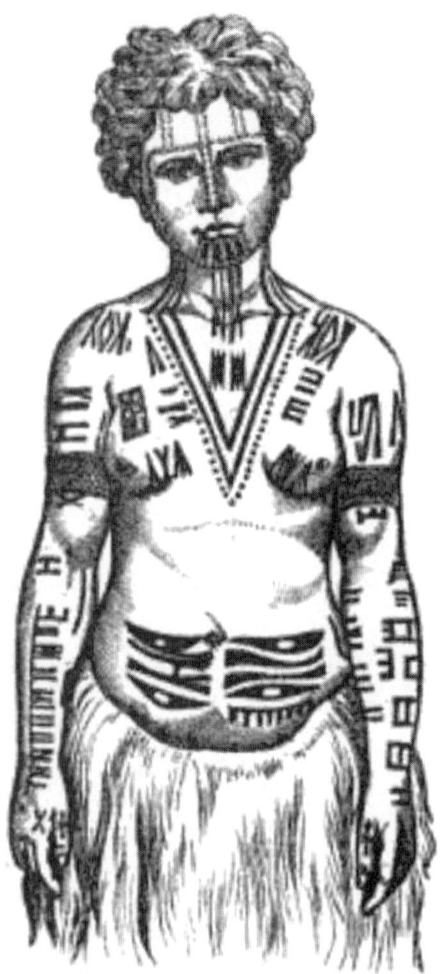

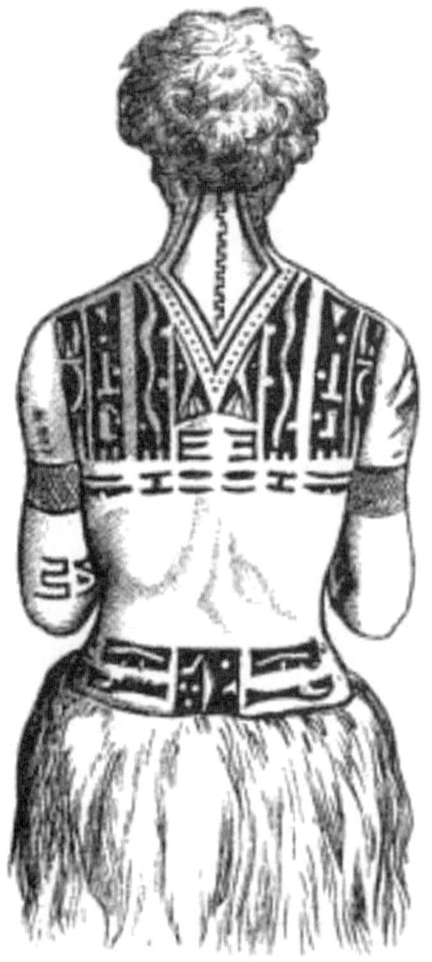

Motu girl

MECHELTA - scarificator, also tattoo tool, Tunis

MEKEO - They are part of the New Guinea people cluster within the Pacific Islanders affinity bloc. This people group is only found in Papua New Guinea. Their primary language is Mekeo. The primary religion practiced by the Mekeo is Protestant Christianity.

MENEHUNE – social class in Tahiti, this term was termed without a pedigree, and the motifs of tattoos that were allowed to get tattooed corresponded to this.

MEMOMINI TRIBE - the Menomini do not tattoo themselves for ornament but only for curative purposes. Persons suffering from chronic headache, for example, often had some local herb-doctor tattoo the figure of a Thunderbird over the seat of affliction. A tattooing instrument composed of several needles

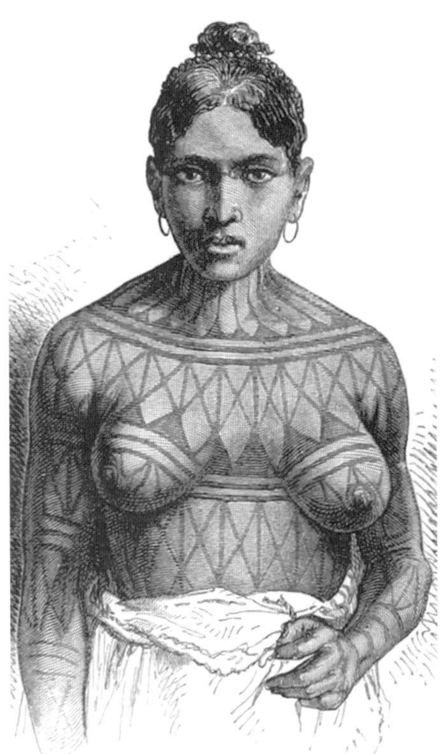

Mundurucú tattoo, illustration by Hercules Florence, ca. 1820

set in a handle made of the thick, strong quill of some large bird, from which the covering had been stripped. The upper end had been folder over and trust into a longitudinal slit made in its own shaft. The needles were fastened in a row in the distal end. In the hollow tube small seeds, shot, or beads, had been placed to cause it to rattle when used. Hawk-bells were attached to the upper or proximal end.

In using the tattooing outfit, a little of the bear´s gall is placed in the bark dish, and dissolved in a quantity of lukewarm water, correspoding in amount to a tablespoonful. To this is added some powdered birch-bark charcoal as pigment, and a portion of the powdered roots. These last are called by the Indians skunk-root, deer´s-ear root, red-top root, black root nad yellow root. The compound is applied in a thick paste over the seat of pain, and the figure desired is pricked in through the paste. The latter is then bandaged over the wound caused by the pricking of the needles, and is allowed to remain for four days.

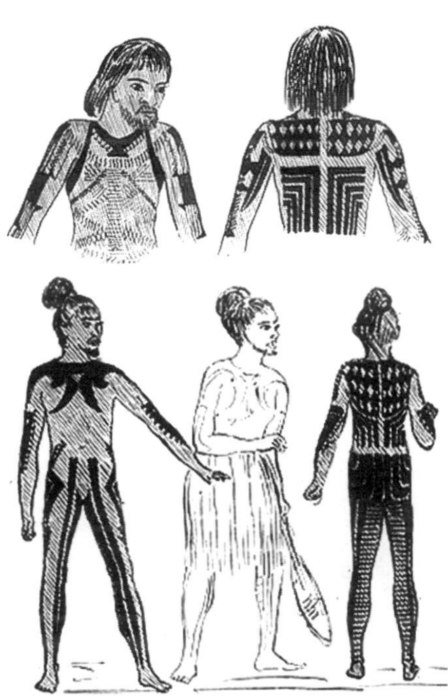

Mwoakilloa (Mokil or Kahlap) and Pingelap Tattoo front and back view

MENTAWAI TRIBE - The Mentawai are famous for their most intricate and elaborate tattoos, which cover the entire body. To the Mentawai islanders, the art of body tattooing is not only an artistic expression but is part of one's life cycle

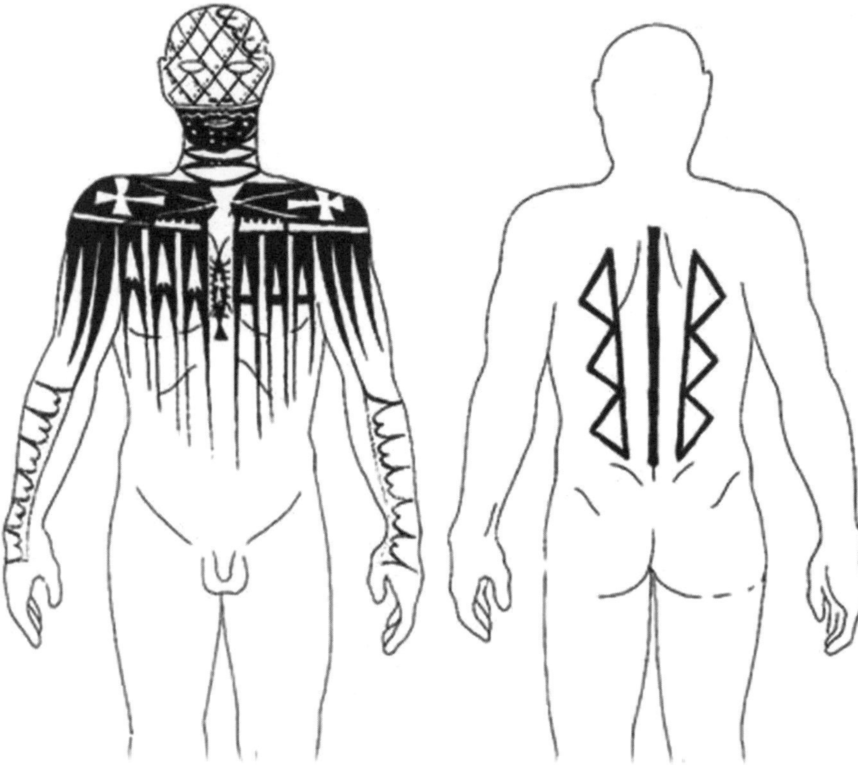

Mohawk and his tattoos

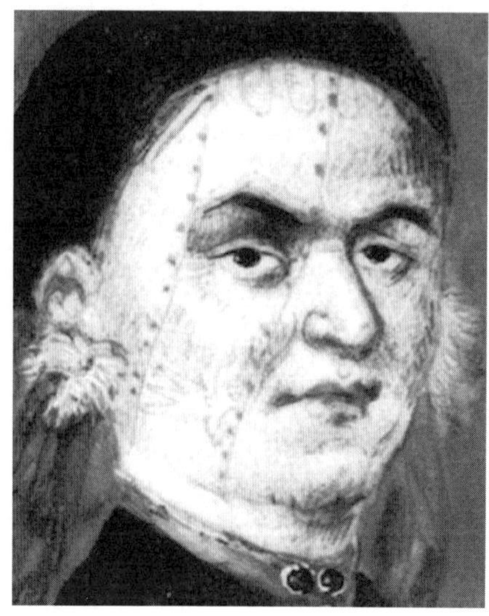

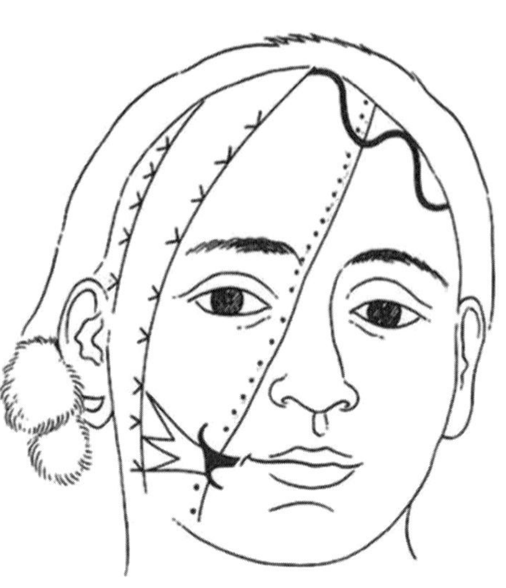

Mohawk Warrior Face Tattoo

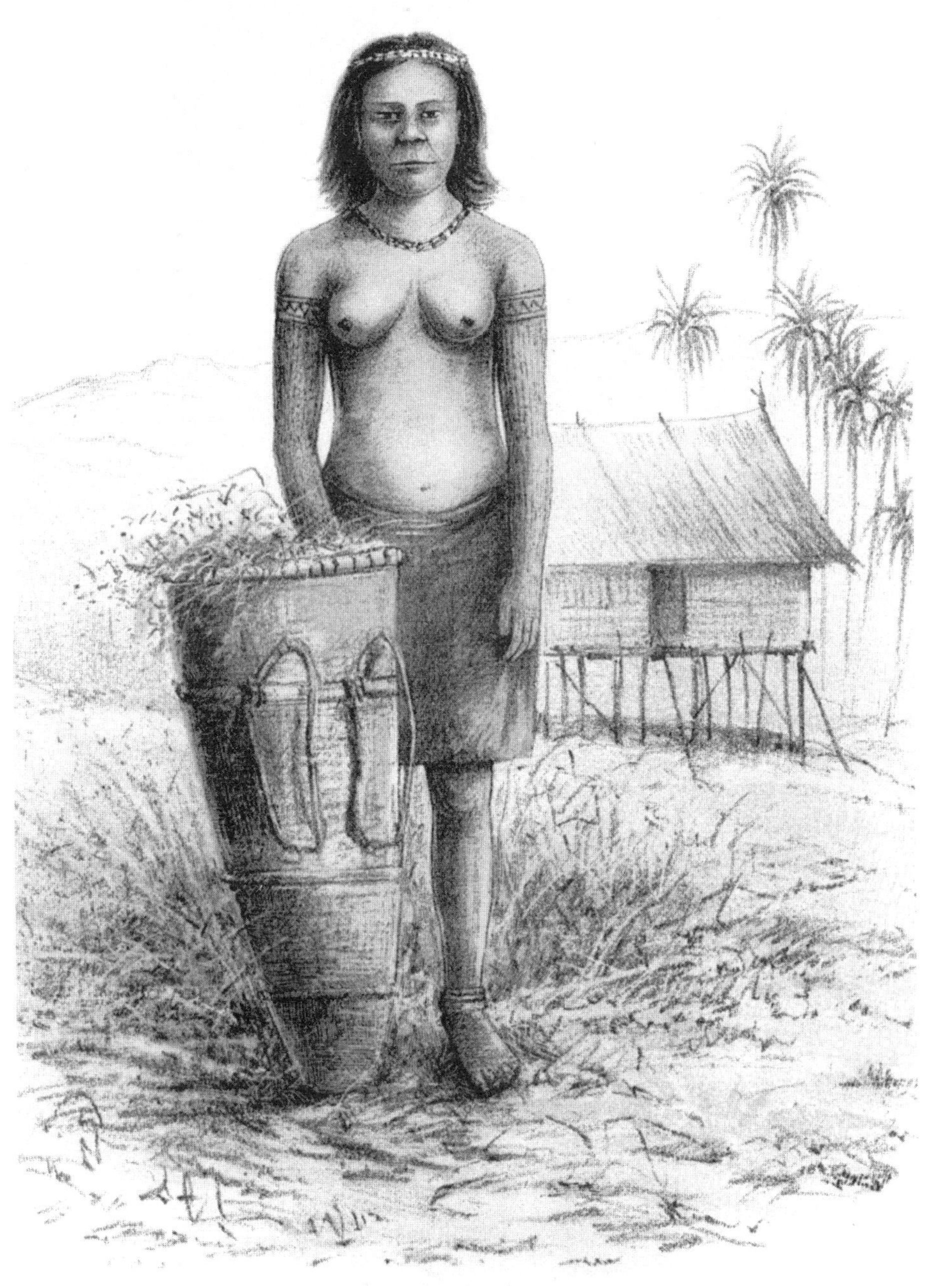

MURUT WOMAN (LAWAS RIVER)

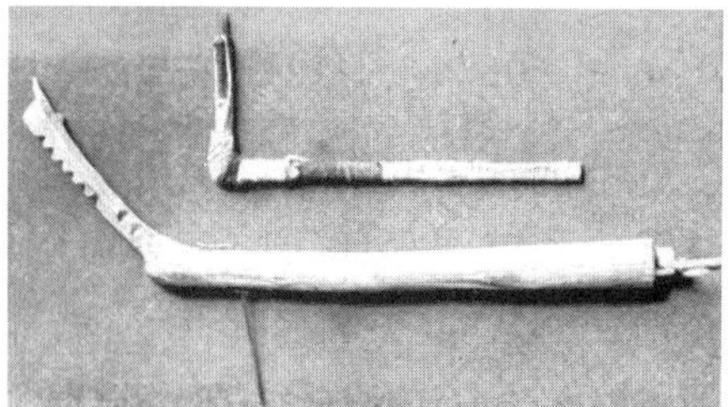

Tattoo tool, Mentawai

where tattoos signify age, social status, as well as profession. At the age of 11 or 12 years, children are given their first tattoos beginning from the upper arms. At age 18 tattoos are applied on the thighs while in the final phase the entire body is tattooed from head to toe. The Mentawai believe that "dressing" themselves up with tattoos forms an essential part of life and their culture, since in the afterlife they will be able to recognize each other and their ancestors through their tattoos. Additionally, to the Mentawai communities, tattoos also symbolize harmony and balance in the natural world. And for this reason, they tattoo animals, flowers, or rock formations on their bodies.

MERTEKA – tattoo ink, Kalinga.

MESH– red color, Haida.

METÁ – The tapu (or taboo) metá (tattoo) did not end until the tarauwana ceremony was over.

MEVALE – Classic tattoo performed by a tattoo comb, Fang tribe, Africa.

MII – black dye used for tattoo, Maisin tribe, Papua New Guinea.

MIŁ-XO΄A΄DIŁ΄E·N - fatty stencil soot mixed with marrow (for tattooing), Hupa.

MIKIRI – a border of a tattoo in Japanese terminology.

MILLBANK – North American Indian tribe from around the Bella Coola River practiced tattoos.

MINYONG - are a sub-group of the Adi people, a tribal people living in Arunachal Pradesh, India. The Minyong are found in East Siang, Upper Siang and West Siang district. Practiced tattoo.

MIS - term for tattoo in Dakhadaev region, Dagestan.

MISPIL – designation for courtesans on the island of Yap, were tattooed on the arms and legs. These tattoos symbolized their social status in society.

MISSISSIPPIAN CULTURE POTTERY - is the ceramic tradition of the Mississippian culture (800 to 1600 CE) found as artifacts in archaeological sites in the American Midwest and Southeast. It is often characterized by the adoption and use of riverine (or more rarely marine) shell-tempering agents in the clay paste. Shell tempering is one of the hallmarks of Mississippian cultural practices. Analysis of local differences in materials, techniques, forms, and designs is a primary means for archaeologists to learn about the life ways, religious practices, trade, and interaction among Mississippian peoples.

MISTICK-OOS - a group of Mistick-oos Indians belonging to the Plains Cree who camped near South Saskatchewan (North America). In 1858, Henry Youle Hind wrote about them: At Plains Cree, it is common to decorate the skin on the arms and chest with a decorative figure, birds, quadrupeds and various symbols.

MITETIC-KATSA - In 1797, L.A. Chapelier made a trip to Foulpoint in the Betsimisaraka area, and recorded several observations of tattoos. "The Malagasy," he wrote, "call the process of tattooing Mitetic-katsa."

MITHRA – a sun god whose followers tattooed a cross on their foreheads, which they also used to decorate their clothing.

MIWOMODOROKETE – Japanese expression for tattoo (mi = body; wo = particles; modorokete = making dots, lines, stains, etc.).

MIWOMODOROKU – Earliest mention of tattooing of the body, Nihonshoki period (97 A.D.)

MO - one of the terms in ancient China (206 BC to 220 AD) for tattoos.

MO – see AVA´BLY AREEMATATOWE

MOAI- are monolithic, stone sculptures scattered around the Easter Island. They look like tall and flat faces. Even though they are known as "heads", they often have neck, shoulders, arms, and body, but, today, these are buried under ground. It is not known yet what does the word actually mean. The creation and purpose of sculptures are shrouded by many theories. It is for sure, though, that it was very difficult and costly to produce them and also that they were transported to locations remote from the place where the material for their production was obtained. Motifs depicting tattoos were often carved on them, mostly on neck, face, and chest.

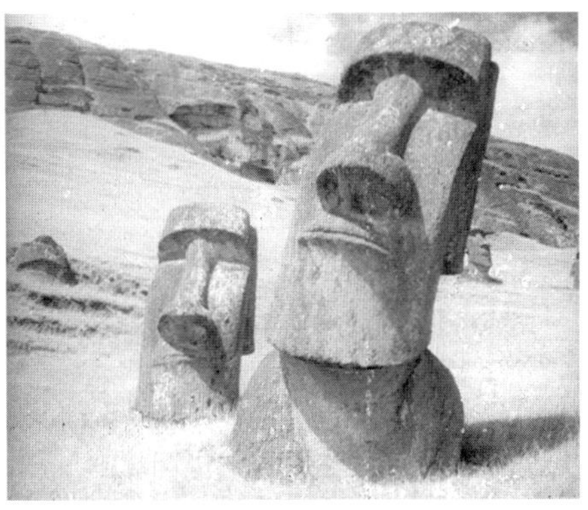

MODOC - An Indian tribe, originally lived in an area that is now in northeastern California and central Southern Oregon. The women tattooed three-blue stripes from mouth to chin.

MOGMOG – island in Micronesia, tattooing was practiced here.

MOHAWK - an Indian tribe from the area of today's New York, men decorated themselves with tattoos on their faces and other places.

MOHO – designation for a completely tattooed man, Marquis.

MOJAVE – Indians, North America, and women tattooed their chins when they were to get married.

MOKOKURI - In New Zealand the curves of the modern tattooing (the tattooing of Mataora) to have superseded a different fashion for marking called mokokuri.

MOLI– Bone tattooing needle, Tahiti.

MOLUCCAS – Indonesian islands where tattoos were widespread. Tattoos were connected with religious rites, which were often part of the offerings. After the prohibition of headhunting from the Dutch colonial government, the tattoos begun to disappear. However, the original inhabitants did not give up and so the secret community of Kakéan raised. Its purpose was to preserve the old traditions, including tattoos. The members of this community were bound by secrecy and that's why the meaning of tattoos is not known well today. Dutch government tried to repress this community as well and maybe for this reason they started to tattoo themselves on less and less visible spots, like under the rectum etc.

MONMON - In Osaka, tattoos were also called monmon - peaks, figures, patterns, circa 1750 and more.

MORI- Unlike women along the south coast of Papua, Maisin women insist that non-standard designs be used on tattoos. Each tattoo, they say, is a unique product of the "ideas" (mori) of their creator.

MORI-BANI – the dreaded warriors who, for their courage and achievements, could have a star symbol tattooed - madu.

MOTKO - a tribe from Port Moresby, New Guinea, women get a tattooed belt with sharp angles at engagement, leading from the armpits to the center of the breasts.

MOTU – tribe on the coast of the Gulf of Papua (New Guinea). The local men decorate their hair with red hibiscus and the women are adorned with rich tattoos on their wedding day. Papuans often decorate their faces with red clay.

MOUTAA ´ANGA – various ways of making motifs on canoes, skins, etc., Bellona Island.

MOZUI – so-called "ink crimes", the term is used in ancient China. Text coming from 6-7. century AD Han Shu (treatise on crime) states that there were five hundred crimes punished by tattoos in order to exclude them from decent society.

MOURI - The spirit of a person, existing in recognizable human form both before and after death. Syns. manu, anana. (After a person dies, the mouri can reveal itself in its former human form but is always facing away and unspeaking. A mouri can also become visible and recognisable before death, having temporarily left the body; such a sighting is an omen of that person's imminent death.

Following the visit to Takuu of a tattooed Maori in recent years, an ethnicity which Takuu speakers pronounce 'Mouri', the term manu has become more common than mouri to refer to the human spirit. If a man accidentally falls from a tree, the trunk must be struck forcefully in order to dislodge his mouri from the point of falling and return it to the victim, Takuu.

MPUNDI WA DINEMBO – Macedonian name for tattoo artist.

MU´URMUT– a Kalinga warrior wearing, among other things, a tattoo called a "dakag".

MUKA– Sometimes the chisel (uhi) was not dipped into the pigment but a wad of scraped flax (muka) with the pigment smeared thereon was drawn over the wound as soon as the incision had been made in the skin.

MUKDĚSI – see MAHDĚSI

MUKDISI - see MAHDĚSI

MUKSI – see MAHDĚSI

MUNDURUCÚ – The Mundurucú tattooing designs consist of fine, widely-spaced parallel lines applied vertically on limbs and torso; bands of lozenges across the upper part of the chest; occasional parallel horizontal lines, and cross-hatchings. Around each eye is tattooed a single line ellipse; curved lines are drawn around the mouth. Lines converging toward the ears across the cheeks give the appearance of wings spread across the face. Both sexes were tattooed but there are slight differences in design for each. The operation begins when the subject is about 8 years old and proceeds gradually over a period of years. It is seldom completed before the subject has reached the age of 20.

MUNGAIYAUWUN – tattoo, Aborigines tribe, South Australia

MUNO – resin that is used as a base for tattoo ink in the Mentawai tribe, Polynesia.

MUNTO-EE-GUN - (sacred cloth) - a designation for a cloth in which a tattoo tools was stored, Cree Indian tribe

MURUT TRIBE – tribe in Borneo practicing tattoos. Tattoos were also a punishment, as a symbol of shame. The man who escaped the fight received a square tattoo on the back of his neck.

MUTHADS – social status of Muthads in India. The Muthads was been classed as degraded Brahmans. They were supposed to have suffered social degradation by their having to tattoo their bodies with figures representing the weapons of the god Siva, and partaking of the offerings made to that god.

MUTLHAVELI - A person who "cuts" tinhlanga, or tattoos; a tattoo artist., Mozambique

MWANE-APUNA - When a man through inheritance or by his own personal gifts achieve the rank of mwane-apuna, or priest and medicine man all in one, he may get the sign of rorofa, two small fish (eiga) tattooed on his cheeks, a sign that he is sacred (apuna) and in intercourse with spirits (ataro), Solomon Group.

MWOAKILLOA - is an inhabited atoll in the central Pacific Ocean. Geographically, it belongs to the Caroline Islands and is a district of the outlying islands of Ponapean of the Federated States of Micronesia.

NA PAELE KULANI – a group of chiefs on the island of Maui, translated as "blackened (tattooed) chiefs", Hawaii.

NAGA TRIBE - the Naga people are an various individuals or ethnic groups conglomerating of several tribes associated to the North Eastern part of India and north-western Myanmar. The tribes have similar cultures and traditions, and form a significant population in the Indian state of Nagaland, with significant population in Manipur, Arunachal Pradesh and in Assam.

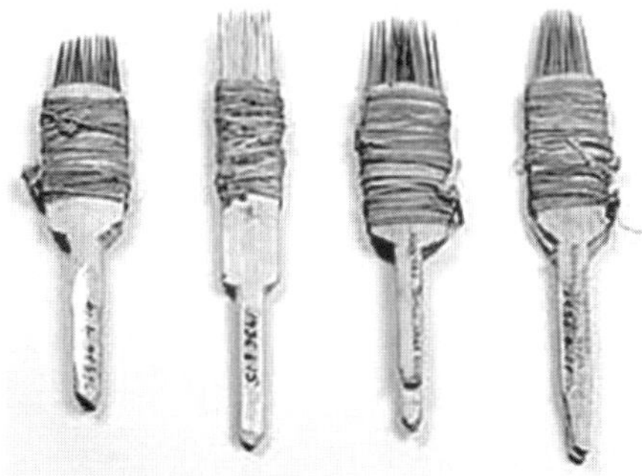

Naga tattooing tools

NANAKO – tattooing, Miriori tribe.

NANAR – "Make marks by teeth", ie tattoo, the Motu tribe.

NAR – tattooing tools, Motu tribe.

NARAHU – pigment or dye with which the process of moko was completed.

NASA– brush from twigs, which painted a tattoo motif, Maisin tribe, Papua New Guinea.

NASKAPI (pronounced NAS-ka-pee)- was a Montagnais word for an Innu band that spoke a slightly different language than the others. Practiced tattooing, lines on the chin.

NASS – or NASS RIVER INDIANS - North American Indian tribe from around the Bella Coola River practicing tattoos.

NATTAMAN TRIBE - The Nattaman women do not, as a rule, cover their breast. The lobes of their ears are much distended, and they tattoo their chins and cheeks in the Paraiyan fashion. This is supposed to be in recollection of their origin.

NATIVE AMERICAN - is a designation used for the indigenous people of the United States.

NÁWA SÚKWIYA or NÁLE SÚKWIYA – Initiation ceremony for the first initiation (scar tattoo), Papua New Guinea.

NCHIKA - a term for the inner thighs, where women of the Makonde tribe tattooed themselves because they believed they would gain in eroticism and thus gain supernatural power to attract men.

NE´ONE´O – In book The Body Decorated, Victoria Ebin states, "On one island, the word ne´one´o, meaning" cry for a long time, "or" menacing, "was used for a full body tattooed person," Marquesas Islands.

NEDEK - Among the Kayans tattooing is always done by a woman, and the position of a tattooist is to a certain extent hereditary. In the old days tattooists are believed to be under the protection of a guardianship spirit, who must be appeased with sacrifices before each process of tattooing or Nedek.

NEEM - tree oil, which can be used just like emu oil and is considered by some to be its vegetarian equivalent. High

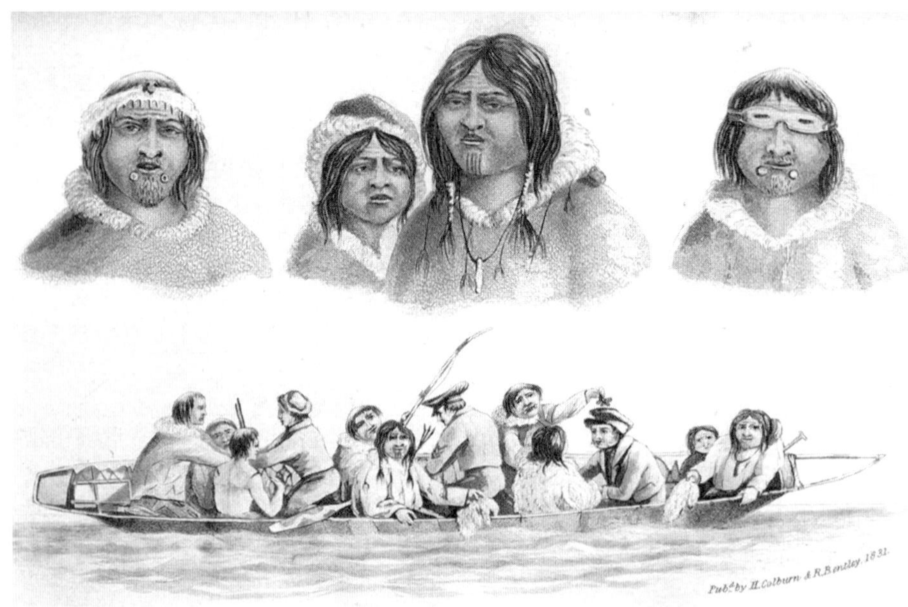

Naskapi

quality oil has been shown to prevent swelling and promote skin regeneration and healing.

NECHTENE – tattoo tools, Tunis.

NEIKALIKIBAI – god of tattoo in Fiji and Polynesia.

NEIRAU – tattoo tool, stick with tattoo needles at the end, Marshall Islands (?)

NEKASH – the skilled operator, Abyssinian.

NEKAŠKY –specialized tattoo artists in Ethiopia who rubbed soot into the skin and punctured it with soot.

NĚNCI- an East Siberian tribe that practiced tattoos. They made perforated needles with which they stretched threads with a dye mixed with soot and oil.

NGADJOES - a tribe from the southeast of Borneo. They practiced tattoos.

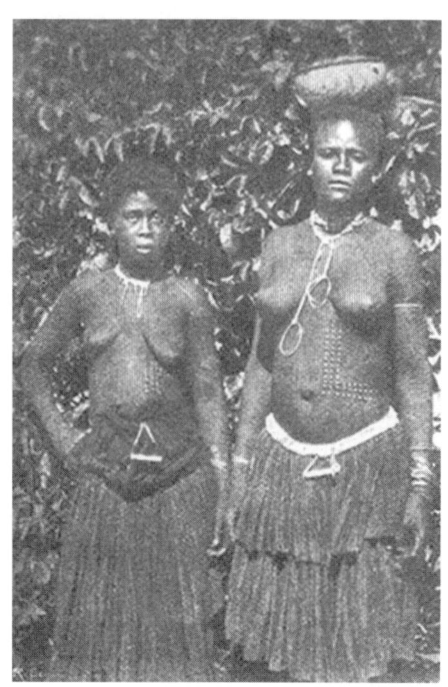

Nhuka

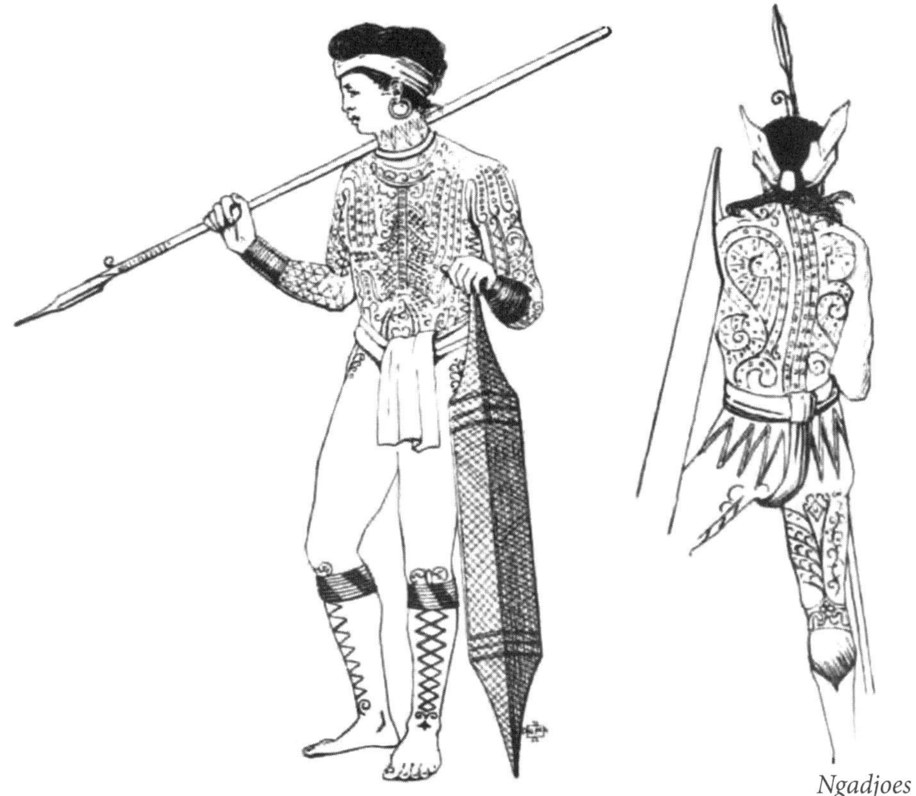

Ngadjoes

NGAPING - the tattoo artist and the client must be cleaned (ngaping) before the tattoo, Borneo.

NGARA´U - the carbon black from which the tattoo pigment was formed, Aitutaki Island.

NGARAHU - Soot from the burnt resin, used in tattooing: Puritia to ngarahu kauri, Maori.

NGARAHU - charcoal, from his carbon black was made a tattoo paint, the island of Magaia.

NGAREHU - blue tattoo pigment, Ngai-Tahu tribe, North Island, New Zealand.

NGUA PENGATAUKUKA MAI SIBA - - Siba is a (mythical?) island from which came the taukuka, a solid black tattoo covering the entire chest. Nobody knew where Siba was. Some kakai (culture heroes) were said to have the art of tattooing there, Bellona Island.

NHABÉZIS - a term for the person who performed the body modification, Nhúngüé tribe, Mozambique

NIEZI - old Chinese term for tattoo

NIEZIE - old Chinese term for tattoo

NIFO - teeth of tattoo chisel, Tonga,

NIHO´I - to draw a tattoo design before tattooing, Marquesas.

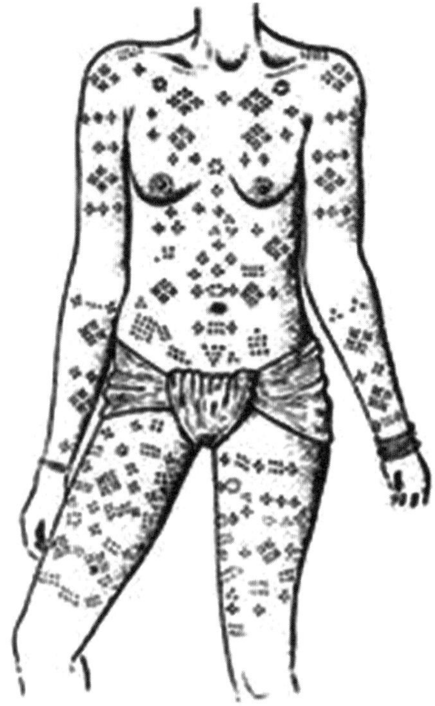

Nhungue

NIHONIREZUMI – translated as "tattooed Japanese." Nihon means "Japanese", ire "introduce" and zumi "colors."

NI´KAGAHI WAU – The feminine cosmic force was typified not only by night but by the heavenly bodies seen by night, as the masculine cosmic force was symbolized by day and the sun. The credential of a man´s attainment to membership in the Ho^N´hewachi was the right to tattoo on a maid certain cosmic symbols of night and day. The women thus tattoed was called a Ni´kagahi wau, woman chief (ni´kagahi, chief; wau - woman), Omaha Indians.

NIKUJUBAN - a flesh-coloured nylon body stocking painted with tattoo designs.

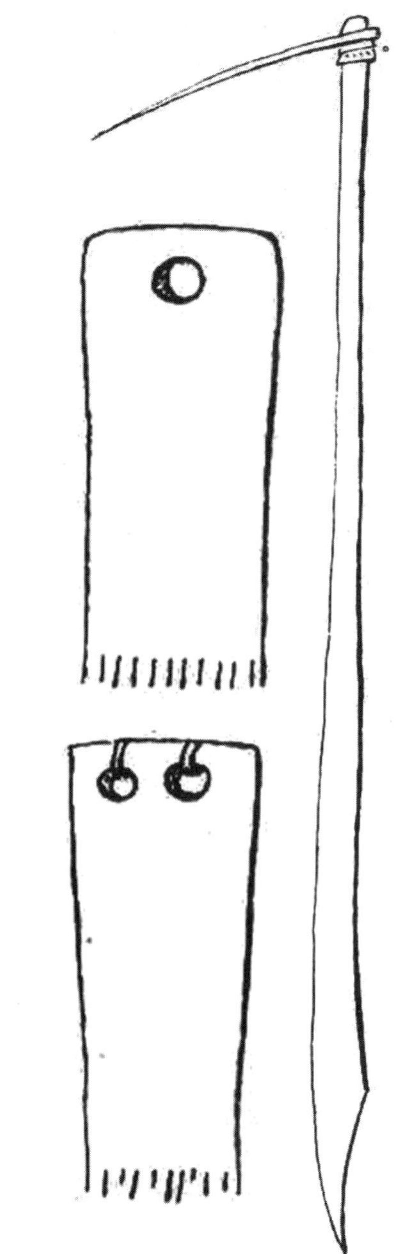

Tattoo chisel from Nukuor atoll

NILGHERRY HILL – tribes in India,

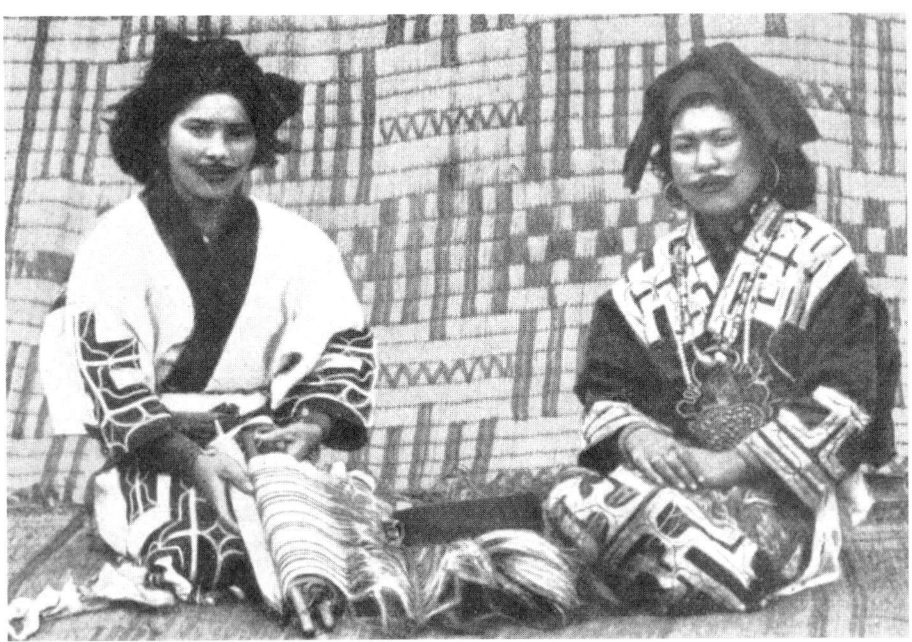

Nui

showing elaborate designs where all women had to be tattooed.

NIRE – the name for a cloth soaked in ash wood that was used to wipe blood off tattoos, Ainu.

NISHTAR - The adasia´s tattooing tools included a blade known as nishtar, which many recalled was burned over a fire and cooled before use.

NIU-MARAUWA – The girl to be tattooed went into the forest and scrapes resin or gum from some bleeding place in the bark of the trunk of a tree, a Barringtonia bearing edible almonds, called gatoga, or another one called maramarangali, a tree resembling the wild almond. The gum is black and burns well, and is used for native torches. Having collected enough she returns to her home. Early the next morning she lights the gum and catches the soot in the concave stem of a fresh coconut leaf called niu-marauwa . This soot scrapes into the half shell of a coconut and mixes it into a paste with a little water. After three days she squeezes the juice of the fruit of the tree aguru into the paste to thin it and make it suitable for tattooing. She takes this to the tattooing artist and the work commences.

NIUUI– coconut milk used during the lulu´u ceremony, Samoa.

NIVKHS – also the Gilyaks are inhabitants of the Russian Far East. They are located in the northern half of the Sakhalin Island (Sakhalin Oblast), it's west and east coasts, catchment area of several rivers (mainly the Tym river), and Amur river catchment (Khabarovsk Krai, Primorsky Krai, Jewish Autonomous Oblast). Unoriginally, a small part of them lives in Ukraine and in the northern part of Japan (Hokkaido Island). The Nivkhs are considered ancestors of the oldest Neolithic inhabitants of the Amur catchment and the Sakhalin Island. The oldest mention is dated back to the 12th century and it comes from a Chinese chronicle where the Nikvhs were called the Gilyaks (???), which were in contact with rulers from the Yuan dynasty. In the 17th and 18th centuries, the Nivkhs were discovered by Russian explorers. In 1643, a Russian named Vassili Poyarkov called them the Gilyaks. During the Second World War, the Japanese moved the Nivkhs (about 100 persons) and the Ainu out from the Japanese part of the Sakhalin Island (or Karafuto) to Hokkaido. Many of the Nivkhs returned to the Sakhalin Island and just a fraction of them remained in Japan after the war.

NIWAREKA - (myth), the wife of Mataora. She left her husband on account of his having beaten her, and she went down to the Underworld (Po) to her father, Uetonga. Her husband followed her and underwent the tattooing process, being the first mortal thus ornamented. Mataora then took his wife back to the world of Day.

NKANA – ash with which the artist covered face or body at the place where the tattoo was performed, Fang tribe, Nigeria.

NKEELEKUT – tattoo artist, Fang tribe, Nigeria.

NKUNA - is a tribe that joined the Vanhlave from Zulu land. Practiced tattoing.

NOBATAMAN – term for tattoo according to English-arabic Vocabulary: Anglo-egyptiansudan.

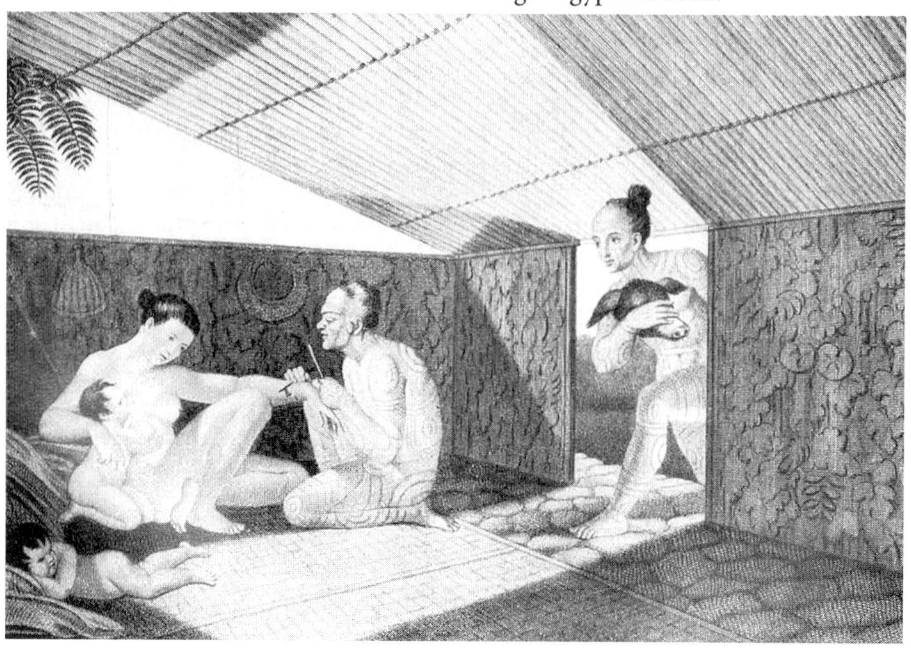

Nuku Hiva tattooing process

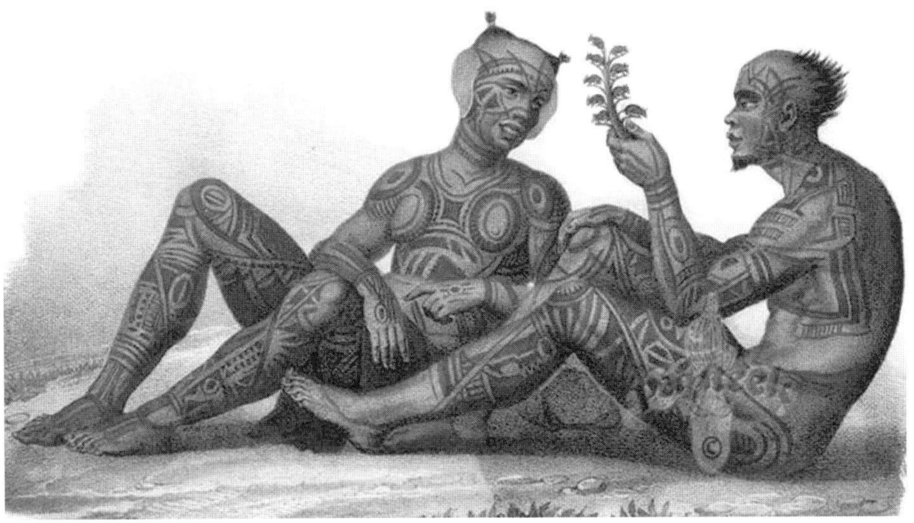

Tatooed Natives of Nuka-Hiva

NOOTKA – a tribe of North America, members tattooed their chest and arms and often had scars running from their chest to their abdomen and down to their arms and legs.

NOMNOM = tattooing, LouIs in the Admiralty Group.

NONI – After the tattoo, the most common medicinal product was noni (morindacitrofolia), which was served in the me΄ae, or holy place; Marquesas.

NOUA – a term denoting the fourth class of the Ariori secret community in Polynesia. Members of this class could tattoo two to three small figures on their shoulders.

NSITI - soot, ashes—(i.e., ground charcoal) still served as coloring agents for tattoo, Mozambique.

NUKU HIVA - is the biggest from the Marquesas Islands in French Polynesia, an overseas collectivity of France in the Pacific Ocean. Formerly, it was known as ÎleMarchand. Nuku Hiva is characterized by small bays leading to deep valleys which go further inland. The biggest bays in the northern part of the island are the Anaho Bay, Hatiheu Bay, and Aakapaa Bay. On the South, there are fewer bays of the bigger Baie du Contrôleur bay) and the Hakaui and Hakatea bays. The middle part of the island is a plateau called Tovi "i. On the east edge of Tovi "I, we can find the Tekao, which is the highest peak of the island reaches up to 1 224 m. In the past, tattoos were widespread in this island, together with its specific style. It is distinguished by triangular shapes of various sizes that fitting into each other with a half-inch gap between them. The only regularity of this arrangement is in placing them within a straight line near a middle part of a leg. Edges looking like flames, teeth, and geometrical lines, occasionally with a natural motif, are break by heavy patterns which gave them an unregular and decorative look.

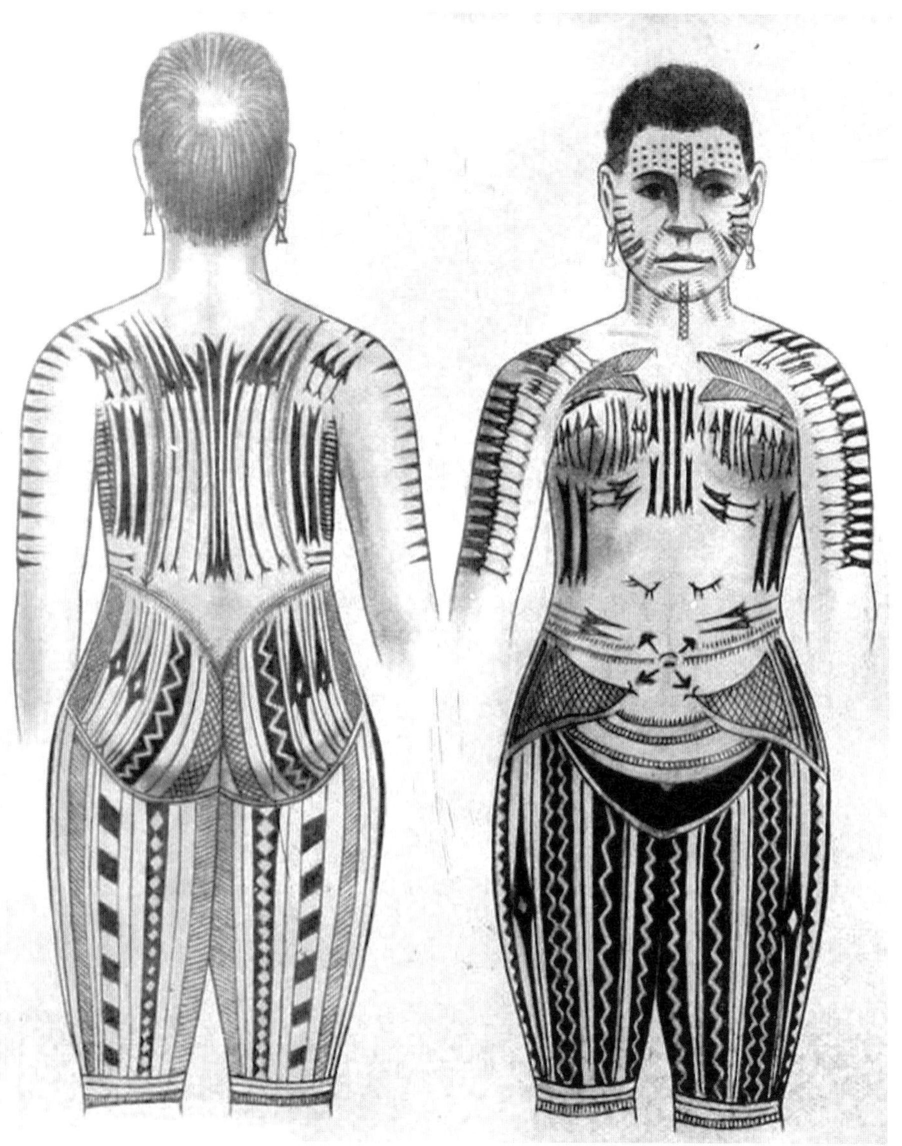

Nukumanu Woman

NUKUMANU - formerly Tasman Islands, is a medium-sized atoll of Papua New Guinea, located in the Southwestern Pacific Ocean. Peoples practiced tattooing.

NUI– term for tattoo, Ainu, Japan.

NUYE - Inuit meaning "tattoo".

NVIRI-OTU – black soot in which a tattoo knife was dipped, Fang tribe, Nigeria.

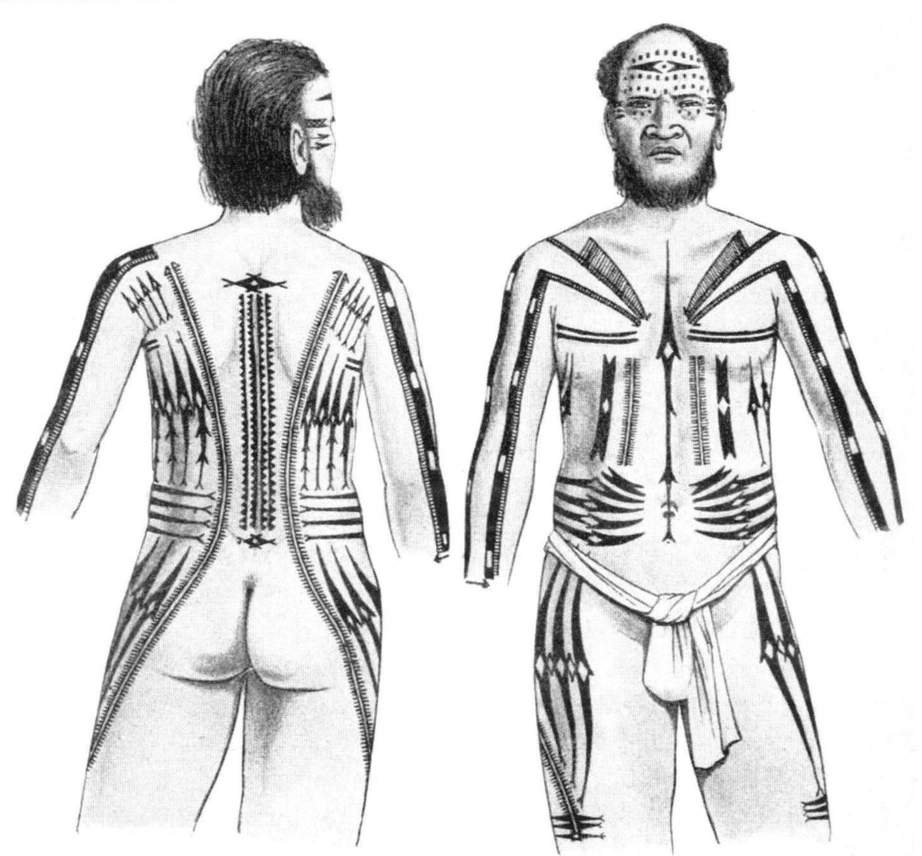

Nukumanu Man

´OLE´AU – tattoo instrument. It is usually used in four different widths, depending on the dimensions of the tattooed area. The device contains a short shank on a bamboo or other light wood called "au", on one end there is a turtle shell vertically bond by coconut shell fibres. On the wide end of this tortoise-shell, there are sharp dorsal ridges that were originally made of killed enemies' bones, Samoa.

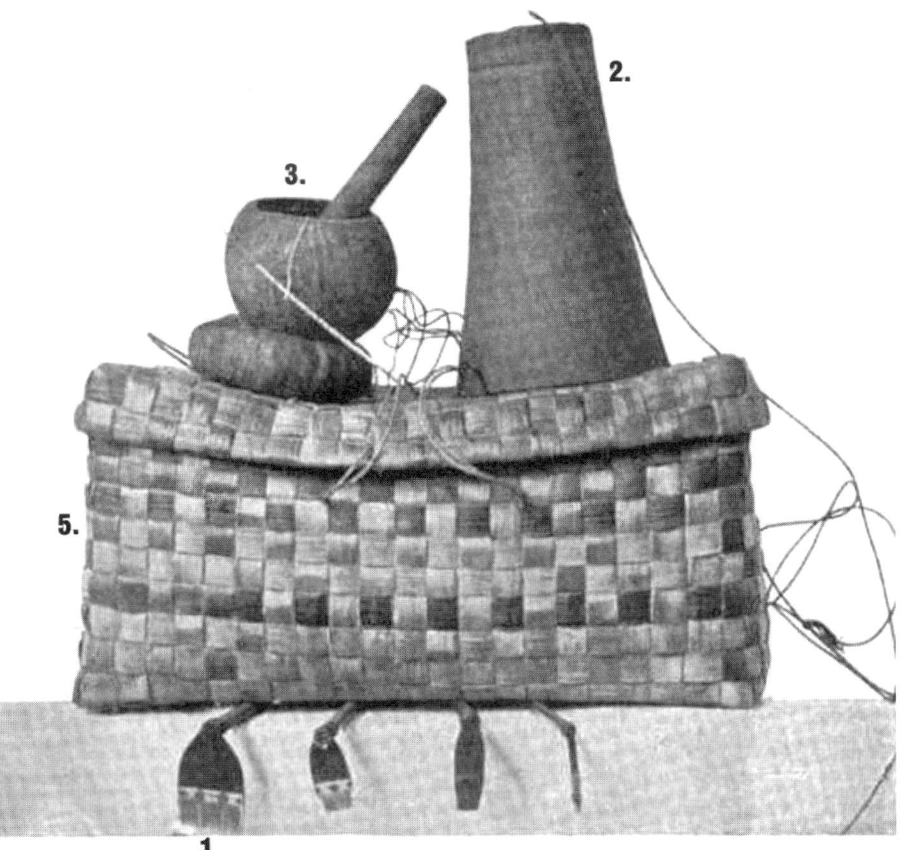

1 . ´o le ´au, 2. Tunuma 3. Ipulama 4. Sausau or ´auta 5 ´ato laupaogo

´O LE TUFUGATOSI´AU (O LETUFUNGATOST AU) – the tattoo tools maker, Samoa.

´OSO TAPU – the food that was brought before the tattoo began, Samoa.

O´ CONNEL, JAMES F. - was an exceptionally significant discoverer and researcher whose voyages and mainly published works have distinctly improved the knowledge about the Earth. The Cook work was significant. He kept careful notes on all the journeys which were printed during his lifetime as well as after his death. He was a member of the Royal Society and was awarded its golden medal. All Cook's expeditions were

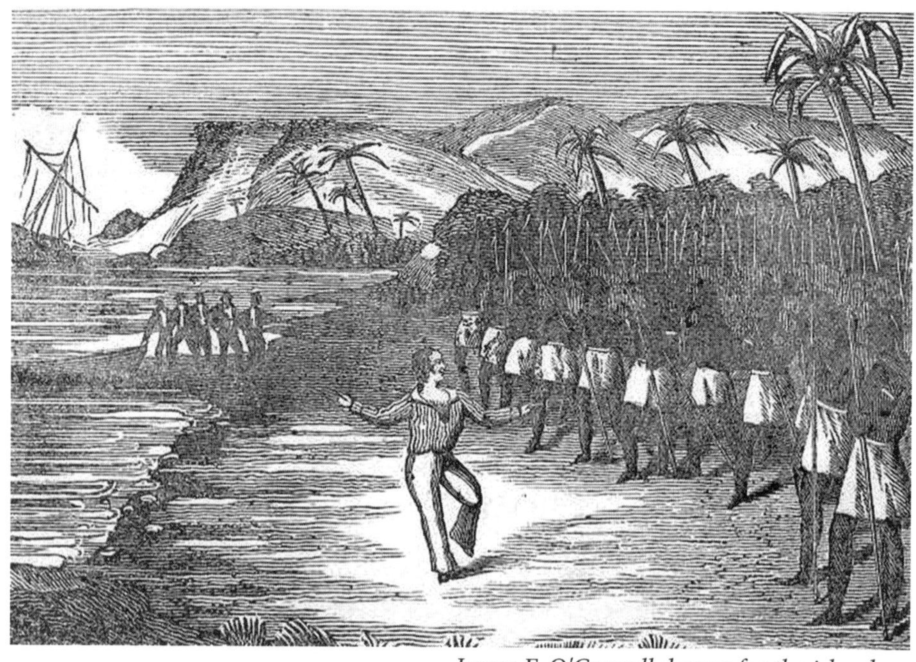

James F. O'Connell dances for the islanders

attended by significant scientists of their time and, thanks to their contribution, humanity has been enriched by a great number of new findings, including tattoos.

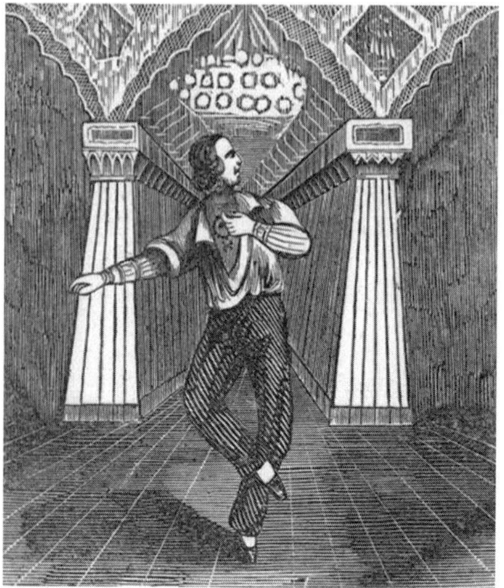

From the book: The life and adventures of James F. O'Connell, the tattooed man

During one of his around-the-globe journeys, this Irishman was captured; he danced an Irish dance to amuse his jailors and discourage them from eating him. The Irishman and other prisoners were taken to a ceremonial banquet and searched. When they were drinking sakau (O'Connel didn't drink it due to its unpleasant taste) and eating a roasted dog, one of the chieftains adopted O'Conell and tattooed him with the traditional Pohnpei patterns. After leaving the tribe, he traveled with a circus as the "Famous Tattooed Man". He danced and showed off his tattoos to the Americans.

O LE LULU´UNGA-O-LE-TATAU – the important ceremony of O le Lulu'unga-

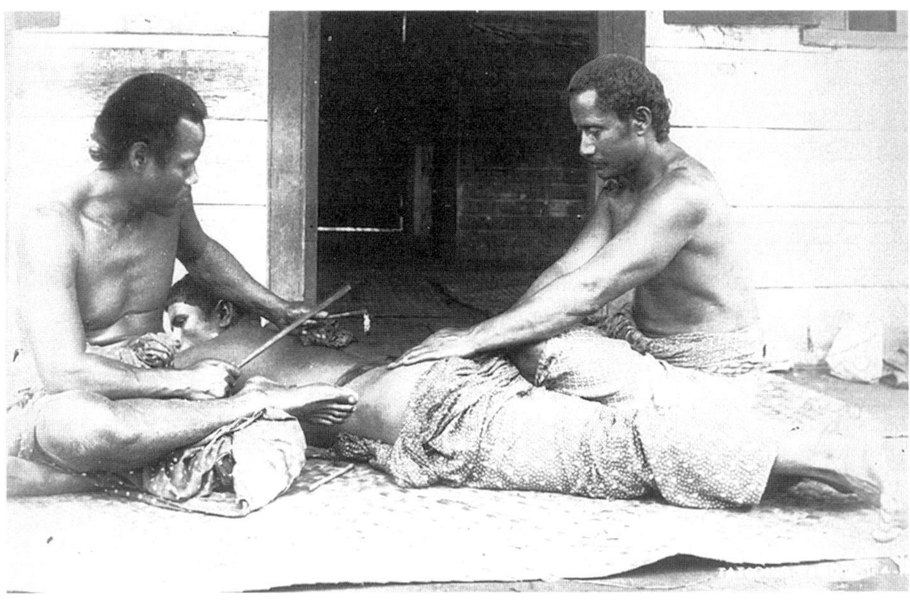

Samoan tatau-tattooing circa 1895.

o-le-tatau, the sprinkling of the tattooed. The evening before this all-important ceremony-or rite, as I almost think it may be considered-was performed, the operators and attendants provided themselves with lighted torches and proceeded to the malae, where they went through a variety of motions until, at a given signal, the torches were all extinguished simultaneously. A water-bottle was then brought out and dashed to pieces in front of the newly tattooed party, after which the torches were relighted and strict search made for the cork of the broken bottle. Much anxiety was felt respecting this cork, or rather plug, since, if lost, it was thought to forebode the death of one of the tattooed party, Samoa.

O LE TA TULAFALE - The operation of tattooing,although most painful, was submitted to by all male on attaining the age of twelve to fifteen and upwards since it was looked upon as an initiation into the state of manhood, to shun which would be a disgrace. Women especially regarded the omission of the custom with disfavour, and freely expressed their contempt for those who failed to comply with this time-honoured custom and observance. Hence it was looked upon as an important period of life, and when a young chief was to be tattooed great preparations were made for the ceremony, and often costly presents were given to the operators. A curious custom prevailed in connexion with the initiation of a young chief to this ceremony. It was customary for a number of young lads, sons of the various Tulafale of the district in which he lived, to be operated upon with him at the same time, in order that they might share the sufferings of their chief (Tale-i-lona-tingd). These lads were not only tattooed gratis at the cost of the chief's family, but, after the distribution of property to the operators had been completed, each young lad was presented with a mat. from the young chief's family, in recognition of the sufferings he had shared with his young master during the operation. This mode of tattooing was, however, rather looked down upon and spoken of contemptuously, being called O le ta Tulafale, and the markings were often carelessly done.

O LE TA TATAU – tattooing in Samoa. The operation of tattooing, although most painful, was submitted to by all-male on attaining the age of twelve to fifteen and upwards since it was looked upon as an initiation into the state of manhood, to shun which would be a disgrace. Women especially regarded the omission of the custom with disfavour, and freely expressed thein contempt of those who failed to could with this time-honoured custom and observance.

O LE TAGA FAI´ASO – designation for the second tattoo session on Samoa on the buttocks and intimate parts. The aso fa'aifo are completed around to the abdomen and the 'asolaititi are finished. Next to be added are the saemutu, which vary in number depending upon social status. A matai will have four an orator three and anyone else would have two. Where it meets the 'ivimutu at the anus it is called tafaufile, where it covers the perineum it is called tasele, where it covers the scrotum it is called tafumiti and the area over the penis is called tafito. Needless to say this is very painful.

O LE TAGA TAPULU - (back and small of the back) In the first session the height to which the tattoo will rise is decided (Ano le Tua), this is always such that the top of the design will show above the lavalava. Then the va'a, pula tama and pula tele are outlined and the design filled in.

O LE TUFUNGA TA TALAU – tattooer, Samoa.

OJIBWE or CHIPPEWA – Native American tribe of North America. They applied therapeutic tattoos, eg against aching teeth.

O – DON - For Osage men, the honor of receiving a warrior tattoo was fraught with extreme difficulty because only those men who had achieved all thirteen sacred war honors (o-don) could ever hope to be tattooed.

ODDÉ – Caste of India. In some places, tattooing on the forehead with a central lines, dots, etc., was universally practised, because, according to the Oddé, they should bear tattoo marks as a proof of their life on earth when they die.

OHEMARA – the second class (seventh degree) of the Ariori company, whose members tattooed rings around their ankles.

OHLONE INDIANS – lived in the Pacific Coast between Baja California and the San Francisco Bay Area. Tattooing was mainly done on women and was mostly decorative, although some men did have tattoos on their arms used to measure disks used for trading. Ohlone tattoos were mostly found on the face, over the neck, breasts and shoulders.

OHO´AU – SEE OHO´AUOPOUA

OHO´AUOPOUA – special tattooing house. The oho´au tiki, together with a sleeping house and a cook house, which

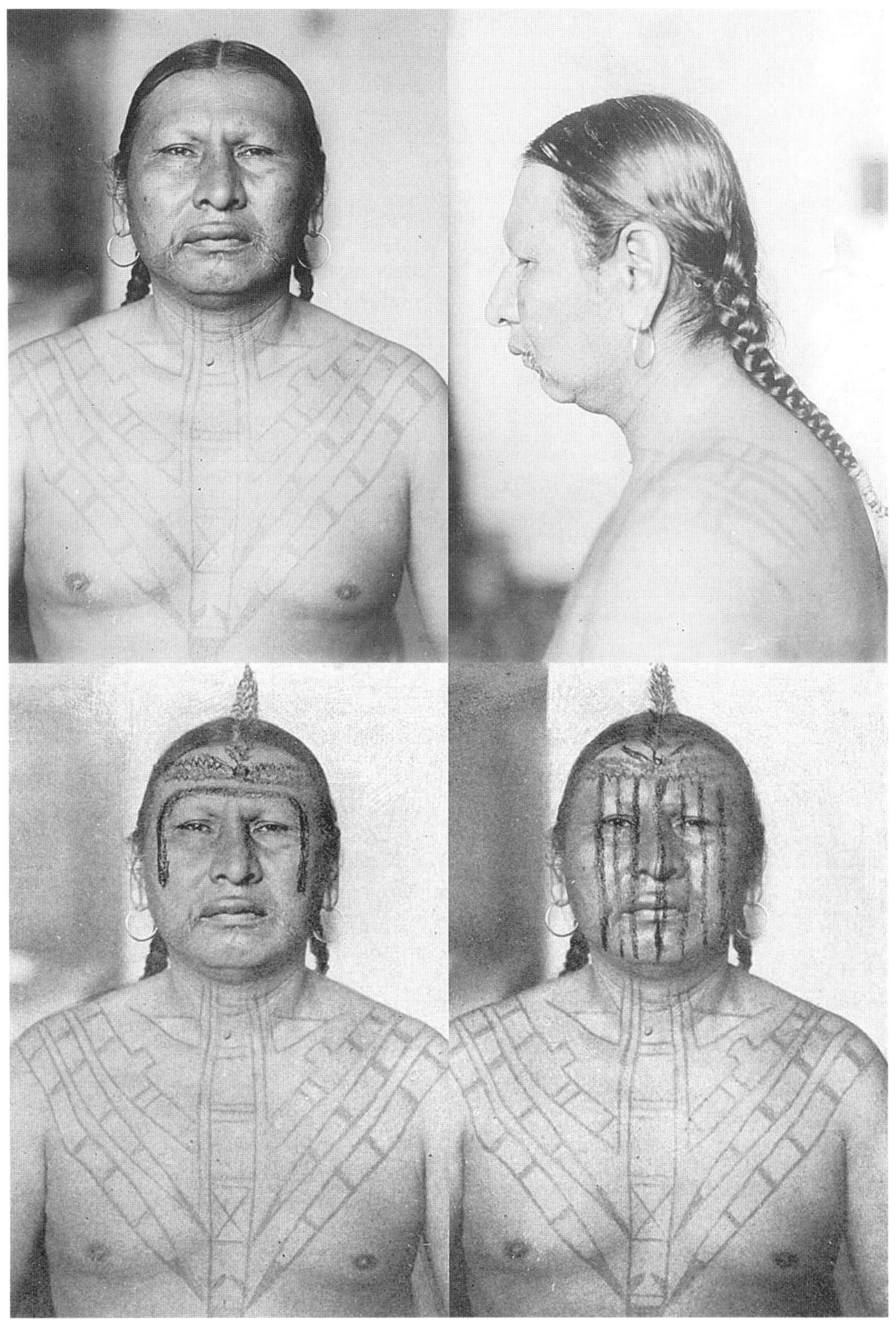

O-don tattoo of an Indian warrior

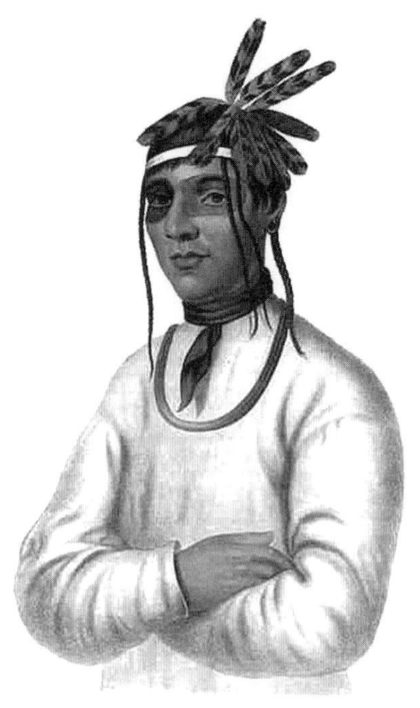

Ojibwe warrior

were placed on a stone paepae near a me'ae (sacred place), or a tohua (public place), was erected for the first-born or adopted boy (matahiapo), other sons usually being ka'ioi and achieving their tattooing piecemeal and gratis in the oho'au of the opou.

OHO´AUTIKI - Preparations for the tattooing of an opou began with the raising of pigs and planting of iite for gifts and payment for tuhuna and ka'ioi. Several days before the beginning of the operation, the father announced that the oho'an tiki, or special house for the occasion, was to be built. About one o'clock on the morning on which the erection of this structure was to take place, two great drums (pahu) and two small ones (hiitii) were beaten on the public festival place, to declare the beginning of the tapu and to summon the ka'ioi. These, usually from forty to eighty in number, immediately gathered at the festival place and together proceeded, under direction of the tuhuna, to raid the place of the opoii's father. They demolished his houses and those of his relatives, with the exception of the sleeping houses ; they seized not only material for the building of the oho'au, but that for making tapa, or the tapa itself in the event of its already having been made.

OJARIKULET INDIANS – see TRIOMETENZEN

OJANAS – Arawak tribe in Surman, magical scarification and tattooing.

OKENGENG – tattoo knife, Fang tribe , Nigéria.

OKU MAEBA – expression for: my tattoo, but the wearer did not mention the tattoo artist, Bellona Island.

OLOMURARO – blue-red pigment for tattoo, Caraja tribe, Brazil.

OMAHA INDIANS - tribe of Northem America, members used to have tattoos on the chest, neck and arms. The charcoal to be used in making the coloring preparation was placed in a wooden bowl and taken to the man who was to do the tattooing. Usually one of the chiefs performed this duty. The figure was first outlined by means of a flattened stick dipped into the solution made from the charcoal; then it was pricked in with needles. Steel needles are now employed; formerly flint points were used. The needles were tied in a bunch, to which small bells were fastened; formerly the rattles of the rattlesnake were used. After

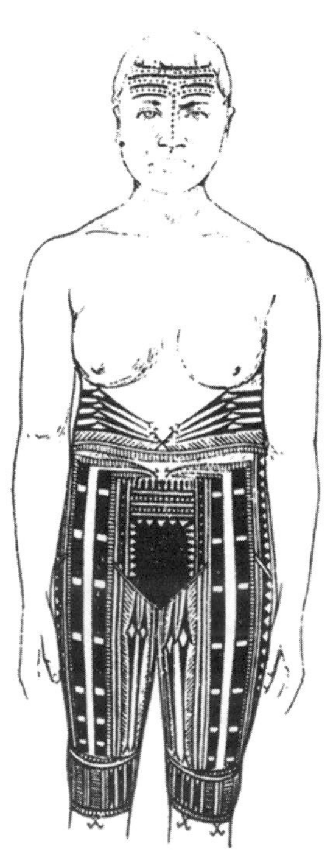
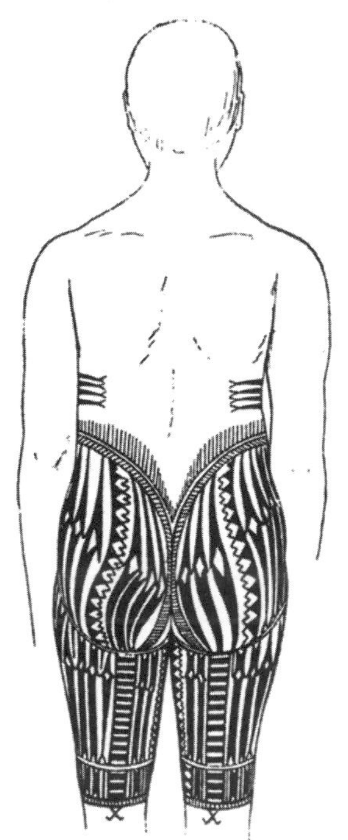
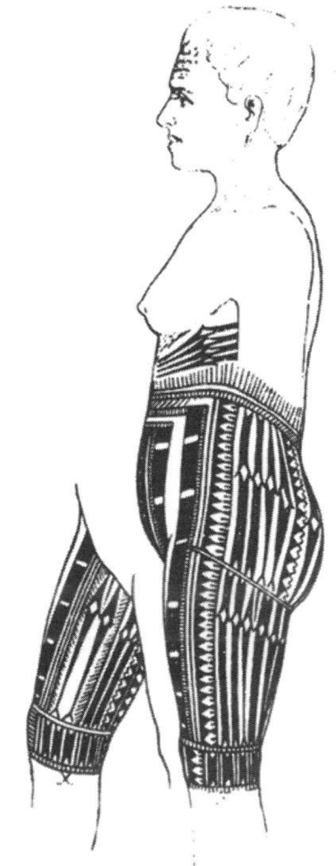

Female tattooing, Ontong Java

the pricking the charcoal was put over the surface, which was then pricked a second time. This completed the tattooing. The round spot was first put on the forehead; this represented the sun.

OMAI - (sometimes referred to as Omiah) was an islander from the southern seas (Tahiti), who in July 1774 aboard the ship HMS Adventure reached London, where he aroused the amazement of people with his tattoos. He was even introduced to the royal couple. The ship belonged to Captain James Cook's expedition.

OMÚRS - Before dádalbai begins the actual tattooing, the woman draws an outline with a coconut leaf omúrs, Palau ins.

ONDONDÓ – a fluid that was supposed to slow down the healing process of a new tattoo to have a plastic shape, Fang tribe, Nigeria.

ONIISONON – The term for "the one who creates art," that is, tattoo artist, enjoyed great recognition and attention, the Yoruba tribe, Africa.

ONTONG JAVA - Atoll or Luangiua is one of the largest atolls on earth. It is sometimes referred to as Lord Howe Atoll, not to be confused with Lord Howe Island.

OÓ-SHE-NAR – pattern sticks for marking off when decorating the face were called Oó - she - nar, Tlingit Indians.

OPATA- a tribe of northwestern Mexico

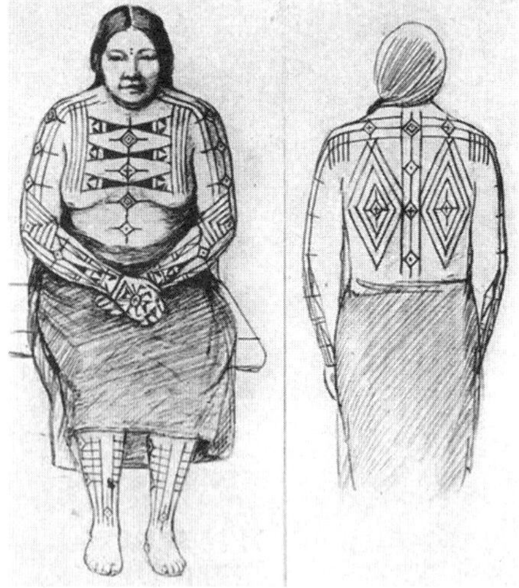

Osage women belonging to a special society had spiders tattooed on the backs of their hands and web-like designs tattooed on their arms and legs

in which women tattooed their chins and around the eyes.

ORO – the great god of Raiateji, Polynesia, who founded the secret community of Ariori.

'OROI TOTO - ('oroi, wipe; this, blood) it was a piece of cloth for wiping blood during tattoos, Aitutaki Island.

OROMO – Ethiopian tribe practicing tattoos.

OROTETEFO - one of the brothers who were commissioned by the god Oro to lead the secret community of Ariori.

OSAGE - (in their language Wa-saw-see). A Native American tribe from Northern America which shaved their heads similarly to the Pawnee and Kansa people. They put an immerse effort into decorating and painting their heads. The way the Osages deformed their skulls is also worth noting. They were doing already at the young age using a wooden plank. However, they did not deform their foreheads like the Flatheads – a Native American tribe from the north of Rocky Mountains - did, they modified the back of their heads instead. In adulthood, they had elongated heads which was perceived as a symbol of men's bravery and beauty.

They also cut their earlobes so they can hang as much tinsels and coins as possible into them. The Osages also wore a lot of necklaces and beads on their necks. Thanks to the warm clime, in which they lived, they basically wore only leggings throughout the year. They had peculiar tattoos on their naked backs, shoulders and arms.

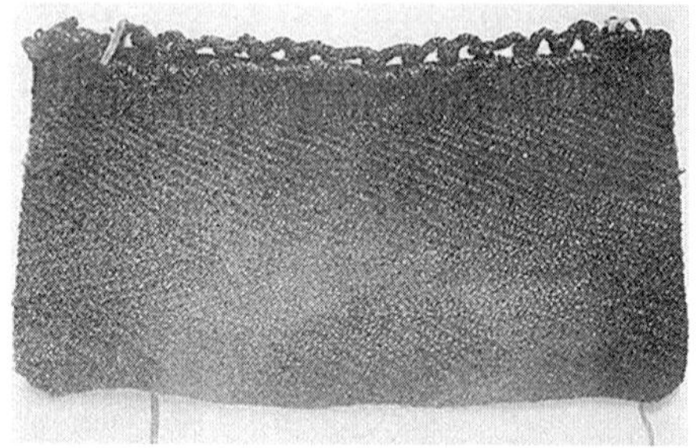

Osage - tattoo bundle

OSHIROI-BORI - Due to the poisonous nature of lead, this lead white was replaced in modern times by titanium, not for use for irezumi purposes but to be used in small quantities for tattooing of the whites in dragoneyes. This tattooing technice is then called oshiroi-bori.

OSIWU – the term for "who tattoo cuts", Bini tribe, Africa.

OSOE - A wooden or iron stick was used as a tattoo tool, to which two iron needles are tied close together. Such an instrument is called Osoe, India.

OTI´ORE – the fourth degree of the Ario´i community. Literally "unfinished". They have light marks on the ankles and wrists and darker on the arms and shoulders.

OTOE (also OTO) – a Native Americans tribe which was a part of the Siouan branch and tribes from around Missouri – a group known as Winnebago. At some point, a large part of the group had split and moved to the southwest. This group was further divided into three group – the Iowa, Missouri and Otoe people, who settled in the Nemaha river valley. They practiced tattoos.

OTOMI (also OTOMÍ) – tribe practicing body painting. The women of this tribe painted their faces yellow and various motifs on their faces in red, with a monkey predominating. They also, for example, made a blue mark on their chest (with small copper needles) that they were already getting married. They also had blue tattoos on their arms and chest, Mexico.

OTORO- a term denoting the third class of the Ariori secret community in Polynesia. Members of this class could tattoo a line on the left side of their buttocks.

OTOSINA - man with the tattooing process finished, Managalasi tribe.

OTTAWA- a term common to the Cree, Algonkin, Nipissing, Montagnais, Ottawa and Chippewa, and applied Ottawa because in early traditional times and also during the historie period they were noted among their neighbors as intertribal traders and barterers. Their bodies were much tattooed in many fashions and designs.

OTU – tattoo ink that was obtained from carbon black, Fang tribe, Nigeria.

OU BA´EMOMOSO - your blue-blacklegs (praisingtattooing), Bellona.

OUCHAM – basic Berber designation for tattoos.

OULED SISI ABID – Algerian Berber tribe. Tattooed cross on the cheek.

OVIEDO DE, GONZALO FERNÁNDEZ (1478 – 1557) - a Spain historian, author of the first and the most complex description of the Mexico conquista. In his four-volume work Historia natural de las Indias, he writes: "…they have images of demons written into their bodies in black that persist the whole life with them; by piercing skin and flesh they capture their cursed beings."

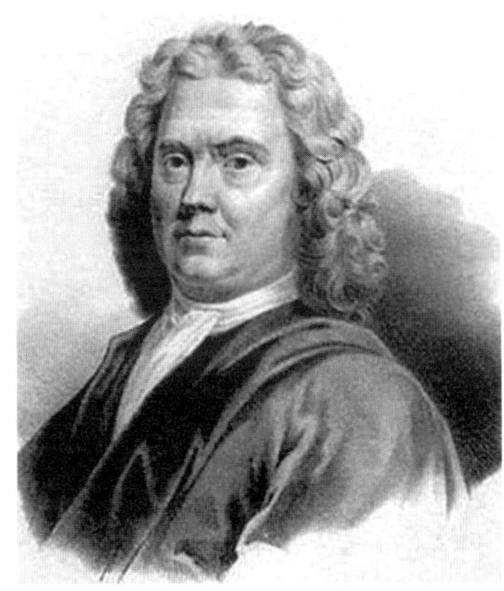

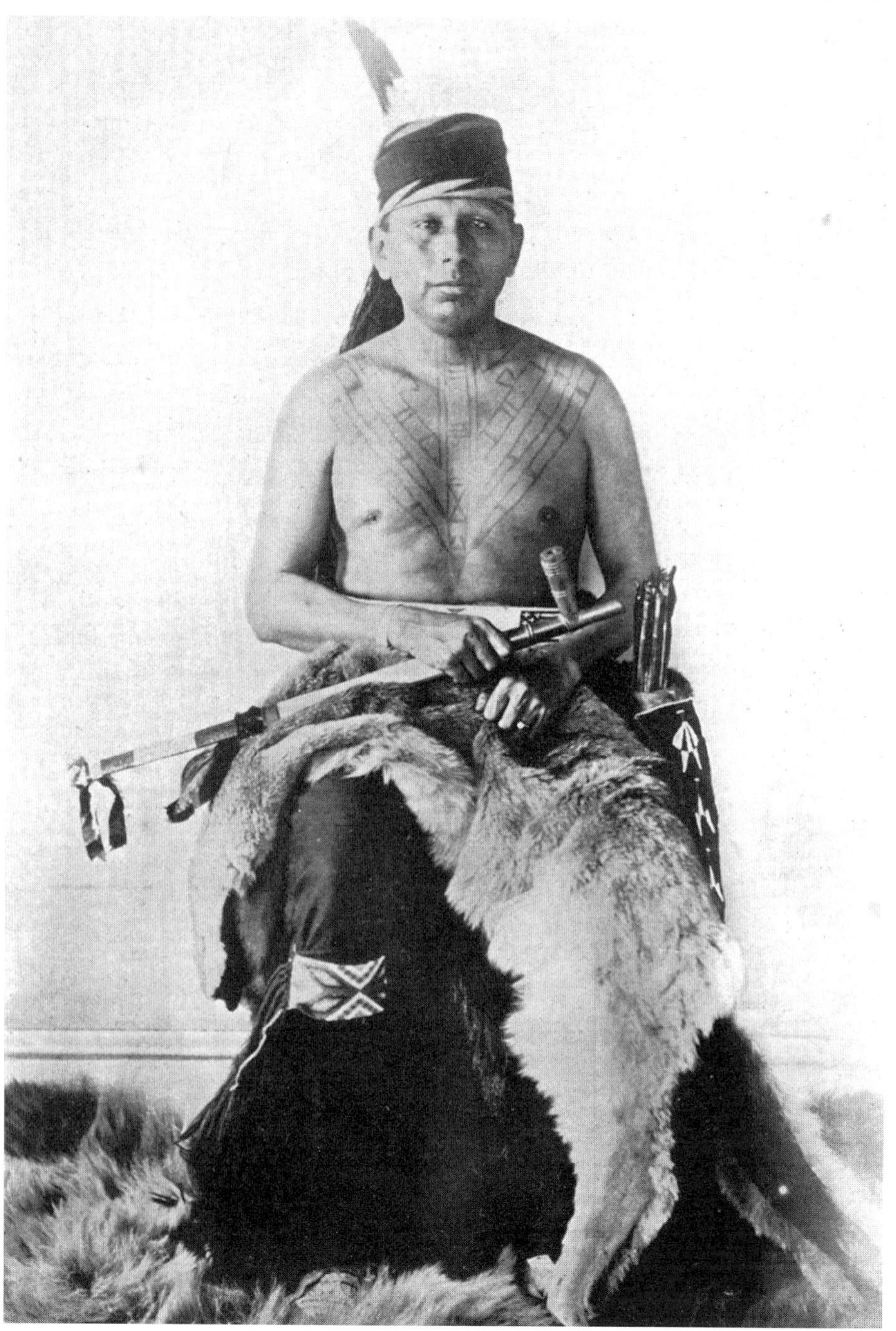

Tattooed Osage

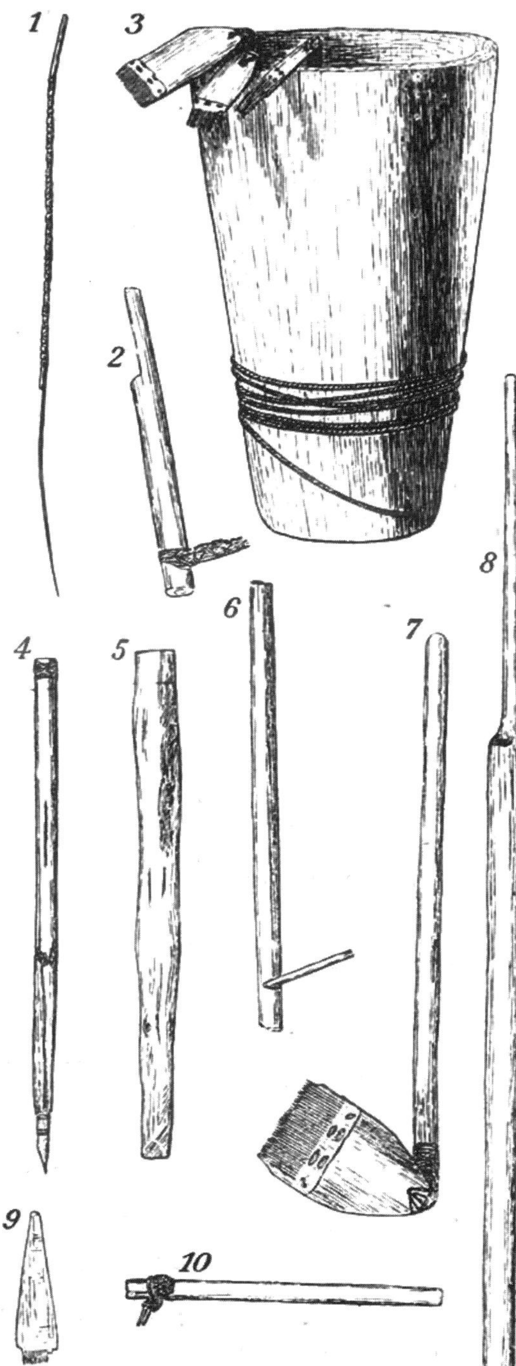

Tattoo instrument, Oceania
1 - Brush for painting the tattoo pattern (djedje), Djalut, Marshall Islands;
2 - Tattoo crest (te neirau), Gilbert Islands;
3 - equipment for storing tattoo combs, Samoa;
4 - tattoo comb, Viti Islands;
5 - Hammer for tattooing (ngi dubb), Djalut, Marshall Islands;
6 - tattoo comb (ngi buromag), Marshall Islands;
7 - Tattoohammer, Samoa;
8 - rod for hammering tattoo coats, Samoa;
9 - Tatauir Crest, Marquesas Islands;
10 - Tattoo Crest, Viti Islands

PA´EHINU – a soot-covered stone laid on a banana leaf and dried in the sun. Soot served as the basis of tattoo ink, Marquesas Islands.

PACHAIKUTHIKIRIDU – or PACHAI-KUTHU-KIRATHU – The Tamil equivalent of tattooing is pachai-kuthu-kirathu, or pricking with green. The marking ink is prepared in the following manner. Turmeric (kappa manja) powder and agathikirai (leaves of Sesbania grandiflora) are rubbed together in a Mostar or on a grinding stone. The

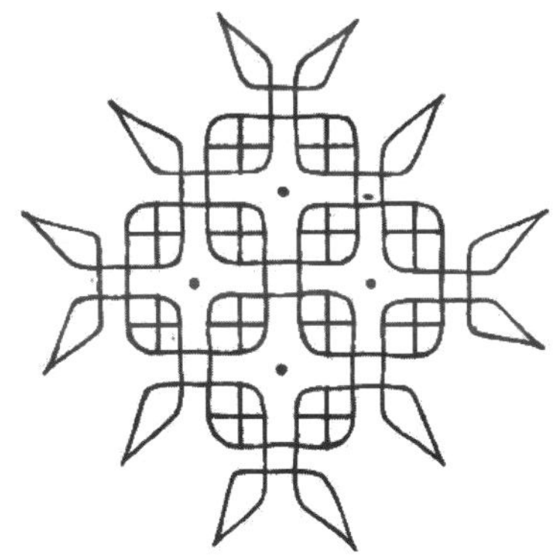

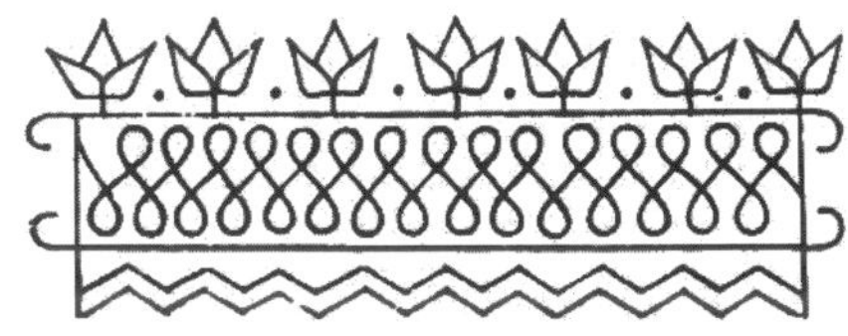

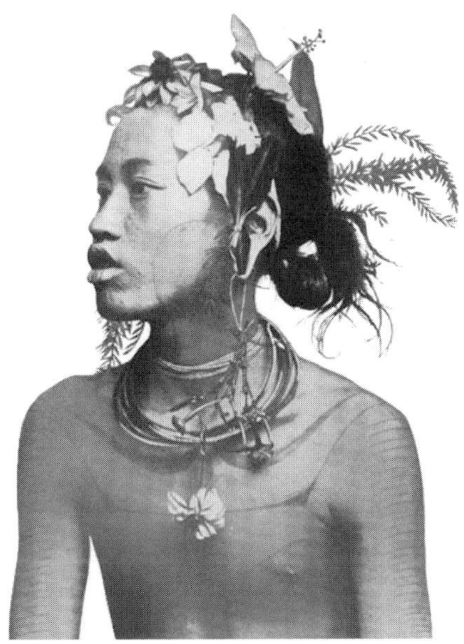

Tattooed man from Pagai Island

mixture is press on a thin cloth, and rolled up in the form of a wick, which is placed in an open lamp charged with castor-oil. The wick is lighted, and the lamp covered with a new earthen pot, on the inside of which the lamp black is deposited. This is scraped off, and mixed with human milk or water.

PAGAI- North Pagai (Indonesian: Pagai Utara) is one of the Mentawai Islands off the west coast of Sumatra in Indonesia. It is south of Sipura and north of South Pagai (or Pagai Selatan) Island.

PAHU - two great drums (pahu) and two small ones (hutu) were beaten on the public festival place, to declare the beginning of the tapic and to summon the ka'ioi.

PAIWAN – tribe practicing tattoos, warriors were tattooed on the chest, shoulders or arms. Women had tattoos

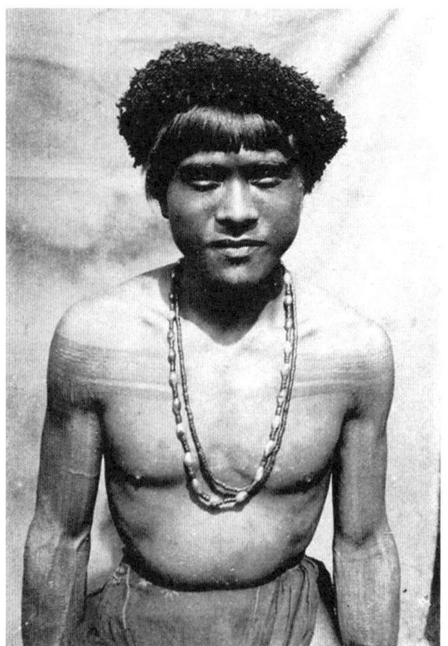
Paiwan man

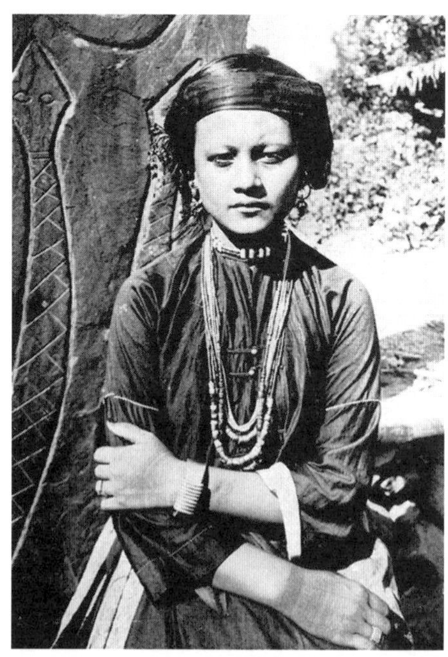
Woman of the Paiwan tribe

only on the back of their hands in the form of circles or squares.

PAKEHA MAORI – a term for Europeans living among the Maori, or white Maori.

PAKIAU – tattoo tool made of short stick with a set of fine teeth from a turtle bones, Tokelau Island.

PAKI PAKI – the preparation of the skull was called Paki Paki, or Popo, which signified taking out the brain. The heads were then steamed in the oven several times, and after each steaming were carefully wiped with the flowers of the kakaho or reed, and every portion of flesh and brain was removed, a small thin manuka stick being inserted between the skin and bone of the nose to preserve its form. This over, the heads were dried in the sun, and afterwards exposed to the smoke of their houses. The eyes were extracted, the sockets filled with flax, and the lids sewn together. The heads thus prepared were exempt from the attacks of insects, being thoroughly impregnated with pyroligneous acid. At the neck, where the head had been severed from the body, the skin was drawn together like the mouth of a bladder tobacco-pouch, leaving an open space large enough to admit the hand, as a portion

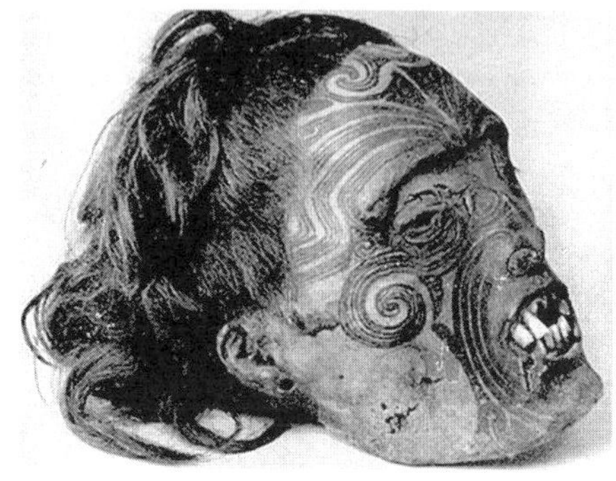

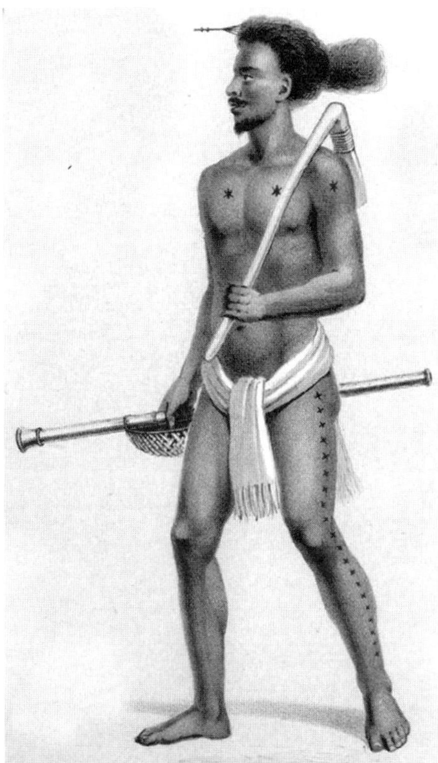

Tattooed man from the Palai island

of the base of the skull was cut away. See MOKOKAI

PAKU - The juice of the banana tree trunk was used as an ointment (paku) to speed healing, Marquesas Islands.

PALAU - (historically Belau, Palaos, or Pelew), officially the Republic of Palau (Palauan: Beluu er a Belau), is an island country located in the western Pacific Ocean. People practiced tattooing.

PANGAN - In the past, eastern groups of Semang people have beenn called Pangan.

PANGWA - African tribe practicing scar tattoo. They cut the skin with a knife and rub the wounds with hot resin.

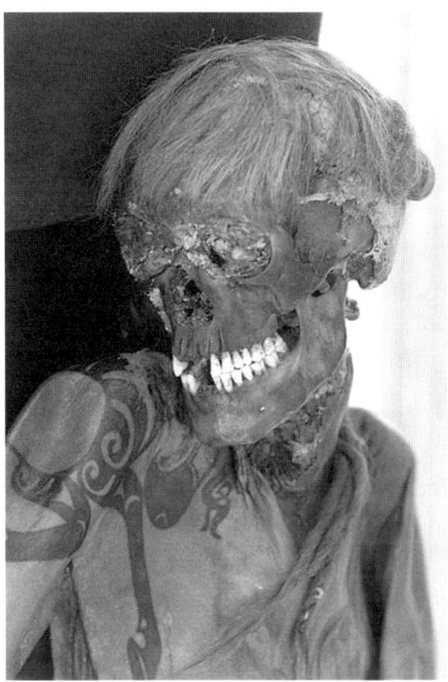

Pazyryk mummy

PAPATEA - Having no tattoo marks on the face, Maori.

PARAKIRI - means dark, distinctly defined tattoo, Maori.

PARANG – for tattooing of fingers, got a tattooist as a reward parang, a short sword, Borneo.

PARARAFA TA TAU - tapping - stick, a small thin wand made of Pathé coconuts, Tikopia.

PARATSI – Before the tattoo can be begun, the skin was scratched with an implement called a paratsi to purify the person (release “bad blood” during ritual purification ceremonies), Kayabi tribe.

PARI-BI-TETÉ - Because of the distinctiveness of the Apiaka facial tattoos, the Apiaká are sometimes referred to as "Black Faces", while the

Mundurukú sometimes call them Paribi-teté, which means "non-Munduruku painted lip Indian".

PARKINSON, SYDNEY (1745 – 1771) – created the first sketches of Maori warriors during Captain Cook's voyage.

PAROJA – Indian tribe from the Orissa region. Women practice facial tattoos and numerous nose and ear piercings.

PAT-IK – a stick which hammered on a handle with tattoo needles, Kalinga.

PAT´AWAT – The Pátawat squaws tattoo in blue free narrow pinnate leaves particularly on their chins, and also lines of small dots on the backs of their hands.

PATASAN - tattoo artist. All had been girls. The sacred artwork was handed from mom to daughter, Hawaii.

PATAWAT - In some tribes of Californian Indians, such as the Karok and Patawat, the women tattooed three narrow leaf-shaped marks on their chins.

PATIK – in some places in the Philippines the term for tattooing (in general).

PAUK-KERSH– tattoo in the language of the Yu´-rok tribe.

PAWNEE PIQUCS – a confederacy belongign to the Caddoan family. Tattooing was seldom practiced. „Pawnee Piqucs "was derived from their custom of „picturing" or tattooing the body.

PAZYRYK MUMMIES - Excavations performed in the last century near Altai in Siberia uncovered several graves. Among other items, tattoos were discovered on two bodies. Bright blue, well-crafted for that time, capturing wild animals and various mythical creatures.

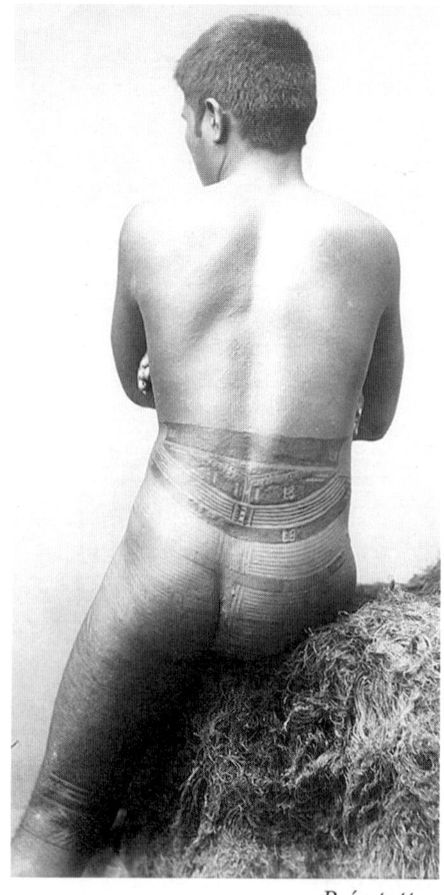

Pe´a tattoo

The depth in the skin into which these tattoos were created points out using the puncture technique instead of cutting, which was common for the Inuit people and different Siberian tribes. Tattoos are located on the shoulders, arms, and legs of the mummies. It is not entirely clear if they served purely decorative purposes, magically protective measures, or both.

PE´A – is the popular name of the traditional male tattoo on Samoa, also known as the malofie. The process is extremely painful.

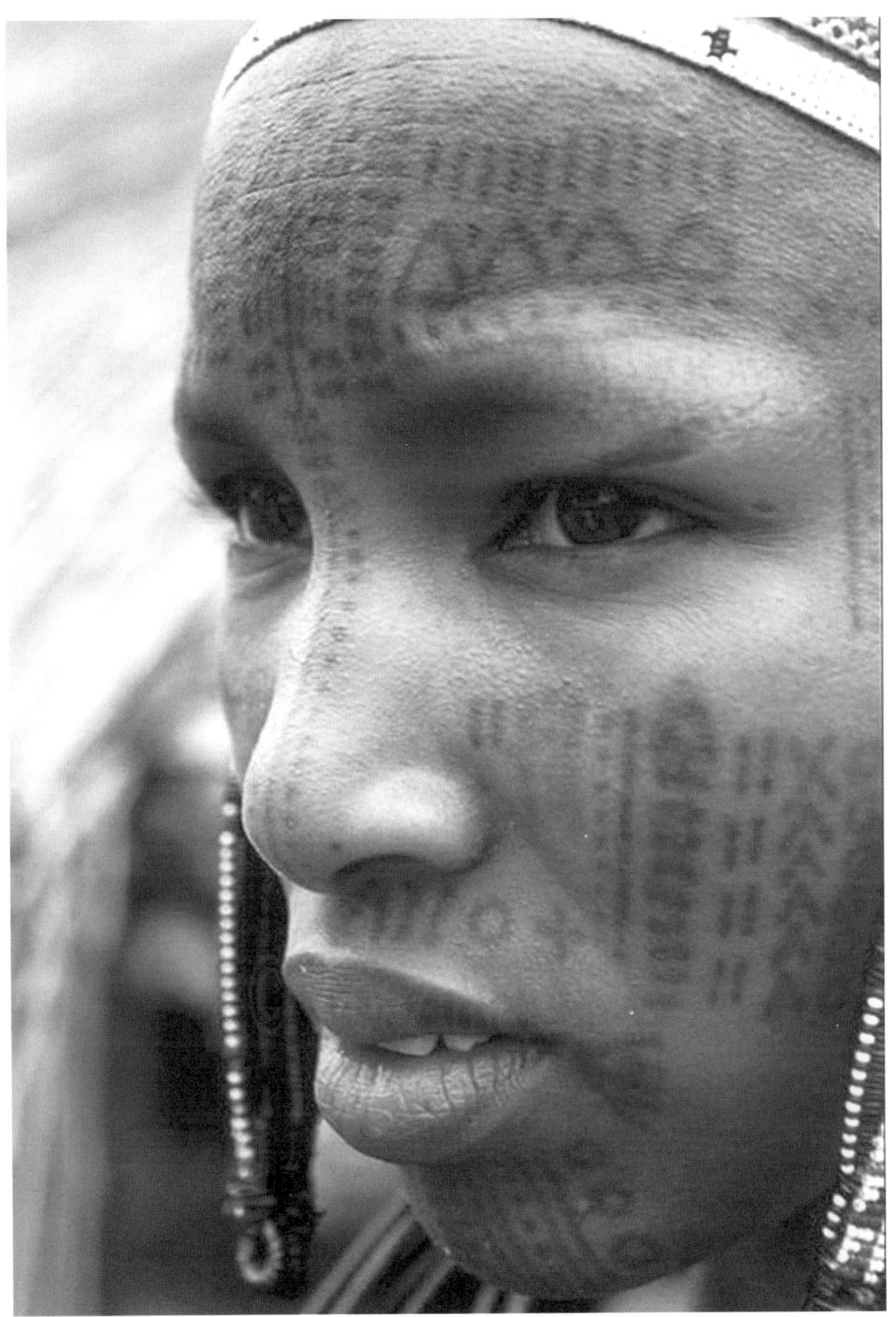

Peul woman covered with facial tattoos

PE´A MUTU – Those who begin the tattooing ordeal but do not complete it due to the pain, or more rarely the inability to adequately pay the tattooist, are called pe'a mutu, a mark of shame.

PEE-CHIM-AH-NACE - the last woman from the Ochapowace reservation (North America) with tattooed lines.

PENAN - Forest nomads are a nomadic group inhabiting mainly the Malaysian state of Sarawak. We can also find them in the Sultanate of Brunei and in Kalimantan, the Indonesian half of Borneo. The Penans are divided into western and eastern branches, divided by the Baam River. Penans practice tattoos and piercings.

PEPAK- an iron striker, tukun or pepak, kept in a wooden case, bungan, Borneo.

PETUN – an Indian tribe from an Iroquois language family. The book Tattoos of North American Indians says: „some have the body and face tattooed {gravee') with figures of serpents, lizards, squirrels, and other animals, and especially the Petun tribe, who nearly all have the bodies so covered with devices. . . . These are pricked into the surface of the flesh in the same manner as the crosses which those have on the arm who return from Jerusalem, and it is forever. These puncturings are done at different times, as they cause great pain, and often make them ill, and they have fever, and lose appetite. Still, they persist until the designs are completed, showing no outward appearance of the pain. Some women, though but few, submit to the operation."

PEUL – French designation for Fulani.

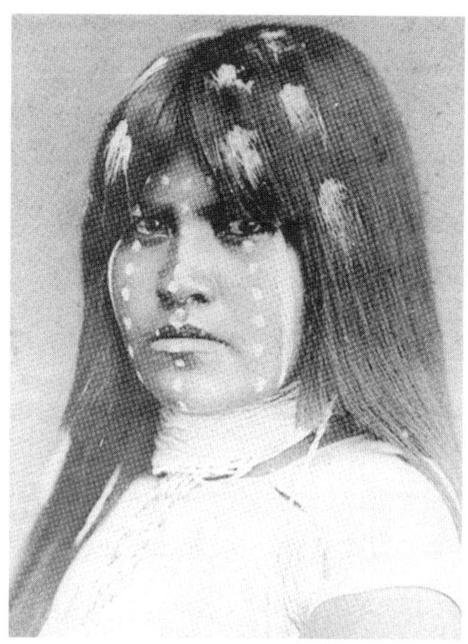

Pima girl- circa 1880

PEULO– see Fulba

PEULH – see Fulba

PHOTOHRAPHI – The older common Greek word for tattoo is photohraphi or mărka. Sometimes syli, scar, and sima, the mark are used.

PI´ILUA – The Siamese sisters, aka the

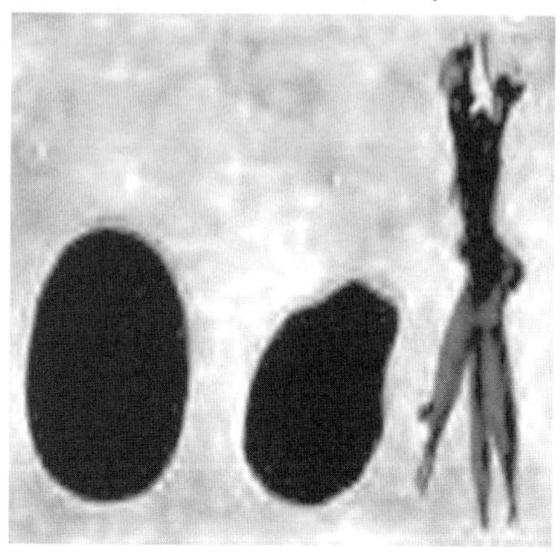

Pima Tattooing outfit

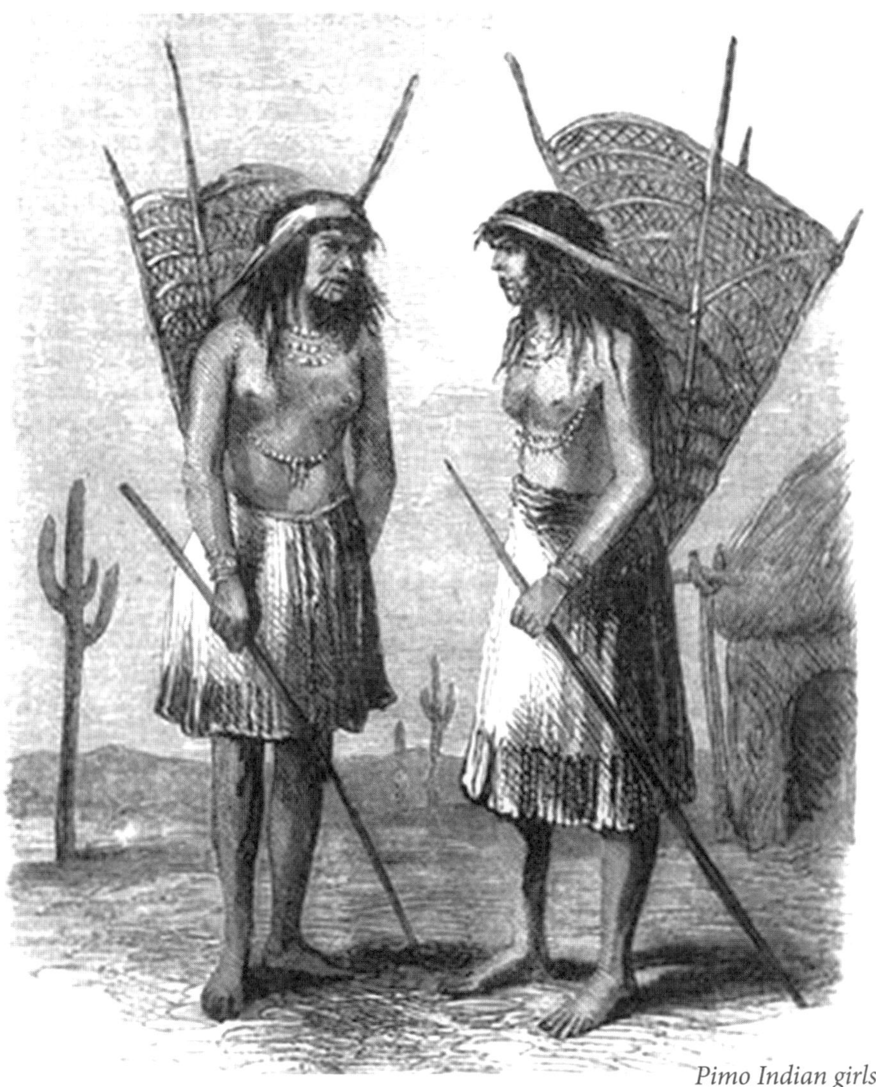

Pimo Indian girls

goddesses of tattoos, brought the first necessary tattoo tools from the islands of Fiji to Samoa. Along the way, they mistook the motto, and instead of "Tattoo a women, not men," they said, "Tattoo the men, not women." Therefore, women in Samoa were not tattooed, while in Fiji they are.

PI or ADUPI – tattoo process, Hidatsa Indian tribe.

PI or KIPI – tattooing, Hidatsa Indian tribe.

PICTI – painting, the Latin word used to name the Celtic nation of Picts, which lived in central and northern Scotland until the 10th century. In 600 AD Isidor

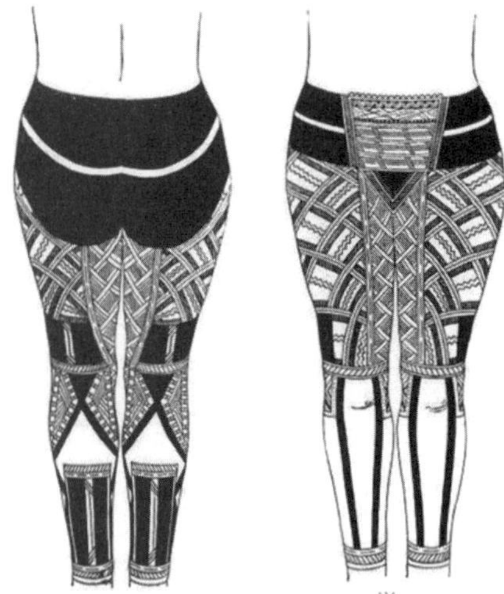

Tattoo, Pohnpei island

of Seville wrote: "The Pict Race bears a name derived from your bodies. They are littered with small needles with squeezed sap from local plants ..."

PICTS– it was the people of present-day Scotland who got their name from the custom of painting their bodies white and pale blue, from pictus - painted in Latin.

PIMA – Among the Pima of Arizona „the older women have tattooed lines on the chin, and frequently a single line from the external angle of each eye backward. The young neither tattoo nor paint."

Dr Frank Russell told us ' of the Arizona Pima :

"A few lines were tattooed on the faces of both men and women. Thorns and charcoal were used in the operation. The thorns were from the outer borders of the prickly-pear cactus; from two to four were tied together with loosely twisted native cotton fiber to enlarge the lower portion to a convenient size for grasping, while the upper end was neatly bound with sinew. The charcoal, from either willow or mesquite wood, was pulverized and kept in balls 2 or 3 cm. in diameter. Both men and women did the work, but the female artist was preferred, as she was more careful. Their fees were small and uncertain.

"[The lines] were drawn on the face first with dry charcoal, then some of the powdered charcoal was mixed with water, and the thorns were dipped into this and pricked into the skin along the outlines. As the operation progressed the face was frequently washed to see if the color was being well pricked in. Two operations were necessary, though it sometimes took more; one operation occupied an entire day. For four days thereafter the face remained swollen, and throughout that period the wound was rubbed with

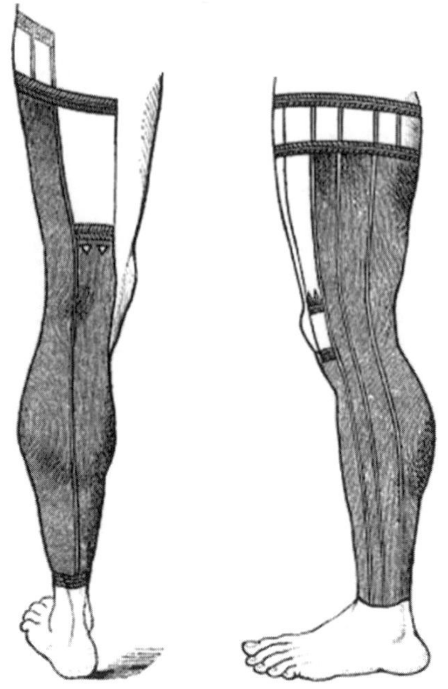

Tattoo pattern, Pohnpei

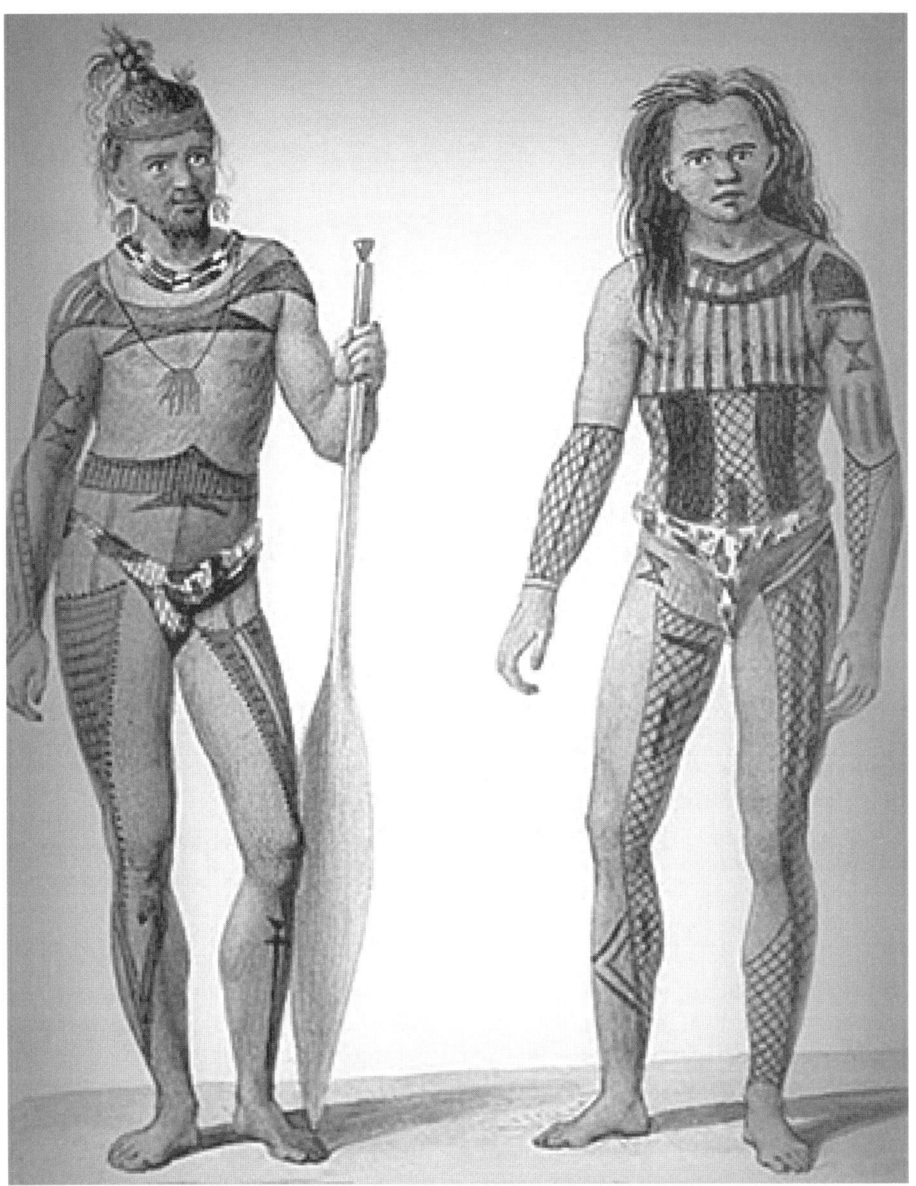

Pingelap and Mwoakilloa Islanders, Micronesia, 1826

charcoal daily. At the end of that time, a wash of squash seeds macerated in water was applied. Sometimes the lips were slow in healing and the individual was compelled to subsist upon Pinole, as the swollen lips and chin forbade partaking of solid food; during this time the squash applications were continued.

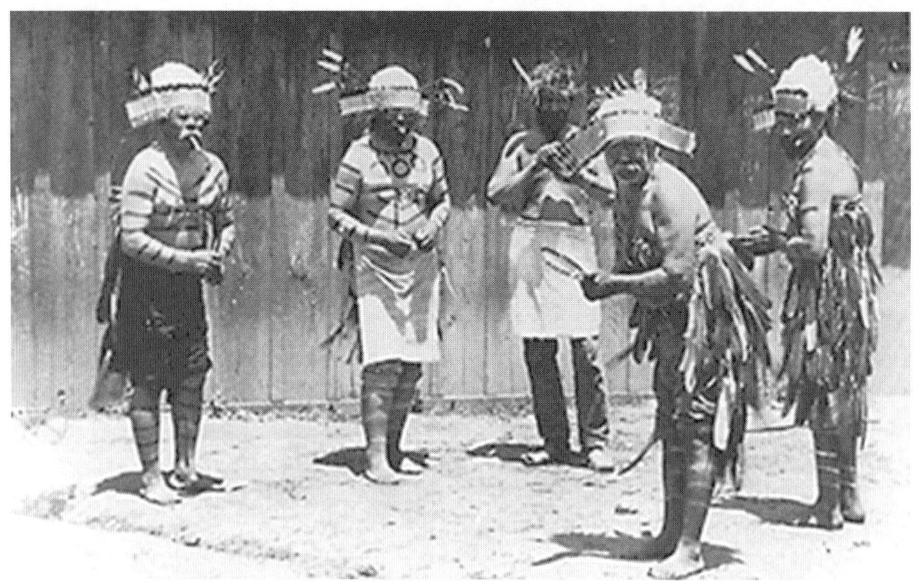

Pomo dancers

"The men were tattooed along the margin of the lower eyelid and in a horizontal line across the temples. Tattooing was also carried across the forehead, where the pattern varied from a wavy transverse line to short zigzag vertical lines in a band that was nearly straight from side to side. Occasionally a band was also tattooed around the wrist. The women had the line under the lids, as did the men; but instead of the lines upon the forehead they had two vertical lines on each side of the chin, which extended from the lip to the inferior margin of the jaw, and were united by a broad bar of tattooing, which included the whole outer third of the mucous membrane of the lip on either side.

"The tattooing was done between the ages of 15 and 20; not it would seem at the time of puberty, but at any time convenient to the individual and the operator. Oftentimes a bride and groom were tattooed just after marriage. All the older Pimas are tattooed, but the young people are escaping this disfigurement. . . .

"The meaning of the designs is unknown. The Pimas aver that the lines prevent wrinkles; thus fortified they retain their youth.

PINGELAP - is an atoll in the Pacific Ocean, part of Pohnpei State of the Federated States of Micronesia, consisting of three islands: Pingelap Island, Sukoru and Daekae, linked by a reef system and surrounding a central lagoon, although only Pingelap Island is inhabited.

PINTADERA – stamp, Central American Aztecs used special clay painting and tattoo stamps, which imprinted the required patterns on the body.

POCKQUEESEGAN - Tattoo operation, which was performed at intervals, lasts

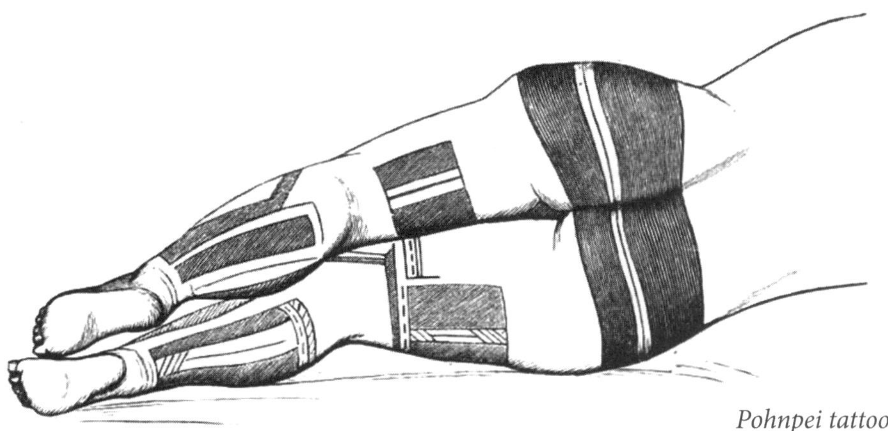

Pohnpei tattoo

two or three days. Every morning the tattooed parts were washed with cold water, in which is infused a herb called Pockqueesegan, Ojibwas.

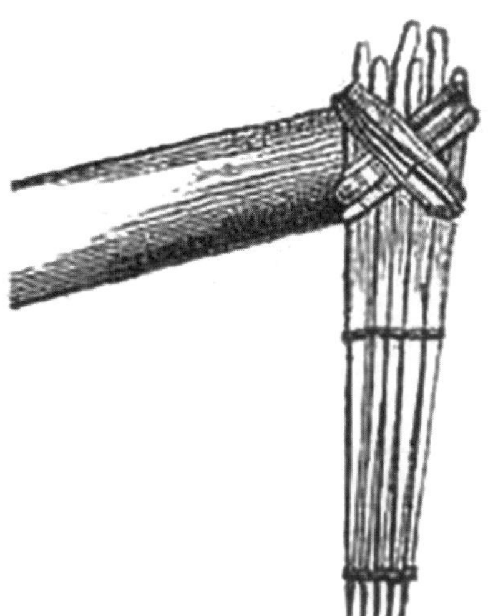

Ponape tattoo instrument

POHNPEI - formerly Ponape, high coral-capped volcanic island, eastern Caroline Islands, Federated States of Micronesia, western Pacific Ocean.

POLOSMAKOVÁ, NATÁLIA – In July 1993, a Russian archaeologist found a frozen tomb in Ukok, high in the Altai steppes on the border with China, in which lay mummified women about 25 years old with a richly tattooed body with similar motifs as in Pazyryk.

POMO – Women of this and others tribes of the Coast Range frequently tattoo a rude representation of a tree or other

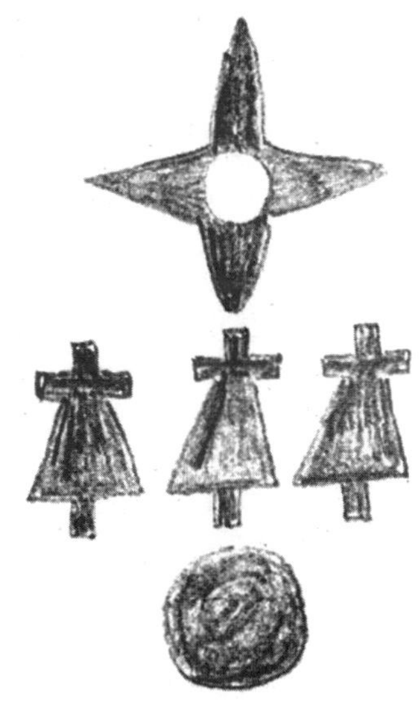

Design tattooed on hand of Ponca girl

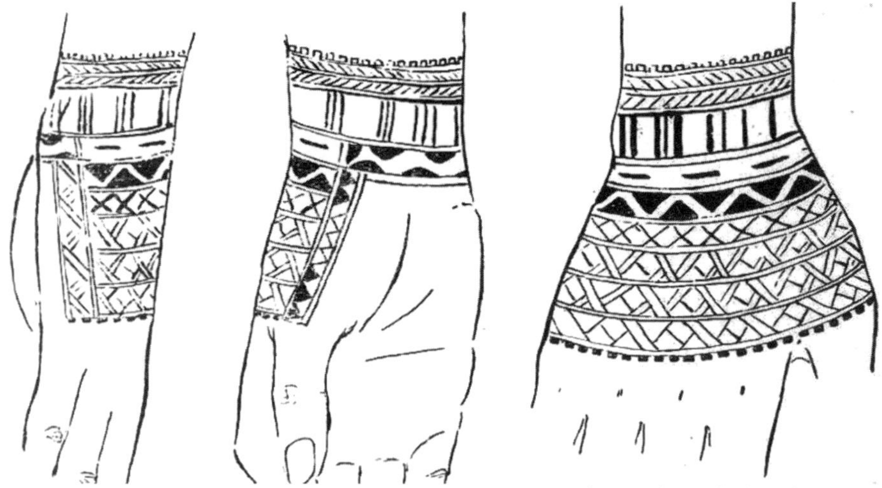

Tattoo marks on the right hand, Ponape

object, covering nearly the whole abdomen and breast.

PONAPE – a Micronesian tribe. They wore tattoos. A famous Czech ethnographic Miloslav Stingl writes about how the authentic Ponape tattoo looked like: "First of all, a Ponapian female tattooist (not only that women tattooed more often, but, within the island, their bodies were decorated by incomparably

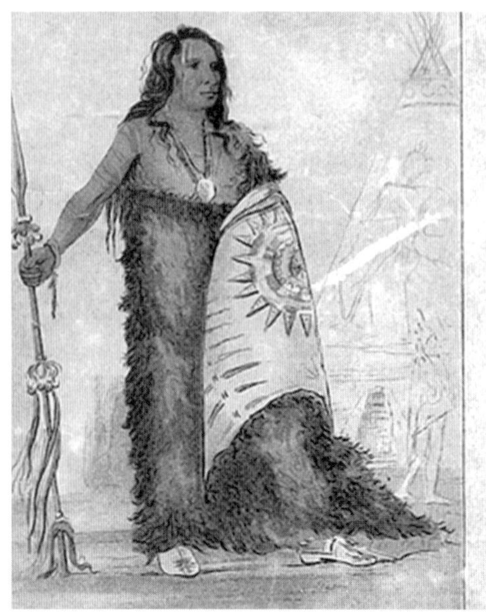

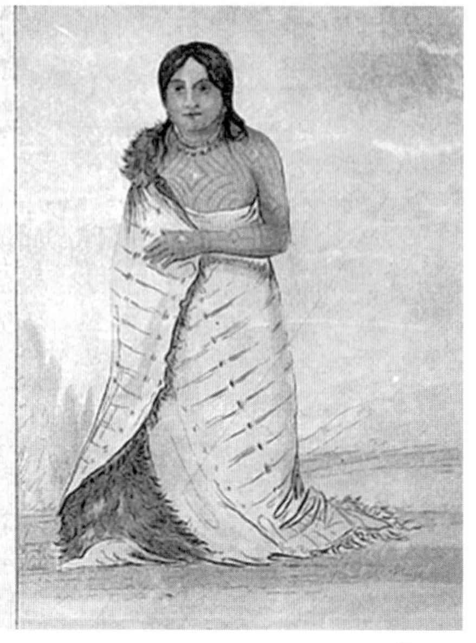

Ponca

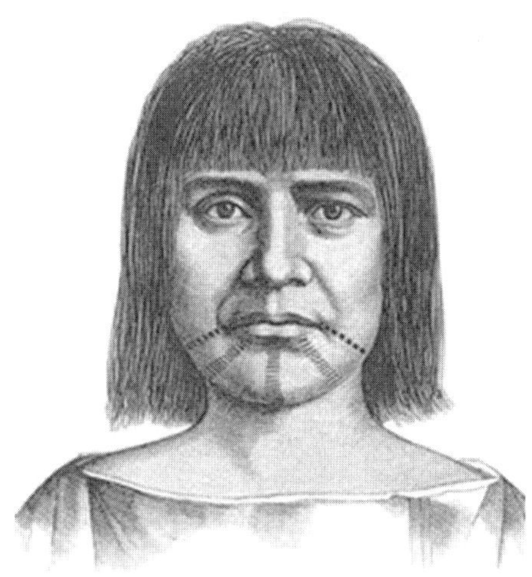

Potter Valley Tattooing

more extensive patterns) used a kaliz, which is some kind of a tattoo pen topped with a sharp thorns of local bushes. The handle of kaliz was often made of bones. The ornament itself was implemented into skin by a homemade “ink” – leneire, made of crushed Aleuritastriloba nut blended with coconut oil. They tattooed the Ponape men’s arms with several strip bracelets, as well as their own arms - similarly with several stripes. While during the decorating of the upper limbs, the tattooist could work according to her own taste, however, the decoration of the lower had a strict order: each leg was always divided into four areas filled with prescribed patterns. For example, the second area always had to be decorated with an ornament called “the tar leaf” (Lap en pan uot). Women used to wore richer tattoos. Almost their entire body was covered in a spectacular ornament, even in areas that cannot be mentioned

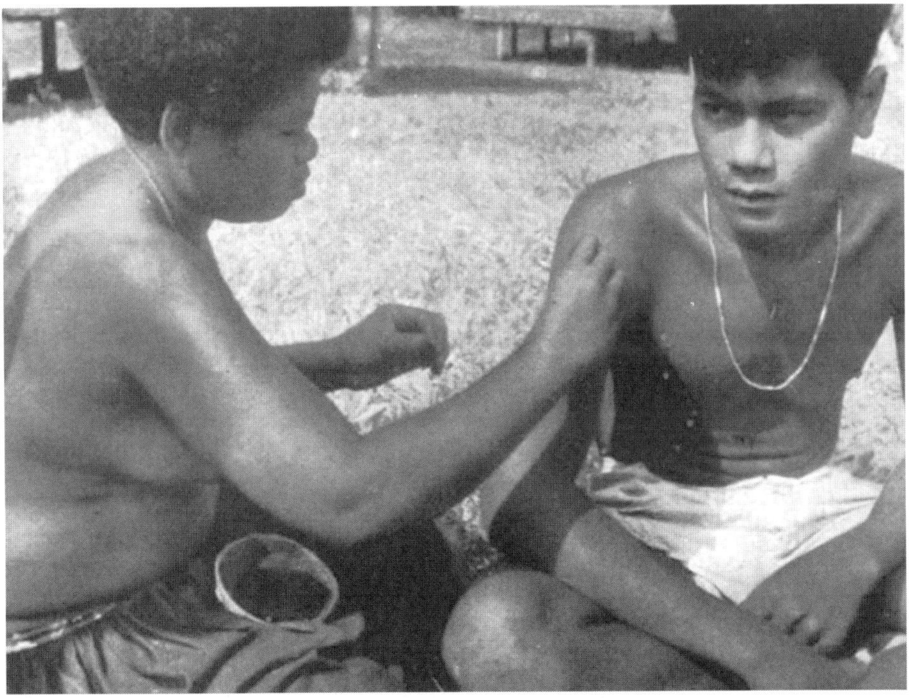

Woman painting design before tattooing, Polynesia

in a decent society at all. The inner part of thighs and a quadrangular area underbelly filled with symmetrical lines and waves were the most complicated part to tattoo."

Moreover, the Ponape men practiced hemicastration – the amputation of one testicle. The Ponapians considered the self-performance of this act an expression of masculinity.

PONCA TRIBE – are a Midwestern Native American tribe of the Dhegihan branch of the Siouan language group. There are two federally recognized Ponca tribes: the Ponca Tribe of Nebraska and the Ponca Tribe of Indians of Oklahoma. Their traditions and historical accounts suggest they originated as a tribe east of the Mississippi River in the Ohio Rivervalley area and migrated west for game and as a result of Iroquois wars. The term Ponca was the name of a clan among the Kansa, Osage, and Quapaws. The meaning of the name is "Cut Throat".

POO – novice of the Ariori community.

POPORO – berries from which juice was obtained, which was mixed into the ash. This mixture served as a color for tattoos on Easter Island

PORONNO – tattooist, (moronno: tattoo; ronno: figures, tattoos), Indie.

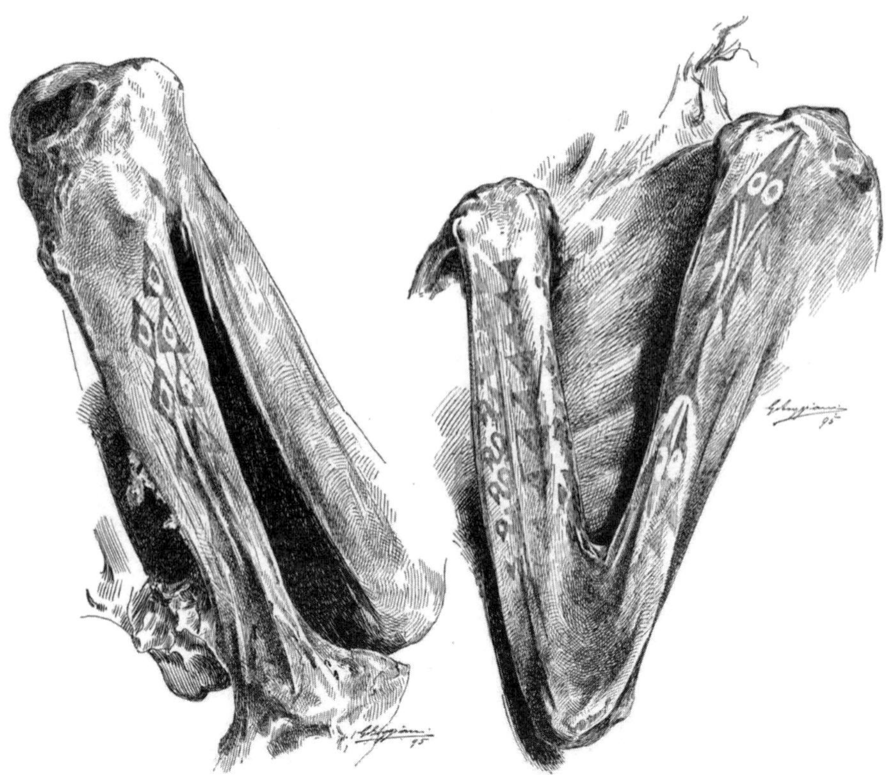

Mummy from Peru, museum of ethnography Rome, painting of the genipa

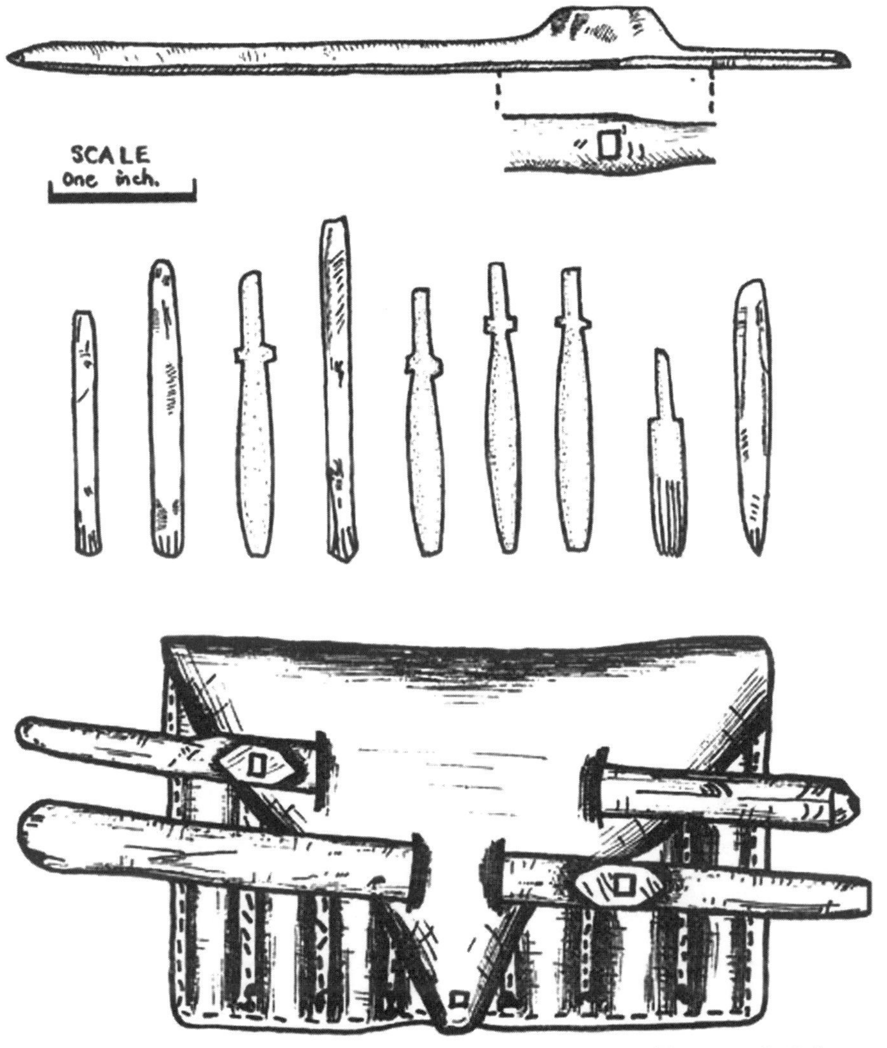

Tattoo tools, Polynesia

QIA – In Viti tattooing was called qia and as it is confined to women, so the operators are always of the same sex. An instrument called a "tooth," consisting of four or five fine bone teeth fixed to a light handle six inches long, is dipped in a pigment made of charcoal and candle-nut oil ; the pattern having been previously marked on the body, the lines are rendered permanent by the blackened comb, which is driven through the skin in the same manner as a fleam, though with less violence. Months are often occupied in the process, which is painful, and only submitted to from motives of pride and fear. Feasts are held also in connection with this. The command of the god affects but one part of the body, and the fingers are only marked to excite the admiration of the chief, who sees them in the act of presenting his food. The spots at the corners of the mouth notify, on some islands, that the woman has borne children, but oftener are for the concealment of the wrinkles of age, Fiji.

QING – one of the ancient Chinese terms for tattoos.

QUAPAW – a tribe lived on the west side of the Mississippi River. Bossu gives interesting details of his adoption by the Arkansas (Quapaw), and the tattooed mark of a roebuck imprinted on his thigh. He was seated on a tiger-skin; some straw was burnt, and the ashes mixed with water. The lines of the roebuck were drawn with this mixture, which was then pricked deep into the flesh with needles, till the blood came, which mixed with the ashes and made a figure which never could be effaced. He was next placed on white skins, and they danced and shouted

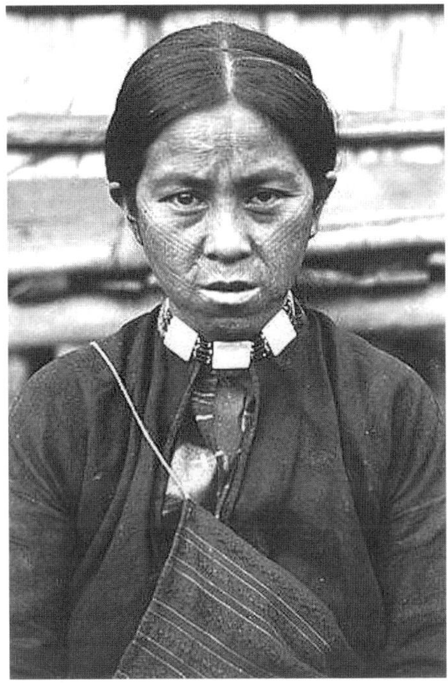

Woman of the Ayatal tribe

for joy before him. The calumet was smoked. They told him that all their allies would welcome him as a brother when he showed his mark. The operation was very painful, and he had a fever from it for a week. It was the mark of a warrior and chief.

QÚ′M - a decoration (e.g. a tattoo), Xoo (last member of the family Bushman languages, southwestern Botswana)

QUWAR – reed scraper used to remove leaking blood during tattooing, Atayal tribe, Taiwan.

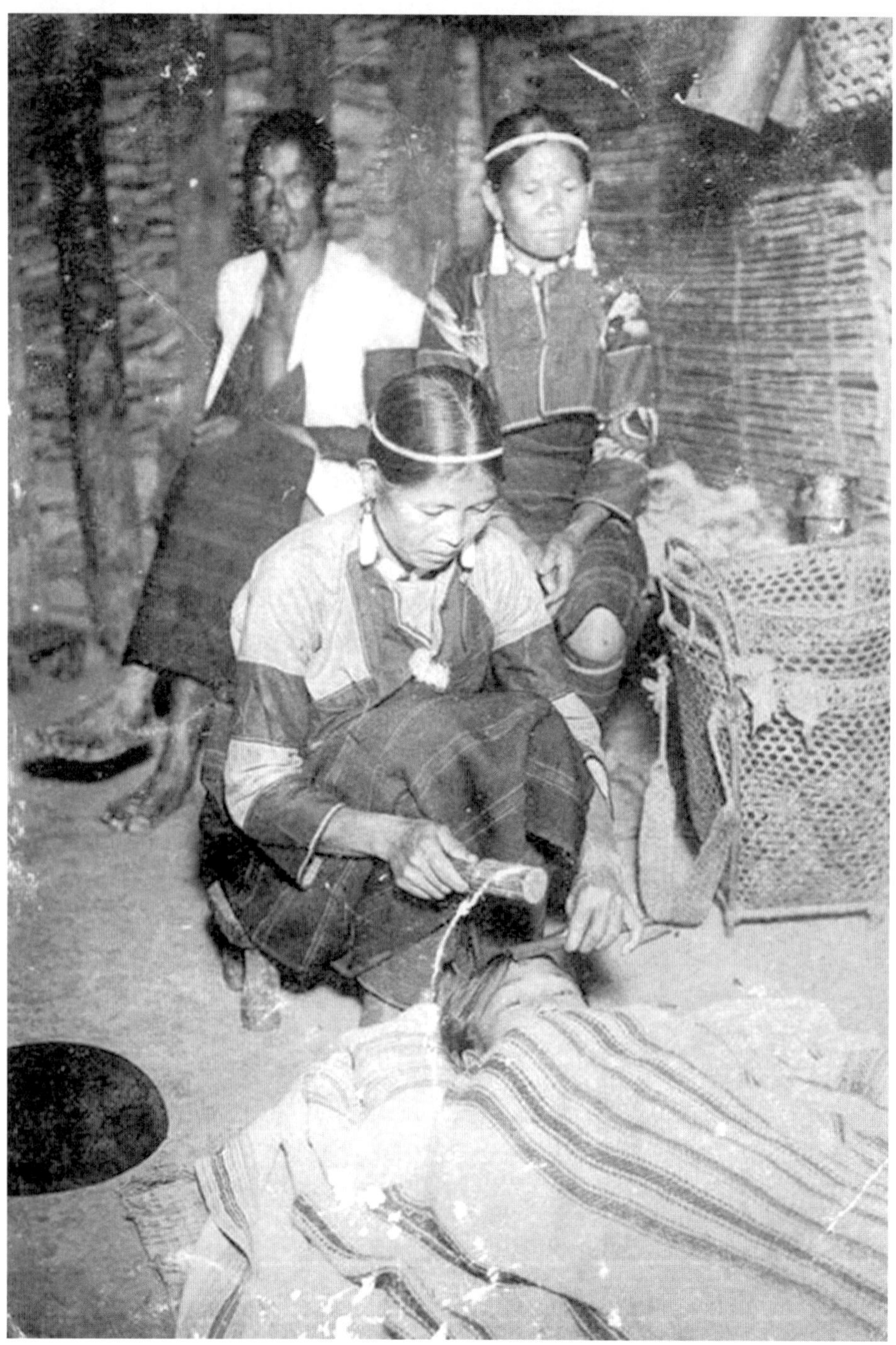

Atayal tattooing process

RAANKE – coconut grater used for final meal after completed tattoo, Marshall Islands.

RABARI– tribal community living in several areas of India and Pakistan. Women wear heavy brass earrings that hang from their ears and stretch their earlobes. They tattoo magic symbols on their breasts, neck and arms. Names such as Desai, Dewasi, Hiravanshi, Rebari, Rebadi and Rayka or Raika are also used for them.

RAIKA – see RABARI

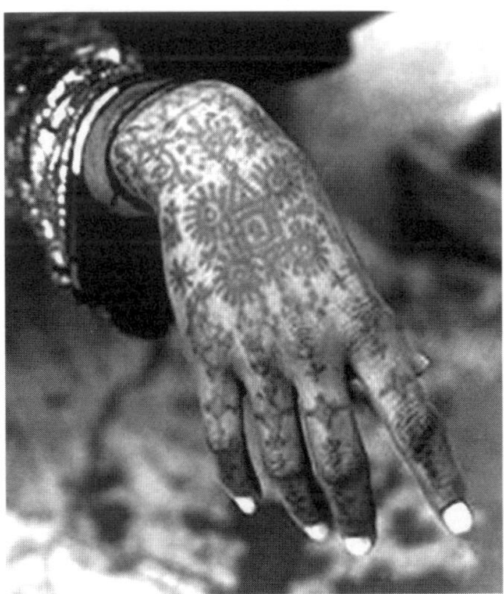

Traditional rabari tattooing

RAKAUPAPA – wooden tool used in tattooing, Aitutaki island.

RAKAUPATUPATU – see RAKAUPAPA

RÁMA - according to legends, the king was physically present in this world. His existence is described by one of the oldest Indian eposes. Rama is one of the most famous persons of Vaishnavism and,

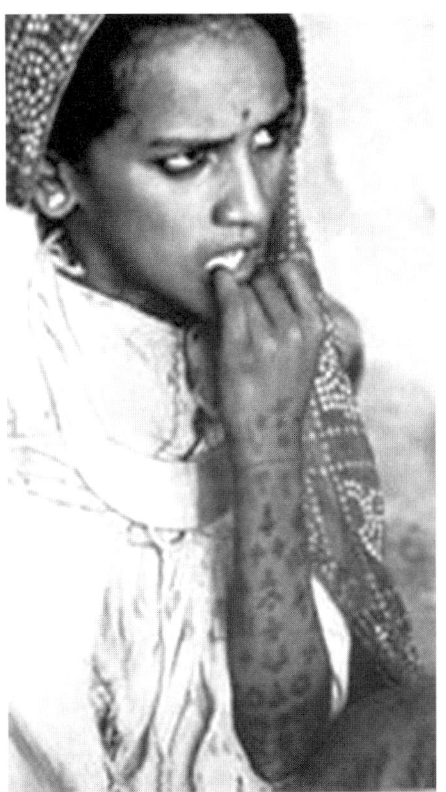

Rabari

according to traditions, he is the seventh incarnation (out of the ten most famous) of god Vishnu. In Reflex journal, his current followers were described as follows: "The followers of the Rama cult worship their god by spending their days working, worshiping and tattooing. Since the young age, every one of them gets the Rama name tattooed on their body. In addition to their bodies, the older members have covered entire faces, including ears, in god's name tattoos. They consider the writing on their skin the most dignified act of worshiping their gods.

RAMNAMI – The Ramnami community, scattered throughout the Indian member states of Bihar and Madhya Pradesh, began a painful custom in the nineteenth century. The name Rama in Sanskrit was tattooed on almost every inch of skin, even on the tongue and inside the lips. This practice was supposed to protect them from fanatical Brahmanas, and it is still practiced today.

RANGI-PARUHI – a person fully tattooed, Maori.

RAPA NUI – see EASTER ISLAND

RAROTONGA - is the most populous island of the Cook Islands.

RATAK - The Ratak Chain (Marshallese: Ratak) is a chain of islands within the island nation of the Marshall Islands. Ratak means "sunrise". It lies to the east of the country's other island chain, the Ralik Chain.

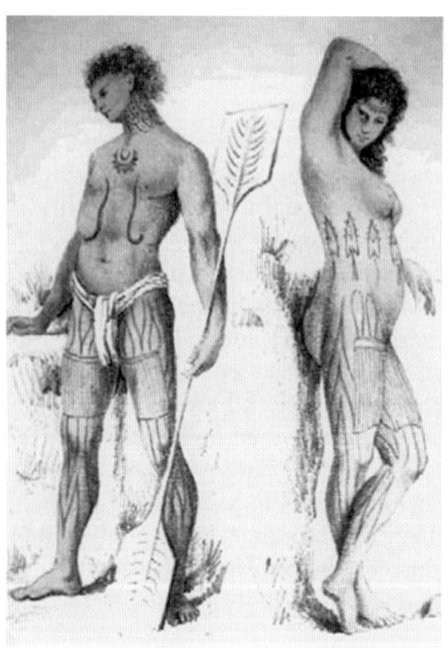

Rapa Nui

RÄWARÄWA – term for tattoo = paint, writing, used in southern Papua New Guinea.

RAYKA – see RABARI

REBARI – see RABARI

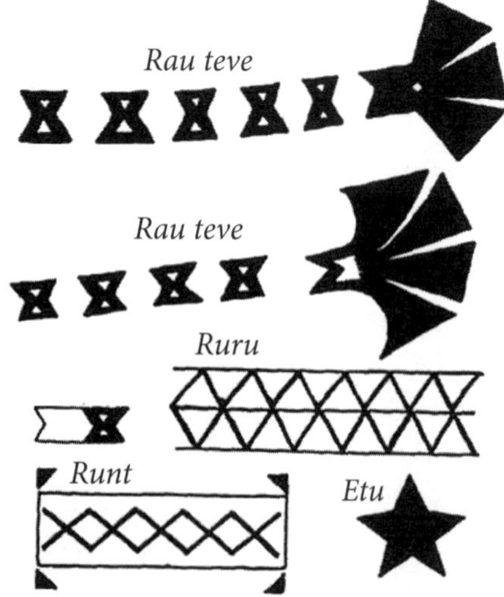

Tattooing motifs from Rarotonga

REBADI – see RABARI

REFU- carbon black used as a dye for tattoos, Tikopia Island.

RELACIÓN DE LAS COSAS DE YUCATÁN - an important source for knowledge of Mayan history written by Diego de Landa, a Franciscen active between 1549 to 1562 in Yucatan. About the tattoos of the ancient Mayas he wrote: "In doing it the craftsman first covers the part he wishes with colour, and then delicately pierces the pictures in the skin, so that the blood and colour leaves the outlines on the body. This they do a little at a time, on account of the pain and because of the disorders that ensue; for the places fester and form matter. But for all this they ridicule those who are not tattooed."

RENNELL ISLAND - locally known as Mugaba, is the main island of two inhabited islands that make up the Rennell and Bellona Province in the Solomon Islands.

RIEO – tattooist, Marshall Islands.

RITUS PAGANORUM - in 787, tattooing at the Council of Celchyth (Chelsea) by Pope Hadrian I was banned as a ritus paganorum, which mangle the divine work.

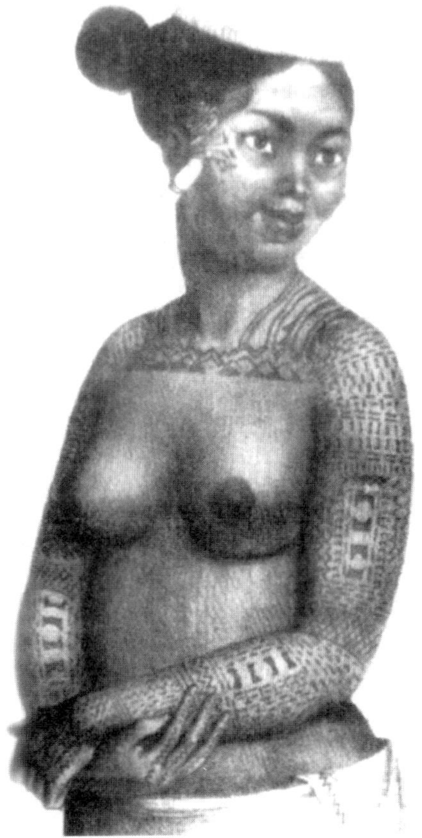

Tattoo ornaments from Ratak

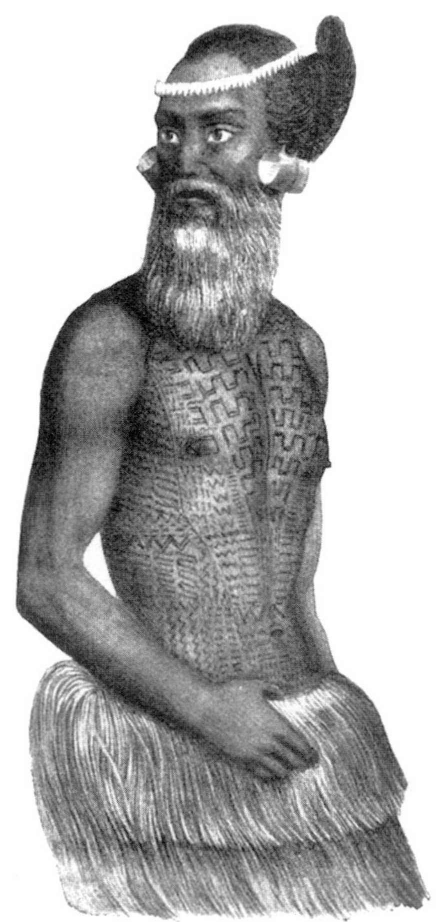

Ratak Tattoo 1815-1818

ROBLEY, HORATIO G. – author of the book Moko or Maori Tattooing.

ROROTEA – untattooed, Mangareva language.

ROTUMA – S. Gardiner wrote in The Natives of Rotuma: The tattooing of the boy followed at the age of thirteen, and, when it was completed, he became a man, if a Chief, however, as soon as it was commenced, he was systematically taken in hand by the women and taught

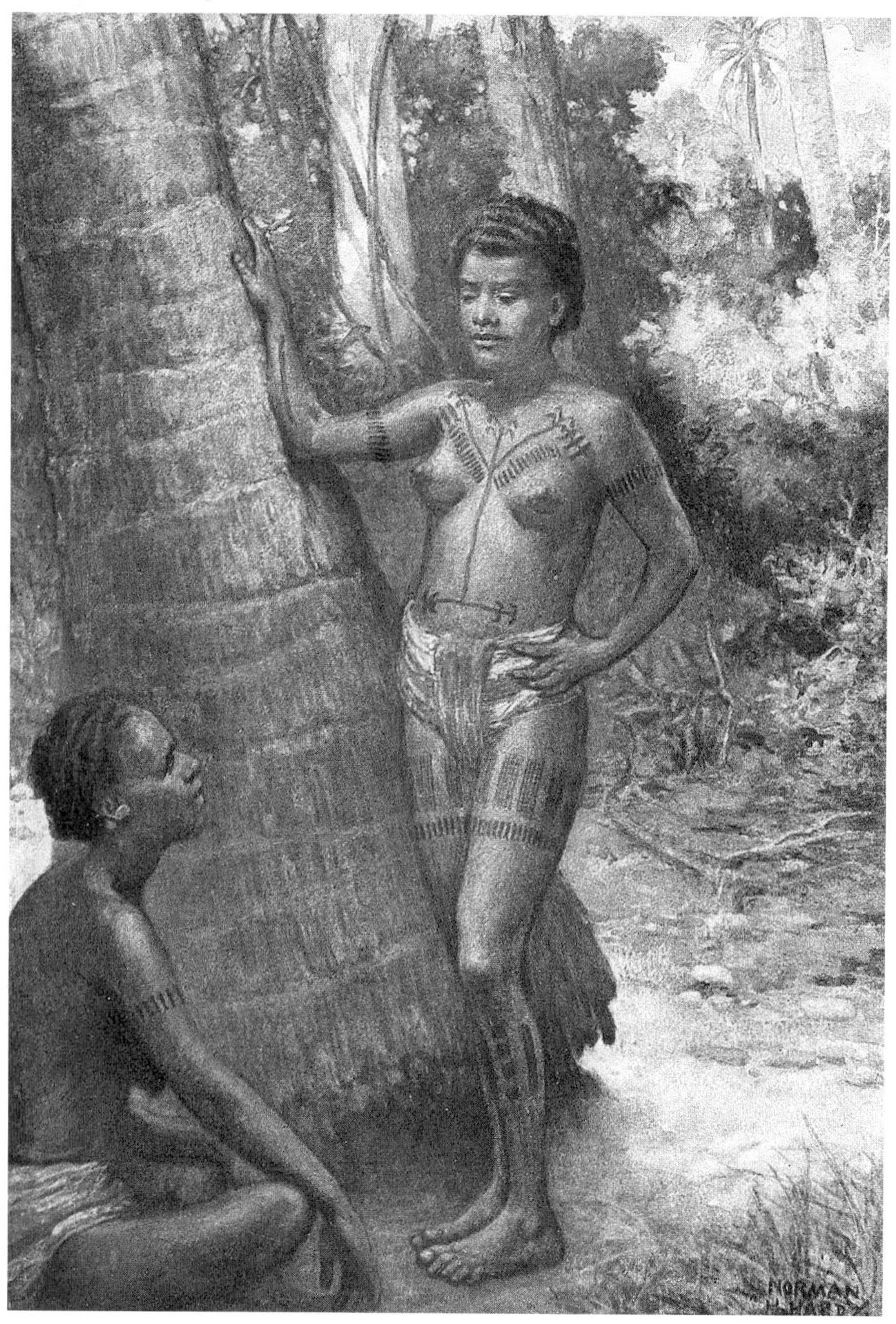

Women of Rennell Island

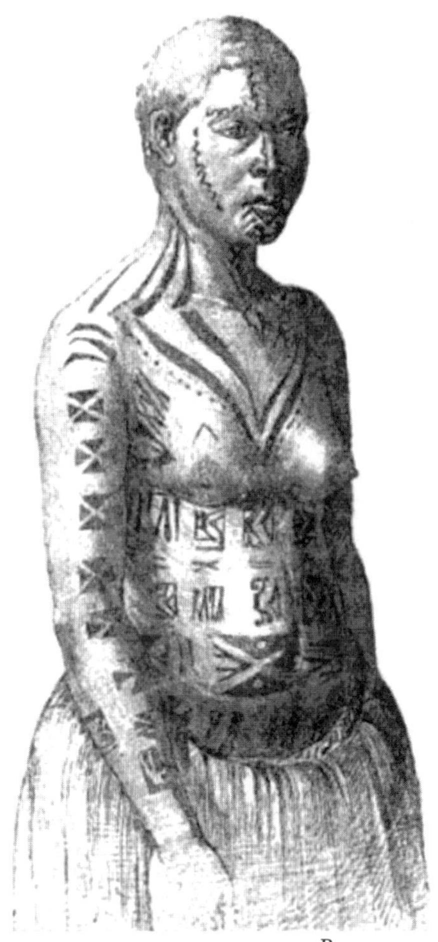
Rawarawa

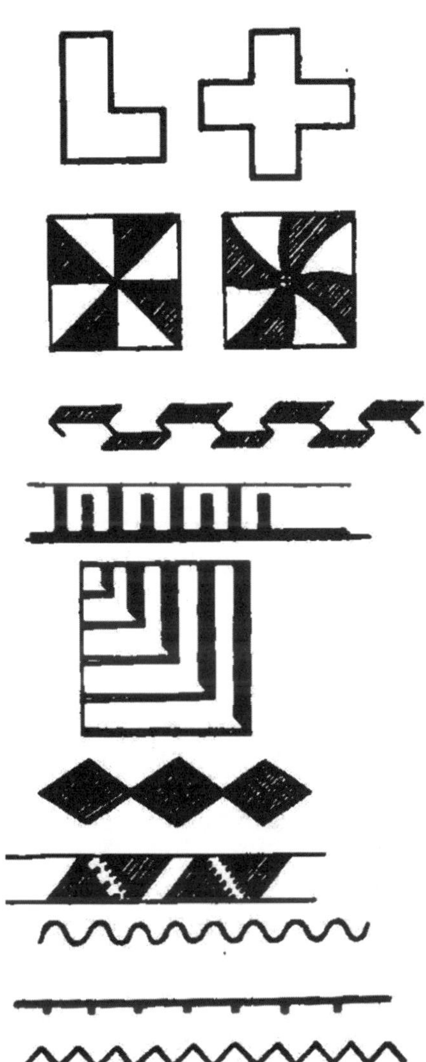
Patterns and tattoo ornaments from Ralik-Ratak

fornication. As different parts of the tattooing were completed, there were feasts, accompanied by various religion ceremonies, in the course of which alle the atua, who had anything to do with the boy´s hoag were called upon, They were in no way accompanied by scenes of unnatural vice.

RUDĚNKO, SERGEJ IVANOVIČ - a prominent Soviet ethno archaeologist who from 1929 to 1949 dealt with the discovery of graves from the Iron Age. In 1947, he found the bodies of a woman and a man in coffins in the second mound, whose arms, back and right leg were decorated with an extraordinary tattoo. It was the finding of a prince from the second kurhan in Pazyryk.

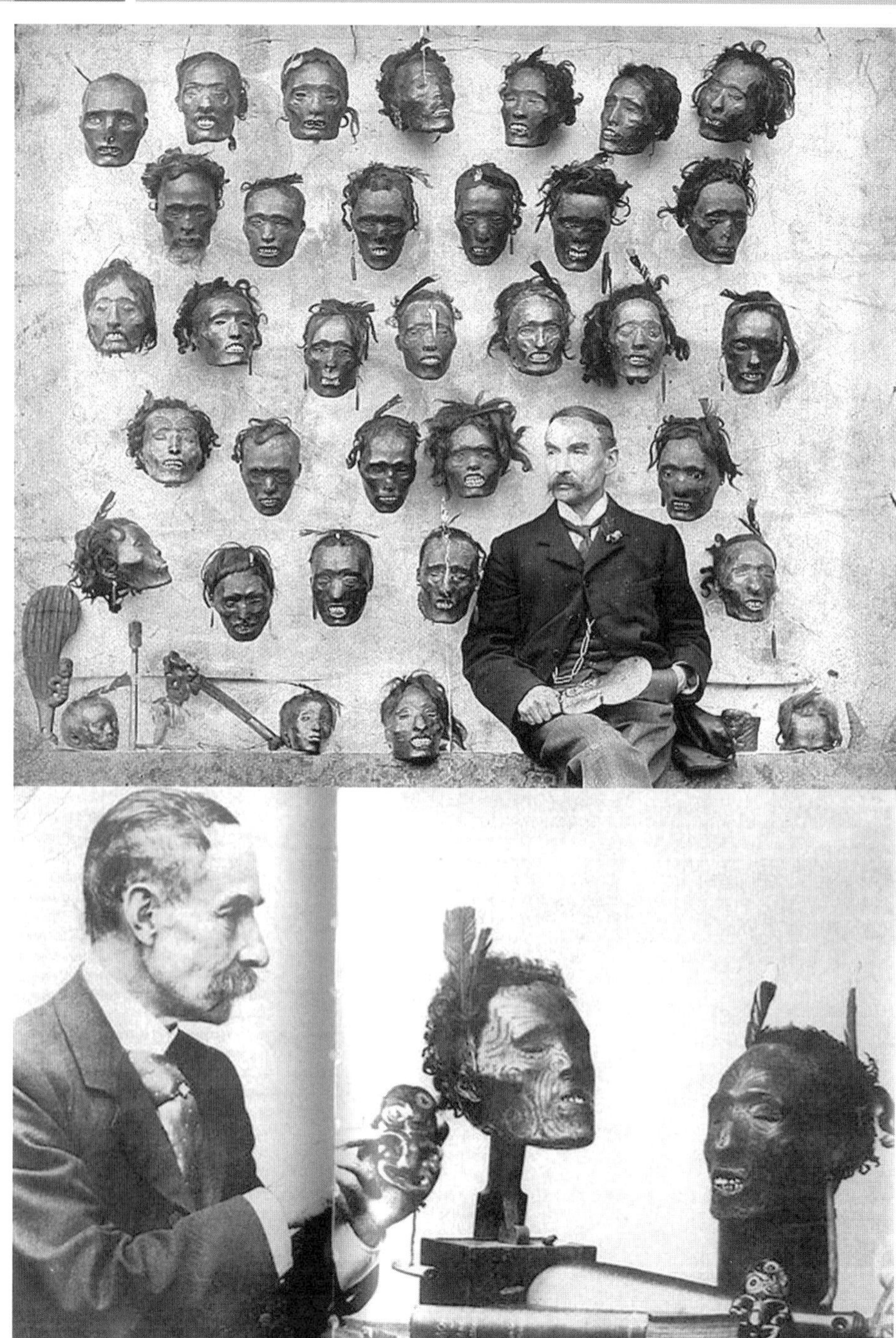

Robley with a collection of Maori heads

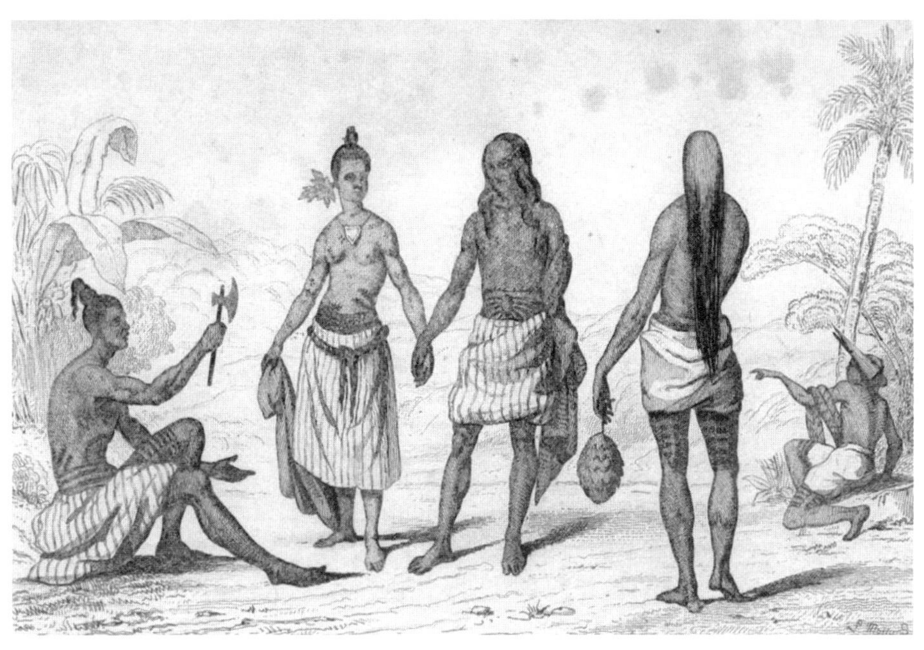

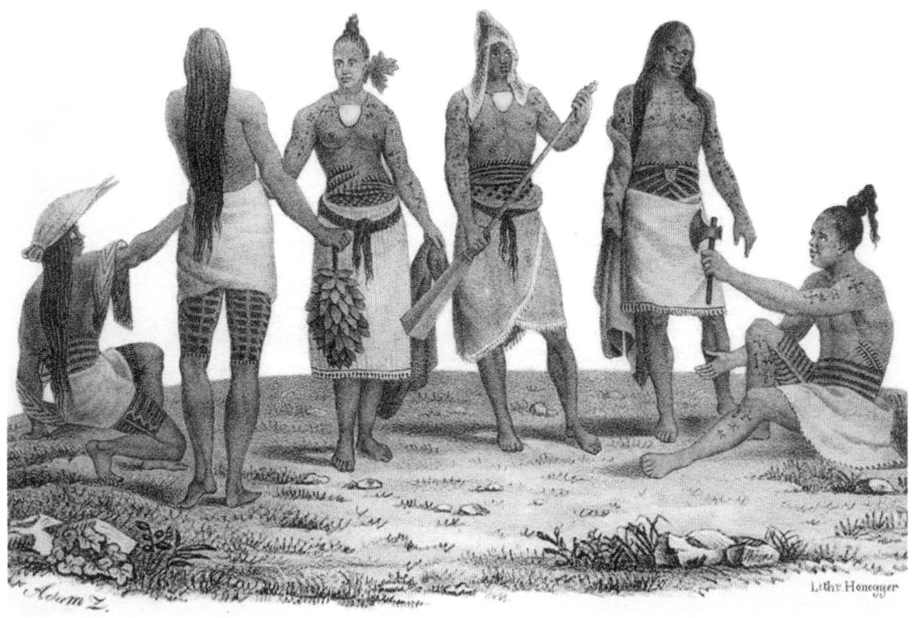

Rotuma tribe

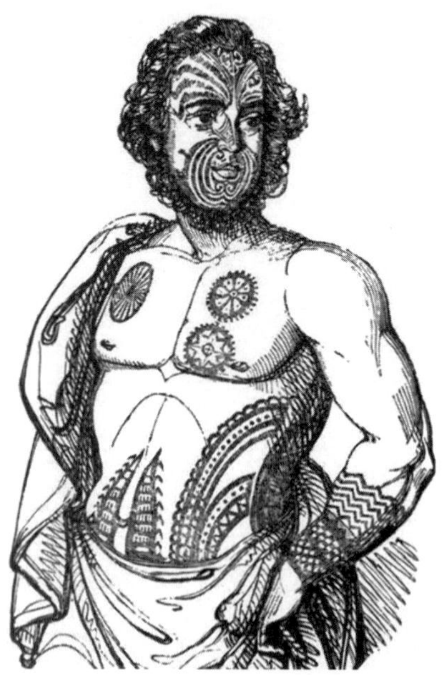
John Rutherford

RUTHERFORD, JOHN - Rutherford became the first extensively tattooed Englishman to return to Bristol from his trip to New Zealand. Craik George Lillie also wrote a book about him, "the White Chief."

RYUKYU - Ainu and Ryukyu are two islands of Japan. Ryukyu tattooing was first mentioned in 1461. The Ryukyu tattoos were done only on the back on hands, including the fingers, the wrists, and the knuckles. They are no examples of facial tattoos. The Ryukyu tattooing symbolized religious beliefs, sexual maturity, indication of marriage, body adornment, distinction of sex, and tribal customs.

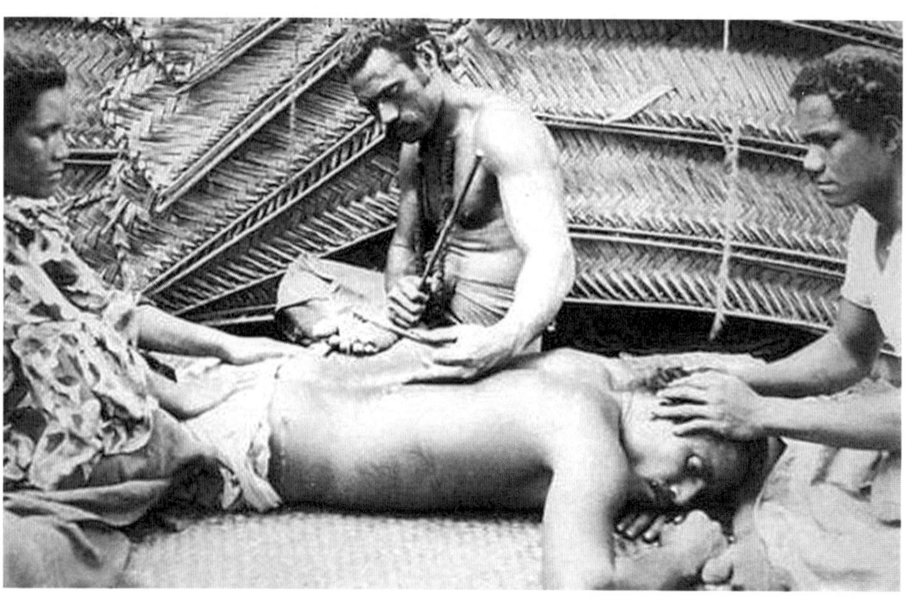
Rapa Nui - tattoo process

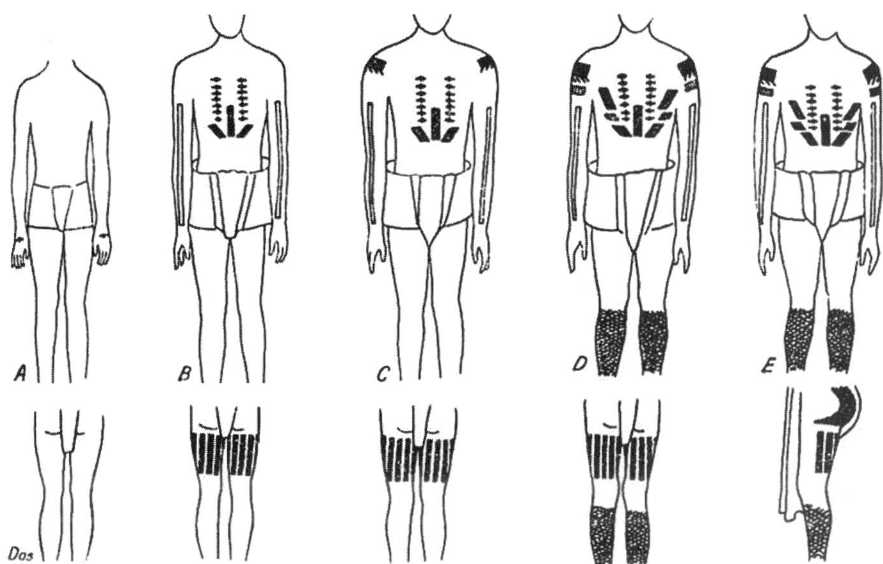

A note on the island of Rennell and its tattoos
Male tattoos vary by age and status
A – teenage boy, te vangoka ; B – single man, te atutahi ; C – married man; D – mature man; E – high ranking man , te akahua ; Crescent moon on the buttocks: te hakasapa ; stripes on the thigh: te tawakatu ; foot motif: te vaeungi.

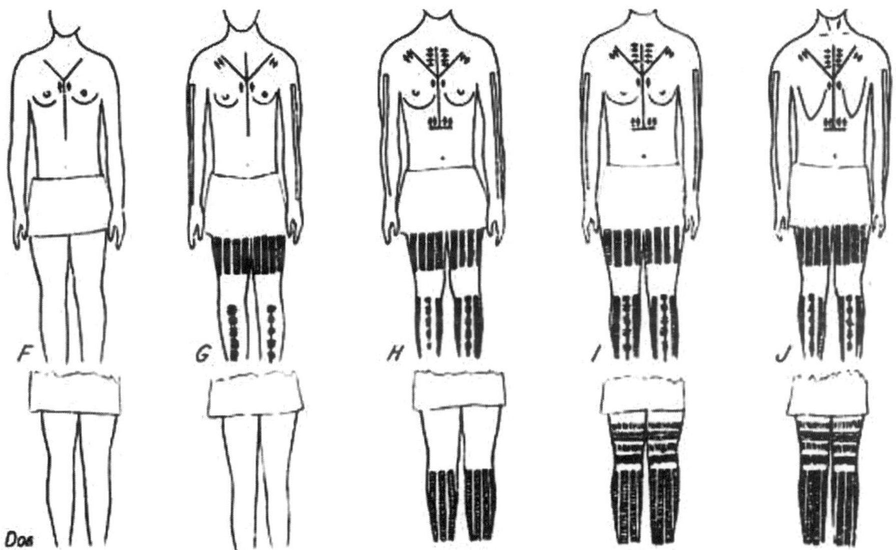

Female tattoo
F - single woman, te atutahi ; G - a married woman ; H - older woman ; I - important woman , huaéha ; J - old woman, haimaatua.

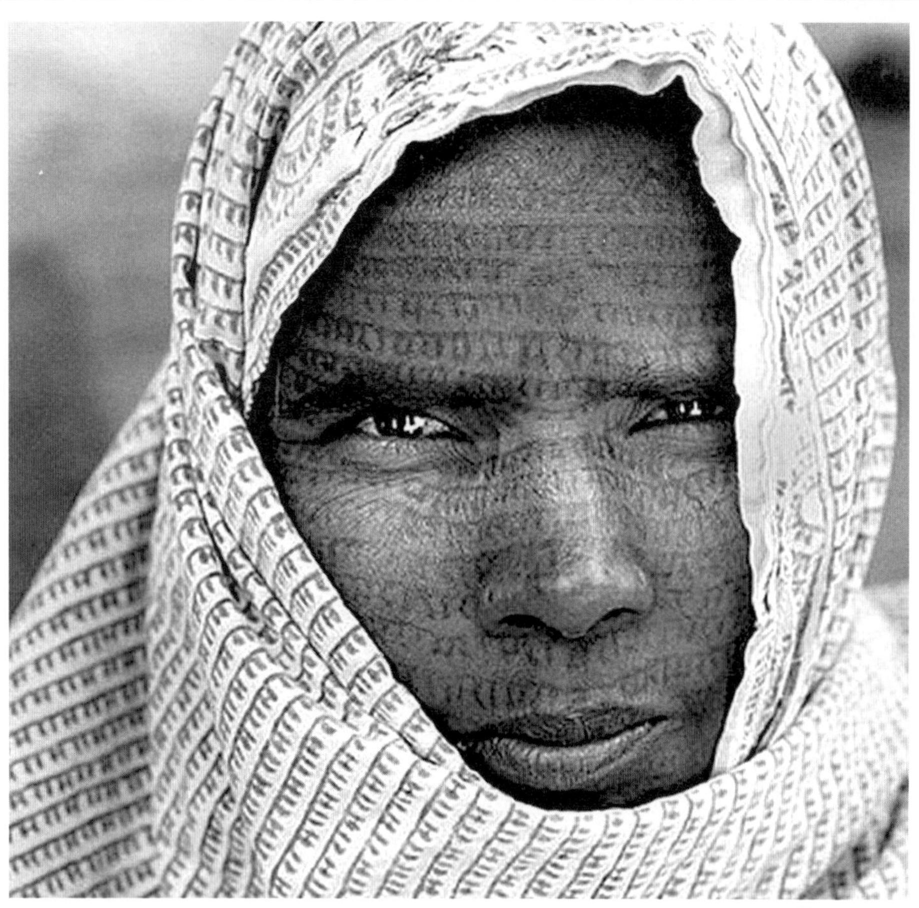

Ramnami

SABARA – see SOURA

SACRAMENNTO INDIANS – many of the women tattooed on their arms and body.

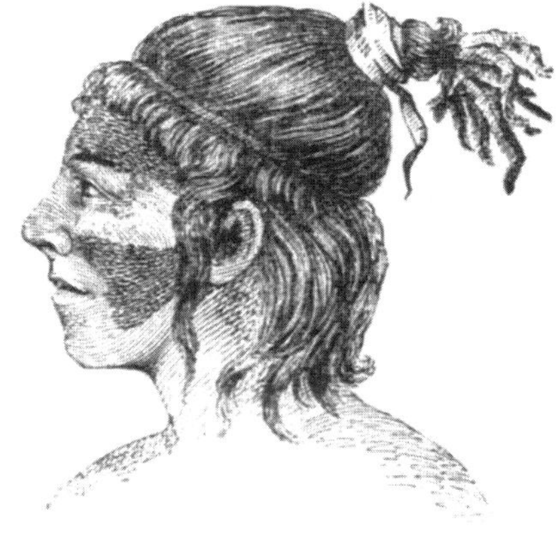

SAGNI – Bontoc women wore tattoos to beautify them and make them look lovely when they perform the traditional dance – the sagni.

SAGNI - The tattooing involved cutting the skin with a small knife called sagni and then rubbing in soot from burnt bamboo.The traditional tattooing among the Pantaron Manobo of Mindanao.

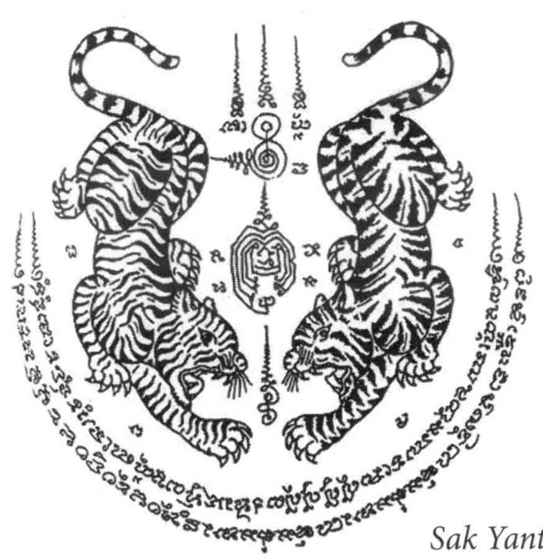

Sak Yant

SAK PHIKAN – a man free from moil, through some infirmity or defect could obtain an exemption tattoo (sak phikan), Tahiland.

SAK YANT – Sak Yants the Thai name for the Tattooing of Sacred geometrical designs on the skin. Yant (or Yantra, as they are call them in the west), are normally tattooed by Buddhist monks, or Brahmin Holy men. The Yant tattoos have developed over the centuries under the influence of several different things The Yantra designs that already existed in Hindu India were adapted by the Thais as Buddhism arrived from neighboring India. Sak- meaning "to tap" or, "to tattoo", and yant - meaning "Yantra". Originally derived from the Sanskrit word "YANTRA".

Sak Yant Thai Tattoo Meanings

The Basics

The lines drawn in the Yant represent the Umbilical Cord of the Buddha, and are traditionally known as 'The Bones of the Yant'. There are many varied forms of Yantra, it appears, such as; Round Yant, Triangular Yant, Four - Sided Yant, and even Pictorial ones.

Round Yant - represents the Face of the Buddha (Pra Pakt Khong Pra Putta Jao) in Brahmin Tradition, Brahma is applied as the meaning.

Triangular Yant - represents the Triple Gem of the Buddha Dharma and Sangha (Pra Put, Pra Tamm, Pra Songk). In Brahmin Tradition the three Lords of Heaven are applied as the meaning (Shiva Brahma, Vishnu)

Four sided Yant - represents the Four

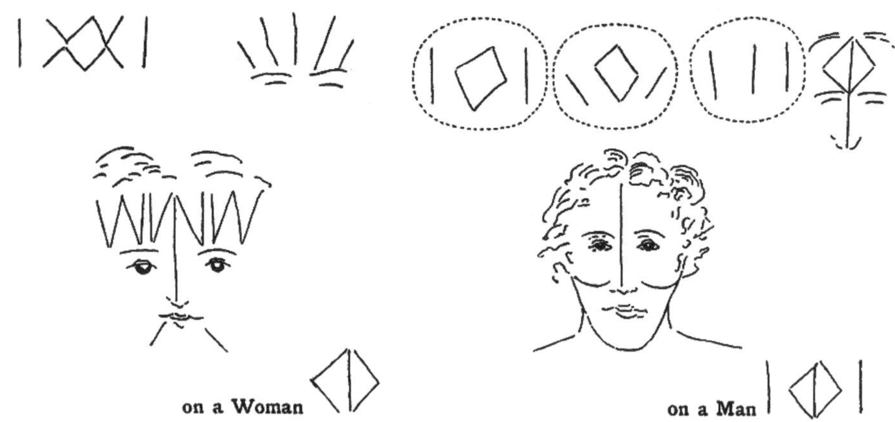

Sakai tattooing

Elements / Continents (Earth, Water, Air and Fire)

Pictorial Yant (Animalistic) - represents various Angels, People, and Mythical Animals (Sathw Himapant)

Onk Pra represents The Buddha Himself.

The Half Moon Symbol to be seen above "Onk Pra" so often represents the Moon Illuminating the way for us in the Dark Hours.

The small Circle (Sun Symbol) to be seen above many Yant means the Sun lighting way in the daytime; and that all Humans and Living beings exist under the influences of the stars and Planets, and that these forces enable us to develop and brings Changes.

The Zig - Zag spiral line on the top of each Yant is called Unaalome. Unaalome represents the Saints who have attained the status of Enlightened beings. The Fetters of desire have been disentangled and discarded. These beings do not waver on their path as normal Humans do (Note the end of the zig zag evolves into a straight line, meaning that he has ceased to enter into diversion and is on a straight, direct path to Nirvana. The spiral in the

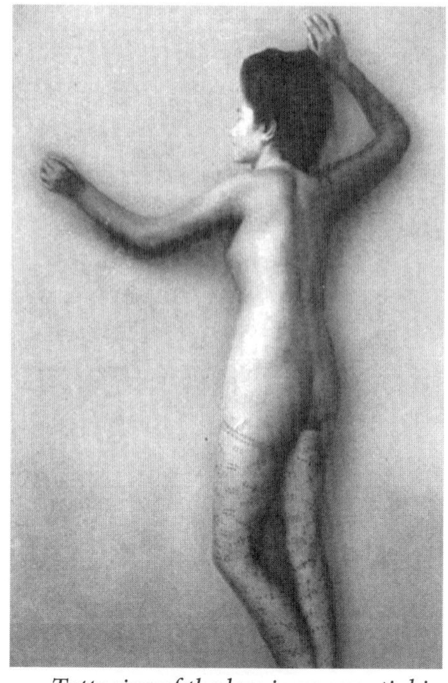

Tattooing of the legs is an essential in Samoa

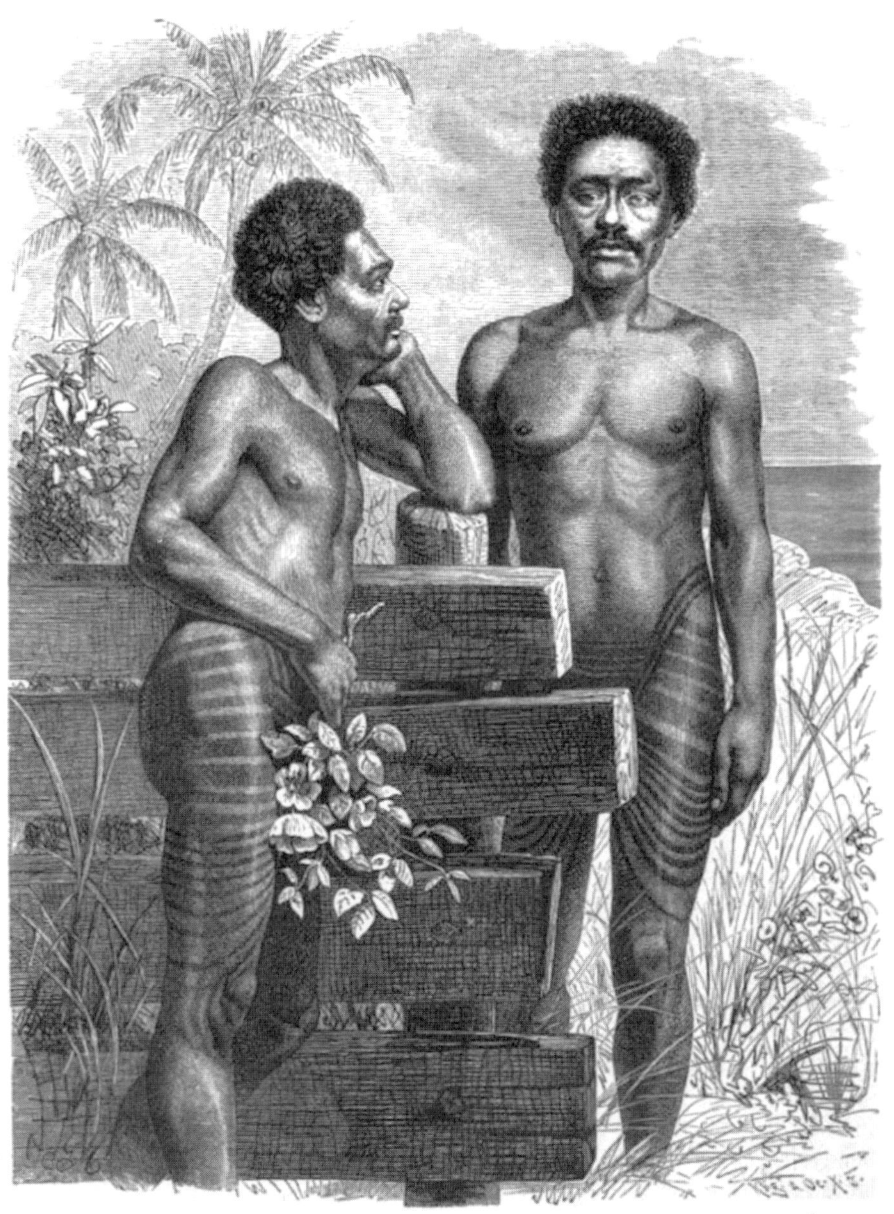

Samoans

middle represents the Crown of the Head of the Buddha. The Line of the Unaalome is straigh and unwavering - Perfect and complete.

SAKA – To alleviate the discomfort and distract the subject into a trance-like state, the beating of the tattoo was usually accompanied with the recitation of a

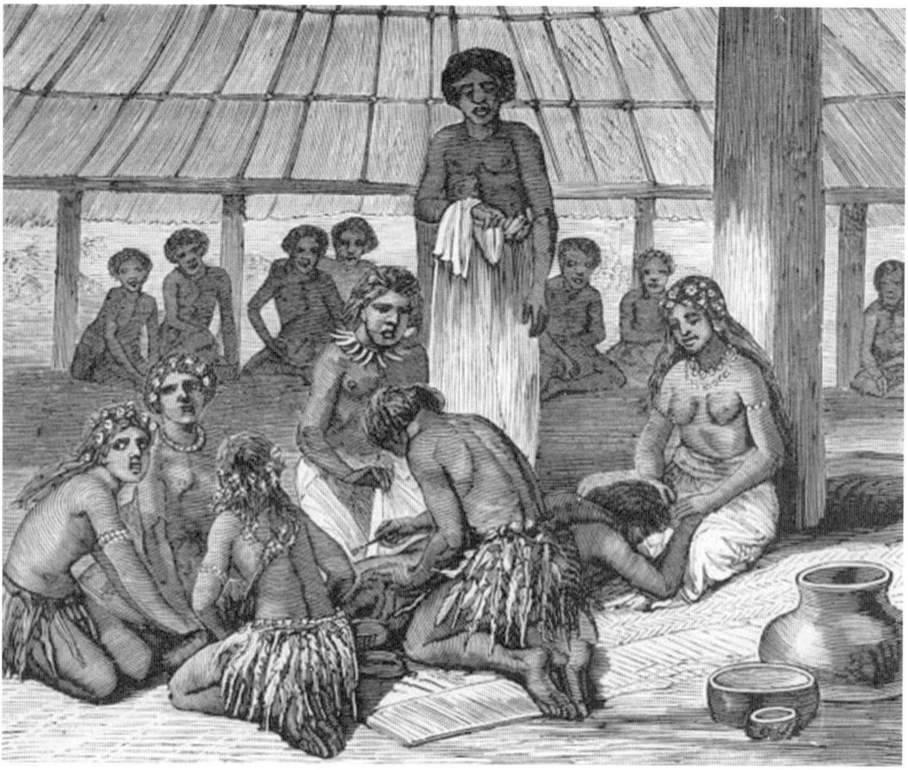

Samoa - tattoo process

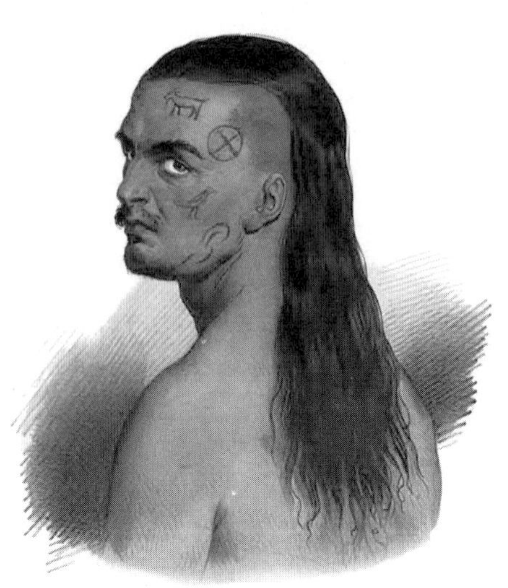

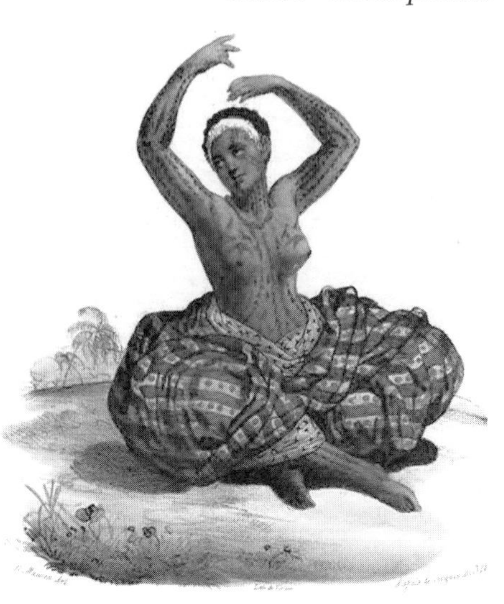

Sandwich Islands

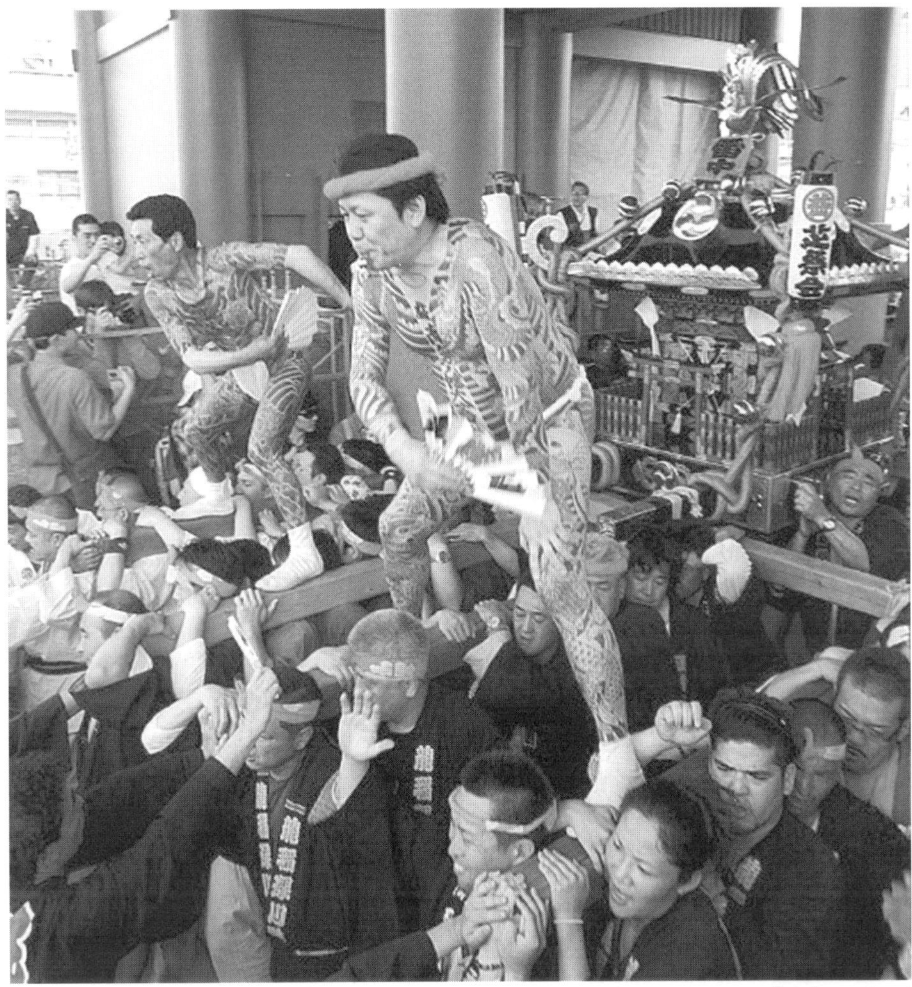

Sanjamatsuri

chant called saka. During the tattooing, saka song was sung to distract the mind of the person under the tattooing mallet. The tattooist (te tipa) sings and his beating of the tattoo accompanies the songs. Bellona.

SAKAI - is one of the tribal communities in Indonesia traditionally living in the interior of Riau, Sumatra. Some of them still leading the nomadic and Hunter-gatherer lifestyle in the remote interior of Sumatra, while most settled into major cities and towns in Sumatra with the rise of industrialisation.

SAKYAN - see SAK YANT

SALAMAJEGA – the tattoos, worn by the Barabaig of Tanzania, are cut into the skin after which the open wound is stained. Worn by both men and women and are traditionally cut in a circular pattern around both eyes, formin the goggles.

SALANUMNIGRUM – eggplant black, eggplant juice served as the basis for the tattoo color, Rapa Nui.

SALAXAR – see JAKUTI

SALINAN TRIBE – Tattooing was practised, principally upon the women.

SAMOANS - the Samoa Island, Polynesia. Artificial cranial deformation belongs among their practices. They laid head of an infant on a "platform" made of a flat volcanic stone and placed two stones to both sides of the head and one on the upper body. So, after some time, the desired flat shape of head was acquired. However, Samoan tattoos are better known. A classic Samoan tattoo spreads from loins to knees and, on back; it reaches high enough to look like some kind of a black belt above the edge of a loincloth. A little lower, on the lower back, it turns into a triangle turned top down and further to a strip, from which some kind of rays stretched out ending on the belly skin above the pelvic bone. Sometimes, several decorative parallel strips can be seen tattooed above the womb and a small square around the navel. Thighs are embellished with extensive areas filled with triangular or ribbon patterns.

SANDWICH ISLANDS - was the name given to the Hawaiian Islands by James Cook in 1778. Tattooing practiced.

SANJA MATSURI - (translate to: "ThreeShrine Festival"), or Sanja Festival held in Japan every Third Saturday in May. The festival is to honor Hinokuma Hamanari, Hinokuma Takenari and Hajino Nakatomo, the free men who established and founded Senso-ji (Tokyo'soldestBuddhist temple). Close to 2 million people attend the free day festival. The parades revolve around mikoshi (portable shrines) with some traditional music and dancing sprinkled about, but one thing you'll also notice are the beautifully adorned skin from Japan's own mafia, theYakuza. Only for this festival are the Yakuza allowed to shine their inked up bodies.

SAORA – see SOURA

SARAWAK - is the largest state in Malaysia, and the seat of the Sarawak Museum. The Sarawak natives adorned themselves with brass jewelry, shells, but also tattoos, especially the people of Kayan, Kenyah, Iban, and Kelabit. Strict rules applied (as with most tribal tattoos) regarding location, shape, and gender.

SAUSAU - tattooing mallet that is part of a set of Samoan tattooing tools. The "sausau" mallet was shaped from a length of hardwood approximately as long as the forearm and about the diameter of the thumb.

SAVARA– see SOURA

SAYAS - monks (tattooist) in Myanmar who create magical tattoos.

SCYTHIAN CHIEFTAIN - is exceptionally preserved individual discovered around 1947 during the excavations of a grave in Kiev. Similarly to the Pazyryk excavations, the body remained relatively untouched due to the combination of subtle embalming and cool climate in the region. Culturally, the

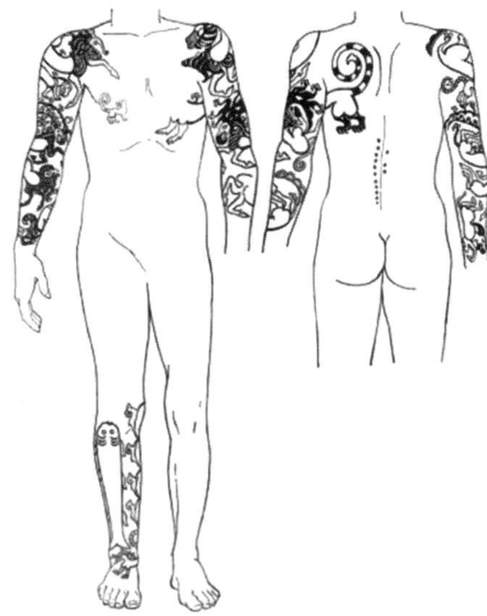

Scythians were connected with the Pazyryk culture which is best seen on decorative animal motifs covering his shoulders, arms, calf of the right leg and partly chest and back.

SDAR – in the Maghreb area, Northern Africa, there is no generally applicable relation between a tattoo and its name. The name may be a mere tautology, so in this case, the drawing has the same name as the part of the body where it is placed: e.g. sdar (chest), other drawings have the similar origin.

SEBASSES - a Native American tribe from the Bella Coola River, practiced tattoos.

SECOYA – also Angotero or Encabellao, ethnic groups living in the Ecuadorian Amazon. Women practiced facial tattoos.

SEIBEI - Seibei, of Choraku-ji Temple, was the first tattooed Yakuza boss. In old times Yakuza were not tattooed. The tattoo on his back was a Ono-no Komachi and cherry blossoms on his waist, hands, and legs. When he took a hot bath and drank, his skin became pink. He was a Yakuza boss in 1827 in Fugieda City, Shizuoka Prefecture.

SELIVIT - When the half of one ikor has been completed the tattooist stops and asks for selivit; this is a present of a few beads, well-to-do people paying eight yellow beads of the variety known as lavany, valued at one dollar apiece, whilst poor people give two beads. It is supposed that if selivit was not paid the artist would be worried by the dogs and fowls that always roam about a Kayan house, so that the work would not be satisfactorily done; however, to make assurance doubly sure, a curtain is hung round the operator and her subject to keep off unwelcome intruders. After selivit has been paid a cigarette is smoked, aind then work recommences in earnest, there being no further interruptions for the rest of the day except for the purpose of taking food, Borneo.

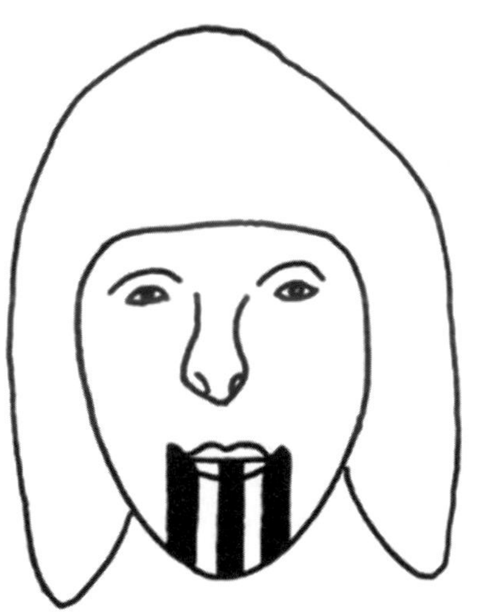

Shasta woman

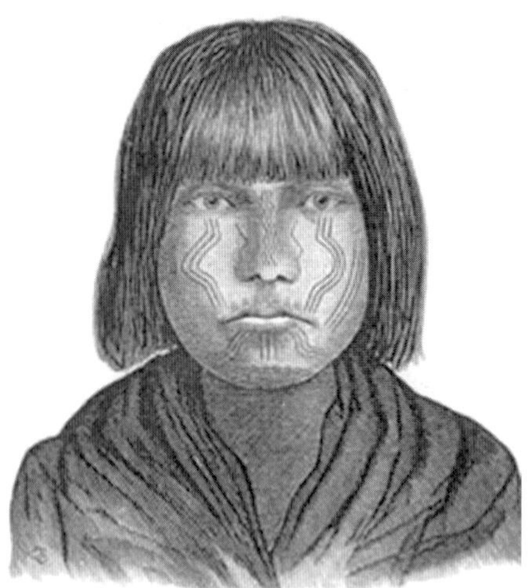

Shasta. Tattoo designs of a Shasta woman, 1900

SENOI - tribe practicing tattoo, Malaysia.

SERAMON – the term for the concentration that each tattooist must have when designing a motif, Maisin tribe, Papua New Guinea.

SERRANOS - an Indian tribe from Southern California (USA), whose people used to tattoo the same patterns on their faces and chins as were drawn or carved on trees.

SHAKKI - is the sound of tebori tattoo, referring to the sound when needles puncture skin. Tattooing by hand in Japan should be done by puncturing the skin with the needles gently, adjusting the strength of the hands. If the tattooist works in a faster sequence, you may hear rhythmic sounds something like "sha, sha, sha;" hence shakki.

SHAMMAR – a tribe located within todays Iraq and Saudi Arabia where women practice tattoos. During the tenth year of age, cheeks, forearms, hands and chest were tattooed. In the next year, they

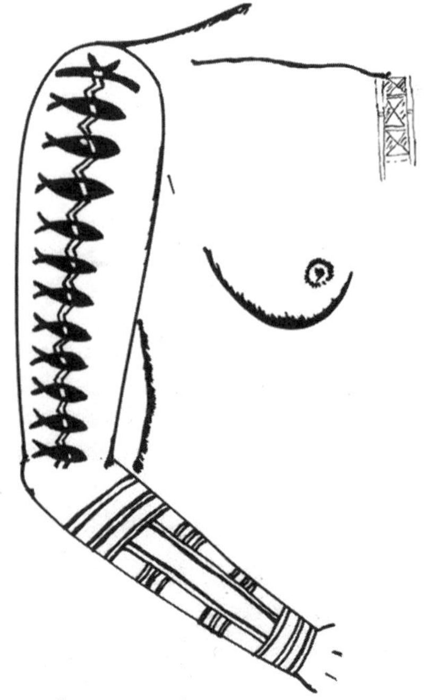

Female tattoo, Sikaiana

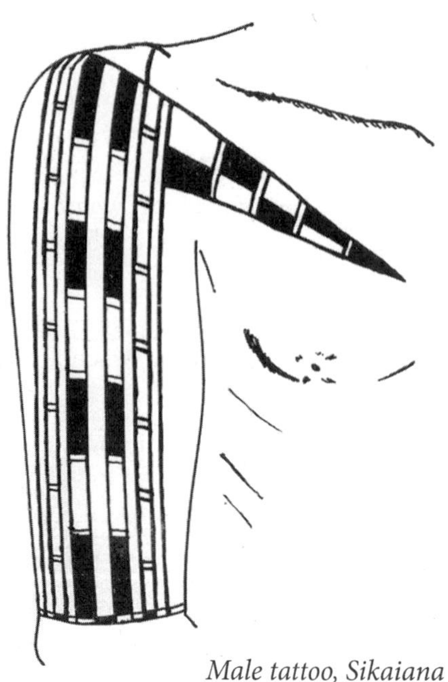

Male tattoo, Sikaiana

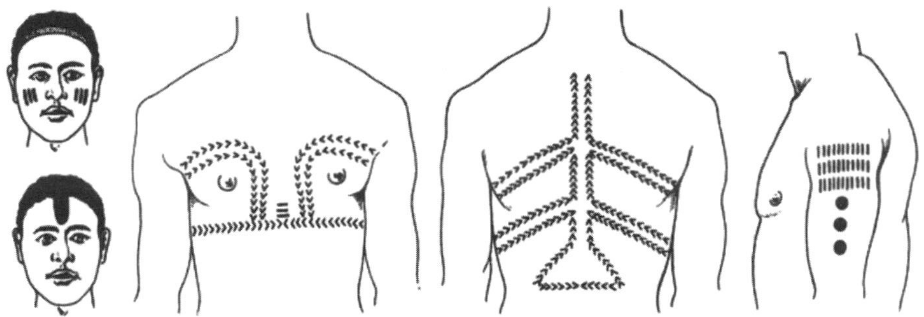

Siera Leone

tattooed thighs and back and when a girl turned nineteen, she got her arms and feet tattooed as well. All of this was simply ornamental but they also used some therapeutic tattoos like a small dot in the inner corner of the eye against eye pain and three dots on right thigh or a linear mark on right leg tattooed for curing the leg pain occurring after a childbirth. Face, hands, arms and legs had been tattooed at some time before the girl got married and thighs, back and belly were tattooed after the marriage all at once, which took for about seven hours and had to be very painful indeed.

SHAN TRIBE – men practised tatttoo; occasionaly one leg has its blue

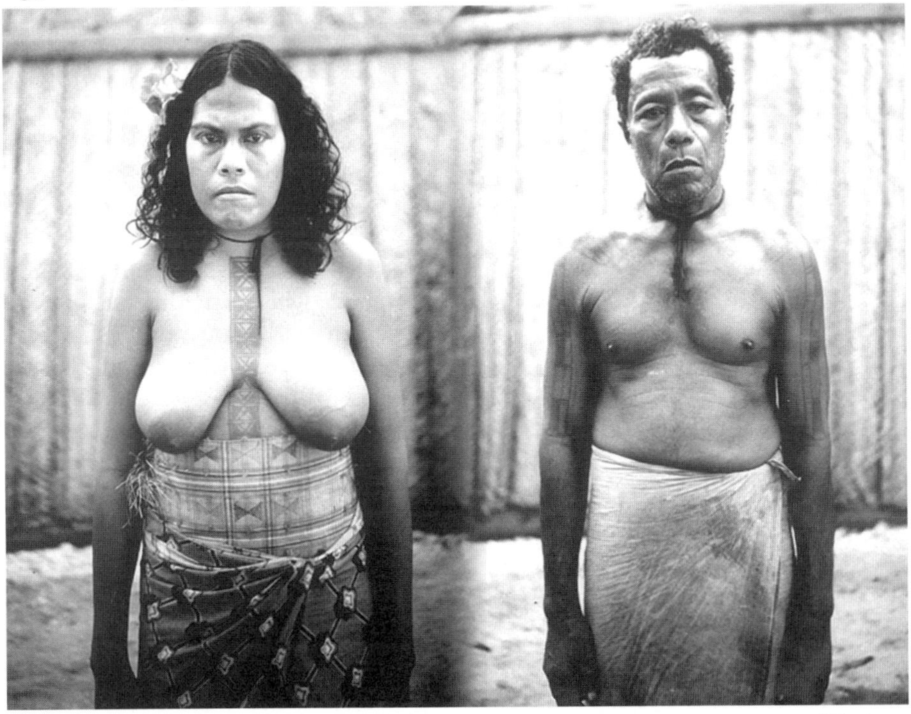

Sikaiana

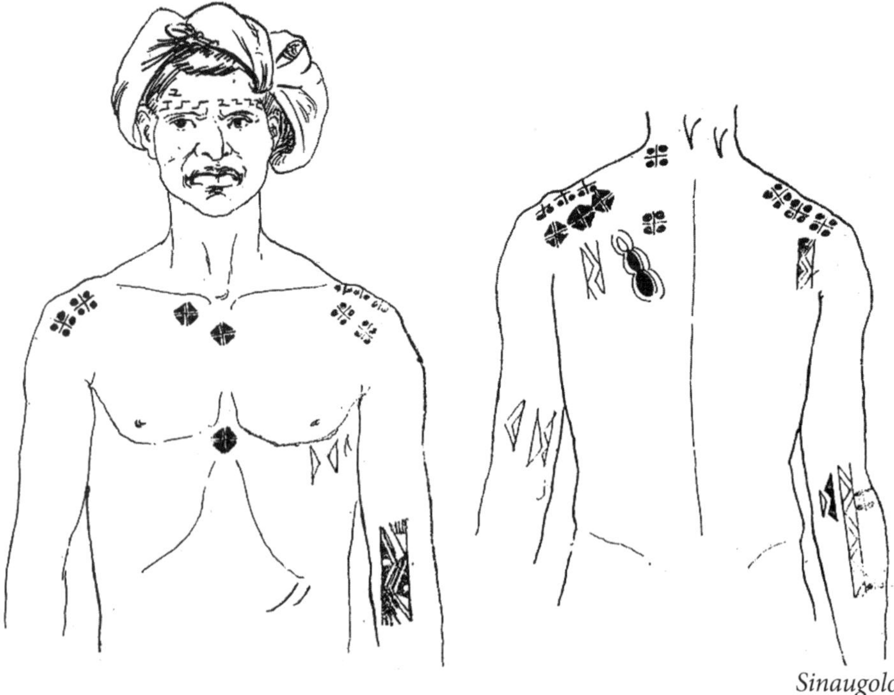

Sinaugolo

decorations; but the rule is to tattoo both legs from waist to knee; the thighs being completely covered with an elaboráte design in dark blue. This ornamentik does not always end at the knees, but may be continued to the ankles. The backs boys was seldom tattooed, though

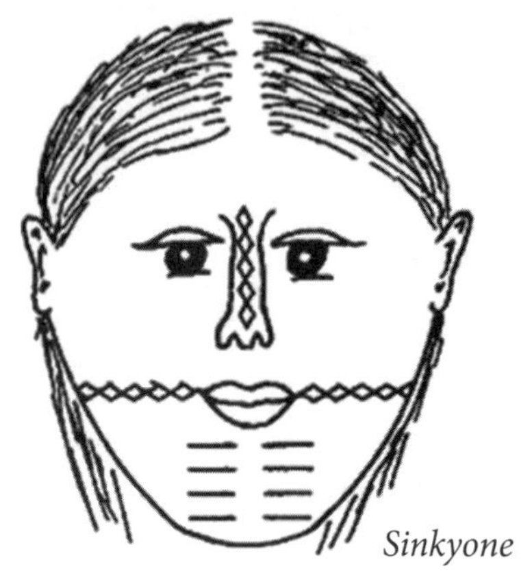

Sinkyone

patterns on the back from the waist to the shoulders, sometiones in blue, more often in red, was addend from time to time. The leg designs were usually much more artistic than those on the back, which have no svetry. Sometimes a design of squares, with a letter in each, may occupy the space under one shoulder-blade, while the other side of the back was perhaps decorated with small circles or Word beasts or birds. Girls and women weared fine circels of cane, which fit tightly round the leg under the knee, five or six, may be worn on each leg, Burma.

SHARATI – Bosnian name for "tattoo process".

SHASTA - The Shastan peoples are a group of linguistically related indigenous from the Klamath Mountains. They traditionally inhabited portions of several regional waterways, including the Klamath, Salmon, Sacramento and McCloud rivers. Shastan lands presently form portions of the Siskiyou, Klamath and Jackson counties.

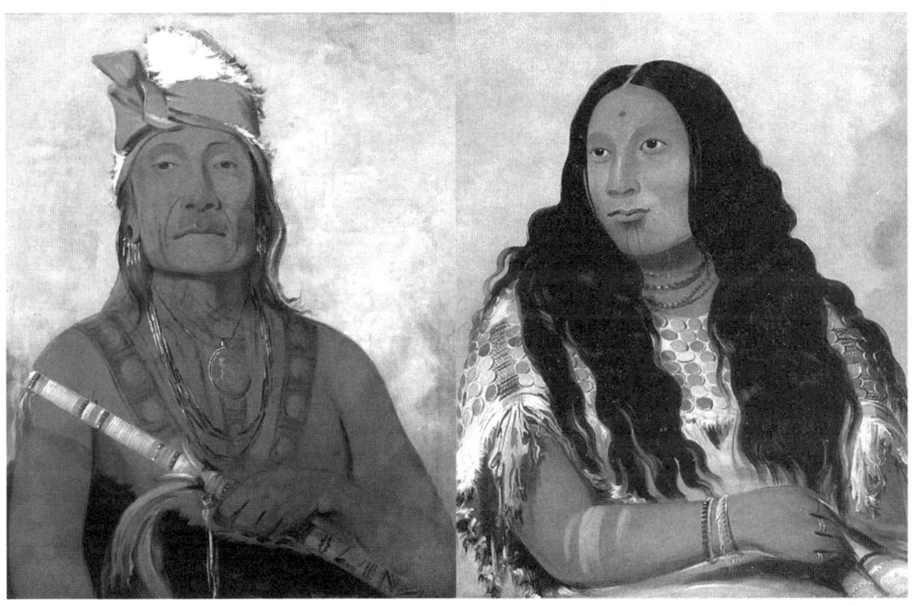

Sioux

Franz Boas wrote: Tattooing as a means of decoration was confined practically to the women. The ornamentation was applied to the chin only, and consisted of three broad vertical marks.

In some cases, narrower lines were put in between the broad ones, or the outer lines were prolonged slightly above the corners of the mouth. Notched or saw-tooth lines were not used, nor were lines ever made on the cheeks or forehead. The tattooing was done when the girl was about ten or twelve years of age. The instrument used was a small, sharp flake of obsidian. The operator was in all cases an old woman who made tattooing her regular trade, and who was paid for the work, when done, by the father of the girl. With the sharp flake, shallow parallel cuts were made close together, and then the coloring-material, either charcoal or blue-clay, was rubbed in. The whole chin was tattooed at once, and, unless the lines were not dark enough, was'not gone over again. Throughout the night on which the tattooing was done, the girl was not allowed to sleep much, and whatever she dreamed was bound to come true. Her dreams were always told to her mother. Men generally had a few short lines tattooed on their hands and arms, not for decoration, but to serve as measures for dentalia, beads, etc.

SHAUSHAUTA – Tattoo, Hausa language, Nigeria.

SHICHI SAMA INOCHI – The section

on tattooing by prostitutes in the Edo seikatsujiten includes for example the note, dating from the Kanei period (1624-1630), that a certain Sakumi of the Nomaya brothel in Osaka, had the characters shichi sama inochi (my life for Mr. Seven) tattooed on the top of her shoulder.

SHISEI - (刺青), translated as "tattoo", is a short story published in 1910 by the famous Japanese novelist Tanizaki Junichir. It is the story of a young tattoo master and a beautiful girl. His work was first included among contemporary works, and retrospectively among the Edo period due to the social unrest of the time.

SIBA- Siba is a (mythical?) island from which came the taukuka , a solid black tattoo covering the entire chest. Nobody knew where Siba was. Some kakai (culture heroes) were said to have learned the art of tattooing there.

SIERE LEONE - a coastal state in West Africa, located on the Atlantic coast in the west and south. Tattooing practiced here.

SIHASAPA - The Sihásapa or Blackfoot Sioux are a division of the Lakota people. Practiced tattoo.

SIIT – needles used for tattooing, these are a series of 5 to 7 reed needles attached to adze, Nags, India also Kalinga, Philippines.

SIKAIANA TRIBE - These are pictures of some traditional tattoos. Not all men were tattooed on the arms. All women were tattooed on the belly and thighes. Missionary teachings opposed tattooing and the last traditional tattoos were

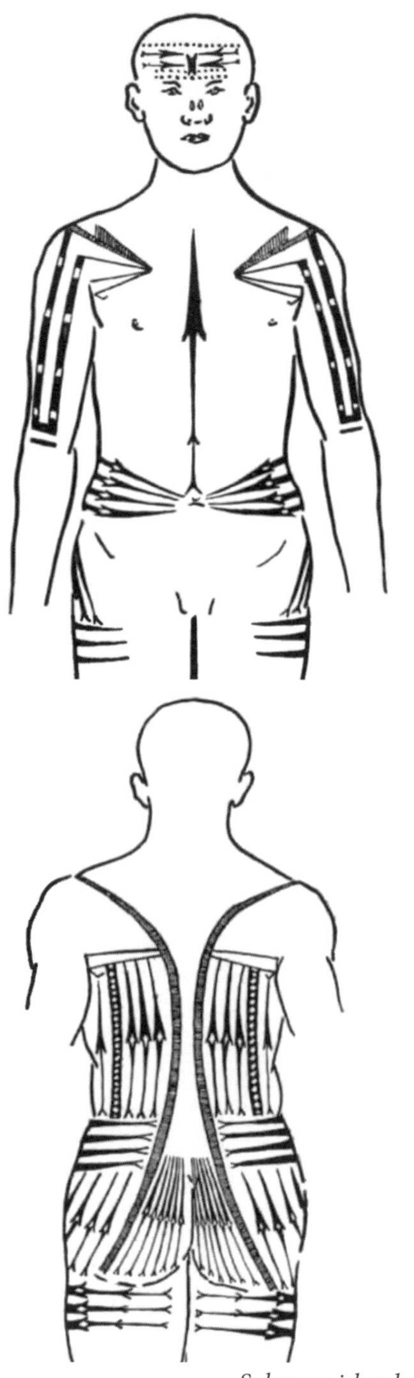

Solomon islands

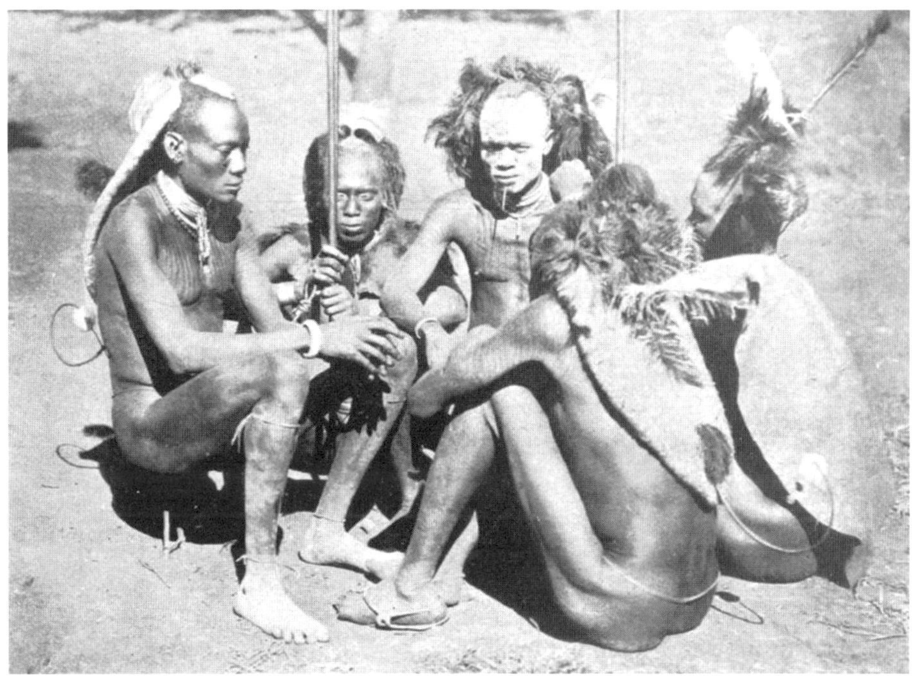

A group of Suk (showing tattooing on arm)

probably done in the 1940s. In the 1980s, there were still some living older women who had stomach and thigh tattoos. There were no living men or women with arm tattoos. Some Sikaiana people, especially men, had a variety of tattoos that were done in different styles and not part of a shared ritual tradition. These pictures were taken in 1933 by the Templeton-Crocker expedition. The drawings were made by Henry Teloto using drawings from government reports.

SIKO HAU – a term for unexpected or accidental nausea associated with vomiting associated with tattoo pain, Tonga.

SINAUGOLO - an inland tribe inhabiting the Rigo District of British New Guinea.

SINKYONE INDIANS - The Eel River Athapaskans include the Wailaki, Lassik, Nongatl, and Sinkyone (Sinkine) groups of Native Americans that traditionally live in present-day Mendocino, Trinity, and Humboldt counties on or near the Eel River and Van Duzen River of northwestern California.

SINU - also SINU SINU - This term is often used to praise tattoos, Bellona.

SINUYE – Inuit literary name for tattoo.

SIPANITI – tattooist of the Mentawai tribe, Indonesia.

SIOUX (DAKOTAS) - an Indian tribe practicing tattoos. He believes that the spirit of the deceased travels through the wasteland on a ghost horse, and then the old woman invites him to show a tattoo: if he has none, he must return and be condemned to the eternal life of a wandering artist.

SKEENAS - a Native American tribe from the Bella Coola River practiced tattoos.

SKIDDEGATES – Indian tribe in the Queen Charlotte Islands practiced tattooing.

SKINNER, ALANSON (1886-1925) - Probably the first anthropologist who described tattoos of eastern Native Americans of Cree tribe and the Saulteaux tribe. The description was elaborated during the summers of 1908 and 1909 when he studied Native Americans living east of York Factory and Norway House. He claimed that tattoos used to be common "but it is already an anachronism in our time. The only motif, preserved until today, is a simple strip around the wrist." In another text about the Saulteaux tribe, he states that he saw an old tattooed woman in Fort Hope. She had "a simple cross, symmetrical on both sides, tattooed on both cheeks like an incantation against toothache and headache." He also noted that "similar symbols used to be placed on legs and wrists against rheumatism." Although he did not present any evidence, Skinner speculated that crosses may come from Roman Catholic missionaries rather than being of indigenous origin.

SOGA´IMITI– Samoan males with a Pe'a are called Soga'imiti and are respected for their courage.

SOKOROS TRIBE – tribe from Chad, practices scar tattoos.

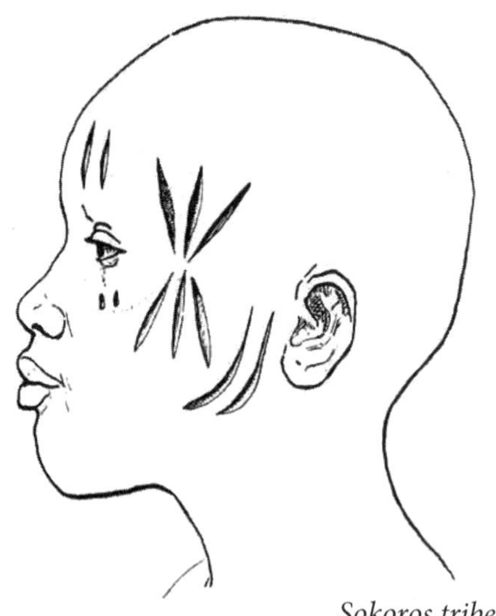

Sokoros tribe

SOLO– Samoa. Towels (solo) are formed of old siapo cloth (ta'afi) that owing to use is frayed and soft. A piece is held by the artist wound round the handle of the instrument in use to keep it from slipping. The bare handle isneverheld.Another solo is held by the assistant. Itisusuallydampenedovernight and is spread over the skin in front or below the part being tattooed. The assistant stretches the skin taut with the solo. Every now and again as the artist lifts his instrument, the assistant wipes off the blood and extra pigment with the towel. He then quickly moves it down away from the tattooing edge and turns the cloth to expose a clean part as he sees fit. The assistant is also called solo and his main duty is to sponge the tattooing.

SOLOMON ISLANDS - country in the southwestern Pacific Ocean. It consists of a double chain of volcanic islands and coral atolls in Melanesia. The country comprises most of the Solomons chain,

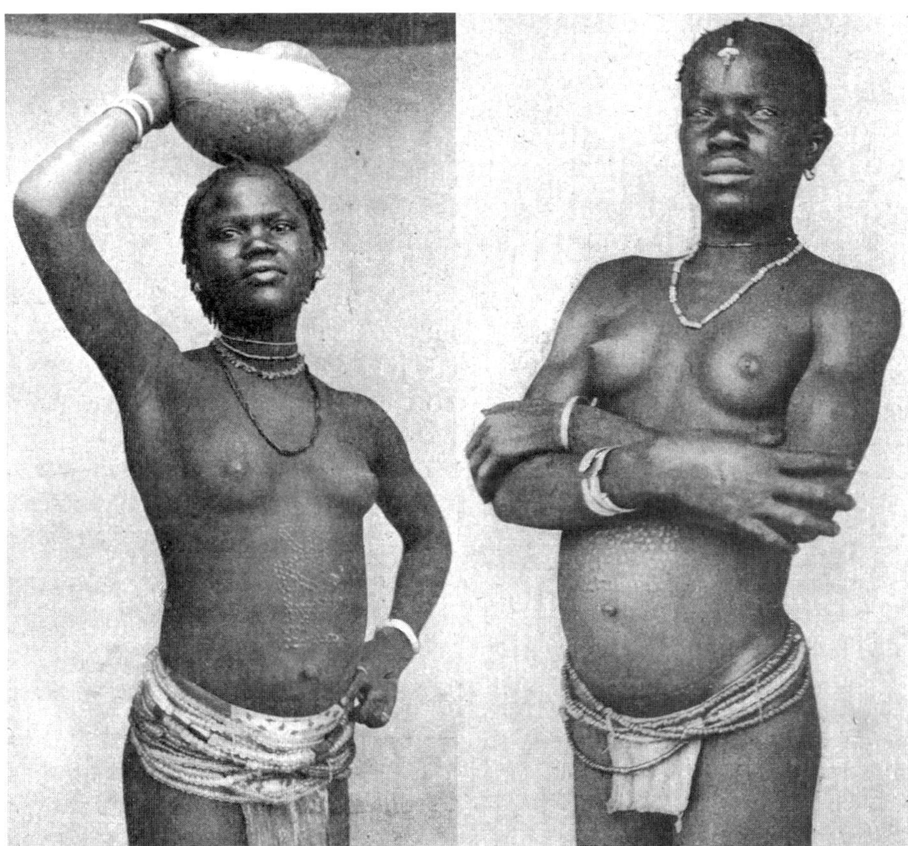

Sereres

with the exception of Buka and Bougainville, two islands at the northwestern end that form an autonomous region of Papua New Guinea.

SONGI ASO – tattoo mallet, Samoa, see AU

SORA – see SOURA

SOURA – also Sora, Saora, Savara, Sabara, tribes from southern India. Women practice facial tattoos.

SUK – Tribe from Afrika. The skin has decorated by a sort of tattoo, in continuos lines or rows of spots round the shoulders and upper arms and extending over the chest. The women generally ornament themselves in the same way over the stomach. These marks do not appeal to be made by raised scars, as is so common elsewhere, but apparently by burning the skin, as the Marsi women do, with some acrid juice.

SUMI (墨) - means a black ink in Japanese. Although there are many kinds of sumi, only few of them is suitable for tattoos. Sumi from Kobaien in the Nara city boasts the highest quality and it is also the most expensive one. Sakurazumi

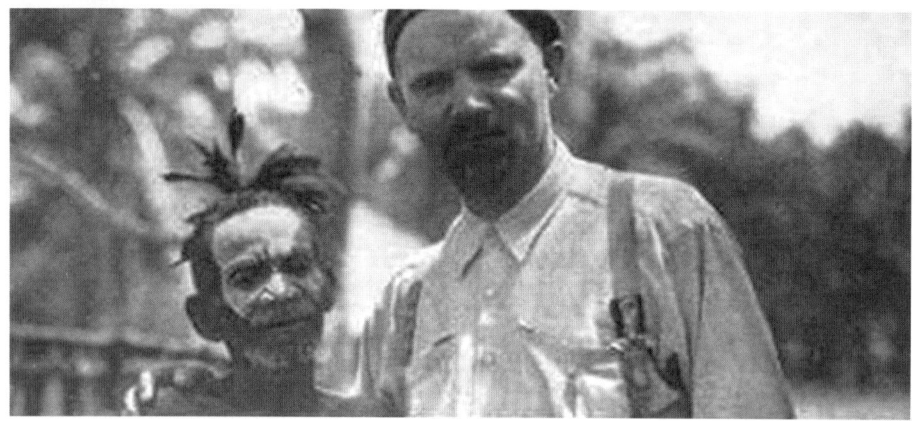

Pavel Šebesta

(桜墨 "cherry blossom ink"), baikaboku (梅花墨 " plum blossom ink") and itsutsuboshi (五つ星 "five stars") are also Kobaien products, most suitable for tebori. Kobaiensumi is made of soot of purely burned vegetable oil – usually sesame or paulownia – with a touch of a glue from vegetable starch. The mixture is wrapped around a stick and dried. If necessary, a tattoo artist grinds it in an inkwell called suzuri until it reaches the correct consistency.

SUSHI-YA-BORI – designation for full back tattoo, Japan.

SUSUKI - by applying tattoos, the girl "became" an adult woman (susuki), Maisin tribe, Papua New Guinea. see IFIIFI

ŠEBESTA, PAVEL (1887-1967) - Trave -ller, ethnographer and anthropologist. During the time spent among Pygmies, he acquired an eloquent nickname "The Father of Pygmies". In his book "Mezi nejmenšími lidmi světa" (Among the Smallest People in the World) he describes his research journeys among Negrito rainforest tribes in Malaysia and the Bambuti Pygmies in Kongo, Africa. His desire for knowledge had no limits. He traveled thousands of kilometers in soggy soil on barely perceptible routes, he daringly sailed through the wild rapids of rivers. Mostly, he traveled alone with a backpack accompanied by several natives. Strong and resistant, used to the hardest challenges, he successfully penetrated into places where no white traveler had stepped before him. He was able to assimilate with natives, gain their trust and affection.

ŠI KA LÄ-LÄGAT – the term for the tattoo artist, Shi Oban on South Pora, Mentawai.

SHILLUKS - An African tribe practicing scar tattoos.

ŠITIE – tattoo of the Siberian peoples.

ŠIT´JO -body decoration performed with a needle and thread is still called with this general Russian term.

ŠODÓ– font path, name for the Japanese art of calligraphy, widely used in tattoos.

ŠU - Japanese tattoo Horimono consists of three parts, one of which is shu, or "coloring".

TA´ANGA – cutting, murder, tattoos, etc. expressions, Rennell and Belona Islands.

TA´UNGA TA TATAU – tattooist, Aitutaki Island.

TA – The instrument is generally known as ta (to strike). There was always an assortment of these toothed ends of varying fineness or coarseness appropriate for all grades of work from the delicate hairlines to solid patches. The flat instruments for straight lines and gradual curves were of human bone, sometimes of the bones of enemy sacrifices (ivi heana). They were about three inches long, flat and slightly wedge-shaped, and toothed or comblike at the end. Instruments for the smaller curves were of the bones of the kena (Sula piscatrix), or of a tapu bird on the small island of Fatu Uku, the leg bones having been used, and according to Langsdorff, wing bones also, Marquesas.

TA-TIKI – (strike-tiki) for the baton, Marquesas.

TA KONA – tattoo tools used on Rapa Nui. It was a comb made of bird bones attached to a wooden stick.

TA MOKO - is a term used by Maori to denote their style of tattooing. The mere tattoo of the face is called moko. The moko uses tattoo motifs to express various meanings.

TA TAU – tattoo process, Tikopia Island.

TA TIPATIPA – term for tattoo on the island of Mangaia.

TAA – tattoos, Rennell and Belona islands.

TAA ´AGA´AGA - (t. 'anga'anga) - o shout and sing to God the cloud of Tehainga'atua while felling a tree in a canoe, or while going to sea, or during a tattoo, Bellona.

TAA BAGE – careless tattoos, Rennell and Belona islands.

TAA GAATAKI - tattoo in imitation, Bellona.

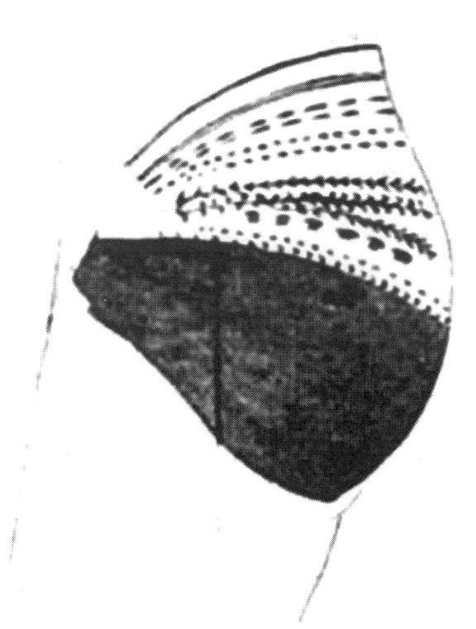

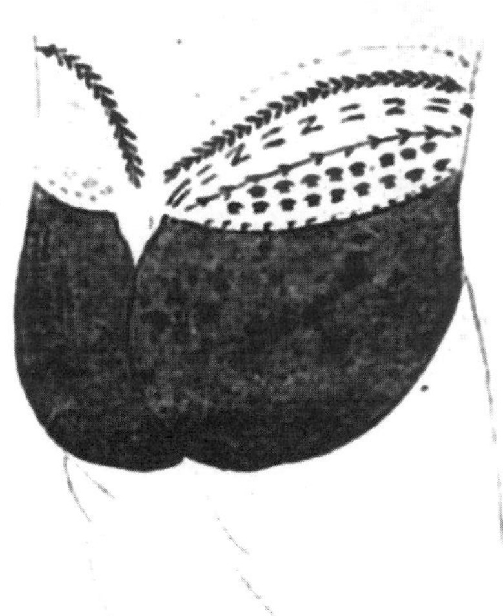

Tattooed Inhabitants of Tahiti, 1823

TAA TATA´O – finishing tattoos, for a darker color, the islands of Rennell and Belona.

TAANGA NGUTU – see TA NGUTA

TAGA O FUSI MA ULUMANU - The fourth session is the tattooing of the ulumanu, from the center of the thigh up to the inner groin. A ribbon (fusi) extending from the perineum and extending to the width of the hand below the knees is added.

TAGA TAPAU – The third session. The lausae, an area of solid tattooing, is added to the thighs beneath the aso e lua.

TAGABILI TRIBE – living in the Philippines. Among other things, they practice tattoos called hakang.

TAGNEGHLI – graphite, which is (was) the basis of color for tattoos on St. Lawrence Island.

TÁGU – a hardwood hammer knocking on a tattoo needle, Carolina Islands.

TAHA MATA KEE – brother of the goddess of tattoo in Polynesia. See KIKIIOANI.

TAHLTAN INDIANS - Emmons in The Tahltan indians wrote: „In the case of both sexes, on the day of birth or shortly afterwards the lobe of the ear and the septum of the nose are pierced formerly with a sharpened claw or bone awl, later with an iron point and a cord of sinew is inserted to keep the aperture open. Later in life the helix of the ear of the man may be perforated at one, two, or three points, according to his social position. On ceremonial occasions an ornament of bone, or of dentalium or haliotis shell, or a silver ring, is worn through the nose.

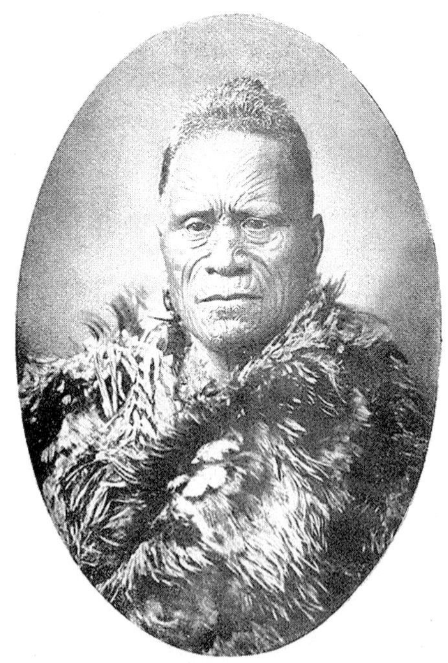

Tawhiao, New Zealand

Pendent from the lobe and from the holes in the helix of the ear, dentalium and haliotis shell and silver rings are likewise worn on dance occasions, although that through the lobe may be of every day use. I saw no evidence of the use of the labret among this people, and they assured me that this custom did not exist among them in early days, and that if a woman were found with the lip pierced, it was because she was of the coast people or related to them. For personal decoration the face was daubed with red ochre or with charcoal, and vermilion procured from traders was used later for the same purpose. No figures, totemic or otherwise, were known.Tattooing was common in the past, but I found no good examples of this form of personal ornamentation, only insignificant

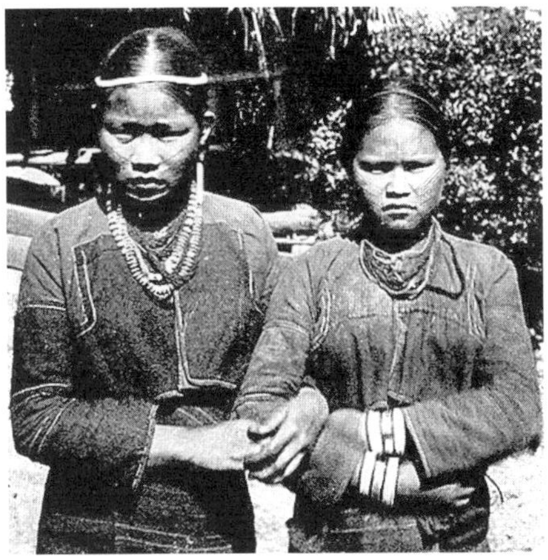

Taiyal belle

geometric figures on the backs of the hands. Formerly it was shown in lines and dots on the forearm, the ankles, the chin, and the face. It was accomplished by means of a fineneedle and a thread of sinew rubbed in powdered charcoal. "

TAHU´A TA TATAU - tattooist, Tahiti.

TAIYAL – In Among the head-hunters of Formosa you can read: The tattooing of the Taiyal is on the face. When a child (whether boy or girl) reaches the age of about five, it has tattooed on its forehead a series of horizontal lines, each line being about half an inch in length. These lines are repeated, one above another, from a point between the eyebrows to one just below the roots of the hair; the design when finished giving the impression of a finely striped rectangle about half an inch in width and two and a half inches in height. Usually, several children are tattooed at the same time, and the occasion is made one of feasting and dancing. The children are by this ceremony formally accepted as members of the tribe, entitled to its rights and privileges, and also expected to bear some share of its duties and responsibilities.

Occasionally one sees the insignia of the successful head-hunter tattooed on the chin of young boys. This indicates that these boys are the sons of famous head-hunters and that their hands have been laid upon heads decapitated by their fathers; or that they have carried these heads in net-bags upon their backs. This, by tribal code, entitles them to the successful head-hunter´s tattoo-mark.

TAITAI – tattooing, Karibati, Oceania.

TAIYA´RU TRIBE – people of Formosa, Vietnam

TAJE – Tattooing of Ioway was under the sponsorship of the Wind Deity, Taje or Tache.

TAMA-NUI – tattoo art learned from Tama-nuim , Polynesia.

TAMDA - a large reddish species of kangaroo, the female of which is called kurlo. A fabulous person from whom the natives derive the usage of tattooing, and who was afterwards transformed into a kangaroo, Aboriginal people.

TANDAN TRIBE – tattooing was popular.

TANIMBAR – archipelago near New Guinea where tattoos were widespread.

TANSY- an herb, it was rubbed into the skin before tattooing in Persia.

TAPA - statuettes from Rapa Nui, which are painted in a stylized tattoo.

TAPAGEBA (TAPANGEBA) - Flat stones used for smoking geemugi resin (pugu) for tattooing, Bellona.

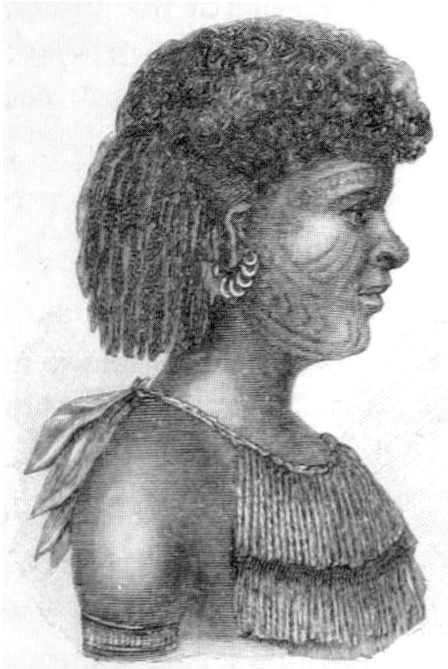

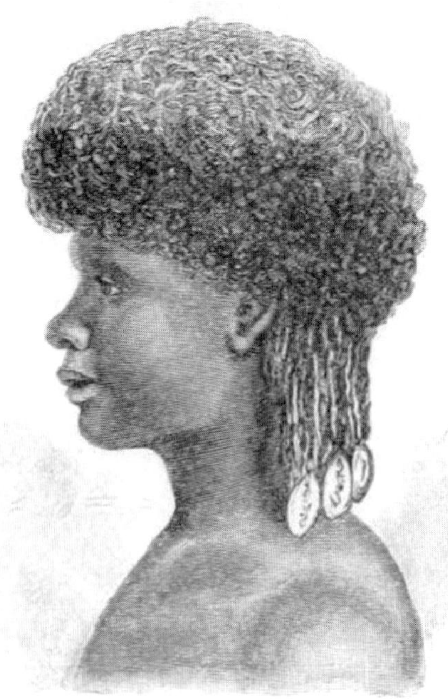

Girl from Tefle

Boy from Tefle

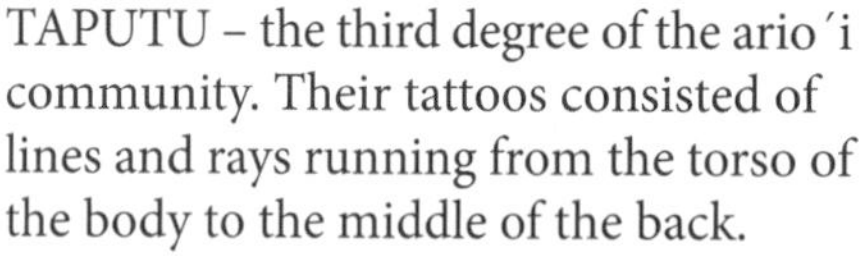

TAPUTU – the third degree of the ario´i community. Their tattoos consisted of lines and rays running from the torso of the body to the middle of the back.

TARA MOEDE – citrus bush thorns used on a tattoo tool, Sumba Island

TARA TUTU – the eighth degree of the Ario´i community. Literally pointed thorn. They were characterized by tattoos in the form of small dots in the popliteal fossa.

TARAHUMARE – This tribe no longer tattoo but this trait was once an important aspect of their culture. In the seventeenth century that the men had marks upon their faces which had been burned deeply into the flesh. The tattooing was done by girls with whom the men were in love, or by girls whom the men had chosen as their future mates. The Indians commonly used thorns to prick dotted wavy lines upon the foreheads and lips of little girls; a round "wheel" was pricked upon both cheeks. Charcoal dust was rubbed into these pricks to produce a permanent design.

TARO-TARO (TAROTARO) – tattooing, Mailu tribe.

TARORO - term for tattoos, tribes around the Mambare River, New Guinea.

TATA – Thorns of wild vine "tata" were used for tattoos, Maisin tribe, Papua New Guinea.

TATAU or TA-TATAU - is the Tahitian mention of tattoos by traditional tools. The name is said to come from the sound made by the instrument during use. Also a tattoo or tattoo motif (in general) on the island of Bellona.

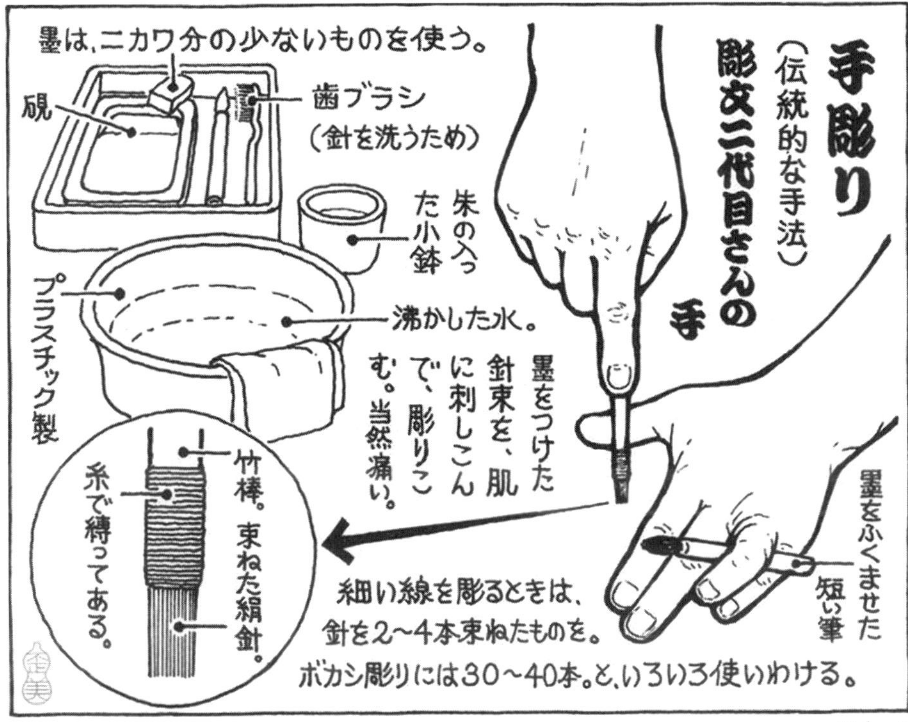

Tebori

TAU – tattoo, Tikopia Island.

TAUA - The high priest in Polynesia was called taua who was considered a divine and sacred person. Taua had many other tasks like preparation of the offerings, ceremonials, sacred chorales, ritual drums and even performing minor surgeries. The taua was also a guardian of the ancient traditions. It was he who preserved the old habits and rituals (like tattooing) and passed them on to future generations.

TAULIPÁNG - forearms of Wapishana and Taulipáng women have been tattooed in recent decades, and facial tattoo with conspicuous curvilinear patterns, often of fishhook shape, was common.

TAUNGO – a tribe from the Middle Myanmar. Thomas Joyce reported that they have a strange habit to tattoo women faces to be all black; black as a polished fireplace door. Inhabitants of Burma say that their king once fell in love to a beautiful local girl and order her to go to the palace with him. The relatives could not refuse and so – in order to make her ugly – they covered her face in tattoos. In his anger, the furious ruler ordered that all women from this tribe would forever wear a black tattoo all over their faces…"

TAVDLORUTIT – tattoo (name of Inuit tattoo designs in Greenland).

TCHINKITANAYANS – Indian tribe, Gulf of Alaska - Tattoos were little used among Tchinkitanayans, several men had tattoos on their arms and legs below the knee, almost all women were tattooed on the same parts of the body.

TCHOUTI – expression for tattoo of Peul tribe, West Africa.

TE AHI TAOKILI – after the turauwano rite, the priest laid small mats across the beach at a certain distance from each other and placed a turmeric root on every one of them. One of the tattooed women bent over every one of these mats, called te ahi taokili, leaned on her hand and tried to kick her leg as high as possible. After this unaesthetic expression of strength, they ate together; the taboo was over and women could return to their homes.

TE ÁNDO – coconut shell soot mixed with tattoo paint, Marshall Islands.

TE FAKAKAI ŊA TAU - Payment is made to the tattooer. It is termed te fakakai ŋa tau, 'the sharpening of the tattooing,' and is regarded as a recompense for the work involved, Tikopia.

TE KAI N ORO – tattoo hammer, Karibati, Oceania.

TE RUA O TE MOKO – the pit of the tattoo, Ngai-Tahu tribe, New Zealand.

TE TINO ʹAHA – body with ʹaha tattoo, Bellona.

TE WAE – coconut, from whose soot a tattoo paint was made, by mixing with salt and water, Karibati, Oceania.

TE WII N TAITAI – tattoo tools, Karibati, Oceania..

TEA – having no tattoo marks on the face, Maori.

TEBORI (手彫り) - traditional Japanese hand tattoo.

TEDEK– tattoo or tedek is a part of the Kayan culture and identity. The Kayas are particularly dond of tattooing with the women more then the man. A Kayan woman is tattooed in complicated serial designs on upper part of the hands and over the whole of each forearm; on both thighs to below the knees, and on the upper part of the feet and toes. Tedek begins when girls are about eight or ten years of age, at first the hand and feet, and afterwards, prior to arriving to the age of puberty the other parts are finished.

TEDJE DEIDEI - this is what the tattooist in southern Hawaii were called.

TEDJE DEIDUA – this is what the tattooist in the north of Hawaii were called.

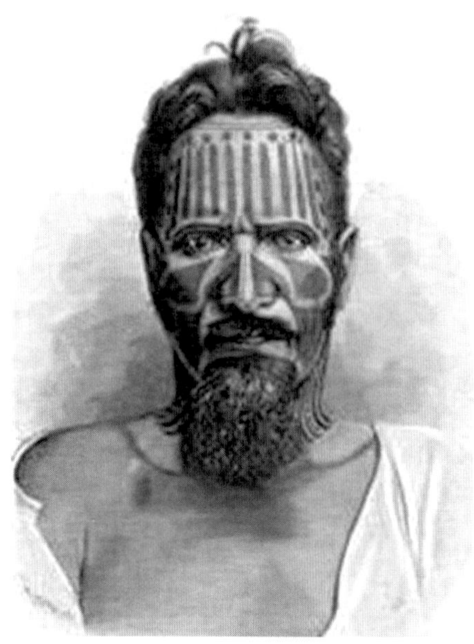

Juan Tepano

TELA FILA - The women of the Malagasy tribe in Madagascar use three needles connected by wire as their main tool in tattooing, which they call the tela fila.

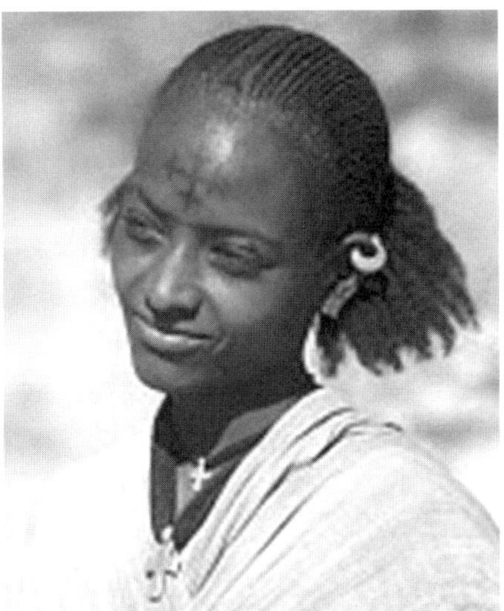

Tigray woman has a cross of the Ethiopian Orthodox Church tattooed on her forehead

TELANG JULAN - Among Kayan women tattooing is universal. They believed that the design act as torches in the next world and that without these to light them would make them forever in total darkness. They also believed that after death the completely tattooed women will be allowed to bathe in the mythical Telang Julan river and that consequently they will be able to pick up any precious articles and stones that are found on the river bed.

TELEFUA – or telenoa, literally naked, a designation for non-tattooed Samoans.

TELENOA – see TELEFUA.

TENBOKU - in old Japanese books, other names appear for tattoos, such as tenboku - celestial black ink.

TENSEI - in old Japanese books, other names appear for tattoos, such as tensei – stipple with blue.

TEPANO, JUAN – (4 March 1867 – 8 November 1947) was a Rapa Nui leader of Easter Island. Tepan had tattoos on his face and neck. The forehead was decorated with six to ten vertical stripes, followed by a tattoo which symbolizing bird on the neck.

TEQUQ – Lampblack or graphite was mixed with urine (tequq), perhaps because it came from the bladder, an organ believed to be one of the primary seats of the life-giving force of the soul, st. Lawrence, Alaska.

TES-KO - tattooing, Chinook Indians.

TEŠIÄ - With the onset of puberty the young people of both sexes receive the tribal tattooing amid similar ceremonies. The outline of a circle is marked on both cheeks with a stamp made out of a piece of gourd (tešiä). Then the place is cut out with a small sharp stone, and cotton lint is put in the wound. After stopping the bleeding, genipa juice rubbed in causes the blue color of the scar, Karajá, Brazil.

TEYE – the well-preserved mummy of the Egyptian lady Teye, with tattoos and the earlobes severely deformed due to the regular wearing of heavy earrings; around 1000 BC, from Der el-Bahri in Thebes.

TĚ-CHE SHOO-DOOK - the soot used for tattooing. It was made by burning pitch under a stone, on which the soot was deposited, Ner´-er´-ner, Ycoastal Yurok.

THELEPALEMÉK – tattooist, Fais Island.

THOMPSON INDIANS - are also known as Ntlakyapamuk. Location the Thompson Indian homeland is the Fraser,

Thompson, and Nicola River Valleys in southwest British Columbia. Language Thompson is a dialect of the Interior division of the Salishan language family.

THRACIANS – were an Indo-European speaking people who inhabited large parts of Eastern and Southeastern Europe in ancient history. Their tattoos served as a sign of dignity.

THRODI – tattooist (female), Fulani tribe, Mali, Africa.

TI – tattoo in Eskimo language.

TIAIRI – The tattoo color. The colouring matter was the kernel of the candle-nut, aleurites triloba, called by natives' tiairi. This was first baked, and then reduced to charcoal, and afterwards pulverized and mixed with oil, Society Islands.

TIFINAGH – an expression for the ancient Berber alphabet, from which many of their tattooed marks are derived.

TIITIIPOO - a god in Polynesia who allegedly invented the tattoo technique together with his brother Matamaatar. See HINAEREER-EMONOI

TIMUCUA – Tattooing was practiced extensively and "all these chiefs and their wives ornament their skin with punctures arranged so as to make certain designs... Doing with this sometimes makes them sick for seven or eight days. They rub the punctured places with a certain herb, which leaves an indelible color." But the strangest of their customs. "For the sake of further ornament and magnificence, they let the nails of their fingers and toes grow, scraping them down at the sides with a certain shell so that they are left very sharp. They are

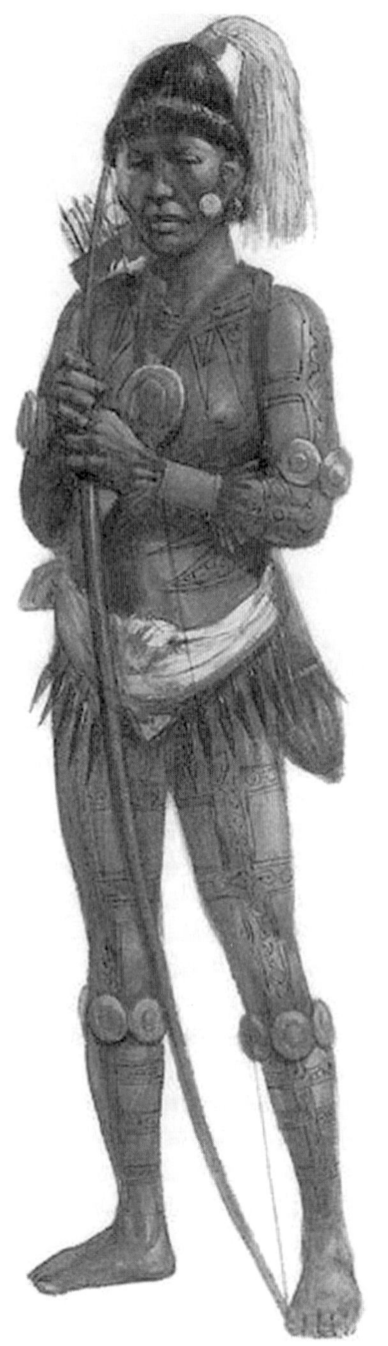

Timucua woman

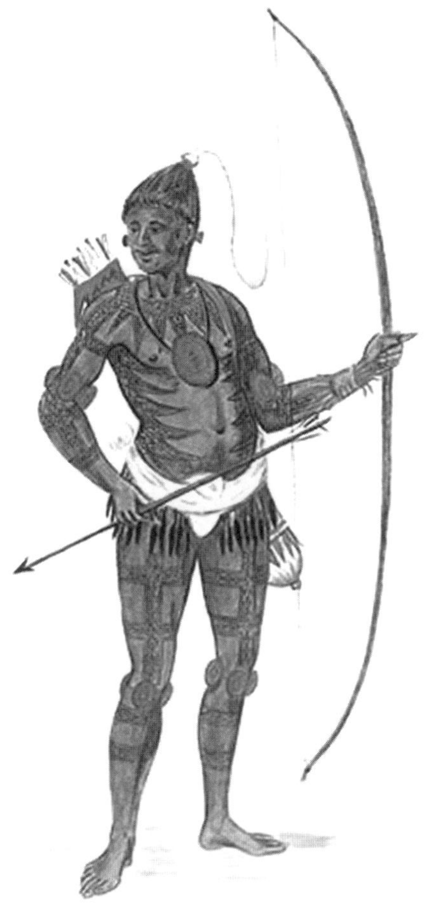

Timucua men, c. 1562 from painting by J. Le Moyne. The men had distinctive hairstyles, wore feather crowns and ear plugs, were heavily tattooed

also in the habit of painting the skin around

TINHLANGA – (from sing. nhlanga). Ornamental cicatrization, keloid scars, or ink-based tattoo, Mozambique. Lenge or Tsopi woman at a glance" from her tattoos, she was more attentive to the enormous diversity of women's body-marking and to the many ways in which

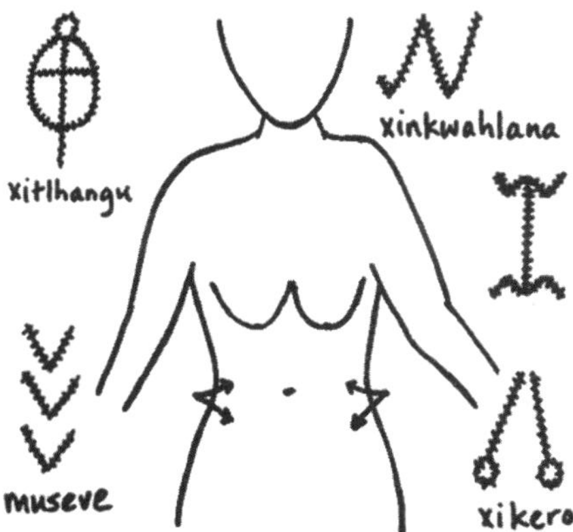

tinhlanga defied classification along strictly ethnic, clan, or family lines. Earthy in her account presents a list of a truly "bewildering" range of tattoo types, designs, and meanings prevalent among Chopi and Lenge women in the 1920s: keloid and incised tattoos of various sizes; images symbolizing seashells, birds, insects, reptiles, plants, arrowheads, body fluids (saliva, tears), lunar and astral bodies, mortar and pestle, a "sacred wand" used in women's harvest ceremonies, and

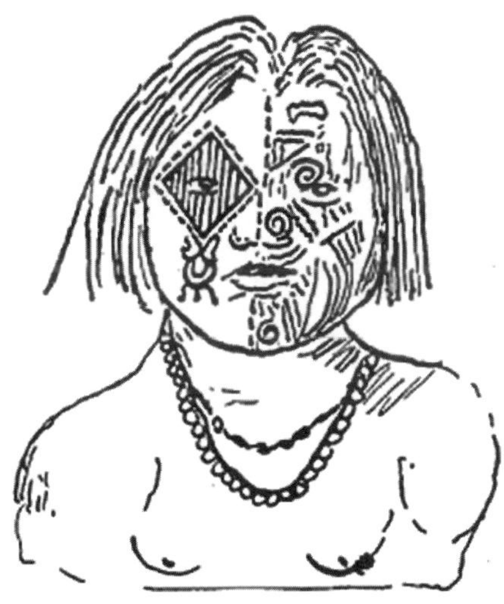

Tattoo adopted by woman of the Tobas tribe

more abstract designs representing such social concerns as marital status, mourning, and protection from witchcraft.

TINHLEKE TA BA-RONGA – tattoo, Khosen tribe, South Africa.

TITI- tattoo in the language of the Mentawai tribe, Polynesia.

TIWANAKU (TIAHUANACO) – an ancient civilization that lived on the territory of today's Peru, most often it is dated to the 3rd century A.D., however, the first villages was built there 3 500 years ago already. Local Natives consider the Tiahuanaco ruins as the seats of their ancestors but which Tiahuanaco nation built them remains a mystery lost in the trammel of speculations to this day. Tattoos were found on the discovered mummies.

TJEN – one of the types of tattoos in ancient China. Tjen was used as a designation for exiles to remote provinces and had a very harsh social impact.

TODA PEOPLE – a nation in India. William H. R. Rivers mentioned their fondness for tattoos: "Only women got tattooed. The patterns consist from circles and dots connected into direct lines, and most of the times they can be seen on chest, shoulders and upper arms. I believe that a peculiar ritual is connected to tattooing but I failed to achieve satisfactory information…"

TOHU - a Polynesian god of tattoos. According to the Polynesian cosmogony, gods practiced tattoos under control of Tohu, the god of tattoos and the creator of multifarious shapes and colours of fish. Two gods, Mata Mata Arahu and Tura'l

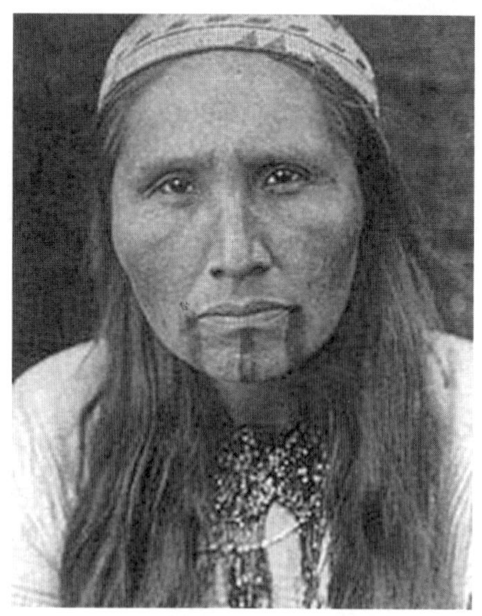

Tolowa tattooing

Po, whose bodies were covered in tattoos, once visited a maiden called Hina at night to seduce her. She succumbed to them and run away with them. When the mortals decided to imitate the gods, Mata Mata Arahu and Tura'l Po, taught them how to imprint tattoos into their skin. Since then, the people tattoo themselves to please the gods and be attractive for others.

TOHUNGA - The Maori tattoo artist is called the tohunga ta moko which means moko specialist.

TOHUNGA-TA-MOKO - is a traditional name for a tattoo expert. The word tohunga mean an expert and it exists in the context of several disciplines like tohunga-whakairo (expert carver) or tohunga-rongoa (a healer, herb grower). Currently, tohunga means a priest (but the word is literally translated as an expert). It is derived from the fact that all arts of tea o Maori (the Maori World)

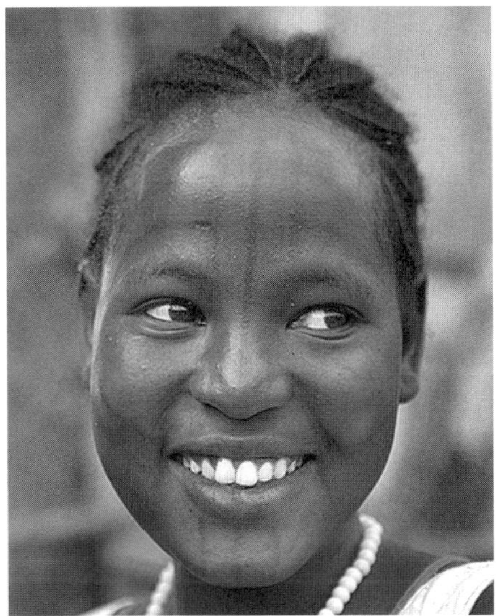

Tsamai woman with tattoos - Ethiopia

are promised to gods and for the completeness of the art procedure, it is necessary to perform rites and contemplations (meditations). So, tohunga is not only an expert of a certain field, but also has a realtions to atua (gods), on which behalf they performed the sacred art and appropriate karakia (long religious singing) and celebrations in order to avoid spiritual raruraru (troubles).

TOKI – edge of tattoo tools, Tikopia Islands..

TOMBOKA - in Sakalavian, it means both "foot" and "tattoo." Tomboka means not only the tattoo process, but also its result.

TOMBOKALANA – the name for tatttoo on Madagaskar, tomboka means too „to mark".

TOMBOTOMBOKA - sometimes also kitomboka fanjaitra, less frequently tselitselika – is a tattoo process using the skin needling in the Sakalava language. The etymology reveals the way in which the tattooing is performed: by small needles (fanjaitra) by which the skin is peeled off, as by punches with miniature pickaxes, which then allows washing with the appropriate mixture and putting the dye particles between skin and dermis.

TONGO – islands of Polynesia, where tattoos were practiced.

TORRES STRAIT- The natives of the Torres Strait betweenNew Guinea and the northern tip of Australia worshiped the shark, which wasa frequent subject of their intricatetattoos.

TORRES STRAIT - The natives of the Torres Strait between New Guinea and the northern tip of Australia worshiped a shark, which was a frequent subject of their intricate tattoos.

TOSI GAHO – paint tattoo outlines, Bellona island.

TOTSIN – tattoo "hammer" of the Atayal tribe from Taiwan. The tattoo tool resembled a toothbrush with four to sixteen needles (atok) arranged in rows and mounted on a wooden handle about 1.5 cm in diameter and 15 cm in length.

TOUGUI - Bleeding of the face or tearing of the skin for the purpose of tattooing, Tonga Island.

TRIOMETEZENS – or OJARIKULETI, an Indian tribe in the Amazon, also practiced facial tattoos.

TSAMAI - An ethnic group in southwestern Ethiopia practicing tattoos.

TSELITSELIKA – tattoo process, see Tombotomboka. Tselitselika refers to the

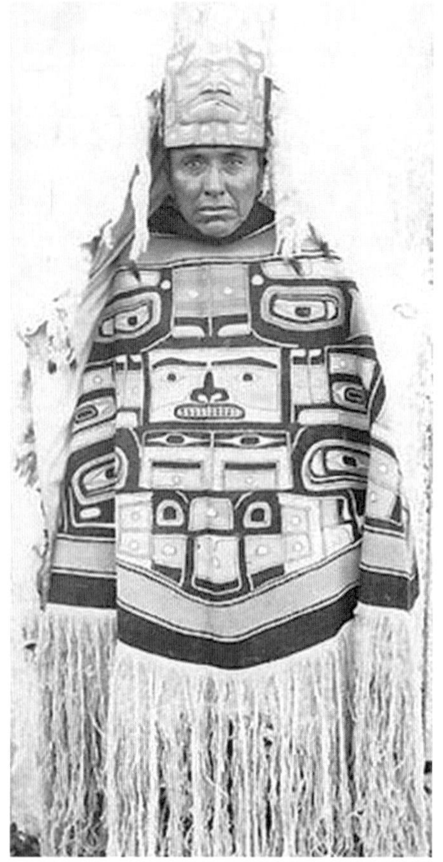

Tahltan, cca 1909

speed of action, the skills of the tattoo artist.

TSIVARIUKA - tattoo in the antanus dialect. For the Antatsim, some of them have special names, some of which do not appear in the Antavaratras, Madagascar.

TSUKI-BORI - a methodology of traditional Japanese hand tattooing that, according to the records of the Tokai Tattoo Club of Japan, is a reference to the "thrust" method of tattooing based in Osaka and western prefectures.

TSUKI-HARI - For bokashi, there are two distinct ways of manipulating the needles. The first of these implies that the needles are inserted perpendicularly into the skin (tsuki-hari). The technique is commonly used for tattooing spaces requiring even colouring.

TU'A – plate of tattoo tool, Tonga.

TU´ATAA – tattooed back, Bellona.

TU´AA TAA– sons or grandsons of persons with taukuka 'ago (chest tattoos) were named tu'aa taa in honor of this person, Bellona Island

TUATUA COCONUT - The handle lashing forms a neat piece of work. The thicker tuatua coconut fibres are used and look like fine copper wire.

TUBATULABAL – an Indian tribe from the Juto-Aztec language family, California, where tattoos used to be only a female ornament.

TUDA– The juice from this plant serves as tattoo paint, Siberut Island.

TUFOU MA FILELEI — tattooist, Fiji.

TUFUGA TA TATAU – tattooist, Samoa.

TUFUNA TA TAU – tattooist, Tikopia.

TUFUNGA TATARU – tattoo master, Samoa.

TUFUNGA TA TATAU - tattooist, Tonga.

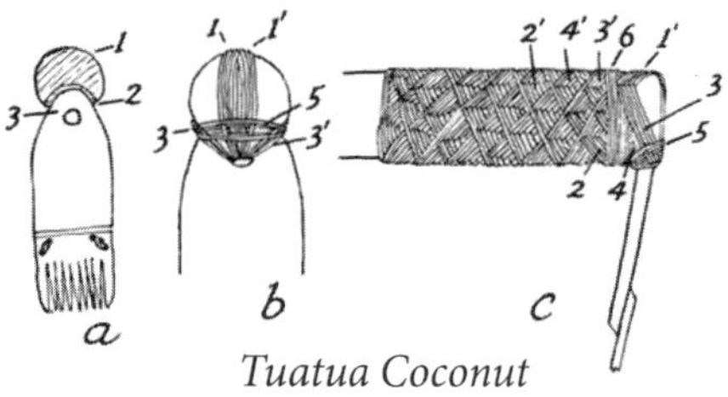

Tuatua Coconut

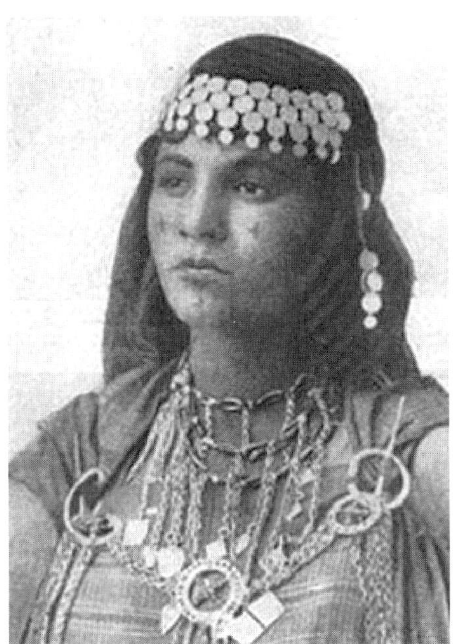
Tunisian face tattoo

TUFUNGA TA´UTAU - tattooist, Gilbert Islands.

TUHUNA - is a traditional Polynesian word for a tattoo master (priest). As in modern cultures, it was necessary to get trained before the man could became a Tuhuna master tattooist. Unlike the North American and Japanese teaching, the taboos connected to the handicraft were taught, too. A man had to master necessary skills before he was respected for his work among villagers.

TUHUNA PATU TIKI – another term for tattooist, Marquesas Islands.

TUHUNGA – tattooist, Samoa.

TU´I - Mallet, used to grind carbon black and mix dye, Samoa.

TUKIPU – full tattooed man, Maori.

TUKUN – an iron mallet that hits a tattoo tool, Borneo.

TUNUMA - is defined in George Milner's dictionary as "cylindrical vessels carved out of a piece of wood and for specific tattoo tools". The German ethnologist Augustin Krämer described Tunuma as a "bottomless beaker" in which tattoo tools were held.

TUPIS – Guarani tribe in eastern Brazil, tattooing of girl at puberty.

TUSI TATAU – 1. To pay for tattooing. 2. Tapa for soaking up blood in a new tattooing, Bellona.

TUTITUI – tar from the Candlenut tree, which was used to burn ngarah.

TWANA – North American Indian tribe that practiced tattoos. Use a needle and thread for this. They blackened the thread with charcoal and drew as deep under the skin.

TZ-HWA - a type of a tattoo in old China. Tz-Hwa was optional, it was a fashion

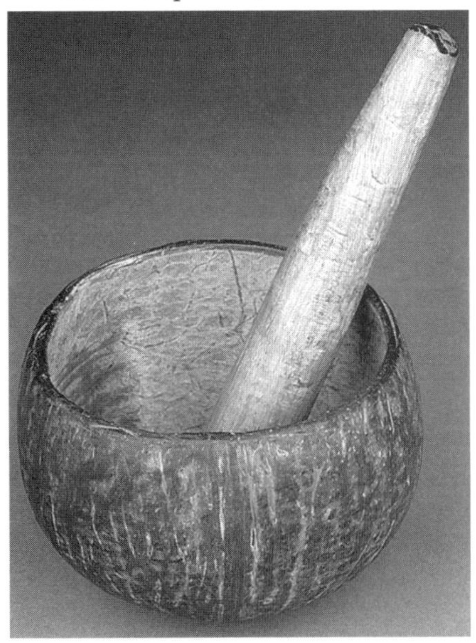
Tunuma

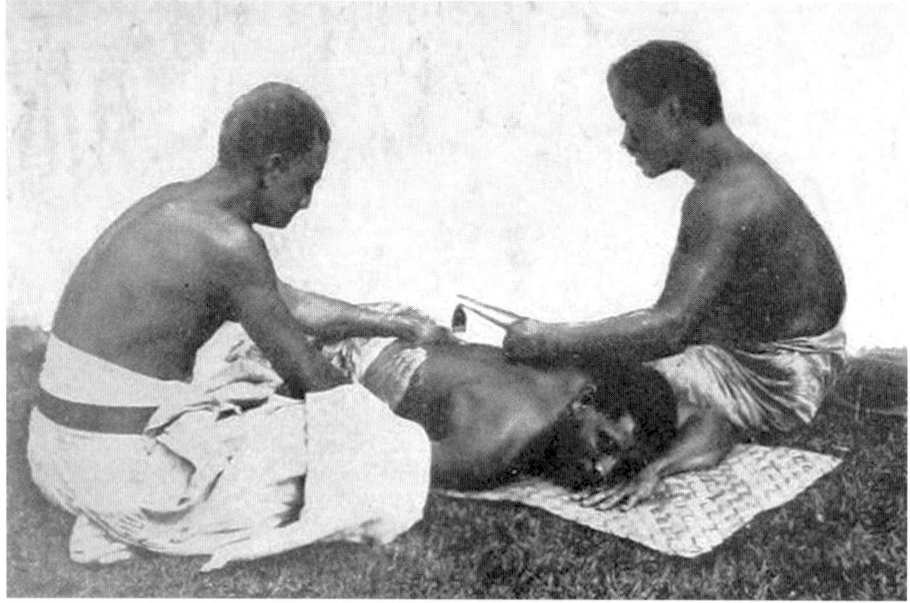

Tattooist, tufuga ta tatau, (left) and assistant (right) tattooing a man's back, 1895 ,photo by Thomas Andrew

that came through Arabia from far Egypt and it consisted of flower and butterfly motifs and delicate ornaments. It, however, never spread too much and the last records of it are from the rule of the Chou dynasty between 300 – 100 B. C. and then it vanished.

TZOW-GWIT-ZOW - The ingredients for tattooing or pricking marks on chest are red ochre (tzow-gwit-zow) or black lead (toong-e-raillery) and indigo bei den Tschuktschi.

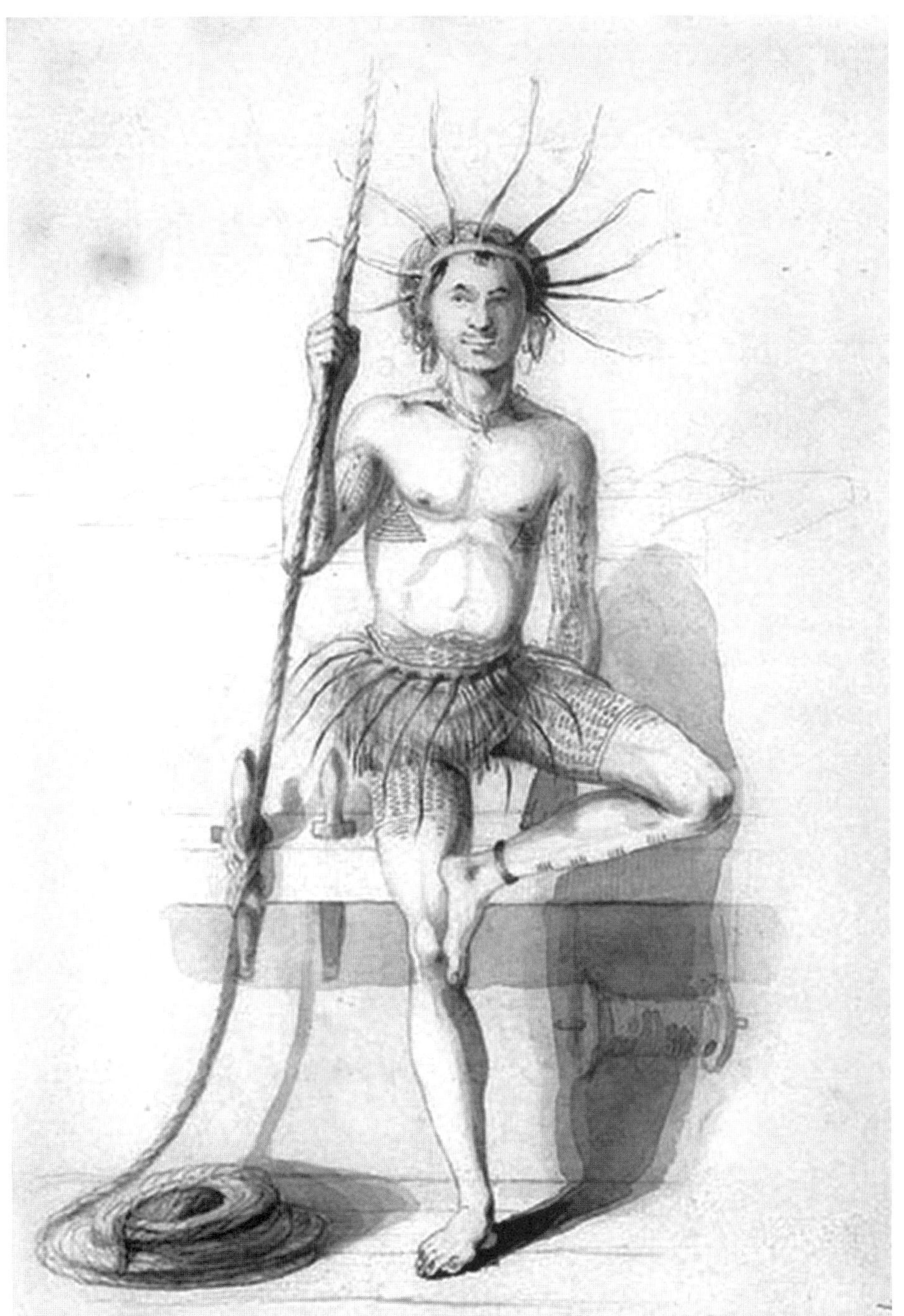

Tuvaluan man in traditional costume, 1841

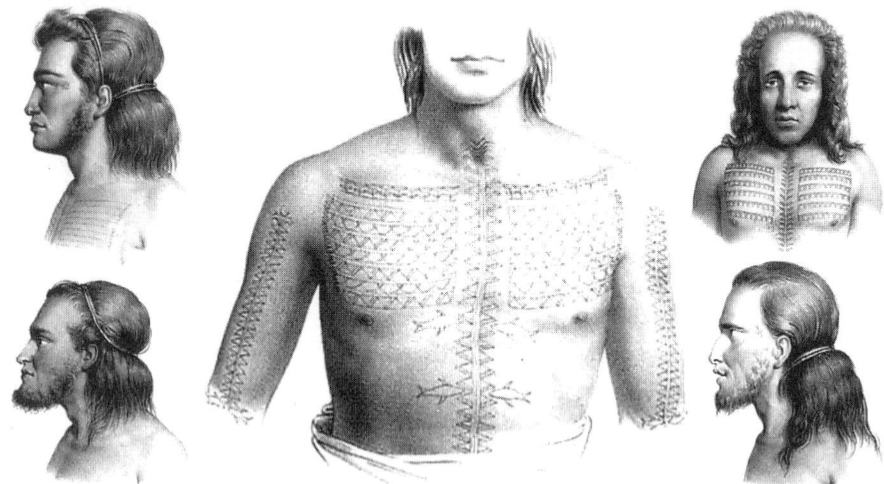

This large finely engraved original lithograph Illustrating different tattoos on Tikopia part of the Solomon Islands group was engraved by Antoine Maurin (1793-1860) and was published in the 1833 edition of Dumont d'Urville Voyage de la corvette l'Astrolabe.The patterns were generally applied in the following order, although this was by no means rigidly adhered to. 1. The face, usually starting with the forehead, the patterns at the eyes, then the cheeks and finally, in the case of women, the jawline. 2. Te tau. The line down the front of the body.3. Fatafata. The male chest design which has not been done in recent times.4. The arms 5. The back.

´UGI (´UNGI) - To be black, dark blue (as tattooing), Ugi may be qualified by sinusinu (glistening, bright, said of taukuka chest tattoo), Bellona.

ÚGO O NA TAUKUKA (´UNGU O N.T.) - 'U. chant danced at the beginning of each raukuka tattooing session (the process might last several months), Bellona.

´UHIMATA - Name of the ceremony in which certain female relatives (as wife, daughter, sister, mother, grandmother, 'igaamutu) wailed and gave gifts to a person about to be tattooed with the tauliuka, done at the moment the mataisau (tattooer) began the tattooing, Bellona.

´ULA – red, scarlet, brown as in skin of Hawaiians.

´UNA - Side tattooing, as of taukuka, Bellona.

U ´I TATAU – tattoo, Rarotongan Island.

UA POU – Ua Pou - tattoo style from the Marquesas Islands. Is put on below the knee only, in horizontal bands of delicately lined patterns, the motives on either side of the center, front and back, being exactly alike. The whole may be conceived of in front and back longitudinal sections of symmetrical halves, which meet in the middle of either

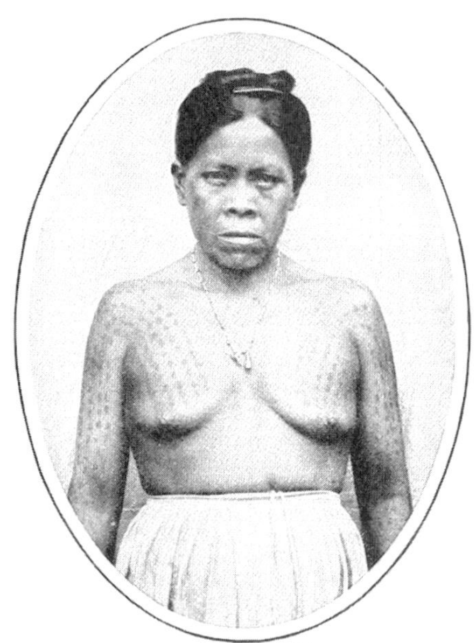

Uanana woman

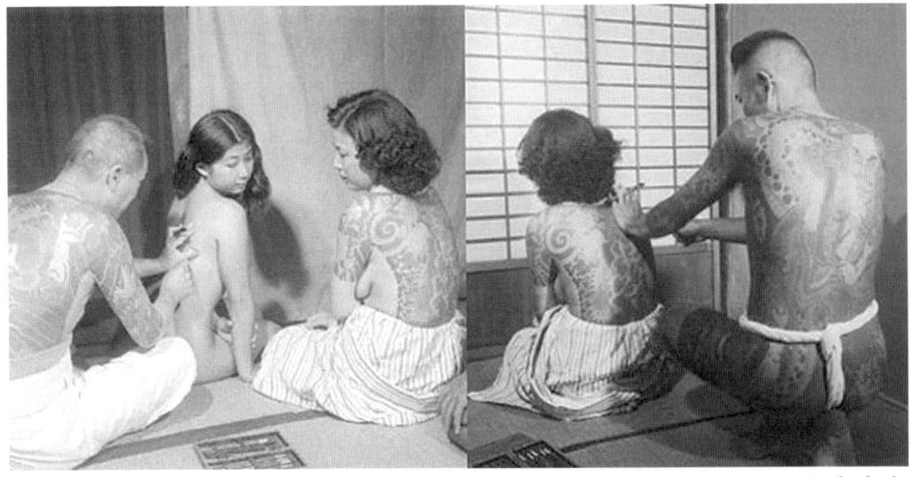

Uchideshi

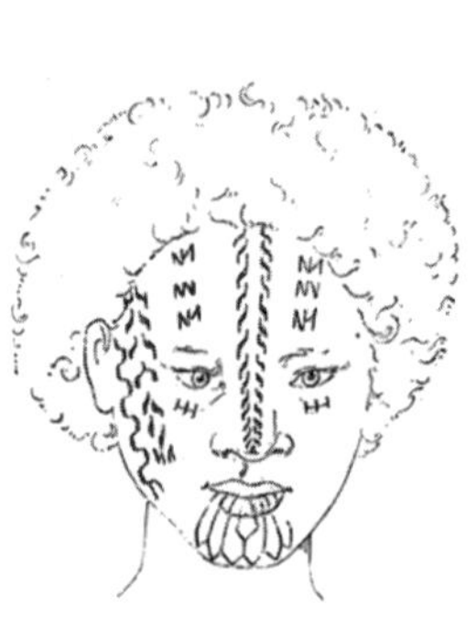

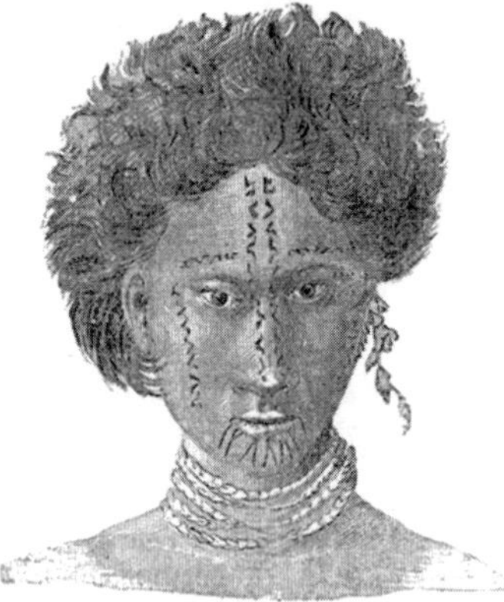

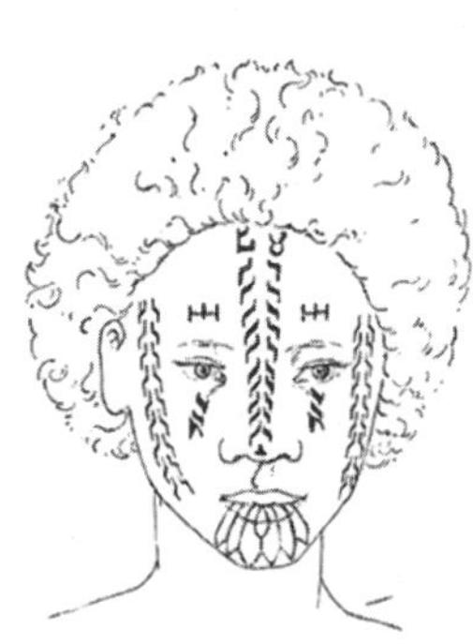

Udu motif on the nose of Hula girls

side of the leg. Naturalistic, geometric, and conventional treatments are all present.

UANANA – also described historically as the Ananas, are an Eastern Tukanoan language group of Amerindians who occupy the banks of the Vaupés River from Uaracapuri Falls in Colombia to Yavarete, Brazil.

UCHIDESHI - a student, who lives with his master - horishi (Japan) and, in addition to studying, holds other work in the house. Uchideshi does not receive any salary, nor does he pay his master for teaching him; as a student he receives food and clothing.

UDAYAR - The tattoo marks on the foreheads of Udayar woman consist of a crescent and dot, and they have a straight line tattooed at the outer corners of the eyes.

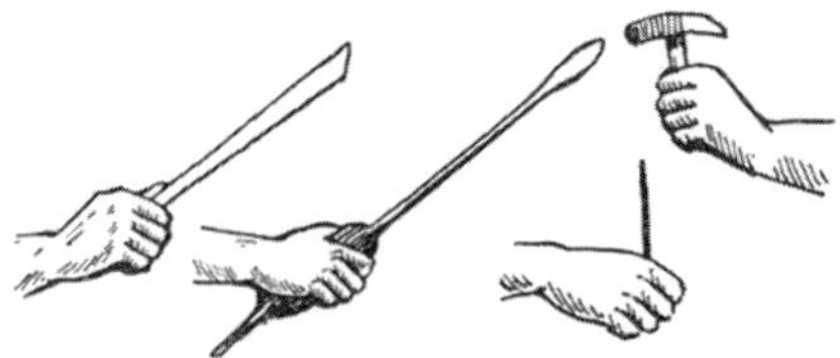

Mallets and methods of holding them

UETONGA - (myth.), a grandson of Ba, the Earth- quake-god. Uetonga dwelt in the Spirit-world (Po) and there taught the art of tattooing to Mataora, who communicated it to men. Uetouga was the father of Niwareka, who was the wife of Mataora — A. H. M., ii. 4. The tattooing on the body of Maui was the work of Uetonga.

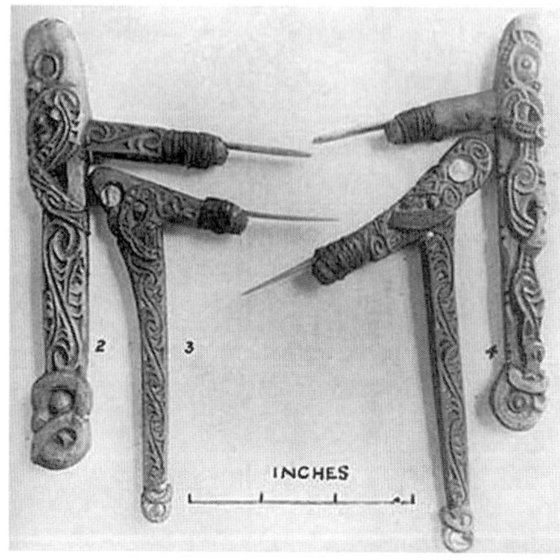

1 - Uhi whaka-tataramoa, 2 - Uhi puru, 3 - Uhi kohiti, 4 - Uhi matarau

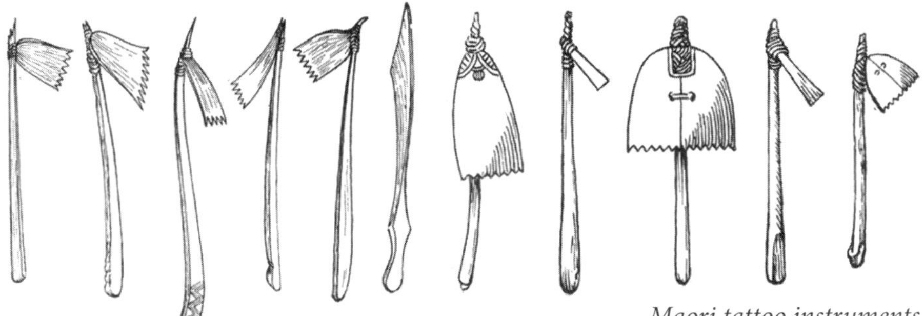

Maori tattoo instruments

UGU O NA TAUKUKA - singing at the beginning of a tattoo on the chest, Bellona Island.

UHI– Hawaiian marking of tattooed symbols.

UHI– tattoo chisel in Maori terminology.

UHI KOHITI - small UHI, for a fine work.

UHI MOLI – tattoo instrument, Hawaii.

UHI PURU – see UHI MATARAU

UHI TAPAHI - cutting chisel, used for cutting the skin only.

UHI WHAKA-TATARAMOA - This is the first implement used. It is used to "clear the way," to cut the skin in preparation for the uhi which implants the pigment.

UHIMATA – tattoo ceremony in which female relatives mourn tattooed people and bring gifts to the person to be tattooed, Bellona Island.

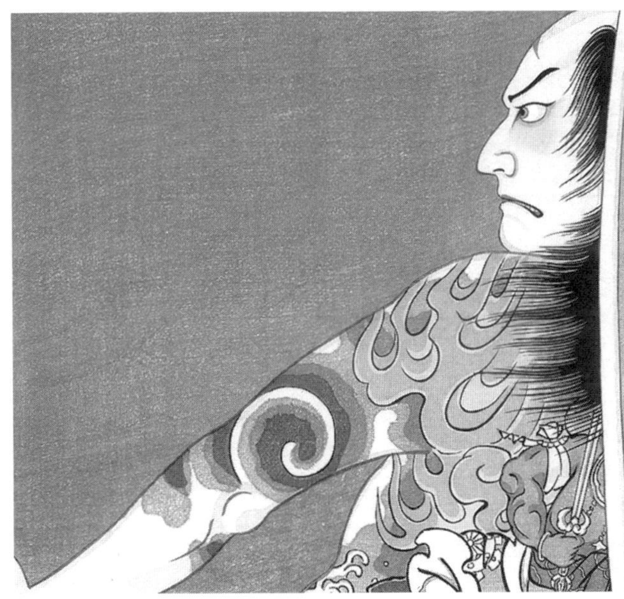

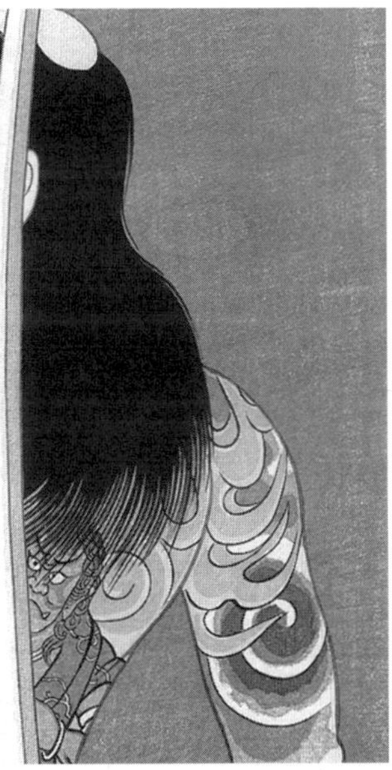

Ukijo-e

UHUUHU – term for tattooing in the southern part of the Solomon Islands.

UIT ULANG – wooden container in which was a mixture for tattooing, Borneo.

UKIYO-E (浮世絵)- pictures of the floating world is a term describing genre pictures (drawings) created using Japanese woodblock prints (sometimes referred to only as wood prints) from the 17th to 20th century. The used technique of printing allowed mass production. It was a color print on wooden blocks using templates. The theme was mainly rural life and the entertainment industry (sumo fighters, courtesans, artists, etc.). Reproductions were available to poorer people who could not afford the original works of the masters. The Ukiyo-e says "life from day to day and enjoys your life free from all doctrines." The Ukiyo-e elements can be found within the traditional Japanese tattoo.

UKIT PEOPLE - is a tribe found in Sarawak, Malaysia. They are a small minority people who until recently were nomads in the rain forests of Borneo.

ULANG or ULANG BRANG– tattoo needles, two or three are used, Borneo.

ULED-ADBDERRAHMAN – tribe from North Africa, refer to tattoos under two names: lusam and ahajam.

ULITHIS – Ulithi women from the Western Pacific got their labia minora tattooed. In some areas, such tattoos were a part of an initiation ritual because it gave the girl the status of an adult woman. This tradition was so strong that when a baby was born to a woman, who have no such tattoo, on the Nakura Island in the Southern Pacific the newborn had to be put to death.

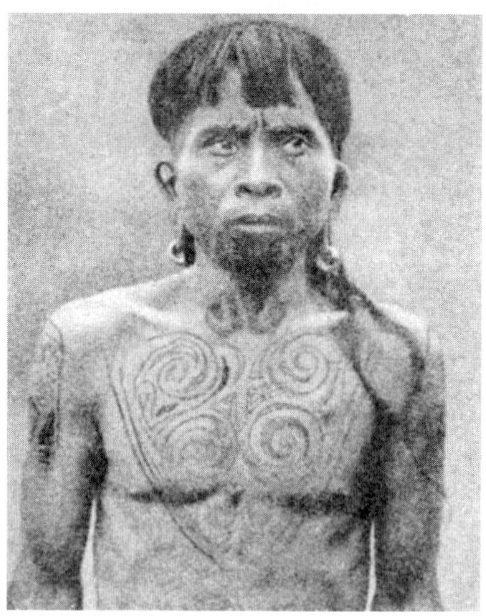

Ukits of the Rejang tattoo extensively. A bold hook pattern covers the chest, and a pattern known as the lizard adorns the sides of the shoulders

'UMAGA - (ending) the final session includes a tattoo of the abdomen and navel. The area that covers the navel is called pute, and is probably the most painful phase of the process.

UMUSAGA - ceremonial sign of finishing the tattoo on Samoa. Naumusaga is a tattooed person anointed with turmeric and egg yolk and gifts are presented to the tattoo artist.

UMUTI - Before the ta-tau (tattoo in Tahiti), the individual purified himself spiritually by walking on hot lava stones during the Umuti ceremony.

URI-URI – tattoo in Daui district, Papua New Guinea.

URUTETEFO – one of the brothers who were commissioned by the god Oro to lead the secret community of Ariori.

UST´ULAGAN – a valley where the tattooed body of a (Scythian) prince from the second kurhan was found in Pazyryk in the mountains of the eastern Altai in southern Siberia (now Russia, near the Mongolian border).

USU– Common name for tattoo, Solomon Islands.

USUZUMI - By diluting the sumi with water, a gray shade was derived called usuzumi,used for instance for carp fins, Japan.

UTE - paper mulberry (Broussonetia papyrifera), which serves as a gift to tuhun, a master of tattoos, Marquis.

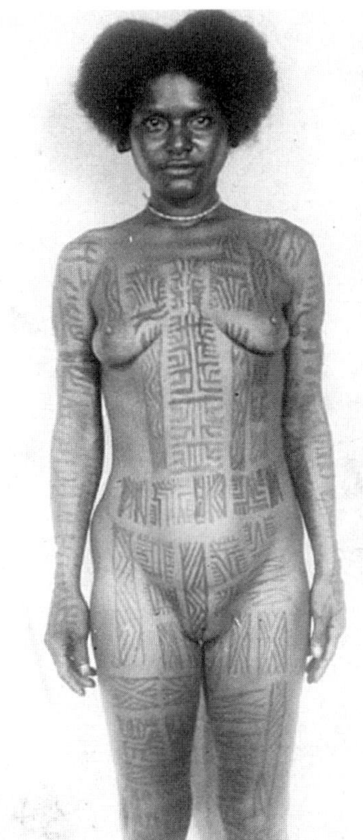

Uri-Uri

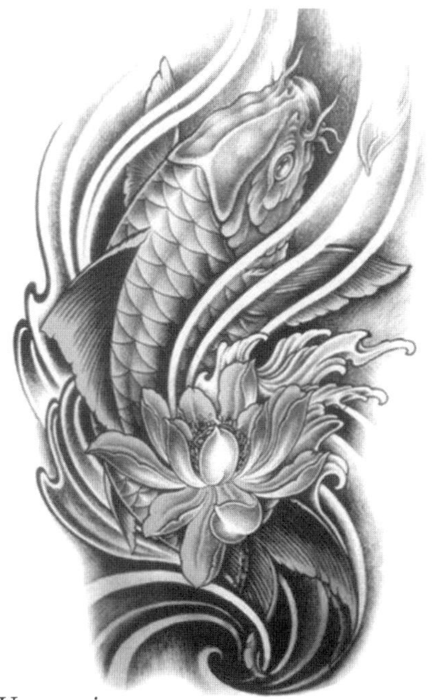

Usuzumi

UZAIRIJ – a Bedouin tribe located on the territory of today's Iran, they practiced tattooing. There is a well-known case of a Bagdad policeman from this tribe. Instead of a dot on the nose, he had a cross with a dot in every angle on each temple. All previous children of his mother have died, he said, and so his mother got him tattooed in this way to survive. He added that the design is also good for his head.

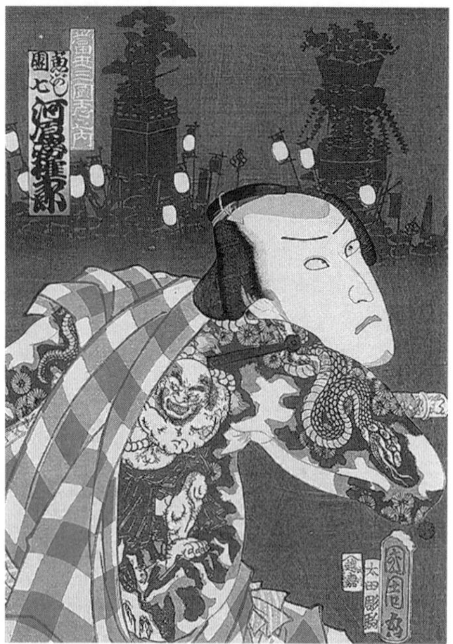

Toyohara Kunichika Snake Tattoo

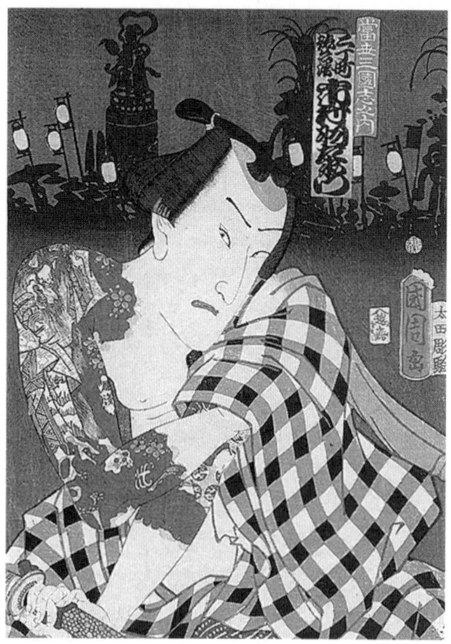

Toyohara Kunichika Wolf Tattoo

VAHA – Unfinished tattoo, Marquesas Islands.

VAIDU - The tattoo artists in Mumbai are often women, professional herbalists known as Vaidu.

VAI TAI - sea water – see TE MAMI

VAITUPU – tattoing in, Ellice Islands.

VARIBORI - tattooing, Tobi island.

VATOTRUKA - people from northwestern Madagascar used juice squeezed from vatotruka (Tristemmavirusanum) for tattoo ink.

VATUKE – see FATUKE

VEI-QIA – term for tattoos in Fiji. Only women could wear tattoos.

VERREE-VERREE – tattoo, Tobi Island.

VILJARU – scar tattoos, Australia.

VISAYA or BISAYA – the name of one of the principal nations of the Philiphines, of their language, and of the peopled by them. The Bisaya Islands include those lying between the two great islands of Luzon and Mindano, as Panay, Leyte etc. The name was given to them from the practise of painting or probably tattooing their person, which obtained among thein inhabitants when they were first seen by the Spaniards, the word bisaya signifying in thein langure „to paint.“

The first tattoos a person received were applied to the legs beginning at the ankles and ending at the waist. Chest tattoo

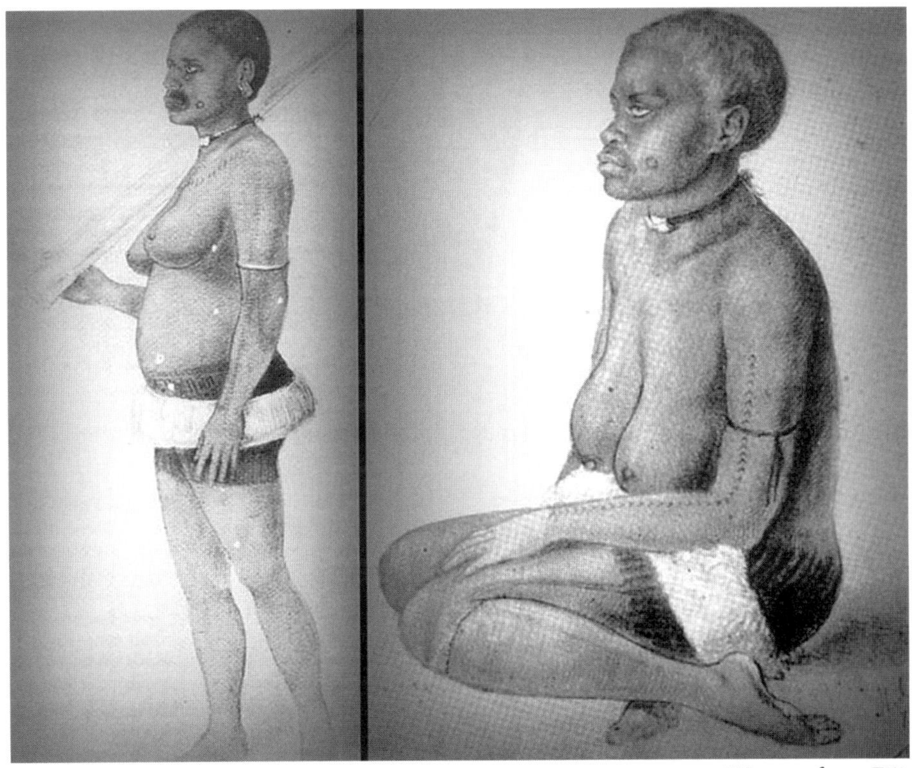

Women from Fiji

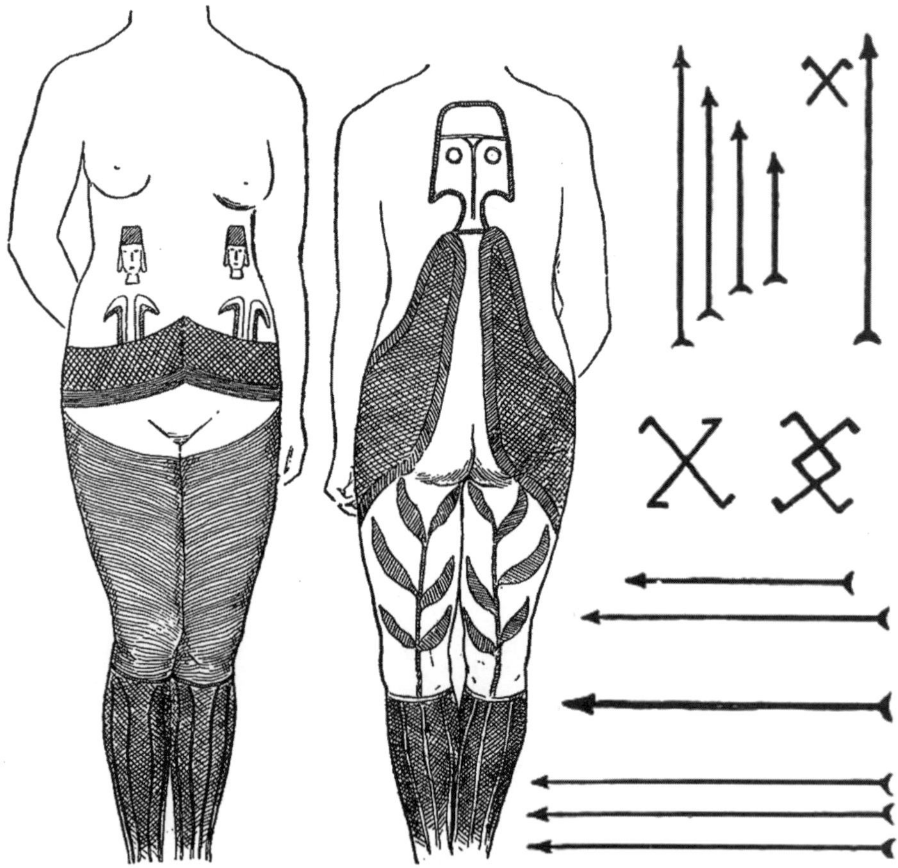

Tattoo of an indigenous woman from Easter Island *Virginian tattoo designs*

which looked like breast-plates, less frequently, tattoos on the abdomen, only came after further action in battle. Fascial tattoos from ear to chin to eye were restricted to the boldest and toughest warriors.

VITI – Viti Levu is the largest island of Fiji. People there practiced tattoos.

VOALITSEKA – squeezed fruit juice, which together with soot or coal dust forms a coloring tincture, Sakalava.

VÚIĚD - For (tattoo) dye vuiěd, were used soot, which is caught through smoking (mangát) in bowls or shards over burning resin (běrór) or derived from oil poured onto burning wood (ilalitl). It is mixed with normal water for use, Palau isl.

VUNIWAI – the circumcision surgeon, Mboumbutho tribe, Melanesia.

VUSKATALATOGA – tattoo without a pattern, Mota tribe.

VUSRAG – tattoo, Mota tribe.

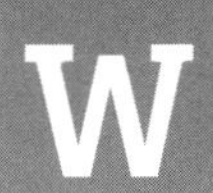

WA – Chinese term for old Japan – see GISHIWAJINDEN

WA´WINA – blue color, e.g. in tattoos, Native American tribe Western Mono, California.

WA´WUNA – charcoal from which blue tattoo ink is made, Western Mono Indian tribe, California.

WA-SAW-SEE – Indian name of the Osage tribe - see OSAGE

WADIGO - Bantu tribe on the equatorial east coast of Africa. Tattoos on the arm and stomach.

WADSCHAGGA – African tribe, practicing scar-tattooing.

WAGIGI TRIBE – belongs to the Bongo tribe group, practiced tattooing, Congo.

WAH-HO´-TE - face tattooing, Mitch-op-do Mi´-du tribe, Chico region, Sacramento Valley, California.

WAH´-KEN SA´TAH - soot for tattooing, Ko´-roo tribe, Sacramento River, Colusa region.

WAH´-KIN - tattoo marks, Ko´-roo tribe, Sacramento River, Colusa region.

WAHEHE (WAHÄHÄ) - people in Southeast Africa. Tattoos are only occasionally common.

WACHANZI TRIBE - they have the same palm leaf on their temple as Bayanzi; vertically on the forehead or a series of parallel cuts from the root of the nose, Congo.

WAI NGAARAHU – pigment for tattooing, Maori.

WAI WHAKATAERANGI – sap mixed with Awe carbon black.

WAIRǍDU - The tattooing was done by special persons who own stamps and stone knives and are called waira˘du, Karajá.

WAITAHOO – beauty of tattooing in, Marquesas Islands.

WAILAKI - An Athapascan tribe or group of many villages of Round valley. Like the Yuki the women have their noses and cheeks as well as their chins tattooed.

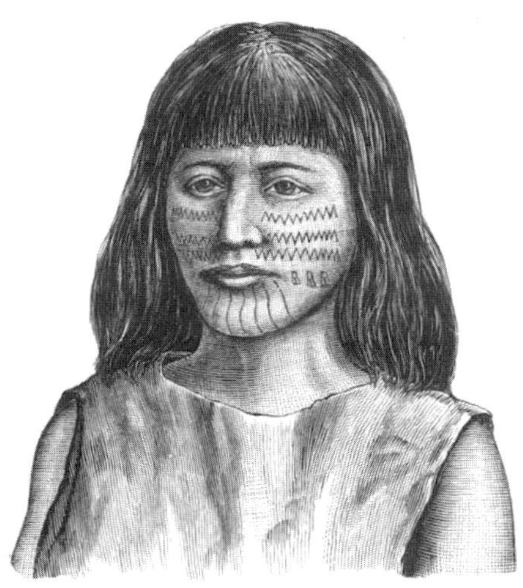

WAIRADU - Tattoo specialist, presses the end of a cut bamboo on the desired location, creating an indented motif. He then incises this with a sharp stone blade and rubs in a blue pigment extracted from the genipa plant, Karajá tribe.

WAIYAU TRIBE – central Africa tribe. Some women have raised lines crossing each other on the arms, which must have cost great pain; they have also small cuts, covering in some cases the whole body.

WAJIJI TRIBE – Tattooing explained as

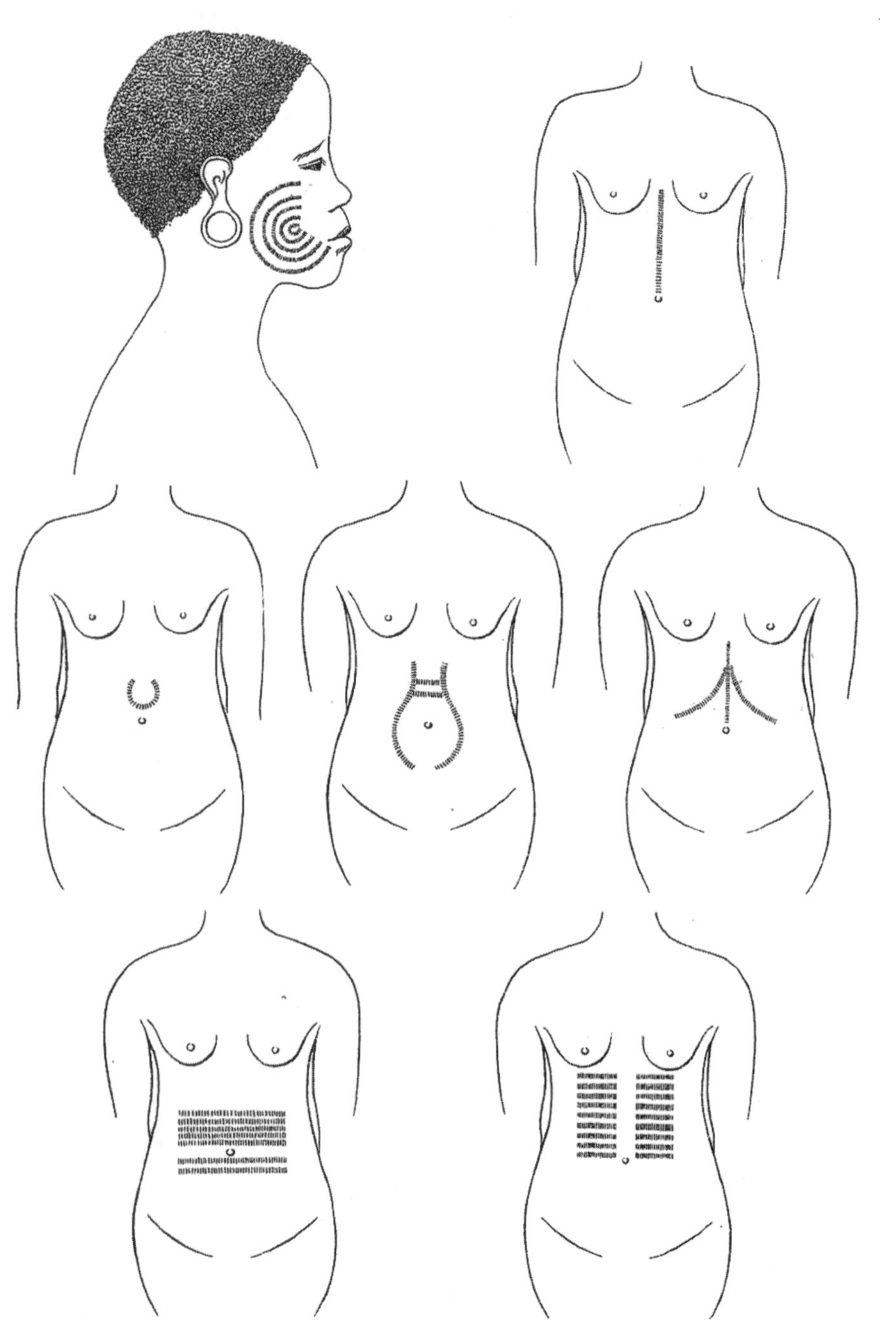

Wadschagga tribe

a protection against the humid atmosphere.

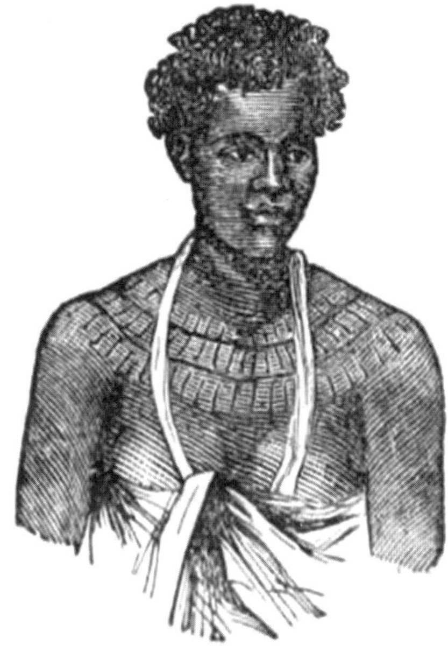

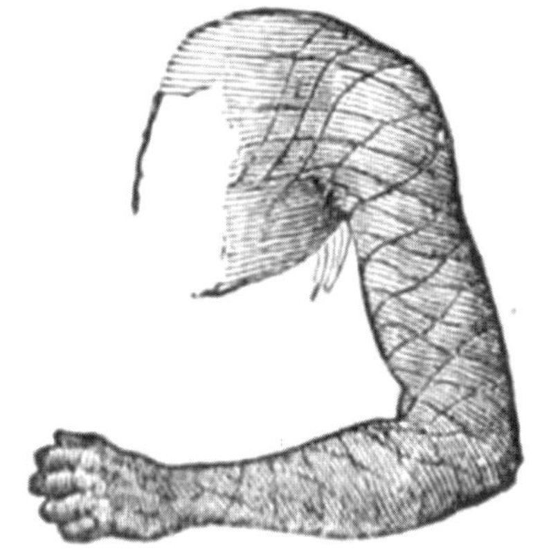

WAKANDA - was the invisible, mysterious, and sacred power that permeatewd all things, including the sacred bundles that housed tattoo instruments, which were derived from the Mysterious power itself. This divin
e

supernatural energy was revered and also feared because it was believed to animate the cosmos, al well as the spiritual and ancestral worlds of the people. Siouan Gross, North America.

WALAPAI TRIBE - tattooing was practiced to a moderate degree, more generally on women than men. Men more often tattoo their forearm or wrist, while women tattoo designs on their forehead or chin as well, and sometimes on their cheeks, calves, or the back or their hands. The most usual tattoo lines run from the lower lip down to the chin, one in the middle and from two to six diagonal lines descending outward from the lower lip.

WALUWA - a tree resin called waluwa is added to the honey. See EKLENG

WAMATIWI – just tattooed girl wearing a skirt called wamatiwi, Maisin tribe, Papua New Guinea.

WAMPUM - the contracted form of New England Algonquian, some of the natives had a set of lines tattooed on the inner side of the left forearm, which indicated the length of 5 shells of the several standards of length. The measures were subdivided, there being lines of moanala long and moanala short, and so on. This was the principal method of estimating the money. The first 5 on the string were measured by holding the tip of the first shell at the thumb nail and drawing the string along the arm and noting tattooed mark reached by the butt of the fifth shell. In like manner the last and intermediate sets of 5 were measured. This shell money was carried in special elk-horn boxes.

WAMWERA - (Mwera, Wamuera) – Tanzanian tribe, practicing scar-tattoo.

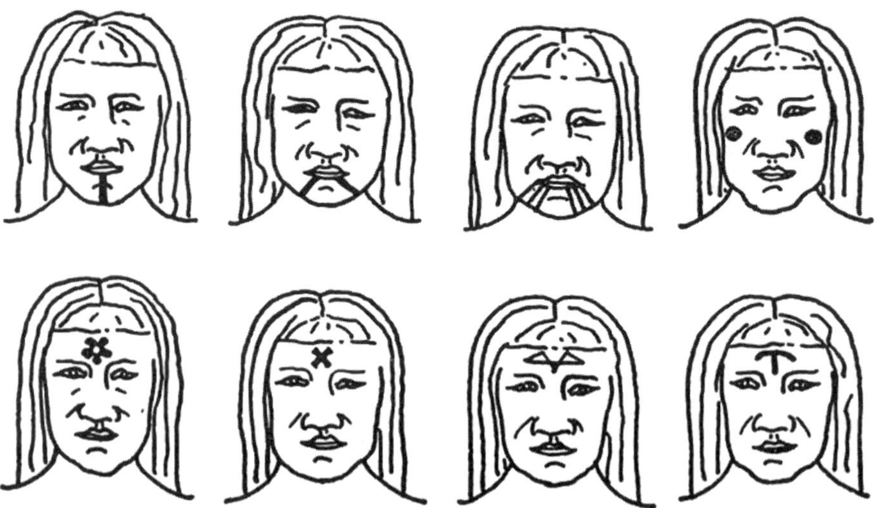

Walapai tribe

WANGATA - African tribe practicing scar tattoo.

WANCHO TRIBE – Wancho girls are tattooed while still very young and the tattoos can have sexual connotations. A girl´s future husband is selected when she is six or seven years old. When a girl reaches adulthood a few zigzag lines are

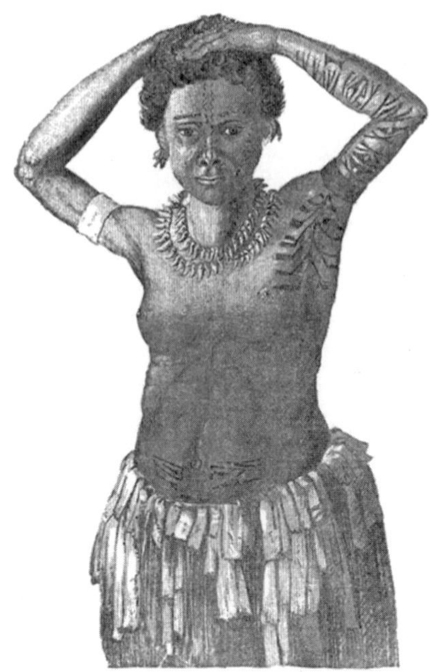

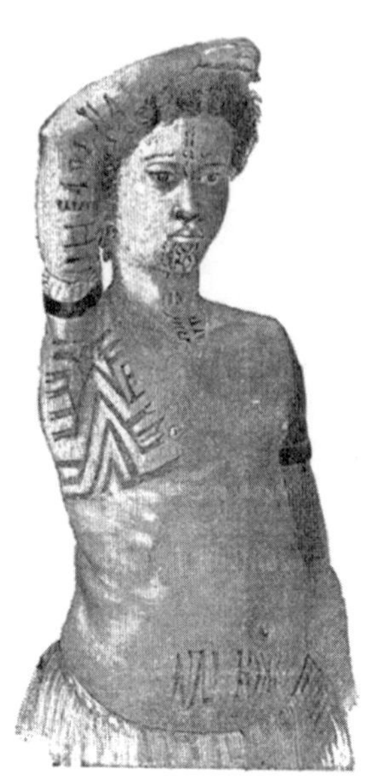

Wamativi

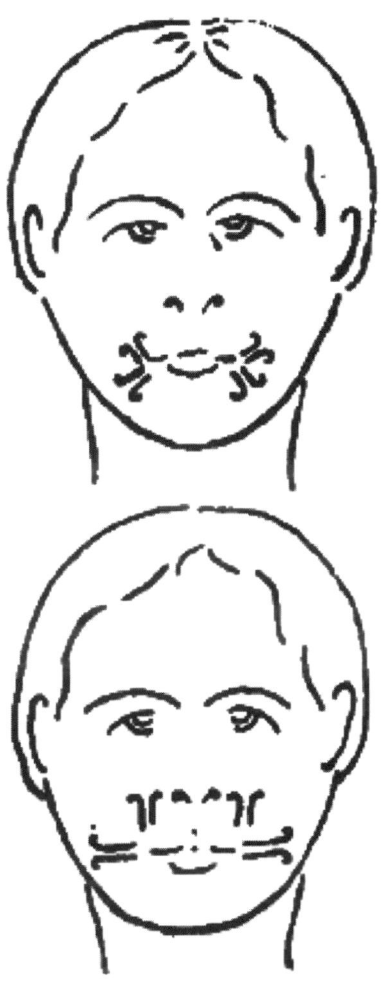
Warawok Murano

tattooed onto her calves. After having sex for the first time, two parallel lines are tattooed on her thighs. The final design, shaped as a large M, is tattooed on her chest when she falls pregnant.

WANKONDE - The Wankonde tattoo extensively about the age of puberty. They make small incisions with a pair of pincers and a knife and rub in wood ashes or charcoal. The Wankonde cut marks like those given in the accompanying illustration over the breast, above the mammae, in both sexes. Some tattoo over the abdomen, others over the hypogastrium, where they make a series of long lines, which are wonderfully straight.

WAPISHANA - see TAULIPÁNG

WARAWOK MURANO - A few men

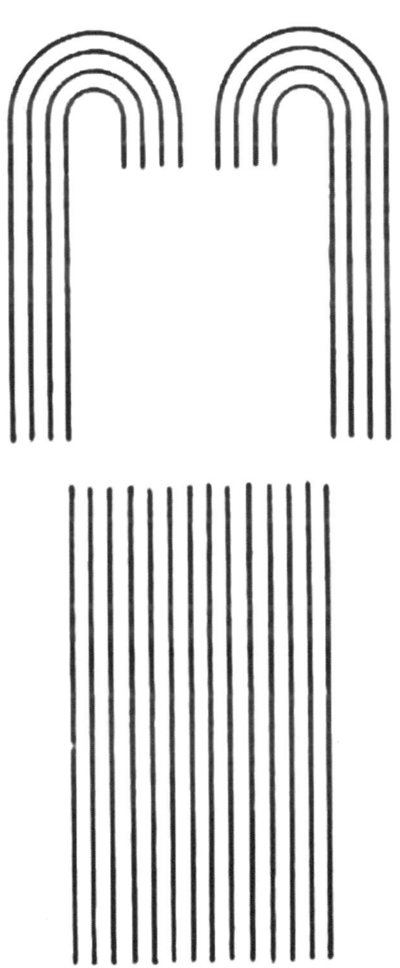
Wankonde

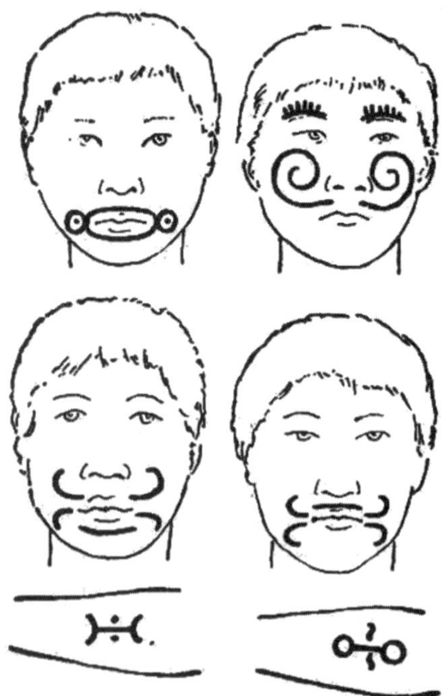

Warau - examples of face and arm tattoo

also have some tattoo marks round the mouth in the scorpion's tail pattern, but the ingredients of the dye differ, being a compound of charred plant roots. These warawok murano, that is, 'men's charms', are hunting charms, Akawaio.

WARRANI PEOPLE – They took tattoos on the site of torn eyebrows. Cactus thorns were used as tools.

WASHAM. DAGG – term for tattoo according to English-Arabic dictionary: Anglo-Egyptian Sudan.

WASHM – The formal name for tattoos in Iraq, although more general is the name Dagg or Daqq.

WASHOO INDIANS - All of the women and a few of the men were tattooed — with the usual blue-black material. The tattooing was mainly in straight and zig-zag lines radiating from the mouth. Cheek lines and vertical nose lines are more common than among the Paiutes. The chin was always tattooed.

WAŠM – the term for tattoos in North Africa, Wasm, an own mark, should not be confused with "wašm" (plural "ušam", for Berbers "elušem") - tattooing.

WATHIN´ETHE - Omaha men who wished to have their daughters tattooed had to present a "wathin´ethe" (long count) of gifts or respectable actions to earn membership into the order of honorary chieftainship known as Hon´hewachi. A partial listing of prescribed wathin´ethe included: eagles, eagle war bones, tobacco pouches, otter skins, buffalo robes, ornamented shirts and leggings...

WATOEPDE - tattoos for Rindi area, Sumba island.

WATUSI TRIBE – some of the women tattooed themselves on the shoulders and breasts in rather a curious fashion.

WA-XO´BE TON-GA - Osage tattooing bundle were wa-xo´be ton-ga (great bundle) imbued with life-giving powers. Tattooing bundle were manufactured and stored with reference to the position of the two great Osage moieties. The outer case was made of woven buffalo hair. This "wallet", which was used to hold the bundle´s sacred contents.

WAXOBE or WAXUBE - Tattooing bundles are one class or category of "sacred" (waxobe - Osage; waxube - Omaha) or "medicine" bundles that may be roughly defined as an object (or cadre

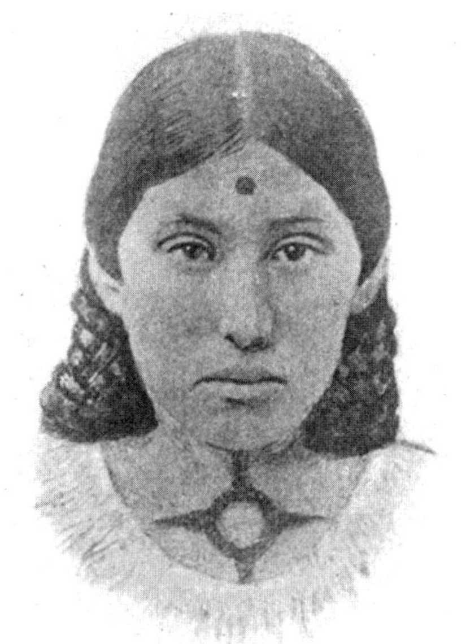

Waxthe´xe

of objects) that is stored in a woven container or skin cover and that functions as a repository for the transfer of supernatural power.

WAXTHE´XE - the name given to the Pole, was the name of ancient Cedar Pole preserved in the Tent of War. The word is difficult to translate. The prefix wa indicates that the object spoken of had power, the power of motion, of life; xthexe means „ mottled as by shadows"; the word has also the idea of bringing into prominence to be seen by all the people as something distinctive.

Xthexe´was the name of the "mark of honor" put on a girl, through certain acts, entrance into the Ho[ŋ]´hewachi, and and so secured the right to have this mark tattooed on the girl. The name of pole, Waxthe´xe, signifies that the power to give the right to possess this "mark of honor" was vested in the Pole. While the mark of honor, as its name shows, was directly connected with Cedar Pole, which was related to thunder and war, the tattooed "mark of honor" among the Omaha was not connected with war, but with achievements that related to hunting and to the maintenance of peace within the tribe.

WE´- YOT - tattooing, Indians on lower Eel River. Both sexes tattoo: the men on their arms and breast; the women from inside the under lip down to and beneath the chin.

WEBORI - Japanese tattoo style, refers to ukiyo-e pictures. They are dragons, carp, Buddha, maple leaves or peonies. See YOUBORI

WEBBER, JOHN - (1752-1793) As the official artist aboard Captain James Cook's third voyage through the Pacific (1776-1780), it was John Webber who visually defined for much of eighteenth-

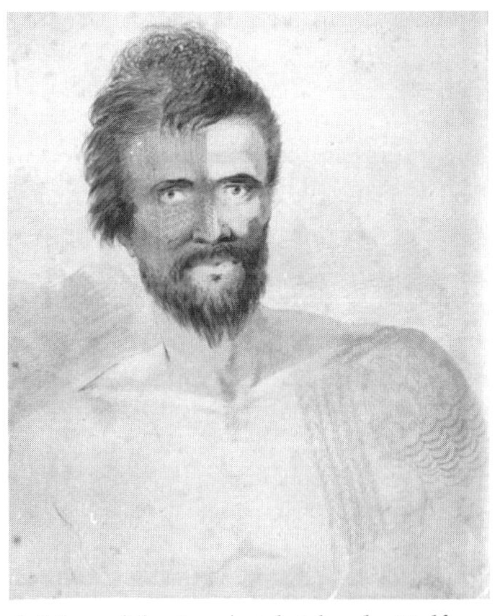

A Man of the Sandwich Islands, Half Face Tattooed by John Webber

century Europe what the distant and exotic peoples and places of this relatively unknown world were like. His commission on this voyage was defined as ethnographic. His work served as a visual history to accompany the written accounts of Cook and his crew. Webber recorded landscapes, scenery, initial contact and other important aspects of society. These images offer a very rare glimpse at life prior to the swift and dramatic changes that would come soon after. The publication and marketing of these well-recorded voyages in the 1785 titled A Voyage to the Pacific Ocean, undertaken by the Command of His Majesty, for making discoveries in the Northern Hemisphere spurred great interest in this part of the globe.

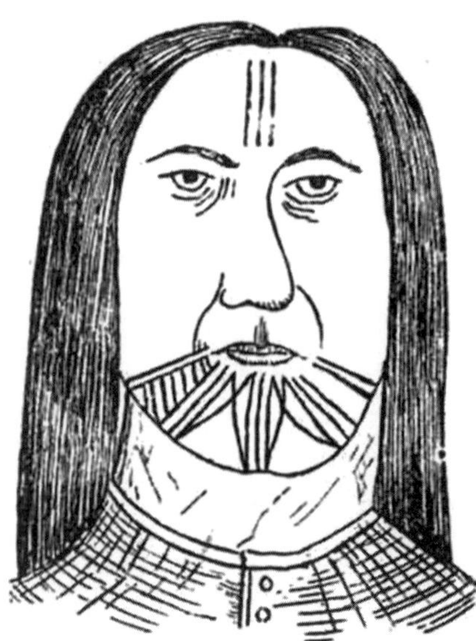

Western Dénés tribe

WEI-HA-HÜH - sharp rattan palm needles on tattoo tool, Konyaks.

WEJT´I - The oldest written mention of Japanese tattoos is a text from 297 AD, which is contained in the Chinese chronicle of Wejťi. „Men, large and small, all tattoo their faces and decorate their bodies with patterns… "

WEFENE-TAPITAPI – tattoo master (women), Santa Anna a Santa Catalina, Solomon Islands.

WEKWIICH - In the language of Kumeyaay tattoos or to be tattooed.

WENSHEN - old Chinese term (wenShen) for tattoo - "body pattern"

WEN-SHIN – or "people with tattooed bodies," a term used in ancient Chinese records of the Ainu tribe.

WENMIAN - one of the ancient Chinese terms for tattoos - literally patterned faces.

WENNA – Tattooing is a very painful affair and so the girl's power (wenna), the Maisin tribe, Papua New Guinea is actually tested.

WENŽIN – Chinese term for tattoo, wen – ornament, žin – person.

WESTERN DÉNÉS – tattooing was formerly very prevalent among these, and not confined to the chest, arms, and legs, as in the neigh-boring heterogeneous tribes, but extended to the face. The face designs were generally lines, single or parallel, on the cheeks, forehead, temples, chin, or radiating from corners of the mouth, and were not totemic. Where figures, these were crosses, fishes, birds, fern-root diggers, etc. The breast was not so commonly tattooed as among the coast tribes, but the devices here were mostly totemic. The symbol of the grizzly bear was greatly honored, and it's marking „cost many a ceremonial banquet." The forearms, inside and out, were more often the seat of a personal totemic design, an animal seen in a dream. Sometimes the marks on arms and legs were intended as a charm against weakness, then being simply one or two transverse lines. The face devices were conventional signs for the otter, a fish, bird, beaver, stick in water, mountain, fern-root digger, marten, lizard, and caribou. See DÉNÉ or SALISH

WESTERN ESKIMO - was a name used formerly for Inuinnaktun (also known as Coppermine or Inuinakton), an Eskimo-Aleut language of Nunavut and the Northwest Territories in Canada, centered on Victoria Island and the adjacent mainland.

WÉXTHEXTHE - tattoo ceremony, Osage.

WHAANNAU – is a Maori-language word for extended family.

WHAKA-IRO – tattooed, Maori

WHAKA-MATAUTAU – tattoo, Tahiti

WHAKAIRO TANGATA - Tattooing by puncture is sometimes referred to as whakairo tangata, the word whakairo carrying the meaning of "to embellish with a pattern." Tuhi means "to delineate," and this term is employed to describe the marking of designs on the skin, as done prior to tattooing by puncture, Maori.

WHAKAIRO TUHI - Maori tradition seems to recognize a period in which tattooing by puncture was unknown to their ancestors. In that far past period we are told a mode of personal decoration consisted of painting various devices on the body. This adornment is described as whakairo tuhi and hopara makaurangi, Maori.

WHATOK SA AWI - The Butbut tribe describe and classify tattoos as those of the past (whatok sa awi) and those of the present (whatok sa sana).

WHATOK SA SANA – see below

WIGREXE – tattoo, Iowa tribe.

WIGREXE - Iowa tattooing bundle.

WICHITA – tribe in New Mexico are known as the "Tattooed People." One curious thing noted by early whites who visited the Wichita was that even though they sometimes acted like Plains Indians, they didn't look much like them. George Catlin was a very famous artist that traveled all over America and lived with different Indians. We know much of what we do about Indians because George Catlin took the time to record and paint

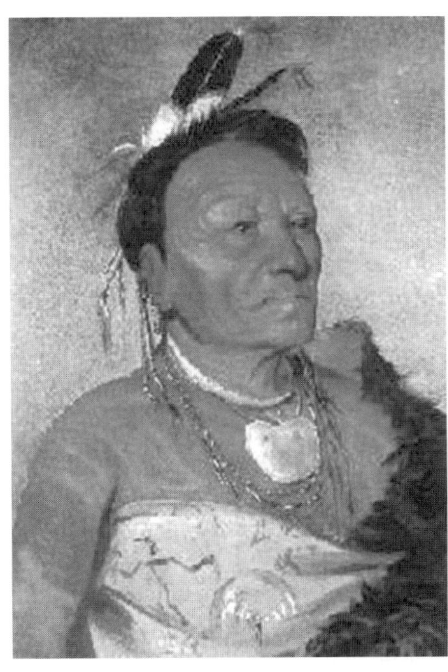

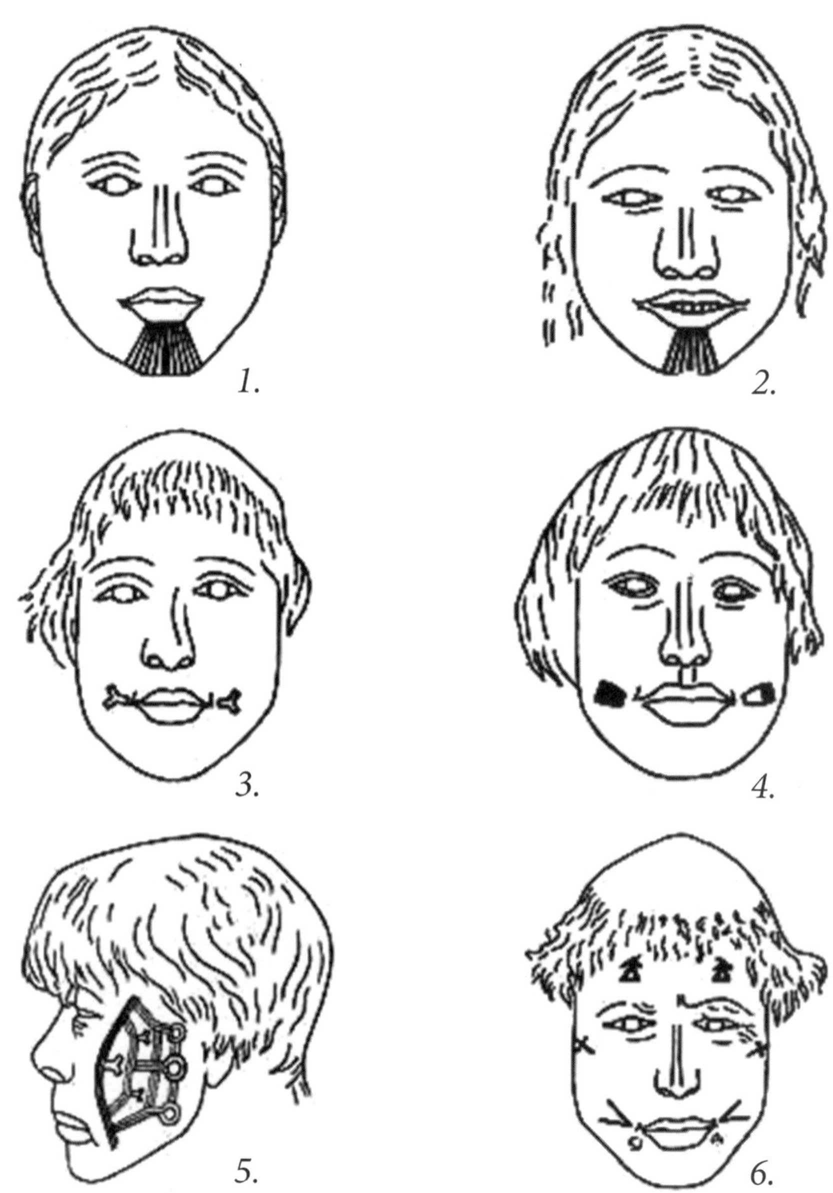

Western Eskimo: 1. Tattooing on the face of an Eskimo woman, in the vicinity of Berong Strait, Alaska; 2. Tattooing on the face of an Eskimo woman, in the vicinity of Berong Strait Alaska; 3. Tattooing on the face of an Eskimo man, in the vicinity of Berong Strait, Alaska; 4. Tattooing on the face of an Eskimo man, in the vicinity of Berong Strait, Alaska; 5. Tattooing on the face of an Eskimo woman, on St. Lawrence Island; 6. Tattooing on the face of an Eskimo man, on Diomede Island, Bering Strait.

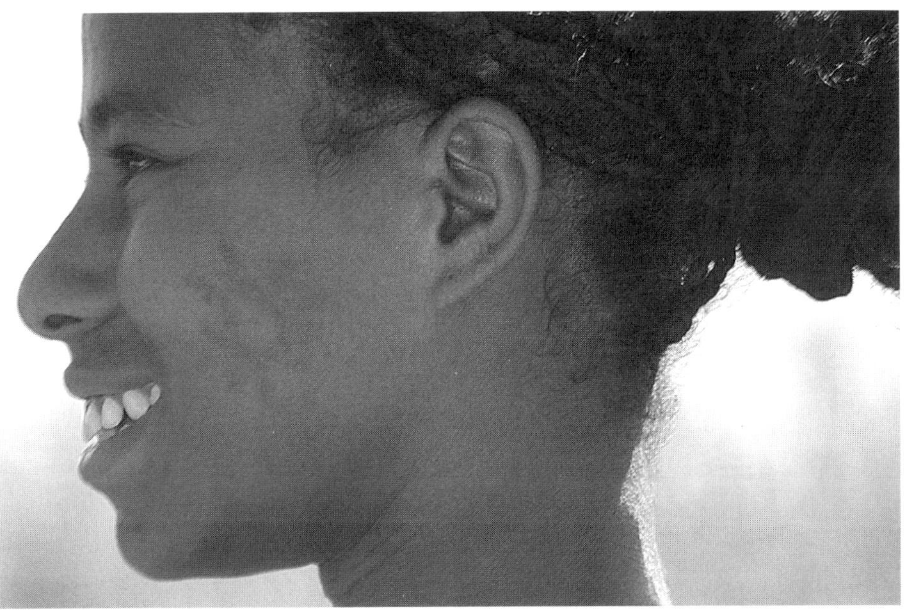

Wollo girl facial tattoo, Ethiopia

their habits and dress. Well, in 1834 he went with Colonel Henry Dodge and his Dragoon Expedition. They came across the Wichita living on the Red River. He painted a few pictures of them and said they were not like other Plains Indians because they were darker, shorter, and stockier. He also said they had many tattoos on their faces and bodies. Even the women, who Catlin thought was pretty, had a bunch of tattoos. They were not of animals or people or other common objects. All the Wichita s tattoos were lines, both solid and dotted, and circles. The Wichita even called themselves the raccoon-eyed people because of the tattooing around their eyes. The kind of clothes they wore was almost simple in comparison to their tattoos.

WIKUNTÉ - spatulas of an unnamed material, bearing split quill rattles used for "laying out the patterns and applying the pigment (wikunté), Iowa Indian.

WILYARU - In the Adelaide district that there are five stages to be passed through, before the native attains the rank of a bourka, or full-grown man. The fourth stage (Wilyaru) is entered about the age of twenty, when the back, shoulders, arms and chest, are tattooed. He is called ngulte. At the time of the operation; yellambambettu, when the incisions have begun to discharge pus; tarkange, when the sores are just healed; mangkauitya, at the time the cuts begin to rise; and bartamu, when the scars are at their highest elevation. Each tribe has a distinctive mode of making their incisions. Some have scars running completely across the chest, from one axillar to the other, whilst others have

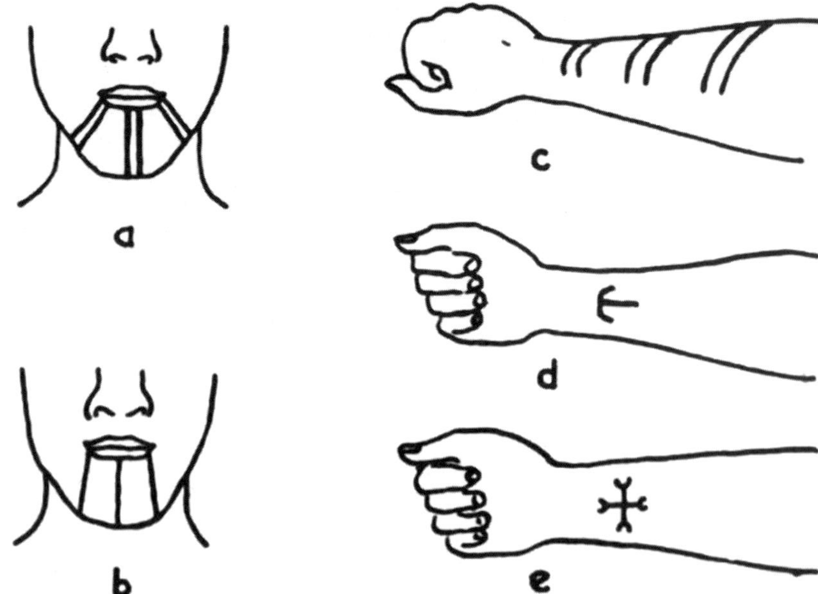

Women's tattoo marks: a,c - Wukchumni; b,d - Telamni; e - Wukchumni

merely dotted lines; some have circles and semicircles formed on the apex of the shoulder, other small dots only, Australia.

WILTAČ — A tattoo; tattooing (What has been tattooed; a tattoo), Hupa Indians.

WINTUNS – girls had three lines running straight down the chin, probably to show to which family they belonged, California tribe.

WISHOSK – was a small tribe on the coast of N. California about Humboldt Bay. The women tattooed their chins.

WIYALKINYE - The Wiyalkinye (youth, who has gone through the ceremony of circumcision and tattooing) must for some months keep out of the sight of women and children, speaking in a low tone of voice, till released by the old men (among the Parnkalla). Wilya, soul or spirit, Australia.

WO-HOT-PIM - tattoo marks, No-to-koi-yo Midoo tribe, Big Meadows, California.

WUKCHUMNI - are a Yokuts tribe of California. Many women used tattooing as a permanent form of personal decoration. It was done of their own volition, usually in young womanhood but before marriage.

WUMUNDE - citrus bush thorns used on a tattoo tool, Sumba Island.

WUS-KWE-PAK-TOE-GUN - or, "keep in a clean place — the designations for religious items, such as the tattoo bag, were referred to by this term, the Cree Indian tribe.

WUSTMAN, ERICH – (1907 -1994) was a German traveler, writer, and ethnographer. He wrote all his life about various people such as the Sami, the Indians, the Faeroes, and the Bedouins. Throughout his travels, he filmed, photographed, recorded speech and songs, collected ethnographic objects for museums, and described countries, people, and culture.

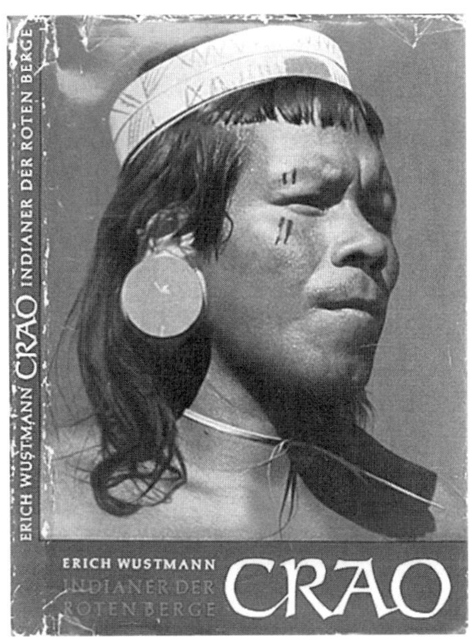

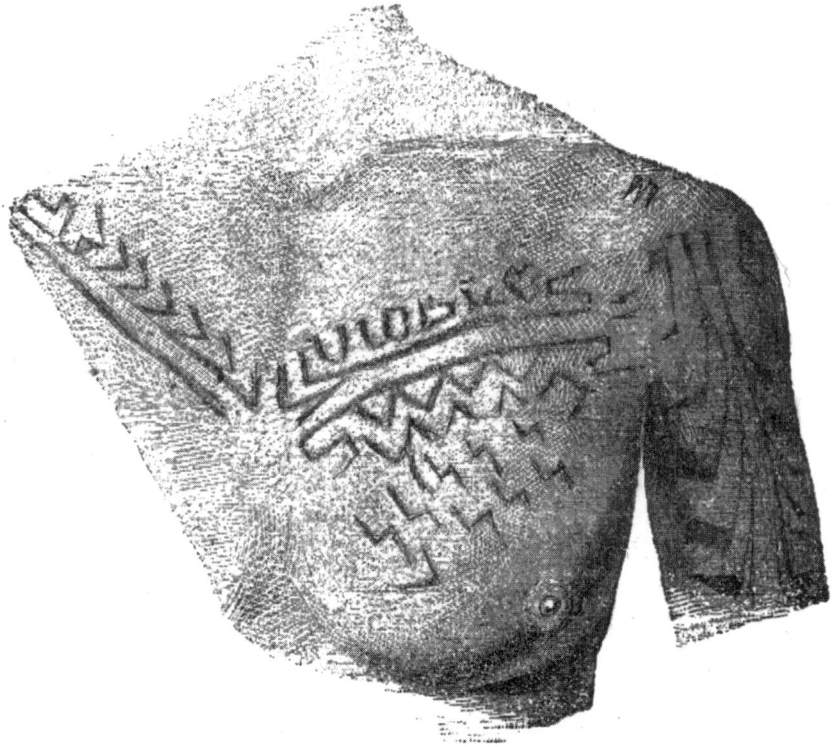

Waara - tattooing from Papua New Guinea

XAM - Tattoos are called xam in both Coos languages

XAM MINH - body tattoo. Since the beginning of recorded history, the Vietnamese have practised the art of tattooing. Fishermen had pictures of sea monsters on their bodies to protect them from sea serpents. The emperors had a dragon tattooed on their thigh until the custom was broken by Emperor Tran Anh-Tong (1293-1314), who refused to be tattooed. In 1323 Emperor Tran Minh-Tong (1314-1329) decreed that his officers should no longer be tattooed. In present times tattooing is practiced by only a few-chiefly among the highland people.

XARIK - tattooing hammer, Sonsorol Islands.

XINGÚ – pronounced "Shin-goo," is a collective term for linguistically diverse but culturally converged groups living in the Amazon on the upper reaches of the Xingú River. They are united by, among other things, uniform body decoration, belief in the first man Mavutsinima, kuarup funerals and huka-huka matches. According to the Czech expert Mnislav Zelený, these are 15 tribes belonging to three language families - Caribbean (eg Kalapalo, Kamayurá), Aravacká (eg Jawalapiti, Waurá) and Žéská (eg Suyá).

XIHUNDLA - The emphasis in oral narratives on the xihundla (secrecy) surrounding the act of cutting tattoos also adds an interesting wrinkle to scholarly explanations of body-marking, in southern Mozambique and elsewhere in Africa, as simply one element of an organized series of initiation rites that adolescent girls underwent at the behest of, or under the strict supervision of, their female elders. According to interviewees, tinhlanga were always done nhoveni (in the bush) or khwatini (in the woods), so

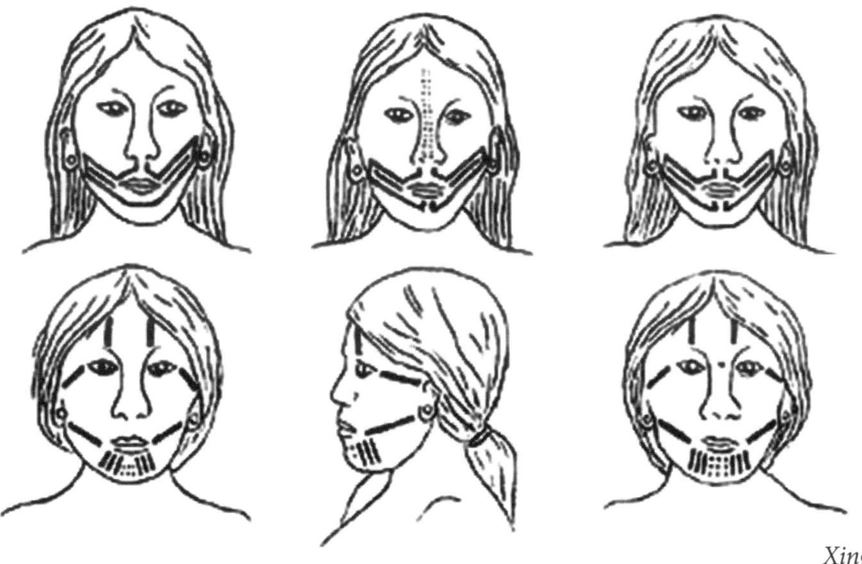

Xingú

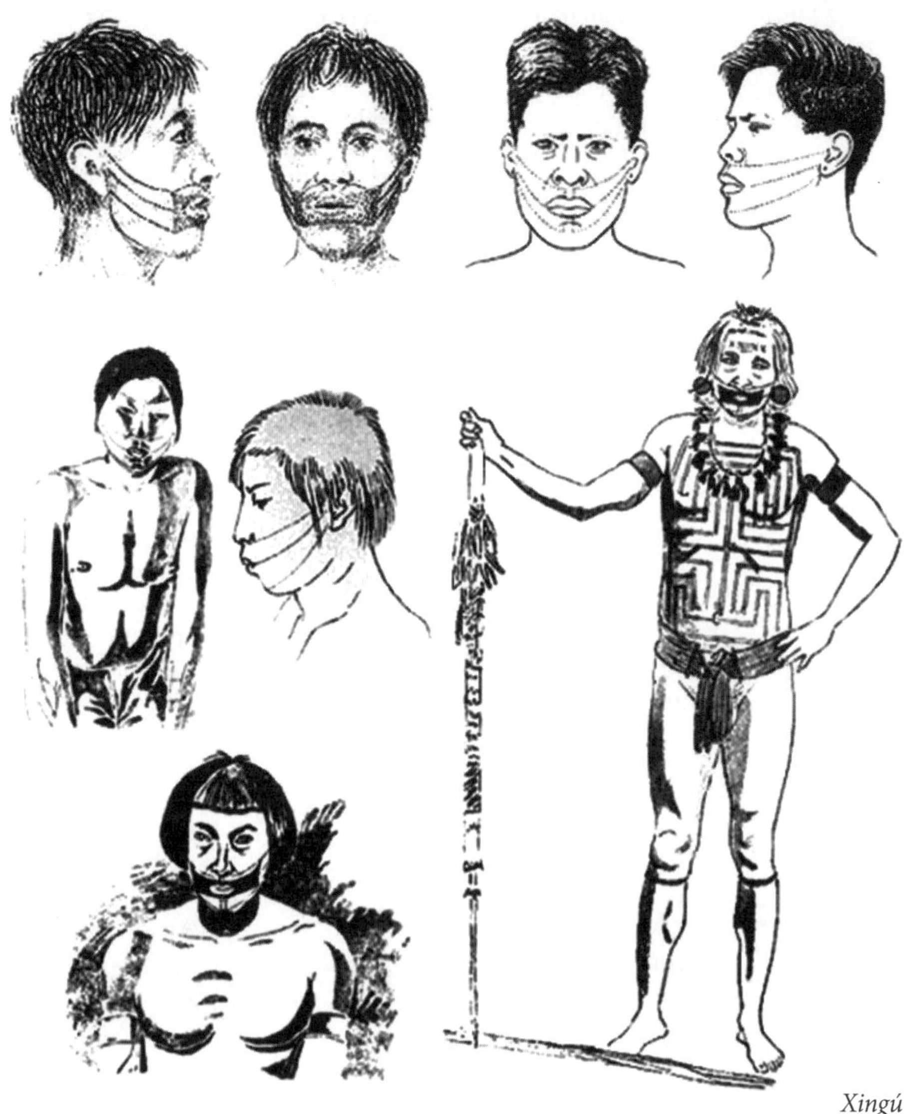

Xingú

that no one—"especially men and children"—would "see all that blood."

XIUMIAN – one of the terms in ancient China (206 BC to 220 AD) for tattoos, translated as "decorate the face".

XTHE-XTHE – Tattooing among Dhegiha Sioux was termed xthe-xthe - „to tattoo," or „to attach symbolism to a person or an object."

YAMACRAW INDIANS - were a small band that existed from the late 1720s to the mid-1740s in the Savannah area, practised tattooing. USA.

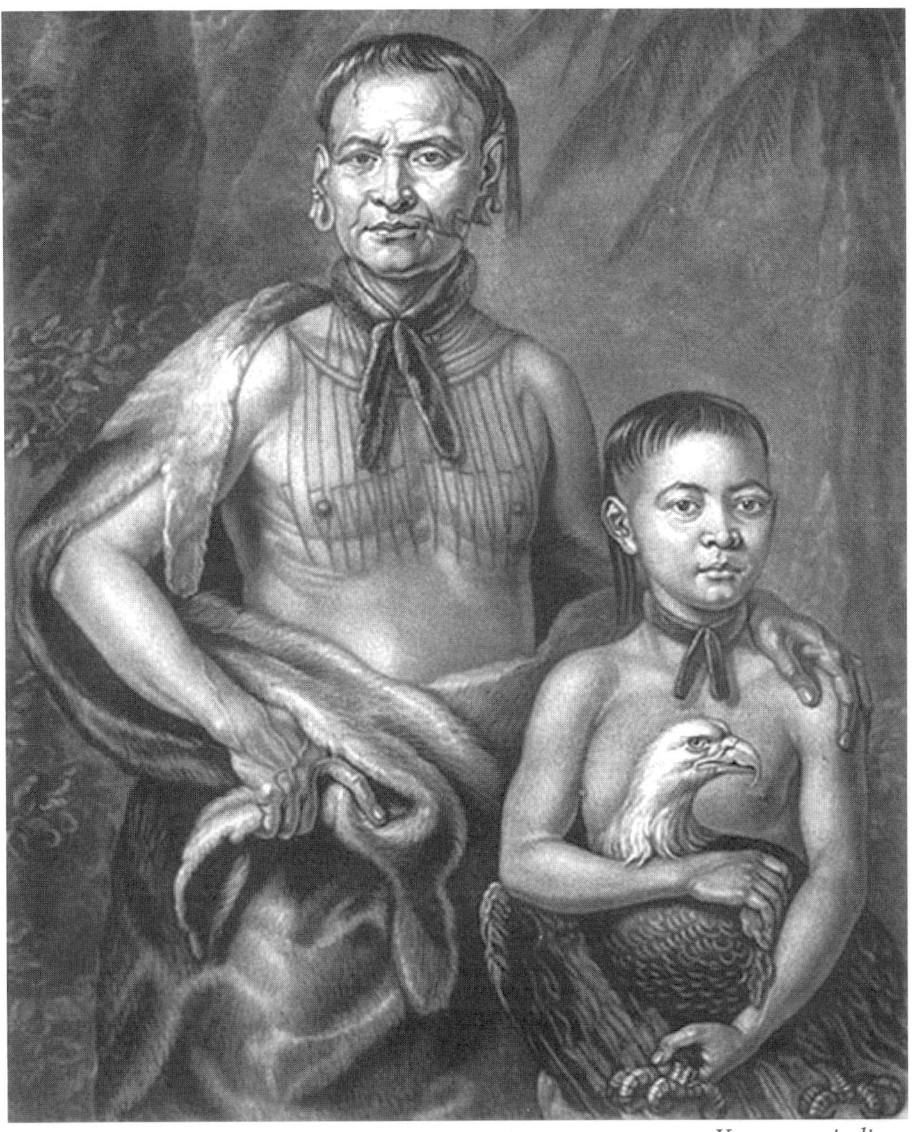

Yamacraw indians

YANG-TSE – area in China. The oldest mention of tattoos in China dates back to about 1100 BC. There were two types of tattoos, Tjen and Tz-Hwa.

YANKTONANAI – Indian tribe, One of the 7 primary divisions or subtribes of the Dakota, North America. They practiced body art.

YANPPAI – acupuncture point where a tattoo was performed against headaches and eye pain, the island of Sv. Lawrence.

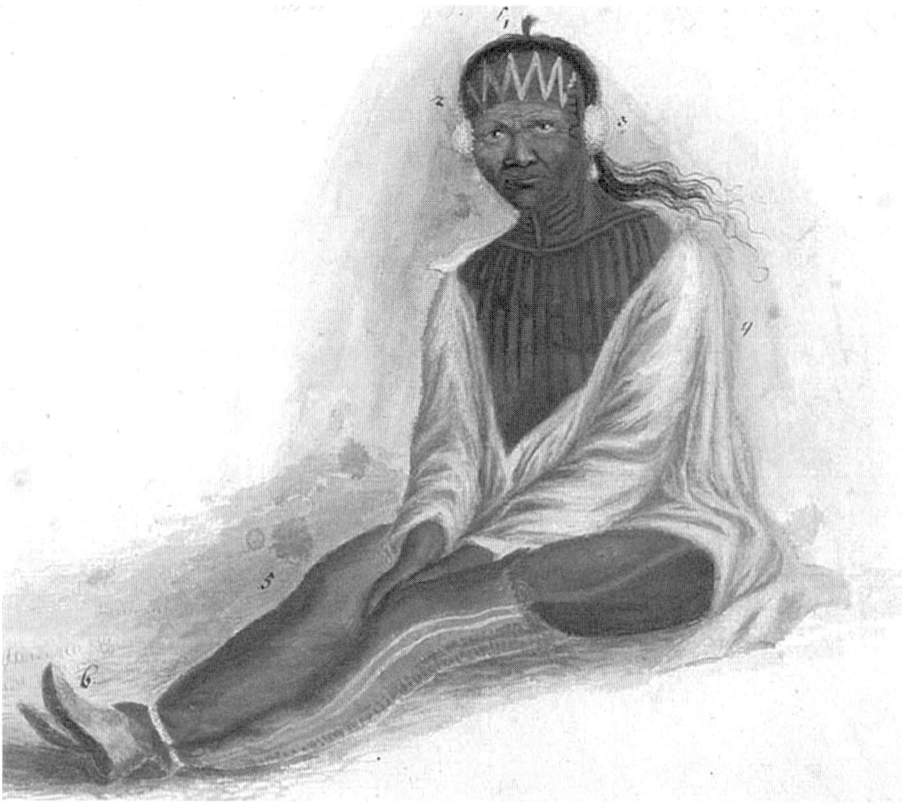

Yuchi Indian

YANTRA - tattoos of the Tai people.

YAP – archipelago, part of the Carolina Islands. The original inhabitants practiced tattoos here.

YAQUI– tribe in Mexico, the Yaqui formerly tattooed the chin and arms.

YAVAPAI - Only women wore tattoos and they were marked after their first menses. Tattooists were women and they plied three or four bundled cactus thorns into the skin to create carbon-based tattoos on the arms, chins, and foreheads of their clients. Sometimes a human figure was tattooed on the wrist to induce conception.

Western Yavapai men possessed facial tattoos that consisted of crosses or circles

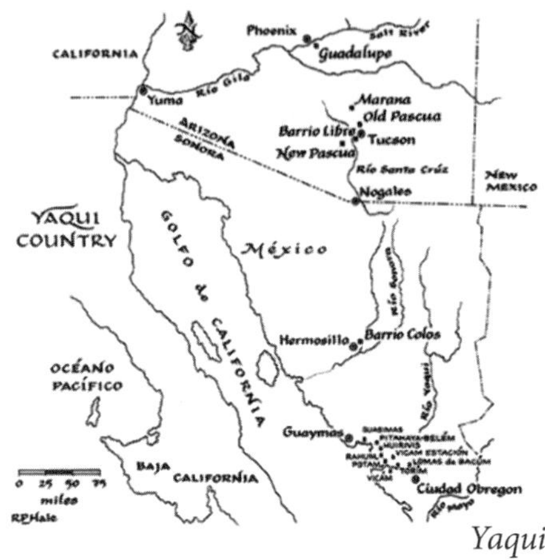

Yaqui

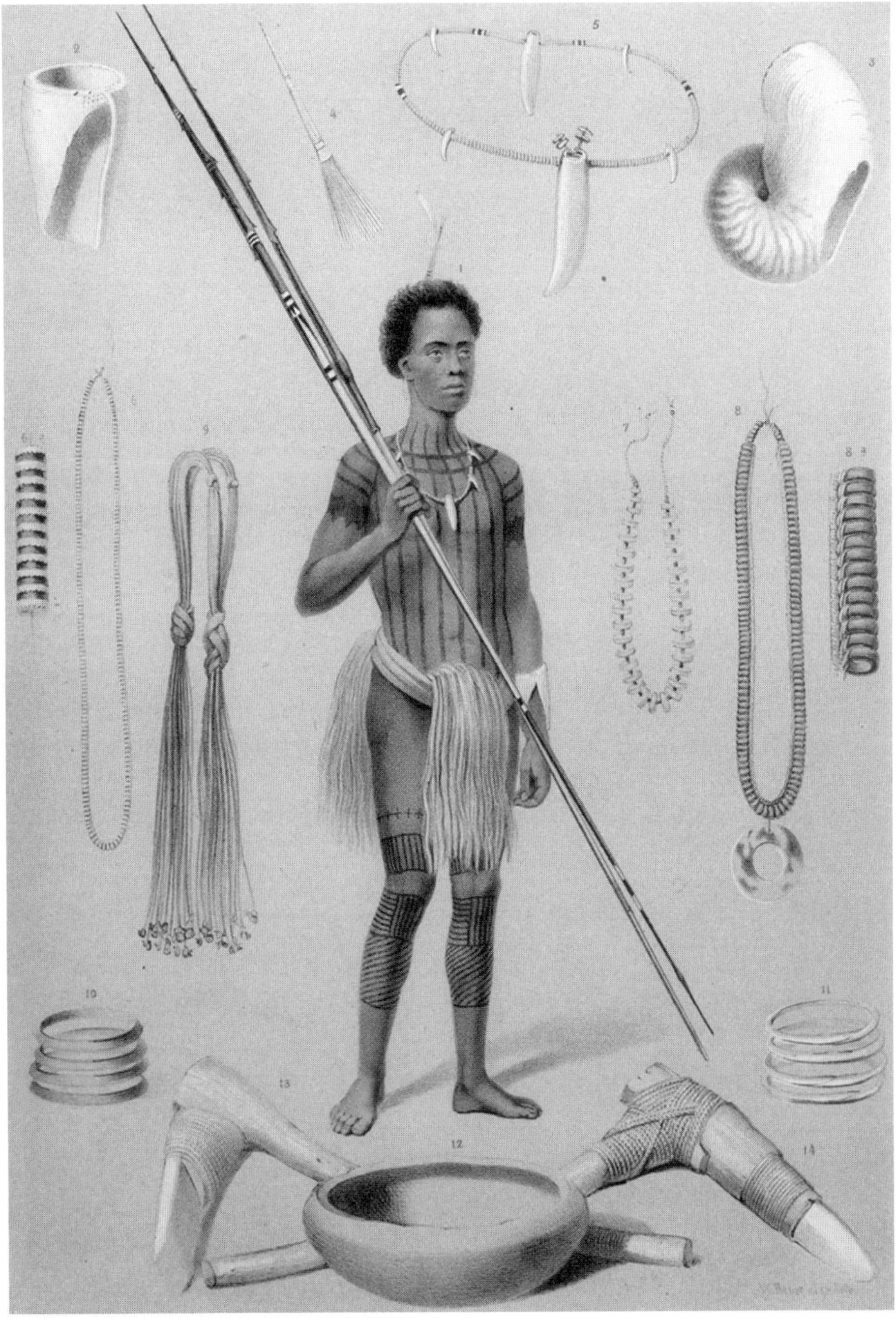

Yap

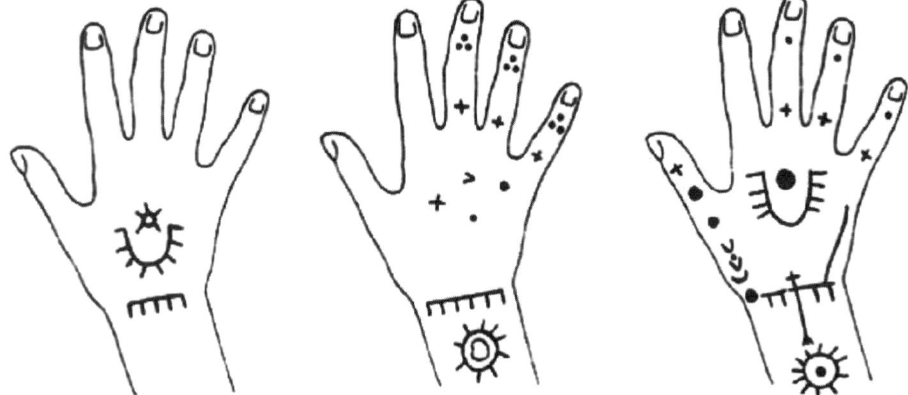

Yezidi men's hand tattoos from Iraq, ca. 1930

on each cheek, wavy or zigzagging lines on the forehead, and a row of dots down the nose. Sometimes they also wore the chin patterns of women, or other motifs on their wrists, calves, or chests

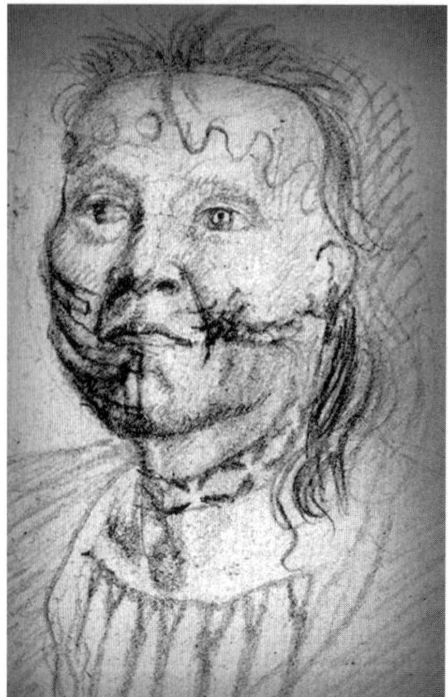

Facial and body tattoos of the Yuchi leader Senkaitschi of Georgia, 1736

YEZIDI – also the YAZIDI, a supporter of the Middle Eastern religion, ethnically Kurdish, practiced tattoos. These were most often ridge or radial motifs.

YUCHI – a Native American tribe from Tennessee, who once practised tattooing. The men painted the face and chest, but the women only the arms and chest. The figures on the chest are pricked in with a needle or other pointed instrument, until they bleed, and in them they

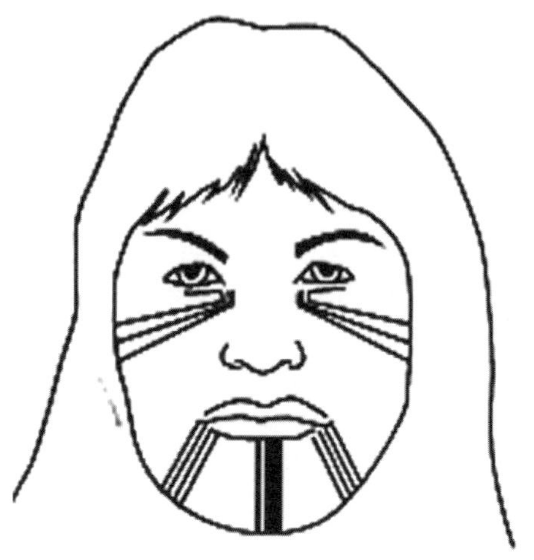

Yuki

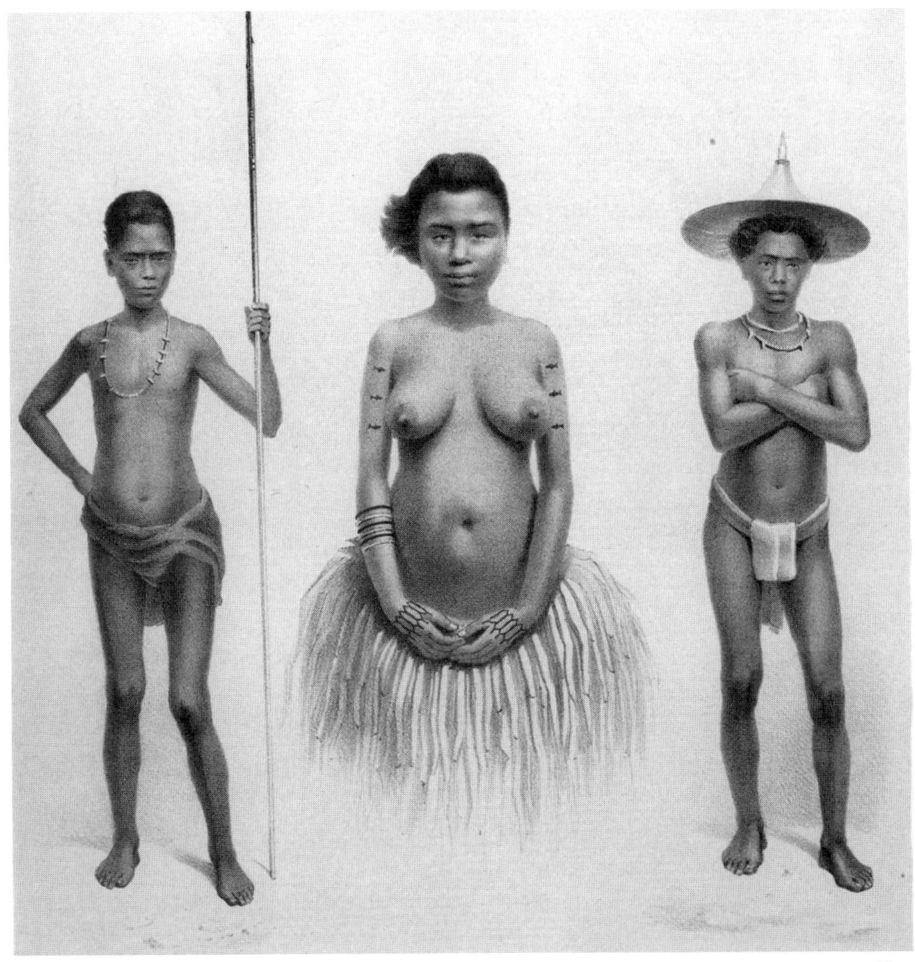

Yap

sprinkle fine powder or charcoal dust, which mixes in the blood, remains in the skin, and appears blue-black.

YUKAR – legendary stories, parts of which were often sung during tattoos, Ainu tribe.

YUKI (also known as Yukiah) - are an indigenous people of California, whose traditional territory is around Round Valley, Mendocino County. Practice tattooing. Tattooing is done with pitch-pine soot a sharp-pointed bone. After the designs have been traced on the skin, the soot is rubbed in dry.

YUPIK – a tribe living in the west and lowest of Alaska. Among other things, they practiced tattoos.

YUP´IK – see Yupik

YUPIIK – see Yupik

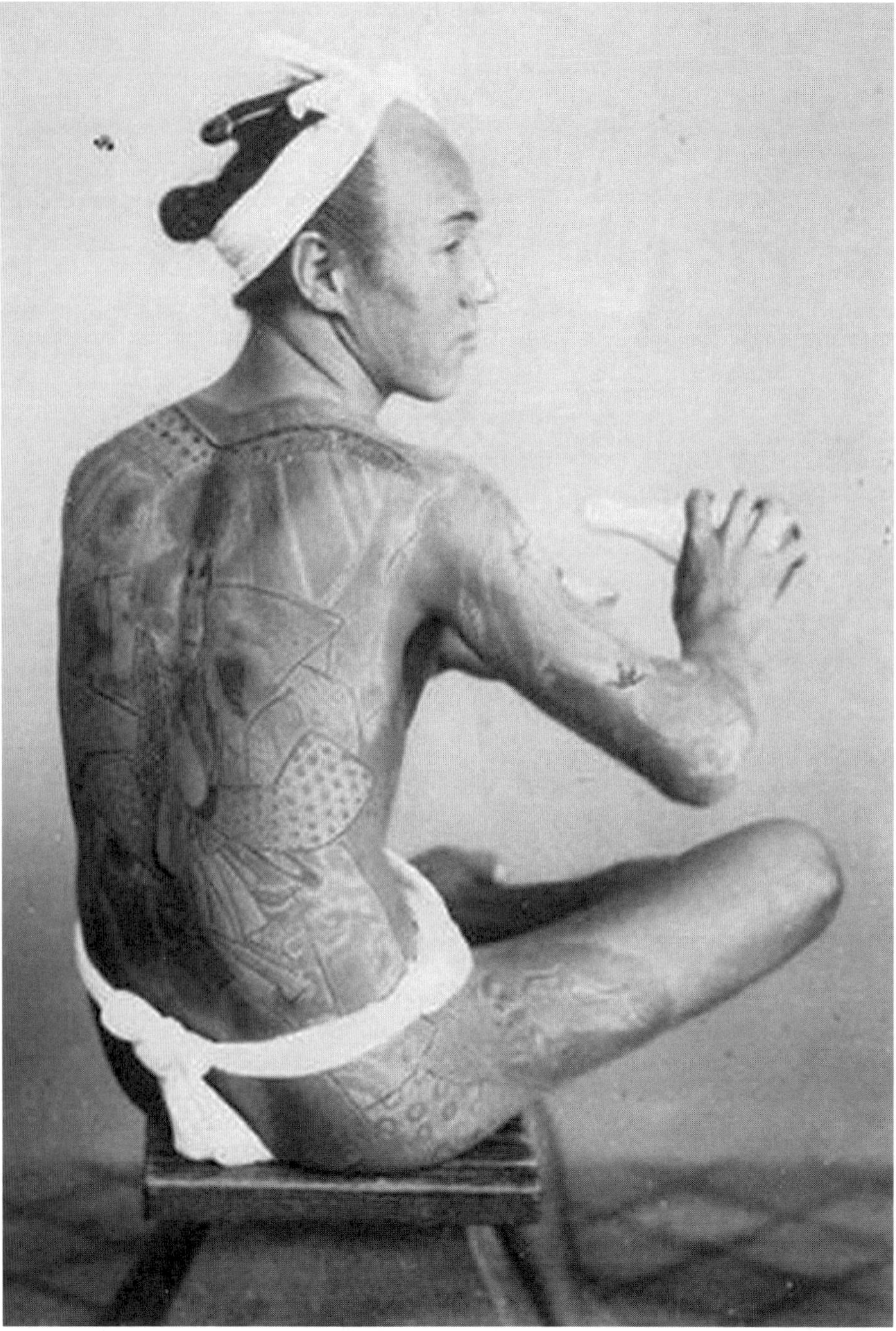

Zenshin-Bori

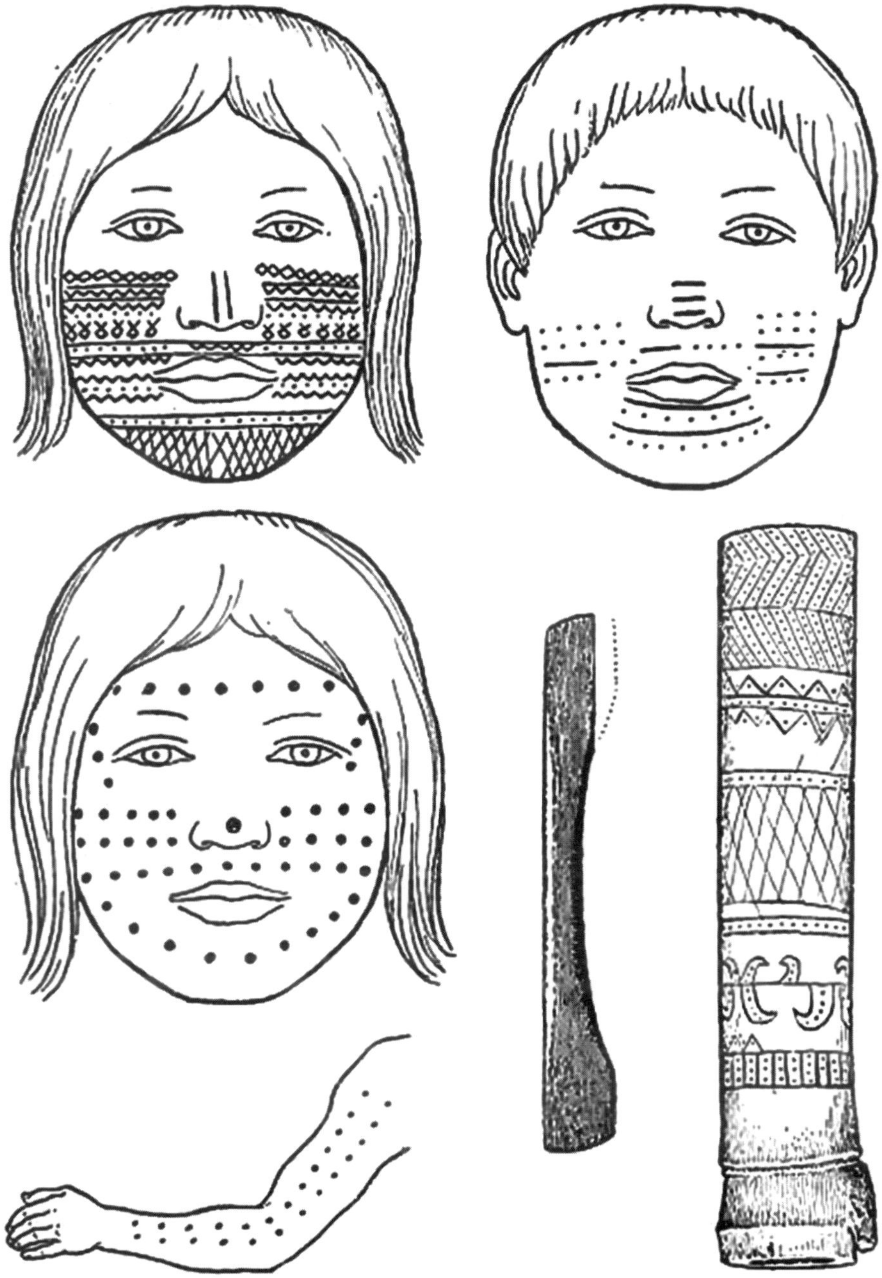

Yuracare

YURACARE TRIBE – see CARIBAN TRIO

ZALIL – an herb that was used as a yellow dye in tattoos, Persia.

ZAUO - tattooing forks were stored in special chests, made of driftwood, zauo. These chests were extremely light and had an arched lid on top, while the bottom side was flat. The lower part of the chest consisted of three parts: the bottom and the long sides were made of one piece, the cross pieces were jammed in-between. On of the two protrudes a bit over the upper rim, which affords the lid more hold, Songosor, Palau.

ZENATAN – tattooing, is characteristic of the Beni Znassen.

ZENSHIN-BORI – term for Japanese full body tattoo.

ZHIN´- GA-WA-DA-IN-GA - The motifs used in tattooing were also related to Wakanda all-encompassing power, and among the Osage many were considered to be "life symbol" (zho´-i-the) of the particular clans who employed then. Life symbols were derived from natural and celestial objects whose supernatural faculties were transmitted in primordial times by Wakanda to sacred religious leaders called „little-old-men" (zhin´-ga-wa-da-in-ga) through visions and dreams.

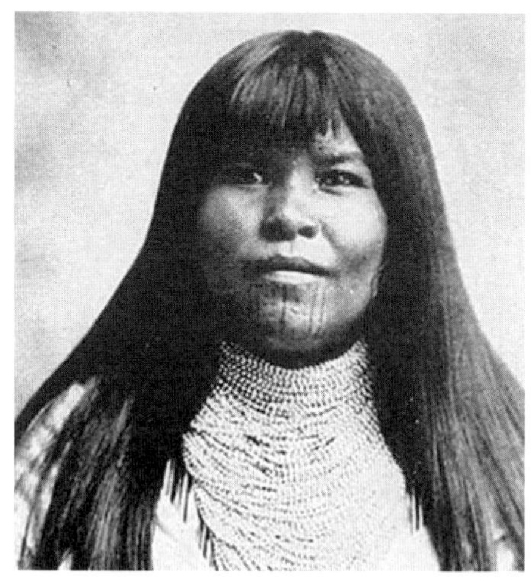

Yuma

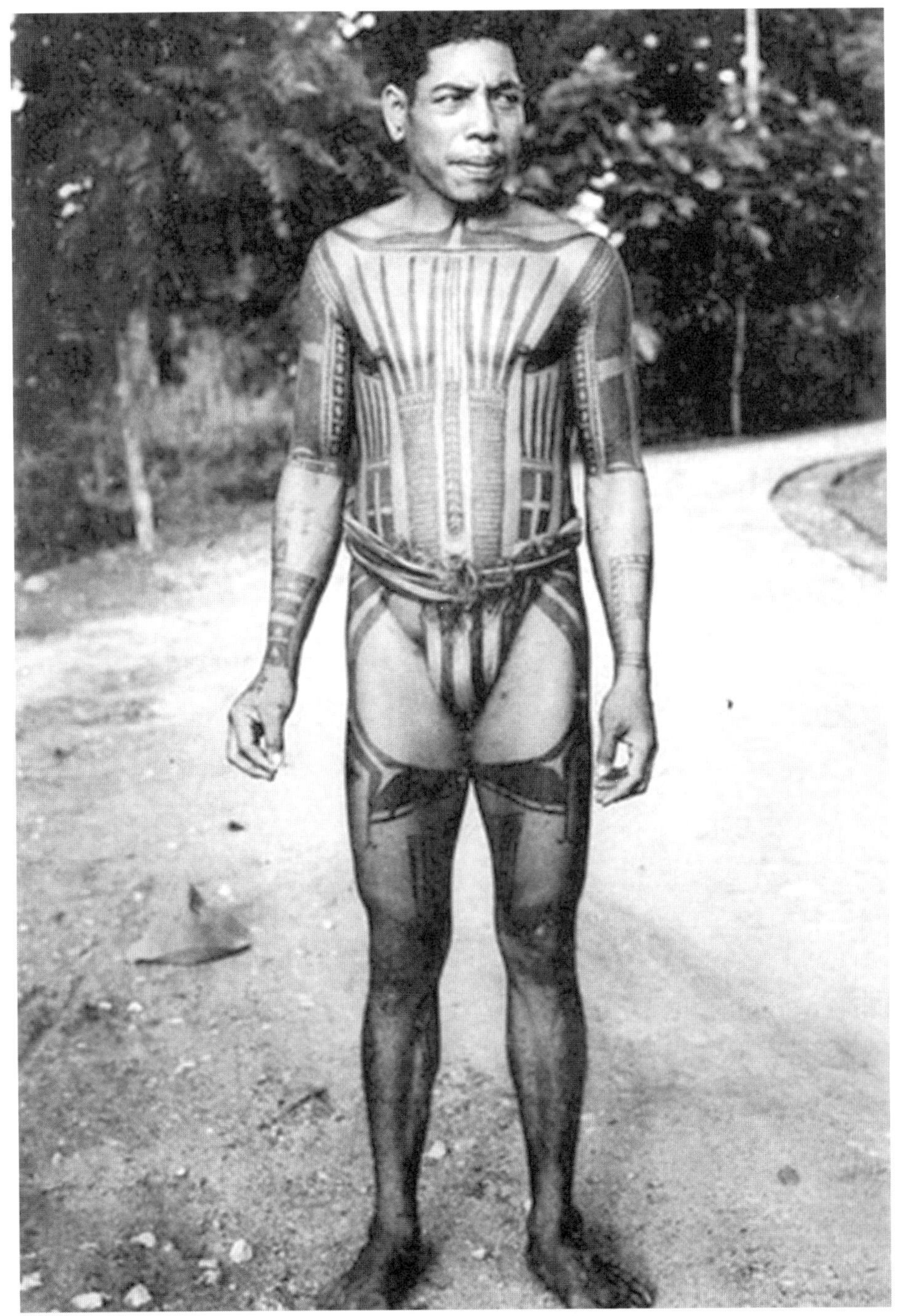

Tattoo of a man from the Yap Archipelago

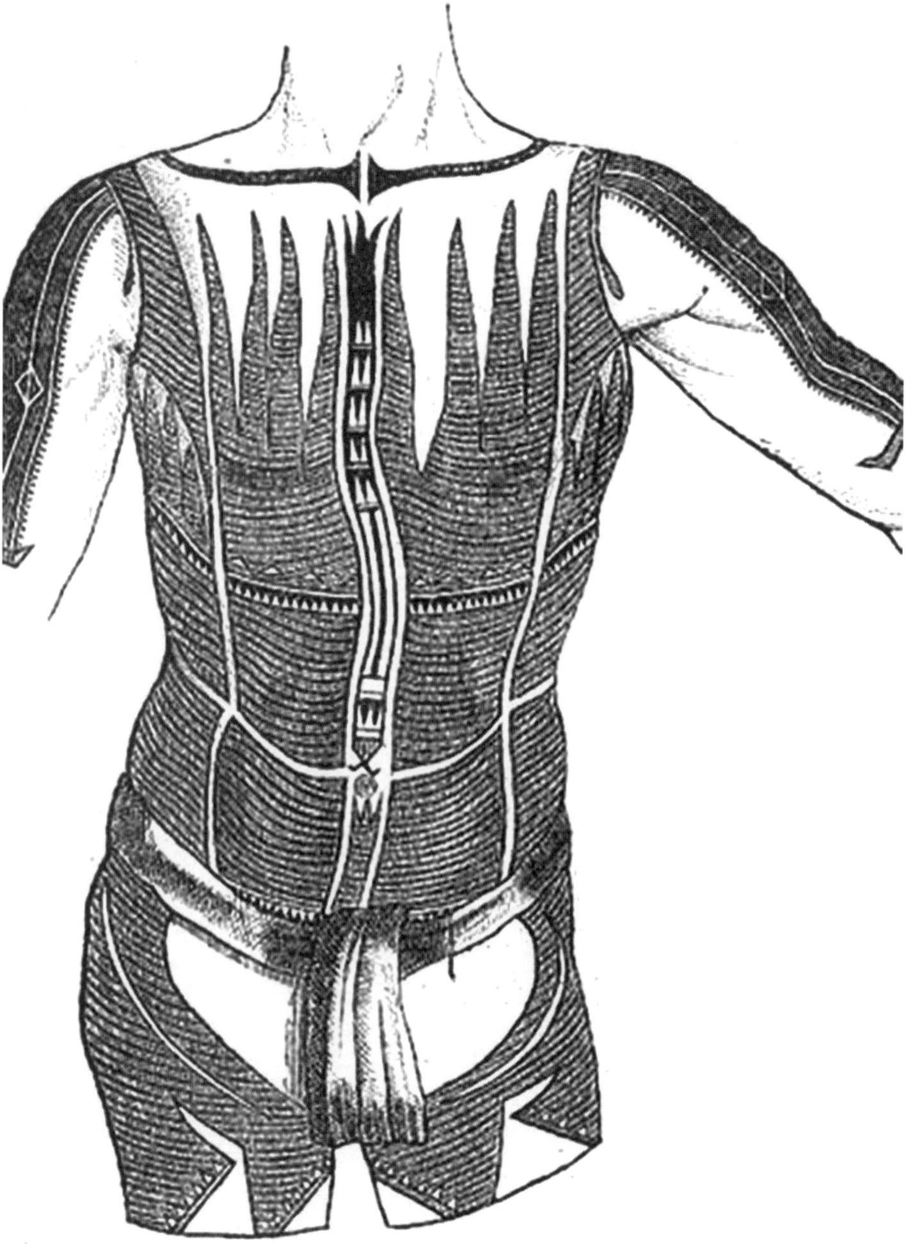

Full body tattoos from the Yap Archipelago, Johann Kubary, 1875

Andersen, Johannes C. – Mýty a legendy Polynésanů, Volvox Globator, 2000

Angas, George French – The New Islandes Illstrated, Thomas M´Lean, London, 1847

Bancroft, Hubert Howe, 1832-1918 - The native races of the Pacific states of North America, Appleton and company, 1875

Bates, Henry Walter, - The naturalist on the River Amazons, A record of adventures, habits of animals, sketches of Brazilian and Indian life and aspects of nature under the Equator during eleven years of travel, London, J. Murray, 1863

Bauron, Pierre – De Carthage au Sahara, 1899

Biggs, Bruce – The complete English-Maori dictionary, Auckland university, 1981

Birket-Smith, Kaj - An ethnological sketch of rennell island a Polynesian Outlier in Melanesia, 1969

Belhassen, Badreddine - Le tatouage maghrébin, Communication & Langages Année 1976

Berchon, Ernest (1825-1895) – Le tatouage aux îles Marquises, V. Masson (Paris), 1860

Boas, Franz – Primitive Art, Dover Publications, 1955

Bohannan, Laura - The Tiv of central Nigeria

Bovin, Mette - Nomades « sauvages » et paysans « civilisés» : WoDaaBe et Kanuri au Borno, Journal des Africanistes Année 1985

Bos, Peter, Konyak, Phejin– Last of the tattooed headhunters, Roli books, 2017

Broek d'Obrenan, Régine Van den - Notes sur l'île Rennel et ses tatouages [Illustrations au trait, d'apres des dessins aquarelles de l'auteur], Journal de la Société des Océanistes Année 1947

Brown, George - Melanesians and Polynesians; their life-histories described and compared, MacMillan and Co, London, 1911

Buck, Peter H. - Arts and Crafts of the Cook Islands, Bishop Museum, 1944

Burch, Ernest S. - Social life in northwest Alaska: the structure of Inupiaq Eskimo nations, University of Alaska Press, 2006

Burrows, Edwin G - Flower in my ear; arts and ethos of Ifaluk Atoll, University of Washington press, 1963

Buschan, Georg - Illustrierte Völkerkunde, in zwei Bänden, 1922

Butt, Audrey J. - Symbolism and ritual among the Akawaio of British Guiana, New West Indian Guide, 1961

The Mazaruni skorpion,

Catlin, George – O-Kee-pa: a religious ceremony; and other customs of the Mandans, 1867

Choris , Luis - Voyage pittoresque autour de monde : avec des portraits de sauvages d'Amérique, 1906

Christian, F. W - The Caroline Islands: travel in the sea of the little lands, New York, 1899

Clayton, Walter - A Vocabulary of the Igorot Language as Spoken by the Bontok Igorots, 1908

Clercq, F. S. A. de - Ethnographische beschrijving van de west- en noord-kust van Nederlandsch Nieuw-Guinea / door F.S.A. de Clercq met medewerking van J.D.E. Schmeltz, 1893

Codrington, Robert Henry - The Melanesians : studies in their anthropology and folklore, 1891

Collocott, E.E.V - Supplementary Tongan Vocabulary, 1886

Crawfurd, John – A Descriptive Dictionary of the Indian Islands and Adjacent Countries, Bradbury and Evans, London, 1856

Crooke, William - Things Indian : being discursive notes on various subjects connected with India, London : J. Murray, 1906

Decary, Raymond - Les tatouages chez les indigenes de Madagascar, Journal des Africanistes Année 1935 5-1 pp. 1-39

Densmore, Frances – YUMAN AND YAQUI MUSIC, Smithsonian institution bureau of American ethnology bulletin 110, 1932

Dinter van, Maarten Hesselt – The world of Tattoo, Kit publishers, 2005

Dobrizhoffer, Martin, 1717-1791 - Geschichte der Abiponer, eine berittenen und kriegerischen Nation in Paraquay. 1783

Dordillon, René - Grammaire et dictionnaire de la langue des Îles Marquises, Paris, 1931

Duke of Mecklenburg-Schwerin, Adolf Friedrich- From the Congo to the Niger and the Nile; an account of the German Central African Expedition of 1910-1911

Elbert, S.H. - Dictionary of the language of Rennell and Bellona, National Museum of Denmark, 1975

Emory, Kenneth – Hawaiing Tattooing, 1946

Eyre, Edward John, 1815-1901 - Journals of expeditions of discovery into central Australia, and overland from Adelaide to King George's Sound, in the years 1840-1

Field, Henry, - Body-marking in southwestern Asia, Peabody museum, 1958

Fiksa, Radek – Piercing, Sowulo Press, 2005

Fiksa, Radek – Tetování, Sowulo Press, 2005

Finch, Otto - Über Bekleidung, Schmuck und Tätowirung der Papuas der Südostküste von NeuGuinea, 1885

Samoafahrten. Reisen in Kaiser Wilhelms-Land und Englisch-Neu-Guinea in den Jahren 1884 u. 1885 an Bord des deutschen Dampfers "Samoa, 1888

Ethnologische Erfahrungen und Belegstücke aus der Südsee: Beschreibender Katalog einer Sammlung, 1883

Fox, C.E. – Social Organization In San Cristoval, Solomon Islands, Journal Of The Anthropological Institute Of Great Britain And Ireland Vol.4, 1918

Fraser, Tolmie W. – Comparative Vocabularies of the Indian Tribes Of British Columbia With A Map Illustrating Distribution, 1884

Fürer-Haimendorf, Christoph von – Through the Unexplored Mountains of the Assam-Burma Border, The Geographical Journal Vol. 91, No. 3 (Mar., 1938), pp. 201-216

Furness, William Henry - The island of stone money, Uap of the Carolines, 1910

Gardiner, J. Stanley - The Natives of Rotuma, The Journal of the Anthropological Institute of Great Britain and Ireland, Vol. 27 (1898),

Gell, Alfred – Wraping in images, Tattooing in Polynesia, Clarendon Press, Oxford, 1993

Clercq, F. S. A. de - Ethnographische beschrijving van de west- en noord-kust van Nederlandsch Nieuw-Guinea / door F.S.A. de Clercq met medewerking van J.D.E. Schmeltz, 1893

Gilbert, Steve – Tattoo history, REsearch 2000

Godden, Gertrude M. - Naga and Other Frontier Tribes of North-East India, The Journal of the Anthropological Institute of Great Britain and Ireland Vol. 26 (1897), pp. 161-201

Guppy, H. B - The Solomon Islands and their natives, 1887

Gupte, B.A. – Notes on female tattoo designs in India, 1902

Haddon, Alfred C - Head-hunters; black, white, and brown, London : Methuen & C, 1091

Hambly W. D. - Origins Of Education Among Primitive Peoples A Comparative Study In Racial Development, 1926

Handy, W.Chatterson – Tattooing in the Marquesas, Bishop Museum, 1922

Haudricourt, A. G., Hollyman K. J. - The New Caledonian Vocabularies Of Cook And The Forsters, BALAD, 1774

Hawkes, Ernest William - The Labrador Eskimo, Ottawa: Government printing bureau, 1916.

Hedley, Charles - The atoll of Funafuti, Ellice group: its zoology, botany, ethnology, and general structure based on collections made by Mr. Charles Hedley, of the Australian museum, Sydney, N.S.W, 1896

Hein, Alois Raimund, 1852 - Die bildenden ku¨nste bei den Dayaks auf Borneo : Ein beitrag zur allgemeinen kunstgeschichte, 1890

Hill-Tout, Charles - British North America, Vol 1, 1907

Hodson, T. C. - The Naga tribes of Manipu, MacMillan and Co, London, 1911

Hoffman, Walter James, 1846-1899 - The graphic art of the Eskimos, 1897

Homes, W.H., Report of the Chief , Twenty-seventh Annual report of the bureau of american ethnology, 1905-1906

Hose Charles, McDougall William – Pagan Tribe of Borneo, 1912

Iluani (The Life and Culture of Kodiak, No. 2 No. 5) , MUNDURUCÚ RELIGION.

Ivens, Walter George - Dictionary and grammar of the language of Sa'a and Ulawa, Solomon Islands; with appendices, Robarts - University of Toronto, 1918,

Melanesians of the south-east Solomon Islands, 1972.

Ivens, H.G. - A vocabulary of the lau language. Big Mala, Solomon Islands, 1934

Jensk, Ernest - The Bontoc Igorot, 1905

Johnson, Samuel - The history of the Yorubas : from the earliest times to the beginning of the British Protectorate, 1901

Johnson, Osa - Bride In The Solomons, Riversidpress, 1944

Journal des Museum Godeffroy – erster band, 1873

Joyce, Thomas Athol, 1878-1942; Thomas, Northcote Whitridge, 1868 –

Women of all nations; a record of their , 1906

Kennedy, Donald Gilbert - Field Notes on the Culture of Vaitupu, Ellice Islands, 1975

Kenneth L. Rehg,Damian G. Sohl - Ponapean-English Dictionary, 1979

Kitamura, Takahiro - Tattoos of the Floating World: Ukiyo-e Motifs in the Japanese Tattoo, Amsterdam Tattoo Museum, 2003

Kjellgren, Eric, with contributions by Jo Anne Van Tilburg and Adrienne L. Kaeppler - Splendid Isolation: Art of Easter Island, The Metropolitan Museum of Art, NY, 2001

Klarr, Caroline Katherine – Hawaiian Hula and Body Ornamentation 1778 to 1858, Easter Island Foundation, 1999

Koch, Gerd - Materielle Kultur Der Gilbert-Inseln: Nonouti, Tabiteuea, Onotoa, 1965

Koch-Grünberg, Theodor, 1872-1924 - Vom Roroima zum Orinoco: Ergebnisse einer Reise in Nordbrasilien und Venezuela in den Jahren 1911-1913, Baessler Institut (Berlin, Germany) 1917

Kramer, Augustin - Die Samoa-inseln: Entwarf einer monographie mit besonderer berücksichtigung Deutsch-Samoas, 1903

Hawaii, Ostmikronesien und Samoa; meine zweite Südseereise 1899.

Zur Tatauierung der Mentawei-Insulaner, 1907

The Samoa Islands: Material Culture, University of Hawaii, 1995

Ergebnissen der Südsee-Expedition 1908–1910 : Zentralkarolinen, Lámotrek-gruppe, Oleai, Feis, 1937

Ergebnissen der Südsee-Expedition 1908–1910: Palau vol 3, 1926

Krutak, Lars and Deter-Wolf, Aaron – Ancient ink, The Archeology of Tattooing, Univeristy of Washington Press, 2017

Kubary, Jan Stanisaw - Ethnographische Beiträge zur Kenntnis des Karolinen Archipels. Veröffentlicht im Auftrage der Direktron des Kgl. Museums für Völkerkunde zu Berlin. Unter Mitwirkung von J.D.E. Schmeltz, 1895

Das Tätowiren in Mikronesien Speciell auf den Carolinen, In Tätowiren narben zeichnen und körperbemalen, Berlin, 1897

Kwiatkowski, P.F. – The Hawaiian Tattoo, Halona Inmc, Hawaii, 1996

Landor, A.H.S. - The Gems of the East: Sixteen Thousand Miles of Research Travel Among Wild and Tame Tribes of Enchanting Islands, 1904

Alone with the hairy Ainu. OR, 3,800 miles on a pack saddle in yezo and a cruise to the Kurile islands. 1893

Light, D.W. – Tattooing Practised Of The Cree Indians, Glenbow-Alberta Institute, Alberta, 1972

Livingstone, David - The last journals of David Livingstone, in Central Africa, 1875

London, Charmian - The log of the Snark, MacMilan company, 1915

Martin, Karl - Reisen in den Molukken, in Ambon, den Uliassern, Seran (Ceram) und] : eine Schilderung von land und Leuten, E.J.Brill, 1894

Martin, Rudolf - Die inlandsta¨mme der Malayischen halbinsel : wissenschaftliche ergebnisse einer reise durch die Vereinigten malayischen staaten, 1905

MacCulloch, J. A - The religion of the ancient Celts, Edinburgh : T. & T. Clark, 1911

Mead, Sidney M; Royal Ontario Museum - Material culture and art in the Star Harbour region, Eastern Solomon Islands, 1973,

Meredith, De Witt. - Hancock, Allan - Voyages of the Velero III : a pictorial version, with historical background, 1939

Métraux, Alfred - Ethnology of Easter Island, Honolulu, Hawaii : Bernice P. Bishop Museum, 1940.

Milne, Leslie - Shans at home, London : J. Murray, 1910

Mooney, James - The ghost-dance religion and the Sioux outbreak of 1890, Washington DC, 1896

Morris, Max – Die Mentawai sprache, Verlag von Conrad Skopnik, 1900

Murray, Alexander Hunter - Journal of the Yukon, 1847-48, Otawa govermment, 1910

Murray, J. - A selection of papers on arcti geografy and etnology, 1875

Oliver, Samuel Pasfield, 1838-1907 – Madagascar; an historical and descriptive account of the island and its former dependencies, Toronto, 1886

Overbergh , Cyrille van - Collection de monographies ethnographiques, publíee, 1907

Parthasarathy, Jakka - The Yerukula: An Ethnographic Study, Anthropological Survey of India, 1988

Passarge, Siegfried - Adamaua : Bericht u¨ber die Expedition des deutschen Kamerun-Komitees in den Jahren 1893-94

Petrie, W. M. Flinders - Naqada and Ballas, 1895

Pita, Graham – Maori Moko or Tattoo, The Bush Press, 2005

Ploss Hermann Heinrich, 1819-1885; Bartels Max (Maximilian), 1843-1904 - Das Weib in der Natur- und Völkerkunde : anthropologische Studien, 1897

Pritchard, W. T. - Polynesian reminiscences; or, Life in the South Pacific islands, 1866

Procházka, Petr – Tanec slunce, Eminent 2006

Racinet, Auguste, 1825-1893 - Le costume historique. Cinq cents planches, trois cents en couleurs, or et argent, deux cents en camaieu. Types principaux du ve^tement et de la parure, rapproche´s de ceux de l'inte´rieur de l'habitation dans tous les temps et chez tous les peuples, avec de nombreux de´tails sur le mobilier, les armes, les objets usuels, les moyens de transport, etc

Ragragio, Andrea Malaya M.; Paluga, Myfel D. - An Ethnography of Pantaron Manobo Tattooing (Pangotoeb): Towards a Heuristic Schema in Understanding Manobo Indigenous Tattoos, Southeast Asian Studies, 2019, Kyoto University.

Rasmussen, Knud - Intellectual culture of the Hudson Bay Eskimos, Nordisk Forlag, 1930

Ratzel, Fridrich - The History of Mankind, MacMillan and co, 1896 – Völkerkunde, 1885, Leipzig

Reitzenstein, von F. - Das Weib bei den Naturvölkern: eine Kulturgeschichte der primitiven Frau, Neufeld & Henius, 1930

Richardson, John, Sir, 1787-1865 - Arctic searching expedition: a journal of a boat-voyage through Rupert's Land and the Arctic Sea, in search of the discovery ships under command of Sir John Franklin. With an appendix on the physical geography of North America

Riedel, J.V.F. - De sluik-en kroesharige rassen tusschen Selebes en Papua, Nijhoff, 1886

Rienzi, Grégoire Louis, Domeny de, 1789-1843 - Océanie, ou, Cinquieme partie du monde : revue géographique et ethnographique de la Malaisie, de la Micronésie, de la Polynésie et de la Mélanésie, 1836

Riria, Ko Te, Sommons David – Maoko Rangatira – Maori Tattoo, Reed Publishing, NZ, 2004

Riviere T, Faublée J. - Les tatouages des Chaouia de l'Aures, Journal des Africanistes Année 1942 12 pp. 67-80

Robley, H.R. – Maorské tetování – Sowulo Press, 2007

Rockhill, William Woodville - Diary of a journey through Mongolia and Tibet in 1891 and 1892, 1894

Roosevelt, Kermit - Head Hunters Of The Amazon, Duffield and company, 1923

Rosenberg, Carl Benjamin Hermann, Baron von - Der Malayische Archipel. Land und Leute in Schilderungen, gesammelt während eines dreissigjährigen Aufenthaltes in den Kolonien, 1878

Roth, H. Ling - The aborigines of Tasmania, 1890

Roth, H. Ling - Great Benin; its customs, art and horrors, 1903

Roth, H. Ling - The natives of Sarawak and British North Borneo; based chiefly on the mss. of the late Hugh Brooke Low, Sarawak government service, vol.2, Truslove & Comba, New York, 1896

Roth, H. Ling - Tatu in the Society Islands, 106

Routledge, Katherine Pease, 1866-1935 - The mystery of Easter island; the story of an expedition, Toronto, 1919

Salvador-Amores. Analy Ikin V. – Batek: Traditional tattoos and Identities in Contemporary Kalinga, North Luzon Phillippines, 2002

Sande, Van der – Nova Guinea, Nederlandsche Nieuw-Guinea-Expeditie, 1903

Sapier, Edward – Hupa Indian tattooing, 1936

Scheerer, Otto – The Nabaloi Dialect, Manila Press, 1905

Schürle, Georg - Die Sprache der Basa in Kamerun : Grammatik und Wörterbuch, 1912

Scott, James George - The Burman, his life and notions, New York : Macmillan, 1896

Scott, William Henry - Barangay Sixteenth Century Philippine Culture And Society, Ateneo de Manila University Press, 1994

Selenka, Emil - Der Schmuck des Menschen, Vitra, Berlin, 1906

Siebold, Heinrich von – Studien über die Aino, auf der insel Yesso, Verlag von Paul Parey, Berlin, 1881.

Sinclair, A.T. – Tattooing The North American Indian, American Anthropologist, 1908

Skinner, Alanson – Material culture art he Menomini, New York, 1921

Indians of Manhattan Island and Vicinity, 1926

Skeat, Walter William - Pagan races of the Malay Peninsula, vol.2, Macmillan and co, 1906

Speck, Frank G. –Ethnology of the Yuchi Indians. Antrhopological Publications of the University Museum, university of Pennsylvania, Philadelphia, 1909.

Spennemann, Dirk HR – Tetování na Marshallových ostrovech, Sowulo Press, 2007

Smeaton, Winifred – Tattooing Among the Arab sof Iraq, American Antthropologist, 1937

Smith, S. Percy- Hawaiki: the original home of the Maori; with a sketch of Polynesian history, Christchurch, N. Z., London, etc., Whitcombe and Tombs limited, 1904

Steinen, Karl von den – Die Marquesaner und ihre Kunst, Band I:Tatauierung, Berlin, 1925

Durch Central-Brasilien : Expedition zur Erforschung des Schingu´ im Jahre, Leipzig, 1884

Stephan, Emil;- Su¨dseekunst. Beitra¨ge zur Kunst des Bismarck-archipels und zur Urgeschichte der Kunst u¨berhaupt. Aus dem Ko¨niglichen Museum fu¨r Vo¨lkerkunde zu Berlin mit Unterstu¨tzung des Reichsmarine-amts, 1907

Swan, James G. – Indiánský kmen Haidů z ostrovů královny Charlotty, Bodyart magazín 2009

Tannenbaum N. - Tattoos: invulnerabilityand power in Shan cosmology. Am. Ethnol.14(4):693–711, 1987

Taplin, George – The folklore, manners, customs, and languages of the South Australian aborigines: gathered from inquiries made by authority of South Australian government, Adelaide, 1879

Taylor, Clyde Romer Hughes - A Pacific bibliography : printed matter relating to the native peoples of Polynesia, Melanesia, and Micronesia, 1965

Taylor, William, E. - Giryama Vocabulary and Collections, Society for promoting Christian knowledge, 1891

Teihet, Jehanne – Dimension of Polynesia, Fine ATS Gallery of San Diego, 1973

Teuira, Henry - Tahitian astronomy. Birth of the heavenly bodies, The Journal of the Polynesian Society, Vol. 16, No. 2(62) (June, 1907), pp. 101-104

Thompson, Edwin Denig - The Assiniboine, University of Regina. Canadian Plains Research Center, 2000

Thurston, Edgar - Ethnographic notes in southern India, 1906

Tickle, Les – Tau Kuka: A Tattooing Of The People Of Bellona Island, Cultural Association of the Solomon Islands, 1977

Tillem, H.F. - Apo-Kajan: Een Filmreis naar en door Centraal-Borneo, van Munster, Amsterdam, 1938

Tregear, Edward - The Maori-Polynesian comparative dictionary, 1891

Trench Gascoigne, Gwendolen Galton - Among pagodas and fair ladies : an account of a tour through Burma, Innes, London, 1896

Turner, Victor Witter - The Forest of Symbols: Aspects of Ndembu Ritual, Cornell University Press, 1967

Vanoverbergh, Morice – Dress and Adornment in the Mountain Province of Luzon, Phillippine Islands. Catholic Anthropological Conference Publications, 1929.

Volz, Wilhelm – Zur Kenntnis de Mentawei-Inseln, Beitrage zur Anthroplgie und Ethnographie von Indonedien, 1906

Vráz E.S. – Cesty a dobrodružství, Touřimský a Moravec, 1939

Wallace, W.J, Taylor, E.S. – Mohave tattooing and face-painting, Soutweat museum, California, 1947

Walter G. - Vocabulary of the Lau Language, Big Mala, Solomon Islands, Ams Pr Inc, 1988

Washington M. - Etnography and philiology of the Hidatsa Indians, 1877

Webb, Wilfred Mark -The heritage of dress; being notes on the history and evolution of clothes, London, The Times Book Club, 1912

Wells, Roger. , Kelly, John W. - English-Eskimo and Eskimo-English vocabularies. Washington: G.P.O., 1890

Westermann, Diedrich - The Shilluk people, their language and folklore, Philadelphia : Board of Foreign Missions of the United Presbyterian Church of N. A., 1912

Wichmann, Arthur - Nova Guinea: résultats de l'expédition scientifique néerlandaise a la Nouvelle-Guinée, 1903

Wilkes, Charles – Narrative of the United States Exploring Expedition during the Years 1838-1842. Lea and Blanchard, Philadelphia, Pennsylvania, 1845.

William, Thomas and James Calvert – Fiji and the Fijians. D. Appletzon and Company, NY, 1859

Williams, William, Bp., 1800-1878 - A dictionary of the New Zealand language, and a concise grammar; to which is added a selection of colloquial sentences, 1852

Wilson, James - A missionary voyage to the southern Pacific ocean, performed in the years 1796, 1797, 1798, in the ship Duff, London Missionary Society, 1799

Wirchow, Rud. – Verhandlungen der Berliner Gesellchaft für Anthropologie, Ethnologie und Urgeschichte, Berlin, 1878

Wolf, Aaron Deter and Diaz-Granados, Carol – Drawing with the needles – Ancient Tattoo Traditions of North America, Univewrsity of texas Press, 2013.

Worcester, Dean C. – The Non-Christian Tribes of Northorn Luzon, The Phillippine Journal of Science, 1906

ANOTHER BOOK BY THE AUTHOR:

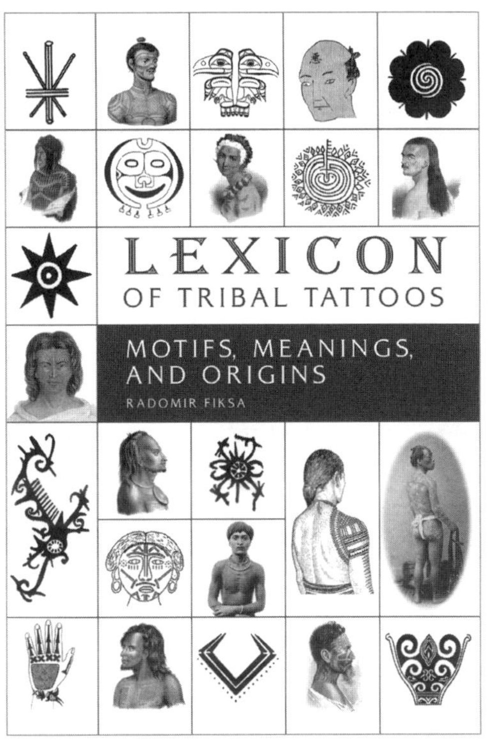

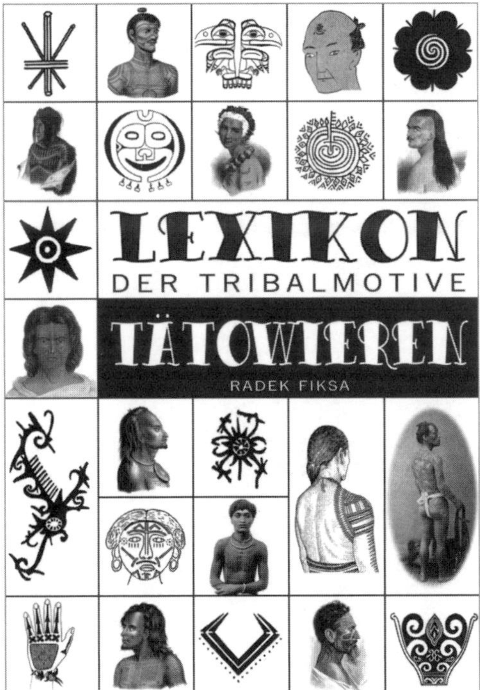

COMING SOON:

PIERCING
ENCYKLOPEDIE / ENCYCLOPEDIA
/czech english version/
RADEK FIKSA

RADEK FIKSA
2. LEXIKON
TETOVÁNÍ
TRIBALOVÝCH MOTIVŮ

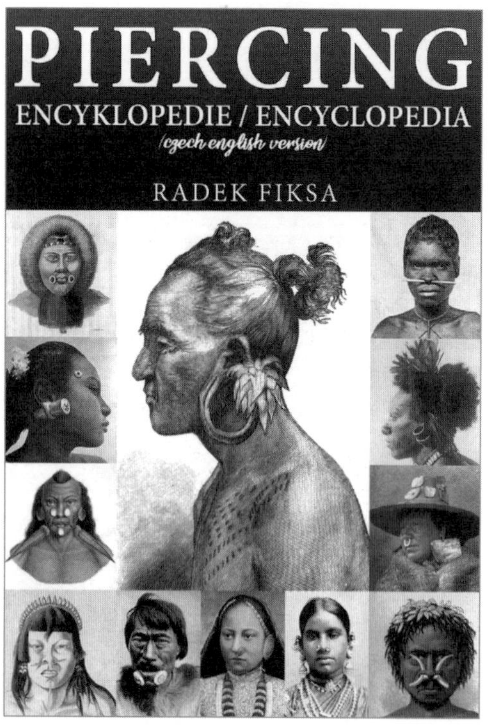

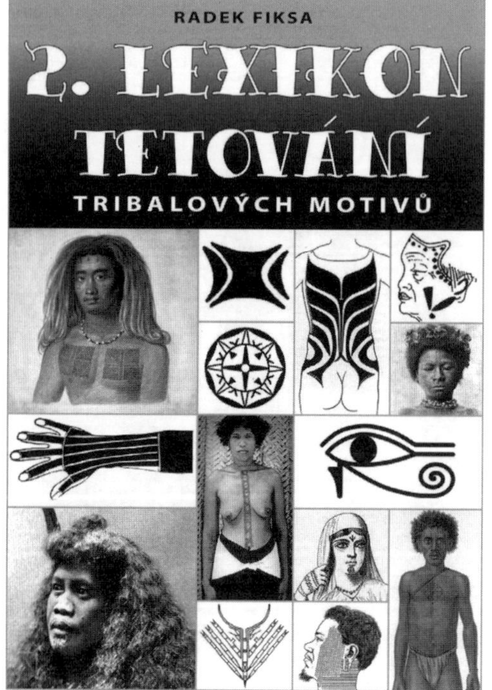